MARKETING RESEARCH WITH SPSS

D0074042

PEARSON
Education

We work with leading authors to develop the
strongest educational materials in marketing,
bringing cutting-edge thinking and best learning
practice to a global market.

Under a range of well-known imprints, including
FT Prentice Hall, we craft high quality print
and electronic publications which help readers
to understand and apply their content, whether
studying or at work.

To find out more about the complete range of our
publishing, please visit us on the World Wide Web at:
www.pearsoned.co.uk

MARKETING RESEARCH WITH SPSS

Wim Janssens

Katrien Wijnen

Patrick De Pelsmacker

Patrick Van Kenhove

Prentice Hall
FINANCIAL TIMES

An imprint of **Pearson Education**

Harlow, England • London • New York • Boston • San Francisco • Toronto • Sydney • Singapore • Hong Kong
Tokyo • Seoul • Taipei • New Delhi • Cape Town • Madrid • Mexico City • Amsterdam • Munich • Paris • Milan

Pearson Education Limited

Edinburgh Gate
Harlow
Essex CM20 2JE
England

and Associated Companies throughout the world

Visit us on the World Wide Web at:
www.pearsoned.co.uk

_____

First published 2008

© Pearson Education Limited 2008

The rights of Wim Janssens, Katrien Wijnen, Patrick De Pelsmacker and Patrick Van Kenhove
to be identified as authors of this work have been asserted by them in accordance with the
Copyright, Designs and Patents Act 1988.

All rights reserved. No part of this publication may be reproduced, stored in a retrieval
system, or transmitted in any form or by any means, electronic, mechanical,
photocopying, recording or otherwise, without either the prior written permission of the
publisher or a licence permitting restricted copying in the United Kingdom issued by the
Copyright Licensing Agency Ltd, Saffron House, 6–10 Kirby Street, London EC1N 8TS.

All trademarks used herein are the property of their respective owners. The use of any
trademark in this text does not vest in the author or publisher any trademark ownership rights
in such trademarks, nor does the use of such trademarks imply any affiliation with or
endorsement of this book by such owners.

ISBN: 978-0-273-70383-9

British Library Cataloguing-in-Publication Data
A catalogue record for this book is available from the British Library

Library of Congress Cataloging-in-Publication Data
Marketing research with SPSS / Wim Janssens . . . [et al.].
     p. cm.
  Includes bibliographical references and index.
  ISBN 978-0-273-70383-9 (pbk. : alk. paper) 1. Marketing research. 2. SPSS for
Windows.   I. Janssens, Wim.
  HF5415.2.M35842 2008
  658.8'30285555—dc22   2007045264

10 9 8 7 6 5 4 3 2
11 10 09

Typeset in 10/12.5pt GraphicSabon Roman by 73
Printed and bound in Great Britain by Ashford Colour Press, Gosport, Hants

The publisher's policy is to use paper manufactured from sustainable forests.

Contents

Preface

Statistical procedures are a 'sore point' in every day marketing research. Usually there is very little knowledge about how the proper statistical procedures should be used and even less about how they should be interpreted. In many marketing research reports, the necessary statistical reporting is often lacking. Statistics are often left out of the reports so as to avoid scaring off the user. Of course this means that the user is no longer capable of judging whether or not the right procedures have been used and whether or not the procedures have been used properly. This book has been written for different target audiences. First of all, it is suitable for all marketing researchers who would like to use these statistical procedures in practice. It is also useful for those commissioning and using marketing research. It allows the procedures used to be followed, understood and most importantly, interpreted. In addition, this book can prove beneficial for students in an undergraduate or postgraduate educational programme in marketing, sociology, communication sciences and psychology, as a supplement to courses such as marketing research and research methods. Finally, it is useful for anyone who would like to process completed surveys or questionnaires statistically.

This book picks up where the traditional marketing research handbooks leave off. Its primary goal is to encourage the use of statistical procedures in marketing research. On the basis of a concrete marketing research problem, the book teaches you step by step which statistical procedure to use, identifies the options available, and most importantly, teaches you how to interpret the results. In doing so, the book goes far beyond what the minimum standard options available in the software packages have to offer. It opts for the processing of data using the SPSS package. At present, SPSS is one of the most frequently used statistical packages in the marketing research world. It is also available at most universities and colleges of higher education. Additionally, it uses a simple menu system (programming is not necessary) and is thus very easy to learn how to use. The book is based on version 15 of this software package.

Information is drawn from concrete datasets which may be found on the website (www.pearsoned.co.uk/depelsmacker). The reader simply has to open the dataset in SPSS (not included) and may then – with the book opened to the appropriate page – practice the techniques, step by step. Most of the datasets originate from actual marketing research projects. Each of the datasets was compiled during the course of interviews performed on consumers or students, and were then input into SPSS. The website also contains a number of syntaxes (procedures in program form).

This book is not however a basic manual for SPSS. The topic is marketing research with the aid of SPSS. This means that a basic knowledge of SPSS is assumed. For the inexperienced reader, the first chapter contains a short introduction to SPSS. This book is also not a basic manual for marketing research or statistics. The reader should not expect an elaborate theoretical explanation on marketing research and/or statistical procedures. The reader will find this type of information in the relevant literature which is referred to in each chapter. The technique used is described briefly and explained at the beginning of every chapter under the heading 'Technique.' The book's primary purpose is to demonstrate the practical implementation of statistics in marketing research, which does more than simply display SPSS input screens and SPSS outputs to show how the analysis should proceed, but also provides an indication of the problems which may crop up and error messages which may appear.

The book starts with a brief introduction to the use of SPSS. The most current data processing techniques are then addressed. The book begins with the simpler analyses. First, descriptive statistics are discussed such as creating visual displays and calculating central tendency and measures of dispersion. After that, we discuss hypothesis testing. The Chi-square test and t-tests are the primary focus, in addition to the most current measures of association. Also, multivariate statistical procedures are discussed at length. The more explorative procedures (factor analysis, cluster analysis, multidimensional scaling techniques and conjoint measurement) as well as the confirmative techniques (analysis of variance, linear regression analysis, logistic regression analysis and linear structural models) are also explained. Some of these techniques require that the reader has more than just the standard modules available within SPSS at his or her disposal. The chapter 'Confirmative factor analysis and path analysis with the aid of SEM' for example requires the separate module 'Amos,' and the chapter 'Multidimensional scaling techniques' makes use of the 'Categories' module.

Each chapter may essentially be read independently from the other chapters. The reader does not have to examine everything down to the very last detail. The 'digging deeper' sections indicate that the text following involves an in-depth exploration that the reader may skip if desired. These areas of text may involve commands in SPSS windows as well as interpretations of SPSS outputs. Grey frames alongside text and figures contain steps which may be immediately relevant within the scope of the technique being discussed, but which may not necessarily be tied to this label under SPSS (see for example the calculation of Cronbach's Alpha values in a chapter on factor analysis). They are labelled as supporting techniques.

The realization of this book would not have been possible without the assistance of and critical commentary from a number of colleagues. A special word of thanks goes to Tammo H.A. Bijmolt, Frank M.T.A. Busing, Ben Decock, Maggie Geuens, Marc Swyngedouw, Willem A. van der Kloot and Yves Van Handenhove for making datasets available and for providing useful tips and advice.

The authors also wish to thank Lien Standaert, Kirsten Timmermans and Ellen Sterckx for their assistance in creating the screenshots. Finally, it would be appropriate to state here that the first two authors mentioned have made an equal contribution toward the creation of this book.

Wim Janssens
Katrien Wijnen
Patrick De Pelsmacker
Patrick Van Kenhove
January 2008

Chapter 0

Statistical analyses for marketing research: when and how to use them

In quantitative marketing research, be it survey or observation based, pieces of information are collected in a sample of relevant respondents. This information is then transformed into variables containing verbal or numerical labels (scores) per respondent. To make sense of this data set, a variety of statistical analytical methods can be used. Statistical analysis normally takes place in a number of steps or stages. The first set of techniques, called **descriptive statistics**, is used to obtain a descriptive overview of the data at hand, and to summarize the data by means of a limited number of statistical indicators. Next, each variable can be studied separately, for instance to compare average scores of a variable for different groups or subsamples of respondents, or to judge the difference between rankings or frequency distributions. These analyses are called **univariate statistics** or **statistical tests**. Finally, in **multivariate statistics**, several variables can be jointly analysed, to assess which variables explain or predict other variables, or how variables are related to one another. Both in univariate and multivariate statistics, not only description is important, but also statistical validation. In other words, results do not only have to be described and to be assessed on what this description means for the marketing problem at hand; it is at least as important to assess how statistically meaningful or significant the results are, in other words how confident the researcher can be that the descriptive conclusions are statistically reliable and valid.

Descriptive statistics

Univariate statistical description usually contains three types of indicators: frequency distributions, central tendency measures and dispersion measures. **Frequency distributions** indicate how scores of individual respondents are distributed over meaningful categories, for instance, how many male and female respondents, or respondents in three pre-defined age groups there are in the sample. **Central tendency measures** summarize the characteristics of a variable in one statistical indicator, for instance the average consumption of coffee per month in kilograms, the average satisfaction score of a sample of customers of a company on a five-point scale (mean), the gender group in which there are the most respondents (mode), or the middle score of a set of scores ranked from low to high (median). **Dispersion measures** provide an indication of the variability in a set of scores on a variable. Respondents can largely agree on certain issues, in which case dispersion will be low, or the scores on a certain variable can substantially vary between them, in which case dispersion will be high. For instance, everyone can consume about the same amount of coffee, or the satisfaction score of a sample of customers can strongly vary, with large numbers of respondents scoring 1 and 2 as well as 4 and 5 on a five-point scale. Descriptive statistics allow summarizing large data sets in a smaller number of meaningful statistical indicators.

Multivariate description can take many forms, depending of the multivariate technique used. They are normally an integral part of the outcome of each analysis, together with the statistical validation measures, that can also be different for each technique.

Univariate statistics

In univariate statistics or statistical tests, a set of observations in one variable is analysed across different groups of respondents, and the statistical meaningfulness of the difference between these groups is assessed, for instance what is the difference in the average consumption of coffee per month in kilograms between men and women, and is this difference statistically meaningful. The choice of the appropriate statistical test is based on three characteristics of the variables in the samples: the measurement level, the number of samples to be compared, and the (in)dependence of these samples. Variables can be measured on a nominal, ordinal or interval/ratio level. Nominal variables are category labels without meaningful order or metric distance characteristics (for instance men and women). Ordinal variables have a meaningful order, but no metric distance characteristics (for instance, preference rank order indications for a given number of brands). In the case of interval/ratio variables, scores have a metrical meaning, for instance the number of kilograms of coffee purchased by a certain person (one person buys one kilogram, the other buys three, and the distance between the two observations is a metrically meaningful 2 kilograms).

Univariate analysis can be carried out on one sample (for instance, is the average satisfaction score of the whole sample of respondents statistically significantly different from the midpoint score 3?), on two samples (for instance, is the average rank order of brand A significantly different between men and women), or on more than two samples (is the average consumption of coffee significantly different between the three age groups in a sample?).

Finally, in the case of two or more samples, these samples can be dependent or independent. In the case of independent samples, the respondents in one subsample are not linked to the respondents in another subsample, for instance men and women, or three age groups that are not in any way related. In dependent samples, the respondents in one subsample are related to those in other subsamples, for instance husbands and wives, sons and daughters, or the same respondents that are measured at different points in time.

Based on these three characteristics, a selection grid for univariate statistical tests can be constructed:

Measurement level	One sample	Two samples		k Samples	
		Independent	Dependent	Independent	Dependent
Nominal	Binomial test (Z-test on proportion) χ^2	χ^2	McNemar	χ^2	Cochran Q
Ordinal	Kolmogorov-Smirnov	Mann-Whitney U	Wilcoxon	Kruskal-Wallis	Friedman
Interval or ratio	t-test Z-test	t-test Z-test	t-test for differences	Analysis of Variance	Repeated measures Analysis of Variance

In each cell, the appropriate statistical test(s) can be found. In Exhibit 1, for each of these cells, a number of examples of marketing research questions are given.

Exhibit 1 Marketing research applications of univariate statistical tests

- Is the percentage of people interested in museums, as measured in a sample of UK citizens, significantly different from the percentage of museum-lovers as measured in an earlier French study?
- Is the average satisfaction score of a sample of customers of a company, measured on a 5-point scale, significantly different from midpoint (3)?
- Is the average number of pairs of shoes bought per family in The Netherlands significantly larger than 6?
- Is the average percentage recall score of radio ads different between men and women in a sample?
- Is there a difference between the preference for different car models between three age groups in France and Germany?
- Is the average consumption of beer per capita per year in Germany significantly different from Belgium?
- Is there a significant difference between the purchase intention (will/will not buy) for a brand of wine in a sample of potential consumers, before and after an advertising campaign for the product?
- Is there a significant difference between the scores on two examinations of a sample of students?
- Is there a difference between the brand attitude scores measured at different points in time (tracking), in a sample of potential customers?
- Is there a difference between sales figures in three samples of shops in which a different sales promotion campaign has been implemented?

Multivariate statistics

Multivariate analytical methods are research methods in which different variables are analysed at the same time. Each of these techniques requires specific types of data, and has its own fields of application to marketing research. Knowing which type of data a certain analytical technique requires is essential for taking the right decisions about data collection methods and techniques, given certain marketing and marketing research problems at hand.

Which multivariate analytical techniques to use depends on a number of criteria. A first important issue is whether a distinction should be made between independent and dependent variables. **Dependent variables** are factors that the researcher wants to explain or predict by means of one or more **independent variables,** factors of which he/she believes can contribute to the explanation in the variation or evolution of the dependent variables. For instance, a brewery may want to study to what extent price, advertising, distribution and sales promotions (independent variables) explain and predict the evolution of beer consumption over a certain period of time (dependent variable). This type of techniques is called **analysis of dependence**. In case the research problem at hand does not require this distinction to be made, another set of techniques, **analysis of interdependence**, is called for. For instance, a bank may ask itself how many fundamentally different customer segments it can define on the basis of multiple customer characteristics. In this example, no distinction between dependent and independent variables is made; the objective is to assess the relationship between variables or observations. Interdependence techniques are also called exploratory, while dependence techniques are called confirmatory. Indeed, the purpose of the former is to look for patterns, for structure in variables and observations, while the objective of the latter is to find proof for a pre-defined model that predicts a criterion using predictors. Therefore, interdependence techniques will be mostly used in the exploratory, descriptive stages of a research project, when looking for patterns and structures. Confirmatory techniques will be mainly used in the conclusive stages of a project, in which conclusive answers are sought about which phenomena and factors explain and predict others.

The second important criterion that is important to select a multivariate analytical technique is only relevant for dependence techniques, namely the measurement level of both the dependent and the independent variables. More particularly, the distinction has to be made between nominal or categorical variables on the one hand, and interval/ratio variables on the other. Multivariate analytical techniques that use ordinal data also exist, but they are beyond the scope of this book, and they will not be discussed further. The figure **Multivariate statistical techniques** provides an overview of the multivariate techniques discussed in this book.

Multivariate statistical techniques

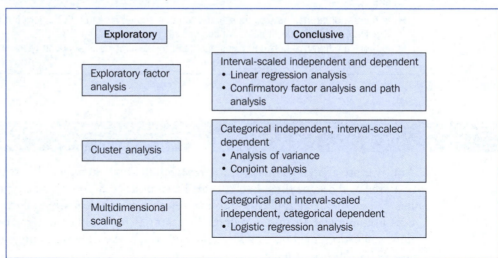

The objective of exploratory factor analysis is a meaningful reduction of the number of variables in a dataset, based on associations between those variables. In the process, meaningful dimensions in a set of variables are found, and the number of factors to use in further analysis is reduced. In cluster analysis the objective is to reduce the number of observations by assigning them to meaningful clusters on the basis of recurrent patterns in a set of variables. The end result of a cluster analysis is a relatively limited number of clusters or groups of respondents or observations, to be used in further analysis. In multidimensional scaling, perceptions and preferences of consumers are mapped, based on the opinion of consumers about products, brands and their characteristics. Again, the result is a more structured insight in the perception and preference of respondents than based on their detailed preference or perception scores.

In linear regression analysis a mathematical relation is defined that expresses the linear relationship between an interval-scaled dependent variable and a number of independent interval-scaled variables. The objective is to find out to what extent the independent variables can explain or predict the dependent variable, and what the contribution of each independent variable is to explaining variations in the dependent one. The data used to apply this technique can be longitudinal (i.e. measured at different points in time), cross-sectional (measures on different respondents or points of observation at one point in time), or both. Logistic regression analysis is a similar technique, but in this case the dependent variable is categorical, and the independent variables can be both categorical and interval-scaled. The objective of analysis of variance and of conjoint analysis is similar, but the measurement level of the variables is different. In both techniques the relative impact of a number of categorical independent variables on an interval-scaled dependent variable is measured. Finally, in confirmatory factor analysis a predefined measurement model (a number of pre-defined factors), and the relation (path) between a number of independent, mediating and dependent interval-scaled variables are statistically tested. In Exhibit 2, for each of these multivariate methods, a number of examples are given of marketing research problems for which they can be used.

Exhibit 2 Marketing research applications of multivariate statistical methods

1. Exploratory factor analysis
   - A car manufacturer measures the reaction of a group of customers to 50 criteria of car quality and tries to find what the basic dimensions of quality are that underlie this measurement
   - A bank measures satisfaction scores of a group of customers on 40 satisfaction criteria and explores the basic dimensions of satisfaction judgments
   - A supermarket asks its customers how they assess the importance of 20 different shopping motives to try to discover a more limited number of basic shopping motivations

2. Cluster analysis
   - A bank tries to identify market segments of similar potential customers on the basis of the similarities in their socio-demographic characteristics (age, level of education . . .) and their preference for certain investments
   - A supermarket chain tries to define different segments of customers on the basis of the similarities in the type of goods they buy, the amount they buy, and the brands they prefer
   - A radio station defines different type of ads based on the characteristics of the ads, the formats and emotional and informative techniques used (image-orientedness, level of informative content, degree of humour, feelings . . .)

3. Multidimensional scaling
   - A car manufacturer wants to find out to what extent potential customers perceive his models and those of competitors similar or dissimilar, and for which models the customer has the greatest preference
   - A fashion boutique wants to find out how it is positioned on various image attributes in comparison with its competitors
   - A furniture supermarket wants to know which type of customers are attracted to what type of characteristics of his shop

4. Linear regression analysis
   - A manufacturer of branded ice cream wants to find out to what extent his price level and advertising efforts have contributed to sales over a period of 36 months
   - An insurance company has collected scores on six components of customer satisfaction and wants to assess to what extent each of them contributes to overall satisfaction

5. Confirmatory factor analysis and path analysis
   - An Internet shop has identified five factors that contribute to 'shop liking', and on the basis of measurements in a sample of potential customers wants to test to what extent these five factors are compatible with the data he collected, to what extent they determine 'shop liking', and to what extent shop liking, in turn, determines purchase intention
   - An advertiser has identified three factors of the attitude of consumers towards advertisements. He wants to find out if these three factors are reflected in the perception of a test sample of customers, and if these factors, together with a brand loyalty measure, determine brand attitudes and buying behaviour

6. Analysis of variance
   - A manufacturer of yoghurt has tested three types of promotions and two types of packaging in a number of shops. He wants to find out to what extent each of these variables have influenced sales and what their joined effect is
   - A manufacturer of shoes wants to find out if the age of his customers (three categories) and the size of the customers' families (single, married or couple with children) has an impact on annual shoe sales

7. Conjoint analysis
   - An airline wants to find out what the impact is of free drinks or not, free newspapers or not, and the availability of mobile phone services on the plane on the customers' preference for a flight
   - A jeweller wants to launch a new type of diamond jewel and tries to find out to what extent colour, clarity, cut and carat have an impact on the propensity to spend a certain amount of money for the new jewel

8. Logistic regression analysis
   - A telecom provider wants to find out to what extent the age of a person, his education level, and the place he lives in determines whether he is a customer or not
   - A hotel wants to know if the country of origin of a traveller, his age, and the number of children he has determines whether he will select his hotel or not for a summer holiday.

Chapter 1
Working with SPSS

Chapter objectives

This chapter will help you to:

- Understand how to construct an SPSS data file
- Create and define variables and labels
- Deal with missing data
- Manipulate data and variables

General

SPSS is a widely distributed software program which allows data to be analysed. This may involve simple descriptive analyses as well as more advanced techniques, such as multivariate analysis. SPSS consists of different modules. This means that in addition to the basic module (Base System), there are also other modules. These are normally destined for more advanced and specialized analyses (for example, the AMOS module is used in Chapter 8, and in Chapter 10, the Categories module is used).

SPSS works with different screens for each type of action (for example data input, output, programming, etc.). This first chapter deals with the Data Editor screen (data input), and several basic topics involving data input and processing will be discussed so that we can quickly begin with the analysis afterwards. Data files are indicated by the extension *.sav*. Starting in Chapter 2, we will also discuss other relevant screens such as the output screen. This is the screen in which all of the results are displayed; this is denoted with the extension *.spo*. For the sake of clarity, it may be said that there are also several other types of screens. For example, there is the 'Chart Editor' which may be used to edit graphs. There is also the syntax screen which will have to be used if the user would like to program the commands instead of clicking on them. This last type of file is indicated with the extension *.sps*. The major advantage of this system is the possibility to move about quickly between input and output.

Additional references may be found at the end of this chapter.

Data input

When SPSS starts up, the user will first see a dialogue window (Figure 1.1) which will ask the user what he would like to do.

Figure 1.1

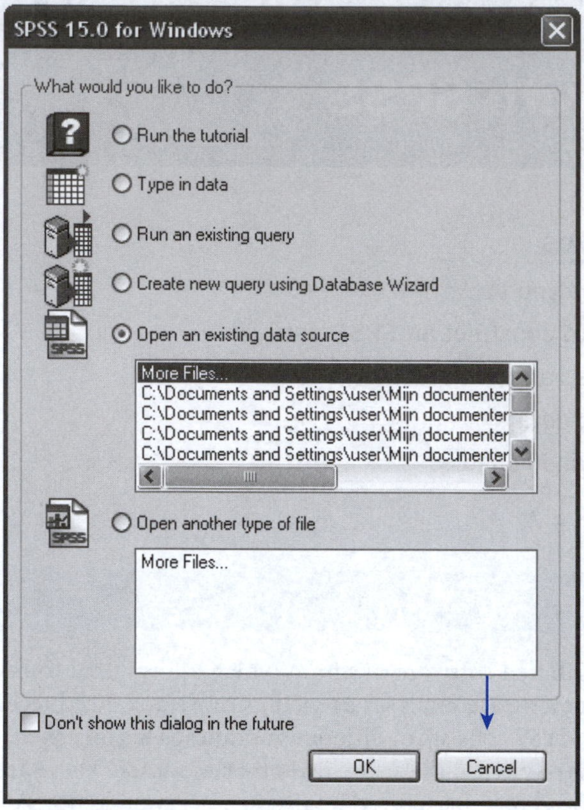

When the user checks 'Type in data' here, and then clicks 'OK', he will enter the data input screen (Data Editor, see Figure 1.2). The same result may be achieved by clicking 'Cancel'.

Figure 1.2

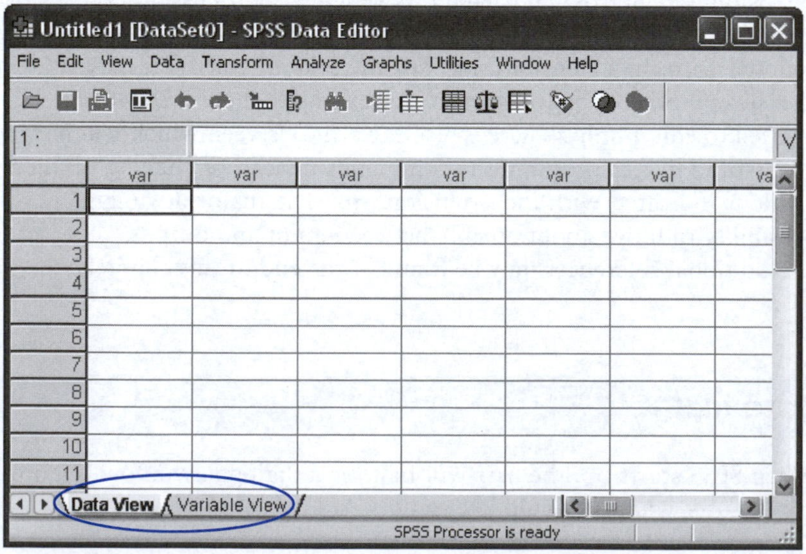

The data input screen in Figure 1.2 consists of two tabs, 'Data View' and 'Variable View'. The user may input the data in the first tab and the characteristics relating to the different variables in the second, such as the name of the variable, the description of the variable, the meaning of each value of the variable, type of variable (numeric, string, etc.), etc.

The user will automatically enter the 'Data View' tab. The tab which is active is indicated with a white tab label (Figure 1.2). To move from one tab to the other, the user just has to click on the tab label.

In order to discuss the different items which are important during the input of data, the following simple example is used here. Suppose the user would like to input the following table into SPSS:

Table 1.1

Name	Gender	Height (cm)	Weight (kg)
Joseph	1	180	75
Caitlin	0	165	67
Charles	1	175	80
Catherine	0	170	70
Peter	1	185	75

There are two methods which may be used to input this data into SPSS: they may be either typed in directly or imported from another application program.

Typing data directly into SPSS

A first step is to go to the 'Variable View' tab (Figure 1.3).

Figure 1.3

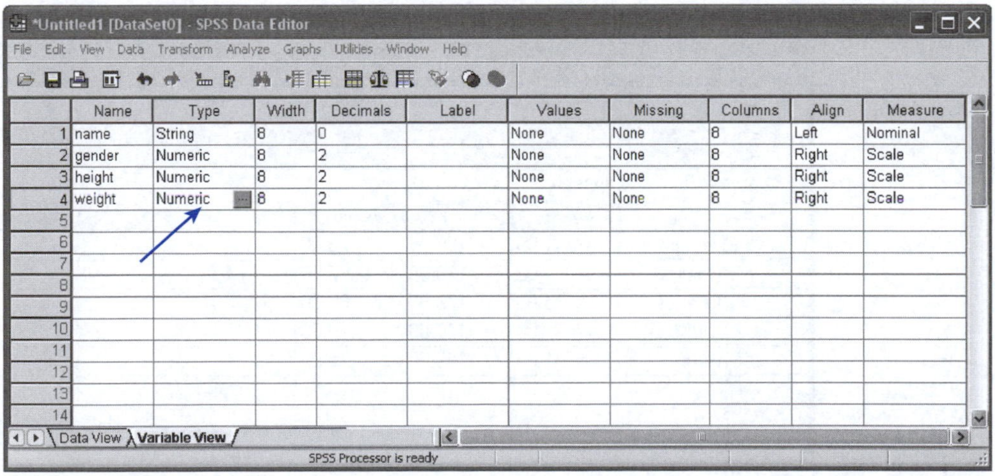

In the first column (Name), you may type the relevant variable name, and the format in the second column (Type). Click on the relevant cell and then on the '. . .' field that appears in the relevant cell.

In the example, a string format (= text format) has been chosen for 'name', and a numerical format has been chosen for the other variables (this allows the software to perform calculations). The use of a string format is only shown here for illustrative purposes since it is advisable to avoid using strings where possible. Using a respondent number can offer advantages if the researcher wishes to sort the observations. For calculations using variables, it is sometimes necessary to have the variables in numerical form. For example, if the researcher were to input gender as 'female/male' instead of '0/1', then during the subsequent analysis, he would not be able to use this variable in the majority of the analyses. The data input is what is truly important here. It is no problem to attach a label to the figures which are input, for example 0 = female and 1 = male. The way in which this is to be done is discussed further below. There are also other columns displayed in Figure 1.3. The number in the 'Columns' column indicates the maximum number of characters which will be shown. If this number is '8' such as in the example, this means that a number containing 8 digits will be displayed in its entirety. A number containing 9 digits will be displayed in an abbreviated scientific notation. 'Decimals' refers to the number of decimals which will be shown. SPSS automatically (default setting) indicates two decimals after the point. Researchers may choose to set these at zero in cases where numbers containing points are not relevant (e.g., gender: 0/1). In this chapter, we will continue to work with the standard setting of two decimals. In the other chapters, we will only work with decimals where necessary. In the column 'Label', a description of the variable may be given if necessary. The code descriptions may be found under 'Values' (e.g. 0 = female, 1 = male, see section on Creating labels). In the 'Missing' column, the numbers which indicate a code for the absence of an observation are displayed (see section on Working with missing values).

When the user then returns to the 'Data View' tab, he or she will see that the names of the four variables have appeared in the heading to replace the grey vars (see previous heading in Figure 1.2). All of the information may then be typed into the 'Data View' tab. For the example referred to above, the user may see an image such as that shown in Figure 1.4.

Figure 1.4

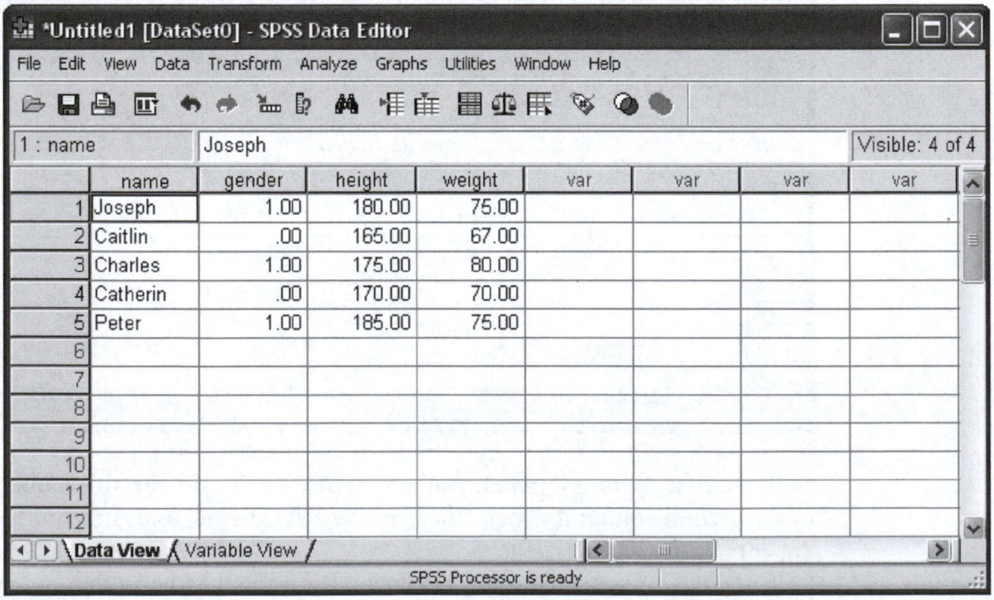

Inputting data from other application programs

If the data are located in application programs other than SPSS (Excel, etc.), these may be imported into SPSS using the path: File/Open/Data. The user then has a choice from among a whole series of possible file types which may be clicked on and loaded. In the event that the user encounters problems with this, the following tips may be helpful. Try to save the original dataset in an older version format (e.g. save files in Excel 4.0 format) and then read them into SPSS. The user must also be aware of headings (variable names) which are sometimes not imported or are imported as a missing value. The latter also applies when a simple Copy-Paste command is performed from another application program.

Data editing

In this section, we will discuss several techniques for performing different data editing activities in SPSS.

Creating labels

In the example, 'gender' is still defined as a 0/1 variable. Let's say that instead of the '0/1', the researcher would prefer to see the 'female/male' coding appear in the Data View screen. This would also allow the labels 'male' and 'female' to appear in the output, which is easier to interpret than '0' and '1'. This is certainly the case when the researcher is working with many different variables.

Figure 1.5

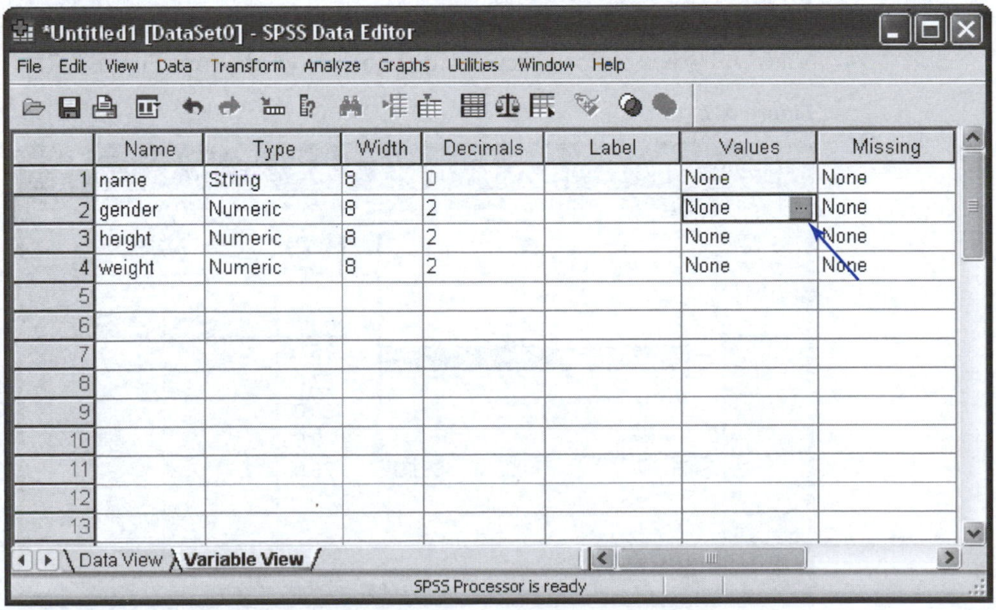

In the 'Variable View' screen (Figure 1.5), go to the line for the variable to be edited, and then to the 'Values' field. Click on this cell and then on the '. . .' which appears.

Figure 1.6

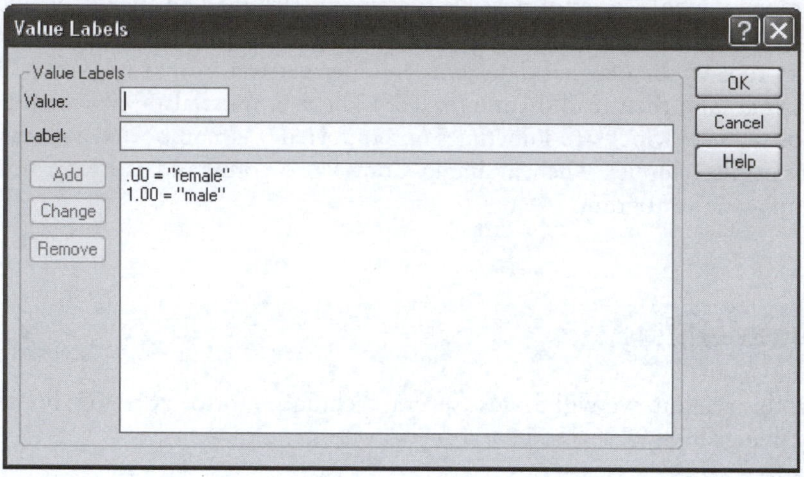

For 'Value' type in '0' and 'female' for 'Value Label' and then click 'Add'. Use the same method for '1' and 'male' (do not forget to click 'Add' each time). This will produce the image that is displayed in Figure 1.6. Now click 'OK'.

If the researcher also prefers to use identical value labels for other variables as for the value labels created for a certain variable, this may be done by simply copying the relevant Values cell in the Variable View window and then pasting this into the Values column for the desired other variables. This is particularly useful in the case of a labeled 7-point scale (1 = totally disagree, 2 = . . . up to 7 = totally agree). Instead of entering this for every variable separately, this may be typed in once and then copied and pasted for all of the other variables.

In order to be able to view the changes made to the data set, first go back to the 'Data View' tab, then choose View/Value Labels from the top (Figure 1.7).

Figure 1.7

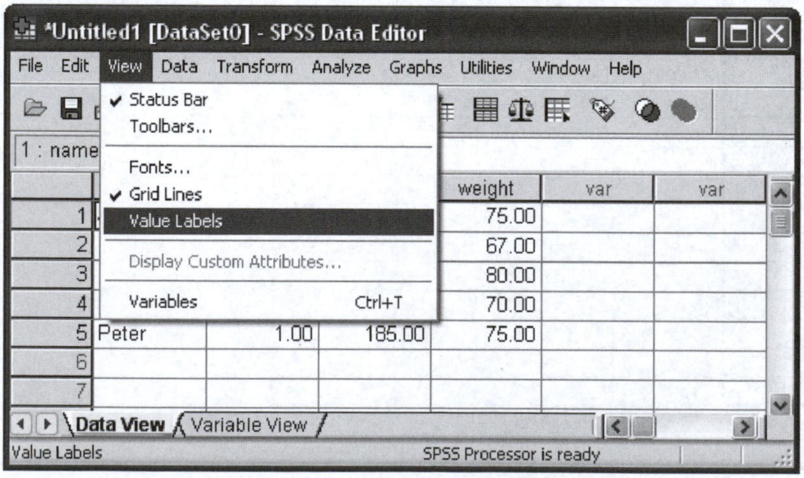

This way, you will activate this function and the label values will be displayed in the data set instead of the numerical values (see Figure 1.12 under 'gender'). In order to turn this function off, you must repeat these steps one more time.

Working with missing values

It occurs regularly that some respondents do not answer all of the questions in a survey. In this case, the researcher would not fill in a value in the 'Data View' screen of SPSS and this would remain an empty cell (SPSS will automatically insert a full stop here and this will be processed as 'System Missing'). If however the user must work with a large amount of data, is unable to fill in the data in one session, or when there are different people who must work with the same data set, it is recommended that a clear indication is provided of whether this involves a value that has not yet been filled in or whether it is a real observation for which no answer was obtained. In this last case, the user can indicate this by using the value '99' for example, or another value that does not occur among the possible answers (this is then called 'User Missing'). The user must however indicate this explicitly in SPSS; failure to do so will result in SPSS treating the value '99' as a normal input. Imagine that the researcher wishes to calculate an average value (mean) later on of a series of values in which '99' occurs a number of times, then SPSS will see this '99' as a real value and include it in the calculations for the average, instead of just neglecting to include these observations in the analyses.

Let's say that in the example, the last respondent, 'Peter', did not provide an answer to the question about his weight; this may be input in one of two ways. First, the cell may simply be left blank, but then it is not 100% clear whether or not the value must be input later or that the value truly is missing. It is better to opt for the second possibility, which would require that, for example, the value '-1' be filled in in the cell. This way there is then a clear indication that it is a missing value. The user must still indicate in SPSS that the value '-1' used is actually a code for missing values.

Figure 1.8

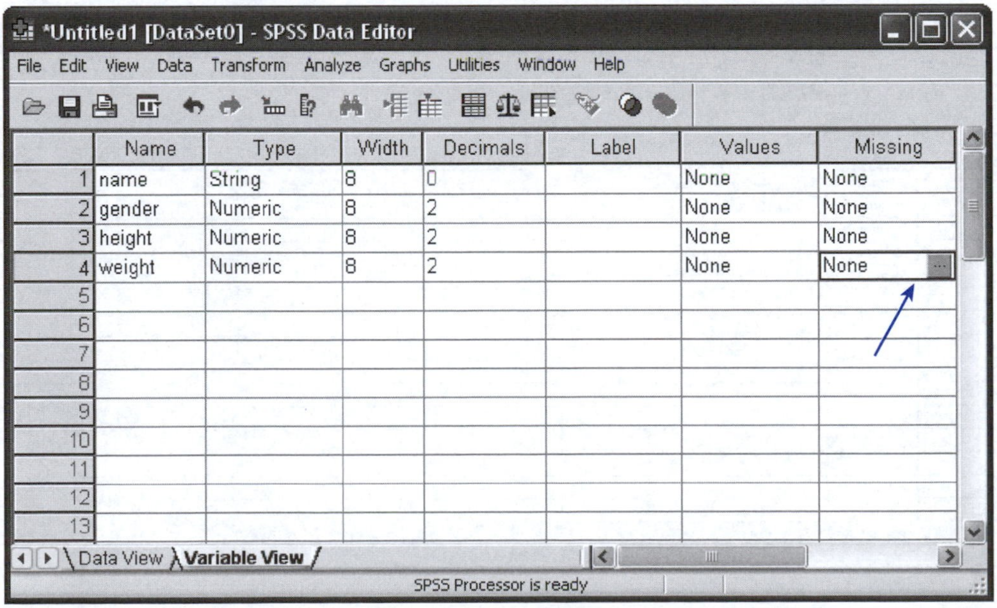

Figure 1.9

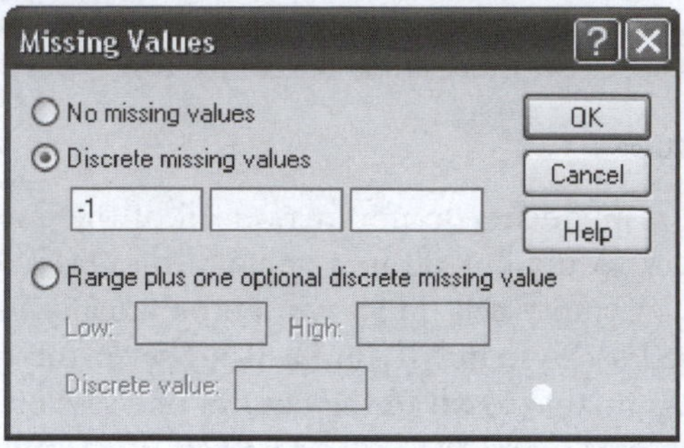

Go to the tab 'Variable View' and then choose the cell which is the result of the combination of the 'weight' row and the 'Missing' column. When you click this cell once, a grey box with three dots will appear (see Figure 1.8). Click on this box so that a dialogue window such as that shown in Figure 1.9 will appear.

Click the option 'Discrete missing values' and fill in one of the three boxes with '-1'. As you might notice, it is possible to indicate three different discrete values as a code, as well as a range of values (plus one discrete value). Now click 'OK' and from now on, SPSS will recognize the value '-1' as a 'missing' value for 'weight.' This setting may be copied to the other variables if desired using a simple Copy-Paste command (in the Variable View tab).

For the further analyses in this chapter, the '-1' will be replaced in the dataset by the original value 75 (Peter's weight).

Creating/calculating a new variable

Suppose that the researcher would like to include an extra column in the example which indicates the 'body-mass index (BMI)'. The BMI is defined as the body weight in kilograms divided by the square of the height in metres.

The path to be followed to calculate an additional variable is Transform/Compute Variable (Figure 1.10).

Figure 1.10

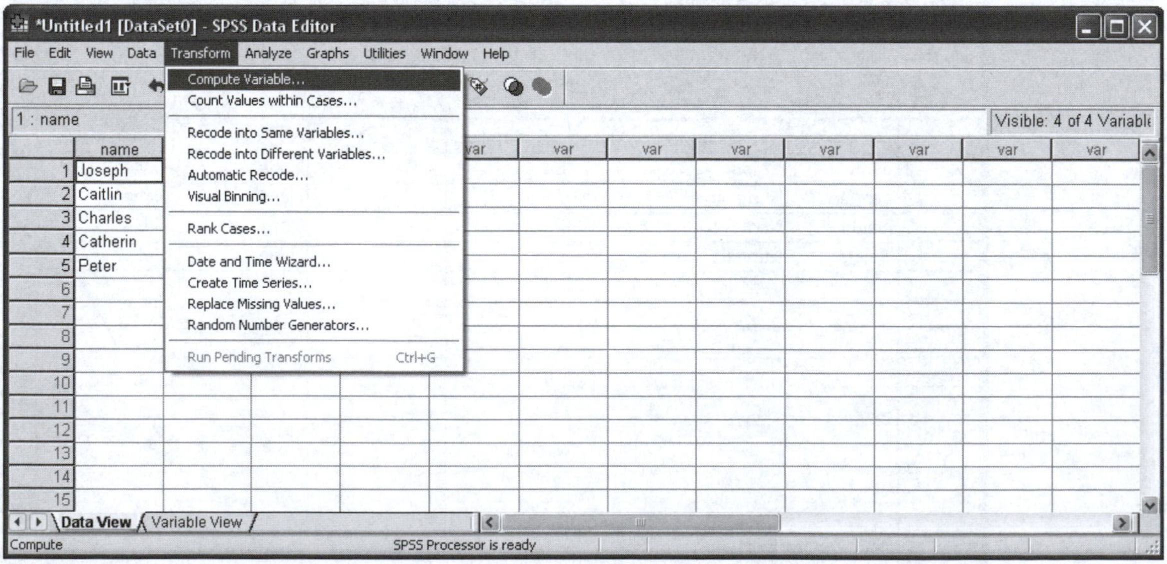

A dialogue window will be displayed such as the one seen in Figure 1.11.

Figure 1.11

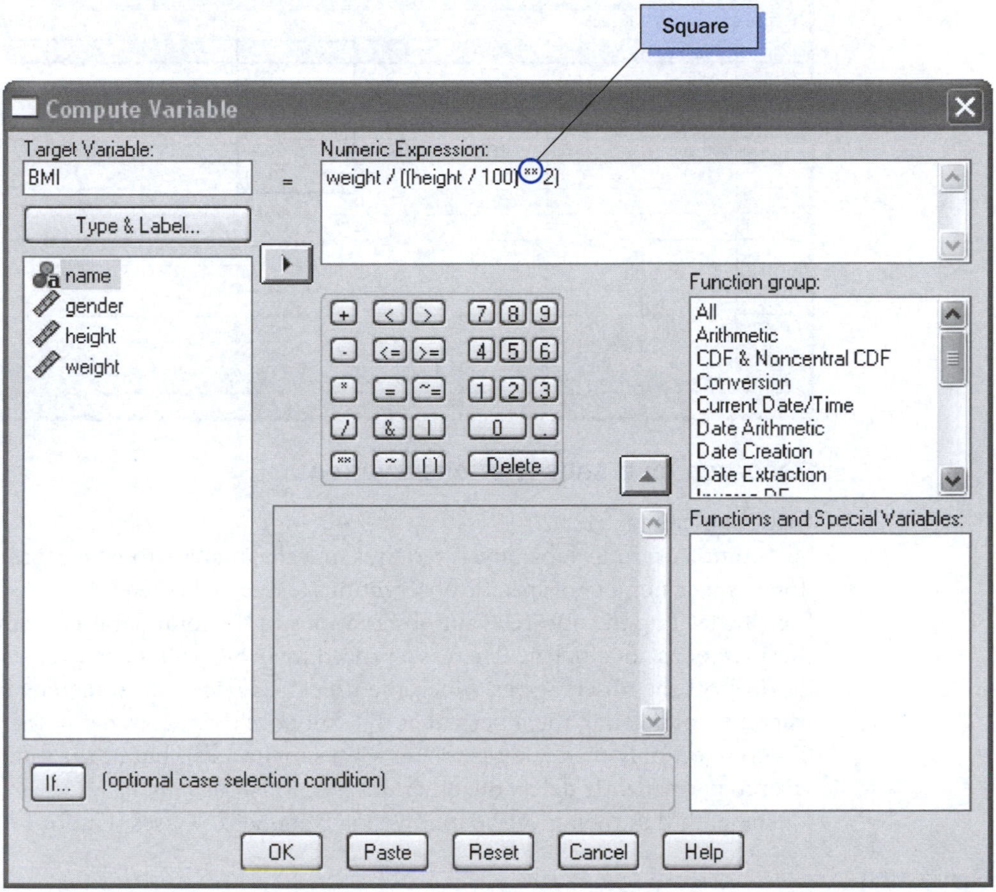

Square

In the 'Target Variable' box, type the name of the new variable you would like to calculate (BMI in this case). In the 'Numeric Expression' field, type the formula which the new variable is equal to (instead of typing in the variable names, you may also select the variable names from the left box and click the ▸ button). Figure 1.11 also demonstrates that, if necessary, the possibility also exists to choose from a number of predefined functions. Then click 'OK'.

The new variable will now be shown in the 'Data View' screen (Figure 1.12).

Figure 1.12

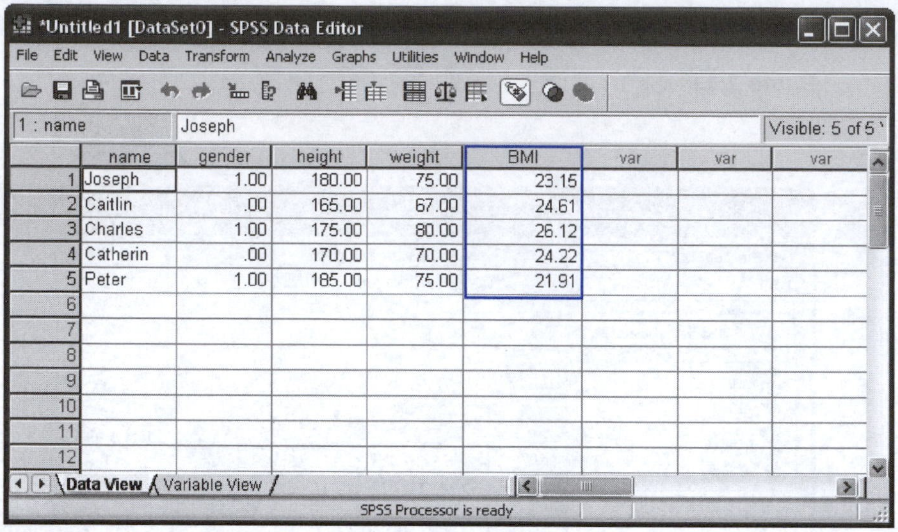

Research on a subset of observations

Selecting cases

Sometimes a certain subanalysis requires that the analysis to be performed may only be done using a number of specific observations (cases). It is then possible to create separate files by deleting the non-relevant observations in the total data file each time, however this method is not efficient. There is a procedure in SPSS which may be used to temporarily turn off the observations which the user does not wish to include in the sub-study (thereby not deleting them permanently). Suppose the researcher in the example would like to select only the male cases (e.g. for a subanalysis), but at the same time, does not wish to permanently delete the other observations (the females).

The path that then must be followed is Data/Select Cases (Figure 1.13).

Figure 1.13

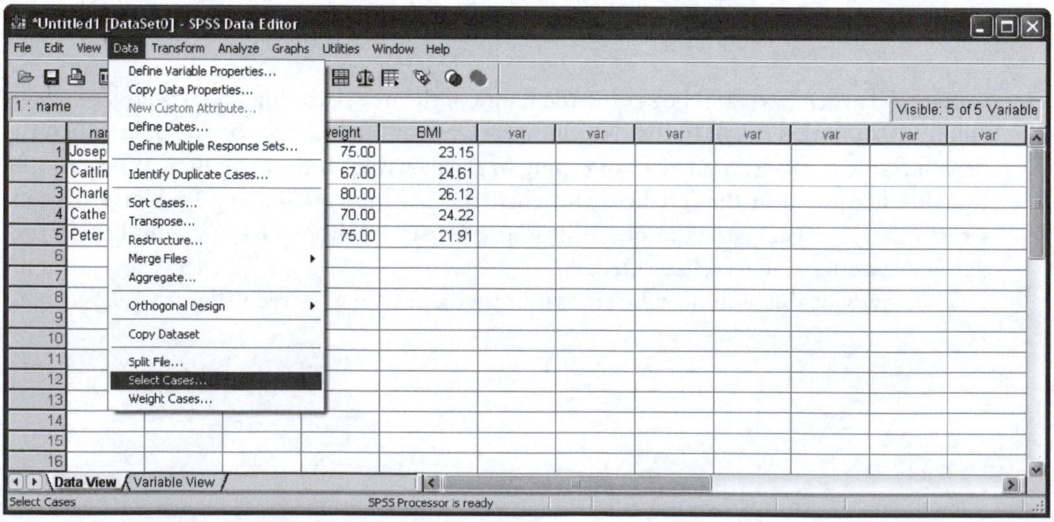

The default setting 'All Cases' must be changed by checking the option 'If condition is satisfied' and then clicking the 'If' button (Figure 1.14).

(Figure 1.14)

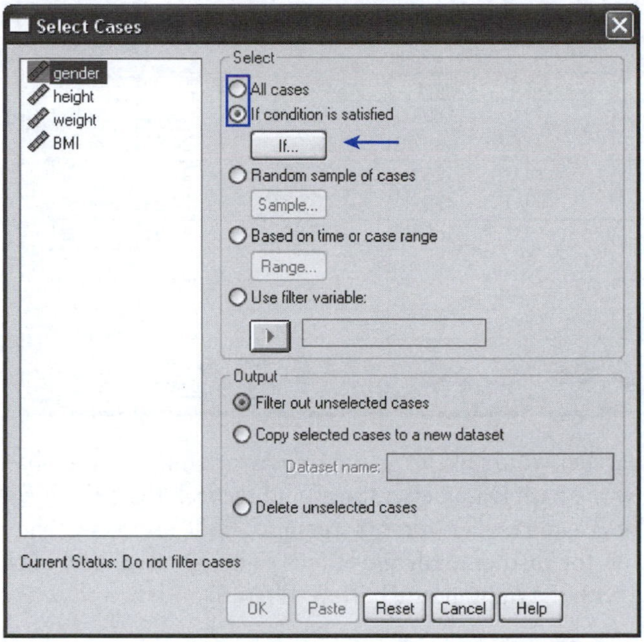

Figure 1.14

This will cause the screen in Figure 1.15 to be displayed.

Figure 1.15

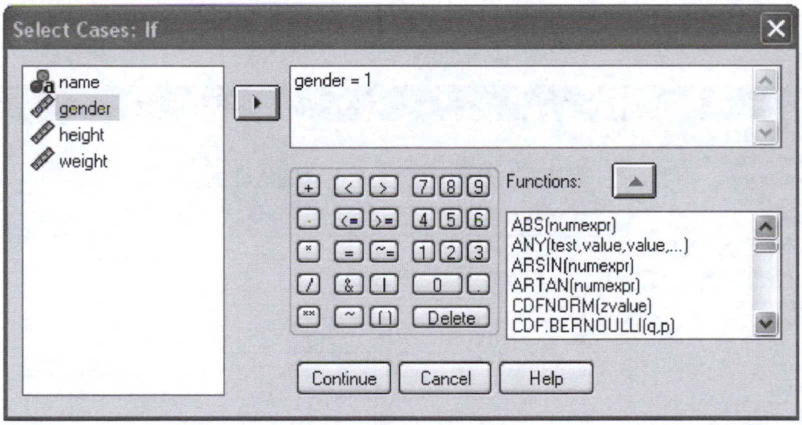

Click on 'gender' and make this equal to 1 (1 is the code for the male gender). Then click on 'Continue' and then on 'OK'.

In the 'Data View' window (Figure 1.16), one will see a slanted line through certain respondent numbers indicating that the observations for the females have been turned off. An extra variable has also been created (filter_$) which indicates whether or not the observation has been selected.

Figure 1.16

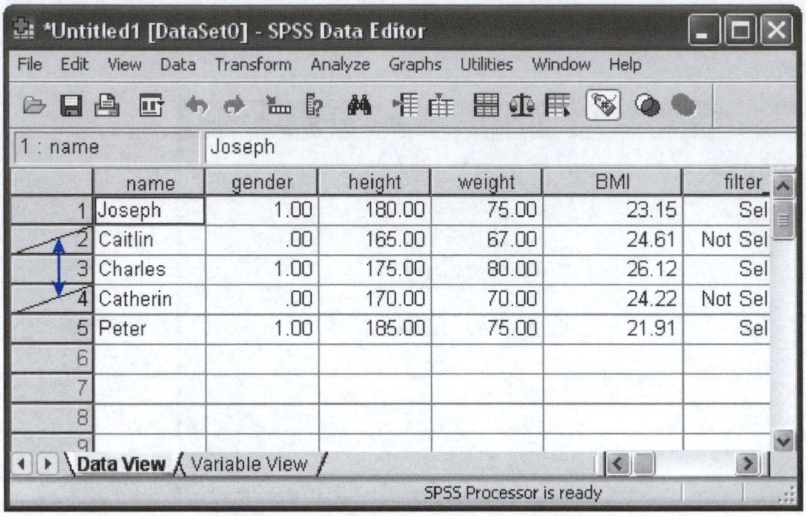

When the researcher would like to go back and work on all of the observations, he will once again follow the path Data/Select Cases and recheck the default setting 'All Cases'. The extra variable created earlier (filter_$) remains. If the user wants, he can use this variable again later on for further analyses. He may also remove it by clicking on the grey variable heading with the right mouse button (filter_$) and then selecting 'Clear'.

Splitting the data file (split file)

Another option is to split the data file. This means that when an analysis is performed, the user will obtain the results for the different groups for the variable for which the file has been split. Suppose that the researcher wishes to perform separate analyses for the women as well as the men.

Figure 1.17

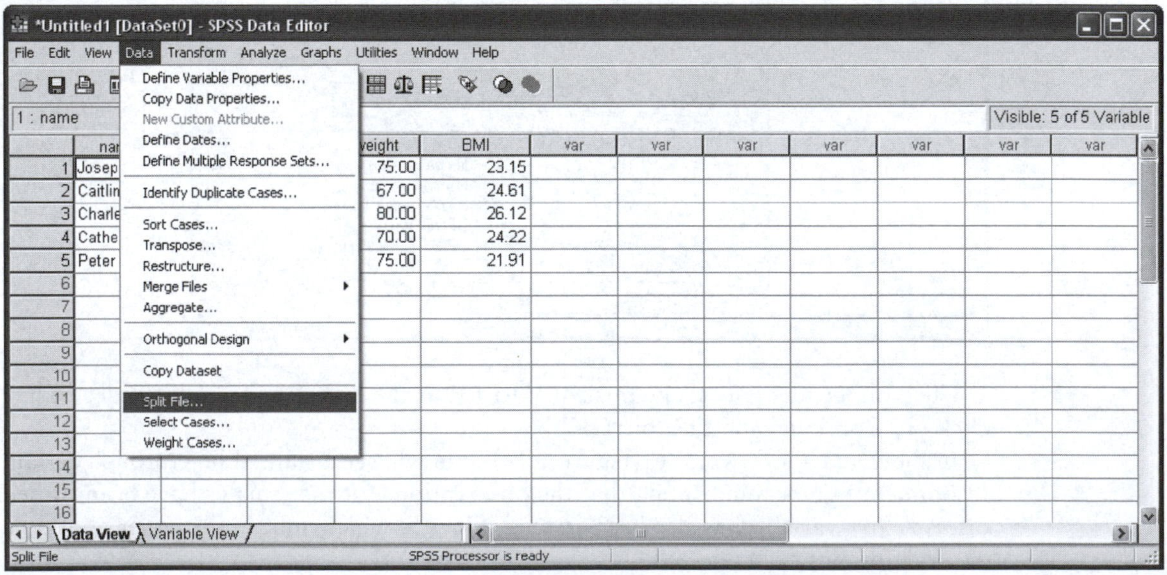

The path which then must be followed is Data/Split File (Figure 1.17).

Figure 1.18

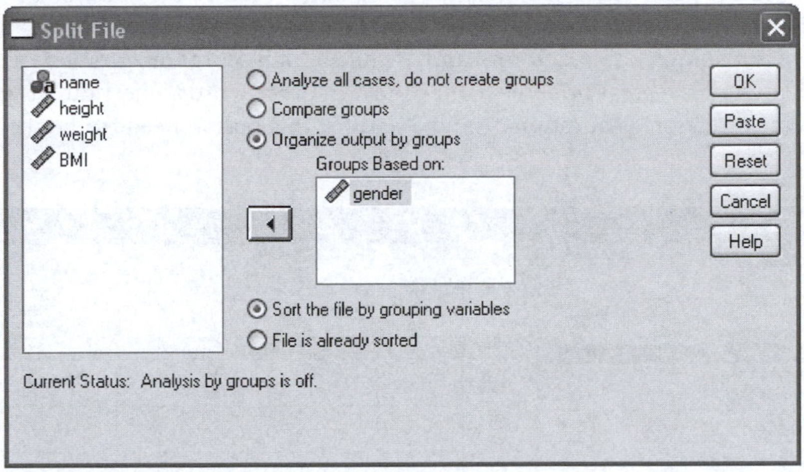

Change the default setting 'Analyze all cases, do not create groups' in 'Organize output by groups'. Next, move 'gender' to the 'Groups Based on:' subscreen. Then click on 'OK' (Figure 1.18).

You can now see that the observations have been ranked by 'gender' in the Data View tab. Now when the researcher performs an analysis (starting from the next chapter), the output for the indicated analysis will be grouped separately for men and women.

Recoding variables

Let's say that these five people must complete a questionnaire. For the sake of simplicity, we assume that this questionnaire consists of three questions (statements) in which their preferences regarding candy are being studied. The three statements must be evaluated on a 7-point scale, ranging from 'totally disagree (1)' to 'totally agree (7)'.

- *Question 1:* When I watch television in the evening, I eat candy on a regular basis.
- *Question 2:* If I'm hungry between meals, I will eat fruit more often than candy.
- *Question 3:* I always like to add extra sugar to my dessert.

Their answers are shown in Table 1.2:

Table 1.2

Name	Question 1	Question 2	Question 3
Joseph	7	3	6
Caitlin	2	5	3
Charles	5	1	5
Catherine	3	6	2
Peter	6	2	6

The data are input in the manner described above. Variable names may not contain spaces in SPSS, therefore type 'question1' for 'Question 1'.

If the researcher wishes to perform an analysis of this data (e.g. calculate an 'average for candy preference'), he must first determine whether the questions were all scaled 'in the same direction'. Take question 2 for example. A high score indicates that these people are not so quick to reach for candy, while a high score for questions 1 and 3 indicates that there is a great preference for candy. In other words, question 2 is not scaled in the same direction as questions 1 and 3 and for this reason needs to be recoded.

Figure 1.19

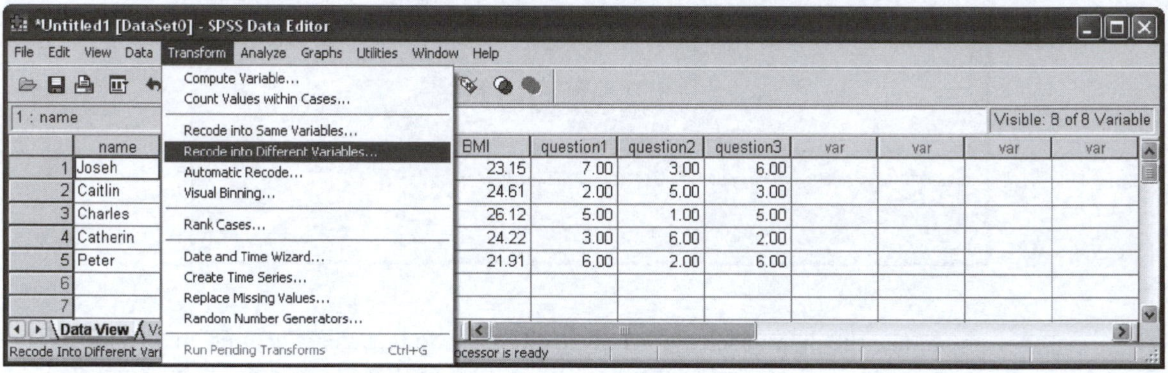

For the purpose of recoding there are two options, namely 'into Different Variables' and 'into Same Variables'. If this last option is chosen, the recoded values are placed in the same variable (column) which means that the original variables are overwritten. If an incorrect recoding takes place by accident, the original data will be lost. To prevent this from happening, it is recommended to convert the recoded values into another variable.

Go to Transform/Recode into Different Variables (Figure 1.19) which will bring up the subscreen Figure 1.20.

Figure 1.20

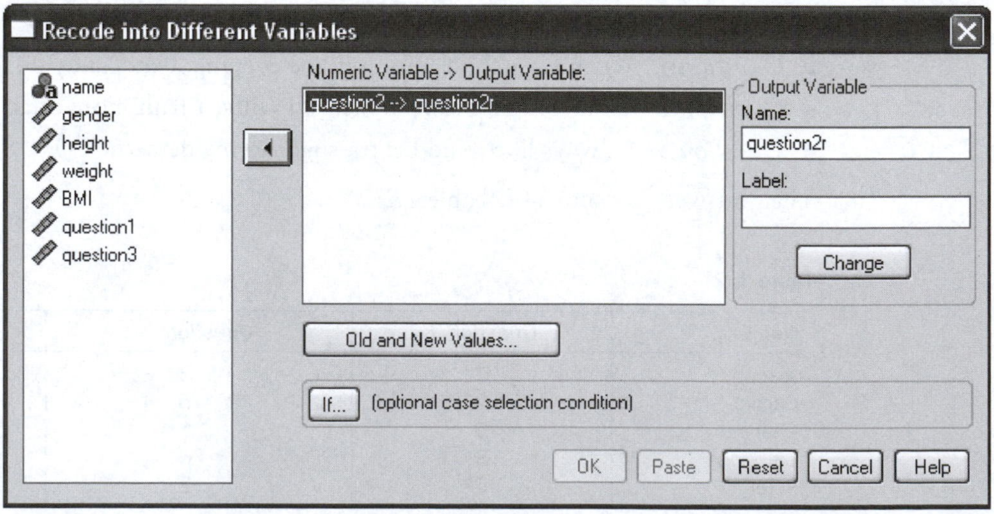

Click on 'question2' in the list of variables on the left and click ▸. Under 'Output Variable' enter the name of the recoded variable (question2r) and click 'Change' so that you see the image as shown in Figure 1.20.

Click on the 'Old and New Values' button so that you see a dialogue window such as that shown in Figure 1.21. For each value to be recoded, the researcher must input the old and the new value.

Figure 1.21

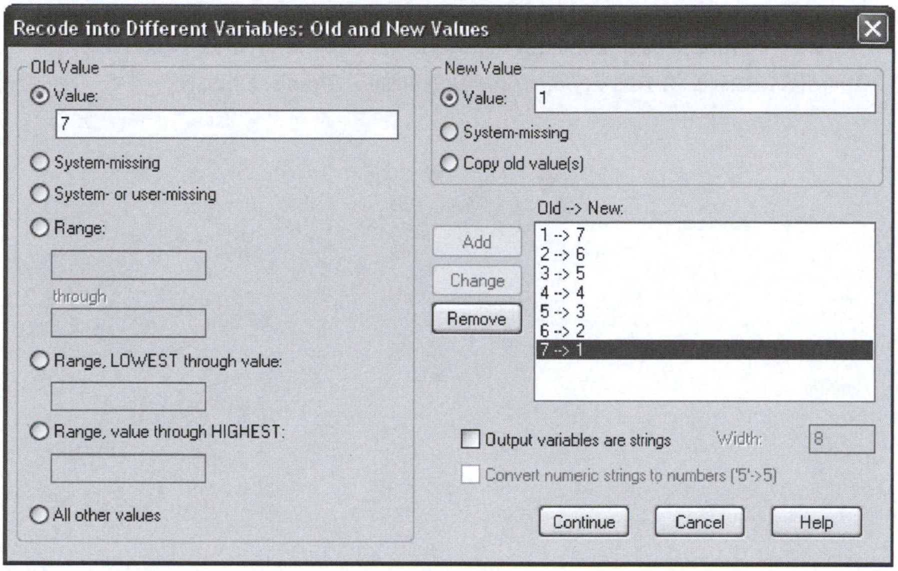

For 'Old Value', fill in the value to be changed (e.g. 7) and under 'New Value', type the new value (1). Next, click on the 'Add' button and in the Old → New window you will now see the recoding. Repeat this for each of the values to be recoded (the 4 to 4 recoding is also necessary since otherwise SPSS will not incorporate this value in the new variable).

Next, click 'Continue' and then 'OK' and you will notice that an extra variable with the recoded values has been created in the 'Data View' tab (see Figure 1.22). The data file as it is now, can also be found on the cd-rom under the name *introduction.sav*.

Figure 1.22

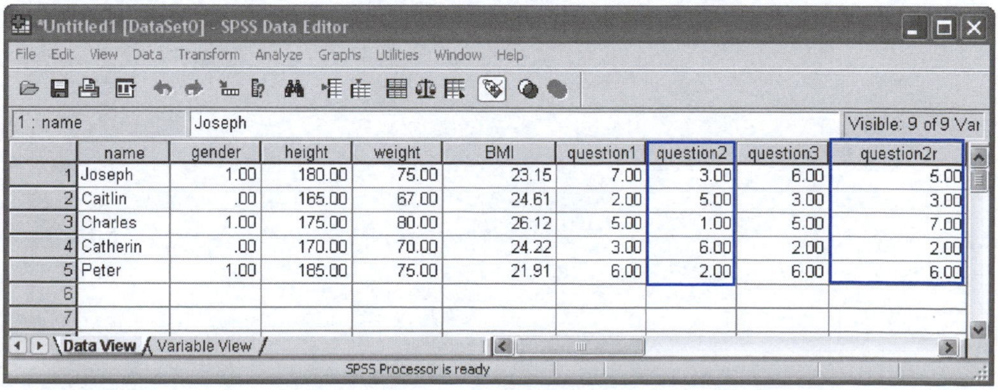

There is one more way to perform the recoding discussed above. A new variable may be calculated for this type of recoding (see above) as 8 minus the original score, such that the score 1 now becomes $8 - 1 = 7$, etc. Now, a useful average of the variables 'question1', 'question2' and 'question3' may be calculated if desired.

Further reading

Field, A. (2005), *Discovering Statistics Using SPSS*. London: Sage Publications.

Green, S.B., Salkind, N.J. and Akey, T.M. (2000), *Using SPSS for Windows – Analyzing and understanding data*. 2nd ed. Englewood Cliffs, N.J.: Prentice Hall.

SPSS Base 13.0 Users Guide (2004), Chicago, Illinois: SPSS, Inc.

Chapter 2

Descriptive statistics

Chapter objectives

This chapter will help you to:

- Create descriptive tables and graphs
- Compose multiple response tables
- Calculate means and standard deviations of a distribution of observations

Introduction

The objective of this chapter is to illustrate several simple procedures which may serve as the basis to describe a dataset. Further reading in this regard may be found at the end of this chapter. In this chapter, we use the dataset *seniors.sav*. In this file, several buying behaviour concepts have been measured for 310 people (aged 20–34, 50–59, and 60–69), as were their preferences for several types of leisure activities. Finally, inquiries were also made about several socio-demographic variables.

The buying behaviour concepts are shown in Table 2.1. Each concept is a mean of a series of statements relevant to that particular concept. These statements were measured on a 7-point Likert scale (1 = totally disagree, 7 = totally agree).

Table 2.1

Name	Variable	Description
Value consciousness	value	Degree to which people strive for an optimal value-for-money relationship
Price consciousness	price	Degree to which consumers focus on finding and paying low prices
Coupon proneness	coup	Tendency to respond to a sale, because the discount coupon has a positive influence on the purchase evaluation
Sale proneness	sale	Tendency to respond to a sale, because a discount off the original price has a positive influence on the purchase evaluation
Price mavenism	primav	Tendency to be a source of information for many products, services and places where lower prices may be found; consumers are eager to transfer this information to other consumers

Table 2.1 *Continued*

Name	Variable	Description
Price-quality schema	priqua	tendency to consider prices as an indicator of quality
Prestige sensitivity	prest	degree to which higher prices are perceived to be a status symbol
Brand consciousness	brand	degree to which the consumer focuses on brands
Importance of convenience	conv	degree to which consumers feel that ease or convenience are important
Impulsiveness	impuls	degree to which consumers are impulse-driven
Risk-aversion (-)	risk	degree to which consumers have a risk preference
Innovativeness	innov	degree to which consumers would like to be innovative or are open to innovation

The leisure activity variables, not tabled, were coded on a 7-point Likert scale (1 = do not like at all, 7 = like very much) and are: drawing-painting [free1], reading [free2], music [free3], sport [free4], studying [free5], television [free6], going out [free7], cultural activities [free8], and walking [free9].

The coding for the socio-demographic variables is shown in Table 2.2:

Table 2.2

Variable name	Description/Coding
Gender	male (0), female (1)
Mrhp	main person responsible for household purchases: no (0), yes (1)
location	I live in the city (1), in the suburbs (2), in the countryside (3)
numfamily	number of persons in the family: 1(1), 2(2), 3(3), 4(4), >5(5)
age	25–34 y (1), 50–59 y (2), 60–69 y (3)
education	elementary school (1), high school (2), higher education (3)
income	< 1250 EUR (1), 1250–1875 EUR (2), 1876–2500 EUR (3), 2501–3750 EUR (4), > 3750 EUR (5), I prefer not to answer (6)

The two extra variables 'rank A' and 'rank AA' will be used in Chapter 3.

Figure 2.1 shows the 'SPSS Data Editor' with the scores for the variables in the *seniors.sav* dataset.

Figure 2.1

	respnr	conv	brand	coup	impuls	innov	prest	price	primav	priqua	risk	sale	value
1	60	4.67	4.00	5.57	6.00	4.40	3.75	4.25	5.33	4.00	4.00	5.50	6.00
2	45	3.00	3.00	3.29	4.00	5.40	2.88	2.88	1.33	3.75	5.40	4.50	5.50
3	36	6.67	2.50	4.29	3.67	5.40	4.75	6.00	1.17	4.50	2.80	5.00	5.83
4	47	2.00	4.00	3.86	3.33	5.80	2.88	3.00	1.00	3.25	5.80	2.33	3.00
5	30	3.67	2.00	3.57	2.67	4.40	1.25	4.25	2.17	2.25	4.00	3.50	3.83
6	144	3.33	4.00	3.71	1.33	3.60	3.13	4.25	3.67	3.75	2.00	4.67	4.83
7	238	5.00	5.50	2.29	2.00	2.20	5.38	2.63	1.67	7.00	2.20	3.83	4.83
8	280	2.67	1.00	5.14	1.33	4.20	2.00	3.50	2.00	3.00	3.60	4.17	4.17
9	297	5.00	4.00	5.29	3.00	2.20	3.13	5.00	3.67	3.50	3.00	4.00	5.50
10	76	2.67	2.50	2.86	3.00	4.20	1.38	3.25	1.67	3.50	3.80	3.17	4.17
11	4	4.33	4.00	3.71	4.00	4.00	3.38	3.88	3.67	4.00	3.40	3.83	4.83
12	50	3.33	2.00	2.00	3.67	3.00	1.13	4.25	1.17	3.50	4.00	2.50	4.50
13	79	2.33	3.50	2.86	3.33	4.20	3.13	5.25	2.83	3.75	4.00	3.50	5.67
14	221	2.00	4.50	2.86	2.00	3.60	5.25	3.88	5.00	4.50	3.60	5.00	4.17
15	264	5.33	4.00	4.00	2.67	3.40	2.63	3.13	3.83	3.00	1.40	3.17	6.33
16	78	5.33	2.50	3.00	4.00	5.40	4.25	4.63	1.17	3.50	6.20	4.17	3.67
17	261	4.67	4.00	5.43	6.00	4.40	3.75	4.25	5.33	4.00	4.00	5.50	5.33
18	277	4.67	5.00	2.43	4.00	4.80	3.75	3.25	3.17	5.25	2.80	2.33	3.33
19	235	2.33	3.50	5.14	2.67	3.20	3.38	4.00	3.83	5.25	2.00	4.33	5.83
20	13	4.33	4.00	2.43	6.67	3.80	3.00	3.63	1.00	6.00	4.80	2.83	4.67
21	57	5.33	2.00	1.43	3.00	4.40	2.25	2.63	2.67	5.00	2.40	1.83	2.17
22	224	2.33	3.00	1.29	2.33	3.20	3.50	2.38	1.33	2.25	3.40	3.17	3.67
23	148	4.33	3.50	2.57	2.33	3.40	2.13	3.63	2.33	4.25	3.00	2.67	5.00
24	266	5.67	3.00	2.57	2.33	4.00	2.13	2.75	2.00	3.00	3.20	2.67	1.83
25	234	7.00	1.00	2.00	2.67	2.80	3.38	4.88	3.17	3.50	2.60	3.83	2.83
26	285	3.00	4.50	3.57	1.67	3.40	3.00	4.38	3.67	5.00	1.80	1.83	5.67
27	296	4.33	4.50	4.57	3.67	3.40	3.00	4.00	3.00	4.50	3.00	3.83	4.33
28	110	4.00	5.50	5.57	3.00	4.00	4.00	4.50	4.00	6.00	1.80	4.67	5.17
29	308	3.67	4.50	5.71	1.33	2.40	1.38	4.50	2.00	4.50	1.40	5.00	5.83
30	135	7.00	5.50	3.43	1.00	3.80	1.63	2.50	1.33	2.50	3.40	3.50	4.33

Frequency tables and graphs

The calculation of frequency tables is on one hand useful in order to quickly be able to obtain a descriptive idea of the dataset you are working with, and on the other hand to determine, for example, whether or not the distribution male/female in the sample corresponds proportionally to the population data. It is also an excellent tool for performing 'data cleaning'. This essentially means that the user must find out if any erroneous (impossible) data have been entered. Sometimes when the user types in scores on a 7-point scale for example, instead of pressing a number once, this is accidentally done twice, and for example '33' would be entered instead of '3'. It goes without saying that further analysis (for example, the calculation of the mean) is then performed on erroneous data and this can distort the entire analysis. For this reason, we cannot emphasize the importance of the process of data cleaning strongly enough. It is therefore always advisable to create a frequency table for each variable and to check this for the presence of 'unexpected' values.

As was mentioned in the description of the dataset, three age groups were surveyed in the example. Suppose the researcher would like to know how many people were surveyed in each of these groups. In order to be able to answer this, a frequency table must be created.

Figure 2.2

SPSS Data Editor — seniors.sav [DataSet1], with the menu path Analyze → Descriptive Statistics → Frequencies... open.

	respnr	conv					prest	price	primav	priqua	risk	sale	value
1	60	4.6					3.75	4.25	5.33	4.00	4.00	5.50	6.00
2	45	3.0					2.88	2.88	1.33	3.75	5.40	4.50	5.50
3	36	6.6					4.75	6.00	1.17	4.50	2.80	5.00	5.83
4	47	2.0					2.88	3.00	1.00	3.25	5.80	2.33	3.00
5	30	3.6			2.67	4.40	1.25	4.25	2.17	2.25	4.00	3.50	3.83
6	144	3.3			1.33	3.60	3.13	4.25	3.67	3.75	2.00	4.67	4.83
7	238	5.0			2.00	2.20	5.38	2.63	1.67	7.00	2.20	3.83	4.83
8	280	2.6			1.33	4.20	2.00	3.50	2.00	3.00	3.60	4.17	4.17
9	297	5.0			3.00	2.20	3.13	5.00	3.67	3.50	3.00	4.00	5.50
10	76	2.6			3.00	4.20	1.38	3.25	1.67	3.50	3.80	3.17	4.17
11	4	4.3			4.00	4.00	3.38	3.88	3.67	4.00	3.40	3.83	4.83
12	50	3.3			3.67	3.00	1.13	4.25	1.17	3.50	4.00	2.50	4.50
13	79	2.3			3.33	4.20	3.13	5.25	2.83	3.75	4.00	3.50	5.67
14	221	2.0			2.00	3.60	5.25	3.88	5.00	4.50	3.60	5.00	4.17
15	284	5.3			2.67	3.40	2.63	3.13	3.83	3.00	1.40	3.17	6.33
16	78	5.33	2.50	3.00	4.00	5.40	4.25	4.63	1.17	3.50	6.20	4.17	3.67
17	261	4.67	4.00	5.43	6.00	4.40	3.75	4.25	5.33	4.00	4.00	5.50	5.33
18	277	4.67	5.00	2.43	4.00	4.80	3.75	3.25	3.17	5.25	2.80	2.33	3.33
19	235	2.33	3.50	5.14	2.67	3.20	3.38	4.00	3.83	5.25	2.00	4.33	5.83
20	13	4.33	4.00	2.43	6.67	3.80	3.00	3.63	1.00	6.00	4.80	2.83	4.67
21	57	5.33	2.00	1.43	3.00	4.40	2.25	2.63	2.67	5.00	2.40	1.83	2.17
22	224	2.33	3.00	1.29	2.33	3.20	3.50	2.38	1.33	2.25	3.40	3.17	3.67
23	148	4.33	3.50	2.57	2.33	3.40	2.13	3.63	2.33	4.25	3.00	2.67	5.00
24	286	5.67	3.00	2.57	2.33	4.00	2.13	2.75	2.00	3.00	3.20	2.67	1.83
25	234	7.00	1.00	2.00	2.67	2.80	3.38	4.88	3.17	3.50	2.60	3.83	2.83
26	285	3.00	4.50	3.57	1.67	3.40	3.00	4.38	3.67	5.00	1.80	1.83	5.67
27	296	4.33	4.50	4.57	3.67	3.40	3.00	4.00	3.00	4.50	3.00	3.83	4.33
28	110	4.00	5.50	5.57	3.00	4.00	4.00	4.50	4.00	6.00	1.80	4.67	5.17
29	308	3.67	4.50	5.71	1.33	2.40	1.38	4.50	2.00	4.50	1.40	5.00	5.83
30	135	7.00	5.50	3.43	1.00	3.80	1.63	2.50	1.33	2.50	3.50	4.33	

Visible: 29 of 29 Variabl

Go to: Analyze/Descriptive Statistics/Frequencies (Figure 2.2).

Figure 2.3

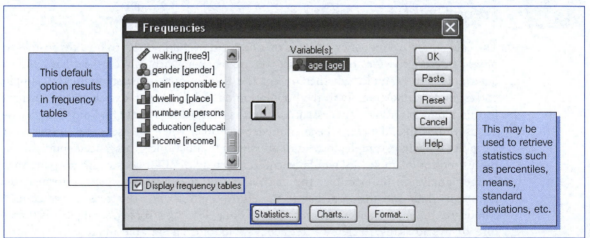

This default option results in frequency tables — points to "Display frequency tables".

This may be used to retrieve statistics such as percentiles, means, standard deviations, etc. — points to "Statistics...".

Click on 'age' and then on ▶, and then click 'OK'. The researcher can select multiple variables at the same time, for example by holding down the 'CTRL' key (for non-sequential variables) or the 'Shift' key (for sequential variables), while indicating the variables. Sequential variables may also be clicked and dragged using the mouse.

The output is obtained in the output window (Figure 2.4).

Figure 2.4

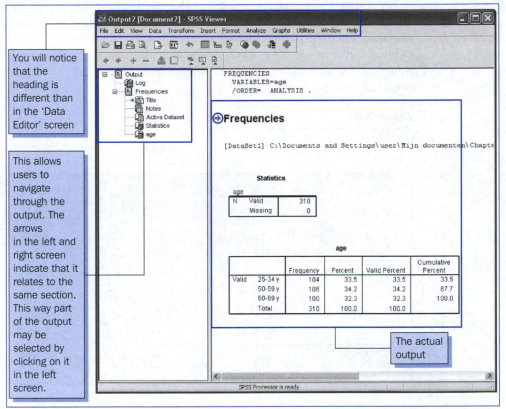

You will notice that the heading is different than in the 'Data Editor' screen

This allows users to navigate through the output. The arrows in the left and right screen indicate that it relates to the same section. This way part of the output may be selected by clicking on it in the left screen.

The actual output

In the further output discussions, only the output in the right subscreen will be shown. If you want to alternate between the 'Output' and the 'Data Editor' windows, you can do this using the Windows toolbar.

The output in the right screen in Figure 2.4 is recaptured in Figure 2.5.

Figure 2.5

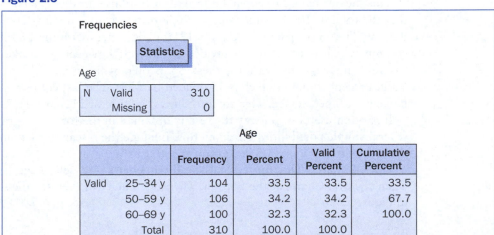

Frequencies

Statistics

Age

N	Valid	310
	Missing	0

Age

		Frequency	Percent	Valid Percent	Cumulative Percent
Valid	25–34 y	104	33.5	33.5	33.5
	50–59 y	106	34.2	34.2	67.7
	60–69 y	100	32.3	32.3	100.0
	Total	310	100.0	100.0	

As you can see, SPSS has considered 310 observations to be valid, because there were no 'missing values' found in any of the observations. Furthermore, it may be determined that 104 '25–34 year olds,' 106 '50–59 year olds,' and 100 '60–69 year olds' were surveyed.

Several percentages have also been calculated. The difference between 'Percent' and 'Valid Percent' is that with the former, missing values are also viewed as being part of the total while the percentages which are shown in the column 'Valid Percent' are calculated for all of the observations which do not contain missing values. In order to illustrate this difference, the frequency table in Figure 2.6 is shown for the variable 'income' from the same study.

Figure 2.6

Income

		Frequency	Percent	Valid Percent	Cumulative Percent
Valid	<1250 EUR	55	17.7	19.7	19.7
	1250–1875 EUR	60	19.4	21.5	41.2
	1876–2500 EUR	54	17.4	19.4	60.6
	2501–3750 EUR	47	15.2	16.8	77.4
	>3750 EUR	10	3.2	3.6	81.0
	I prefer not to answer	53	17.1	19.0	100.0
	Total	279	90.0	100.0	
Missing	99.00	31	10.0		
Total		310	100.0		

Given the fact that this is fairly personal information that people are not generally quick to disclose, a number of missing values may be expected here (even in the event that the additional option 'I do not wish to answer this' is offered in the questionnaire). In fact, it appears that there were 31 respondents in the total dataset (= 10%) who did not fill in an answer (these 'missings' were coded as '99').

This means that 279 people did provide a response. In the 'Percent' column, we see that the total of 100% is made up of 90% respondents who answered and 10% who did not. The 55 people in the class '<1250 EUR' agrees with the 17.7% in the Percent column which is equal to 55 divided by 310. If however we make an abstraction from the missing observations, these 55 people will agree with the 19.7% in the Valid Percent column (which is 55 divided by 279). The last column shows the cumulative (valid) percentage. This column shows the sum of 21.5 and 19.7, or 41.2.

It is often useful to portray the results obtained in the form of a graph. SPSS offers several simple possibilities for doing this. Imagine the researcher would like to display the results from Figure 2.5 in a graph as well.

Go to Analyze/Descriptive Statistics/Frequencies and select age (see Figure 2.3). Then click on Charts at the bottom. The researcher will then see the screen as shown in Figure 2.7.

Figure 2.7

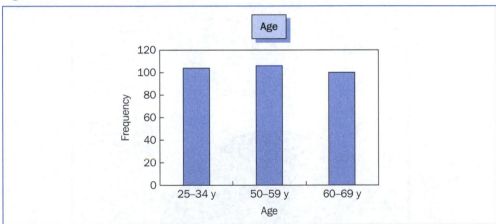

Change the default setting under 'Chart Type' from 'None (no graphs)' into 'Bar Charts'. Now click on 'Continue' and then 'OK' (in the main window). The researcher will then see a bar chart like the one shown in Figure 2.8.

Figure 2.8

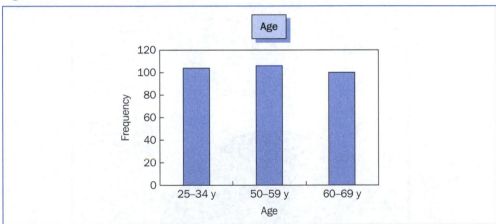

These figures may be illustrated in other ways as well. This is demonstrated here using a pie chart (Figure 2.9) for the education variable. Follow the steps again as described for the creation of a bar chart, but this time indicate 'Pie charts' in the window in Figure 2.7. Once this graph has been created (Figure 2.9) in the output window, you may adjust and revise it by double-clicking on the graph. You will now see an image such as that displayed in Figure 2.10.

Figure 2.9

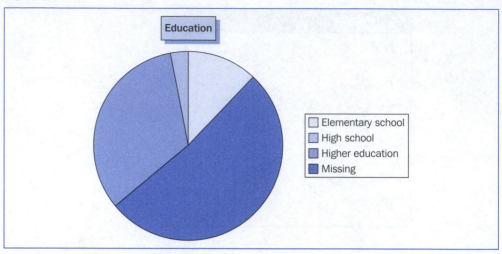

Figure 2.10

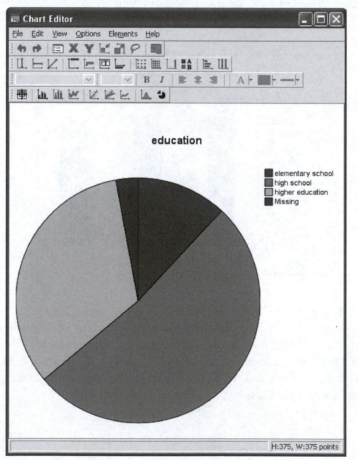

Continue now with Elements/Show Data Labels (Figure 2.11).

Figure 2.11

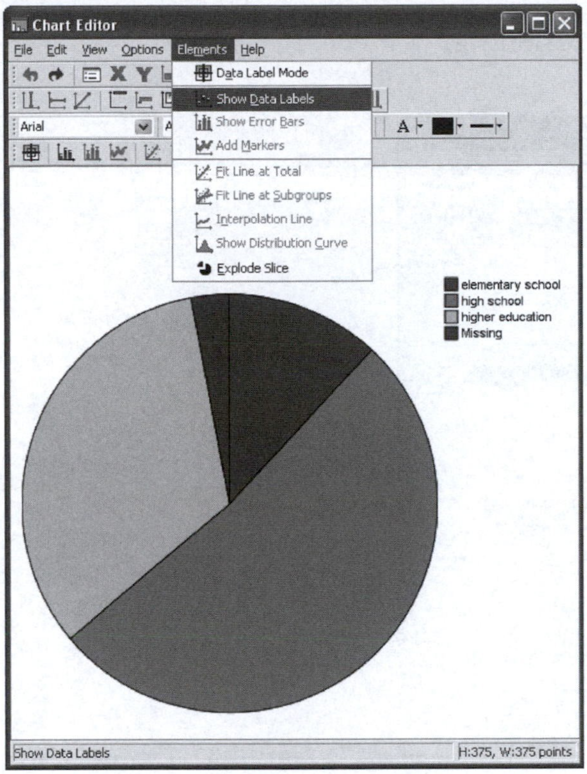

You will now see a window such as that shown in Figure 2.12.

Figure 2.12

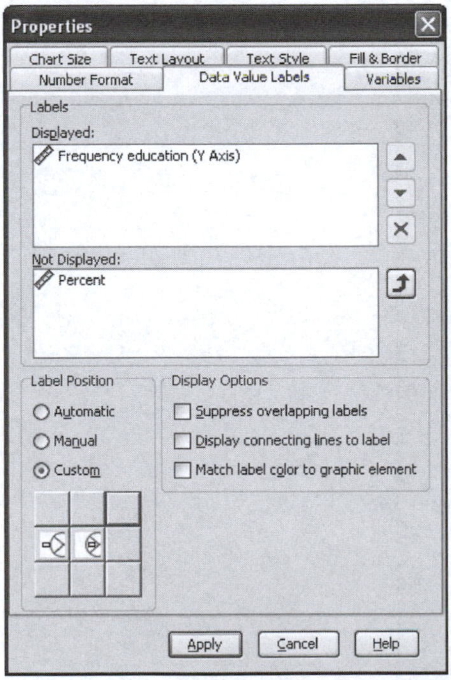

If you want to see percentages in the graph as well as a reference to the different types of education, you must select 'Percent' and move this to the 'Displayed' box by clicking on the green arrow (Figure 2.13).

Figure 2.13

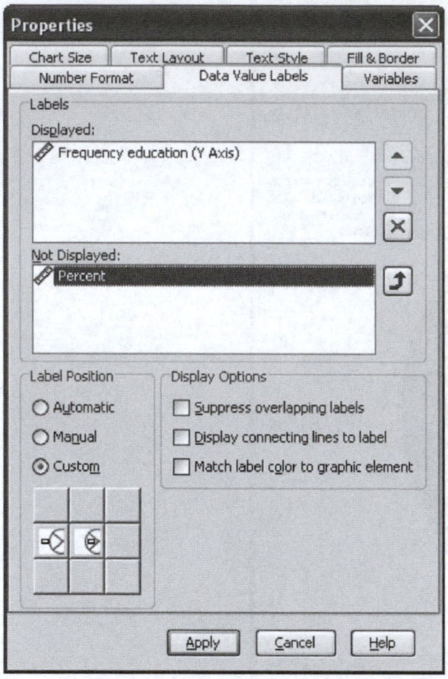

It is not desirable to see a display of the frequency of the responses here. For this reason, the option 'Frequency education' must be selected and moved to the 'Not Displayed' box using the red cross (Figure 2.14).

Figure 2.14

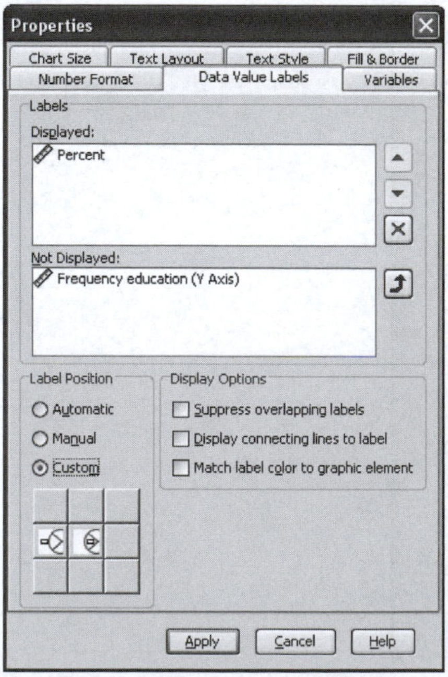

You will now see a pie chart with four pie pieces, which are actually the three types of education plus the portion with the missing values (Figure 2.15).

Figure 2.15

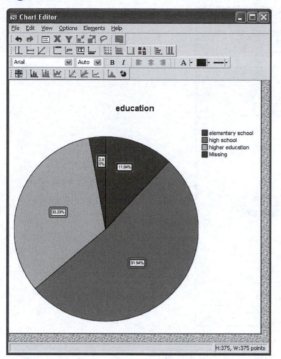

If the researcher prefers to remove this last part from the graph, he must do the following. Double click on the Chart which will cause the 'Properties' window to appear (Figure 2.16).

Figure 2.16

Go to the subscreen 'Categories', select 'Missing' and move this with the red cross to the 'Excluded' box (Figure 2.17).

Figure 2.17

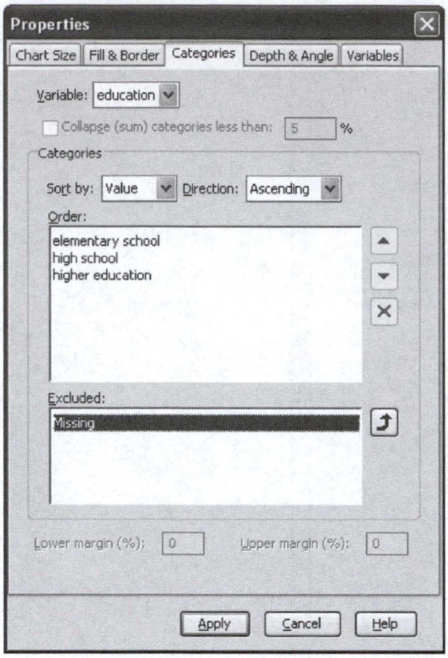

Click on 'Apply' and Figure 2.18 will appear.

Figure 2.18

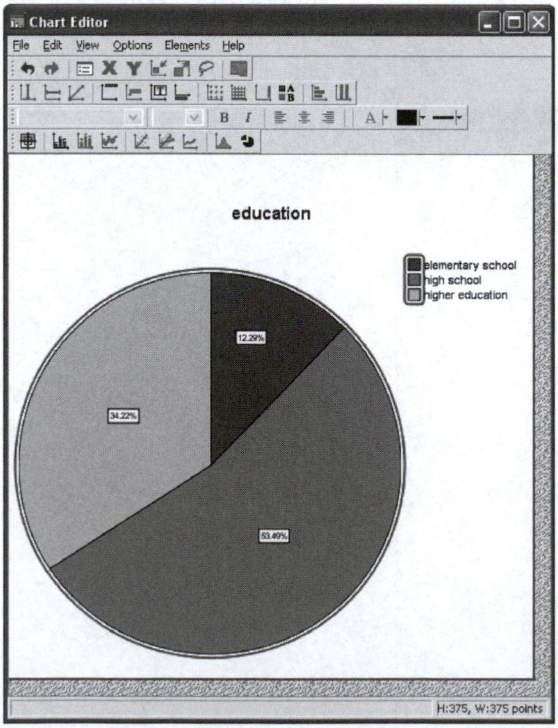

You will notice that only the three educational levels are shown, from which it appears that people with a secondary education comprise just over half of the respondents who were prepared to indicate their level of education on the survey.

Figure 2.7 also includes the option 'Histograms' with the option 'With normal curve'. Just like a 'bar chart', a histogram is a way to display frequencies in graphic form. A 'Bar chart' will however show the number of observations for every observed possible response. This can lead to a potentially confusing situation. For example, when the 'importance of convenience' variable is examined, it becomes clear that nearly all of the observations have a different value. When an organised display and an idea of the distribution is the objective here, this may best be obtained by creating a histogram. The researcher must then check 'Histograms' for 'Chart type' (Figure 2.8). If he would also like to compare the distribution obtained with the normal distribution, the option 'with normal curve' must be indicated. For the variables (Figure 2.3), the user may choose 'importance of convenience' only. In Figure 2.19, the relevant histogram with normal distribution may be found.

Figure 2.19

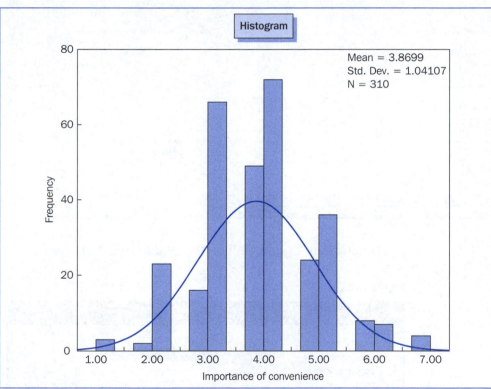

SPSS has created a number of groups itself and at first sight the distribution is not really normal (the frequencies which should be expected from the normal distribution (the curve) do not differ very much from the actual observed frequencies). If you would like to change the number of groups, just double-click on the X-axis.

Statistical tests which formally test this graphic assumption are for example the Kolmogorov-Smirnov test (with Lilliefors correction) and the Shapiro-Wilk W test. Although univariate tests form the subject of the subsequent chapters, the normality test will be treated here.

Go to Analyze/Descriptive Statistics/Explore (Figure 2.20)

Figure 2.20

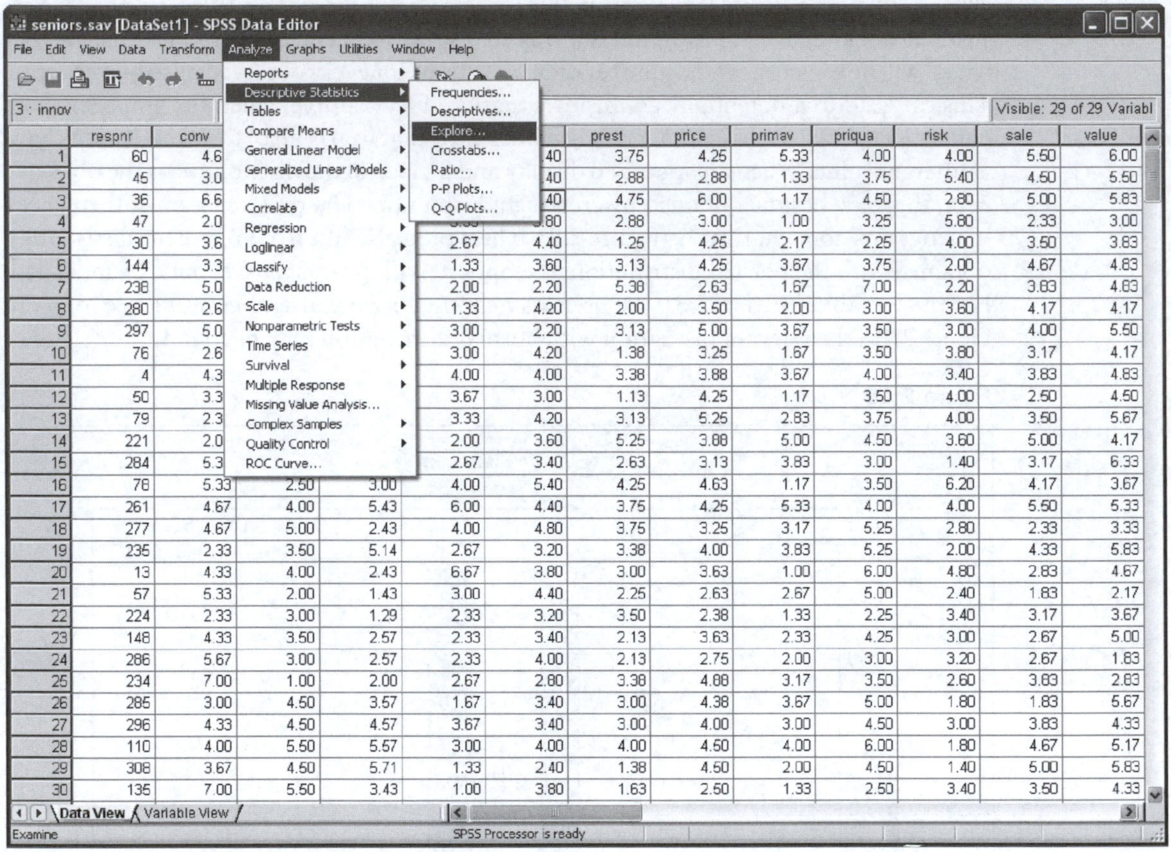

The subscreen 'Explore' will be displayed (Figure 2.21).

Figure 2.21

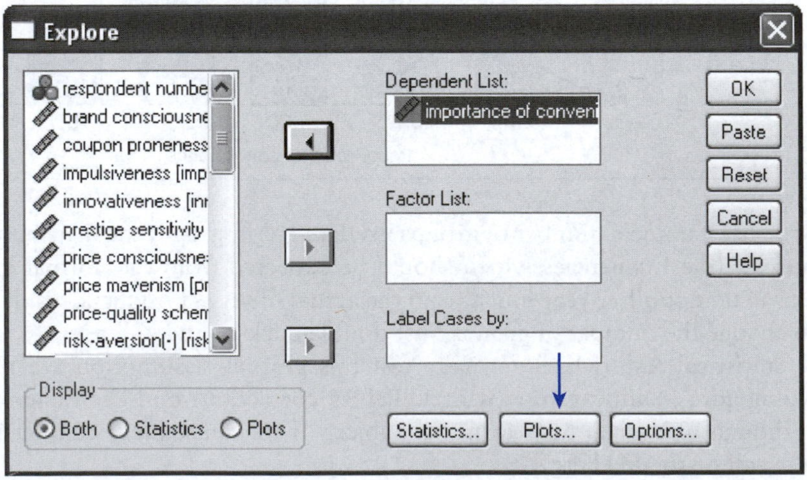

Move the 'importance of convenience' variable to the 'Dependent List'. Next, click on 'Plots' and check the 'Normality plots with tests' option on the next subscreen (Figure 2.22).

Figure 2.22

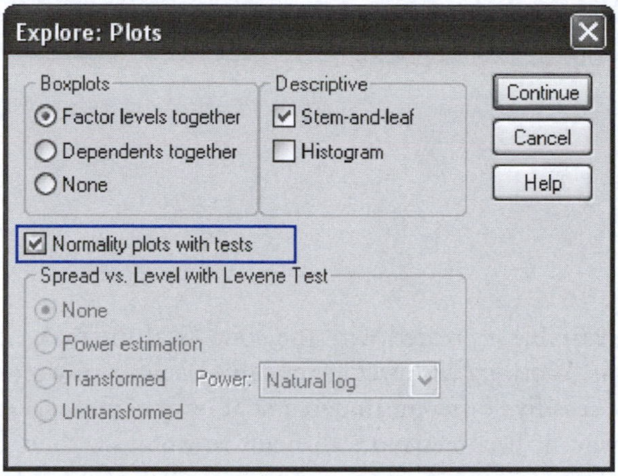

Click on 'Continue' and then 'OK'.

The null hypothesis to be tested is that the data are normally distributed. Figure 2.23 shows the selected output of the normality tests.

Figure 2.23

	Kolmogorov-Smirnov[a]			Shapiro-Wilk		
	Statistic	df	Sig.	Statistic	df	Sig.
Importance of convenience	.102	310	.000	.985	310	.003

Tests of Normality

[a]Lilliefors Significance Correction

In the Kolmogorov-Smirnov test (with Lilliefors correction) as well as in the Shapiro-Wilk test, under 'Sig.', it must be determined if the null hypothesis for normality should be rejected or not. This appears to be the case with both tests, since both significance levels (respectively <.001 and .003) are less than .05. The 'importance of convenience' variable is therefore not normally distributed. The previously mentioned deviation from normality on the basis of the graphic output is therefore statistically confirmed. The performance of these types of normality tests is certainly relevant. As we will see in the upcoming chapters, the normal distribution of (obtained) variables can sometimes be an underlying assumption in the technique used.

The Lilliefors correction relates to the fact that the standard Kolmogorov-Smirnov test assumes an a priori known mean and a standard deviation (which is not the case for example with a sample involving an estimate). This is why a correction must be made which is automatically generated by SPSS. Recently, there has been evidence of a marked preference for the Shapiro Wilk's W test because this test possesses better statistical properties (more power).

Multiple response tables

In questionnaires, one often sees a question for which there is more than one response. Take the following question, for example:

Below you will find a number of car brands. Please indicate which brand you find attractive (more than one answer is possible).

- BMW
- Opel
- Mercedes
- Ford
- Renault

For each brand, a variable is created with the code '0' if the make is not indicated, and '1' in the event it is. Working with frequency tables is not really recommended here because the user then sees five different (independent of one another) frequency distributions and in this way, it becomes more difficult to obtain a total overview of the choices of car make. This is possible using the 'Multiple Response' option.

Suppose that the above question on make is answered by 20 respondents. The responses obtained may be found in the data file *car makes.sav*. This file is illustrated in Figure 2.24.

Figure 2.24

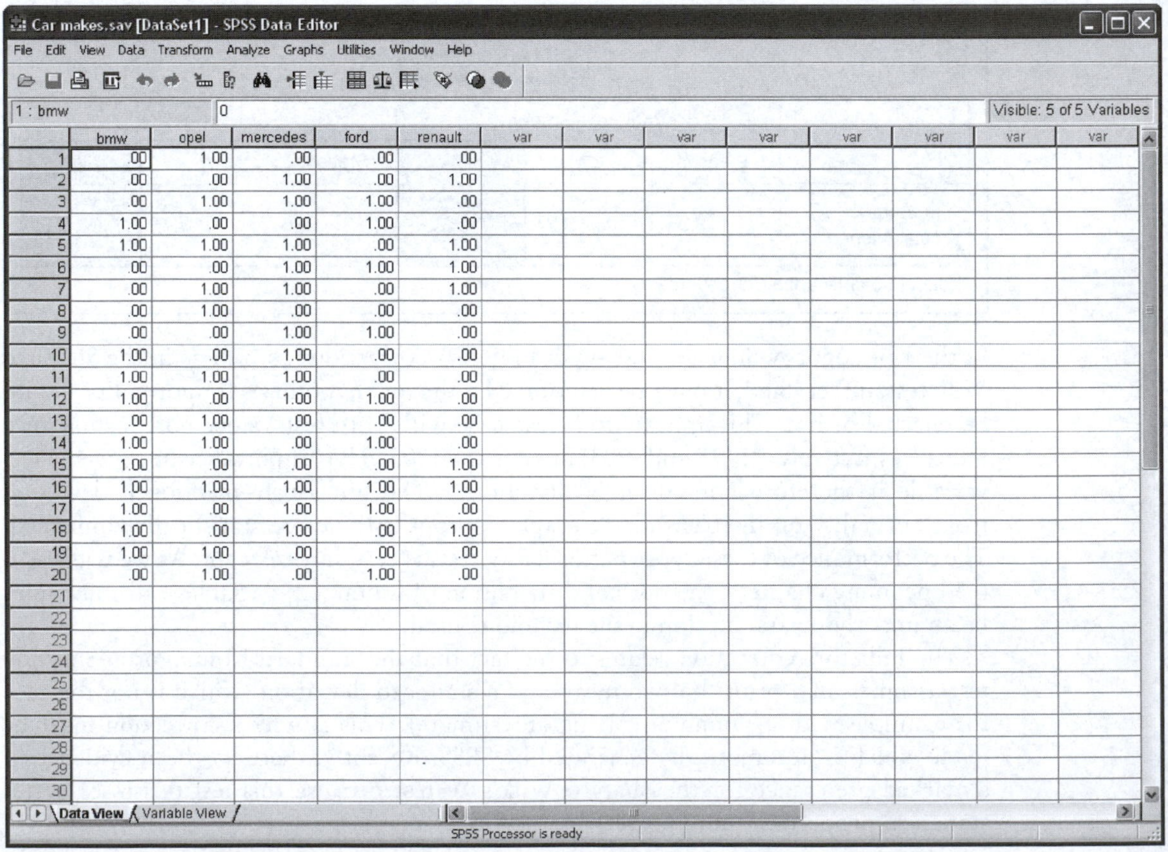

	bmw	opel	mercedes	ford	renault
1	.00	1.00	.00	.00	.00
2	.00	.00	1.00	.00	1.00
3	.00	1.00	1.00	1.00	.00
4	1.00	.00	.00	1.00	.00
5	1.00	1.00	1.00	.00	1.00
6	.00	.00	1.00	1.00	1.00
7	.00	1.00	1.00	.00	1.00
8	.00	1.00	.00	.00	.00
9	.00	.00	1.00	1.00	.00
10	1.00	.00	1.00	.00	.00
11	1.00	1.00	1.00	.00	.00
12	1.00	.00	1.00	1.00	.00
13	.00	1.00	.00	.00	.00
14	1.00	1.00	.00	1.00	.00
15	1.00	.00	.00	.00	1.00
16	1.00	1.00	1.00	1.00	1.00
17	1.00	.00	1.00	1.00	.00
18	1.00	.00	1.00	.00	1.00
19	1.00	1.00	.00	.00	.00
20	.00	1.00	.00	1.00	.00

For a 'Multiple Response' analysis, the five variables must be defined as one group.

Figure 2.25

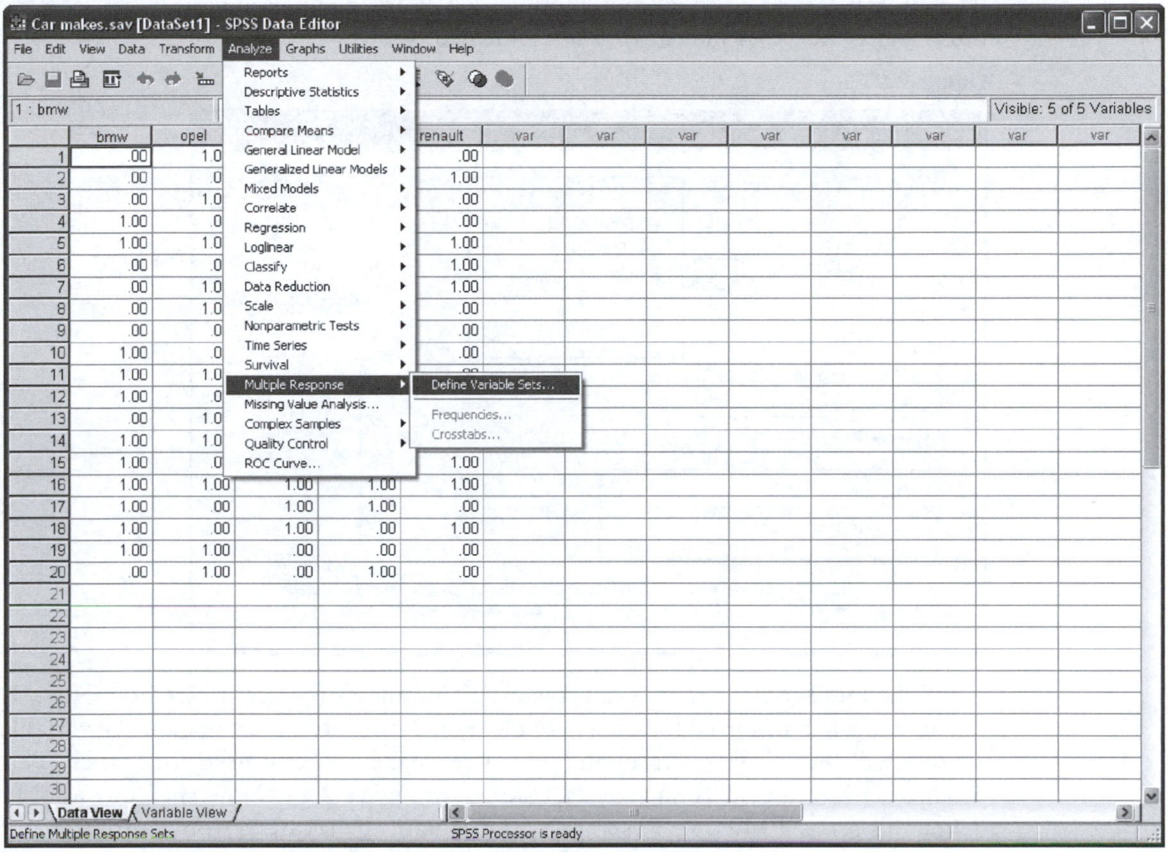

Go to Analyze/Multiple Response/Define Variable Sets (see Figure 2.25). This results in the dialogue window shown in Figure 2.26.

Figure 2.26

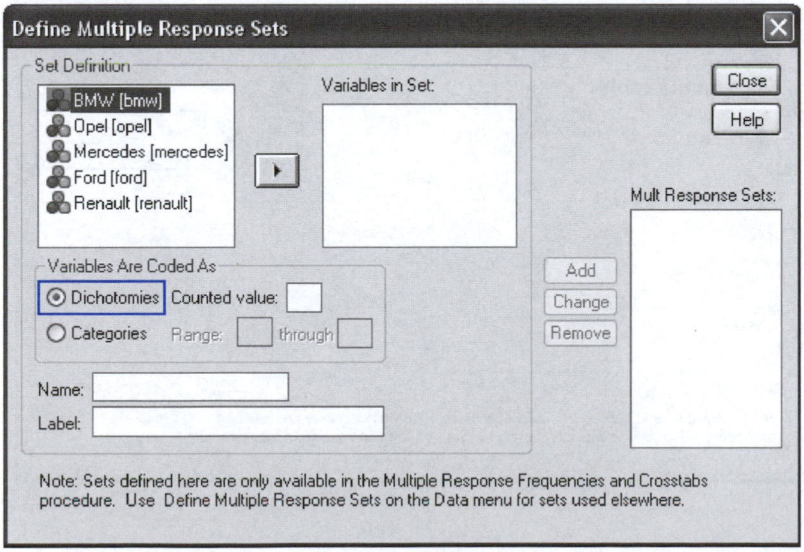

The five brands are shown in the 'Set Definition' screen. Select these and move them to the 'Variables in Set' window. For 'Variables Are Coded As', make sure that 'Dichotomies' is indicated. Dichotomous variables are in fact used here, which is to say those which are either indicated or not indicated.

Figure 2.27

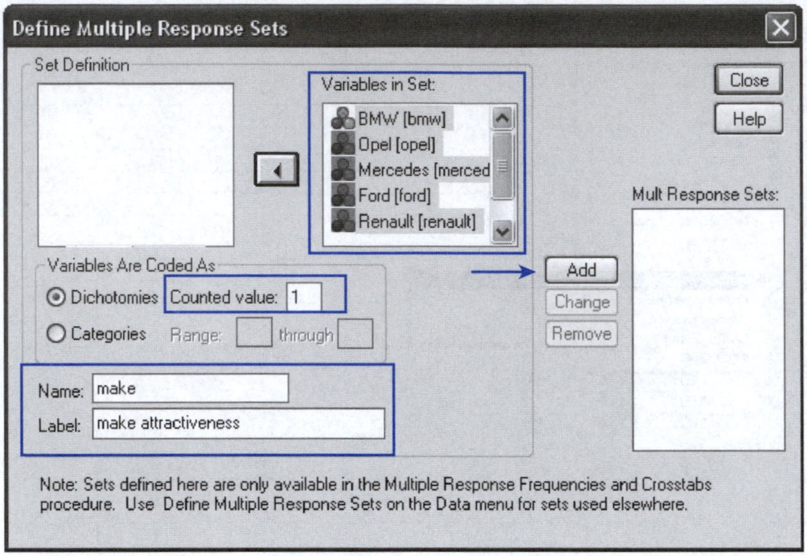

Fill the number '1' in for 'Counted value'. This allows the user to see how often '1' (make indicated) occurred for each variable. For 'Name', fill in a name for the variable set selected ('make' in this case) and the name 'make attractiveness' for 'Label'. This produces a screen display such as that shown in Figure 2.27. Now click on 'Add' to define this set as a Multiple Response set (automatically set by SPSS by putting '$' for the set name ($make), see Figure 2.28). Then click on 'Close'.

Figure 2.28

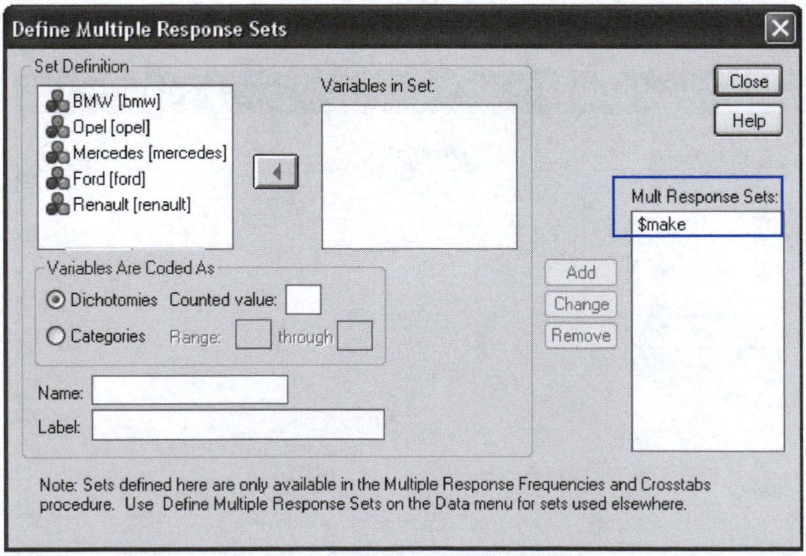

In order to now show the frequency distribution of the group of variables, the following steps must be taken. Go to Analyze/Multiple Response/Frequencies (Figure 2.25).

Figure 2.29

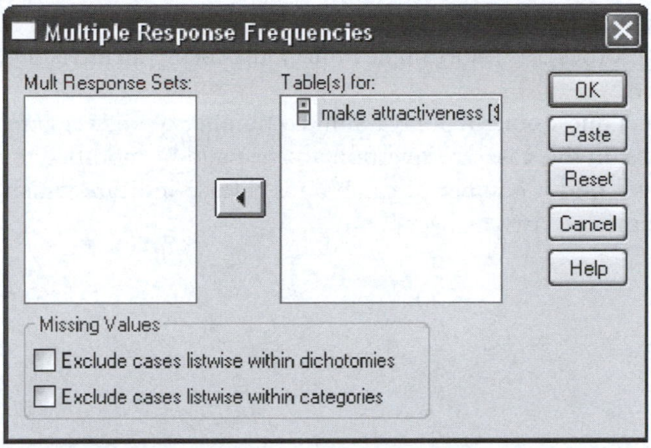

Move the set 'make attractiveness' from the 'Multiple Responses Set' window to the 'Table(s) for:' window so that the screen looks like Figure 2.29. Now click on 'OK'. The output will appear as shown in Figure 2.30.

Figure 2.30

Case Summary

| | Cases | | | | | |
| | Valid | | Missing | | Total | |
	N	Percent	N	Percent	N	Percent
$make[a]	20	100.0%	0	.0%	20	100.0%

[a]Dichotomy group tabulated at value 1.

$make Frequencies

| | | Responses | | Percent of Cases |
		N	Percent	N
make attractiveness[a]	BMW	11	22.0%	55.0%
	Opel	11	22.0%	55.0%
	Mercedes	12	24.0%	60.0%
	Ford	9	18.0%	45.0%
	Renault	7	14.0%	35.0%
Total		50	100.0%	250.0%

[a]Dichotomy group tabulated at value 1.

The number 20 in the cell of 'valid cases' as shown in Figure 2.30 refers to the number of persons in the data set who had indicated a particular brand once (in the example this was the case with all twenty respondents). Of these 20, 11 (55%) indicated BMW (among others). The number '50' is shown in the cell of 'Total Responses'. This refers to the number of times that a make was indicated (the number of scores of '1' in the data set). Mercedes was for example indicated as being an attractive make 12 of the 50 times (24%).

Sometimes in a questionnaire, only a limited number of answers are permitted from the list of choices. In this case, the question above could be modified to read as follows:

Below you will find a number of car brands. Please indicate which make you find attractive (maximum of two answers).

- BMW (1)
- Opel (2)
- Mercedes (3)
- Ford (4)
- Renault (5)

In this case, only two variables must be created; here, 'choice1' and 'choice2'. The answers may be found under *car makes2.sav* (Figure 2.31). This means that for each variable, there is a value of 1 (BMW) through 5 (Renault) possible.

Figure 2.31

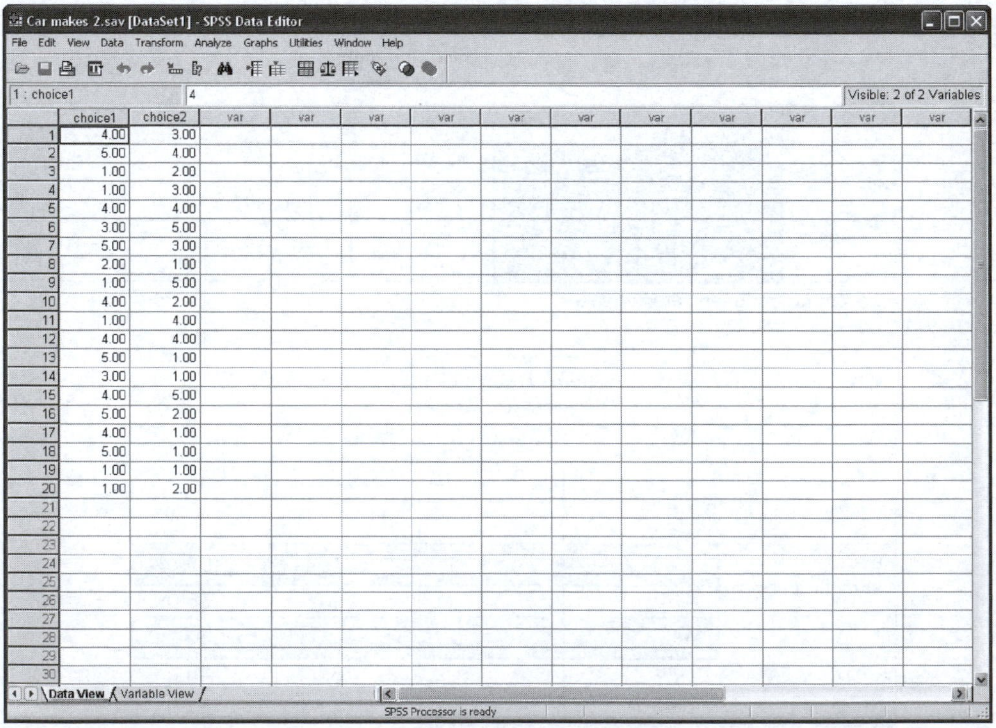

The procedure is analogous to the previous one, but instead of the five variables, now there are only two variables entered into a set. For the 'Variables Are Coded As' subscreen, the user must now indicate 'Categories' and a '1' for 'Range' and after 'through' the user must type '5'. This will produce an image such as the one shown in Figure 2.32.

Figure 2.32

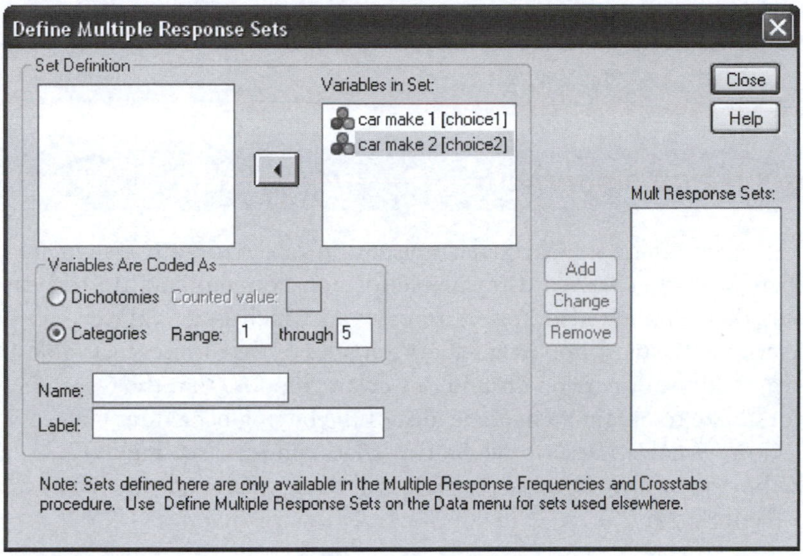

Now click on 'Add' and then 'Close'. Follow the rest of the procedure such as is described for Figure 2.29. The output is shown in Figure 2.33.

Figure 2.33

Case Summary

	Cases					
	Valid		Missing		Total	
	N	Percent	N	Percent	N	Percent
$make[a]	20	100.0%	0	.0%	20	100.0%

[a]Group

$make Frequencies

		Responses		Percent of Cases
		N	Percent	N
make attractiveness[a]	BMW	12	30.0%	60.0%
	Opel	5	12.5%	25.0%
	Mercedes	5	12.5%	25.0%
	Ford	10	25.0%	50.0%
	Renault	8	20.0%	40.0%
Total		40	100.0%	200.0%

[a]Group

Given the fact that all of the 20 respondents gave two answers, there are thus 40 answers in total. This does not have to be the case of course: someone may provide only one or even no answer at all. In the example, it appears that 60% of the respondents indicated BMW as being an attractive car. In 30% of the cases in which a car brand was indicated as being attractive, the answer provided was BMW.

Mean and dispersion

Frequency tables are particularly useful in order to gain insight into nominal data. There are better standards available for non-nominal data. In this case it is desirable (and this certainly also applies to cases in which large datasets are used) to quickly determine the most important characteristics of the different variables, for instance the mean and the dispersion around this mean. Suppose that the researcher in the example would like to obtain an average idea of the buying behaviour concepts.

Go to Analyze/Descriptive Statistics/Descriptives (see Figure 2.25) and select all of the buying behaviour concepts. You will then see a window such as the one illustrated in Figure 2.34.

Figure 2.34

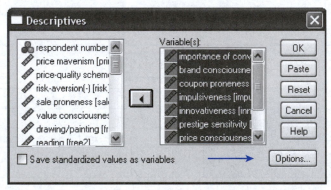

You will also notice the option at the bottom 'Save standardized values as variables'. Using this option, it is possible to standardize each variable selected, in other words, to subtract the mean value from every observation and to divide it by the standard deviation. A standardized variable always has a mean of 0 and a variance of 1. This can prove useful when two variables which have been measured on a different scale (for example, one variable is measured in milligrams and the other in kilometers) must be given an equal 'weight' in later analyses (for example a cluster analysis, Chapter 9). After standardization, the standardized variables may then be used (SPSS creates these and places a 'z' in front of the original variable name) instead of the original variables. An example of this type of standardization may be found in Chapter 7: Exploratory factor analysis.

The output may be adjusted by clicking on 'Options'.

Figure 2.35

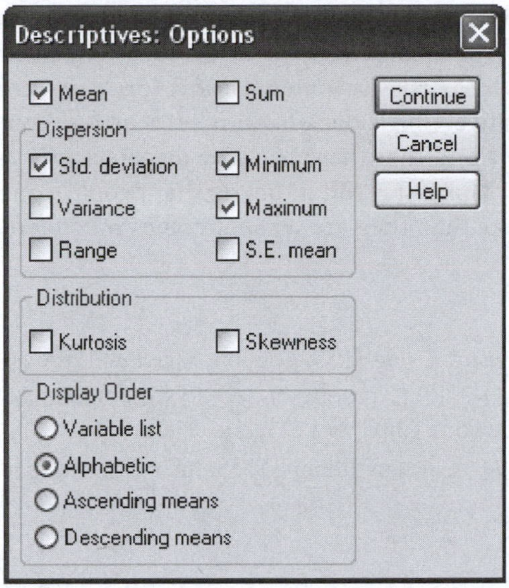

As Figure 2.35 indicates, the standard output consists of the mean value, the standard deviation, the minimum (lowest value) and the maximum (highest value). If you also indicate the option 'Alphabetic' in the 'Display Order' field, the output will be ranked in alphabetical order with regard to the buying behaviour concepts. Click on 'Continue' and then on 'OK'.

Figure 2.36

Descriptive Statistics

	N	Minimum	Maximum	Mean	Std. Deviation
brand consciousness	310	1.00	7.00	3.4500	1.17067
importance of convenience	310	1.00	7.00	3.8699	1.04107
coupon proneness	310	1.00	7.00	3.6768	1.42772
impulsiveness	310	1.00	6.67	3.0225	1.16624
innovativeness	310	1.00	6.60	3.6826	.90315
prestige sensitivity	310	1.00	6.88	2.7373	1.09947
price consciousness	310	1.00	6.88	3.9073	.95613
price mavenism	310	1.00	6.83	2.6298	1.15699
price-quality scheme	310	1.00	7.00	3.6694	1.35055
risk-aversion(–)	310	1.00	6.20	3.1942	1.13221
sale proneness	310	1.00	6.83	3.5799	1.17567
value consciousness	310	1.00	7.00	4.5495	1.19129
Valid N (listwise)	310				

The output will then be generated as it appears in Figure 2.36. Note that across the entire sample, the respondents apparently strive fairly strongly to achieve an optimal value-for-money relationship (value consciousness = 4.5495). The inclination to act as a source of information for third parties is somewhat low (price mavenism = 2.6298). You will also note that a relatively high dispersion is present for 'coupon proneness' (standard deviation = 1.4277) and that there is a low dispersion for 'innovativeness' (standard deviation = .9032). This last result indicates that people's opinions on 'innovativeness' are much more alike than they are when it comes to 'coupon proneness'.

Further reading

Field, A. (2005), *Discovering Statistics Using SPSS*. London: Sage Publications.

Green, S.B., Salkind, N.J. and Akey, T.M., (2000), *Using SPSS for Windows – Analyzing and understanding data,* 2nd ed. Englewood Cliffs, N.J.: Prentice Hall.

SPSS Base 13.0 Users Guide (2004), Chicago, Illinois: SPSS, Inc.

Chapter 3

Univariate tests

Chapter objectives

This chapter will help you to:

- Select univariate statistical tests on the basis of the measurement level of the variables and the number and nature of the samples
- Conduct χ^2 analyses and tests
- Set up a Binomial test
- Deal with different types of t-test
- Conduct ordinal tests such as the Wilcoxon test, the Mann-Whitney U test, Kruskal-Wallis test, and the Friedman test
- Use the McNemar test
- Get insight into the Cochran Q test and repeated measure analysis of variance

General

Interesting insight is often extracted from the descriptive analysis, however the question remains to what degree these results are statistically significant, or to what degree may they be attributed purely to coincidence? This may be determined with the aid of tests. This chapter discusses and illustrates several statistical tests. Part of this chapter will focus on the further discussion of the dataset *seniors.sav* (see Chapter 2 for a description of the data).

This chapter discusses univariate tests, which refers to a situation involving a single variable. When the effect of several independent variables on one or more dependent variables is investigated later on, this is referred to as a multivariate test. This type of test will be discussed in separate chapters. Table 3.1 provides an overview of the tests for nominal, ordinal and interval/ratio-scaled data as they will be discussed in this chapter. A further discussion of these techniques may be found in the references at the end of this chapter.

Table 3.1

Measurement level	One sample	Two samples		k Samples	
		Independent	Dependent	Independent	Dependent
Nominal	Binomial test (Z-test on proportion) χ^2	χ^2	McNemar	χ^2	Cochran Q
Ordinal	Kolmogorov-Smirnov	Mann-Whitney U	Wilcoxon	Kruskal-Wallis	Friedman
Interval or ratio	t-test Z-test	t-test Z-test	t-test for differences	Analysis of Variance	Repeated measures Analysis of Variance

One sample

Nominal variables: Binomial test (z-test for proportion)

The binomial test may be applied if one wishes to compare a certain sample proportion of a nominal variable with an assumed proportion. Suppose that in a Dutch study, the proportion of women in the sample was 69% (and thus 31% were men). The researcher would like to find out whether the percentage of women in the Belgian *seniors.sav* sample (via frequencies, one can determine that this is 64.8%), differs statistically significantly from this 69%. The following steps must then be taken.

Figure 3.1

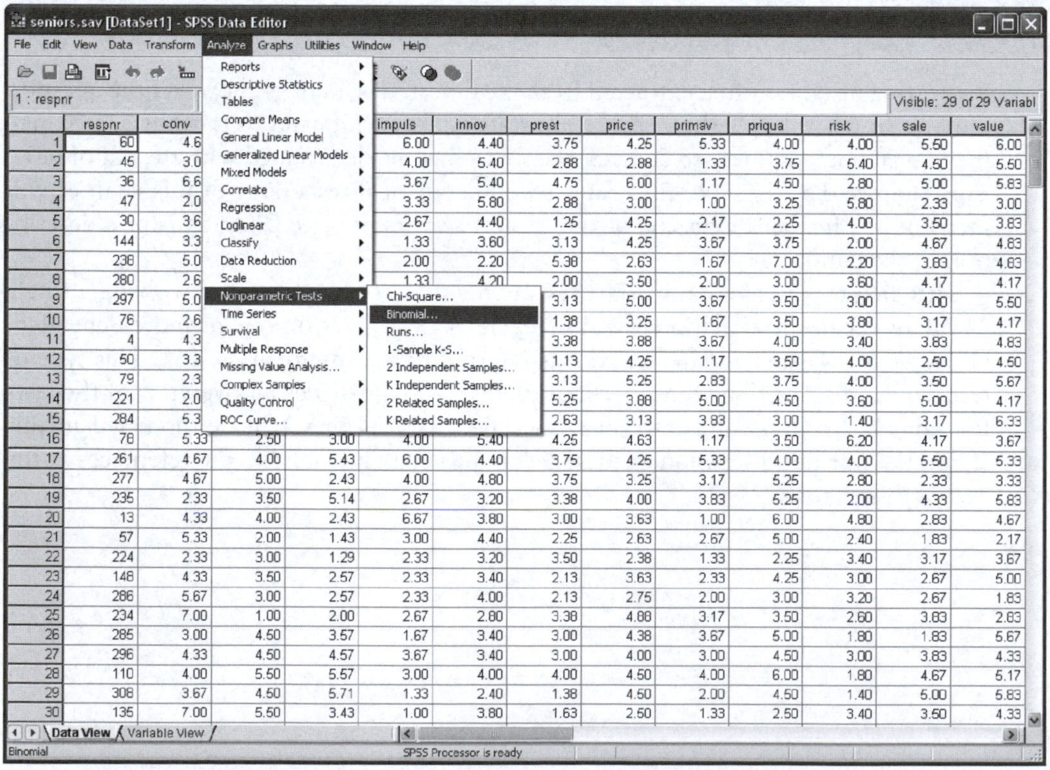

Go to Analyze/Nonparametric Tests/Binomial (Figure 3.1).

Figure 3.2

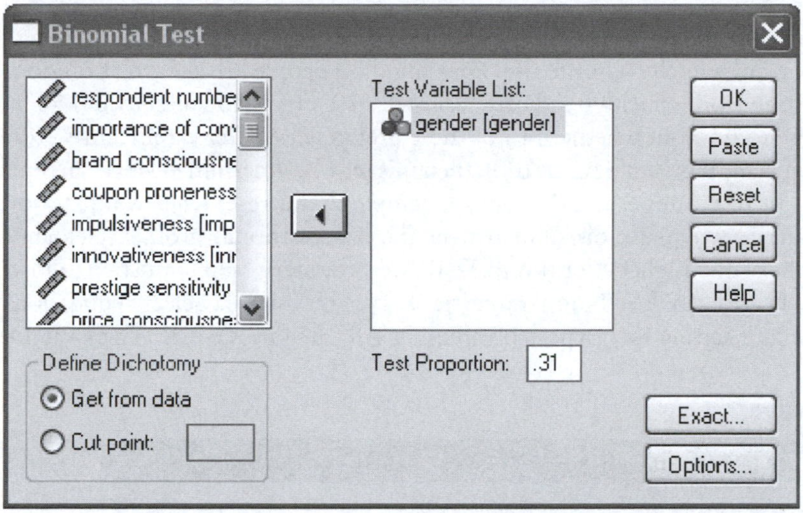

In the subscreen (Figure 3.2) select 'gender' and fill in the value '.31' for 'Test Proportion'. This test proportion refers to the proportion of the variable with which the value '0' (the first observation for the 'gender' variable in the data file) agrees (this is men in the example, so $1 - .69 = .31$). Click 'OK'.

Figure 3.3

Binomial Test

		Category	N	Observed Prop.	Test Prop.	Asymp. Sig. (1-tailed)
Gender	Group 1	Male	109	.35	.31	.065[a]
	Group 2	Female	201	.65		
	Total		310	1.00		

[a]Based on Z Approximation.

The output of this analysis may be found in Figure 3.3. This figure shows that the sample is composed of 35% men and 65% women. You will also note that the test proportion equals the 31% indicated. In hypothesis tests, a null hypothesis is first stated in advance (here: equal proportions). Under this null hypothesis, a distribution of the test statistic is determined with critical values. When the test statistic calculated exceeds this critical value or values, one can assume with a certain confidence that the test statistic calculated originates from another distribution than that used for the test statistic under the null hypothesis, meaning that the null hypothesis may be rejected. SPSS shows the significance level, or in other words, the probability that the calculated test statistic originates from the distribution under the null hypothesis. The number .05 is often used as the critical significance level. Because the significance level in this example is .065 and thus larger than .05, the null hypothesis of equal proportions may not be rejected at the 95% significance level. One may thus assert that the proportion of women in our Belgian sample does not differ significantly from those in the previous Dutch study.

Nominal variables: χ^2 test

Suppose that an automobile manufacturer plans to launch a new car on the market, but is not sure which colour to use. Four hundred people are chosen at random from the target group from which 90 indicate 'yellow', 120 'blue', 100 'green' and 90 'red'. If we would like to find out whether or not these preferences differ significantly from what could be expected a priori (4 times 100), then this may be determined via a Chi-square or goodness-of-fit test. Suppose in the senior example that a researcher wants to know whether the sample is equally distributed over the 3 educational groups (elementary school, high school and higher education). To do this, the steps below must be followed.

Go to Analyze/Nonparametric Tests/Chi-Square. Select 'education'. Note that the default setting for 'Expected values' is 'All categories equal'. Click on 'OK' (Figure 3.4).

Figure 3.4

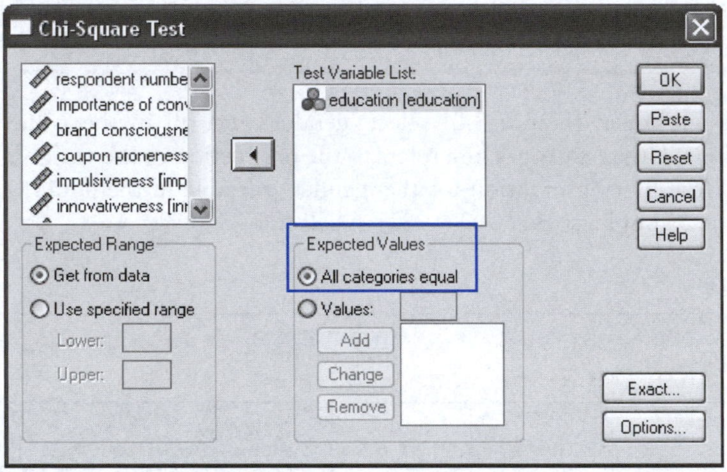

The following output is then obtained (Figure 3.5).

Figure 3.5

Education

	Observed N	Expected N	Residual
Elementary school	37	100.3	−63.3
High school	161	100.3	60.7
Higher education	103	100.3	2.7
Total	301		

Test Statistics

	Education
Chi-Square[a]	76.731
df	2
Asymp. sig.	.000

[a] 0 cells (.0%) have expected frequencies less than 5. The minimum expected cell frequency is 100.3.

You will note that of the 310 respondents, there were 9 who did not fill in an answer for this question, which means that the total number of valid respondents is 301. The frequency which may be expected per group is indeed 100.3 (=301/3). The null hypothesis that the three educational groups were interviewed uniformly is rejected here (sig. < .001). Persons who had a maximum of elementary school were for example clearly underrepresented (37 versus 100.3). The relevance of this test will be proven even further when it is used to determine whether the sample used is representative of the population with regard to certain socio-demographic variables, for example. Suppose that, with regard to their education, the approximately 5 million people in the total population may be broken down into 1.3 million with a maximum of an elementary school education, 2.7 million with a high school education and 1 million which have completed a programme in higher education. The researcher now wishes to determine whether the sample is representative for the total population with regard to educational level. The method is analogous to the previous one used (see Figure 3.4) with the difference that for 'Expected Values,' the user indicates his own expected frequencies (Figure 3.6).

Figure 3.6

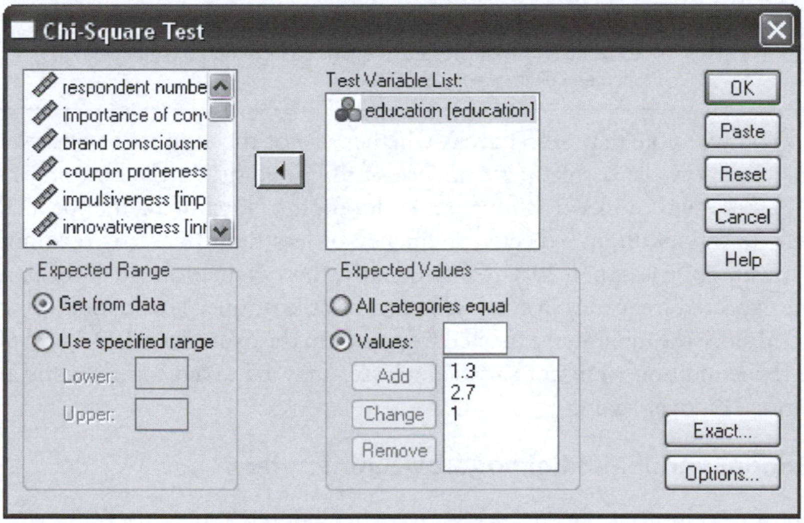

Under 'Expected Values', check the box for 'Values'. Next, input the relevant value and click on 'Add'. If the researcher were to input more than three values (thus more than the three educational groups), SPSS would display an error message in the output and fail to calculate the test statistic.

An output such as the one shown in Figure 3.7 is then obtained.

As one can see in Figure 3.7, SPSS calculates (rescaled on the basis of the sample) the expected number of respondents itself (e.g., 78.3 = (1.3/5)* 301). Since the null hypothesis (sample respondents are distributed over the different educational levels on the basis of the actual situation in the population) must be rejected (sig. <.001), it must be determined that the sample drawn is not representative for the population with regard to educational level (too few people interviewed with a maximum of an elementary school diploma and too many people with a higher education diploma). This conclusion does not necessarily have to be considered negative if in fact the priority in the study was to interview three specific age groups of equal size (as indeed was the case in the study).

Figure 3.7

NPar Tests
Chi-Square Test
Frequencies

Education

	Observed N	Expected N	Residual
Elementary school	37	78.3	−41.3
High school	161	162.5	−1.5
Higher education	103	60.2	42.8
Total	301		

Test Statistics

	Education
Chi-Square[a]	52.197
df	2
Asymp. sig.	.000

[a]0 cells (.0%) have expected frequencies less than 5. The minimum expected cell frequency is 60.2.

You will note that SPSS checks whether or not the number of observations is satisfactory to allow the correct performance of this analysis. At the bottom of Figures 3.5 and 3.7, these two checks are shown under footnote a. First of all, it appears that there are no cells (=0%) with an expected frequency of less than five. It is recommended that this percentage be less than 20%. Consequently, there is no problem in the example. Secondly, the expected frequency in every cell must be at least one. This condition has also been satisfied since the minimum expected frequency in the example is 100.3 and 60.2 respectively. If this condition were not satisfied, classes may be taken together and the analysis performed all over again.

Ordinal variables: Kolmogorov-Smirnov test

For an example applied to normality, see Chapter 2, pp. 35–37.

Interval scaled variables: Z-test or t-test for the mean

Z-tests are actually identical to t-tests, with the exception that a known variance is assumed for the former which is then also used in the test statistic to be calculated. Usually the variance (of the variables) is not known in advance, for which reason t-tests are usually the ones which will have to be used.

Suppose that a similar study of buying behaviour of seniors had already been conducted in the Netherlands. For the age group of 60–69 year olds, buying behaviour concepts were also measured there. The Dutch average score for 'value consciousness (aiming for an optimal value-for-money relationship)' was 3.8. The researcher would now like to know what the Belgian score was for similar seniors and whether or not this deviates significantly from the Dutch average. The first step is of course the selection of the 60–69 year olds (see Chapter 1). The following steps must then be taken:

Figure 3.8

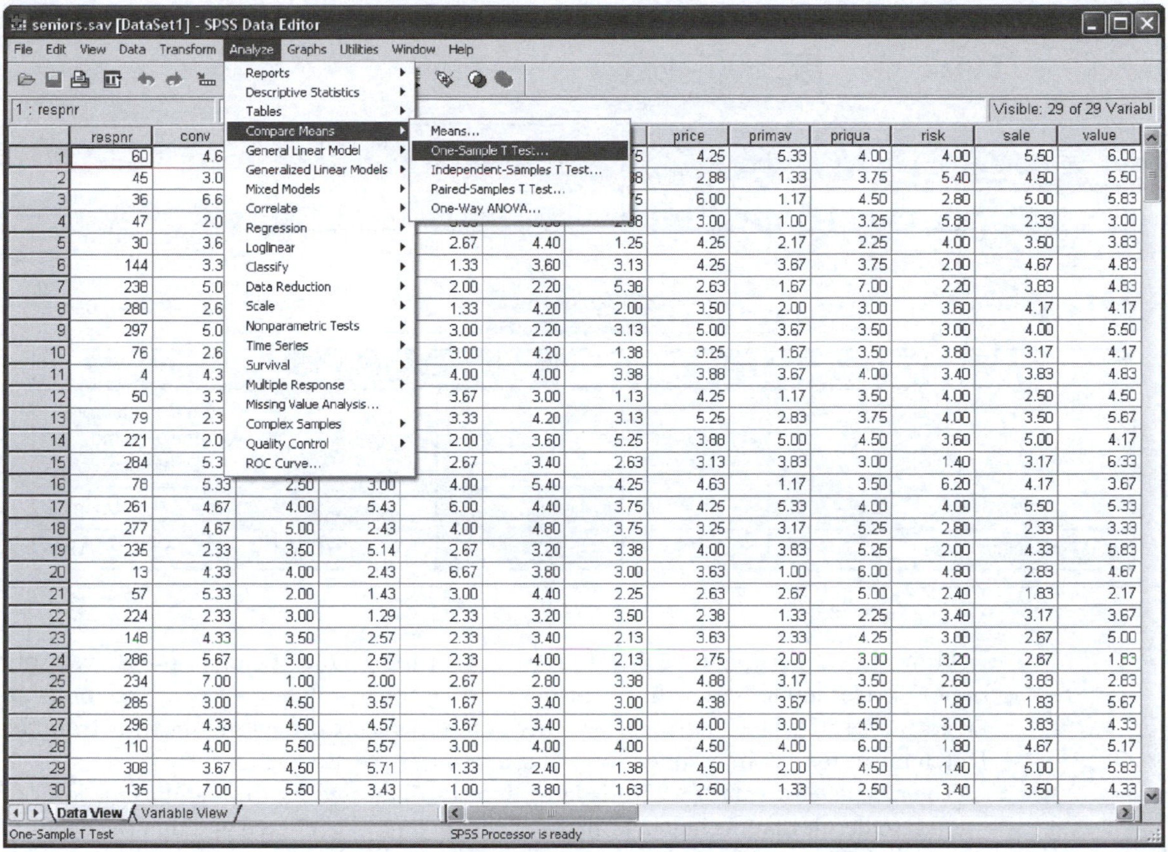

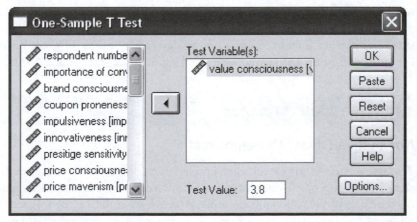

Go to Analyze/Compare Means/One Sample T-Test (Figure 3.8).

Figure 3.9

On the subscreen shown in Figure 3.9 select 'value consciousness' and for 'Test Value', fill in the reference value, which in this case is 3.8 (default value = 0). Now click 'OK'.

Figure 3.10

T-Test

One-Sample Statistics

	N	Mean	Std. Deviation	Std. Error Mean
Value consciousness	100	4.7701	1.08677	.10868

One-Sample Test

	Test Value = 3.8					
					95% Confidence Interval of the Difference	
	t	df	Sig. (2-tailed)	Mean Difference	Lower	Upper
Value consciousness	8.926	99	.000	.97010	.7545	1.1857

From the output (Figure 3.10), it appears that the average Belgium 60–69 year old senior strives quite seriously to achieve an optimal value-for-money relationship (average = 4.77). The question is whether or not this score differs significantly from the Dutch mean for a comparable group of seniors, i.e., the assumed 3.8.

The calculated t-value (8.926) is large enough (indicated by the significance level of <.001) to decide that the null hypothesis of equality may be rejected and that the Belgium figure of 4.77 thus differs significantly from the Dutch 3.8. This involves a two-sided t-test in which the goal is to find out if one score differs from another, without having to specify a direction. If the only objective is to test whether the Belgian score is higher than the Dutch value, then it is sufficient to perform a (less strict) one-sided t-test. This may not be performed as standard in SPSS. However, the two-sided significance level may be divided by two in order to arrive at the one-sided significance level. In this way, a two-sided significance level of .08 will not be significant with a 95% confidence level, however, this will be the case with a one-sided significance level (.08/2 = .04 < .05).

Two dependent samples

Nominal variables: McNemar test

This test is particularly useful when applied to before-and-after experiments, in which the same group of people is measured at two different points in time. This will be illustrated on the basis of the following example. At a wine exhibition, people may buy a specific wine at one of the stands. One hundred test persons are first asked if they would buy the wine purely on the basis of its appearance, smell, etc., however, they may not taste it. Of the 100 test persons surveyed, 30 answer 'yes'. After that, they may taste a glass of wine after which they will then again be asked if they would buy the wine. Of the 30 people who answered 'yes', 25 abide by their opinion [B], 5 decide not to buy the wine anymore [A]. Of the 70 people who originally decided not to buy the wine, there are now 15 [D] who have changed their mind and now wish to buy it. This may be shown as follows:

Table 3.2

		After	
		Will not buy	Will buy
Before	Will buy	5 [A]	25 [B]
	Will not buy	55 [C]	15 [D]

Before trying to determine if this change of opinion as the result of having tasted the wine is significant, it is useful to examine the structure of the data. The table above cannot automatically be read into SPSS; an SPSS datafile usually contains observations per subject (respondent). In this example, the researcher must provide two values per person (= observation) each time, one to indicate the decision to buy or not to buy before tasting, and one for the decision to buy or not to buy after tasting. This results in 100 rows, each with three columns of cells; one for the number of the observation, one for no/yes (0/1) to buying before tasting and one for no/yes (0/1) to buying after tasting. Another possibility is to weigh each 'before-after' combination, but this procedure is not discussed here. Please consult the references at the end of this chapter.

Once these data have been entered into SPSS, the analysis may be performed. This SPSS datafile is named *wine.sav* (see Figure 3.11).

Figure 3.11

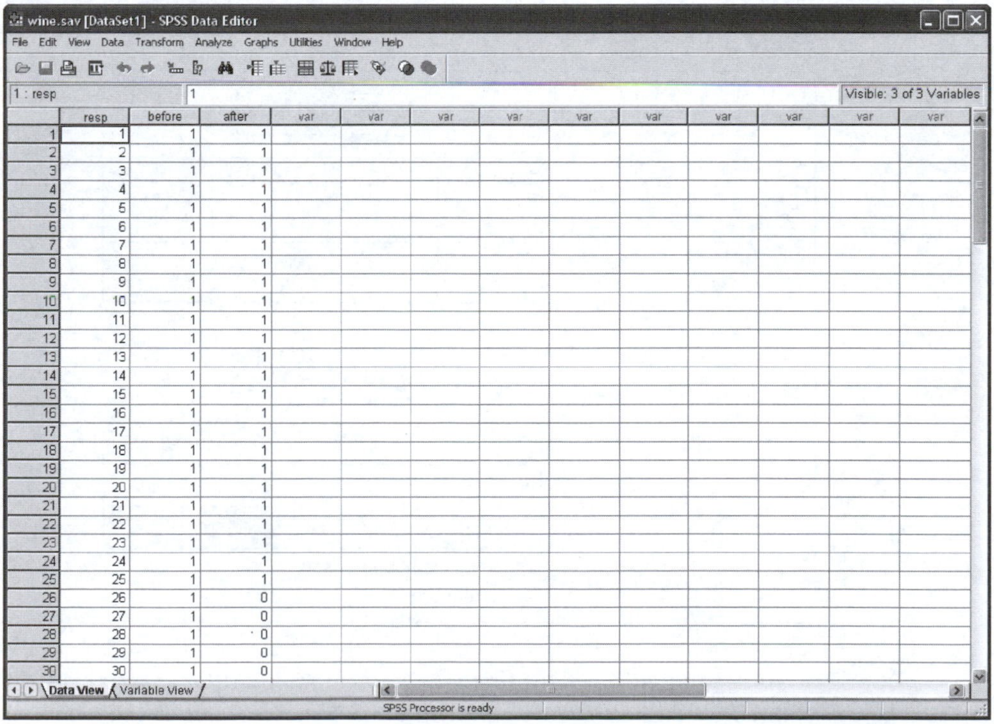

Go to Analyze/Nonparametric Tests/2 Related Samples.

Figure 3.12

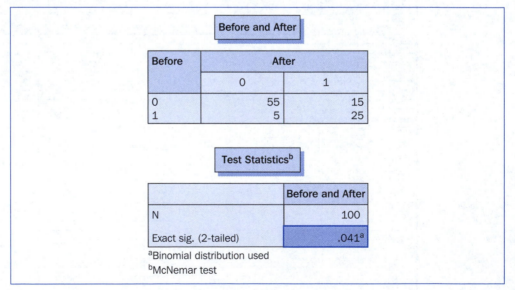

On the subscreen shown in Figure 3.12 click on the variables 'before' and 'after' (respectively to purchase or not to purchase (0/1) before and after having tasted the wine) and then click on ▶ to move this pair of variables to the 'Test Pair(s) List' window. Turn off the option 'Wilcoxon' under 'Test Type' and tick the box 'McNemar'. The window will now look like the one shown in Figure 3.12. Click 'OK'. This will produce the output shown in Figure 3.13.

Figure 3.13

Before and After

Before	After	
	0	1
0	55	15
1	5	25

Test Statistics[b]

	Before and After
N	100
Exact sig. (2-tailed)	.041[a]

[a]Binomial distribution used
[b]McNemar test

As seen in Figure 3.13, first an overview table of the answers is shown which corresponds to the information in Table 3.2. The researcher may now deduce from the results obtained in 'Test statistic' that the null hypothesis that no change has occurred as a result of the tasting may be rejected (sig. = .041 < .05). Both samples therefore differ significantly from one another and as a result, the change in opinion observed is significant.

Ordinal variables: Wilcoxon test

A rank ordering is a typical ordinal variable. Respondents were asked to taste 5 drinks (A, B, C, D and E) and rank these according to their preference (see *seniors.sav*). The most preferred drink gets a ranking 1, the second most preferred drink a ranking 2, and so on. Variable [rank A] contains the ranking (1 to 5) of each respondent for drink A. E.g. respondent 1 ranked drink A fourth, . . . Suppose that after the drinking experiment, some information is given to the respondents about the ingredients of drink A. Suppose that one of the ingredients is perceived as rather unhealthy. Does this influence the ranking? Respondents are asked to rank the 5 drinks again from 1 (most preferred) to 5 (least preferred): see variable [rank AA] for the new ranking of drink A.

The null hypothesis is that both rankings for [rank A] and [rank AA] are equal.

Figure 3.14

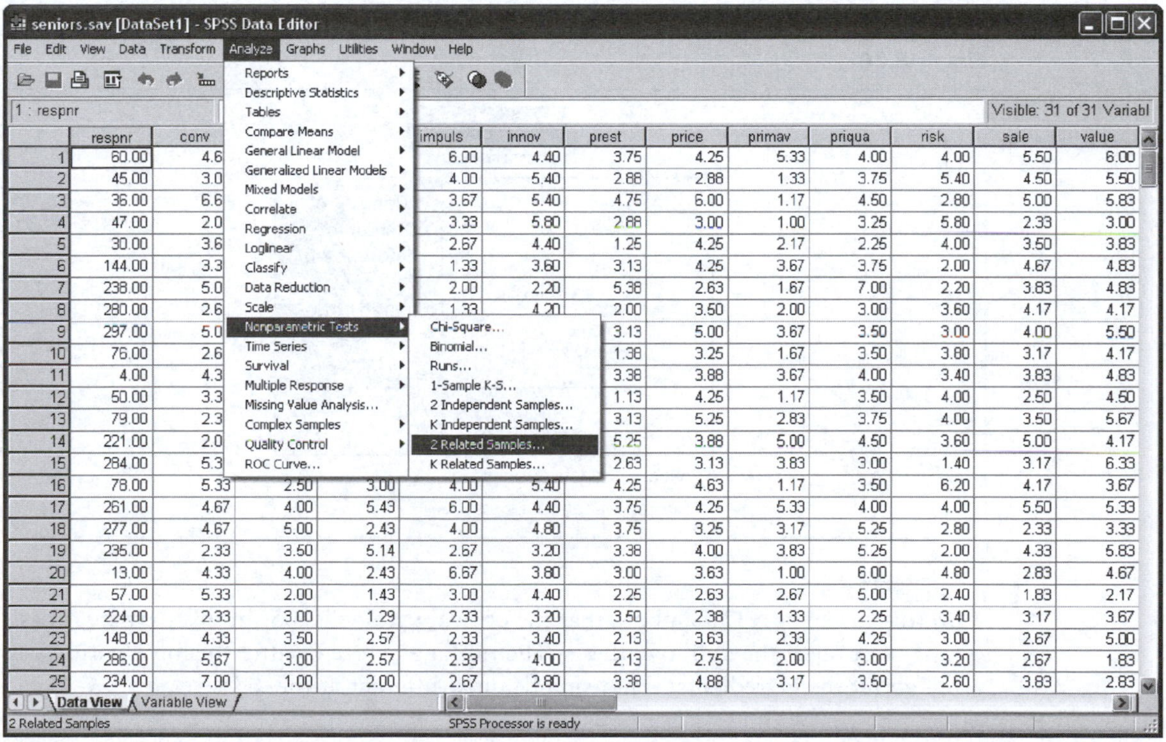

Go to Analyze/Nonparametric Tests/2 Related Samples (Figure 3.14).
Take the variables [rank A] and [rank AA] to the 'Test Pair(s) List' and select as 'Test Type' 'Wilcoxon'. Next click 'OK'.

Figure 3.15 shows the 'Mean Rank'. The 'mean rank' for respondents who changed their opinion in either or both directions (negative ranks and positive ranks), are being compared.

Figure 3.15

		N	Mean Rank	Sum of Ranks
Ranks				

		N	Mean Rank	Sum of Ranks
Ranking of drink A after information about ingredients – Ranking of drink A	Negative Ranks	37[a]	38.03	1407.00
	Positive Ranks	38[b]	37.97	1443.00
	Ties	235[c]		
	Total	310		

[a]Ranking of drink A after information about ingredients < Ranking of drink A
[b]Ranking of drink A after information about ingredients > Ranking of drink A
[c]Ranking of drink A after information about ingredients = Ranking of drink A

Figure 3.16 shows the relevant Z-value, and most important the p-value (asymptotic significance).

Figure 3.16

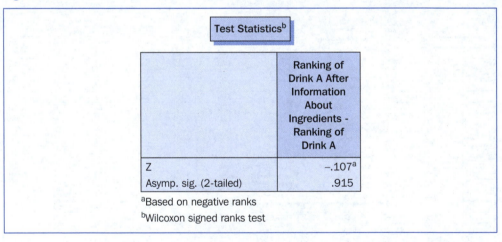

Test Statistics[b]	Ranking of Drink A After Information About Ingredients - Ranking of Drink A
Z	−.107[a]
Asymp. sig. (2-tailed)	.915

[a]Based on negative ranks
[b]Wilcoxon signed ranks test

In this case p = .915. Suppose that the critical p-value is .05. In this particular case, we may not reject the null hypothesis. The ranking before or after the information was given about the ingredients, is not significantly different at the .05 level.

Interval scaled variables: t-test for paired observations

Suppose that the following data are gathered. Each respondent is asked to state his gender and preference for car A [p_car_a] and car B [p_car_b]. These preferences are rated using a number on a 10-point Likert scale (1 = total aversion and 10 = absolute preference).

The data were entered into SPSS (Figure 3.17). The datafile is named *car.sav*.

Figure 3.17

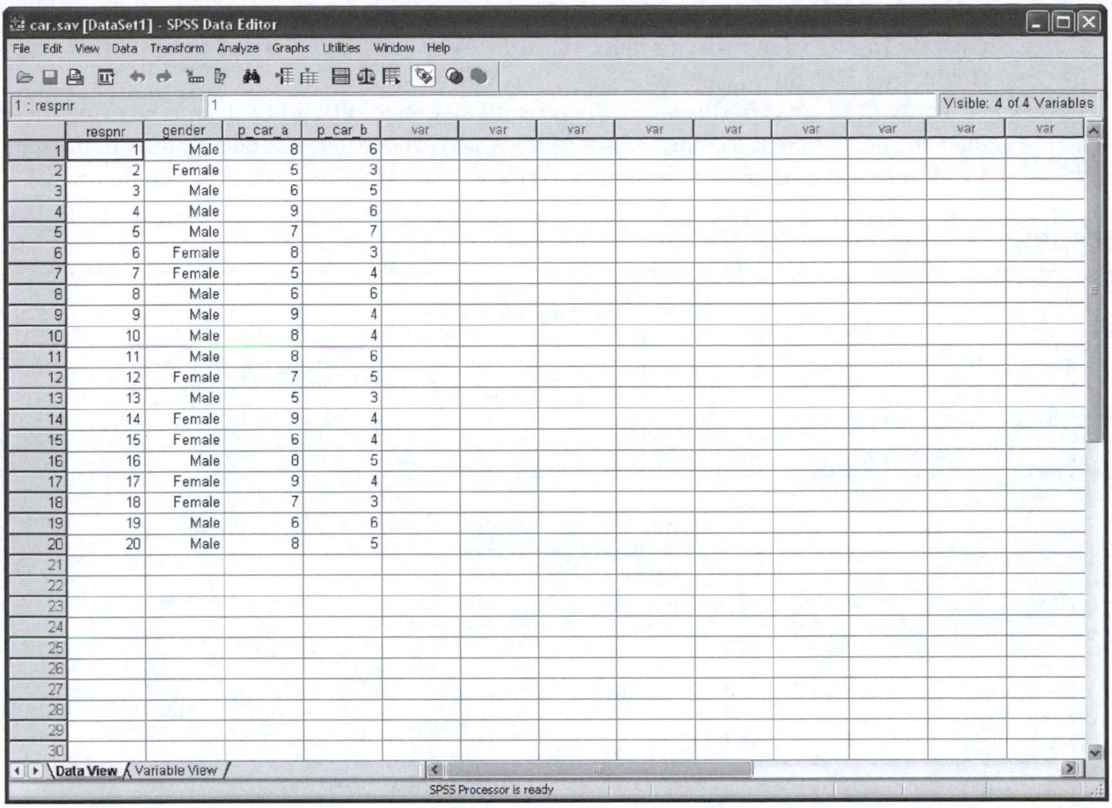

	respnr	gender	p_car_a	p_car_b
1	1	Male	8	6
2	2	Female	5	3
3	3	Male	6	5
4	4	Male	9	6
5	5	Male	7	7
6	6	Female	8	3
7	7	Female	5	4
8	8	Male	6	6
9	9	Male	9	4
10	10	Male	8	4
11	11	Male	8	6
12	12	Female	7	5
13	13	Male	5	3
14	14	Female	9	4
15	15	Female	6	4
16	16	Male	8	5
17	17	Female	9	4
18	18	Female	7	3
19	19	Male	6	6
20	20	Male	8	5

The researcher would like to find out whether a significant difference exists among all of the respondents between the preference for car A and car B. Given the fact that the same respondent must provide an opinion for both cars each time, this involves the use of paired observations. In order to determine whether the means are equal to one another, a test must be performed to find out whether the difference between the means is equal to zero. In order to perform this analysis, the following steps must be taken.

Go to Analyze/Compare Means/Paired Samples T Test.

Figure 3.18

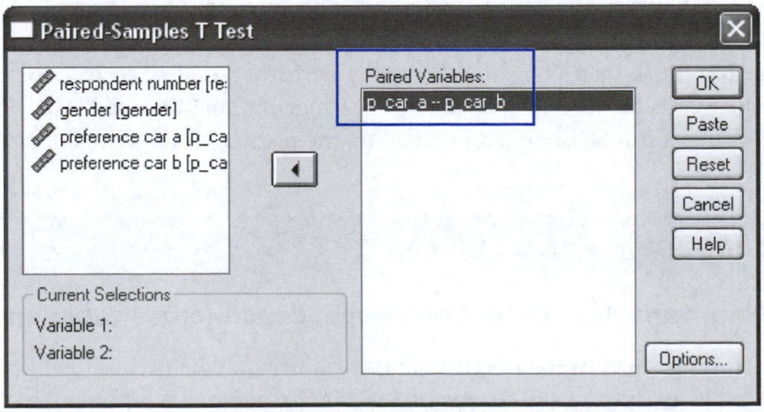

On the subscreen shown in Figure 3.18 click on [p_car_a] so that this variable name will follow the indication for 'Variable 1:' in the 'Current Selections' subwindow. Now click on [p_car_b] in order to place this after 'Variable 2:'. Click ▶ to move this set to the 'Paired Variables' window. Now click 'OK'.

You will see that in this way, it is possible to create different sets and to bring these over to the 'Paired Variables' window. This way, the difference test may be performed for different sets in one single analysis. You will see an output as shown in Figure 3.19.

Figure 3.19

Paired Samples Statistics

		Mean	N	Std. Deviation	Std. Error Mean
Pair 1	Preference car a	7.20	20	1.399	.313
	Preference car b	4.65	20	1.226	.274

Paired Samples Test

		Paired Differences					t	df	Sig. (2-tailed)
					95% Confidence Interval of the Difference				
		Mean	Std. Deviation	Std. Error Mean	Lower	Upper			
Pair 1	Preference car a - Preference car b	2.550	1.701	.380	1.754	3.346	6.706	19	.000

The null hypothesis is that the means are equal to one another. In the example, the null hypothesis may then be formulated as determining whether the mean difference between [p_car_a] and [p_car_b] is equal to zero. This null hypothesis is rejected because the significance level ($<.001$) is less than the usual cut-off level of .05. Therefore, we can say with more than 95% certainty that the mean (here, the mean of the differences) differs from the assumed average (here: 0). In other words, there is a difference in the preference between car A and car B. It must be noted that the example is based on a two-sided test. If you want to determine whether the preference for car A is higher than the preference for car B, then you should actually perform a one-sided test. SPSS only performs two-sided tests however, which are more stringent than one-sided tests. The p-value for a one-sided test can be obtained by dividing the p-value of the two-sided test by two.

Two independent samples

Nominal variables: χ^2 test of independence (cross-table analysis)

The relationship between two nominal variables may be determined on the basis of the cross-table analysis. Take for example 100 test persons who have, in addition to their gender, also been asked whether or not they would buy the latest CD of a well-known crooner. The answers may be presented as follows:

Table 3.3

	Male	Female	Total
Buying	15	30	45
Not buying	40	15	55
Total	55	45	100

The question may now be asked whether there is a connection between the gender of the test persons and whether or not they would buy the CD. The two (independent) samples which are drawn here are the male and the female. The 'buy' variables in this example only have two possible values (buy and not buy), but may also take on additional values. By calculating percentages for each column, it may be determined that women are relatively more inclined to buy the CD. If we now want to find out whether or not this relationship between gender and buying intention (or the difference between men and women and their buying preferences) is statistically significant, we will find out to what degree the observed frequencies deviate from the expected frequencies. These expected frequencies are the frequencies which one would expect to see if the categories of the row and column variables were independent of one another. Just like the McNemar analysis (section 3.3.1), 100 rows will also have to be entered here with 3 columns, e.g. for a respondent number (not required), male/female (0/1) and no/yes (0/1) to indicate whether they would buy the CD (see *cd.sav*, Figure 3.20).

Figure 3.20

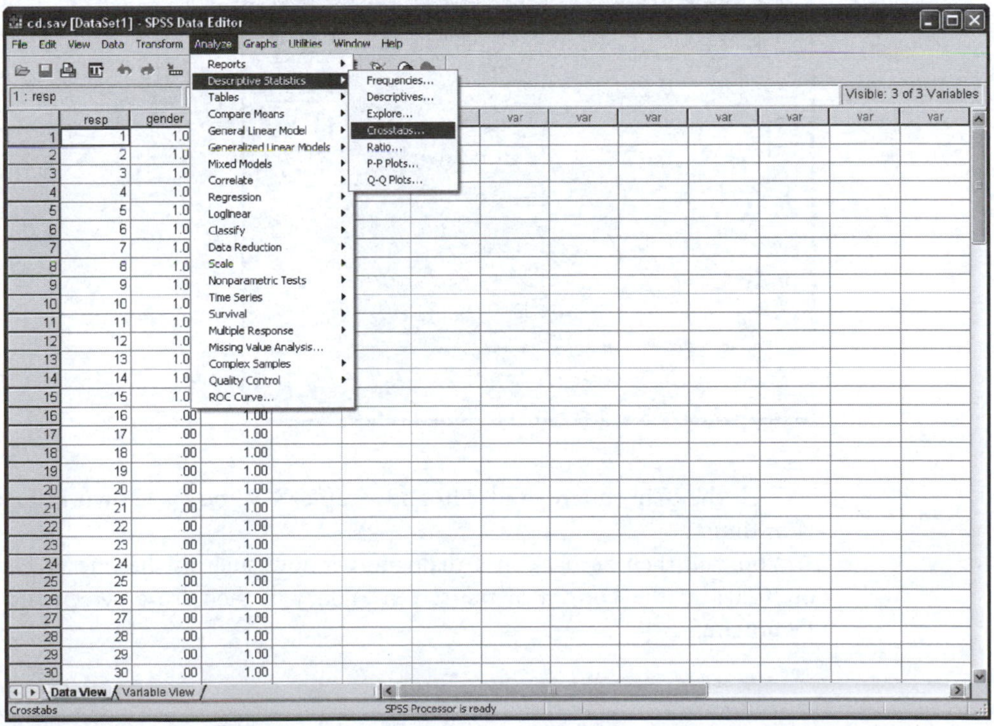

Go to Analyze/Descriptive Statistics/Crosstabs (Figure 3.20).

Figure 3.21

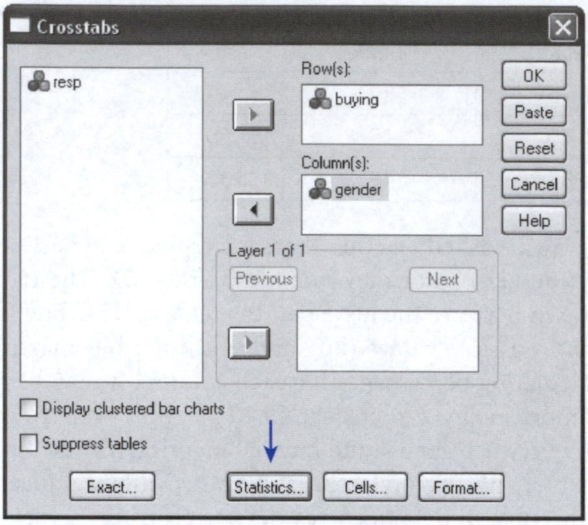

Move the dependent variable [buying] to the 'Row(s)' window and the independent variable [gender] to the 'Column(s)' window. Now click on 'Statistics'.

Figure 3.22

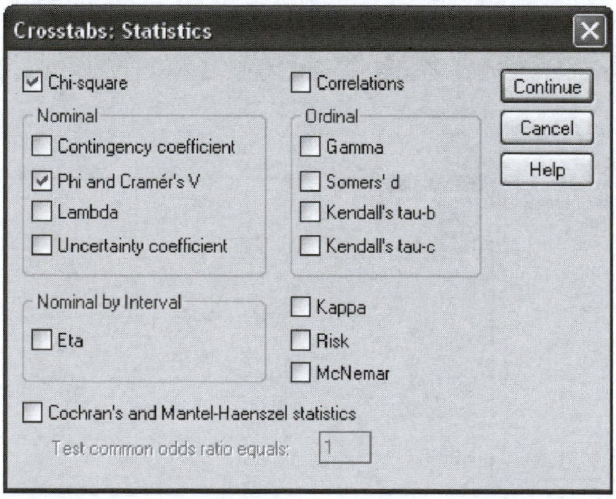

Tick the 'Chi-square' and 'Phi and Cramer's V' boxes shown in Figure 3.22. Click 'Continue'.

You will then be back in a dialogue window such as the one in Figure 3.21. Click on 'Cells' at the bottom of the screen. You will then see a screen such as the one in Figure 3.23.

Figure 3.23

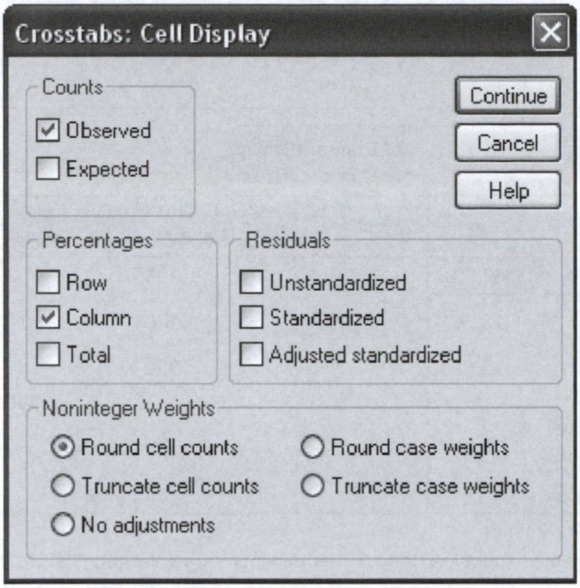

Crosstabs: Cell Display

Counts
- ☑ Observed
- ☐ Expected

[Continue]
[Cancel]
[Help]

Percentages
- ☐ Row
- ☑ Column
- ☐ Total

Residuals
- ☐ Unstandardized
- ☐ Standardized
- ☐ Adjusted standardized

Noninteger Weights
- ◉ Round cell counts
- ○ Truncate cell counts
- ○ No adjustments
- ○ Round case weights
- ○ Truncate case weights

Under 'Percentages', click on 'Column' (make sure that the independent variable is selected as a column variable). This produces a window such as the one shown in Figure 3.23. Click 'Continue' and on 'OK' in the main window. You will see an output like the ones shown in Figures 3.24 to 3.26.

Figure 3.24

			Gender		Total
			Female	Male	Female
Buying	Don't buy cd	Count	15	40	55
		% within gender	33.3%	72.7%	55.0%
	Buy cd	Count	30	15	45
		% within gender	66.7%	27.3%	45.0%
Total		Count	45	55	100
		% within gender	100.0%	100.0%	100.0%

Buying* Gender Crosstabulation

Figure 3.24 provides a picture similar to that displayed in Table 3.3. The column percentages differ considerably between the men and the women. In order to find out if this difference is also statistically significant, we must look at the Pearson Chi-square in Figure 3.25.

Figure 3.25

Chi-Square Tests

	Value	df	Asymp. Sig. (2-sided)	Exact Sig. (2-sided)	Exact Sig. (1-sided)
Pearson Chi-Square	15.519[b]	1	.000		
Continuity correction[a]	13.968	1	.000		
Likelihood ratio	15.887	1	.000		
Fisher's exact test				.000	.000
Linear-by-linear association	15.364	1	.000		
N of valid cases	100				

[a]Computed only for a 2 x 2 table
[b]0 cells (.0%) have expected count less than 5. The minimum expected count is 20.25

The number 15.519 with a significance level of $< .001$ means that the null hypothesis, that there is no significant relationship, is rejected. Women thus appear to be significantly more inclined to buy the CD than men. The Cramer's V in Figure 3.26 tells us something about the strength of the significant relationship.

Figure 3.26

Symmetric Measures

		Value	Approx. Sig.
Nominal by Nominal	Phi	−.394	.000
	Cramer's V	.394	.000
N of valid cases		100	

[a]Not assuming the null hypothesis
[b]Using the asymptotic standard error assuming the null hypothesis

A value of zero indicates no relationship; a value of one indicates a perfect relationship. The value of .394 obtained in the example indicates that the significant relationship is not that strong.

Finally it is important to note that SPSS also checks whether the number of observations is sufficient in order to correctly perform the analysis. At the bottom of Figure 3.25, two checks are shown in footnote b which had already been discussed in the nominal variables section. Because there are no cells in the example (=0%) which have an expected frequency lower than five (the recommendation is that this percentage should be lower than 20%), and the minimal expected frequency is 20.25 (this should be at least 1), the conditions have been met here such that there is no problem in the example. In cases where these conditions are not satisfied, you may take the (relevant) columns and rows (in the event that there are more than two rows and/or columns) together and perform the analysis over again.

Ordinal variables: Mann-Whitney U test

Suppose that we would like to test the difference in ranking of drink A between male and female respondents (see *seniors.sav*). Respondents were asked to taste 5 drinks (A, B, C, D and E). The most preferred drink gets a ranking 1, the second most preferred drink a ranking 2, and so on. Variable [rank A] contains the ranking (1 to 5) of each respondent for drink A. E.g. respondent 1 ranked drink A fourth, . . . A typical test to examine the difference in ranking given by 2 groups (e.g. male/female) is the Mann-Whitney U test. It tests the null hypothesis that both groups (male versus female respondents) have, on average, the same ranking. All scores for both groups are combined and an overall ranking is calculated. The mean rank for each group is next calculated and both mean ranks are compared. The null hypothesis is that both mean rankings are equal.

Go to Analyze/Nonparametric Tests/2 Independent Samples (Figure 3.27).

Figure 3.27

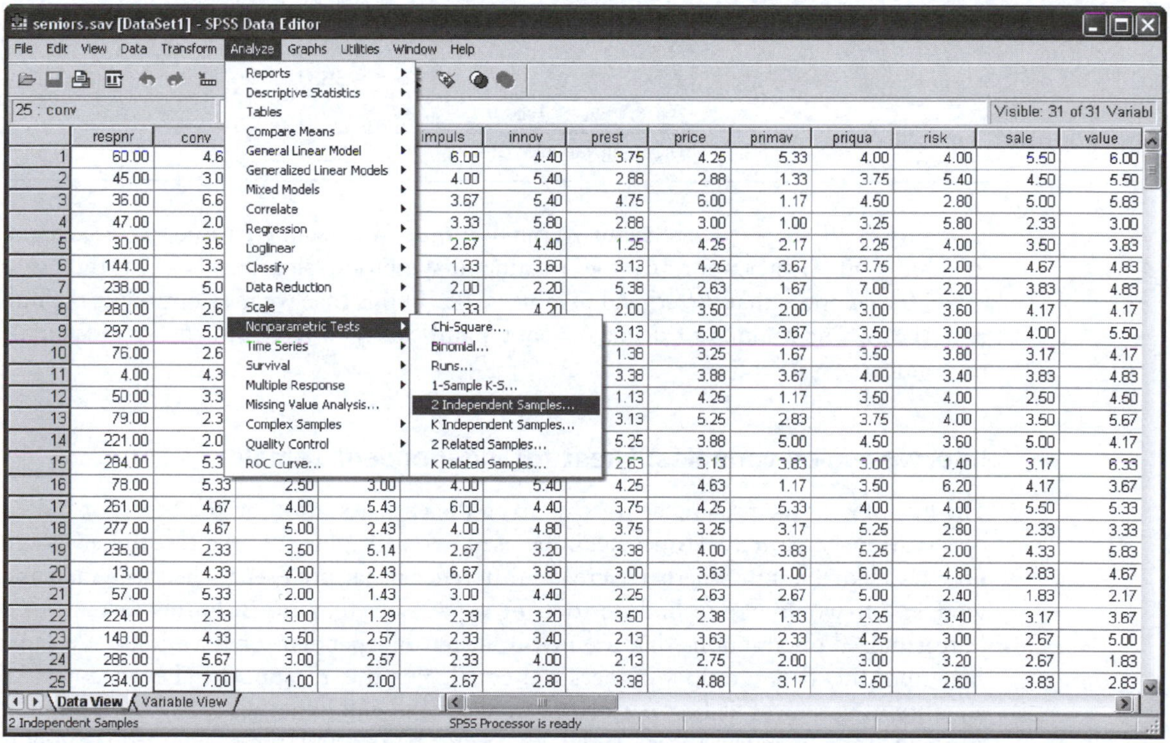

Take the variable [rank A] to the 'Test Variable List' and 'gender' to 'Grouping Variable'. Next click 'Define Groups'. For group 1 indicate '0' (male respondents) and for group 2 indicate '1' (female respondents). Next click continue. For 'Test Type' indicate 'Mann-Whitney U'. Next click 'OK'.

Figure 3.28

	Gender	N	Mean Rank	Sum of Ranks
Ranking of drink A	Male	109	152.92	16668.00
	Female	201	156.90	31537.00
	Total	310		

Figure 3.28 shows the 'Mean Rank' for both male and female respondents. In this example, male respondents have a slightly lower ranking compared to female respondents. A lower ranking for males would mean that on average they have a higher preference for drink A compared to female respondents.

Figure 3.29

Test Statistics[a]

	Ranking of Drink A
Mann-Whitney U	10673.000
Wilcoxon W	16668.000
Z	−.383
Asymp. sig. (2-tailed)	.701

[a]Grouping variable: Gender

Figure 3.29 shows the relevant Mann-Whitney U calculated value, its associated Z-value and most important the p-value (asymptotic significance). In this case p = .701. Suppose that the critical p-value is .05. In this case we may not reject the null hypothesis. The ranking of drink A is not significantly different for male and female respondents.

Interval scaled variables: t-test for independent samples

The example of the preference for cars from the earlier section on the t-test for paired observations, *car.sav*, will once again be used here. Imagine that the researcher would now also like to know whether there is a difference in car preferences between men and women. He would like to find this out for car A as well as car B. In this case, it is no longer paired observations that are involved, but independent observations. We must first find out if the group variances are equal. For this reason, the 'Levene's test of equality of variances' is first performed in SPSS (the null hypothesis, H_0: both populations have the same variances). If this H_0 cannot be rejected, the t-value from the output must be read in the case of equal variances; in the other case, the t-value must be read from the output for unequal variances. The following steps must be followed.

Go to Analyze/Compare Means/Independent-Samples T-Test to display the subscreen shown in Figure 3.30.

Figure 3.30

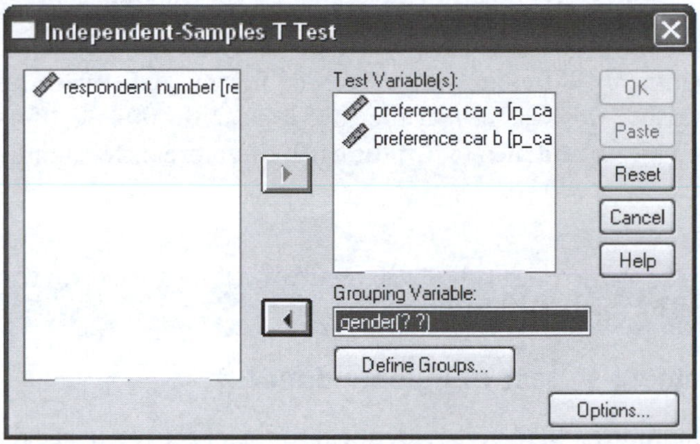

Figure 3.31

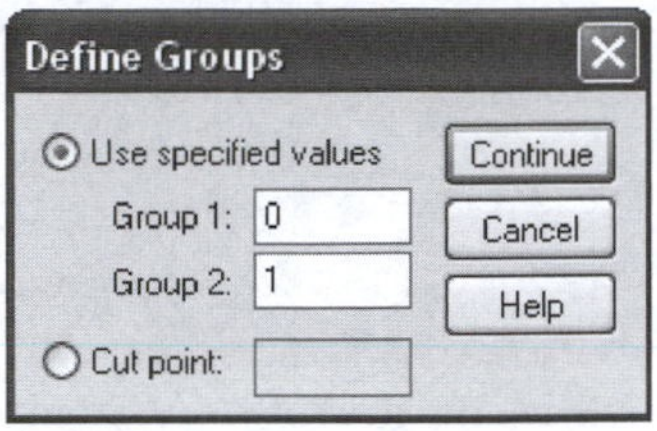

Move 'preference car A' and 'preference car B' to the 'Test Variable(s)' subwindow. Next, move 'gender' to the 'Grouping Variable' cell. Now click 'Define Groups'.

In the subwindow that now appears (Figure 3.31), fill in a '0' for 'Group1' (0 is the code for female) and a '1' for 'Group2' (male). Click on 'Continue' and then on 'OK' in the main window.

You will now see the following output (Figure 3.32).

Figure 3.32

Group Statistics

	Gender	N	Mean	Std. Deviation	Std. Error Mean
Preference car a	Female	8	7.00	1.604	.567
	Male	12	7.33	1.303	.376
Preference car b	Female	8	3.75	.707	.250
	Male	12	5.25	1.138	.329

Independent Samples Test

		Levene's Test for Equality of Variances		t-Test for Equality of Means					95% Confidence Interval of the Difference	
		F	Sig.	t	df	Sig. (2-tailed)	Mean Difference	Std. Error Difference	Lower	Upper
Preference car a	Equal variances assumed	.178	.678	−.512	18	.615	−.333	.651	−1.702	1.035
	Equal variances not assumed			−.490	12.923	.632	−.333	.680	−1.804	1.137
Preference car b	Equal variances assumed	2.110	.164	−3.309	18	.004	−1.500	.453	−2.452	−.548
	Equal variances not assumed			−3.633	17.963	.002	−1.500	.413	−2.368	−.632

In this part we verify whether the group variances are equal

In this part we verify whether the averages between females and males are equal

For both car A and car B, it appears that the null hypothesis of equal variances may not be rejected (.678 > .05 and .164 > .05, respectively). This means that the t-test output for 'Equal variances assumed' must be checked every time. This shows that there was no significant difference in preference for car A between men and women (.615 > .05), yet that this was in fact the case for car B (.004 < .05). The preference scores for women (3.75) and men (5.25) for car B therefore differ significantly from one another.

K independent samples

Nominal variables: χ^2 test of independence

The analysis technique applied here is identical to the procedure discussed in the section on cross-table analysis. Once again, we have two nominal scaled variables, however this time the relationship may be tested between more than two (independent) samples, for example, the differences in CD buying intentions among three age categories.

Ordinal variables: Kruskal-Wallis test

This test is an extension of the 'Two independent sample case'. Go to Analyze/Nonparametric Tests/K Independent Samples.

The relevant test is the 'Kruskal-Wallis test'. The procedure is analogous to the one described earlier (see Two independent samples: ordinal variables).

Interval scaled variables: Analysis of variance

Analysis of variance is the topic of the next chapter; you may find detailed information regarding this technique there.

K dependent samples

Nominal variables: Cochran Q

If a researcher would like to find out if there is a significant difference between more than two dependent samples of variables which have been measured nominally (here: 0/1), he may use the Cochran Q test. Suppose the researcher assembles 30 test persons to whom he then shows three posters, one after the other. The test persons may indicate whether they find the poster good (=0) or bad (=1) (in this type of analysis, the value '0' is used to indicate the level that reflects success). The dataset *poster.sav* contains the answers from the 30 respondents. The question is whether a significant difference exists among the three posters in terms of the proportion of respondents who feel a certain poster is good. The analysis may be performed as follows.

Go to Analyze/Nonparametric Tests/K Related Samples (Figure 3.33).

Figure 3.33

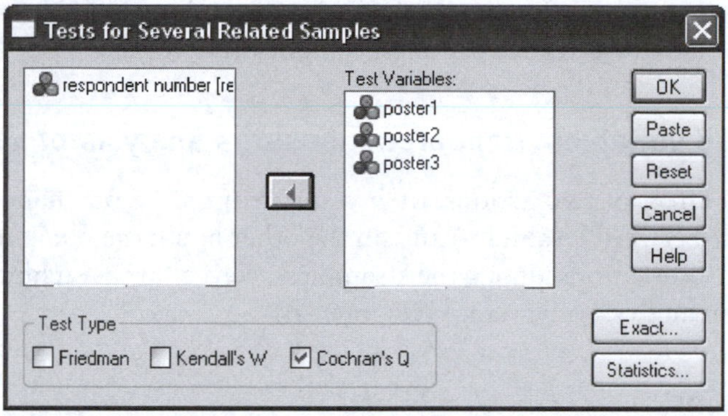

Select the three different poster (variables). Tick Cochran's Q under 'Test Type'. Now click 'OK'. You will see the output displayed in Figure 3.34.

Figure 3.34

Frequencies

	Value	
	0	1
Poster1	10	20
Poster2	19	11
Poster3	11	19

Test Statistics

N	30
Cochran's Q	6.636[a]
df	2
Asymp. sig.	.036

[a] 0 is treated as success

The null hypothesis that there are no differences between the three posters is rejected (sig. = 0.036 < .05). On the basis of the frequencies, one may decide that poster 2 is considered to be the best. If one would like to know if the differences between 2 groups are significant each time, then the previously discussed McNemar test will have to be consulted.

Ordinal variables: Friedman test

This test is an extension of the 'Two related sample case'. Click Analyze/ Nonparametric Tests/K Related Samples.

The relevant test is the 'Friedman test'. The procedure is analogous to the one described earlier (see Two related samples: ordinal variables).

Interval scaled variables: Repeated measures analysis of variance

In this case, the effect of two actions are investigated: on the one hand, the treatment effect (difference between k samples) and on the other hand, the blocking effect (difference between n observations among the k samples). This analysis technique is discussed in the chapter on analysis of variance (Chapter 4).

Further reading

Field, A. (2005), *Discovering Statistics Using SPSS*. London: Sage Publications.

Green, S.B., Salkind, N.J. and Akey, T.M. (2000), *Using SPSS for Windows – Analyzing and understanding data, 2nd ed.* Englewood Cliffs, N.J.: Prentice Hall.

SPSS Base 13.0 Users Guide (2004), Chicago, Illinois: SPSS, Inc.

Analysis of variance

Chapter objectives

This chapter will help you to:

- Understand when and how to use analysis of variance
- Carry out and interpret one-way analysis of variance and analysis of variance based on full factorial designs
- Carry out and interpret repeated measure analysis of variance

Technique

In the section about the t-tests (see Chapter 3), we mentioned that when the number of samples was more than two, another technique must be applied, namely the analysis of variance. The analysis of variance is thus an extension of the t-test in cases where there are more than two samples involved. An analysis of variance may therefore be used to determine the significance level of the difference between more than two means, as well as to find out what the effect of one or more nominal independent variables is on an interval-scaled dependent variable. Ultimately, both approaches come down to the same thing. The nominal independent variables are also called factors. The different values that these nominal variables may take on are referred to as levels.

Analysis of variance (or ANOVA) may take on various forms. For instance, you might have several independent variables (each with several levels of measurement) and/or there might be several dependent variables (MANOVA – M stands for Multivariate) involved. In addition, an additional independent variable (covariate) may be included in the analysis (ANCOVA – COVA stands for Covariance). Several observations per respondent may also be analysed (Repeated Measures). What it amounts to each time is the comparison of a variance caused by one or more independent factors with the unexplained variance. If the former is relatively large, then one may say that the factor results in a significant difference.

When we work with more than one independent variable, these types of analyses are indicated in a specific manner. For example, determining the effect of the independent variables 'colour' (red, green, blue) and 'upholstery' (leather and no leather) on the preference for a car will be expressed as a 3×2 experimental design (two independent variables, the first of which is measured on three levels, the other measured on two levels).

The following types of analysis will be discussed in this chapter:

- analysis of variance as a test of difference or one-way ANOVA (example 1)
- covariance analysis or ANCOVA (example 2)

- analysis of variance for a complete factorial $2 \times 2 \times 2$ design (example 3)
- multivariate analysis of variance or MANOVA (example 4)
- analysis of variance using repeated measures (example 5)
- analysis of variance using repeated measures and a between-subjects factor (example 6)

An additional discussion on the various forms which an analysis of variance may take on may be found in the references mentioned at the end of this chapter.

Example 1

Analysis of variance as a test of difference or one-way ANOVA

Managerial problem

Suppose that three marketing promotional tools were tested for a new brand of soup: one large poster (display) of the product in the shop (R1), a tasting in the shop (R2) and decoration around the product stand (R3). Each of these special promotions was tried out in five different stores (15 stores in total). These stores must be comparable so that no 'hidden factors' get included in the analysis by mistake. Suppose that the five shops in which a poster is used are also shops which were recently renovated and the other ten shops come across as being old-fashioned. If we find a significant difference between the shops with and without a poster, the question is whether this difference has its origin in the way the poster is used or in the renovated look in the shops. Table 4.1 illustrates the sales data gathered after one month.

Table 4.1

Shop/Promotion	R1	R2	R3
Shop 1	7	15	9
Shop 2	4	13	7
Shop 3	4	17	5
Shop 4	5	11	10
Shop 5	6	13	8

This example therefore attempts to determine the effect of one factor or independent variable (promotion), measured on three levels. These data are entered into SPSS as shown in Figure 4.1 (datafile *soup.sav*).

Problem

Perform a one-way ANOVA to determine the effect of the different promotions on the sales. Using post-hoc tests, also find out whether the effect differs between each pair of promotions.

Figure 4.1

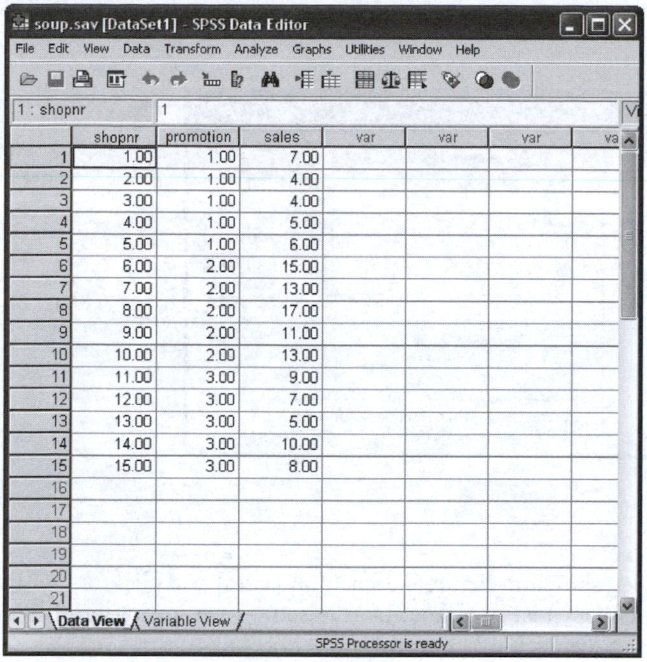

Solution

SPSS commands

Figure 4.2

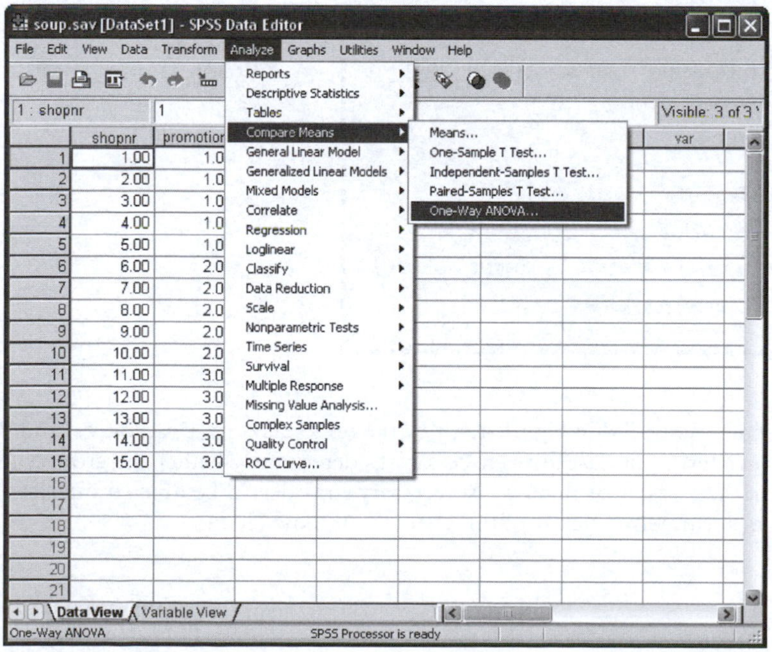

Go to Analyze/Compare Means/One-Way ANOVA (Figure 4.2)

Figure 4.3

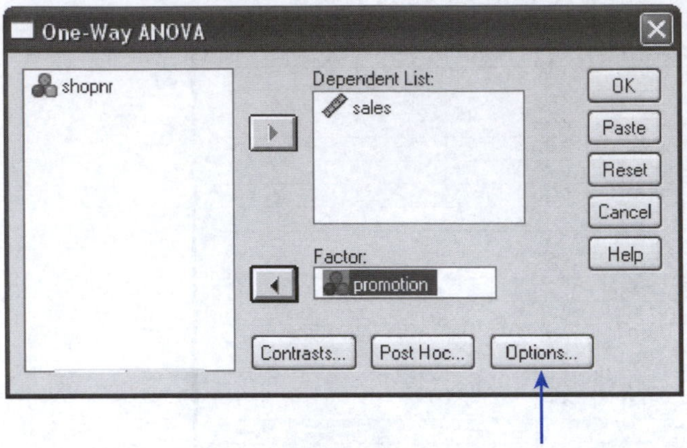

In the subscreen shown in Figure 4.3 click on [sales] and click on ▸ to move this variable to the 'Dependent List' window. Do the same with 'promotion' by moving it to the 'Factor' window. Now click on Options.

Figure 4.4

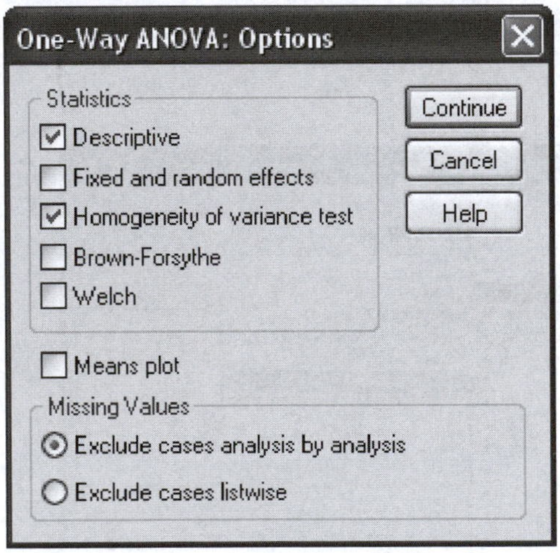

Under 'Statistics' in Figure 4.4, tick the boxes next to 'Descriptive' and 'Homogeneity of variance test'. This last test is necessary to determine whether the group variances are equal or not. The result of this test is necessary in order to be able to interpret the further test results accurately. Click 'Continue' and then 'Post Hoc'.

Figure 4.5

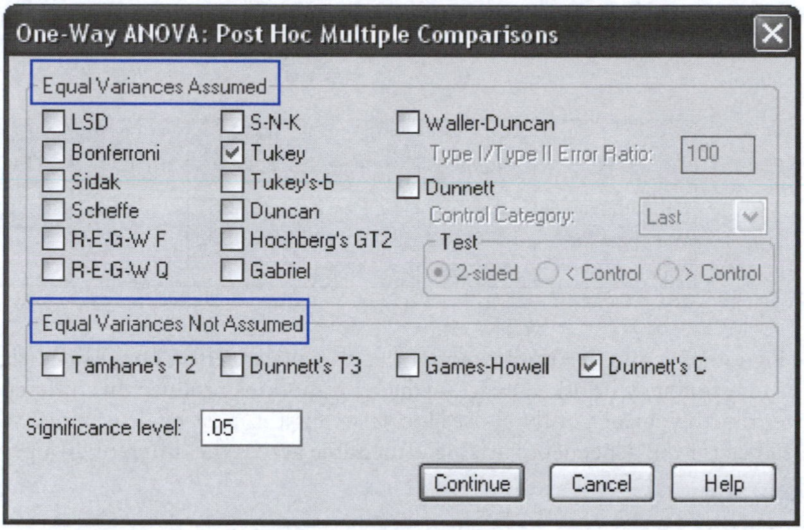

In this screen (Figure 4.5), the researcher must indicate which extra tests he would like to perform in order to find out which levels (different promotions) are the ones that are responsible for any factor effect (the act of running the promotion). In other words, these extra tests are necessary if one would like to know for which promotions the average sales differ significantly from one another.

Because it is not yet known whether there are equal variances between the different groups or not, a test has been selected for 'Equal Variances Assumed' as well as 'Equal Variances Not Assumed'. In Figure 4.5, 'Tukey' and 'Dunnett's C' have been chosen, respectively. The other tests each have their own characteristics, but are, in general, of equal merit. Click on 'Continue' and then on 'OK' in the main window.

Interpretation of the SPSS output

Figure 4.6

Descriptives

Sales

	N	Mean	Std. Deviation	Std. Error	95% Confidence Interval for Mean		Minimum	Maximum
					Lower Bound	Upper Bound		
Display	5	5.2000	1.30384	.58310	3.5811	6.8189	4.00	7.00
Tasting	5	13.8000	2.28035	1.01980	10.9686	16.6314	11.00	17.00
Decoration	5	7.8000	1.92354	.86023	5.4116	10.1884	5.00	10.00
Total	15	8.9333	4.11386	1.06219	6.6552	11.2115	4.00	17.00

Figure 4.6 shows the descriptive results. A tasting seems to stimulate sales the best (average sales = 13.8), followed by 'decoration' (7.8). The use of a 'display' apparently has the least impact (5.2). Figure 4.7 provides an idea of the significance of the differences in the means between the three groups.

Figure 4.7

ANOVA

Sales

	Sum of Squares	df	Mean Square	F	Sig.
Between groups	194.533	2	97.267	27.528	.000
Within groups	42.400	12	3.533		
Total	236.933	14			

Figure 4.7 shows that the promotion has a significant effect on the sales (sig. $< .001 < .05$). The question may be asked exactly which promotions produce this difference. This may be determined by means of the 'Post Hoc' tests. First it must be determined whether the error variance for the dependent variable is the same across the different groups.

Figure 4.8

Test of Homogeneity of Variances

Sales

Levene Statistic	df1	df2	Sig.
.701	2	12	.515

Given the fact that this is also the null hypothesis and this may not be rejected here (.515 > .05, see Figure 4.8), in the 'Post Hoc' tests (Figure 4.9), we must look at the 'Tukey' test and not the 'Dunnett C' (see Figure 4.5 where 'Tukey' is chosen in the case of a situation with equal variances).

Figure 4.9

Multiple Comparisons

Dependent Variable: Sales

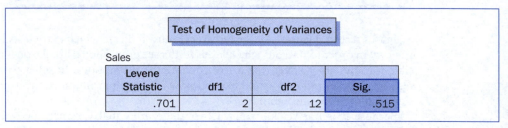

	(I) Promotion	(J) Promotion	Mean Difference (I-J)	Std. Error	Sig.	95% Confidence Interval Lower Bound	95% Confidence Interval Upper Bound
Tukey HSD	Display	Tasting	-8.60000*	1.18884	.000	-11.7717	-5.4283
		Decoration	-2.60000	1.18884	.114	-5.7717	.5717
	Tasting	Display	8.60000*	1.18884	.000	5.4283	11.7717
		Decoration	6.00000*	1.18884	.001	2.8283	9.1717
	Decoration	Display	2.60000	1.18884	.114	-.5717	5.7717
		Tasting	-6.00000*	1.18884	.001	-9.1717	-2.8283
Dunnett C	Display	Tasting	-8.60000*	1.17473		-12.7867	-4.4133
		Decoration	-2.60000	1.03923		-6.3038	1.1038
	Tasting	Display	8.60000*	1.17473		4.4133	12.7867
		Decoration	6.00000*	1.33417		1.2450	10.7550
	Decoration	Display	2.60000	1.03923		-1.1038	6.3038
		Tasting	-6.00000*	1.33417		-10.7550	-1.2450

*The mean difference is significant at the .05 level

When the two-by-two tests are examined in combination with the mean scores, we notice that it is in fact the tasting that causes the significant differences. The null hypothesis is still that there is no significant difference between both groups. When the significance level is less than .05, this null hypothesis may be rejected and we may decide that the means for both groups differ significantly from each other. Therefore, the average sales in the stores in which a tasting was held differed significantly from the mean sales in the other two groups of stores. This may be seen from the significance level which may be found in the 'Sig.' column. The difference between 'tasting' on the one hand, and 'display' and 'decoration' on the other is significant ($< .001$ and $.001$, respectively, both $< .05$). This significant difference is also indicated by a '*' in the 'Mean Difference (I-J)' column). Because each case involves two-by-two comparisons, each relationship may be found twice in Figure 4.9. With the exception of the sign of the difference and the direction of the confidence intervals, the comparison between 'tasting' and 'display' is obviously the same as the comparison between 'display' and 'tasting'.

Example 2

Analysis of variance with a covariate (ANCOVA)

Technique: supplement

Determining whether or not the effect of a certain factor on a variable to be explained is significant is actually a matter of studying the variance explained by the factor, as opposed to the unexplained variance. If this ratio is large enough, this indicates that it is meaningful to include this factor in the analysis. However, when it may be assumed that there are other variables which have a linear relationship to the variable to be explained, it is recommended that this is included in the relevant analysis of variance. Suppose that we take the intention to buy a durable product as the dependent variable, then we may expect that income has a positive influence on this dependent variable. Under these circumstances, it is recommended that this interval-scaled variable is included in the analysis of variance as a covariate. A portion of the variance of the dependent variable is then explained by the covariate.

An extra assumption (in addition to the minimum requirement that the dependent variable is interval-scaled, a normal distribution of the error term, homogeneity of the variances and independence of the observations) which must be checked using ANCOVA as compared with ANOVA, is the homogeneity of the regression slopes across the various experimental groups. What is important here are the regressions (relationships) between the dependent variable on the one hand, and the covariate on the other hand for each experimental group. This will be discussed in the example below both graphically as well as formally.

Managerial problem

Suppose that the manager of an electronics store chain would like to find out whether or not spraying a perfume (lavender oil) in the retail stores will result in higher sales. To do this, he selects 30 different stores which are similar in nature. In 10 of the stores, no perfume is sprayed, and this group of stores also serves as the benchmark for the study. In 10 other stores, he only sprays a very limited quantity of lavender oil. In the remaining stores, he allows a substantial quantity to be sprayed. With regard to the stores where the lavender oil is sprayed, previous research had already shown that the limited spraying usually led to a subconscious fragrance perception, while for the stores where a significant quantity was sprayed, this usually led to a conscious perception of a fragrance; in other words, people who entered the store immediately noticed the lavender fragrance.

As is the case with ANOVA, this study must also involve comparable stores, so that no 'hidden factor' is included in the analysis. One factor which the researcher cannot get around is that the stores do have different surface areas and that previous research had already proven that larger stores can lead to more sales. In order to free the experiment with the fragrances from any potentially biasing effect of store size, this last aspect is included as a covariate in the gathering and analysis of data (here the covariate is actually used more as a control variable).

Unlike the first section of this chapter (relating to ANOVA) in which there had been no a priori expectations of the direction of the differences between the levels of the factor, the researcher does have these in part now. The researcher's expectation here is that the benchmark group will experience the poorest sales (due to the lack of pleasant lavender fragrance) in comparison with the stores in which a lavender fragrance is in fact used. What the researcher has not yet figured out himself however (where he has no a priori expectation) is the question of whether or not the group in which a high dose of lavender fragrance is used will perform better than the group in which a lower dose of lavender fragrance is used. After all, the strong presence of fragrance can put the customers in a better frame of mind, however it can also create a negative effect because a number of customers might experience this as inappropriate and/or bring about a feeling of being manipulated. Whether or not there are a priori expectations is important to the selection of the sort of testing system that will be used to determine the differences between the groups. If there are a priori expectations, the choice will be made for contrasts, and in the case of no a priori expectations, post-hoc tests will be chosen. The difference between these two situations lies in the fact that post-hoc tests are more conservative (stricter). To a certain extent, this may be compared with one-sided and two-sided hypothesis tests, in which one-sided tests are less stringent and two-sided tests are more conservative.

Problem

Perform an ANCOVA and find out if the use of a low, high or no dose of lavender fragrance has an effect on sales. Next, using contrasts, find out whether low and high doses lead to better sales when compared with a situation in which no lavender fragrance is used. Finally, using post-hoc tests, find out whether there is a difference in sales between the low and high dose groups. While you are doing this, keep in mind the possibility of a linear influence of store surface area on the sales. The data are in the file *fragrance.sav*, an illustration of which may be found in Figure 4.10. 'Sales' are the sales on a weekly basis, 'fragrance' indicates the experimental group to which the store belongs (0 = no lavender fragrance, 1 = low dose of lavender fragrance, 2 = high dose of lavender fragrance). 'Size' is the store surface area expressed in m^2.

Figure 4.10

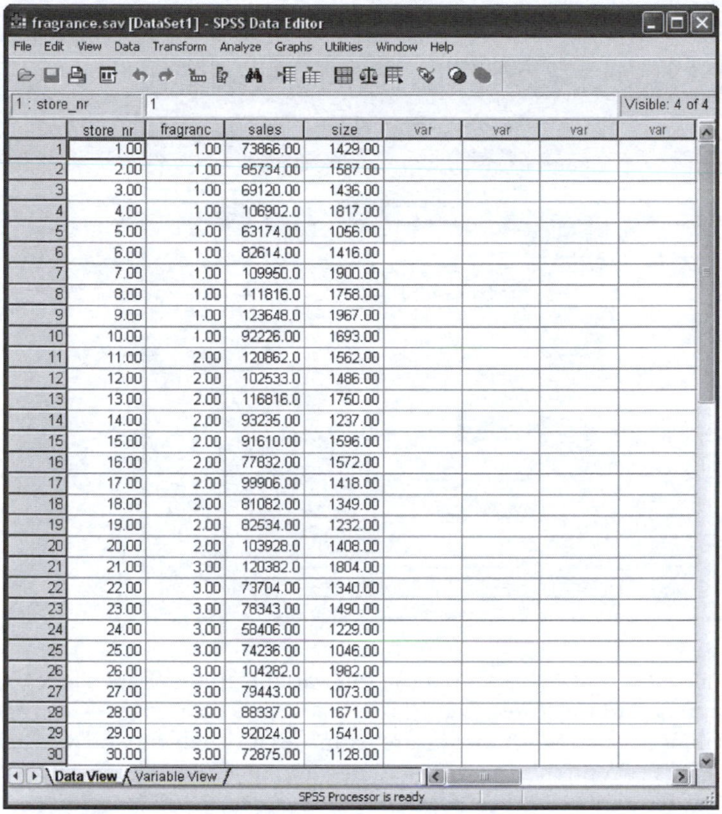

	store_nr	fragranc	sales	size	var	var	var	var
1	1.00	1.00	73866.00	1429.00				
2	2.00	1.00	85734.00	1587.00				
3	3.00	1.00	69120.00	1436.00				
4	4.00	1.00	106902.0	1817.00				
5	5.00	1.00	63174.00	1056.00				
6	6.00	1.00	82614.00	1416.00				
7	7.00	1.00	109950.0	1900.00				
8	8.00	1.00	111816.0	1758.00				
9	9.00	1.00	123648.0	1967.00				
10	10.00	1.00	92226.00	1693.00				
11	11.00	2.00	120862.0	1562.00				
12	12.00	2.00	102533.0	1486.00				
13	13.00	2.00	116816.0	1750.00				
14	14.00	2.00	93235.00	1237.00				
15	15.00	2.00	91610.00	1596.00				
16	16.00	2.00	77832.00	1572.00				
17	17.00	2.00	99906.00	1418.00				
18	18.00	2.00	81082.00	1349.00				
19	19.00	2.00	82534.00	1232.00				
20	20.00	2.00	103928.0	1408.00				
21	21.00	3.00	120382.0	1804.00				
22	22.00	3.00	73704.00	1340.00				
23	23.00	3.00	78343.00	1490.00				
24	24.00	3.00	58406.00	1229.00				
25	25.00	3.00	74236.00	1046.00				
26	26.00	3.00	104282.0	1982.00				
27	27.00	3.00	79443.00	1073.00				
28	28.00	3.00	88337.00	1671.00				
29	29.00	3.00	92024.00	1541.00				
30	30.00	3.00	72875.00	1128.00				

Solution

SPSS commands

Figure 4.11

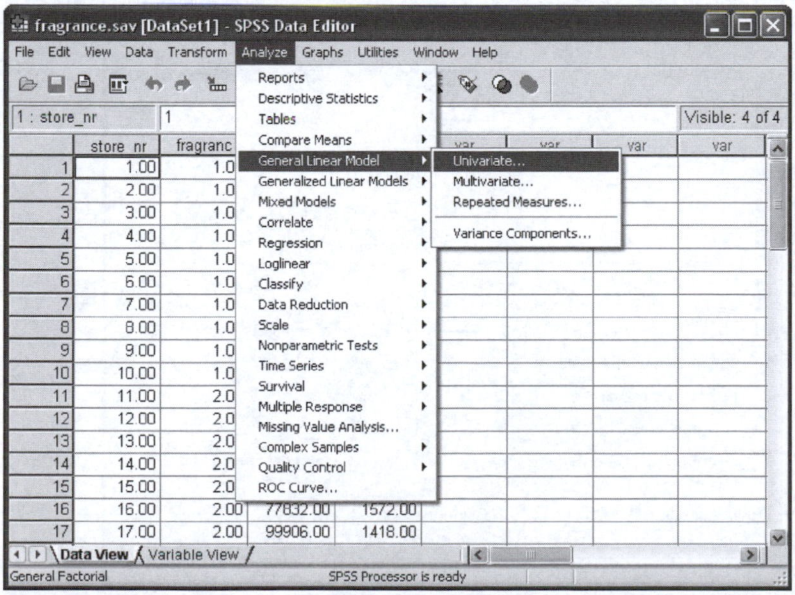

Go to Analyze/General Linear Model/Univariate as shown in Figure 4.11.

Figure 4.12

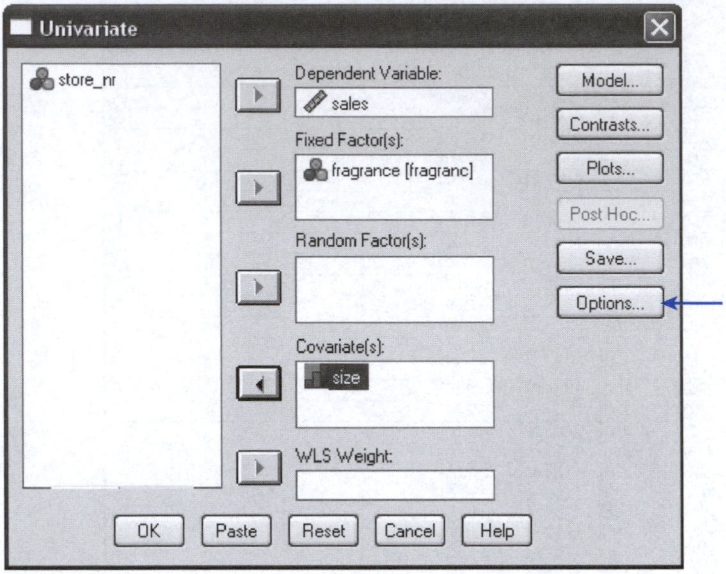

Click on 'Sales' and click ▶ to move this variable to the 'Dependent Variable' window. Move 'fragrance' to the 'Fixed Factor(s)' window and 'size' to the 'Covariate(s)' window.

You will notice that when the researcher moves a variable to the 'Covariate(s)' window, the 'Post Hoc . . .' option turns grey and may no longer be selected. In order to be able to use post hoc tests anyway, click 'Options'.

Figure 4.13

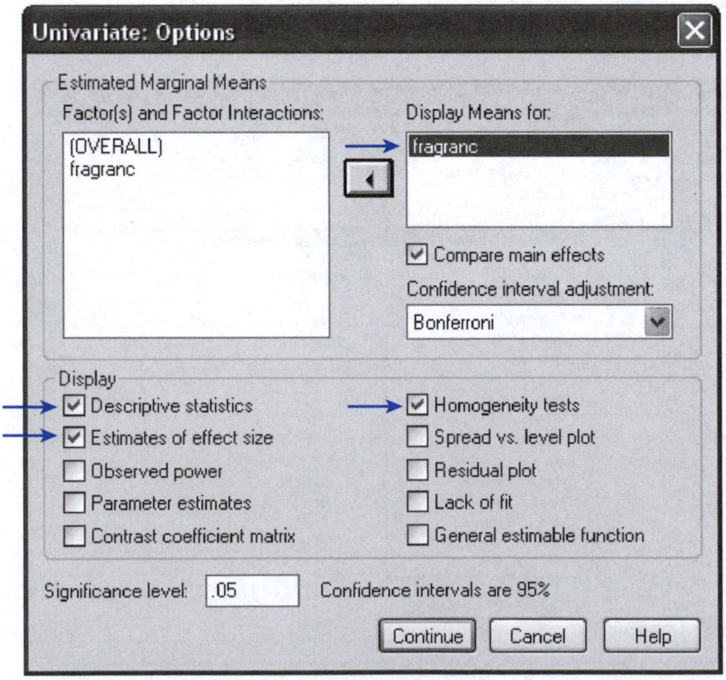

As seen in Figure 4.13, move the 'fragranc' variable from the 'Factor(s) and Factor Interactions' window to the 'Display Means for' window by clicking ▶. Now tick the box for the option 'Compare main effects'. Under 'Confidence interval adjustment' select 'Bonferroni' instead of the default option '(LSD) none'. This way, the post hoc tests will still be performed.

In the lower half of this same 'Options' window, under 'Display', indicate the options 'Descriptive statistics', 'Estimates of effect size' (to get an idea of the strength of the relationships found) and 'Homogeneity tests' (to test the assumption of the equality of group variances).

Next, click on 'Continue' and on 'Contrasts' in the 'Univariate' window. You will now see the image such as the one shown in Figure 4.14a. Click on the drop down symbol in the 'Change Contrast' section and change the option from 'None' to 'Simple'. Under 'Reference Category' change the option 'Last' to 'First' (no lavender fragrance is coded with '0' and the other two levels have the higher coding '1' and '2', therefore no lavender fragrance is the reference category). In this way, SPSS will test group 2 (low dose) and group 3 (high dose) against the first group (no lavender fragrance). Now click on 'Change', so that the changes also become visible in the 'Factors' window, as shown in Figure 4.14b.

Figure 4.14a

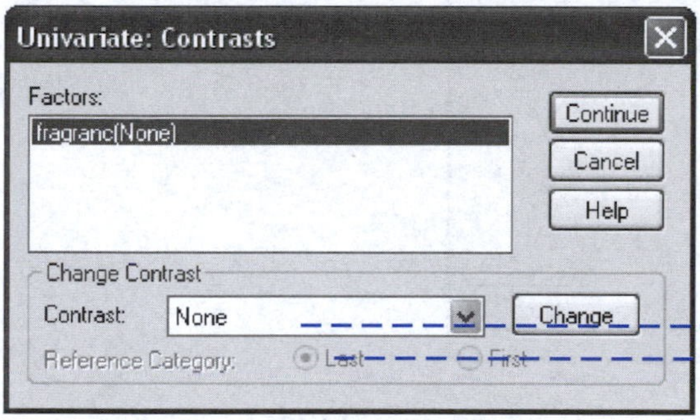

Figure 4.14b

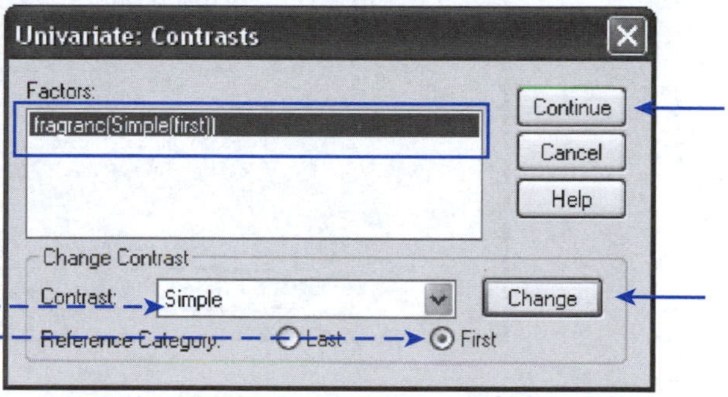

Now click 'Continue' and then 'Plots' in the 'Univariate' window shown in Figure 4.15.

Figure 4.15

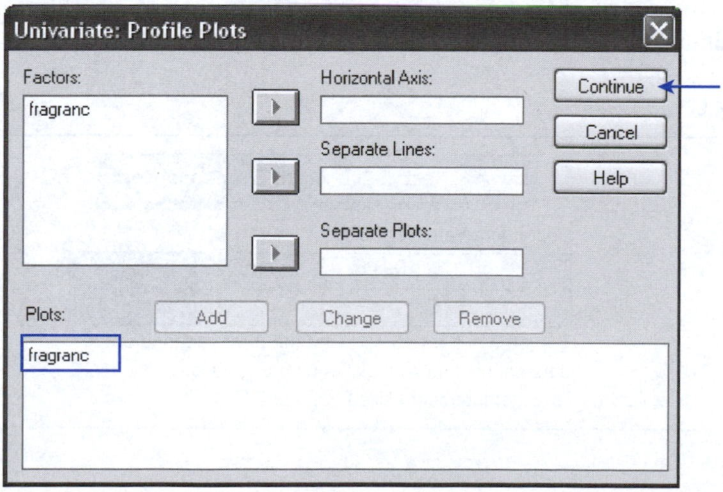

Move the variable 'fragranc' from the 'Factors' window to 'Horizontal Axis' in order to create a graphic image of the sales as a function of the quantity of lavender fragrance used, and then click on the 'Add' button. You will then see an image like the one shown in Figure 4.15.

Next click 'Continue' and then on 'Save' in the main window.

Figure 4.16

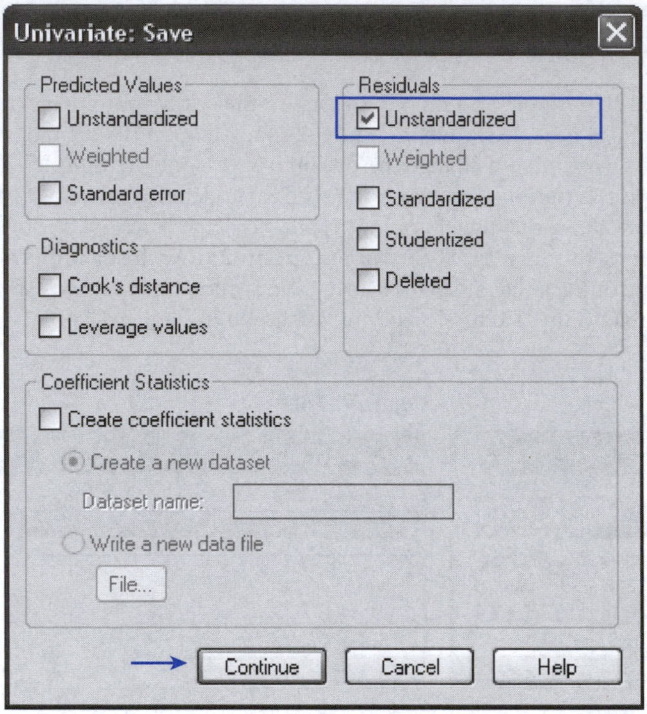

As shown in Figure 4.16, tick the option 'Unstandardized Residuals'. This will add an extra variable to the dataset which will be used to test several assumptions.

Click 'Continue' and then on 'OK' in the main window.

Interpretation of the SPSS output

First, the different assumptions for ANCOVA are checked. An initial assumption is that the error variance for the different experimental groups must be equal. This may be determined by examining the Levene's Test of Equality of Error Variances.

Figure 4.17

Levene's Test of Equality of Error Variances[a]

Dependent Variable: Sales

F	df1	df2	Sig.
1.225	2	27	.309

Tests the null hypothesis that the error variance of the dependent variable is equal across groups.

[a] Design: Intercept+size+fragranc

As shown in Figure 4.17, the null hypothesis of equal variances may not be rejected ($p = .309 > .05$), meaning that this assumption is satisfied. If this assumption had not been satisfied, the researcher could consider remedying interventions such as a transformation of the dependent variable (this is certainly the case when the inequality of the error terms is coupled with a non-normal distribution of the residuals) or the researcher may consider a non-parametric analysis of variance, such as Friedman's non-parametric ANOVA. Please refer to the specialised literature for further information in this regard.

Furthermore it is also assumed that the residuals are distributed normally. To determine this, a normality test must be performed on the unstandardized residuals, a new variable which was created via Figure 4.16. (This test may also be done on the standardized residuals. The result is the same). The normality of the residuals may then be tested here via Analyze/Descriptives/Explore, in which the option 'Normality plots with tests' is ticked under 'Plots' (see also Chapter 2, Frequency tables and graphs). An output like the one shown in Figure 4.18 will be obtained.

Figure 4.18

Tests of Normality

	Kolmogorov-Smirnov[a]			Shapiro-Wilk		
	Statistic	df	Sig.	Statistic	df	Sig.
Sales	.114	30	.200[*]	.965	30	.417

[*]This is a lower bound of the true significance
[a]Lilliefors significance correction

Figure 4.18 shows that the normality assumption has been satisfied since neither the significance level for the Kolmogorov-Smirnov statistic, with Lilliefors Correction (.200), nor for the Shapiro-Wilk's statistic (.417) is less than .05, therefore, the null hypothesis for normality cannot be rejected. Furthermore it is assumed that this experimental set-up was performed in such a manner that the independence of the observations may be assumed. Also, the scaling level of the dependent variable does not present a problem, since the dependent variable 'sales' is ratio-scaled.

With regard to ANCOVA, an extra assumption must be checked, namely the assumption of equality of the slope of the regression lines between the dependent variable and the covariate over the different experimental groups (a positive relationship in the one group and a negative relationship in the other group at the same time is not allowed). This assumption may be graphically determined and also tested formally. With regard to the graphic standpoint, we have plotted the regression line for each of the three experimental groups.

Go to Graph/Interactive/Scatterplot.

Figure 4.19

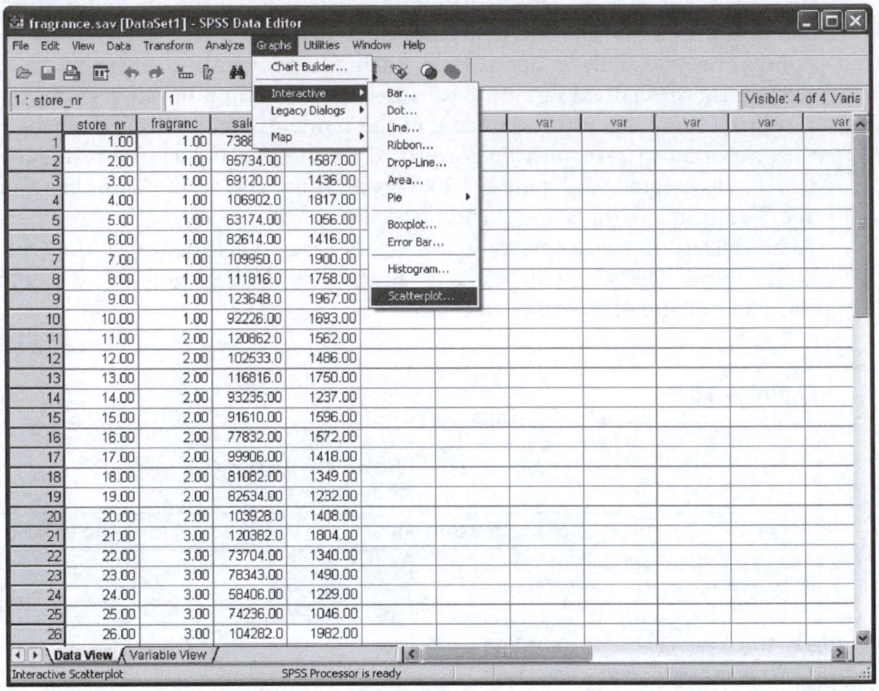

In the 'Assign Variables' tab (Figure 4.20), move the dependent variable 'sales' to the Y-axis and the covariate 'size' to the X-axis.

Figure 4.20

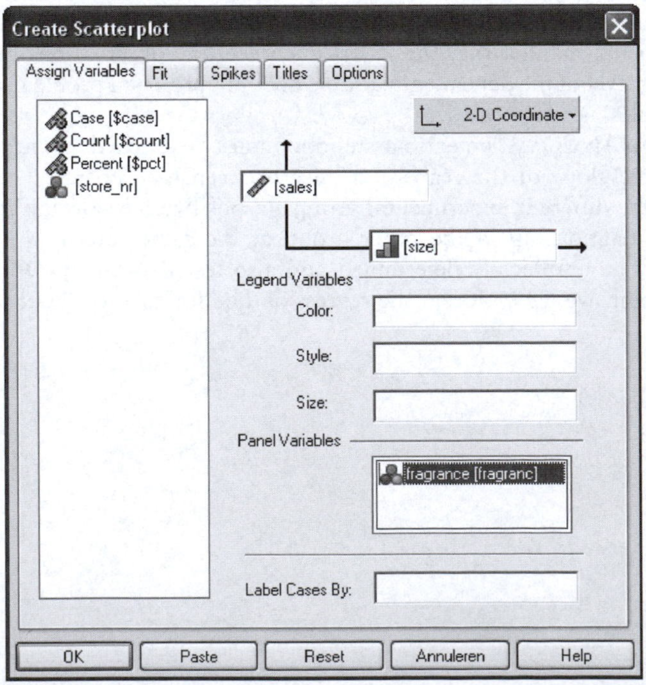

Now move the experimental group variable 'fragrance' to the 'Panel Variables' window. If this last variable has not yet been defined as a categorical variable, SPSS will give a warning as shown in Figure 4.21, in which it will ask you to convert the scale variable to a categorical variable. Click on 'Convert'. You will then see an image such as the one shown in Figure 4.20. Now click the 'Fit' tab.

Figure 4.21

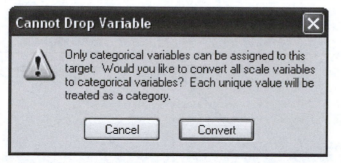

Figure 4.22

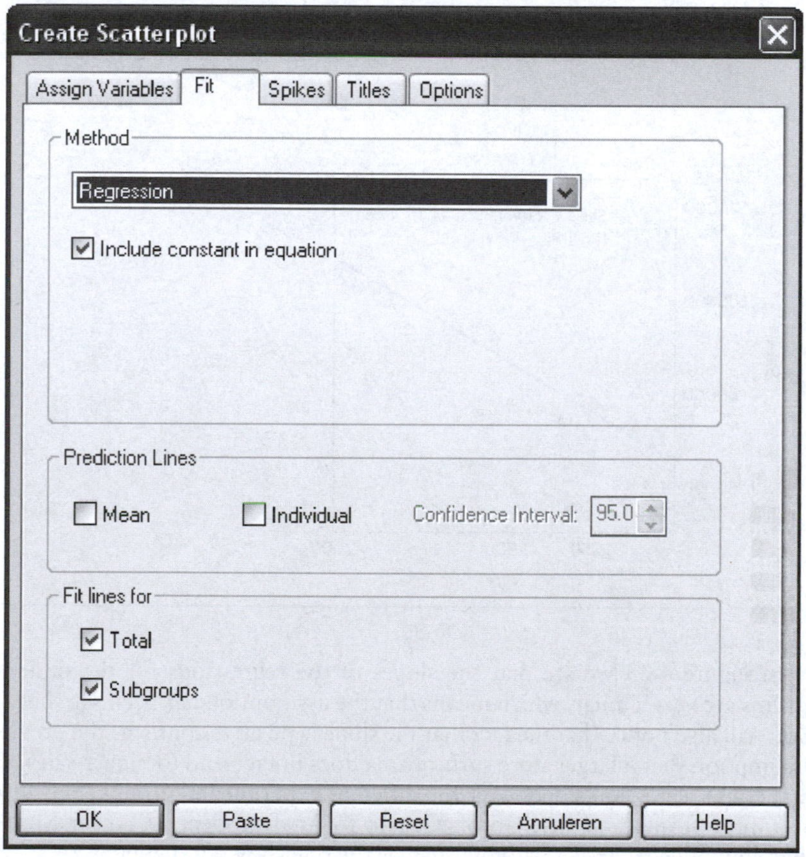

The default setting in the 'Fit' tab is 'Regression', which is what the researcher was aiming for, so this means that no changes should be made here. The 'Subgroups' option under 'Fit lines for' ensures the creation of regression plots for each group. Click 'OK'. You will then see an output like the one shown in Figure 4.23.

Figure 4.23

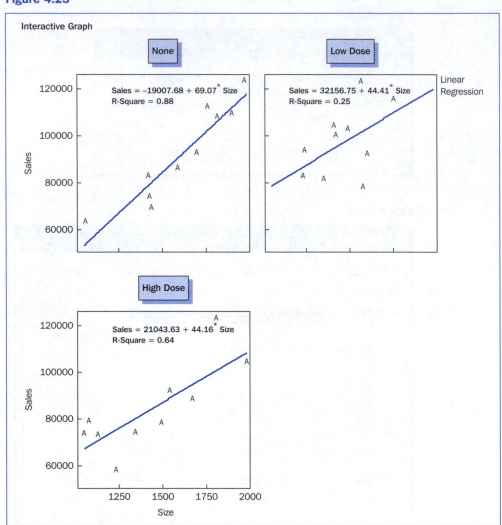

In Figure 4.23 we see that the slopes of the regressions for the different experimental groups are very similar, which means that the assumption has been satisfied in graphic terms. You will also notice that the fact that the slope is positive confirms the previously formulated assumption that a larger store surface area does in fact lead to higher sales. This assumption, that equal regression slopes over the different experimental groups, may also be determined in a more formal manner. Go once again to Analyze/General Linear Model/Univariate, so that you will again see a window such as the one shown in Figure 4.24.

Figure 4.24

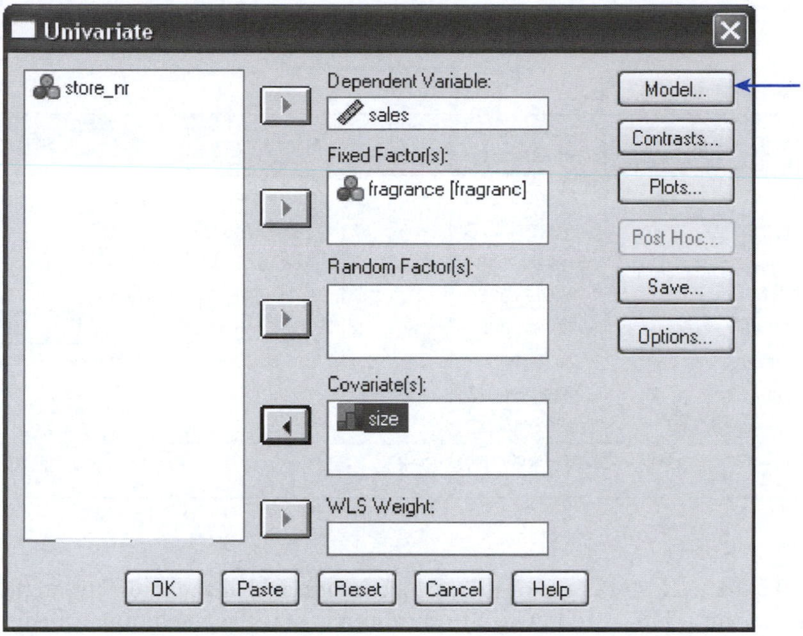

Click on 'Model'.

Figure 4.25

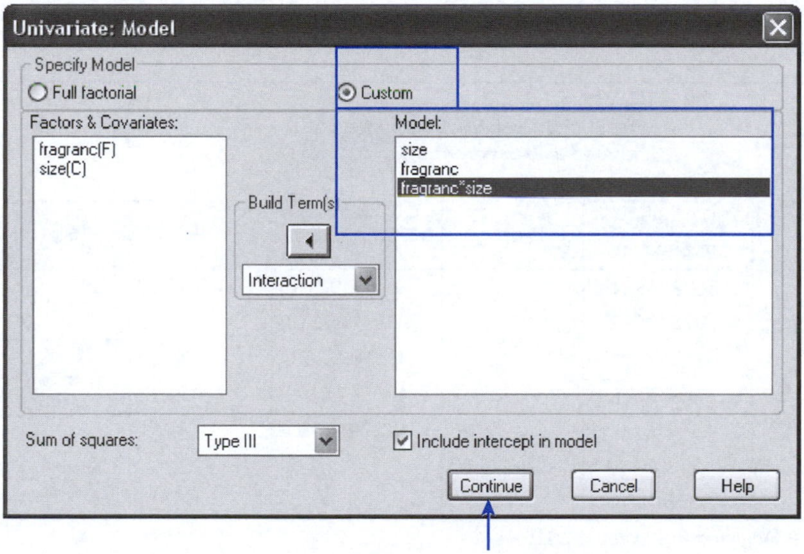

Next, change the 'Full Factorial' option to 'Custom'. Under 'Factors & Covariates', you must now indicate 'fragranc' and click ▶ to move this variable to the 'Model' window. Do the same for 'size'. In order to select the interaction term between both variables, click on 'fragranc', while pressing the Ctrl key and then click on 'size' so that both are selected (Figure 4.25) Now click ▶, 'Continue' and then 'OK'.

Figure 4.26

Tests of Between-Subjects Effects

Dependent Variable: Sales

Source	Type III Sum of Squares	df	Mean Square	F	Sig.	Partial Eta Squared
Corrected model	6432917308[a]	5	1286583462	10.562	.000	.688
Intercept	78221745.3	1	78221745.29	.642	.431	.026
Fragranc	328389950	2	164194974.9	1.348	.279	.101
Size	3761779330	1	3761779330	30.882	.000	.563
Fragranc * Size	269169060	2	134584530.2	1.105	.348	.084
Error	2923496505	24	121812354.4			
Total	2.580E+011	30				
Corrected Total	9356413813	29				

[a]R Squared = .688 (Adjusted R Squared = .622)

Figure 4.26 shows the output, which indicates that the interaction effect studied is not significant (.348 > .05), which in turn means that the assumption of equal slopes has not been violated, and confirmation is provided of the graphic analysis (the Partial Eta Squared is not relevant here).

Now that all of the assumptions have been checked, we can go back and view the actual main output of the ANCOVA analysis. The most important table for this is shown in Figure 4.27.

Figure 4.27

Tests of Between-Subjects Effects

Dependent Variable: Sales

Source	Type III Sum of Squares	df	Mean Square	F	Sig.	Partial Eta Squared
Corrected model	6163748248[a]	3	2054582749	16.732	.000	.659
Intercept	97849992.0	1	97849992.00	.797	.380	.030
Size	5329592884	1	5329592884	43.402	.000	.625
Fragranc	961089488	2	480544744.2	3.913	.033	.231
Error	3192665565	26	122794829.4			
Total	2.580E+011	30				
Corrected total	9356413813	29				

[a]R Squared = .659 (Adjusted R Squared = .619)

In Figure 4.27, we see that both the covariate 'size' ($p < .001$) as well as the fragrance variable 'fragranc' ($p = .033 < .05$) are significant. For purposes of comparison, a similar table is shown in Figure 4.28, but without the covariate 'size' (you may do this quite simply yourself by performing the same analysis again, without the covariate).

Figure 4.28

Tests of Between-Subjects Effects

Dependent Variable: Sales

Source	Type III Sum of Squares	df	Mean Square	F	Sig.	Partial Eta Squared
Corrected model	834155363[a]	2	417077681.7	1.321	.283	.089
Intercept	2.487E+011	1	2.487E+011	787.889	.000	.967
Fragranc	834155363	2	417077681.7	1.321	.283	.089
Error	8522258449	27	315639201.8			
Total	2.580E+011	30				
Corrected total	9356413813	29				

[a] R Squared = .089 (Adjusted R Squared = .022)

In comparing the two, you will see that without correcting the analysis for the biasing effect of store size, there would be no significant effect from the fragrance variable 'fragranc' (.283). In other words, by controlling the store-size effect, we obtain a purer image of the effect of the experimental variable, and this appears to be significant.

Now that we know that the fragrance variable exerts a significant influence on sales, we are interested in finding out which level of this variable (none/low/high) has the most effect. To do this, we need to examine Figure 4.29 and Figure 4.30.

Figure 4.29

Descriptive Statistics

Dependent Variable: Sales

Fragrance	Mean	Std. Deviation	N
None	91905.00	20410.06580	10
Low dose	97033.80	14615.06458	10
High dose	84203.20	17797.37921	10
Total	91047.33	17962.04217	30

Figure 4.30

Estimates

Dependent Variable: Sales

Fragrance	Mean	Std. Error	95% Confidence Interval	
			Lower Bound	Upper Bound
None	86201.931[a]	3609.552	78782.391	93621.472
Low dose	99068.322[a]	3517.791	91837.399	106299.244
High dose	87871.747[a]	3548.177	80578.364	95165.130

[a] Covariates appearing in the model are evaluated at the following values: size = 1499.1000

At first glance, these figures which show the means and standard deviations appear to show conflicting results. For example, Figure 4.29 shows that the mean sales for a high dose (84203.20) lie under those of the benchmark group (reference category) (91905.00). Figure 4.30 however indicates that precisely the opposite is the case: the sales for the high dose group (87871.747) are higher than those for the benchmark group (86201.931). The essential difference between both tables is that the means in Figure 4.30 are estimated for a mean covariate score (i.e., 1499.100 m^2 as the mean size of the store), while this was not the case in Figure 4.29 (normal means, without taking the covariate into consideration). This means that it is primarily the output in Figure 4.30 which is relevant in order to be able to estimate the mean sales for each experimental group. The plot of the averages which is obtained in the process (Figure 4.31) shows the means as given in Figure 4.30.

Figure 4.31

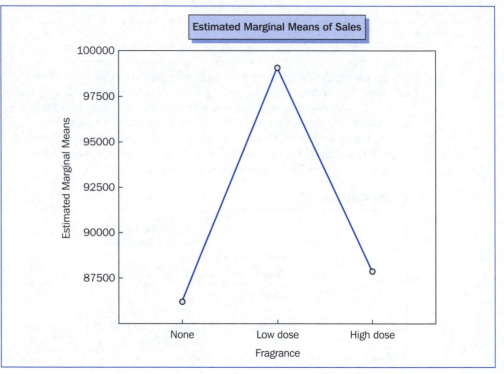

You will notice that the sales per group lie in the expected direction: in comparison with the benchmark group, the sales are higher in both the low dose group as well as in the high dose group, although this is only a relatively small amount of additional sales for the last group.

The formal tests between the averages are shown in Figures 4.32 and 4.33. We had expected a priori that group 2 (low dose) and group 3 (high dose) would each lead to significantly higher sales when compared with group 1 (no lavender fragrance). These a priori expectations have been tested using contrasts, as shown in Figure 4.32. Here we see that significantly more was sold in group 2 than in group 1 (additional sales = 12866.390; p = .018 < .05), but that this was not the case for group 3 (additional sales = 1669.815; p = .749 > .05).

Figure 4.32

Contrast Results (K Matrix)			

Fragrance Simple Contrast[a]			Dependent Variable
			Sales
Level 2 vs. Level 1	Contrast estimate		12866.390
	Hypothesized value		0
	Difference (Estimate – Hypothesized)		12866.390
	Std. error		5092.974
	Sig.		.018
	95% confidence interval for difference	Lower bound	2397.631
		Upper bound	23335.149
Level 3 vs. Level 1	Contrast estimate		1669.815
	Hypothesized value		0
	Difference (Estimate – Hypothesized)		1669.815
	Std. error		5155.824
	Sig.		.749
	95% confidence interval for difference	Lower bound	–8928.133
		Upper bound	12267.763

[a]Reference category = 1

With regard to the difference in additional sales between the low and high dose groups, the researcher actually had no a priori expectations (these could have been higher as a result of the stimulus from the stronger fragrance, but they also could have been lower, because it could have been perceived as manipulation). If we have no expectations about the direction of the difference, we can have a look at the post-hoc tests (Pairwise Comparisons) in Figure 4.33.

Figure 4.33

Pairwise Comparisons						

Dependent Variable: Sales

(I) Fragrance	(J) Fragrance	Mean Difference (I-J)	Std. Error	Sig.[a]	95% Confidence Interval for Difference[a]	
					Lower Bound	Upper Bound
None	Low dose	–12866.390	5092.974	.054	–25899.018	166.238
	High dose	–1669.815	5155.824	1.000	–14863.272	11523.641
Low dose	None	12866.390	5092.974	.054	–166.238	25899.018
	Nigh dose	11196.575	4961.903	.098	–1500.650	23893.799
High dose	None	1669.815	5155.824	1.000	–11523.641	14863.272
	Low dose	–11196.575	4961.903	.098	–23893.799	1500.650

Based on estimated marginal means
[a]Adjustment for multiple comparisons: Bonferroni

Here we see that there is a weak significant difference in sales between the low and high dose group (p = .098 < .10). You will also notice that the contrasts do test statistically less stringently than the post-hoc tests. In Figure 4.33, we see that the difference between the benchmark group and the low dose group is only slightly significant with p = .054 (in other words, significance level of 90% instead of 95%), while the contrasts had indicated earlier that the p-value there was .018. If we adhere strictly to the p < .05 rule, post-hoc testing would see it as a non-significant difference, while in terms of contrast testing, it is in fact significant.

On the basis of the above findings, the researcher can decide that the use of a low dose of lavender fragrance leads to significant additional sales with respect to a situation in which lavender fragrance is not used (on a 95% level), as well as when compared with the use of a strong lavender fragrance (on a 90% level).

Example 3

Analysis of variance for a complete 2 × 2 × 2 factorial design

Managerial problem

When a researcher would like to test the effect of different levels of several factors on a dependent variable, a factorial design will be necessary. In the following example, the effect of three dichotomous variables on a dependent variable will be determined, in this case the attitude with regard to an advertisement (Attitude towards the ad, or Aad). When more than one independent variable is studied, interaction effects are possible, which means that the effect of a certain variable will depend in part on the level of another variable; in other words, combinations of the independent variables may have a significant influence on the dependent variable.

Prior research has indicated that for new products, it is better to use a rational rather than an emotional advertisement (consumers prefer clear, rational information), while for existing products, an emotional advertisement is the better choice. The question now is whether or not the media context in which the advertisement will be shown is also important. In other words, does it matter whether an advertisement is shown in a rational or in an emotional context? One might also ask oneself if the interaction between the different factors has an influence on Aad. Given the fact that there are three independent variables (type of brand, type of ad, type of context), each of which is measured on two levels, this is referred to as a 2 × 2 × 2 factorial design.

In other words, there are eight different possible combinations. For each of these combinations, an advertisement was created. Each advertisement was shown to a different group of approximately 25 test persons. Each of the groups was compiled at random. Next, they were asked to fill out a questionnaire which included a number of statements which measured one aspect of Aad, the comprehension of the advertisement [m_aad_be] (7-point Likert-type scale). This variable is calculated as the mean of the relevant statements for this concept.

In Figure 4.34, part of the dataset *context.sav* is shown. This dataset shows the different factors and the 'comprehension' variable.

Figure 4.34

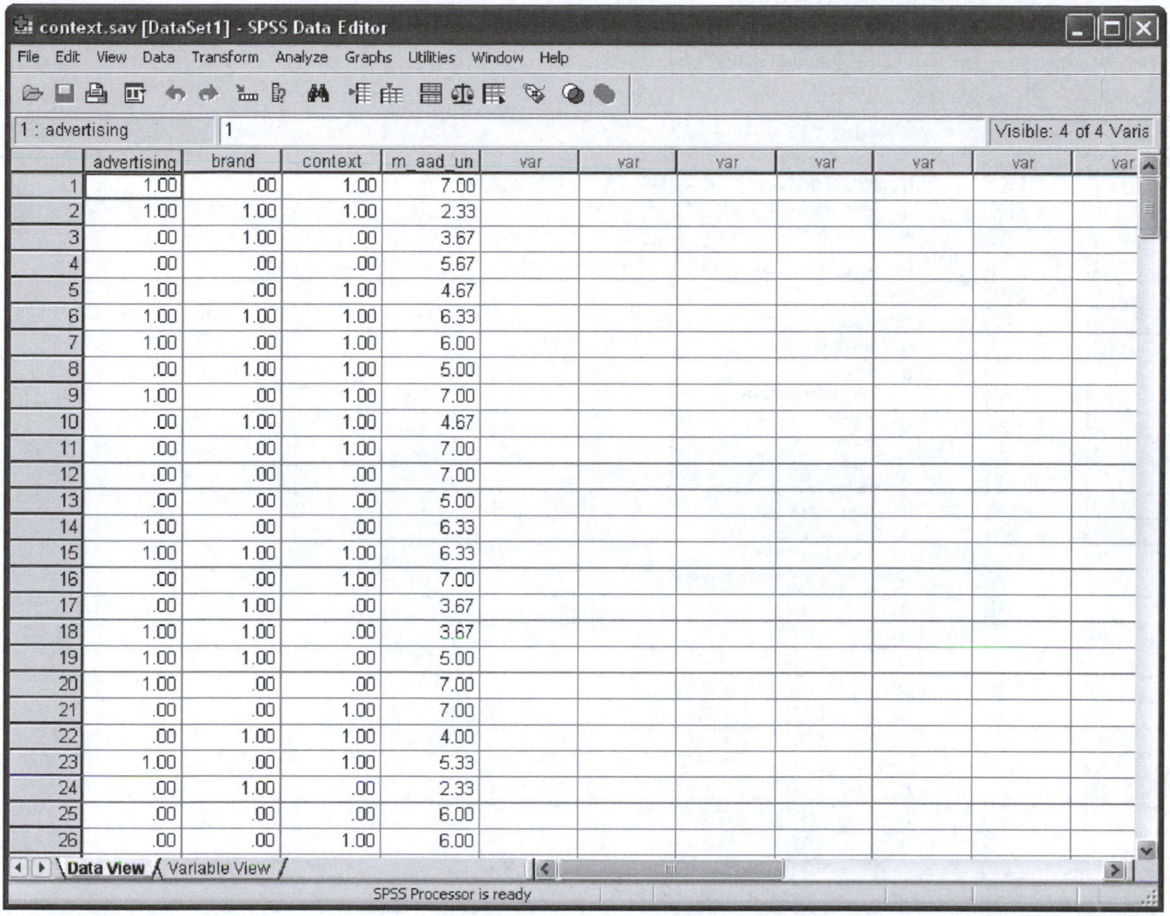

	advertising	brand	context	m_aad_un	var	var	var	var	var	var	var
1	1.00	.00	1.00	7.00							
2	1.00	1.00	1.00	2.33							
3	.00	1.00	.00	3.67							
4	.00	.00	.00	5.67							
5	1.00	.00	1.00	4.67							
6	1.00	1.00	1.00	6.33							
7	1.00	.00	1.00	6.00							
8	.00	1.00	1.00	5.00							
9	1.00	.00	1.00	7.00							
10	.00	1.00	1.00	4.67							
11	.00	.00	1.00	7.00							
12	.00	.00	.00	7.00							
13	.00	.00	.00	5.00							
14	1.00	.00	.00	6.33							
15	1.00	1.00	1.00	6.33							
16	.00	.00	1.00	7.00							
17	.00	1.00	.00	3.67							
18	1.00	1.00	.00	3.67							
19	1.00	1.00	.00	5.00							
20	1.00	.00	.00	7.00							
21	.00	.00	1.00	7.00							
22	.00	1.00	1.00	4.00							
23	1.00	.00	1.00	5.33							
24	.00	1.00	.00	2.33							
25	.00	.00	.00	6.00							
26	.00	.00	1.00	6.00							

Problem

Find out if the different dichotomous variables (new versus existing brand 'brand', emotional versus rational advertisement [advertising] and emotional versus rational context 'context') have a significant influence on the understanding of the advertising message [m_aad_un]. Also find out if there are interaction effects between the different independent variables and present these in graphic form.

Solution

SPSS commands

Figure 4.35

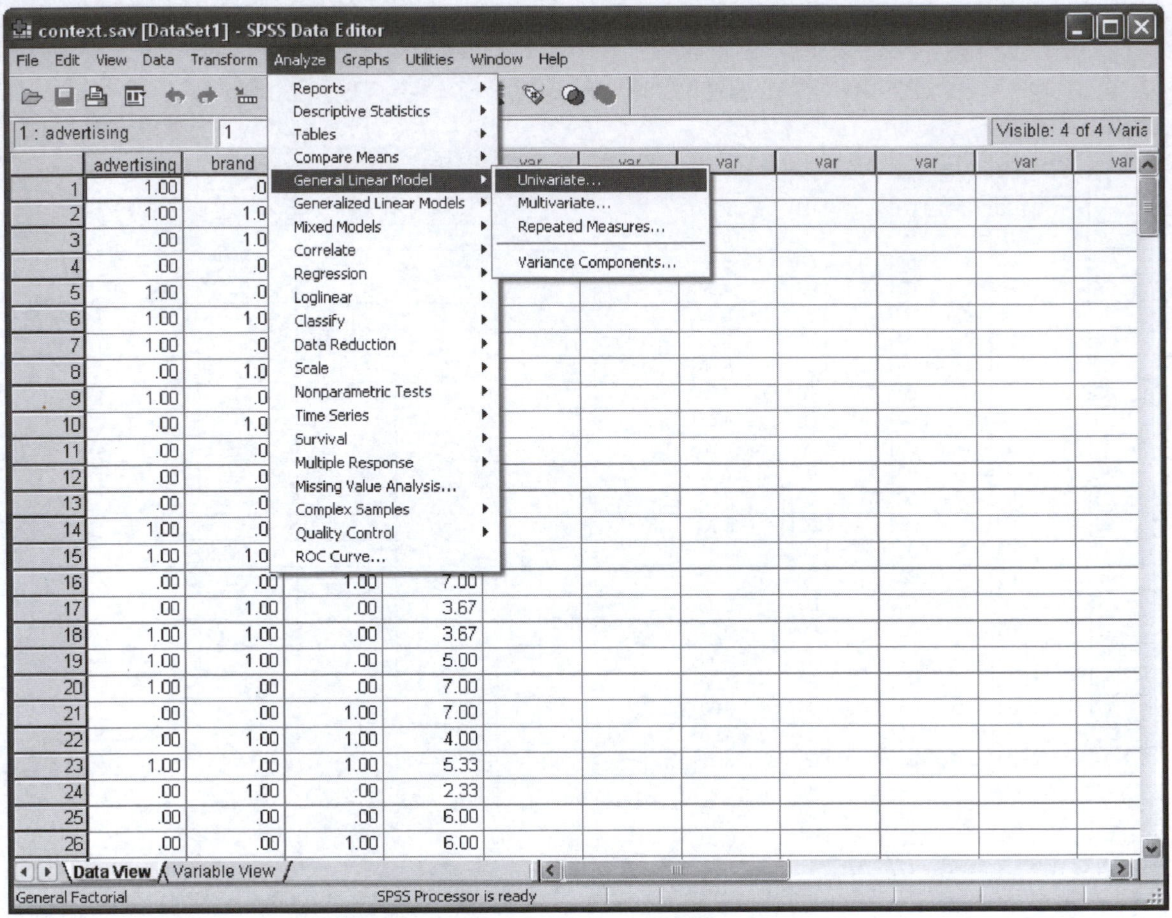

Go to Analyze/General Linear Model/Univariate (Figure 4.35).

Figure 4.36

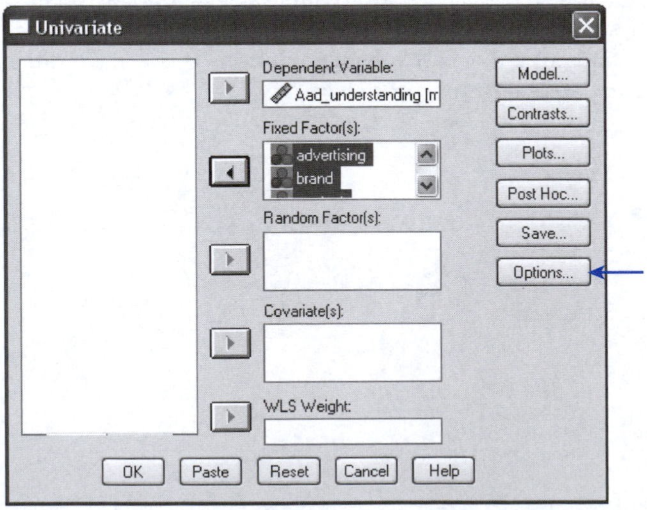

Click on 'Aad understanding' [m_aad_un] and then on ▶ to move this variable to the 'Dependent Variable' window. Move all variables of the subscreen 'advertising', 'brand', and 'context' to the 'Fixed Factor(s)' window. Next, click on Options to display the window as shown in Figure 4.37.

Figure 4.37

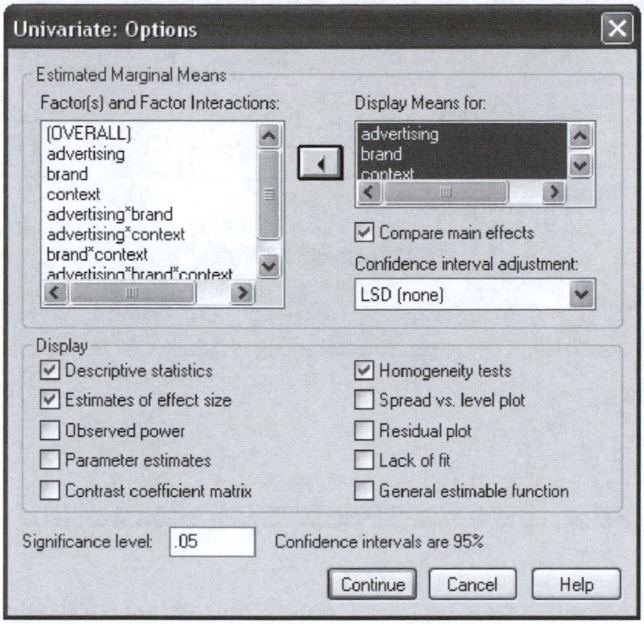

Select 'Factor(s) and Factor Interactions' as options as shown in Figure 4.37 and move these to the 'Display Means for' subwindow. In this subwindow, tick the option 'Compare main effects'. Under 'Display', indicate 'Descriptive statistics', 'Estimates of effect size', and 'Homogeneity tests'.

Next, click on 'Continue' and then on 'Save'.

Figure 4.38

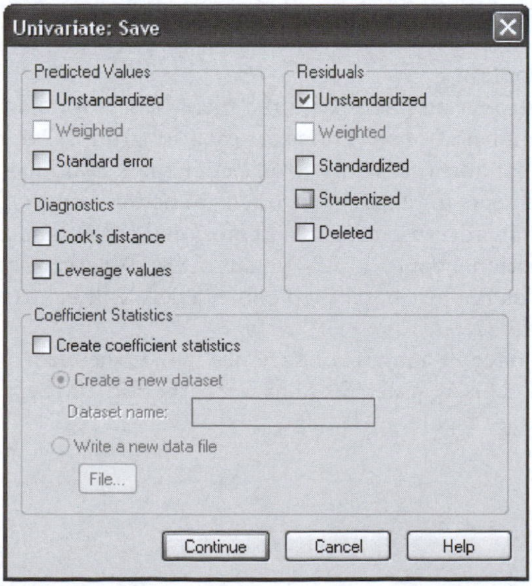

Under 'Residuals', indicate 'Unstandardized' (Figure 4.38). Then click on 'Continue' and then on 'Plots'.

Figure 4.39

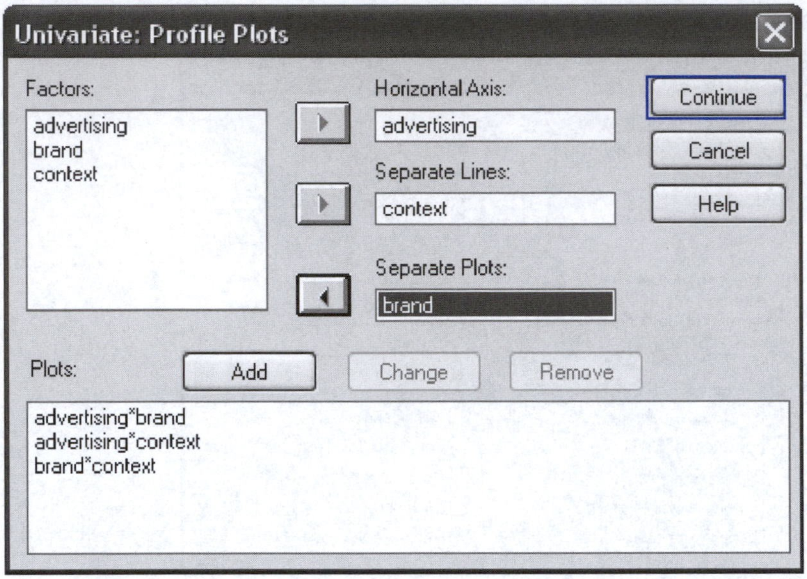

In order to obtain a graphic representation of the interaction effects, the researcher may create 'plots' (Figure 4.39). In the example, there are three second-order interaction effects which may be analysed. There is also one third-order interaction effect (advertising × brand × context).

Move [advertising] to 'Horizontal Axis' and [brand] to 'Separate Lines'. Now click on 'Add' so that 'advertising*brand' appears in the 'Plots:' subwindow. Do the same for advertising and context as well as for brand and context. For the third-order interaction effect, move [advertising] to 'Horizontal Axis', [context] to 'Separate Lines' and [brand] to 'Separate Plots'. This will create the image seen in Figure 4.39. Now click 'Add', 'Continue' and then 'OK' which will produce the output as shown in Figure 4.40.

Interpretation of the SPSS output
In Figure 4.40, the researcher sees an image with the mean scores for Aad understanding, standard deviations and a number of observations for each subgroup. One sees for example that, on the face of it, rational advertisements score better than emotional advertisements (5.39 versus 4.89), advertisements for existing products do better than those for new products (5.55 versus 4.72), and an advertisement in an emotional context hardly scores better than an advertisement in a rational context (5.20 versus 5.08). Whether or not these differences are significant (and thus not attributable to coincidence) will be discussed in further detail later (see also Figure 4.43).

One of the assumptions made in analysis of variance is that the error variance is equal across the different groups. This is tested in SPSS with the aid of the Levene's Test of Equality of Error Variances (see Figure 4.41).

Figure 4.40

Descriptive Statistics

Dependent Variable: Aad_understanding

Advertising	Brand	Context	Mean	Std. Deviation	N
Emotional	Existing	Emotional	5.7126	1.15633	29
		Rational	4.9583	1.23495	32
		Total	5.3169	1.24748	61
	New	Emotional	4.1012	1.36486	28
		Rational	4.7727	1.24848	33
		Total	4.4645	1.33545	61
	Total	Emotional	4.9211	1.49241	57
		Rational	4.8641	1.23564	65
		Total	4.8907	1.35617	122
Rational	Existing	Emotional	5.8889	1.08396	30
		Rational	5.6667	1.21411	31
		Total	5.7760	1.14782	61
	New	Emotional	5.0323	1.37263	31
		Rational	4.9425	1.52250	29
		Total	4.9889	1.43532	60
	Total	Emotional	5.4536	1.30247	61
		Rational	5.3167	1.40811	60
		Total	5.3857	1.35196	121
Total	Existing	Emotional	5.8023	1.11395	59
		Rational	5.3069	1.26619	63
		Total	5.5464	1.21576	122
	New	Emotional	4.5904	1.43583	59
		Rational	4.8522	1.37440	62
		Total	4.7245	1.40497	121
	Total	Emotional	5.1963	1.41684	118
		Rational	5.0813	1.33528	125
		Total	5.1372	1.37384	243

Figure 4.41

Levene's Test of Equality of Error Variances[a]

Dependent Variable: Aad_understanding

F	df1	df2	Sig.
1.496	7	235	.169

Tests the null hypothesis that the error variance of the dependent variable is equal across groups

[a]Design:
Intercept+advertising+brand+context+advertising * brand+advertising * context+brand * context+advertising * brand * context

In this case, it may be concluded that the null hypothesis of equal variances may not be rejected (sig. = .169 > .05) and that as a result, this assumption has been satisfied. For this reason, in Figure 4.38, the user was asked to save these residuals as a new variable in the dataset. Via Analyze/Descriptive Statistics/Explore (Plots) this normality may be determined (see also Chapter 2). Figure 4.42 shows that the null hypothesis of Normality is rejected (Kolmogorov-Smirnov: p = .004 < .005 en Shapiro-Wilk: p = .001 < .005).

A chart displaying the histogram with a normal curve can also be examined. This graph can be obtained by following Analyze/Descriptive Statistics/Frequencies and by clicking on 'Charts' and indicating 'Histogram with normal curve'.

Figure 4.42

	Kolmogorov-Smirnov[a]			Shapiro-Wilk		
	Statistic	df	Sig.	Statistic	df	Sig.
Residual for m_aad_un	.072	243	.004	.977	243	.001

[a]Lilliefors significance correction

If the previous two assumptions have not been satisfied, then one may consider transformations of the dependent variable. It is recommended to consult the specialised literature available on this topic for this (see reference list at the end of this chapter).

Figure 4.42 *Continued*

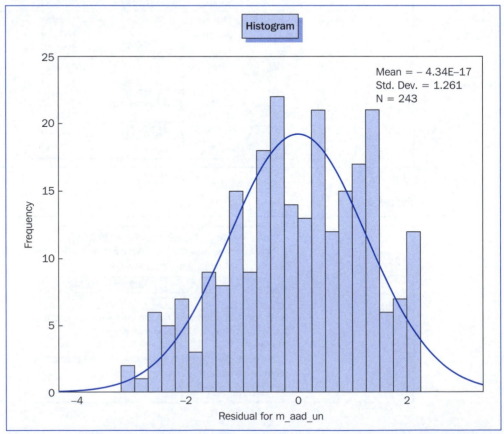

However, based on the histogram as shown in Figure 4.42 (continued) the researcher decides that the normality is substantially present. Therefore he decides to continue working with the variables as they are. A third assumption involves the independence of the error terms, in other words that the one observation does not influence the other. A good experimental design can prevent problems in this regard. This is assumed in the example.

The main output of the ANOVA is shown in Figure 4.43. When one examines the main effects, one sees that two of the three main effects are significant, namely 'advertising' (sig. = .003 < .05) and 'brand' (sig. = .001 < .05). The other main effect, 'context', is not significant (sig. = .549 < .05). More important than these main effects in fact are the interaction effects. There are three second-order interaction effects. One of these ('brand' * 'context') appears to be significant. This means that specific combinations (of the levels) of these factors will differ significantly from the other combinations.

Figure 4.43

Tests of Between-Subjects Effects

Dependent Variable: Aad_understanding

Source	Type III Sum of Squares	df	Mean Square	F	Sig.	Partial Eta Squared
Corrected Model	72.145[a]	7	10.306	6.297	.000	.158
Intercept	6388.823	1	6388.823	3903.568	.000	.943
advertising	14.927	1	14.927	9.120	.003	.037
brand	43.205	1	43.205	26.398	.000	.101
context	.590	1	.590	.360	.549	.002
advertising * brand	.177	1	.177	.108	.742	.000
advertising * context	.199	1	.199	.122	.728	.001
brand * context	9.196	1	9.196	5.619	.019	.023
advertising * brand * context	6.334	1	6.334	3.870	.050	.016
Error	384.616	235	1.637			
Total	6869.667	243				
Corrected Total	456.761	242				

[a]R Squared = .158 (Adjusted R Squared = .133)

A better indication of the interaction effect may be found in Figures 4.44 through 4.46.

Figure 4.44

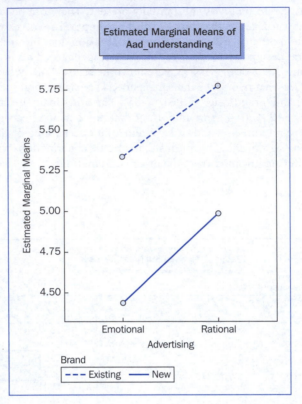

Figure 4.45

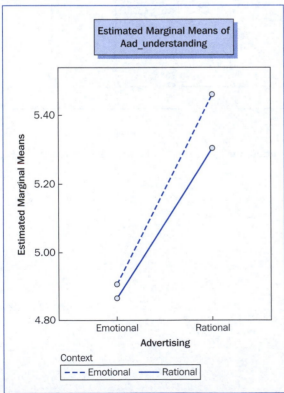

Figure 4.46

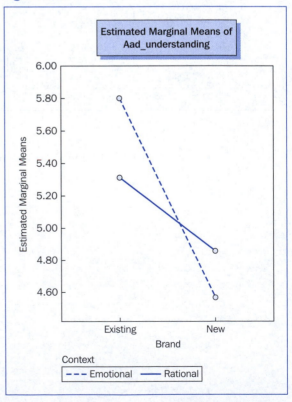

If the two lines in the figures are parallel to one another, then this indicates that there is no interaction effect present. In other words, when the differences between the scores at different levels of a certain factor are equal to those of another factor, then one can say that there are no interaction effects present. Figure 4.44 shows that the effect of an existing or new brand is no different for an emotional advertisement than it is for a rational advertisement. The combination of types of advertisements and context types (Figure 4.45) also fails to lead to significant differences. Be sure to also note the scale on the vertical axis; SPSS always creates the best possible graphic 'fit', which results in the distances in the graph always being relative.

In Figure 4.46, the significant interaction effect between 'brand' and 'context' is shown. You will notice that the lines do not run parallel to one another and even cross, so that the effect of the 'context' is factor-dependent on the level of the 'brand' factor. The significant interaction effect observed earlier in Figure 4.43 is thus confirmed graphically. With the significant interaction effects, the question is which combinations of factor levels are the ones that result in significance. The output section on 'Estimated Marginal Means' provides a better picture of this. Figure 4.47 shows the relevant section on the 'brand' * 'context' interaction effect.

Figure 4.47

Pairwise Comparisons

Dependent Variable: Aad_understanding

(I) Advertising	(J) Advertising	Mean Difference (I-J)	Std. Error	Sig.	95% Confidence Interval for Difference[a]	
					Lower Bound	Upper Bound
Emotional	Rational	−.496[*]	.164	.003	−.820	−.173
Rational	Emotional	.496[*]	.164	.003	.173	.820

Based on estimated marginal means
[*]The mean difference is significant at the .05 level
[a]Adjustment for multiple comparisons: Least Significant Difference (equivalent to no adjustments)

It may be useful here to look at the non-overlapping confidence intervals, in other words, those situations in which there is no overlap with another factor level combination within a 95% confidence interval. A graphic representation simplifies the interpretation. Go to Graphs/Legacy Dialogs/Error Bar (Figure 4.48).

Figure 4.48

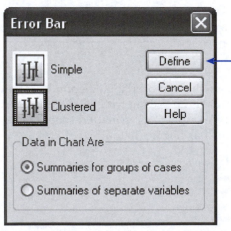

	advertising	brand	cont			var	var	var	var
1	1.00	.00							
2	1.00	1.00	1.00	2.33					
3	.00	1.00	.00	3.67					
4	.00	.00	.00	5.67					
5	1.00	.00	1.00	4.67					
6	1.00	1.00	1.00	6.33					
7	1.00	.00	1.00	6.00					
8	.00	1.00	1.00	5.00					
9	1.00	.00	1.00	7.00					
10	.00	1.00	1.00	4.67	.11				
11	.00	.00	1.00	7.00	2.04				
12	.00	.00	.00	7.00	1.29				
13	.00	.00	.00	5.00	-.71				
14	1.00	.00	.00	6.33	.44				
15	1.00	1.00	1.00	6.33	1.39				
16	.00	.00	1.00	7.00	2.04				
17	.00	1.00	.00	3.67	-.43				
18	1.00	1.00	.00	3.67	-1.37				
19	1.00	1.00	.00	5.00	-.03				
20	1.00	.00	.00	7.00	1.11				
21	.00	.00	1.00	7.00	2.04				
22	.00	1.00	1.00	4.00	-.77				
23	1.00	.00	1.00	5.33	-.33				
24	.00	1.00	.00	2.33	-1.77				
25	.00	.00	.00	6.00	.29				
26	.00	.00	1.00	6.00	1.04				

Figure 4.49

Change 'Simple' to 'Clustered' on the subscreen shown in Figure 4.49 because we want to see two factors displayed at the same time. Now click 'Define'.

Figure 4.50

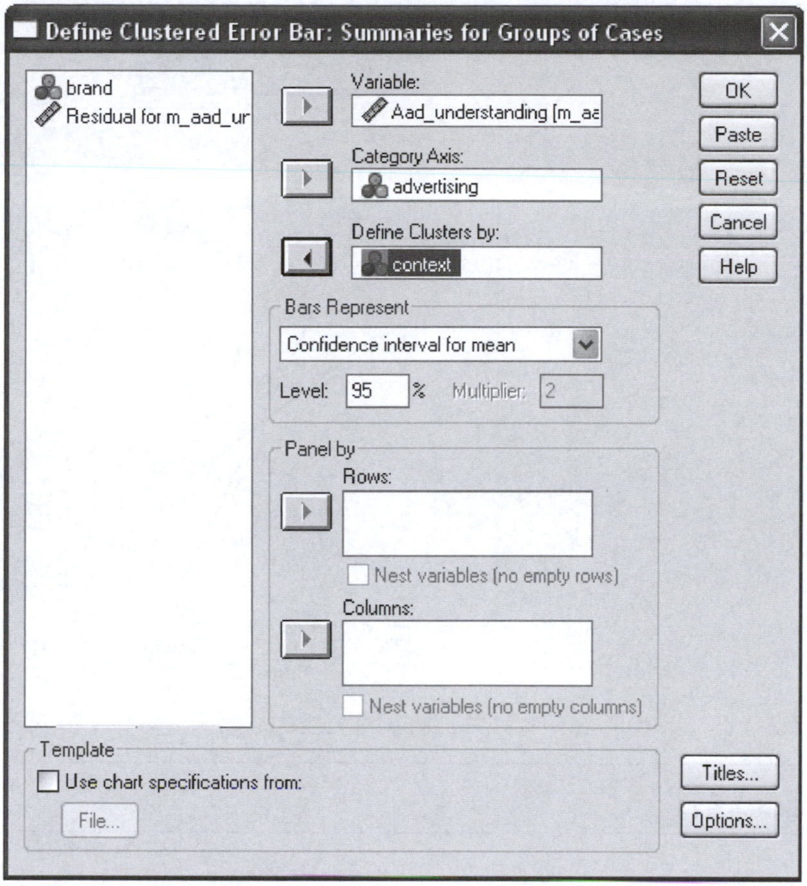

Move 'Aad_understanding' to 'Variable', 'brand' to 'Category Axis' and 'context' to 'Define Clusters by' (Figure 4.50). Now click 'OK'. You will see the output as shown in Figure 4.52.

In order to ensure that the user understands this, Figure 4.46 has been repeated in Figure 4.51. Both figures are the graphic representation of the data found in Figure 4.47.

The apparent conclusion in Figure 4.51 that it is better to use an emotional context for an existing brand and that it is better to use a rational context for a new brand, must be qualified. As one can see in Figure 4.52, for each brand type (new or existing), the two confidence intervals overlap one another in part each time. On the basis of this graphical representation of the confidence intervals one can however say that an emotional context scores significantly better for an existing brand than a new brand, and also scores better than a rational context does for a new brand (the intervals do not overlap). In case intervals overlap, a t-test has to be performed to test the difference between the conditions under study.

The fact that there is also a significant main effect from the factor 'brand' is less crucial information because of the interaction between 'brand' and 'context'.

The researcher also sees in Figure 4.43 that there is another significant third-order interaction effect present ($.05 = .05$).[1] Figures 4.53 through 4.57 display this effect.

Figure 4.51

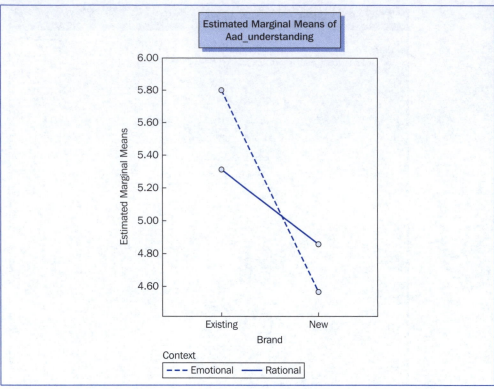

Figure 4.52

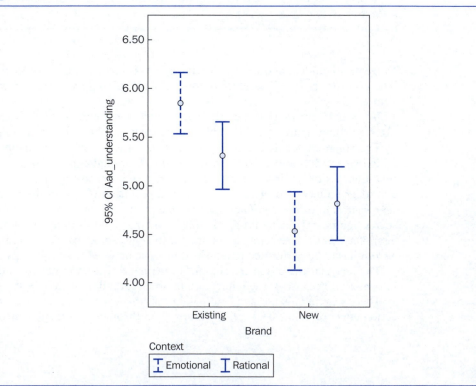

Figure 4.53

8. Advertising * Brand * Context						

Dependent Variable: Aad_understanding

Advertising	Brand	Context	Mean	Std. Error	95% Confidence Interval	
					Lower Bound	Upper Bound
Emotional	Existing	Emotional	5.713	.238	5.245	6.181
		Rational	4.958	.226	4.513	5.404
	New	Emotional	4.101	.242	3.625	4.578
		Rational	4.773	.223	4.334	5.211
Rational	Existing	Emotional	5.889	.234	5.429	6.349
		Rational	5.667	.230	5.214	6.119
	New	Emotional	5.032	.230	4.580	5.485
		Rational	4.943	.238	4.475	5.411

The nature of the third-order interaction effect may best be analysed graphically. The Figures 4.55 and 4.57 have been created as described for Figures 4.48 and 4.50. However, one must choose the other group each time for [brand] (via Data/Select Cases).

Figure 4.54

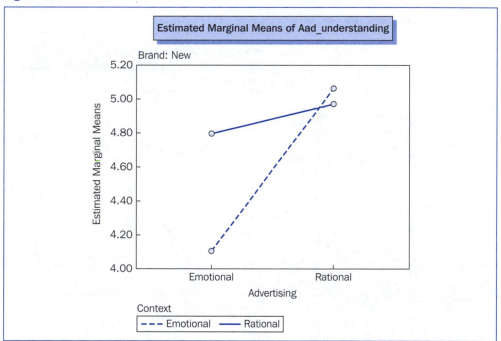

Figure 4.55

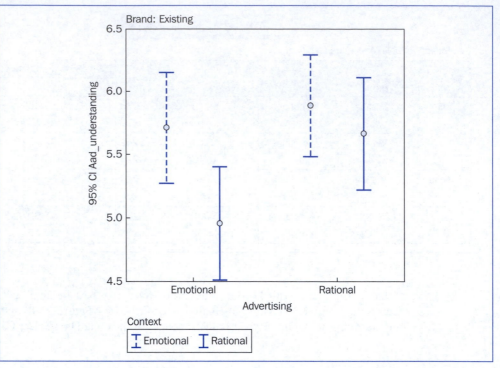

Figure 4.56

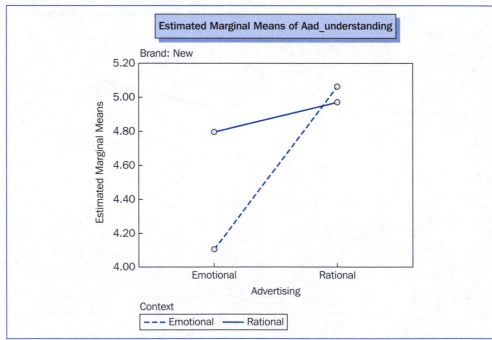

Figure 4.57

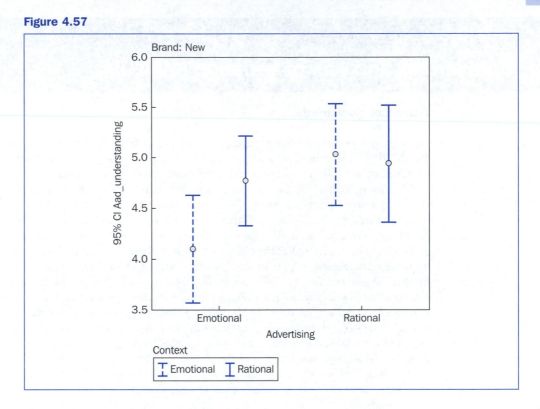

The first impression one obtains from Figure 4.54, that it is best to use an emotional context for an existing brand, requires a bit of modification. Figure 4.55 demonstrates that the only significant conclusion which may be made is that for an existing brand, a rational advertisement in an emotional context scores higher than an emotional advertisement in a rational context. This interaction changes completely when one examines the situation in the case of a new brand. In this case, it may be concluded significantly that a rational advertisement in an emotional context scores better than an emotional advertisement in an emotional context. In the figures (e.g. Figure 4.57), one must pay special attention to the accuracy of the graphs. In Figure 4.57, it seems like the 'error bars' just barely overlap, but the numbers in Figure 4.53 show that there is still a slight lack of overlapping, which therefore implies a significant difference (upper limit of emotional advertisement in an emotional context = 4.578 and the lower limit of rational advertisement in an emotional context = 4.580).

A general decision which may be made here is that the context into which an advertisement is introduced has a significant influence on the understanding of an advertisement for both new and existing products.

Example 4

Multivariate analysis of variance (MANOVA)

Technique: supplement

If researchers would like to determine whether or not one or more categorical variables have an effect on several dependent variables, they perform a multivariate analysis of variance (MANOVA). The dependent variables are thus simultaneously tested in determining whether or not there are differences between the different categorical groups.

The question may be asked why a separate ANOVA is not performed each time for each dependent variable instead of a multivariate ANOVA. There are two important reasons for this. First of all, the performance of different ANOVAs can increase the chance of a Type I error substantially: the more dependent variables, the more separate ANOVAs and consequently the higher the chance of incorrectly rejecting a null hypothesis. A second, more intrinsic reason is that the multivariate test produces important extra information. Instead of determining for each dependent variable whether or not there are group differences (and whereby abstractions are made for the possible connections between the dependent variables), with a MANOVA, we find out whether or not there are group differences between the variable combinations (results) which are created by the different dependent variables. It is important to note here that it is not always meaningful to perform a MANOVA, particularly if the dependent variables are strongly correlated (perform a single ANOVA with one of the perfectly correlated variables as a dependent variable), or if they have a zero correlation (then only separate ANOVAs should be performed).

A typical sequence in the analysis is to first perform a MANOVA and then to perform the univariate ANOVAs as post-hoc analysis in order to better be able to interpret the MANOVA results. This is also the approach which will be applied in the following example.

There are also several assumptions which apply to a MANOVA analysis. The observations must be independent, the samples involved must be random and must be taken from the population to be studied, the dependent variables should be at least interval-scaled, the dependent variables must be multivariate normally distributed, and finally, the variances and the co-variances of and between the dependent variables must be equal for the different groups being studied. These assumptions will be studied in the following example.

Finally it must be noted that just like covariates may be added to an ANOVA (ANCOVA), this may also be done with a MANOVA (MANCOVA). The inclusion of covariates compensates for the error variance which may be attributed to the covariance of the covariate with the dependent variable. The working out of a MANCOVA will not be discussed in a separate example, but the interpretation for the covariates is analogous to the ANCOVA case (see example 2 in this chapter).

Managerial problem

In this example, we would like to find out if a difference exists between groups with different personal values with respect to their attitudes regarding Fair Trade shops (e.g., Oxfam World Shops). People's personal values may be measured in a variety of ways, however the most well-known measuring tool is the Rokeach Value Survey (RVS). This scale consists of 18 statements with regard to instrumental values (actions) and 18 which concern terminal values (achievement). A factor analysis was performed on these 36 items (see Chapters 7 and 8) to discover the underlying dimensions in these personal values. There were 6 dimensions found (competence, feeling of public obedience, emotional peace, comfort, being nice and idealism). Next, a cluster analysis was performed on these dimensions (see Chapter 9). After these manipulations, it appeared that on the basis of personal values, there were four distinct groups of people which could be identified:

- *Cluster 1:* value-conscious people (relatively high for all values)
- *Cluster 2:* ascetic idealists (relatively high for idealism and low for comfort)
- *Cluster 3:* hedonistic egoists (relatively low for idealism and high for comfort)
- *Cluster 4:* value sceptics (relatively low for all values)

The survey also contained several questions about the respondents' attitudes toward Fair Trade stores. A factor analysis indicated three underlying dimensions, namely 'staff professionalism' (personal service and knowledge), 'shop sophistication' (fair-trade stores are not austere and have a broad assortment of products), and 'shop familiarity', whereby low scores indicate the less accessible aspect of Fair Trade shops (too unfamiliar and too alternative). High scores for each of the dimensions were indicative of a positive attitude with regard to FT shops. Information was studied for each dimension on the basis of two items. Scores were given on a −2 (totally disagree) to +2 (totally agree) Likert type of scale and the mean was then taken of these.

Problem

Perform a MANOVA to determine whether or not there is a difference between the four value groups with regard to the attitude towards Fair Trade shops, measured by the three dimensions: 'Staff professionalism', 'Shop sophistication' and 'Shop familiarity'. The mean scores for the three dimensions as well as the value group to which the respondent belongs may be found in '*FTshops_RVSgroups*' displayed in Figure 4.58.

Figure 4.58

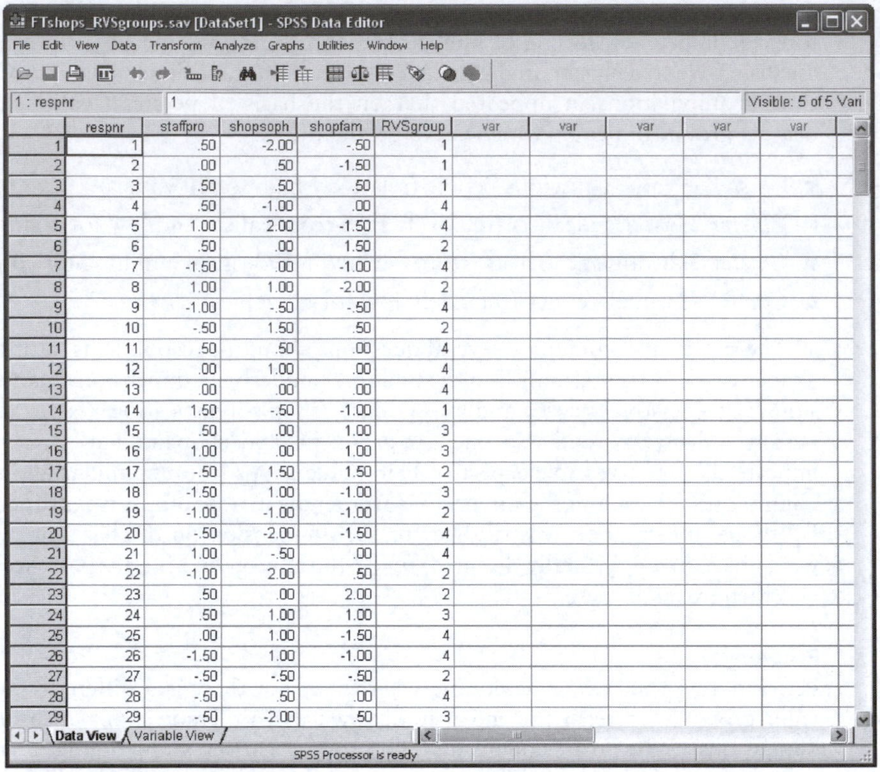

Solution

SPSS commands

Figure 4.59

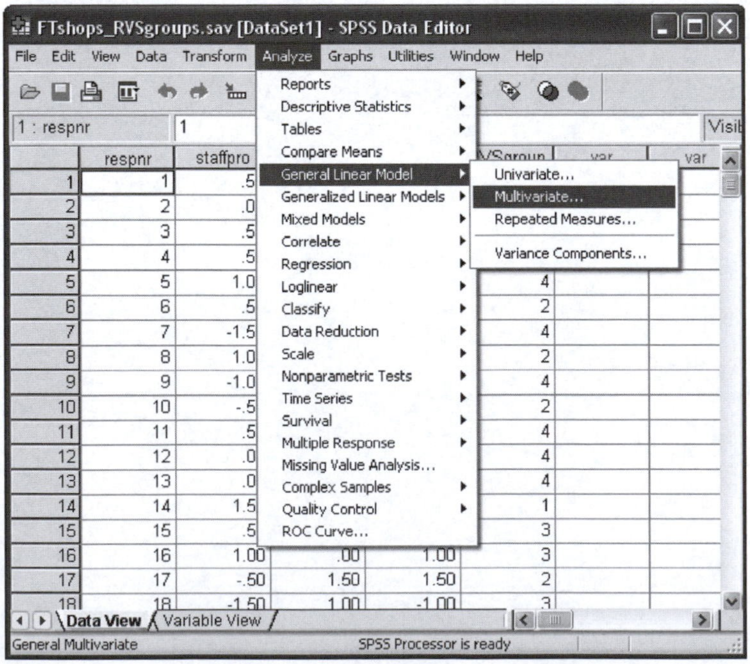

Go to Analyze/General Linear Model/Multivariate (Figure 4.59).

Figure 4.60

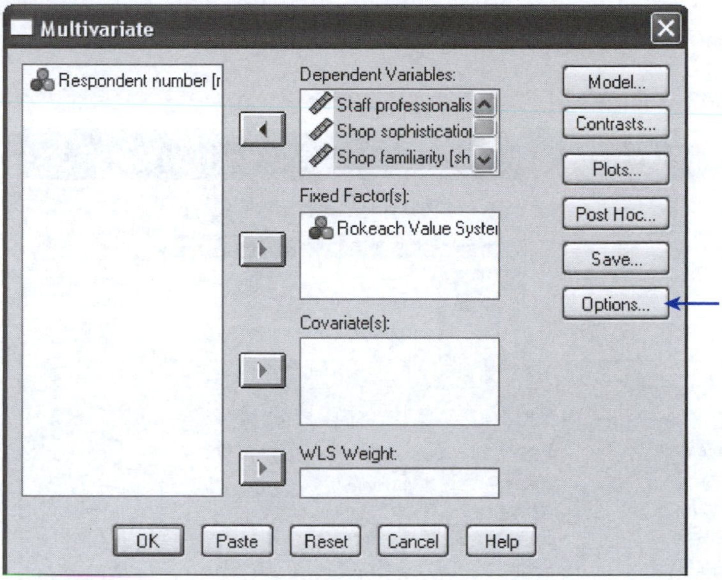

Move the three dependent variables ('staffpro', 'shopsoph' and 'shopfam') from the resulting window to the 'Dependent Variables' window and move the group variable (rvsgroup) to the 'Fixed Factor(s)' window. You will then see an image like the one shown in Figure 4.60. Next click on 'Options'.

Figure 4.61

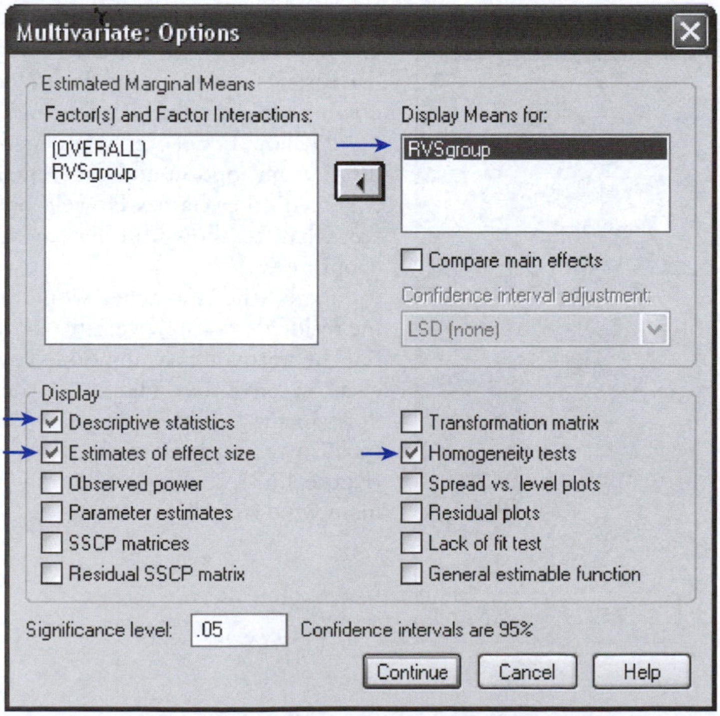

In the 'Options' window move the variable from the 'Factor(s) and Factor Interactions' window to the 'Display Means for' window by selecting this variable and then clicking ▶. Tick the options 'Descriptive statistics', 'Estimates of effect size' and 'Homogeneity tests' in the 'Display' window. You will then see an image like the one shown in Figure 4.61. Now click 'Continue'.

Figure 4.62

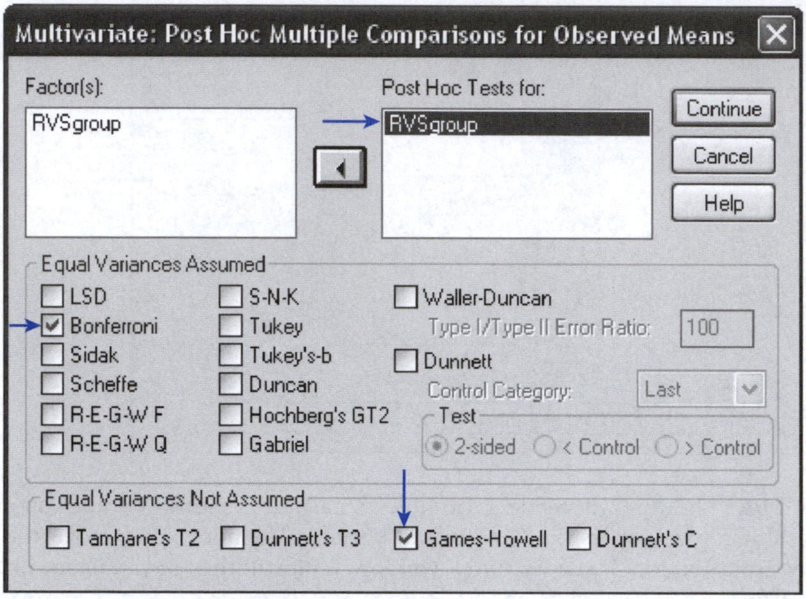

Figure 4.63

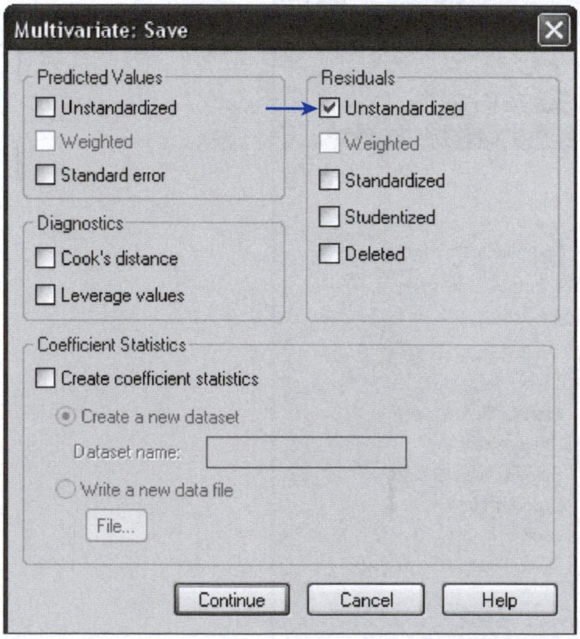

In order to see the 'Post hoc' window, you must click on 'Post Hoc' in the main window (see Figure 4.60). Move the variable 'rvsgroup' from the 'Factor(s)' window to the 'Post Hoc Tests for' window by selecting this variable and then by clicking on ▶. For 'Equal Variances Assumed', select the 'Bonferroni' option and for 'Equal Variances Not Assumed', the 'Games-Howell' option so that you see what is shown in Figure 4.62. Now click 'Continue'.

Finally, the researcher would also like to save the residuals as a new variable in the dataset and to test the normality assumption. To do so, you must click on 'Save' (see Figure 4.60) in the main window. In the 'Multivariate: Save' window, tick the box 'Unstandardized' in the 'Residuals' subwindow (Figure 4.63), click 'Continue' and then 'OK' in the main window.

Interpretation of the SPSS output

First of all, the assumptions from the MANOVA must be checked. In addition to the fact that the observations must be at least interval-scaled, independent and taken from the population at random (this is what we assume has happened), there are still two other conditions, namely multivariate normality and homogeneity of the covariance matrices. SPSS does not provide a way to test the multivariate normal distribution. The univariate normality may however be determined. These different univariate normal distributions are however no guarantee for a multivariate normality, however this is the best approximation to this available here. As was seen previously (in Chapter 2), the univariate normality may be tested and may also be determined graphically. The formal testing may be performed by following the Analyze/Descriptive Statistics/Explore path, and by ticking the box for the option 'normality plots with tests' under 'Plots'. This allows the researcher to perform a formal test as well as to see several graphs (including a Q-Q plot and a Box plot). A third method of determining the distribution of the variables in graph form is via Analyze/Descriptive Statistics/Frequencies and by choosing the Histogram option under 'Charts' and ticking the box for the 'With normal curve' option. The formal output is shown in Figure 4.64.

Figure 4.64

		Tests of Normality				
	Kolmogorov-Smirnov[a]			Shapiro-Wilk		
	Statistic	df	Sig.	Statistic	df	Sig.
Residual for staffpro	.097	244	.000	.982	244	.004
Residual for shopsoph	.090	244	.000	.982	244	.003
Residual for shopfam	.065	244	.014	.989	244	.062

[a]Lilliefors Significance Correction

From the Shapiro-Wilk's statistics (Figure 4.64), it appears that the only variable (residuals) for which the null hypothesis for normality may not be rejected is the 'shop familiarity' variable (p = .062 > .05). It is however the case that when large samples are used, both test statistics (both the Kolmogorov-Smirnov test with Lilliefors corrections as well as the Shapiro-Wilk's test) are extremely sensitive to minor deviations from normality. A rejection of the null hypothesis is thus no indication that the deviation would be large enough to cause a distortion of the statistical analyses which were to be performed on the data. This is why it is important (certainly with larger samples, n > 200) to perform a graphic inspection of the normality in addition to the formal testing. In this example, we are working with 244 observations which would mean that a graphic inspection is recommended such as that compiled in Figure 4.65. In Figure 4.65, for each error term (residual) of a dependent variable, three plots are shown. At the far left, one sees the Q-Q plot. When all of the observations are plotted along the straight line, there is a normal distribution. A Box plot is shown in the middle in which the coloured rectangle reflects the 50% of the observations in the middle and the black line in this rectangle in turn splits these observations into two 25% segments and this consequently represents the median. This 50% range is also called the 'interquartile range'. The T-shaped ends on the top and bottom (whiskers) each represent the 25% of the observations which lie at the ends of the distribution. The range of the whiskers cannot however be longer than one and a half times the length of the interquartile range. Observations falling outside of this range are referred to as outliers (e.g. by tiny circles). If the distances in the rectangle and the whiskers with respect to the median are equal along the top and the bottom and there are also no outliers, then this indicates a

Figure 4.65

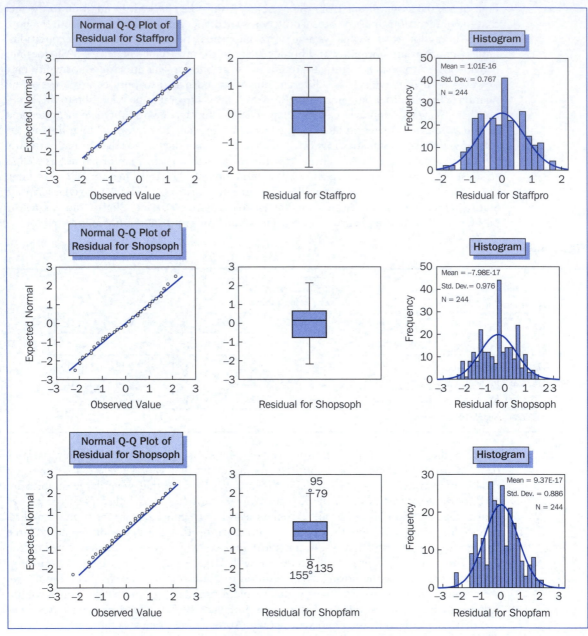

symmetric distribution. This is still no guarantee for a normal distribution, however it can at any rate give the researcher an idea of the possible deviations. Finally, a histogram is shown at the far right, in which the form of the normal distribution is drawn. It goes without saying that the histogram and the line of the normal distribution must coincide as much as possible. If we look at Figure 4.65, it appears that the graphic inspection indicates normality for all three of the variables: in the Q-Q plots, the observations lie on the straight line (or in any case, extremely close to it). The symmetry in the Box plots indicates a symmetric distribution and when the histograms with normal distribution are examined, one sees that the distribution fits in closely with a normal distribution. On the basis of the formal testing and particularly for the graphic inspection, in performing his further analysis, the researcher assumes a normal distribution of the three residual series.

A subsequent assumption which must be verified is that of the equality of the variance-covariance matrices of the variables across the groups (also the null hypothesis). This is done on the basis of the Box's Test, which also assumes multivariate normality. Figure 4.66 shows that the null hypothesis from the Box's Test may not be rejected ($p = .974 > .001$).

Figure 4.66

Box's Test of Equality of Covariance Matrices[a]	
Box's M	8.482
F	.460
df1	18
df2	134892.6
Sig.	.974

Tests the null hypothesis that the observed covariance matrices of the dependent variables are equal across groups.
[a]Design: Intercept+RVSgroup

The reason why the cut-off has been set at .001 here (instead of .05) is that the Box's M test is an extremely sensitive test statistic and this is why we allow more room for the null hypothesis to be accepted. In the event there are equal group sizes, some statisticians postulate that the assumption of equality of the variance-covariance matrices may be left for what they are, and researchers may assume that the Hotelling's and Pillai's statistics (see Figure 4.71) are solid. In the event of unequal group sizes, it is recommended to test Box's Test against .001. In our example, this is recommended because Figure 4.67 shows that the group 'Value sceptics' contains nearly two times as many subjects as the 'Ascetic idealists' group (89 versus 46). When there are unequal group sizes and the Box's Test null hypothesis is still rejected, one can subsample if necessary in order to arrive at equal group sizes. It is important to remember however that this goes hand in hand with a loss of information.

Figure 4.67

Between-Subjects Factors		Value Label	N
Rokeach Value system Group	1	Value conscious people	60
	2	Ascetic idealists	46
	3	Hedonic egoists	49
	4	Value sceptici	89

Consequently, the assumption of equal variance-covariance matrices has been satisfied. You will also notice that the Levene's tests in Figure 4.68 show that for each of the residuals, there are equal group variances, which lends a certain support to the assumption of equal covariance matrices across the groups.

Figure 4.68

Levene's Test of Equality of Error Variances[a]				
	F	df1	df2	Sig.
Staff professionalism	.643	3	240	.588
Shop sophistication	1.405	3	240	.242
Shop familiarity	.511	3	240	.675

Tests the null hypothesis that the error variance of the dependent variable is equal across groups.
[a]Design: Intercept+RVSgroup

We may now proceed with the inspection of the core results of the MANOVA. The researcher finds descriptive statistics in Figure 4.69 and Figure 4.70.

Figure 4.69

Descriptive Statistics				
	Rokeach Value System	Mean	Std. Deviation	N
Staff professionalism	Value conscious people	.1750	.78018	60
	Ascetic idealists	.1739	.80428	46
	Hedonic egoists	−.1020	.77041	49
	Value sceptici	−.1742	.75038	89
	Total	−.0082	.78432	244
Shop sophistication	Value conscious people	.1833	.99561	60
	Ascetic idealists	.4674	1.02957	46
	Hedonic egoists	−.0204	1.01530	49
	Value sceptici	−.1517	.92750	89
	Total	.0738	1.00241	244
Shop familiarity	Value conscious people	.0083	.83611	60
	Ascetic idealists	.2174	1.00914	46
	Hedonic egoists	.0102	.83846	49
	Value sceptici	−.1573	.89059	89
	Total	−.0123	.89572	244

In addition to the average scores, Figure 4.69 also shows the standard deviations and the number of respondents per variable and per group.

Figure 4.70

Dependent Variable	Rokeach Value System group	Mean	Std. Error	95% Confidence Interval	
				Lower Bound	Upper Bound
Staff professionalism	Value conscious people	.175	.100	−.021	.371
	Ascetic idealists	.174	.114	−.050	.398
	Hedonic egoists	−.102	.110	−.319	.115
	Value sceptici	−.174	.082	−.335	−.013
Shop sophistication	Value conscious people	.183	.127	−.066	.433
	Ascetic idealists	.467	.145	.182	.753
	Hedonic egoists	−.020	.140	−.297	.256
	Value sceptici	−.152	.104	−.357	.053
Shop familiarity	Value conscious people	.008	.115	−.218	.235
	Ascetic idealists	.217	.131	−.041	.476
	Hedonic egoists	.010	.127	−.241	.261
	Value sceptici	−.157	.094	−.343	.029

Rokeach Value System Group

Figure 4.70 also shows the standard error and the confidence interval. It should come as no surprise that the mean scores in both tables are equal. On the basis of an inspection of these tables, the researcher will notice that in general, 'Value conscious people' and 'Ascetic idealists' will produce higher scores than 'Hedonic egoists' and 'Value sceptics', or at least they will do so for the first two variables ('Staff professionalism' and 'Shop sophistication'). For 'Shop familiarity', 'Ascetic idealists' in particular score high and 'Value sceptics' score low. It is important here to note that this involves relatively small differences and that in the further discussion, 'high' and 'low' scores are relative.

Figure 4.71

Multivariate Tests[c]

Effect		Value	F	Hypothesis df	Error df	Sig.	Partial Eta Squared
Intercept	Pillai's Trace	.015	1.172[a]	3.000	238.000	.321	.015
	Wilks' Lambda	.985	1.172[a]	3.000	238.000	.321	.015
	Hotelling's Trace	.015	1.172[a]	3.000	238.000	.321	.015
	Roy's Largest Root	.015	1.172[a]	3.000	238.000	.321	.015
RVSgroup	Pillai's Trace	.109	3.017	9.000	720.000	.002	.036
	Wilks' Lambda	.892	3.103	9.000	579.380	.001	.037
	Hotelling's Trace	.121	3.169	9.000	710.000	.001	.039
	Roy's Largest Root	.113	9.036[b]	3.000	240.000	.000	.101

[a]Exact statistic
[b]The statistic is an upper bound on F that yields a lower bound on the significance level
[c]Design: Intercept+RVSgroup

Information on the central null hypothesis of the MANOVA, namely whether or not there are group differences between the variable combinations may be found in Figure 4.71. Four test statistics are given, e.g. Pillai's Trace, Wilks' Lambda, Hotelling's Trace and Roy's Largest Root, each of which test the null hypothesis in their own specific manner. Each of the four test statistics has its own characteristics in terms of statistical power. The four often confirm one another and one often encounters Wilks' Lambda as the test statistic used. For a detailed description of the differences between the four test statistics, we refer the reader to the specialised literature (at the end of this chapter). In our example, the four test statistics confirm one another (all of the p-values, $< .05$), therefore the null hypothesis that there are no differences between the groups is rejected.

In order to interpret this significant effect further, a follow-up analysis of this MANOVA may be performed. One possibility is the performance of univariate ANOVAs for each of the dependent variables. SPSS performs these automatically in the MANOVA, and the results are displayed in Figure 4.72.

Figure 4.72

Tests of Between-Subjects Effects

Source	Dependent Variable	Type III Sum of Squares	df	Mean Square	F	Sig.	Partial Eta Squared
Corrected model	Staff professionalism	6.422[a]	3	2.141	3.591	.014	.043
	Shop sophistication	12.806[b]	3	4.269	4.428	.005	.052
	Shop familiarity	4.349[c]	3	1.450	1.825	.143	.022
Intercept	Staff professionalism	.075	1	.075	.127	.722	.001
	Shop sophistication	3.270	1	3.270	3.392	.067	.014
	Shop familiarity	.088	1	.088	.111	.739	.000
RVSgroup	Staff professionalism	6.422	3	2.141	3.591	.014	.043
	Shop sophistication	12.806	3	4.269	4.428	.005	.052
	Shop familiarity	4.349	3	1.450	1.825	.143	.022
Error	Staff professionalism	143.062	240	.596			
	Shop sophistication	231.366	240	.964			
	Shop familiarity	190.615	240	.794			
Total	Staff professionalism	149.500	244				
	Shop sophistication	245.500	244				
	Shop familiarity	195.000	244				
Corrected total	Staff professionalism	149.484	243				
	Shop sophistication	244.172	243				
	Shop familiarity	194.963	243				

[a]R Squared = .043 (Adjusted R Squared = .031)
[b]R Squared = .052 (Adjusted R Squared = .041)
[c]R Squared = .022 (Adjusted R Squared = .010)

Given the possibility of Type I errors occurring from performing different ANOVAs, the critical p-value must be divided by the number of tests that are performed. In concrete terms, this means that the usual cut-off of .05 must be converted into 0.017 (=.05/3). Figure 4.72 shows that there are significant group differences for the variables 'Staff professionalism' (p = .014 < .017) and 'Shop sophistication' (p = .005 < .017), but not for 'Shop familiarity' (p = .143 > .017), which means that post-hoc tests for this last variable are not as meaningful. There are other methods which may be used to correct for the possible Type-I error (e.g. Holm correction). Further information may be found in the specialized literature (at the end of this chapter).

Figure 4.73

Multiple Comparisons

Dependent Variable		(I) Rokeach Value System group	(J) Rokeach Value System group	Mean Difference (I-J)	Std. Error	Sig.	95% Confidence Interval Lower Bound	95% Confidence Interval Upper Bound
Staff professionalism	Bonferroni	Value conscious people	Ascetic idealists	.0011	.15131	1.000	-.4014	.4036
			Hedonic egoists	.2770	.14866	.382	-.1184	.6725
			Value sceptici	.3492*	.12897	.044	.0061	.6922
		Ascetic idealists	Value conscious people	-.0011	.15131	1.000	-.4036	.4014
			Hedonic egoists	.2760	.15850	.498	-.1457	.6976
			Value sceptici	.3481	.14020	.082	-.0249	.7210
		Hedonic egoists	Value conscious people	-.2770	.14866	.382	-.6725	.1184
			Ascetic idealists	-.2760	.15850	.498	-.6976	.1457
			Value sceptici	.0721	.13734	1.000	-.2933	.4375
		Value sceptici	Value conscious people	-.3492*	.12897	.044	-.6922	-.0061
			Ascetic idealists	-.3481	.14020	.082	-.7210	.0249
			Hedonic egoists	-.0721	.13734	1.000	-.4375	.2933
	Games-Howell	Value conscious people	Ascetic idealists	.0011	.15559	1.000	-.4057	.4079
			Hedonic egoists	.2770	.14919	.253	-.1126	.6666
			Value sceptici	.3492*	.12834	.037	.0149	.6834
		Ascetic idealists	Value conscious people	-.0011	.15559	1.000	-.4079	.4057
			Hedonic egoists	.2760	.16179	.327	-.1474	.6993
			Value sceptici	.3481	.14279	.078	-.0261	.7222
		Hedonic egoists	Value conscious people	-.2770	.14919	.253	-.6666	.1126
			Ascetic idealists	-.2760	.16179	.327	-.6993	.1474
			Value sceptici	.0721	.13579	.951	-.2829	.4271
		Value sceptici	Value conscious people	-.3492*	.12834	.037	-.6834	-.0149
			Ascetic idealists	-.3481	.14279	.078	-.7222	.0261
			Hedonic egoists	-.0721	.13579	.951	-.4271	.2829
Shop sophistication	Bonferroni	Value conscious people	Ascetic idealists	-.2841	.19242	.847	-.7959	.2278
			Hedonic egoists	.2037	.18905	1.000	-.2992	.7067
			Value sceptici	.3350	.16401	.253	-.1013	.7713
		Ascetic idealists	Value conscious people	.2841	.19242	.847	-.2278	.7959
			Hedonic egoists	.4878	.20157	.098	-.0484	1.0240
			Value sceptici	.6191*	.17829	.004	.1448	1.0934
		Hedonic egoists	Value conscious people	-.2037	.18905	1.000	-.7067	.2992
			Ascetic idealists	-.4878	.20157	.098	-1.0240	.0484
			Value sceptici	.1313	.17466	1.000	-.3334	.5959
		Value sceptici	Value conscious people	-.3350	.16401	.253	-.7713	.1013
			Ascetic idealists	-.6191*	.17829	.004	-1.0934	-.1448
			Hedonic egoists	-.1313	.17466	1.000	-.5959	.3334
	Games-Howell	Value conscious people	Ascetic idealists	-.2841	.19891	.485	-.8042	.2361
			Hedonic egoists	.2037	.19380	.720	-.3025	.7099
			Value sceptici	.3350	.16182	.169	-.0866	.7566
		Ascetic idealists	Value conscious people	.2841	.19891	.485	-.2361	.8042
			Hedonic egoists	.4878	.20996	.100	-.0615	1.0371
			Value sceptici	.6191*	.18086	.005	.1449	1.0932
		Hedonic egoists	Value conscious people	-.2037	.19380	.720	-.7099	.3025
			Ascetic idealists	-.4878	.20996	.100	-1.0371	.0615
			Value sceptici	.1313	.17522	.877	-.3272	.5898
		Value sceptici	Value conscious people	-.3350	.16182	.169	-.7566	.0866
			Ascetic idealists	-.6191*	.18086	.005	-1.0932	-.1449
			Hedonic egoists	-.1313	.17522	.877	-.5898	.3272
Shop familiarity	Bonferroni	Value conscious people	Ascetic idealists	-.2091	.17465	1.000	-.6737	.2556
			Hedonic egoists	-.0019	.17160	1.000	-.4584	.4546
			Value sceptici	.1656	.14887	1.000	-.2304	.5617
		Ascetic idealists	Value conscious people	.2091	.17465	1.000	-.2556	.6737
			Hedonic egoists	.2072	.18296	1.000	-.2795	.6939
			Value sceptici	.3747	.16183	.129	-.0558	.8052
		Hedonic egoists	Value conscious people	.0019	.17160	1.000	-.4546	.4584
			Ascetic idealists	-.2072	.18296	1.000	-.6939	.2795
			Value sceptici	.1675	.15853	1.000	-.2542	.5893
		Value sceptici	Value conscious people	-.1656	.14887	1.000	-.5617	.2304
			Ascetic idealists	-.3747	.16183	.129	-.8052	.0558
			Hedonic egoists	-.1675	.15853	1.000	-.5893	.2542
	Games-Howell	Value conscious people	Ascetic idealists	-.2091	.18382	.668	-.6906	.2725
			Hedonic egoists	-.0019	.16124	1.000	-.4230	.4192
			Value sceptici	.1656	.14340	.656	-.2075	.5388
		Ascetic idealists	Value conscious people	.2091	.18382	.668	-.2725	.6906
			Hedonic egoists	.2072	.19101	.700	-.2931	.7074
			Value sceptici	.3747	.17621	.153	-.0874	.8368
		Hedonic egoists	Value conscious people	.0019	.16124	1.000	-.4192	.4230
			Ascetic idealists	-.2072	.19101	.700	-.7074	.2931
			Value sceptici	.1675	.15251	.691	-.2307	.5657
		Value sceptici	Value conscious people	-.1656	.14340	.656	-.5388	.2075
			Ascetic idealists	-.3747	.17621	.153	-.8368	.0874
			Hedonic egoists	-.1675	.15251	.691	-.5657	.2307

Based on observed means.
*The mean difference is significant at the .05 level

In order to now know between which value groups exact differences exist, we can examine Figure 4.73 (multiple comparisons). You will also notice that here the researcher has elected to use 'Post Hoc' tests rather than 'Contrasts'. As was previously mentioned (e.g. in the section on ANCOVA), contrasts are performed when one has a certain expectation beforehand with regard to the direction of the differences. Although we could assume that people with higher values will also take a more positive attitude towards Fair Trade shops, this may not be expected as a matter of course according to the researcher, and for this reason he opts for more conservative post-hoc tests. In Figure 4.73 a reference is made to the Bonferroni statistics (for equal variances) and to the Games-Howell statistic (for unequal variances). The choice between these two depends on whether or not the group variances are equal. The test for equality of group variances is requested in Figure 4.62, and from the output in Figure 4.68, it seems that for each of the three variables, one may assume equal variances. As a result, one should examine the Bonferroni window in Figure 4.73. It appears that for 'staff professionalism', 'Value conscious' people score .35 higher than 'Value sceptics' ($p = .044 < .05$) and also .35 better than 'Ascetic idealists' ($p = .082 < .10$, significant at 90%). Furthermore, with regard to 'Shop sophistication', it appears that 'Ascetic idealists' score .62 better than 'Value conscious' people ($p = .004 < .05$) and .49 better than 'Hedonic egoists' ($p = .098 < .10$).

Example 5

Analysis of variance with repeated measures

Managerial problem

Within the context of analysis of variance, 'repeated measures' means that different observations are registered for each person. In a repeated measures set-up, there are two types of factors which may occur, namely the 'between-subjects' factors and the 'within-subjects' factors. The first type remains constant for each subject (for example, man or woman), while the second type changes within the subjects (e.g., the two factors in the following example). This section describes how one may analyse repeated measures with 'General Linear Model (GLM) – Repeated measures'.

As far as the within-subject effects are concerned, there are two approaches used in this model, the univariate and the multivariate approaches. The approach which is chosen usually has to do with the evaluation of one of the underlying conditions which the data must satisfy. This condition is the 'sphericity assumption' and means that the population variance of the differences between the scores for each of the two levels of a within-subject factor is the same, independent of which of the two levels are chosen. This assumption is also only meaningful if there are more than two levels in a within-subject factor.

When this assumption is satisfied, the usual univariate test is used (sphericity assumed). When this sphericity assumption is violated however, we must examine the corrected univariate tests (Greenhouse-Geisser, Huynh-Feldt, and Lower bound). Another possibility consists of choosing the multivariate approach, because it is not based on the sphericity assumption. The reason why the corrected univariate and/or multivariate results are not always examined lies in the fact that when the sphericity assumption is not violated, the normal univariate test is more powerful.

A repeated measures set-up must be balanced. This means that there must be an observation for each subject and for each experimental condition. If an observation is lacking for a specific experimental condition for one person, then that subject will be excluded from the analysis (and the observations for the three remaining experimental conditions for this subject will also be lost). This has to do with the estimation method that is used. If it occurs, this problem can be compensated by an alternative analysis method (mixed models), however, we will not delve deeper into this topic here.

The example worked out below involves a researcher who is interested in comparative advertising (a form of advertising in which two brands are positioned in opposition to one another), and more specifically in the effect of two factors on Aad (attitude towards the advertisement). The first factor, 'emotional appeal' [appeal] involves the ad's **emotional** or **rational** quality, the other factor, 'involvement' [involv] relates to the nature of the product, or with the **high** or **low level of involvement** with the product which is being advertised. The researcher would also like to know whether there is a significant interaction effect. He creates four advertising messages which are a combination of the factors mentioned above. Pre-testing suggests that his experimental set-up is fine (the emotional advertisement is perceived by a number of test persons as being emotional). Aad is measured on the basis of a number of items (statements evaluated on a 7-point Likert scale) from which a mean is taken. Due to budget and time constraints, he can only interview fifty people. Splitting this group in four to expose each group to one advertisement would produce groups which are too small. For this reason, he decides to expose each of the fifty people to all four of the advertisements. In this analysis there are thus two within-subject factors which are each measured on two levels. With this method, the between-subject variance is eliminated. This way, it is only the variance between the combinations (each time within one respondent) that will be relevant. There are however two important aspects which the researcher must pay attention to. The first are the order effects (for example the tendency to give lower or higher scores to the first advertisements) which may be avoided by changing the order in which the advertisements are offered to each respondent. Then there are the carry-over effects (influence of a previous advertisement on each of the subsequent ones), which may be compensated for by leaving a sufficient amount of time between the evaluations of each of the four advertisements.

In this set-up, a subject (respondent) is exposed to a number of different subsequent experimental conditions (combinations of levels of the factors chosen). For each experimental condition, a variable is created in SPSS. The datafile which is used in the following example is *comparative advertising.sav* (Figure 4.74).

Figure 4.74

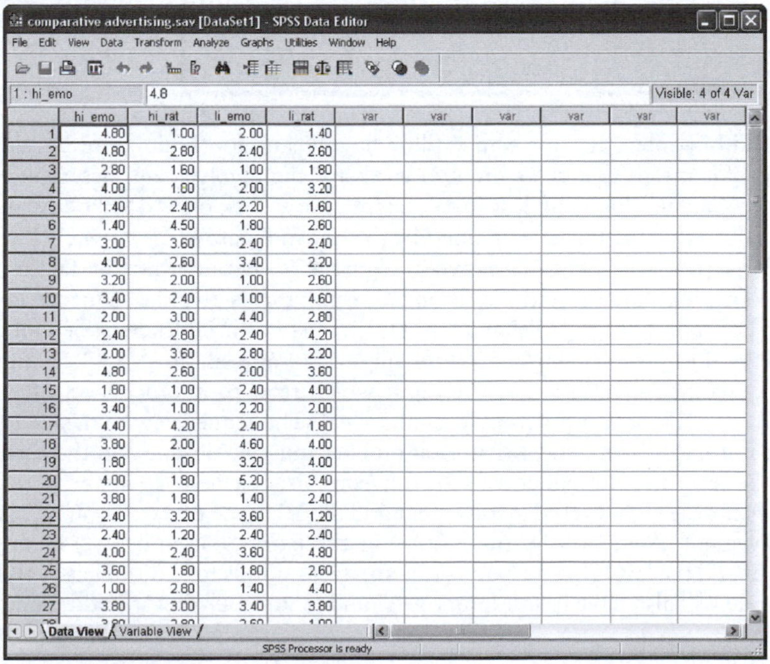

Problem

Perform a repeated-measures analysis and find out if the type of appeal [appeal] and the degree of involvement [involv] influence Aad. Determine if there are interaction effects and present these in graphic form.

Solution

SPSS commands

Go to Analyze/General Linear Model/Repeated Measures.

Figure 4.75

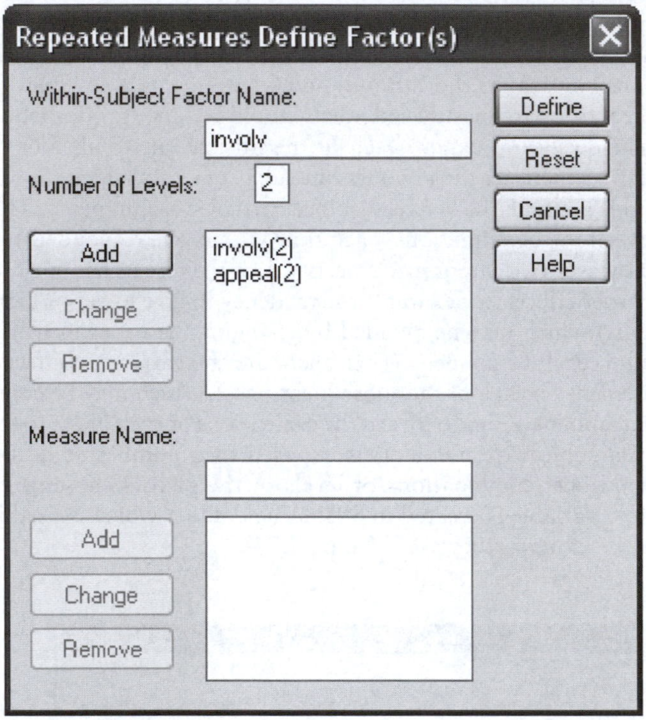

For 'Within-Subject Factor Name' fill in 'involv' and for 'Number of Levels' fill in the number 2 (this means that there are two levels for the involvement factor (indicated here with 'involv'), namely high and low involvement). Now click on 'Add'. Follow the same steps for 'appeal' so that the image will look like the one in Figure 4.75. Now click on 'Define'.

The screen will appear as shown in Figure 4.76. Because the first factor given in the previous step was 'involv' and the second 'appeal', this is also the sequence in which the pairs must be input. For '_?_(1,1)' and '_?_ (1,2)', the two variables must be input which have the same level of involvement but a different level of appeal. For '_?_(2,1)' and '_?_ (2,2)', the two remaining variables must be input which refer to another level of involvement (and which also still have a different level of appeal). The sequence within each factor is in and of itself not important, except that each number must be unique and the further output must also be interpreted analogously. In the example, the first '1' in the pairs (1,1) and (1,2) stands for the high level of involvement and the '2' in the pairs (2,1) and (2,2) stands for low involvement. Analogously, the last '1' in the pairs (1,1) and (2,1) stands for emotional appeal and the last '2' in the pairs (1,2) and (2,2) stands for rational appeal. Later in the output, one will also have to interpret the '1' and '2' for each factor in the same way. Given this

Figure 4.76

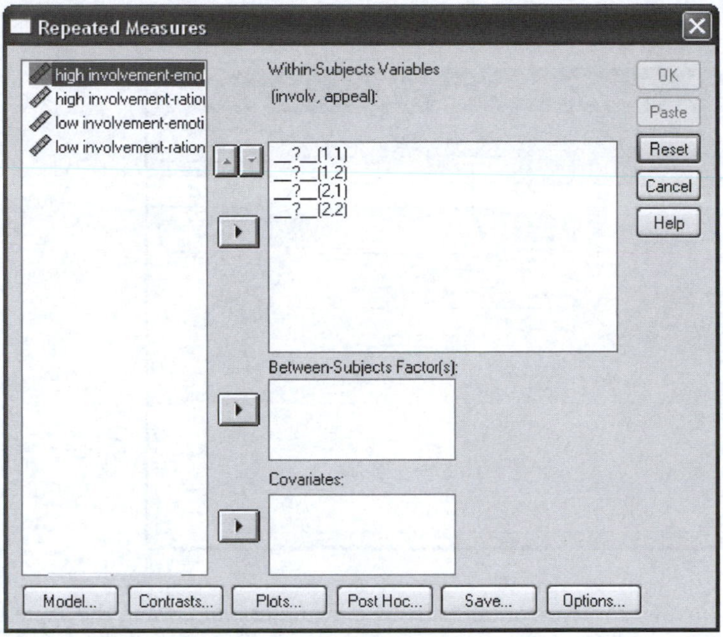

![Repeated Measures dialog box]

sequence discussion, all four of the variables in Figure 4.76 may be selected (by holding the Ctrl-key down) and moved to the 'Within-Subjects Variables' subwindow by clicking on thereby creating an image as seen in Figure 4.77. The variables may also be selected one by one and moved to the corresponding line in the 'Within-Subjects Variables' subwindow.

Figure 4.77

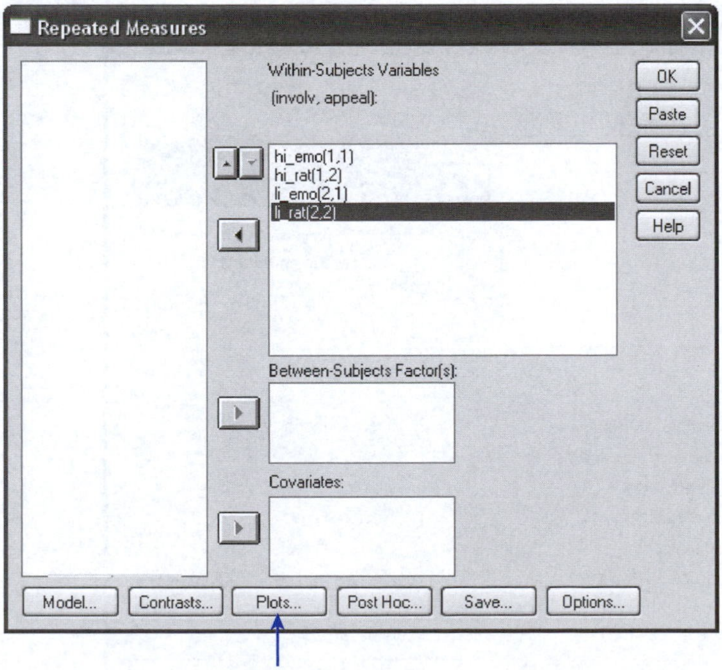

![Repeated Measures dialog box with variables selected]

Now click on 'Plots'.

Figure 4.78

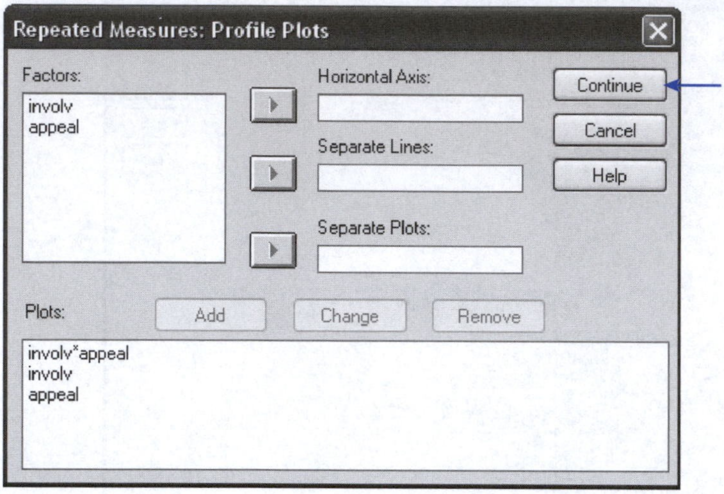

Move 'involv' to 'Horizontal Axis' by clicking [▶] and doing the same for 'appeal' and 'Separate Lines'. Click on 'Add'. This way, a graphic image of the interaction effects will be shown in the output. Now move 'involv' and 'appeal' respectively to 'Horizontal Axis' (remember to click 'Add' each time) so that the main effects are visually presented as well. This results in a screen like the one shown in Figure 4.78. Now click on 'Continue' and 'Options' to open the subscreen shown at Figure 4.79.

Figure 4.79

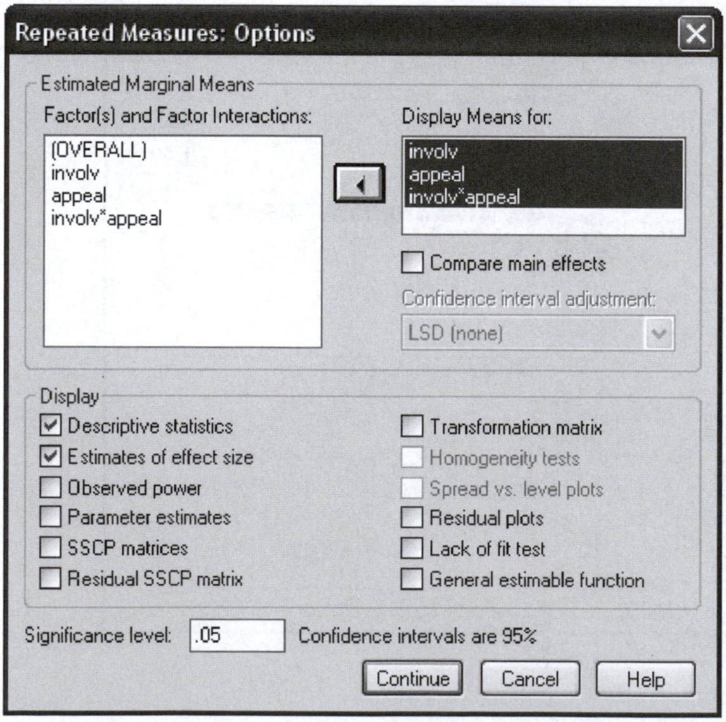

Select 'involv', 'appeal' and 'involv*appeal' and move these to the 'Display Means for' subwindow by clicking ▶. Under 'Display', tick the 'Descriptive statistics' and 'Estimates of effect size' boxes. Now click on 'Continue' and 'OK'. 'Post Hoc' tests are not meaningful here because each factor only has two levels.

Interpretation of the SPSS output

Figure 4.80

Within-Subjects Factors

Measure: MEASURE_1

Involv	Appeal	Dependent Variable
1	1	hi_emo
	2	hi_rat
2	1	li_emo
	2	li_rat

Figure 4.80 shows a control and overview of the input variables and combinations (see also Figures 4.75 through 4.77) while Figure 4.81 provides descriptive statistics for the different variables (experimental conditions).

Figure 4.81

Descriptive Statistics

	Mean	Std. Deviation	N
High involvement-emotional	3.1760	1.15680	50
High involvement-rational	2.5300	1.15745	50
Low involvement-emotional	2.9960	1.08834	50
Low involvement-rational	2.5920	1.00201	50

The emotional advertisement for a product with a high involvement has, for example, the highest Aad score (3.18), but also a relatively high standard deviation (1.16).

In this example, there are no between-subject factors. If there is a similar factor in the analysis, the 'Test of Between-Subject Effects' segment of the output may be used to determine significance level.

Figure 4.82 shows the influence of the within-subject factors. In this figure, four multivariate tests are shown. Wilk's Lambda is the most commonly used test statistic, however it is of course better for all four of the statistics to provide the same image. There is no significant interaction effect ($.444 > .05$) and it is therefore useful to examine possible main effects. The effect of appeal is the only one which appears to be significant (sig. $< .001 < .05$), while that of involvement is not. The multivariate output is examined here. As was already mentioned above, the output to be examined depends on the sphericity assumption. A test for this is shown in Figure 4.84.

Figure 4.82

Multivariate Tests[b]

Effect		Value	F	Hypothesis df	Error df	Sig.	Partial Eta Squared
Involv	Pillai's Trace	.003	.137[a]	1.000	49.000	.712	.003
	Wilks' Lambda	.997	.137[a]	1.000	49.000	.712	.003
	Hotelling's Trace	.003	.137[a]	1.000	49.000	.712	.003
	Roy's Largest Root	.003	.137[a]	1.000	49.000	.712	.003
Appeal	Pillai's Trace	.194	11.777[a]	1.000	49.000	.001	.194
	Wilks' Lambda	.806	11.777[a]	1.000	49.000	.001	.194
	Hotelling's Trace	.240	11.777[a]	1.000	49.000	.001	.194
	Roy's Largest Root	.240	11.777[a]	1.000	49.000	.001	.194
Involv * appeal	Pillai's Trace	.012	.596[a]	1.000	49.000	.444	.012
	Wilks' Lambda	.988	.596[a]	1.000	49.000	.444	.012
	Hotelling's Trace	.012	.596[a]	1.000	49.000	.444	.012
	Roy's Largest Root	.012	.596[a]	1.000	49.000	.444	.012

[a]Exact statistic
[b]Design: Intercept
   Within Subjects Design: involv+appeal+involv*appeal

Figure 4.83

Tests of Within-Subjects Effects

Measure: MEASURE_1

Source		Type III Sum of Squares	df	Mean Square	F	Sig.	Partial Eta Squared
Involv	Sphericity Assumed	.174	1	.174	.137	.712	.003
	Greenhouse-Geisser	.174	1.000	.174	.137	.712	.003
	Huynh-Feldt	.174	1.000	.174	.137	.712	.003
	Lower-bound	.174	1.000	.174	.137	.712	.003
Error(involv)	Sphericity Assumed	62.068	49	1.267			
	Greenhouse-Geisser	62.068	49.000	1.267			
	Huynh-Feldt	62.068	49.000	1.267			
	Lower-bound	62.068	49.000	1.267			
Appeal	Sphericity Assumed	13.781	1	13.781	11.777	.001	.194
	Greenhouse-Geisser	13.781	1.000	13.781	11.777	.001	.194
	Huynh-Feldt	13.781	1.000	13.781	11.777	.001	.194
	Lower-bound	13.781	1.000	13.781	11.777	.001	.194
Error(appeal)	Sphericity Assumed	57.341	49	1.170			
	Greenhouse-Geisser	57.341	49.000	1.170			
	Huynh-Feldt	57.341	49.000	1.170			
	Lower-bound	57.341	49.000	1.170			
Involv*appeal	Sphericity Assumed	.732	1	.732	.596	.444	.012
	Greenhouse-Geisser	.732	1.000	.732	.596	.444	.012
	Huynh-Feldt	.732	1.000	.732	.596	.444	.012
	Lower-bound	.732	1.000	.732	.596	.444	.012
Error(involv*appeal)	Sphericity Assumed	60.230	49	1.229			
	Greenhouse-Geisser	60.230	49.000	1.229			
	Huynh-Feldt	60.230	49.000	1.229			
	Lower-bound	60.230	49.000	1.229			

In the example however, this type of test is useless because there are only two levels for each within-subjects factor. This may also be observed on the decimal point in the Sig. column in Figure 4.84.

Figure 4.84

Mauchly's Test of Sphericity[b]

Measure: MEASURE_1

Within Subjects Effect	Mauchly's W	Approx. Chi-Square	df	Sig.	Epsilon[a]		
					Greenhouse-Geisser	Huynh-Feldt	Lower-bound
Involv	1.000	.000	0	.	1.000	1.000	1.000
Appeal	1.000	.000	0	.	1.000	1.000	1.000
Involv * appeal	1.000	.000	0	.	1.000	1.000	1.000

Tests the null hypothesis that the error covariance matrix of the orthonormalized transformed dependent variables is proportional to an identity matrix.

[a]May be used to adjust the degrees of freedom for the averaged tests of significance. Corrected tests are displayed in the Tests of Within-Subjects Effects table.

[b]Design: Intercept
   Within Subjects Design: involv+appeal+involv*appeal

However, if there were more than two levels per factor, we would have to look at this significance level in order to know which output should best be analysed. If the sig. level > 0.05, sphericity is assumed and it would be best for the researcher to look at the first line in Figure 4.83 under 'Sphericity Assumed' for each factor. If this is not the case, he can look at the other three adjusted univariate tests in Figure 4.84, or at the multivariate test in Figure 4.82, because sphericity is not a condition here. Because there are only two levels per factor (and the sphericity-requirement is not meaningful here), one sees that the F-values (and significance levels) are the same in the univariate and the multivariate approaches. You will also notice that for this reason, there is no difference between each of the univariate results.

The significant main effect in emotional appeal indicates that this effect may not be attributed to coincidence. Appeal '1' (= emotional stimulus, see Figure 4.80 and the discussion for Figures 4.76 and 4.77) has a significantly higher Aad score than Appeal '2' (= rational stimulus).

Figure 4.85

2. Appeal

Measure: MEASURE_1

Appeal	Mean	Std. Error	95% Confidence Interval	
			Lower Bound	Upper Bound
1	3.086	.119	2.846	3.326
2	2.561	.097	2.366	2.756

Figure 4.85 shows that the average scores are 3.086 and 2.561 respectively. The fact that this is also a significant effect may incidentally also be determined when we look at the confidence levels which do not overlap one another in Figure 4.85 ([2.846, 3.326] and [2.366, 2.758]).

Figure 4.86

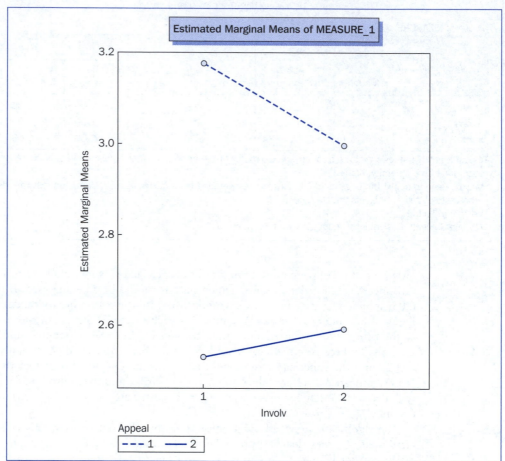

In Figure 4.86, the significant effect is shown graphically. For the sake of clarity: the '1' next to appeal stands for an emotional and the '2' for a rational stimulus. The '1' for involvement indicates a high and the '2' a low involvement. The fact that there are no significant interaction effects may also be seen in Figure 4.87. After all, the lines run nearly parallel. Figures 4.86 and 4.87 may also be edited in SPSS Chart Editor (double-click on the Figure in the SPSS output screen). This way, we can give the numbers used a more meaningful label, among other things.

On the basis of the findings above, the researcher may conclude that it is better to use an emotional advertisement in comparative advertising, regardless of the fact whether it concerns a product with a high or low level of involvement.

Figure 4.87

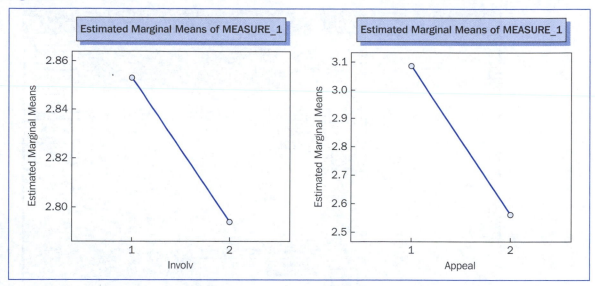

Example 6

Analysis of variance with repeated measures and between-subjects factor

Managerial problem

In the previous example, an analysis of variance with repeated measures was performed, yet without a between-subjects factor (= a factor which remains constant for each subject). In this example, this factor will be added to the data from the previous example. The datafile which will be used is the same as the one used in the previous example, but with the addition of a single between-subjects variable, namely gender. This new file is named *comparative advertisement_with_gender.sav*.

Problem

Perform a repeated measures analysis and find out if the emotional appeal [appeal] and the degree of involvement [involv] as well as the sex of the respondent [gender] influence Aad. Also determine whether or not there are interaction effects and present these graphically.

Solution

SPSS commands

The SPSS commands are analogous to those used in the previous example and will not be repeated here. There is however one difference. In the main window, in addition to the 'Within-subjects' variables, we must now obviously also stipulate the 'Between-Subjects' variable. This may be done by moving the variable 'gender' to the 'Between-Subjects Factor(s)' window. The image shown in Figure 4.88 will appear.

Figure 4.88

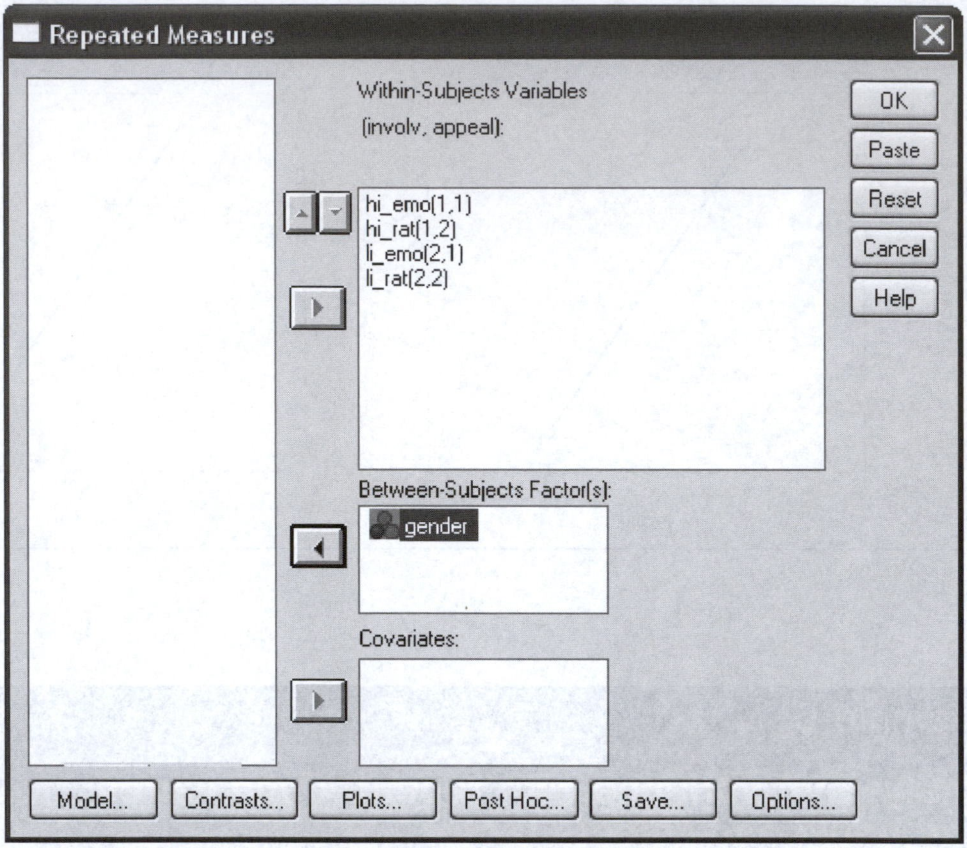

Under 'Plots', the researcher may request the desired graphics.

Figure 4.89

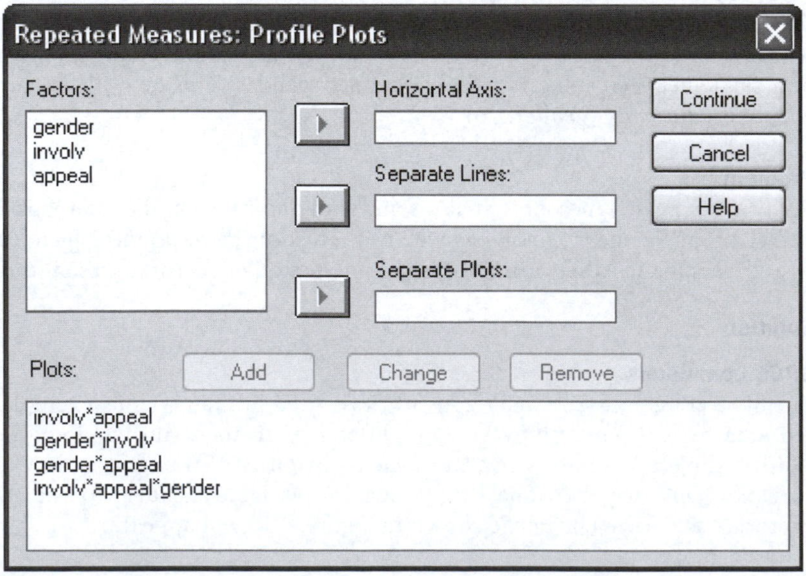

In this example, we assume that the researcher is interested in all of the interaction effects (four in total, namely three second-order and one third-order interaction effect). Although some of them might appear to be insignificant later and an inspection of the graph will contribute very little added value, the researcher will indicate this now for information. An alternative is to first examine the outputs and only request graphs for the relevant (significant) interaction or other effects. As indicated in Figure 4.89, the desired interaction effects are selected by indicating the desired variables for 'Horizontal Axis', 'Separate Lines' and 'Separate Plots' and by clicking 'Add'.

Now click on 'Continue' and then on 'Options' in the 'Repeated Measures' window.

Figure 4.90

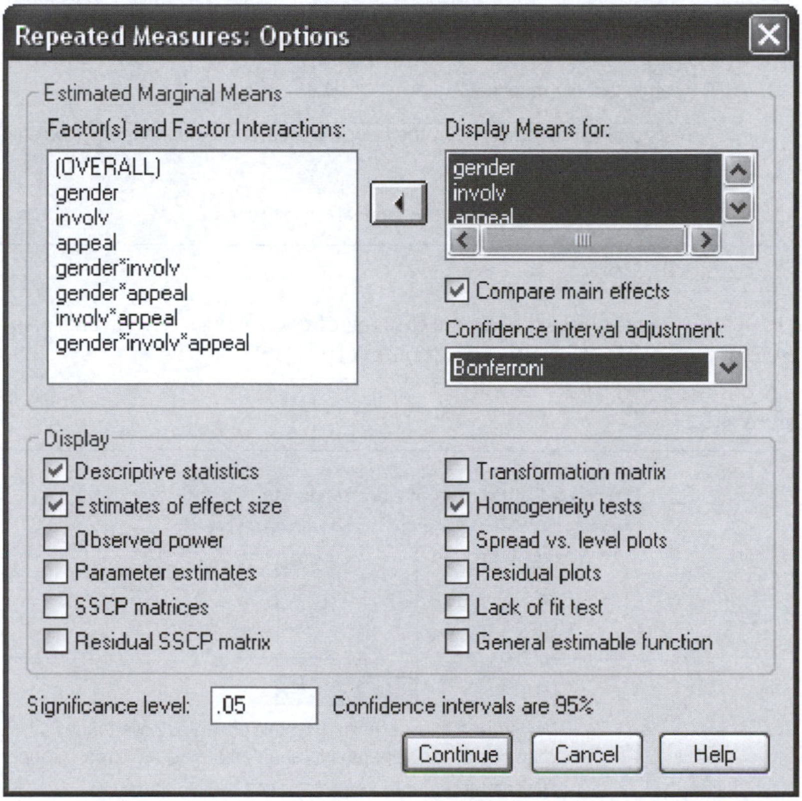

Move all of the variables from the 'Factor(s) and Factor Interactions' window to the 'Display Means for' window. Tick the option 'Compare main effects' and select 'Bonferroni' under 'Confidence interval adjustment'. In the 'Display' window, tick the boxes for the 'Descriptive statistics', 'Estimates of effect size' and 'Homogeneity tests' options. Now click 'Continue' and 'OK'. The 'Post Hoc' option is not used here considering there are only two levels involved for each variable.

Interpretation of the SPSS output

Before examining the main output from the analysis, we must first check to see whether the error variances are homogeneous across the groups.

Figure 4.91

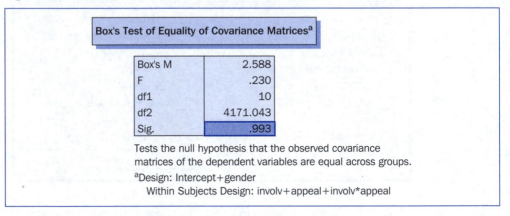

	F	df1	df2	Sig.
Levene's Test of Equality of Error Variances[a]				
Hoge betrokkenheid-emotioneel	.187	1	48	.668
Hoge betrokkenheid-rationeel	.109	1	48	.743
Lage betrokkenheid-emotioneel	.661	1	48	.420
Lage betrokkenheid-rationeel	.001	1	48	.981

Tests the null hypothesis that the error variance of the dependent variable is equal across groups.
[a]Design: Intercept+gender
  Within Subjects Design: involv+appeal+involv*appeal

In Figure 4.91, this appears to be the case (all of the p-values >.05). This also appears to be the case in Figure 4.92 in a multivariate context (p = .993 > .05).

Figure 4.92

Box's Test of Equality of Covariance Matrices[a]

Box's M	2.588
F	.230
df1	10
df2	4171.043
Sig.	.993

Tests the null hypothesis that the observed covariance matrices of the dependent variables are equal across groups.
[a]Design: Intercept+gender
  Within Subjects Design: involv+appeal+involv*appeal

If this were not the case, the researcher could consider a transformation of the variables. Further information on this topic may be found in specialized literature (see the end of this chapter).

If the researcher would like to have an idea whether the Between-Subjects factor 'gender' is significant (making an abstraction of the other factors), then from Figure 4.93 it appears that this is not the case. There appears to be no difference between men and women in this regard (p = .187 > .05).

Figure 4.93

Tests of Between-Subjects Effects

Measure: MEASURE_1
Transformed Variable: Average

Source	Type III Sum of Squares	df	Mean Square	F	Sig.	Partial Eta Squared
Intercept	1349.019	1	1349.019	1142.175	.000	.960
Gender	2.119	1	2.119	1.794	.187	.036
Error	56.693	48	1.181			

The central output is found in Figure 4.94.

Figure 4.94

Multivariate Tests[b]

Effect		Value	F	Hypothesis df	Error df	Sig.	Partial Eta Squared
Involv	Pillai's Trace	.000	.000[a]	1.000	48.000	.998	.000
	Wilks' Lambda	1.000	.000[a]	1.000	48.000	.998	.000
	Hotelling's Trace	.000	.000[a]	1.000	48.000	.998	.000
	Roy's Largest Root	.000	.000[a]	1.000	48.000	.998	.000
Involv * gender	Pillai's Trace	.019	.936[a]	1.000	48.000	.338	.019
	Wilks' Lambda	.981	.936[a]	1.000	48.000	.338	.019
	Hotelling's Trace	.020	.936[a]	1.000	48.000	.338	.019
	Roy's Largest Root	.020	.936[a]	1.000	48.000	.338	.019
Appeal	Pillai's Trace	.105	5.624[a]	1.000	48.000	.022	.105
	Wilks' Lambda	.895	5.624[a]	1.000	48.000	.022	.105
	Hotelling's Trace	.117	5.624[a]	1.000	48.000	.022	.105
	Roy's Largest Root	.117	5.624[a]	1.000	48.000	.022	.105
Appeal * gender	Pillai's Trace	.159	9.054[a]	1.000	48.000	.004	.159
	Wilks' Lambda	.841	9.054[a]	1.000	48.000	.004	.159
	Hotelling's Trace	.189	9.054[a]	1.000	48.000	.004	.159
	Roy's Largest Root	.189	9.054[a]	1.000	48.000	.004	.159
Involv * appeal	Pillai's Trace	.025	1.225[a]	1.000	48.000	.274	.025
	Wilks' Lambda	.975	1.225[a]	1.000	48.000	.274	.025
	Hotelling's Trace	.026	1.225[a]	1.000	48.000	.274	.025
	Roy's Largest Root	.026	1.225[a]	1.000	48.000	.274	.025
Involv * appeal * gender	Pillai's Trace	.023	1.149[a]	1.000	48.000	.289	.023
	Wilks' Lambda	.977	1.149[a]	1.000	48.000	.289	.023
	Hotelling's Trace	.024	1.149[a]	1.000	48.000	.289	.023
	Roy's Largest Root	.024	1.149[a]	1.000	48.000	.289	.023

[a]Exact statistic
[b]Design: Intercept+gender
   Within Subjects Design: involv+appeal+involv*appeal

For reasons discussed in the previous example, only the 'Multivariate Tests' output is discussed here. From this, it appears that 'appeal' remains a significant factor ($p = .022 < .05$) however, even more importantly, that there is also an interaction effect between 'appeal' and 'gender' (p = .004 < .05). The other factors do not appear to be significant (all of the p-values > .05). Both significant effects will then be examined.

Figure 4.95

Estimates

Measure: MEASURE_1

Appeal	Mean	Std. Error	95% Confidence Interval	
			Lower Bound	Upper Bound
1	2.964	.120	2.723	3.205
2	2.604	.104	2.395	2.812

From Figure 4.95, it appears that an 'emotional appeal' (1) leads to a higher Aad score than a 'rational appeal' (2) (2.964 versus 2.604). Figure 4.96 shows the difference between the two (.360) and confirms that the significance level is p = .022.

Figure 4.96

Pairwise Comparisons

Measure: MEASURE_1

(I) Appeal	(J) Appeal	Mean Difference (I-J)	Std. Error	Sig.[a]	95% Confidence Interval for Difference[a]	
					Lower Bound	Upper Bound
1	2	.360*	.152	.022	.055	.666
2	1	−.360*	.152	.022	−.666	−.055

Based on estimated marginal means
*The mean difference is significant at the .05 level
[a]Adjustment for multiple comparisons: Bonferroni

Even more interesting is the interaction effect between 'gender' and 'appeal'. The means may be found in Figure 4.97, and Figure 4.98 represents this in graphic form.

Figure 4.97

5. Gender * Appeal

Measure: MEASURE_1

Gender	Appeal	Mean	Std. Error	95% Confidence Interval	
				Lower Bound	Upper Bound
Female	1	3.303	.135	3.031	3.575
	2	2.485	.117	2.249	2.721
Male	1	2.625	.198	2.228	3.022
	2	2.722	.171	2.378	3.066

From this, it appears that an advertisement that is emotional and shown to women leads to a higher Aad score than the other combinations. In Figure 4.97, the 95% confidence intervals provide an indication of the significance of this difference: the interval for female and appeal 1 is [3.031, 3.575]. The lower bound of this interval is higher than the upper bounds of the other combinations (in other words, the confidence intervals do not overlap one another). There is only a marginal overlap (3.066 < 3.031) for male and appeal 2 and we can say that these two experimental pairs probably differ from one another (a formal t-test should confirm this). The 'gender × appeal' interaction effect is in turn not moderated by the level of the product involvement since the third-order interaction effect does not appear to be significant (p-value = .289, see Figure 4.96).

Figure 4.98

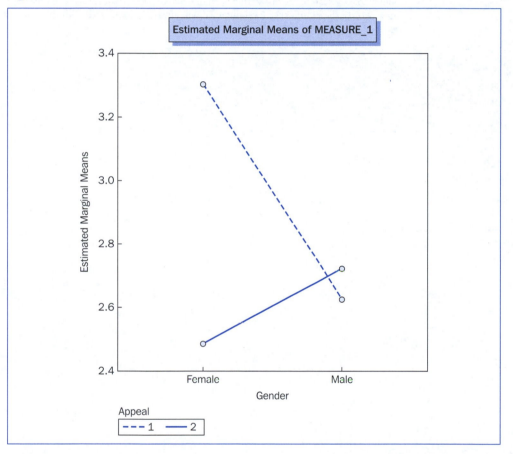

One could conclude that if the target group consists predominantly of women, an emotional comparative advertisement is recommended, regardless of the level of product involvement.

Further reading

Green, S.B., Salkind, N.J. and Akey, T.M. (2000), *Using SPSS for Windows – Analyzing and understanding data,* 2nd ed., Englewood Cliffs, NJ.: Prentice Hall.

Iacobucci, D. (1994), 'Analysis of Experimental Data', in Richard P. Bagozzi (ed.) (1994), *Principles of Marketing Research.* Cambridge, Massachusetts: Basil Blackwell.

Neter, J., Kutner, M.H., Nachtsheim, C.J. and Wasserman, W. (1996), *Applied Linear Statistical Models,* 4th ed., Boston, MA.: WCB/McGraw-Hill.

Endnote

1 In this book, a critical value of .05 is generally used. However, this should not be viewed as an absolute guideline. In research, the distinction is often made between significance at levels of 1%, 5% and 10%. In other words, the significance level obtained will always be compared with the numbers .01, .05 and 0.1.

Chapter 5

Linear regression analysis

Chapter objectives

This chapter will help you to:

- Understand when and how to use regression analysis
- Know when regression analysis can be carried out in a meaningful and valid way, and when the assumptions for using the regression model are met
- Conduct a linear regression analysis and interpret the results and the statistical validity
- Apply and interpret a stepwise regression analysis (next to the enter method)
- Deal with categorical variables in the regression model

Technique

Regression analysis is a technique which is used to determine the causality between one dependent interval- or ratio-scaled variable (the explained variable) and one or more independent interval- or ratio-scaled variables (the explanatory variables), in other words, one tries to explain the variation in one dependent variable as much as possible on the basis of the variation in a number of relevant independent variables. If there is only one independent variable, then this is a 'simple regression', while 'multiple regression' is the term used when multiple independent variables are involved.

A linear regression model in its general form is expressed as follows:

$$Y = b_0 + b_1 X_1 + b_2 X_2 + \cdots + b_n X_n + \varepsilon$$

where Y = dependent variable
X_i = independent variable
b_i = parameter to be estimated, coefficient
ε = disturbance term

The data set upon which a regression analysis is performed may be structured in different ways:

- **Time series**: with this set-up, there are observations at several (consecutive) moments in time for one subject.

   Example: data to explain or predict a firm's turnover on the basis of other variables may be presented in the following way:

Table 5.1

	Dependent variable	Independent variable		
	Turnover	Marketing expenditures	. . .	Season Factor
Quarter 1				
Quarter 2				
Quarter 3				
. . .	. . .	. . .	. . .	. . .

It is important to note here that the term 'time series analysis' is usually used when the dependent variable as a delayed variable, is included in the model as an independent variable. In the example, this would mean that the turnover from the previous quarter would represent an extra independent variable.

- **Cross-section data**: here we have observations for a single point in time for several subjects.

   Example: data to explain or predict consumers' buying intentions on the basis of other variables may be presented in the following manner:

Table 5.2

	Dependent variable	Independent variable		
	Buying intention	Brand appreciation	. . .	Advertisement appreciation
Subject 1				
Subject 2				
Subject 3				
. . .	. . .	. . .	. . .	. . .

- **Panel data**: here we see observations at multiple (consecutive) points in time for several subjects.

   Example: data for the family consumption to be explained or predicted on the basis of other variables may be presented as follows:

Table 5.3

		Dependent variable	Independent variable		
Family	Period	Family consumption	Available family income	. . .	Number of family members
1	1				
1	2				
1	3				
2	1				
2	2				
2	3				
3	1				
. . .	. . .	. . .	. . .	. . .	. . .

A regression analysis will estimate the parameters for the variables (b_i) in such a manner that the best possible fit is obtained between the actual and the predicted values for the dependent variable. The traditional way in which these coefficients are determined is 'the least squares method': the parameters of the equation are defined in such a way that the sum of the square of each of the residuals (deviation between the actual and predicted value) is as small as possible.

In determining the importance of each of the variables included in the model, we can arrive at situations in which keeping one or more variables in the model is no longer appropriate. With regard to this problem, there are various approaches which may be used:

- **Enter**: in this method, all of the variables indicated by the researcher are included in the model. The researcher may then, after examining the analysis output, choose to eliminate variables which do not contribute significantly to the explanation of the model, to then perform a second analysis on the basis of the 'Enter' method. Within this context, a 'General-to-Specific' approach is also referred to (GTS).

- **Forward**: this is an automatic form of a 'Specific-to-General' (STG) approach, in which SPSS essentially starts with a model with one variable, and ends with a model with multiple variables. This is a technique which may be used to determine in a step-by-step manner for each variable which is not yet included in the model, whether or not this variable provides a significant explanation for the dependent variable, and includes the most significant variable in the (new) model, until there is no single variable left in a certain step which makes a significant contribution to the model.

- **Backward**: this is a 'General-to-Specific' approach in which SPSS essentially starts with a model with multiple variables, and ends with a model with fewer variables. It is a technique which is used to calculate the significance levels for all of the variables step-by-step, and removes the most non-significant ones from the (previous) model, until all of the remaining variables in a certain step make a significant contribution to the explanation of the dependent variable.

■ **Stepwise**: a shortcoming of the 'Forward' method is the following: suppose that the researcher has already included two significant variables in the model and that, by adding a third variable, one of those two will no longer be significant, meaning that the final model will contain a non-significant variable, which makes the model incorrect. One solution to this problem is the application of the 'Stepwise' procedure, which is a combination of the 'Forward' and the 'Backward' methods: each step involves the addition of that variable to the model which explains the most in the dependent variable and removes those variables from the model which no longer make a significant contribution. The final model then consists only of significant variables.

There are a number of assumptions which lie at the basis of the performance of a regression analysis. Failure to satisfy these assumptions makes the outcome of the analysis either less valid or invalidates it entirely and/or makes it unreliable. There are nine assumptions which may be summarized as follows:

1 There must be a **causality** present, whereby the dependent variable is explained by the independent variable(s).

2 **All of the relevant** (independent) **variables** must be taken into consideration.

3 The dependent and independent variables must be at least **interval** scaled. If the dependent variable is dichotomous in nature, then logistic regression is the technique preferred (see Chapter 6). Nominal independent variables may be converted into dummy variables, which could constitute part of the regression-equation (see Chapter 5, Example 3: 'The presence of a nominal variable in the regression model').

4 There must be a **linear relationship** between the dependent and the independent variables. In the event there is a non-linear relationship present, the researcher may employ the transformation of the variables previously added to the model (e.g. by taking the square root or the logarithm) or by adding extra variables (e.g. a quadratic term). This last method is explained further under 'Linear relationship between the dependent and independent variables' discussed later in the current chapter.

5 An **additive relationship** is assumed. Modifying this additive relationship by adding an interaction term occurs under 'Additive relationship between the dependent and independent variables' later in the current chapter.

6 The **residuals** must satisfy the following characteristics:

   a) they are independent from one another;
   b) they are normally distributed;
   c) they have the same variance for each value of the independent variable (homoscedasticity assumption, and if this is not satisfied, then this is referred to as heteroscedasticity);
   d) no relationship may exist between the subsequent residuals (if this does occur, then this is referred to as autocorrelation). This is particularly relevant within the context of time series.

7 There must be a **sufficient number of observations** in order to be able to provide a good indication of the 'fit'. The rule of thumb is: at least five times as many observations as variables.

8 **No multicollinearity**: in other words, a high degree of correlation between the independent variables is not permitted.

9 **Attention for outliers.** Outliers are exceptionally high or low values. Although the presence of outliers may not be seen as a violation of the assumptions, it is still important to pay attention to them. Two different approaches may be adopted. One may either dictate that a similar observation provides valuable information that must definitely be included in the estimation of the model. Or, one could reason that this outlier biases the model too sharply and it would be better to leave it out of the dataset. This last solution must be accompanied by the necessary caution and foundation because one might otherwise risk criticism for having manipulated the analysis. It is therefore advisable to first try to estimate the model as accurately as possible, for example by finding out whether a very important variable was not omitted inadvertently, a factor which might explain the outliers.

The performance of a regression analysis is essentially a fixed procedure, which is performed in the following three steps:

1 **Check the assumptions listed above.** If the assumptions have not been satisfied, depending on the assumption violated, one must take appropriate action.

2 **Check the meaningfulness of the model.** The null hypothesis in a regression model is: all of the coefficients (b_i) are equal to zero. The model which has been designed is only meaningful if this hypothesis may be rejected.

3 **Interpret the coefficients obtained for the independent variables.** For each of the estimated parameters (b_i), one will have to find out whether or not a significant contribution is being made to the model and whether the sign is meaningful (e.g. in explaining the turnover on the basis of the marketing expenditures, one would expect a positive sign for this). The relative importance of the variables in their influence on the dependent variable is an important point of interest.

For a more in-depth discussion of this technique, the reader may consult reference works which are indicated at the end of this chapter.

Example 1

A cross-section analysis

Managerial problem

A pizza restaurant would like to find out to what degree various factors contribute to the overall customer satisfaction [satisfaction]. Based on discussions with its technical and commercial staff, there are five factors which could potentially play a role: reception [reception], service [service], waiting time [waiting time], food quality [quality] and price [price]. In addition to an indication for the overall degree of satisfaction with the restaurant, 107 restaurant visitors have indicated for each of these factors how satisfied they were (1 = very dissatisfied, ..., 7 = very satisfied). The answers obtained were then input into the SPSS data editor, an excerpt of which is shown in Figure 5.1. If the reader sees numbers instead of words under the variable names [satisfaction], [reception], [service], [waiting time], [quality] and [price], then he may obtain the labels by choosing View/Value Labels.

Figure 5.1

	resp_nr	satisfaction	reception	service	waitingtime	quality	price
1	16	very dissatisfied	dissatisfied	very satisfied	very dissatisfied	dissatisfied	dissatisfied
2	14	dissatisfied	dissatisfied	neutral	very dissatisfied	very dissatisfied	very dissatisfied
3	28	dissatisfied	dissatisfied	rather dissatisfied	rather dissatisfied	dissatisfied	very dissatisfied
4	58	dissatisfied	dissatisfied	rather dissatisfied	rather dissatisfied	dissatisfied	very dissatisfied
5	7	rather dissatisfied	neutral	rather satisfied	satisfied	rather dissatisfied	rather satisfied
6	17	rather dissatisfied	neutral	rather dissatisfied	rather dissatisfied	dissatisfied	very dissatisfied
7	29	rather dissatisfied	rather dissatisfied	rather satisfied	rather satisfied	neutral	dissatisfied
8	35	rather dissatisfied	neutral	rather satisfied	neutral	rather dissatisfied	very dissatisfied
9	36	rather dissatisfied	rather dissatisfied	neutral	neutral	rather dissatisfied	dissatisfied
10	50	rather dissatisfied	rather dissatisfied	satisfied	very satisfied	rather dissatisfied	very dissatisfied
11	52	rather dissatisfied	neutral	neutral	satisfied	rather dissatisfied	dissatisfied
12	54	rather dissatisfied	dissatisfied	satisfied	rather satisfied	dissatisfied	very dissatisfied
13	64	rather dissatisfied	dissatisfied	satisfied	rather satisfied	rather dissatisfied	dissatisfied
14	105	rather dissatisfied	dissatisfied	rather dissatisfied	rather dissatisfied	rather dissatisfied	very dissatisfied
15	1	neutral	rather dissatisfied	rather satisfied	satisfied	rather dissatisfied	very dissatisfied
16	4	neutral	rather satisfied	satisfied	very satisfied	rather dissatisfied	rather satisfied
17	12	neutral	rather dissatisfied	neutral	rather satisfied	rather dissatisfied	dissatisfied
18	26	neutral	rather dissatisfied	rather dissatisfied	satisfied	rather dissatisfied	very dissatisfied
19	32	neutral	neutral	rather dissatisfied	rather satisfied	rather dissatisfied	very dissatisfied
20	39	neutral	rather satisfied	neutral	very satisfied	rather dissatisfied	rather dissatisfied
21	40	neutral	rather satisfied	neutral	very satisfied	rather dissatisfied	neutral
22	60	neutral	neutral	rather satisfied	satisfied	very dissatisfied	dissatisfied
23	61	neutral	rather dissatisfied	neutral	rather satisfied	rather dissatisfied	dissatisfied
24	62	neutral	neutral	rather satisfied	rather satisfied	rather dissatisfied	neutral
25	87	neutral	rather satisfied	neutral	very satisfied	rather dissatisfied	neutral
26	97	neutral	rather dissatisfied	satisfied	very satisfied	neutral	very dissatisfied
27	99	neutral	neutral	neutral	satisfied	neutral	dissatisfied
28	101	neutral	dissatisfied	satisfied	rather satisfied	rather dissatisfied	very dissatisfied

Problem

Develop the following regression model on the basis of the data above (*Pizza.sav*):

$$\text{Overall satisfaction} = b_0 + b_1 \text{ reception} + b_2 \text{ service}$$
$$+ b_3 \text{ waiting time} + b_4 \text{ food quality} + b_5 \text{ price} + \varepsilon$$

Use the three-step procedure (check assumptions, check usefulness of the model and interpretation of the coefficients) and choose the 'Enter' method (GTS).

Later in this chapter, you will find two variations on this question, namely the application of the 'Stepwise' method (*Pizza Stepwise method.sav*) and the introduction of a nominal independent variable in the model (*Pizza incl gender.sav*).

For the application of the different procedures, there are thus different datasets used, which only differ from one another to a limited degree. The difference between the datasets *Pizza.sav* and *Pizza Stepwise method.sav* is the filter variable 'filter_$' (which eliminates outliers from the analysis), and between *Pizza.sav* and *Pizza incl gender.sav* the variable [gender].

Solution

SPSS commands

Figure 5.2

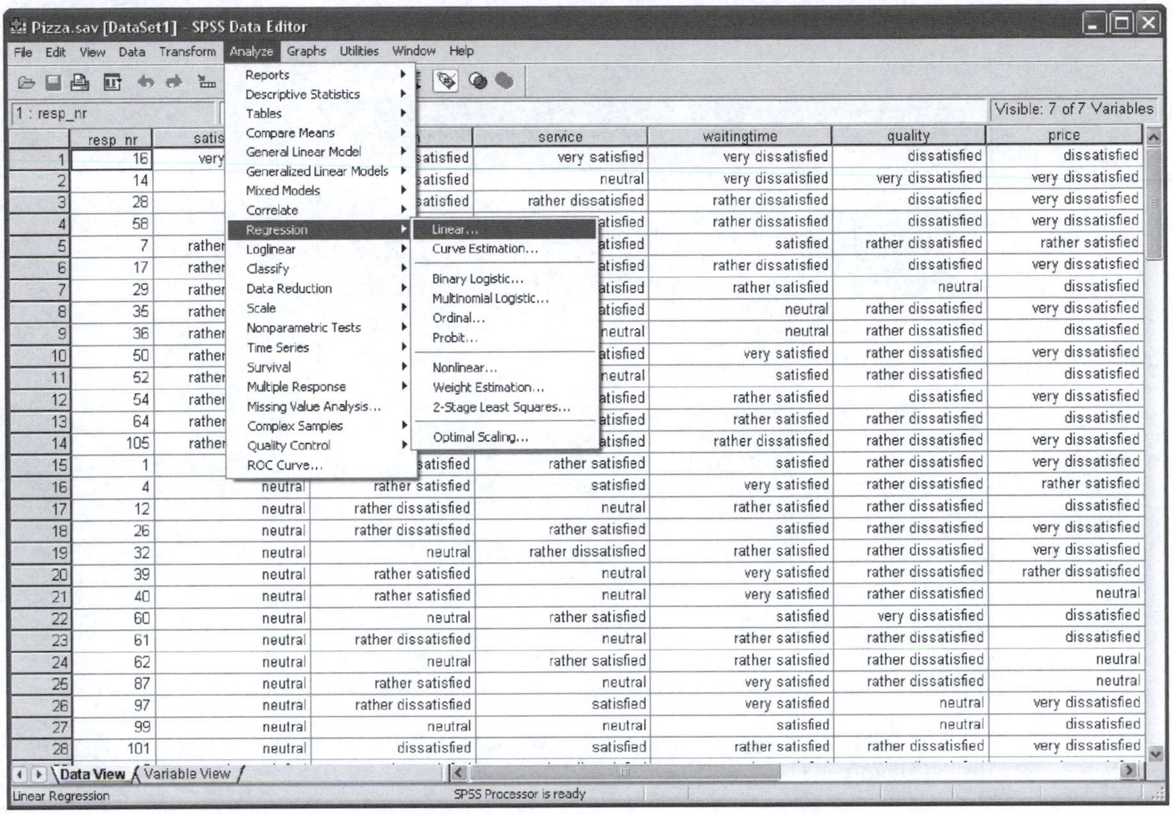

Go to Analyze/Regression/Linear (Figure 5.2).

Figure 5.3

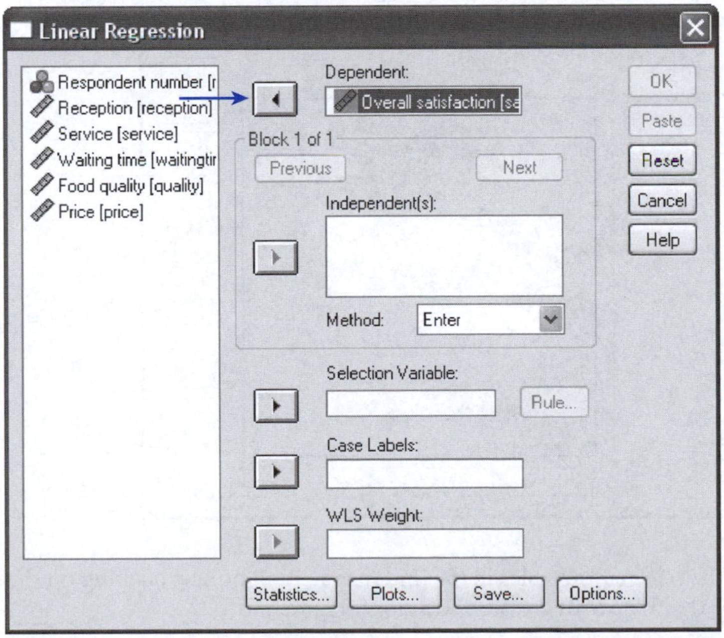

Click on the dependent variable 'overall satisfaction' [satisfaction], and move this to the 'Dependent' box by clicking on the arrow ▸ at the top of the dialogue window (Figure 5.3).

Figure 5.4

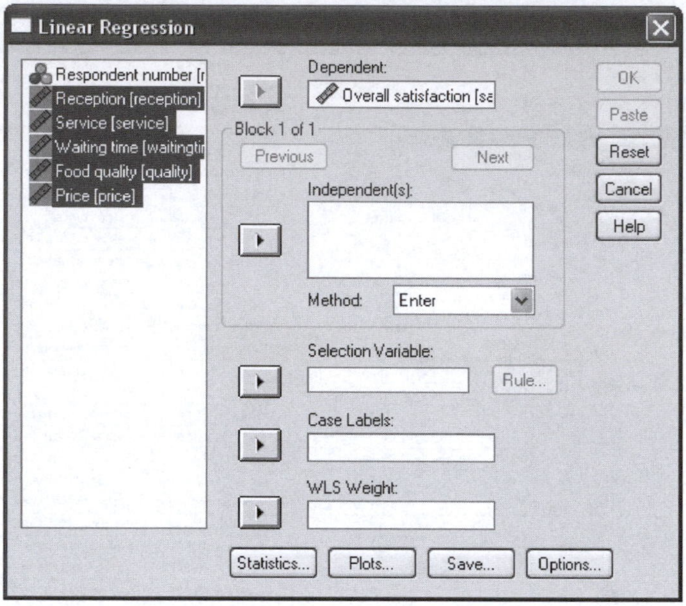

Now select the independent variables [reception], [service], [waiting time], [quality], and [price] (Figure 5.4).

Figure 5.5

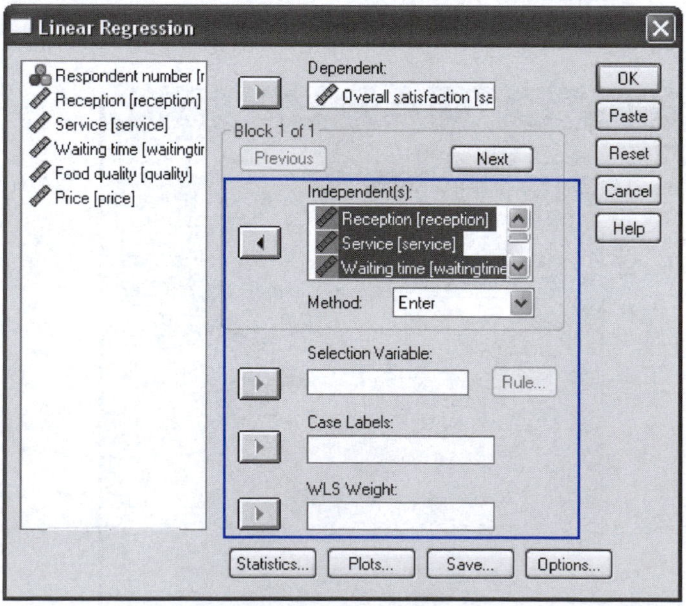

Place the selected variables in the 'Independent(s)' box by clicking on the arrow ▸ in the middle of the 'Linear Regression' window (Figure 5.5).

The pull-down menu for 'Method' contains the 'Enter' method as its default setting. Nothing should be changed here considering the fact that this method is indicated in the 'Problem' section.

'Selection Variable' offers the possibility to perform the analysis for only a portion of the respondents, e.g. only for those persons with a respondent number under 50.

The labels (e.g. 'male' and 'female') for the variable entered under 'Case Labels' (e.g. 'gender') will be used for the identification of the respondents, e.g. in a scatterplot. Figure 5.35 will illustrate this in further detail.

The input of the above specifications and working with the default statistical indicators ('Estimates' and 'Model fit' in Figure 5.7) is sufficient to obtain a basic regression output. In this chapter, we go one step further however, considering the accompanying statistics and graphs provide good insight into whether or not the assumptions have been satisfied.

Figure 5.6

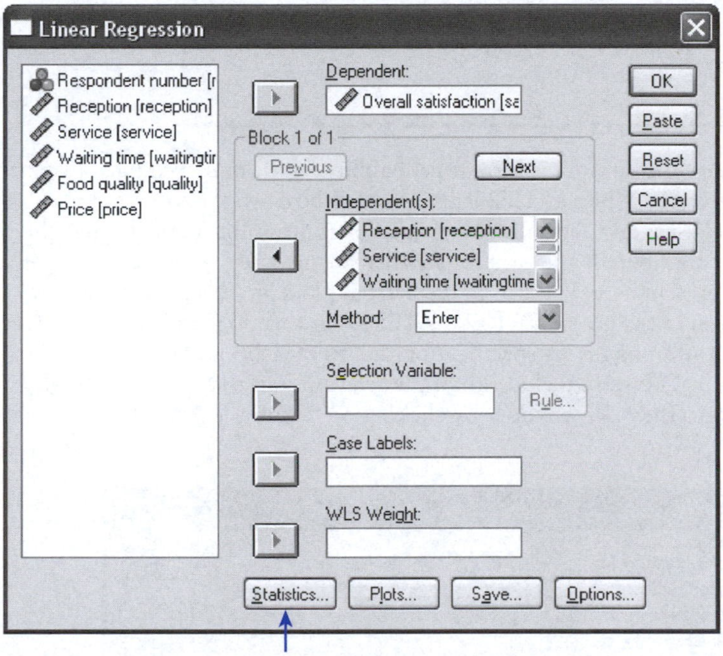

Figure 5.7

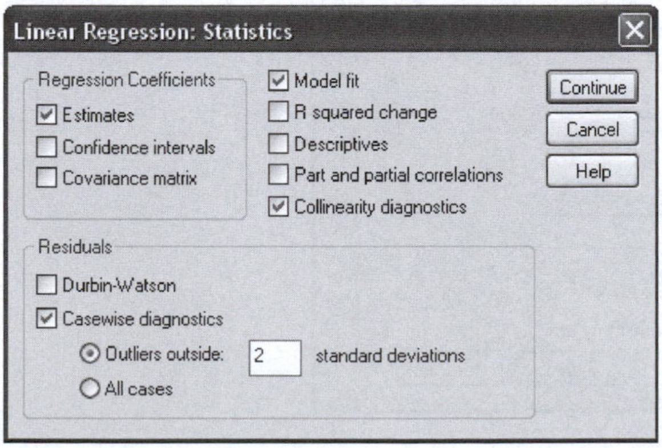

Click on the 'Statistics' button at the bottom of the dialogue window (Figure 5.6) and the 'Linear Regression: Statistics' window (Figure 5.7) will appear.

Choose the following statistics: 'Estimates', 'Model fit', 'Collinearity diagnostics' and 'Casewise diagnostics/Outliers outside 2 standard deviations'.

'Estimates' results in the estimated regression coefficients. 'Model fit' is related to the determination of the meaningfulness of the model, 'Collinearity diagnostics' results in the discovery of multicollinearity, and 'Casewise diagnostics/ Outliers outside 2 standard deviations' in the tracking down of outliers.

'Durbin-Watson' provides diagnostic data on autocorrelation and is only relevant in the context of time series analysis.

Click on 'Continue' to return to the main window (Figure 5.6). In the main window, select 'Plots' and the window 'Linear Regression: Plots' (Figure 5.8) will appear.

Figure 5.8

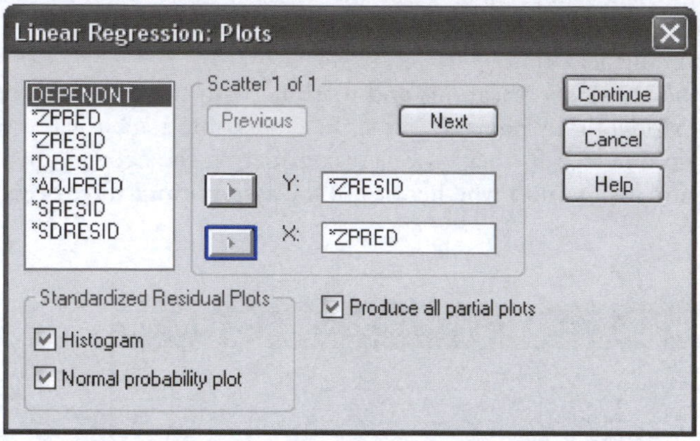

Indicate 'Histogram', 'Normal probability plot', and 'Produce all partial plots'. Move 'ZRESID' to the Y box and 'ZPRED' to the X box.

If the 'Histogram' and the 'Normal probability plot' indicate that the residuals are not normally distributed, then there is either an incorrect specification, collinearity or other problem present here. Patterns in the 'Partial plots' indicate heteroscedasticity. The presence of a pattern in the graph (ZPRED, ZRESID) in turn indicates the presence of heteroscedasticity and/or an incorrect specification due to measurement errors, an incorrect functional form, or the failure to include all of the relevant variables in the model.

Return to the main window by clicking on 'Continue' and click on 'Save' (Figure 5.9).

Figure 5.9

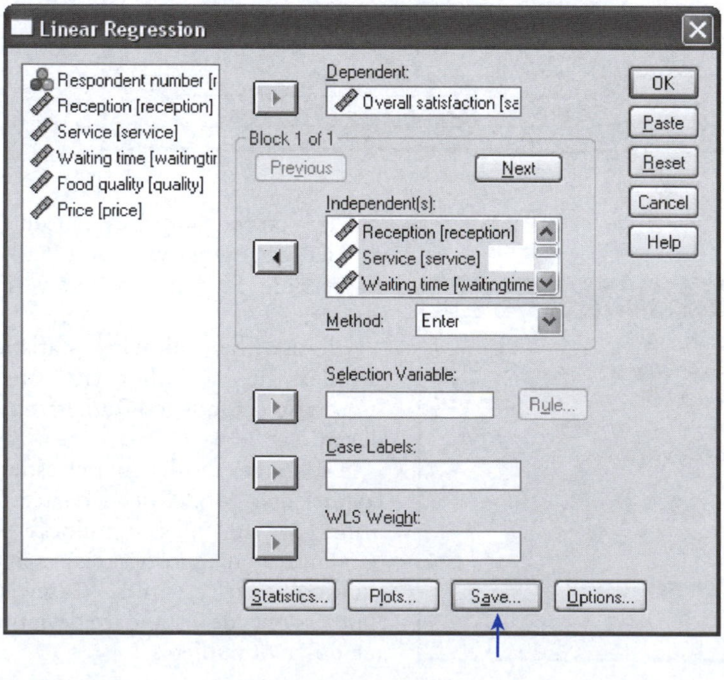

Figure 5.10

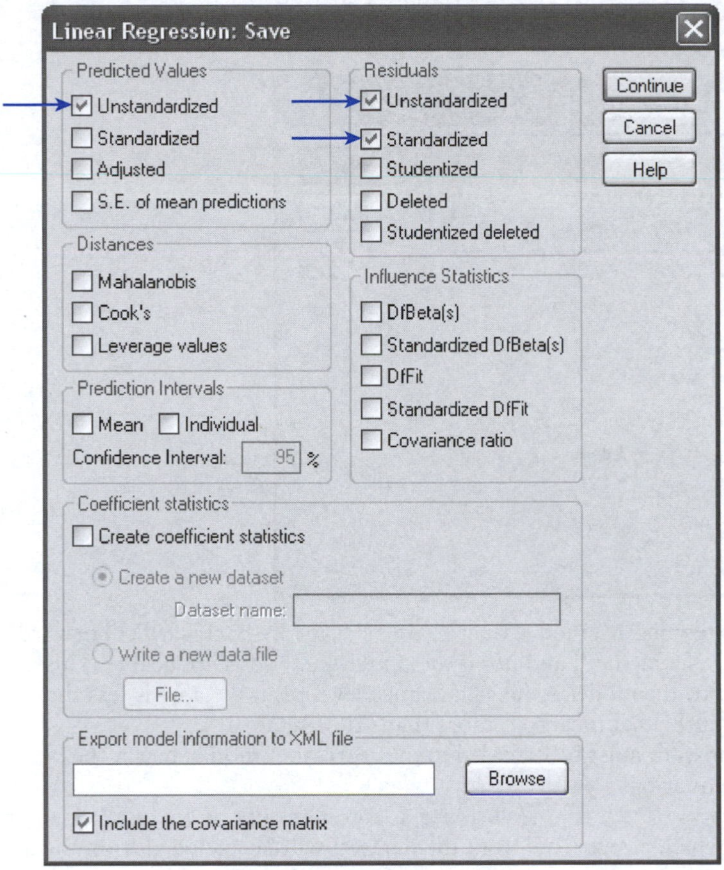

In the 'Linear Regression: Save' window (Figure 5.10), tick the boxes for 'Unstandardized Predicted Values', 'Unstandardized Residuals', and 'Standardized Residuals'.

The 'Unstandardized Residuals' are used in 'White's test' which formally determines the presence of heteroscedasticity.

The 'Unstandardized Predicted Values' and the 'Unstandardized Residuals' form the input for the 'Reset test'. This last test will formally test for an incorrect specification of the model, such as an incorrect functional form or the lack of relevant independent variables.

The 'Standardized Residuals' are part of the Kolmogorov-Smirnov test (with Lilliefors correction) and the Shapiro-Wilk's W test, which determine whether the residuals are normally distributed or not. It is worth noting here that these types of tests may also be applied to 'Unstandardized Residuals'.

Return to the main window (Figure 5.9) and click 'Options'. The window 'Linear Regression: Options' (Figure 5.11) will appear.

Figure 5.11

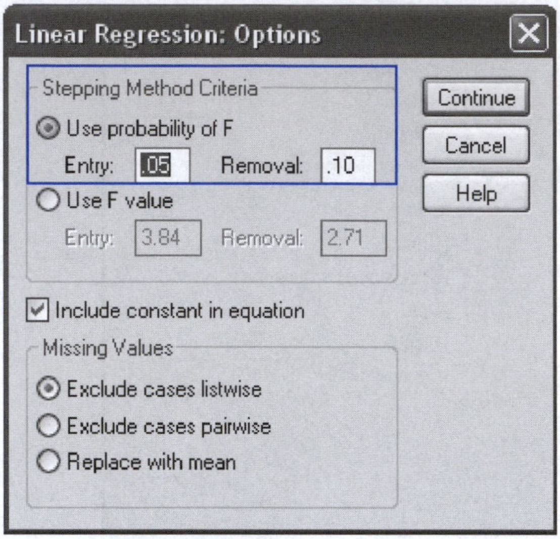

The 'Stepping Method Criteria' are relevant if 'Backward', 'Forward' or 'Stepwise' is indicated as a method, and not if the 'Enter' method is applicable. This way a variable will be added to the model if the significance level of its F-value is less than .05 ('Entry'), and removed if this significance is more than .10 ('Removal').

If a constant must be included in the regression model, check the box for 'Include constant in equation'.

The option 'Exclude cases listwise' is automatically ticked in SPSS, and refers to the situation in which a case (row from the dataset) will be excluded from the analysis, if it has a 'system missing' or a 'user missing' (see Chapter 1) for one or more of the variables included in the analysis.

Return to the main window by clicking on 'Continue', and then click 'OK' (Figure 5.12).

Figure 5.12

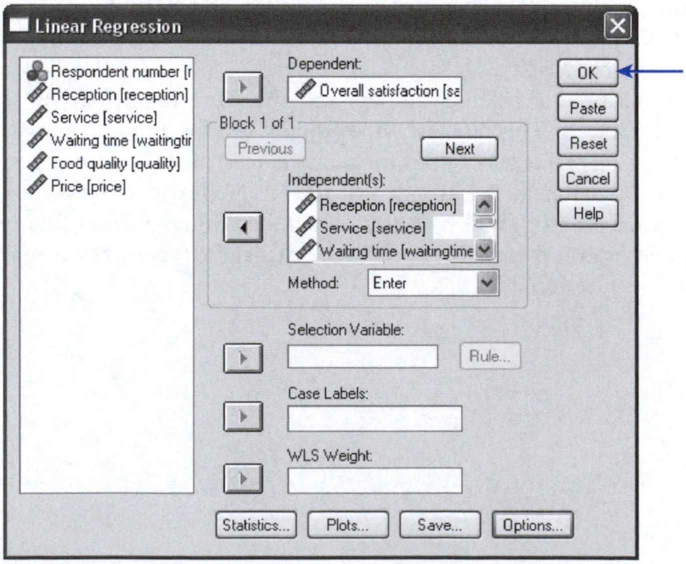

The SPSS output window (Figure 5.13) will appear. The output in this window will be used in the following section of this chapter to check the assumptions and the meaningfulness of the model and to interpret the regression coefficients which have been obtained.

Figure 5.13

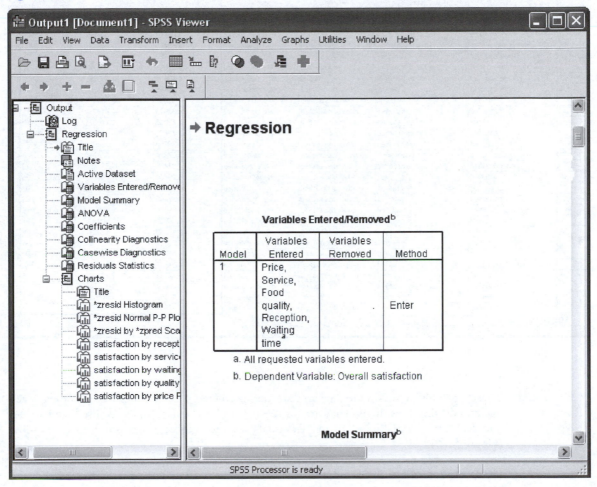

In addition to generating the output window, three variables are added to the dataset ([PRE_1], [RES_1], and [ZRE_1]; Figure 5.14).

Figure 5.14

*Pizza.sav [DataSet1] - SPSS Data Editor

File Edit View Data Transform Analyze Graphs Utilities Window Help

1 : resp_nr 16 Visible: 17 of 17 Variabl

	service	waitingtime	quality	price	PRE_1	RES_1	ZRE_1
1	very satisfied	very dissatisfied	dissatisfied	dissatisfied	3.46390	-2.46390	-2.86875
2	neutral	very dissatisfied	very dissatisfied	very dissatisfied	2.09905	-.09905	-.11532
3	rather dissatisfied	rather dissatisfied	dissatisfied	very dissatisfied	2.63473	-.63473	-.73903
4	rather dissatisfied	rather dissatisfied	dissatisfied	very dissatisfied	2.63473	-.63473	-.73903
5	rather satisfied	satisfied	rather dissatisfied	rather satisfied	5.12192	-2.12192	-2.47058
6	rather dissatisfied	rather dissatisfied	dissatisfied	very dissatisfied	3.09633	-.09633	-.11216
7	rather satisfied	rather satisfied	neutral	dissatisfied	4.76606	-1.76606	-2.05624
8	rather satisfied	neutral	rather dissatisfied	very dissatisfied	4.24685	-1.24685	-1.45172
9	neutral	neutral	rather dissatisfied	dissatisfied	3.88031	-.88031	-1.02496
10	satisfied	very satisfied	rather dissatisfied	very dissatisfied	4.81923	-1.81923	-2.11815
11	neutral	satisfied	rather dissatisfied	dissatisfied	4.47005	-1.47005	-1.71160
12	satisfied	rather satisfied	dissatisfied	very dissatisfied	3.78798	-.78798	-.91745
13	satisfied	rather satisfied	rather dissatisfied	dissatisfied	4.35852	-1.35852	-1.58174
14	rather dissatisfied	rather dissatisfied	rather dissatisfied	very dissatisfied	3.07624	-.07624	-.08876
15	rather satisfied	satisfied	rather dissatisfied	very dissatisfied	4.37499	-.37499	-.43660
16	satisfied	very satisfied	rather dissatisfied	rather satisfied	5.79696	-1.79696	-2.09223
17	neutral	rather satisfied	rather dissatisfied	dissatisfied	4.05978	-.05978	-.06960
18	rather satisfied	satisfied	rather dissatisfied	very dissatisfied	4.37499	-.37499	-.43660
19	rather dissatisfied	rather satisfied	rather dissatisfied	very dissatisfied	3.89678	.10322	.12018
20	neutral	very satisfied	rather dissatisfied	rather dissatisfied	5.00936	-1.00936	-1.17521
21	neutral	very satisfied	rather dissatisfied	neutral	5.13839	-1.13839	-1.32544
22	rather satisfied	satisfied	very dissatisfied	dissatisfied	3.85181	.14819	.17254
23	neutral	rather satisfied	rather dissatisfied	dissatisfied	4.05978	-.05978	-.06960
24	rather satisfied	rather satisfied	rather dissatisfied	neutral	4.81342	-.81342	-.94707
25	neutral	very satisfied	rather dissatisfied	neutral	5.13839	-1.13839	-1.32544
26	satisfied	very satisfied	neutral	very dissatisfied	5.26074	-1.26074	-1.46789
27	neutral	satisfied	neutral	dissatisfied	4.91156	-.91156	-1.06134
28	satisfied	rather satisfied	rather dissatisfied	very dissatisfied	4.22949	-.22949	-.26719

Data View / Variable View

SPSS Processor is ready

These variables contain the unstandardized predicted values, and the unstandardized and standardized residuals. They are the result of ticking 'Unstandardized Predicted Values and Residuals' and 'Standardized Residuals' in the 'Linear Regression: Save' window (Figure 5.10).

Interpretation of the SPSS output

STEP 1: Checking the assumptions

Assumption 1: Causality

The researcher would like to determine the effect of a number of (independent) variables on another (dependent) variable. Based on empirical findings, the technical staff has proposed a model form in which the reception, service, waiting time, the food quality and the price lie at the basis of the overall satisfaction.

Assumption 2: All of the relevant variables must be taken into consideration

The failure to include all of the relevant independent variables can bias the regression results. Three possible ways of finding out whether variables are missing are:

a) Inspection of the (ZPRED, ZRESID) graph

The presence of a pattern in the (ZPRED, ZRESID) graph indicates a possible lack of a relevant variable in the model. If for example the points form different groups (clusters), then it is possible that a categorical variable, which contains as many categories as there are groups, is missing from the model.

Figure 5.15

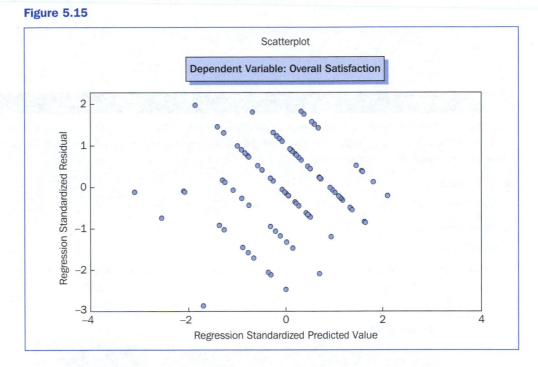

The current graph (Figure 5.15) does not appear to contain such a pattern, and leads one to suspect that all of the relevant independent variables are part of the model.

b) Formal test: Reset test

If the (ZPRED, ZRESID) graph indicates the presence of a pattern, then the lack of relevant variables may be formally tested using the 'Reset test'. The extensive explanation of this test falls outside of the scope of this book, however.[1]

c) Intuition, previous research, . . .

In addition to the (ZPRED, ZRESID) graph and the 'Reset test', the researcher may decide to rely on his or her intuition or the results of previous research. This way he may be able to sense that the interior of the restaurant might have a considerable influence on the overall satisfaction. A question which attempts to gauge the satisfaction with the interior may then also be included in a future study.

Assumption 3: Dependent and independent variables must be at least interval scaled

The scales used are the 7-point Likert scales, and are thus, strictly speaking, ordinal scales. However, the 'assumption of equal appearing intervals' permits Likert scales with five or more possible answers to be treated as interval scales.

Assumption 4: Linear relationship between the dependent and independent variables
A bias of the regression results will be the result of the application of a linear regression model whereas the correct form is not linear in nature (e.g. square or logarithmic). An inspection of the (ZPRED, ZRESID) graph, the application of the 'Reset test' and allowing intuition to play a role are also ways of tracking down an incorrect functional form.

In this example, it would appear that working with a linear relationship is advisable, since the (ZPRED, ZRESID) graph does not display a pattern (e.g., a parabola) that would indicate a non-linear relationship.

Digging Deeper

It is also possible to determine a non-linear relationship on the basis of the 'Model comparison approach'. An example is set out below in which the 'Price' variable is no longer a linear one, but can exert a quadratic influence on the overall satisfaction score:

- **'Full model'**

  Overall satisfaction $= b_0 + b_1$ price $+ \cdots + b_5$ waiting time $+ \mathbf{b_6 \ price^2} + \varepsilon$

- **'Restricted model'**

  Overall satisfaction $= b_0 + b_1$ price $+ \cdots + b_5$ waiting time $+ \varepsilon$

In SPSS (Transform/Compute) the new variable [price2] will be created and calculated as the square of the original price variable (Figure 5.16).

Figure 5.16

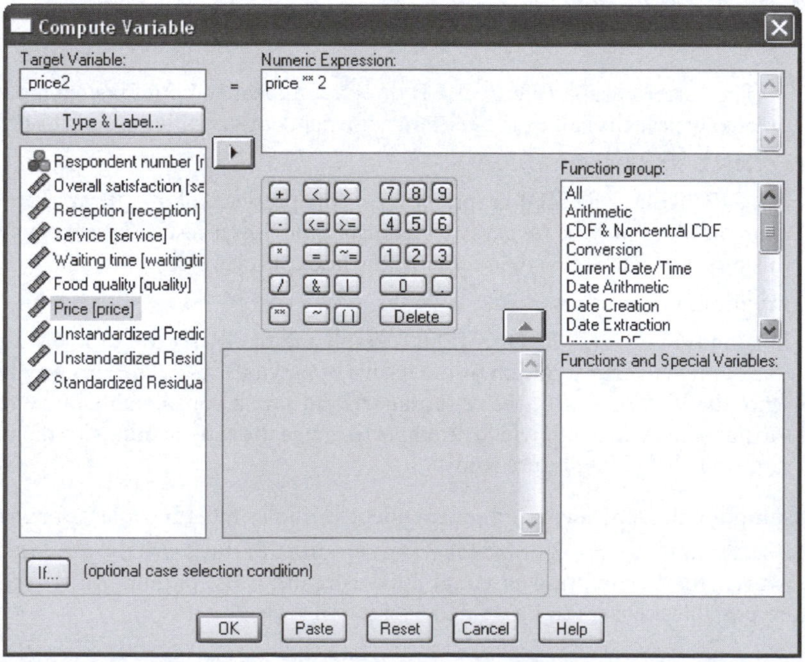

Within the main window of the linear regression (Figure 5.17), there are then two blocks defined: the first block contains the five original variables and the second block, which is obtained by clicking on the 'Next' button, only contains the variable [price2]. In the 'Statistics' subwindow, the 'R squared change' is additionally ticked.

Figure 5.17

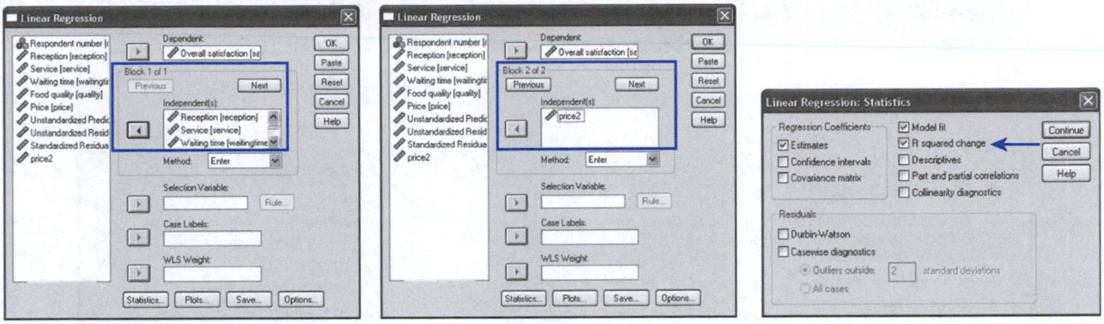

The limited output which is displayed here (Figure 5.18) shows that the addition of the variable [price2] to the 'restricted' model does not lead to a significant improvement in the model (.478 > .05). The [price] variable will therefore exert a linear rather than a quadrative influence on the dependent variable.

Figure 5.18

Model Summary[c]									
			Adjusted R Square	Std. Error of the Estimate	Change Statistics				
Model	R	R Square			R Square Change	F Change	df1	df2	Sig. F Change
1	.758[a]	.575	.554	.859	.575	27.361	5	101	.000
2	.760[b]	.577	.552	.861	.002	.508	1	100	.478

[a]Predictors: (Constant), Price, Service, Food quality, Reception, Waiting time
[b]Predictors: (Constant), Price, Service, Food quality, Reception, Waiting time, price2
[c]Dependent Variable: Overall satisfaction

Assumption 5: Additive relationship between the dependent and the independent variables

Digging Deeper

On the basis of the 'Model comparison approach', not only the linearity of relationships may be tested, but also their additivity. In the example below, a test is performed to determine whether an interaction exists between the variables 'Price' and 'Service':

■ **'Full model'**

Overall satisfaction = $b_0 + b_1$ price $+ \cdots + b_5$ waiting time $+ b_6$ price $\times$ service $+ \varepsilon$

■ **'Restricted model'**

Overall satisfaction = $b_0 + b_1$ price $+ \cdots + b_5$ waiting time $+ \varepsilon$

The same approach is applied as was used for the introduction of the quadratic term. The new variable is now [priceser] and is calculated as the product of the two original variables 'Price' and 'Service' (Figure 5.19).

Figure 5.19

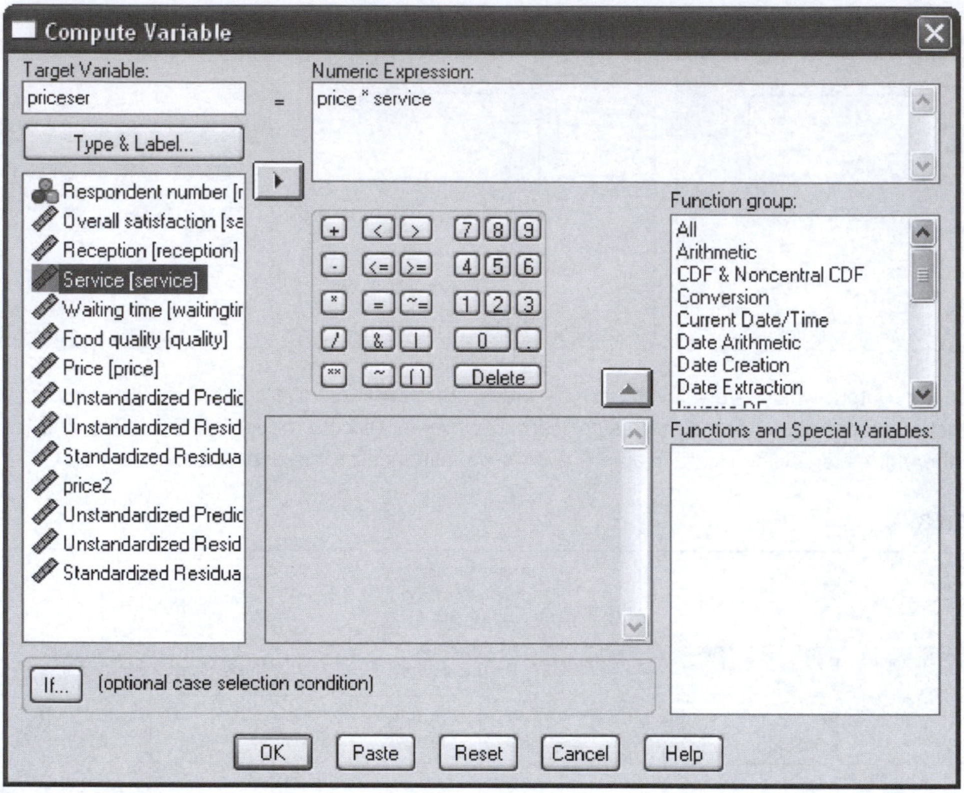

The introduction of an interaction between 'Price' and 'Service' does not lead to a significant improvement in the model either (.403 > .05; Figure 5.20). The additive model ('Restricted model') is thus chosen.

Figure 5.20

					Change Statistics				
Model	R	R Square	Adjusted R Square	Std. Error of the Estimate	R Square Change	F Change	df1	df2	Sig. F Change
1	.758[a]	.575	.554	.859	.575	27.361	5	101	.000
2	.760[b]	.578	.553	.860	.003	.706	1	100	.403

Model Summary[c]

[a]Predictors: (Constant), Price, Service, Food quality, Reception, Waiting time
[b]Predictors: (Constant), Price, Service, Food quality, Reception, Waiting time, priceser
[c]Dependent Variable: Overall satisfaction

Assumption 6: Residuals

The residuals must satisfy the following four characteristics:

a) Independence

This assumption means that each observation must be made independently of the others. In the current example, there must be special care taken to ensure that the people who fill in the questionnaire cannot be influenced by the way in which the others have filled in their questionnaires. The researcher assumes that efforts have been made to ensure that this occurs, such as preventing two questionnaires from ever being filled in simultaneously.

b) Normality

Figure 5.21

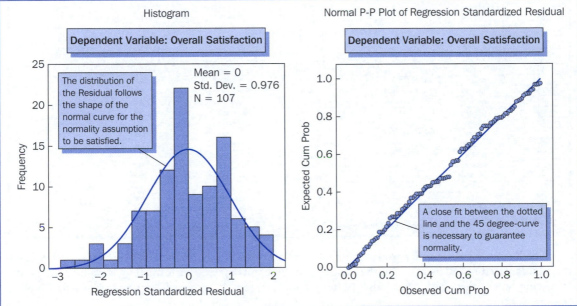

Figure 5.21 displays a histogram of the standardized residuals. As one may observe visually, the residuals are 'more or less' normally distributed. The 'normal probability plot' also displays this visually.

Supporting technique

The normality of the residuals may also be tested formally on the basis of a non-parametric test: the Kolmogorov-Smirnov test (with Lilliefors correction) and the Shapiro-Wilk's W test. It is worth noting here that if the normality assumption is not satisfied, transformations such as the taking of the inverse or the logarithm, or taking the square root may also offer a solution.

Figure 5.22

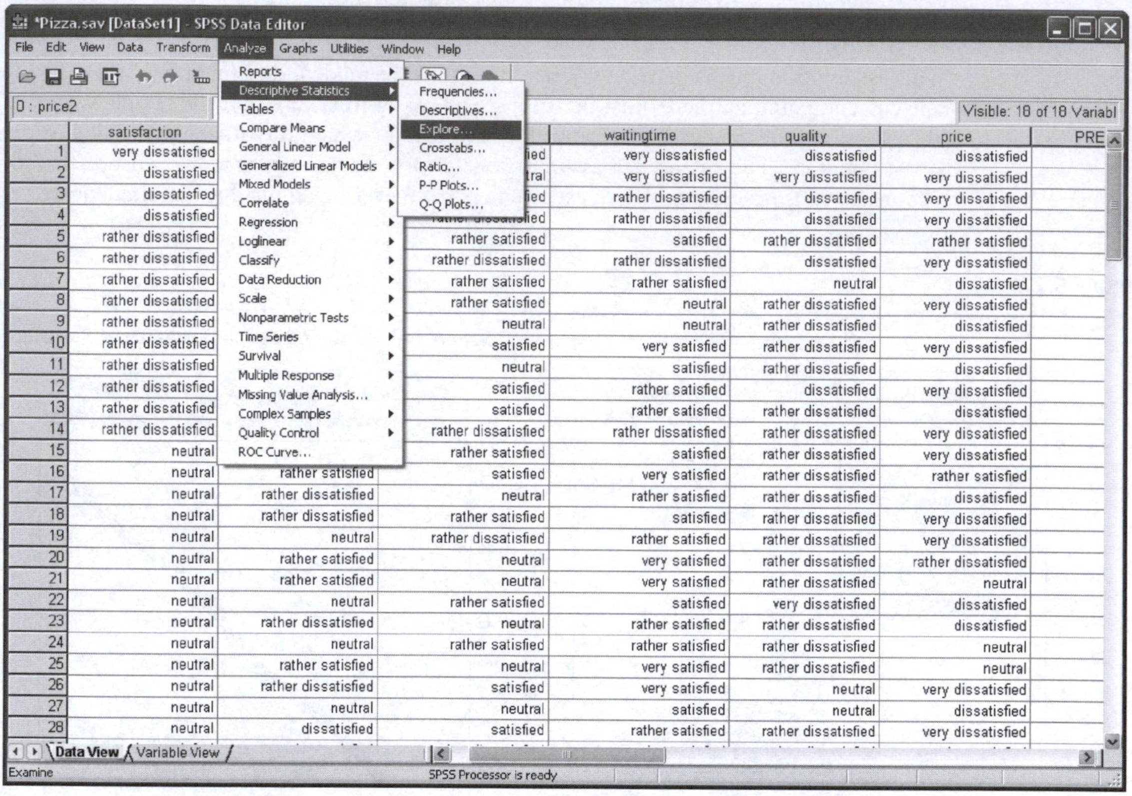

The Kolmogorov-Smirnov test (with Lilliefors correction) and the Shapiro-Wilk's W test both employ the standardized residuals added to the dataset and these tests may be performed by running through the following steps (these steps may also be found in Chapter 2): Analyze/Descriptive Statistics/Explore (Figure 5.22).

Figure 5.23

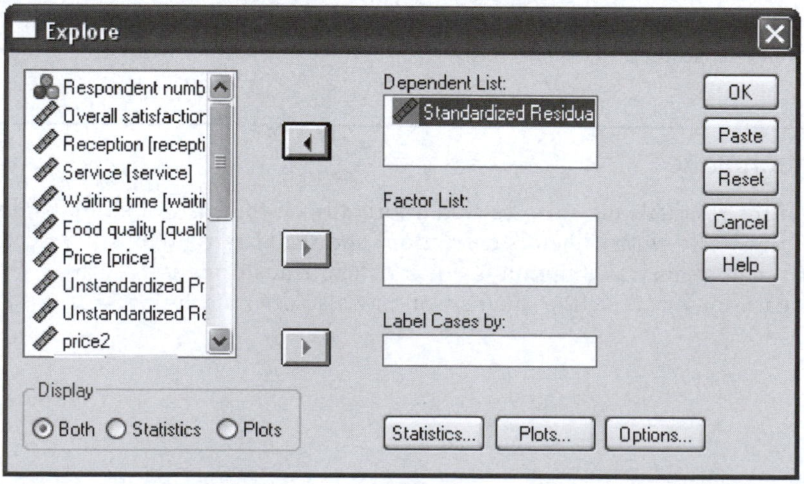

In the 'Explore' window (Figure 5.23), the variable [ZRE_1] is then selected and moved to the 'Dependent List'. In the 'Explore: Plots' window (Figure 5.24), the option 'Normality plots with tests' is ticked.

Figure 5.24

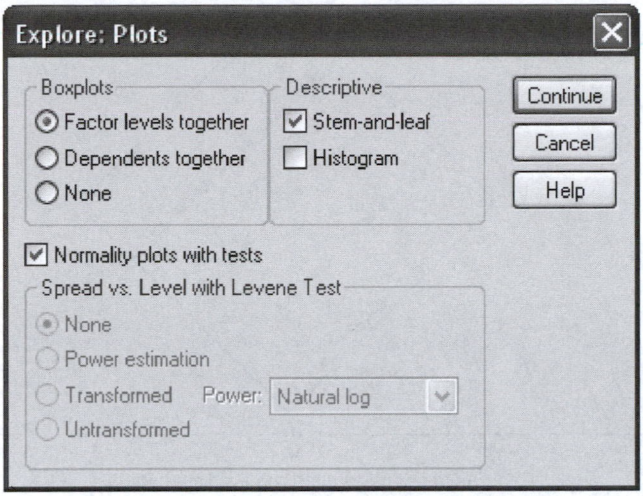

In the output obtained (Figure 5.25), it is primarily the values found under the column title 'Sig.' which are important, and this applies to the Kolmogorov-Smirnov test (with Lilliefors correction) as well as the Shapiro-Wilk's W test.

Figure 5.25

Tests of Normality						
	Kolmogorov-Smirnov[a]			Shapiro-Wilk		
	Statistic	df	Sig.	Statistic	df	Sig.
Standardized residual	.057	107	.200[*]	.986	107	.302

[*]This is a lower bound of the true significance
[a]Lilliefors significance correction

These values are respectively: .200 and .302. Since these values are greater than .05, the null hypothesis which corresponds to a normal distribution of the variable is accepted. Therefore, the conclusion on the basis of the histogram and the normal probability plot is formally confirmed here: the standardized residuals are normally distributed.

c) Homoscedasticity

The presence of a pattern in the (ZPRED, ZRESID) graph can indicate that the statement 'the residual has the same variance for every value of the independent variable' does not

Figure 5.26

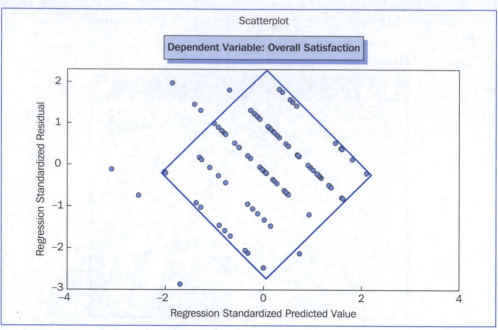

apply, and that heteroscedasticity is present. Patterns which clearly indicate that the homoscedasticity assumption has not been satisfied include the triangle, which opens to the left or right, and the diamond. This last pattern appears to be present in the current exercise (Figure 5.26).

Figure 5.27

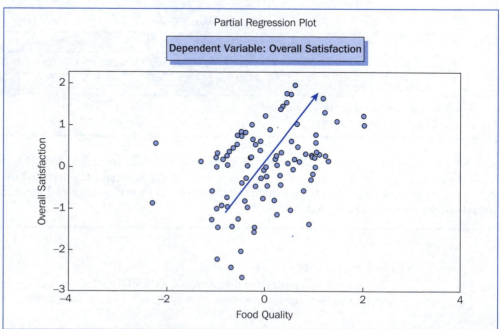

Figure 5.27 *Continued*

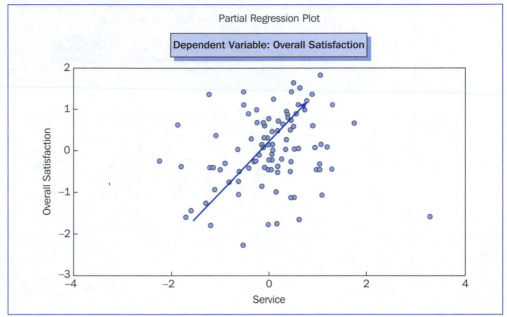

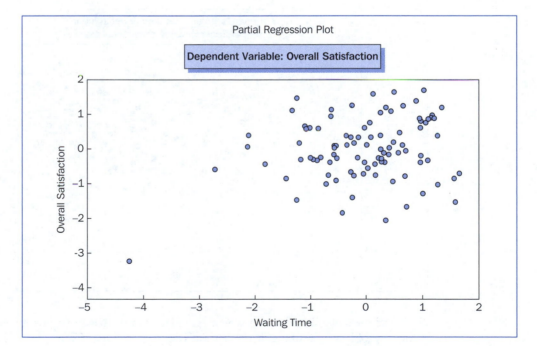

Figure 5.27 *Continued*

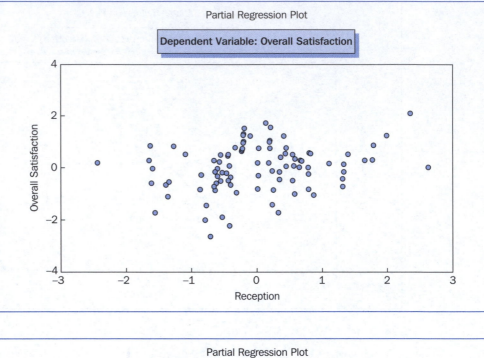

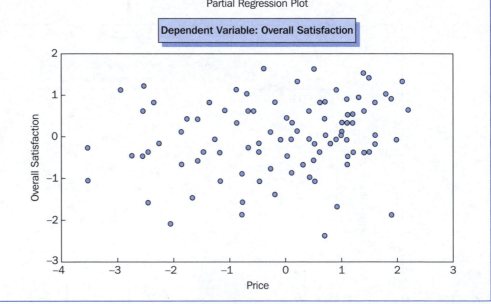

The researcher can discover which variables lie at the basis of a possible heteroscedas-ticity problem by looking at the 'Partial Regression Plots' (Figure 5.27). This way, the positive patterns for the variables 'food quality' and 'service' show their contribution to this problem. The graphs linked to the variables 'waiting time', 'reception' and 'price' do not demonstrate a pattern, and are therefore not responsible for the possibly violated homoscedasticity requirement.

A formal test which is used to detect the presence of heteroscedasticity is 'White's test'. However, the detailed description of this test falls outside of the scope of this book.[2]

If the form of a partial regression plot brings the constancy of the variance into question, then it is best to take remedying measures such as: a non-linear transformation of the dependent variable Y in $Y^{1/2}$ or log Y, or by applying the more complex 'weighted least squares' (WLS) procedure. These procedures are also not treated in any further detail in the current book.[3]

d) Autocorrelation

Given the fact that the example is not based on time series, this point is irrelevant.

Assumption 7: Sufficient number of observations

Keeping the previously stated rule of thumb in mind of at least five times as many observations as parameters to be estimated (6), the researcher may decide that the number of observations is more than sufficient (5*6 = 30 whereas there are 107 respondents).

Assumption 8: No multicollinearity

A number of factors may point to multicollinearity: e.g., a significant F-value in the 'ANOVA' table (see Step 2), whereas not one of the t-values corresponding to the coefficients is significant (see Step 3). A more formal indicator is the bivariate correlation coefficient; a correlation between two variables of .60 or more indicates a (multi) collinearity problem.

Supporting technique

The bivariate correlations may be calculated via: Analyze/Correlate/Bivariate (Figure 5.28).

Figure 5.28

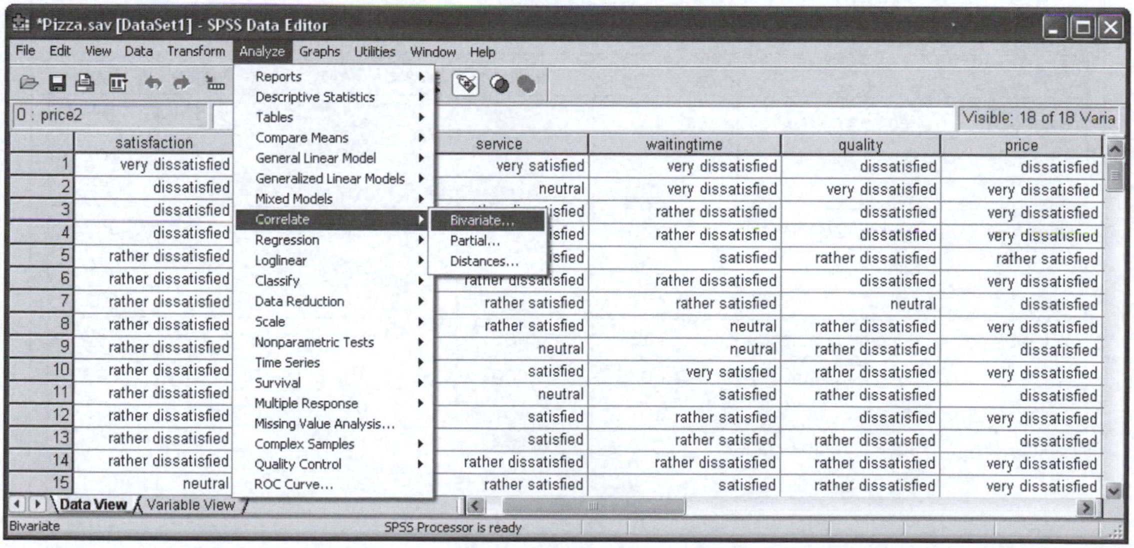

Select the five independent variables in the 'Bivariate Correlations' window (Figure 5.29) and move them to the 'Variables' box using the arrow ▶.

Figure 5.29

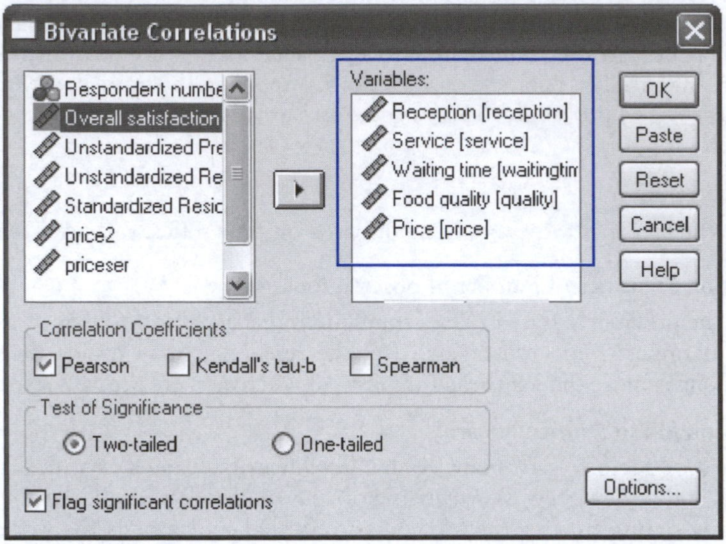

Since the independent variables are all interval-scaled, tick the box for the 'Pearson' correlation coefficient.

Select 'Two-tailed Test of Significance', since it must be tested whether or not the correlation differs significantly from zero, with H_0: correlation = 0. Indicate 'Flag significant correlations' if the output must mark the correlations which differ significantly from zero with a '*' (*: significant on the .05 level; **: on the .01 level). Click 'OK' to obtain the output.

Figure 5.30

Correlations

		Reception	Service	Waiting Time	Food Quality	Price
Reception	Pearson correlation	1	.273**	.413**	.242*	.462**
	Sig. (2-tailed)		.004	.000	.012	.000
	N	107	107	107	107	107
Service	Pearson correlation	.273**	1	.486**	.326**	.392**
	Sig. (2-tailed)	.004		.000	.001	.000
	N	107	107	107	107	107
Waiting time	Pearson correlation	.413**	.486**	1	.435**	.443**
	Sig. (2-tailed)	.000	.000		.000	.000
	N	107	107	107	107	107
Food quality	Pearson correlation	.242*	.326**	.435**	1	.402**
	Sig. (2-tailed)	.012	.001	.000		.000
	N	107	107	107	107	107
Price	Pearson correlation	.462**	.392**	.443**	.402**	1
	Sig. (2-tailed)	.000	.000	.000	.000	
	N	107	107	107	107	107

**Correlation is significant at the 0.01 level (2-tailed)
*Correlation is significant at the 0.05 level (2-tailed)

All of the correlations differ significantly from zero, but not one of them is greater than .60 (Figure 5.30). In all likelihood, multicollinearity is therefore not a problem.

Digging Deeper

In addition to the calculation of the bivariate correlations, there are other techniques used to detect multi-collinearity: 'condition index' and 'tolerance'. Both statistics have been included in the SPSS output, since the option 'Collinearity diagnostics' has been ticked in the 'Linear Regression: Statistics' window (Figure 5.7).

Figure 5.31

Collinearity Diagnostics[a]

Model	Dimension	Eigenvalue	Condition Index	Variance Proportions					
				(Constant)	Reception	Service	Waiting Time	Food Quality	Price
1	1	5.730	1.000	.00	.00	.00	.00	.00	.00
	2	.148	6.223	.02	.00	.01	.00	.01	.78
	3	.051	10.647	.00	.55	.00	.00	.42	.01
	4	.034	12.913	.04	.35	.19	.04	.52	.06
	5	.022	16.041	.18	.00	.07	.92	.01	.04
	6	.015	19.692	.76	.09	.72	.03	.04	.11

[a]Dependent Variable: Overall satisfaction

■ **Condition index** (Figure 5.31): a condition index of 30 or more indicates a strong presence of multi-collinearity. The researcher can thus decide that the problem does not present itself here (maximum value is 19.69, < 30).

In the presence of a multicollinearity problem, one can determine which specific variables are responsible for this by examining the rows with a low (nearly zero) Eigenvalue. For each row in question, one must then look at the values in the columns (i.e. 'Variance Proportions' per variable). If there are two or more columns with high (nearly one) 'Variance Proportions', then the variables linked to these will be the ones responsible for the multicollinearity.

Figure 5.32

Coefficients[a]

Model		Unstandardized Coefficients		Standardized Coefficients	t	Sig.	Collinearity Statistics	
		B	Std. Error	Beta			Tolerance	VIF
1	(Constant)	−.172	.548		−.313	.755		
	Reception	.231	.090	.195	2.571	.012	.732	1.366
	Service	.265	.099	.205	2.680	.009	.719	1.391
	Waiting time	.179	.085	.175	2.106	.038	.606	1.649
	Food quality	.442	.106	.313	4.181	.000	.750	1.334
	Price	.129	.059	.176	2.176	.032	.644	1.552

[a]Dependent Variable: Overall satisfaction

■ **Tolerance** (or its opposite, the 'Variance Inflation Factor'; Figure 5.32): the proportion of the variance in an independent variable which is independent of each one of the other independent variables. A tolerance of .50 or less indicates a multicollinearity problem, a tolerance of .30 or less indicates a serious multicollinearity problem. This problem does not occur in the current example since all of the values are greater than .50 (minimum value is .606).

The values 30 and .30 for the 'condition index', and 'tolerance' respectively, are target values and must not be adhered to strictly in the interpretation of the output.

In the presence of a multicollinearity problem, the researcher may adopt various strategies including:

a) Removing one or more independent variables. It would be best to choose those variables which are strongly correlated to the other independent variables.

b) Merging strongly correlated independent variables, by calculating a mean score.

c) Working with factor scores which arise from an exploratory factor analysis. These scores are uncorrelated by definition (see Chapter 7).

Assumption 9: Outliers

In the 'Linear Regression: Statistics' window (Figure 5.7), the option 'Casewise diagnostics – outliers outside 2 standard deviations' is indicated. This produces a table with observations for which the difference between the actual and the predicted value for the dependent variable does not lie in a range of two standard deviations of the mean residual.

Figure 5.33

		Casewise Diagnostics[a]		
Case Number	Std. Residual	Overall Satisfaction	Predicted Value	Residual
1	−2.869	1	3.46	−2.464
5	−2.471	3	5.12	−2.122
7	−2.056	3	4.77	−1.766
10	−2.118	3	4.82	−1.819
16	−2.092	4	5.80	−1.797

[a]Dependent Variable: Overall satisfaction

The respondents which may be found in rows '1', '5', '7', '10' and '16' of the 'Data View' window are thus outliers (Figure 5.33), and the 'Scatterplot' (Figure 5.34) provides visual confirmation of this.

Figure 5.34

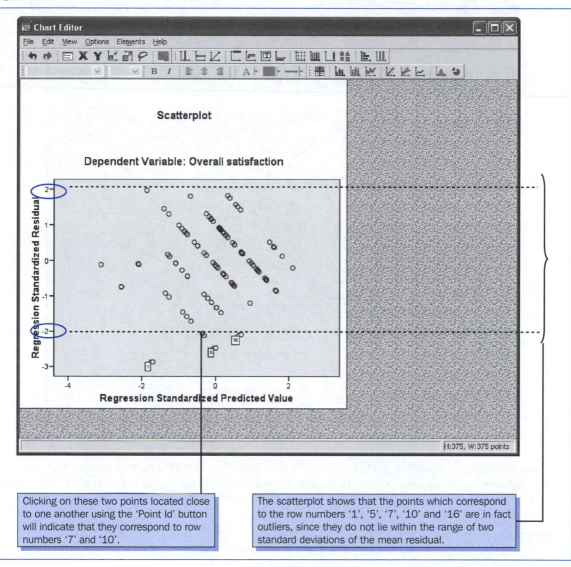

Clicking on these two points located close to one another using the 'Point Id' button will indicate that they correspond to row numbers '7' and '10'.

The scatterplot shows that the points which correspond to the row numbers '1', '5', '7', '10' and '16' are in fact outliers, since they do not lie within the range of two standard deviations of the mean residual.

With regard to the scatterplot, it is worth noting that the 'SPSS Chart Editor' (double-click on the plot with the left mouse button in the output window; Figure 5.34), may be used to assign labels to points by activating the 'Point Id' button (click the icon in the upper left of the 'SPSS Chart Editor' window), and then by clicking on the points in the plot with the left mouse button.

Digging Deeper

'Case Number' in Figure 5.33 corresponds to the row number in the 'Data View' window and **not** to the respondent number (see the values under the variable name [resp_nr] in Figure 5.1).

Figure 5.35

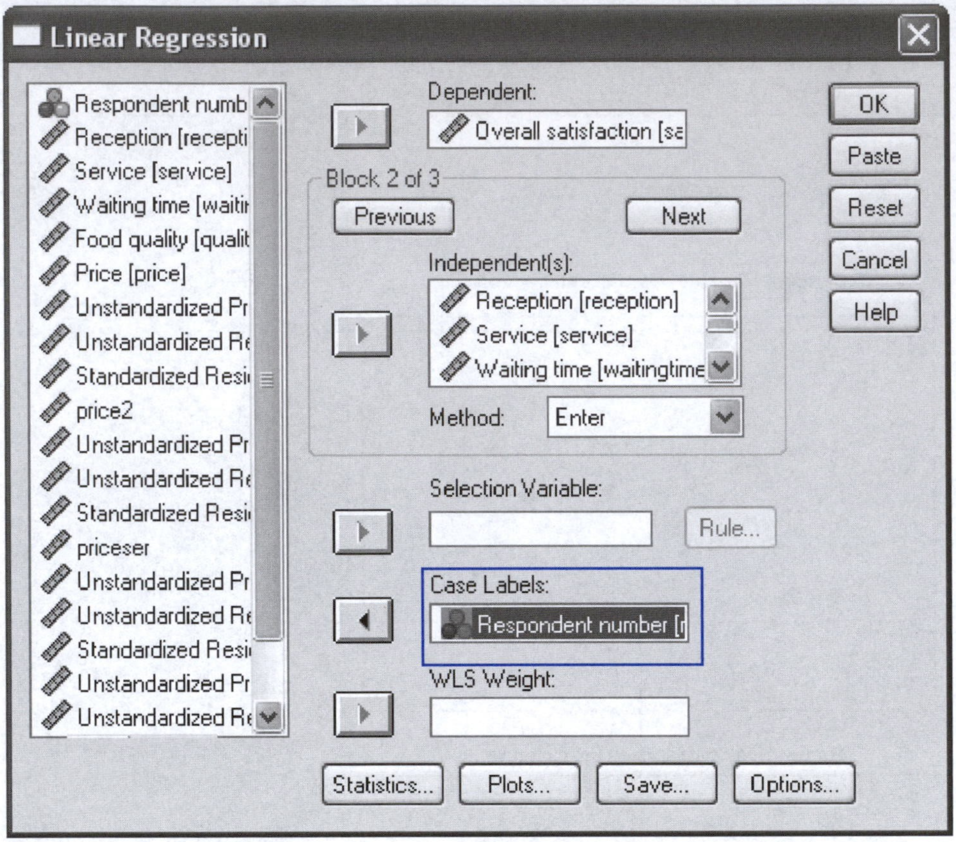

The definition of a variable, e.g. [resp_nr], in the 'Case Labels' box of the 'Linear Regression' main window (Figure 5.35) will add an extra column to the 'Casewise Diagnostics' table, namely 'Respondent number' (Figure 5.36).

Figure 5.36

Casewise Diagnostics[a]

Case Number	Respondent Number	Std. Residual	Overall Satisfaction	Predicted Value	Residual
1	16	−2.869	1	3.46	−2.464
5	7	−2.471	3	5.12	−2.122
7	29	−2.056	3	4.77	−1.766
10	50	−2.118	3	4.82	−1.819
16	4	−2.092	4	5.80	−1.797

[a]Dependent Variable: Overall satisfaction

In this way, SPSS provides an additional characterization of the outliers on the basis of the appropriate label for this variable: '16', '7', '29', '50', and '4'. In addition, the labels in the new 'Scatterplot' will now no longer correspond to the row numbers, but instead to the respondent numbers (Figure 5.37). The researcher may remove all of the labels in the scatterplot at once by selecting Elements/Hide Data Labels in the 'SPSS Chart Editor'.

Figure 5.37

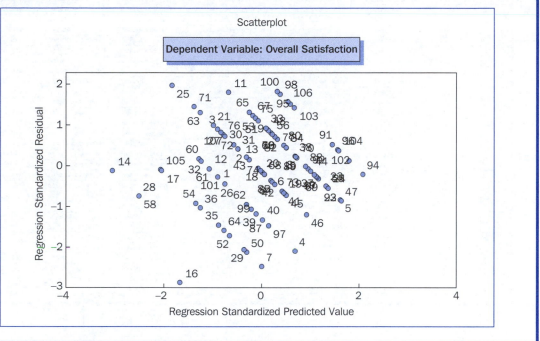

In the presence of outliers, it is advisable to perform two analyses: (1) on the original dataset, excluding the outliers (Data/Select Cases – If the condition is satisfied[4] (Figure 5.38); the resulting dataset (Figure 5.39) forms the basis for steps 2 and 3 which are set out below);

Figure 5.38

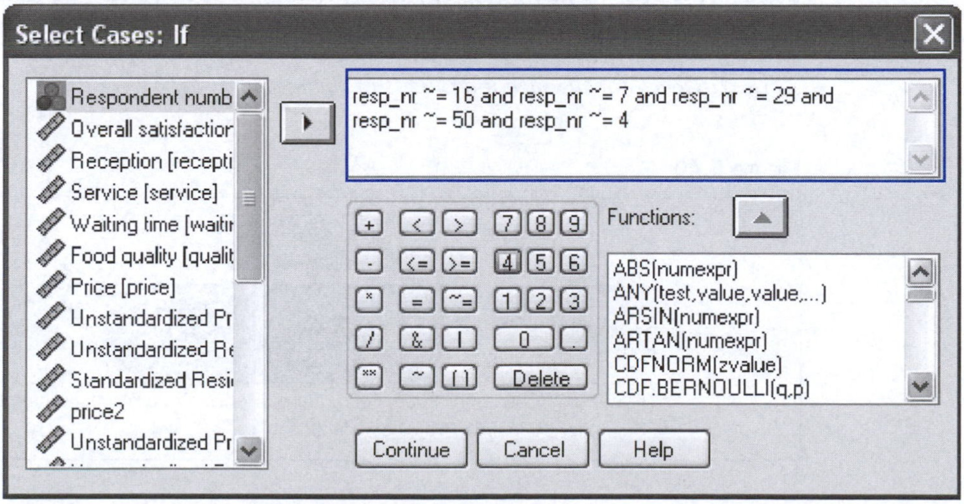

Figure 5.39

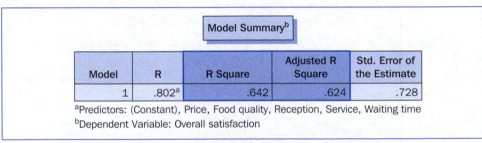

	resp_nr	satisfaction	reception	service	waitingtime	quality	price
1	16	very dissatisfied	dissatisfied	very satisfied	very dissatisfied	dissatisfied	dissatisfied
2	14	dissatisfied	dissatisfied	neutral	very dissatisfied	very dissatisfied	very dissatisfied
3	28	dissatisfied	dissatisfied	rather dissatisfied	rather dissatisfied	dissatisfied	very dissatisfied
4	58	dissatisfied	dissatisfied	rather dissatisfied	rather dissatisfied	dissatisfied	very dissatisfied
5	7	rather dissatisfied	neutral	rather satisfied	satisfied	rather dissatisfied	rather satisfied
6	17	rather dissatisfied	neutral	rather dissatisfied	rather dissatisfied	dissatisfied	very dissatisfied
7	29	rather dissatisfied	rather dissatisfied	rather satisfied	rather satisfied	neutral	dissatisfied
8	35	rather dissatisfied	neutral	rather satisfied	neutral	rather dissatisfied	very dissatisfied
9	36	rather dissatisfied	rather dissatisfied	neutral	neutral	rather dissatisfied	dissatisfied
10	50	rather dissatisfied	rather dissatisfied	satisfied	very dissatisfied	rather dissatisfied	very dissatisfied
11	52	rather dissatisfied	neutral	neutral	satisfied	rather dissatisfied	dissatisfied
12	54	rather dissatisfied	dissatisfied	satisfied	rather satisfied	dissatisfied	very dissatisfied
13	64	rather dissatisfied	dissatisfied	satisfied	rather satisfied	rather dissatisfied	dissatisfied
14	105	rather dissatisfied	dissatisfied	rather dissatisfied	rather dissatisfied	rather dissatisfied	very dissatisfied
15	1	neutral	rather dissatisfied	rather satisfied	satisfied	rather dissatisfied	very dissatisfied
16	4	neutral	rather satisfied	satisfied	very satisfied	rather dissatisfied	rather satisfied
17	12	neutral	rather satisfied	neutral	rather satisfied	rather dissatisfied	dissatisfied
18	26	neutral	rather dissatisfied	rather satisfied	satisfied	rather dissatisfied	very dissatisfied
19	32	neutral	neutral	rather dissatisfied	rather satisfied	rather dissatisfied	very dissatisfied
20	39	neutral	rather satisfied	neutral	very satisfied	rather dissatisfied	rather dissatisfied
21	40	neutral	rather satisfied	neutral	very satisfied	rather dissatisfied	neutral
22	60	neutral	neutral	rather satisfied	satisfied	very dissatisfied	dissatisfied
23	61	neutral	rather dissatisfied	neutral	rather satisfied	rather dissatisfied	dissatisfied
24	62	neutral	neutral	rather satisfied	rather satisfied	rather dissatisfied	neutral
25	87	neutral	rather satisfied	neutral	very satisfied	rather dissatisfied	neutral
26	97	neutral	rather dissatisfied	satisfied	very satisfied	neutral	very dissatisfied
27	99	neutral	neutral	neutral	satisfied	neutral	dissatisfied
28	101	neutral	dissatisfied	satisfied	rather satisfied	rather dissatisfied	very dissatisfied

and (2) on a new dataset which only contains the outliers. In this last dataset, we are in search of what makes these outliers so special. It is important to note however that for the performance of statistical analyses on the outliers dataset, the number of cases must be sufficiently large, which is not the case in the current example (five cases is too few).

Reanalyze the dataset *Pizza.sav* on the basis of the outlier analysis. Make sure that the respondents with numbers '16', '7', '29', '50' and '4' are no longer included in the analysis, and that the variables [price2] and [priceser], which could still be part of 'Block 2' (Figure 5.17) are removed.

STEP 2: Check for the meaningfulness of the model

Figure 5.40

				Model Summary[b]	

Model	R	R Square	Adjusted R Square	Std. Error of the Estimate
1	.802[a]	.642	.624	.728

[a]Predictors: (Constant), Price, Food quality, Reception, Service, Waiting time
[b]Dependent Variable: Overall satisfaction

The 'Model Summary' table (Figure 5.40) indicates that 64.2% of the variation in the dependent variable may be explained by the variation in the independent variables included in the model (see 'R Square', also referred to as the 'coefficient of determination'). It is however better to look at the 'Adjusted R Square': this statistic corrects for the number of independent variables in the regression model. After all, the 'R Square' would continue to increase purely through the addition of independent variables to the regression model. In this exercise, 'R Square' and 'Adjusted R Square' do not differ strongly from one another, and the value .62 is a good score for a commercial cross-section analysis (.50 is the lower bound). In the case of time series, one should aim for higher values (.80).

Figure 5.41

ANOVA[b]

Model		Sum of Squares	df	Mean Square	F	Sig.
1	Regression	91.453	5	18.291	34.497	.000[a]
	Residual	50.900	96	.530		
	Total	142.353	101			

[a]Predictors: (Constant), Price, Food quality, Reception, Service, Waiting time
[b]Dependent Variable: Overall satisfaction

It is recommended to perform the interpretation of the 'Adjusted R Square' **after** the procedure for the p-value (Sig.) in the 'ANOVA' table (Figure 5.41). This p-value provides an insight into the need to reject or accept the following null hypothesis: H_0: 'Adjusted R Square' = 0, or in other words, $b_0 = b_1 = b_2 = b_3 = b_4 = b_5 = 0$. If the p-value is greater than .05, then the null hypothesis is valid, resulting in the model not being meaningful. A further interpretation of the 'Adjusted R Square' (Figure 5.40) and the 'Coefficients' table (Figure 5.42) is in that case unnecessary.

Figure 5.42

Coefficients[a]

Model		Unstandardized Coefficients B	Std. Error	Standardized Coefficients Beta	t	Sig.
1	(Constant)	.087	.470		.185	.853
	Reception	.171	.077	.156	2.225	.028
	Service	.423	.092	.357	4.577	.000
	Waiting time	.077	.082	.076	.928	.356
	Food quality	.379	.091	.293	4.148	.000
	Price	.143	.052	.212	2.775	.007

[a]Dependent Variable: Overall satisfaction

By contrast, a p-value less than .05, such as is the case in the current example, leads to a rejection of the null hypothesis. The model is meaningful; in other words, a good fit is present between the model and the data, and further interpretation is allowed.

STEP 3: Interpretation of the regression coefficients
On the basis of the 'Coefficients' table (Figure 5.42), the concrete values for the b's in the regression model may be filled in:

$$\text{Overall satisfaction} = .087 + .171 \text{ reception} + .423 \text{ service} + .077 \text{ waiting time}$$
$$+ .379 \text{ quality} + .143 \text{ price} + \varepsilon$$

For example, the regression coefficient of the variable 'Reception' indicates that an increase in the satisfaction regarding the reception with one unit leads to an increase in the overall satisfaction with .171 units. However, this type of interpretation of regression coefficients should be performed **after** the interpretation of the p-values, with H_0: $b_i = 0$. Given the fact the 'Enter' method is being applied, variables with p-values greater than .05 may be part of the model: this means that the null hypothesis is valid and that the relevant b's do not differ significantly from zero. A next step can involve the repetition of the analysis, but without these variables. In the current example, it is only $b_{\text{waiting time}}$ (.077) which does not differ significantly from zero (p-value = .356 > .05), which can lead to the estimation of the following model:

$$\text{Overall satisfaction} = b_0 + b_1 \text{ reception} + b_2 \text{ service} + b_3 \text{ quality} + b_4 \text{ price} + \varepsilon \quad (1)$$

It is worth noting here that the tendency to remove all of the variables with a p-value greater than .05 can lead to the creation of regression models purely on the basis of statistical values, and not on the basis of a certain underlying theory. This is an incorrect approach since the goal of regression analysis concerns proving/supporting a certain theory and/or intuition. It is therefore also necessary before the start of a regression analysis (1) to assign an expected sign to every independent variable and (2) to have an idea of the size of the expected effect, supported by these theoretical grounds and/or on the basis of previous empirical observations. In the current example, one may expect the following symbols:

- **Reception** (+): the more satisfaction there is with the reception in the restaurant, the greater the overall satisfaction with the restaurant
- **Service** (+): the more satisfaction there is with the service in the restaurant, the greater the overall satisfaction with the restaurant
- **Waiting time** (+): the more satisfaction there is with the waiting time in the restaurant (the customer should not have to wait too long for his meal), the greater the overall satisfaction with the restaurant
- **Food quality** (+): the more satisfaction there is with the food quality in the restaurant, the greater the overall satisfaction with the restaurant
- **Price** (+): the more satisfaction there is with the price in the restaurant (the price is not too high), the greater the overall satisfaction with the restaurant

An important step is then the comparison of the regression results obtained (b's or beta's) with these expectations.

The 'General-To-Specific' approach which is indicated in the 'Problem' section leads here to **the estimation of the above model (1); the model that excludes the 'waiting time' variable.**

The next step is then to remove the 'Waiting time' variable from the list of independent variables in the 'Linear Regression' window (Figure 5.43).

Figure 5.43

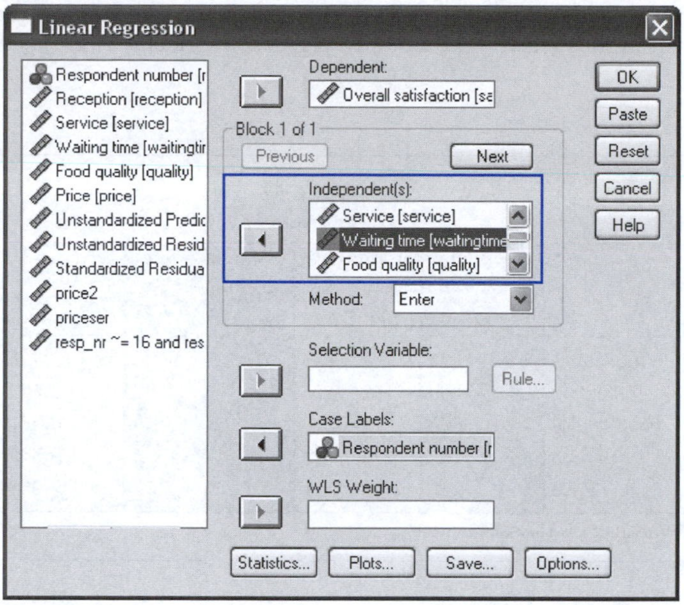

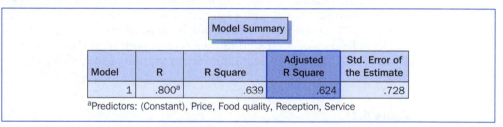

This re-estimation normally goes hand in hand with a new check of the assumptions (e.g., all of the statistics and conclusions based on the residuals must be re-examined, since a new estimation is involved here), however that has been left out here because the approach is analogous to what has been worked out above. The new estimates for steps 2 and 3 follow below.

Figure 5.44

			Model Summary		

Model	R	R Square	Adjusted R Square	Std. Error of the Estimate
1	.800[a]	.639	.624	.728

[a]Predictors: (Constant), Price, Food quality, Reception, Service

The 'Adjusted R Square' indicates that 62.4% of the variation in the dependent variable 'Overall satisfaction' is explained by the variation in the four independent variables 'Price', 'Food quality', 'Reception', and 'Service' (Figure 5.44).

Figure 5.45

			ANOVA[b]			

Model		Sum of Squares	df	Mean Square	F	Sig.
1	Regression	90.996	4	22.749	42.967	.000[a]
	Residual	51.357	97	.529		
	Total	142.353	101			

[a]Predictors: (Constant), Price, Food quality, Reception, Service
[b]Dependent Variable: Overall satisfaction

It is meaningful to interpret the 'Adjusted R Square' and the regression coefficients, given the fact that the p-value in the 'ANOVA' table (.000; Figure 5.45) is less than .05. There is a good fit between the data and the assumed regression model.

Figure 5.46

		Unstandardized Coefficients		Standardized Coefficients		
Model		B	Std. Error	Beta	t	Sig.
1	(Constant)	.191	.456		.418	.677
	Reception	.183	.076	.167	2.421	.017
	Food quality	.398	.089	.308	4.462	.000
	Service	.461	.083	.388	5.543	.000
	Price	.150	.051	.222	2.954	.004

Coefficients[a]

[a]Dependent Variable: Overall satisfaction

The four regression coefficients appear to differ significantly from zero (p-values < .05; Figure 5.46), and they have the theoretically expected sign (b or beta > 0; Figure 5.46). Therefore, the reception, the service, the food quality and the price are the determining factors for the overall satisfaction with the pizza restaurant.

Given the size of 'beta' (the 'standardized' regression coefficient), this is an indication of the share the factor has in the determination of the overall satisfaction, it appears that the 'Service' variable has the greatest impact (.388) and the 'Reception' variable has the least impact (.167) on the overall satisfaction. If the researcher were to plot (e.g., on the basis of the spreadsheet program Excel) this importance with regard to the mean satisfaction score (Figure 5.47), and were to do this for each of the four factors, then Figure 5.48 would be the result.

Figure 5.47

Descriptive Statistics

	N	Minimum	Maximum	Mean	Std. Deviation
Reception	102	2	6	4.02	1.081
Service	102	3	7	5.29	1.001
Food quality	102	1	6	3.45	.919
Price	102	1	5	3.29	1.755
Valid N (listwise)	102				

Figure 5.48

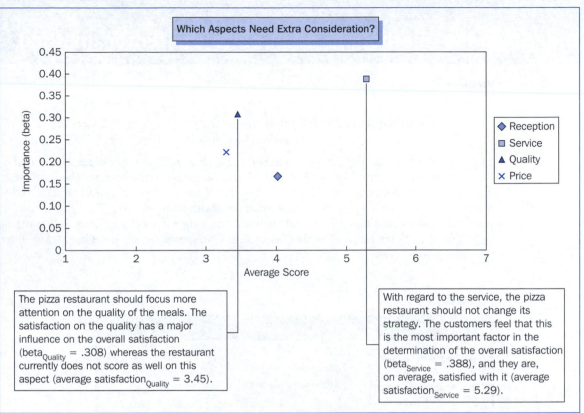

Which Aspects Need Extra Consideration?

The pizza restaurant should focus more attention on the quality of the meals. The satisfaction on the quality has a major influence on the overall satisfaction (beta$_{Quality}$ = .308) whereas the restaurant currently does not score as well on this aspect (average satisfaction$_{Quality}$ = 3.45).

With regard to the service, the pizza restaurant should not change its strategy. The customers feel that this is the most important factor in the determination of the overall satisfaction (beta$_{Service}$ = .388), and they are, on average, satisfied with it (average satisfaction$_{Service}$ = 5.29).

We already mentioned above that the standardized beta coefficients, and more specifically, the order of these coefficients, reflects the relative importance of the independent variables in the determination of the dependent variable. For example, 'Service' has the highest beta value and therefore has the most important influence, and 'Reception' has the lowest beta value and thus the least amount of influence of the four variables. It may be noted that the beta coefficients merely provide an idea of the order of the independent variables related to their importance, and that for example we may not necessarily refer to a variable that is x-times more important than another variable (e.g., the 'Service' variable is .388/.167 or 2.3 times more important in the influence over the dependent variable 'Overall satisfaction' than the variable 'Reception'). In addition, one may ask oneself whether the different beta values differ significantly from one another and whether the reported difference in importance of the variables is actually realistic. There are procedures which exist to determine whether two betas (or two b's) differ from one another significantly or not[5], but they are not dealt within this book.

Two variations of the original problem follow below, whereby the result will be limited to the indication of the important dissimilarities with the example set out above. With regard to the interpretation of the SPSS output, attention will only be paid to the meaningfulness of the model (Step 2) and the interpretation of the regression coefficients (Step 3). It is important to note that the calculation of every such problem requires a check of the assumptions (Step 1).

Example 2

The 'Stepwise' method, in addition to the 'Enter' method

Problem

The model to be estimated is identical to that in the original problem, namely:

$$\text{Overall satisfaction} = b_0 + b_1 \text{ reception} + b_2 \text{ service} + b_3 \text{ waiting time}$$
$$+ b_4 \text{ quality} + b_5 \text{ price} + \varepsilon$$

The dissimilarity is that the 'Stepwise' method is used instead of the 'Enter' method, and that the *Pizza Stepwise method.sav* instead of the *Pizza.sav* dataset is the basis for the analyses. It must also be said here that the *Pizza Stepwise method.sav* dataset contains the filter variable 'filter_$'. This variable will exclude the respondents with numbers '16', '7', '29', '50' and '4' from the analyses (analogous to the calculation of the original problem; Figure 5.39), after it was defined as 'filter variable' in the 'Select Cases' window (Data/Select Cases – Use filter variable; Figure 5.49).

Figure 5.49

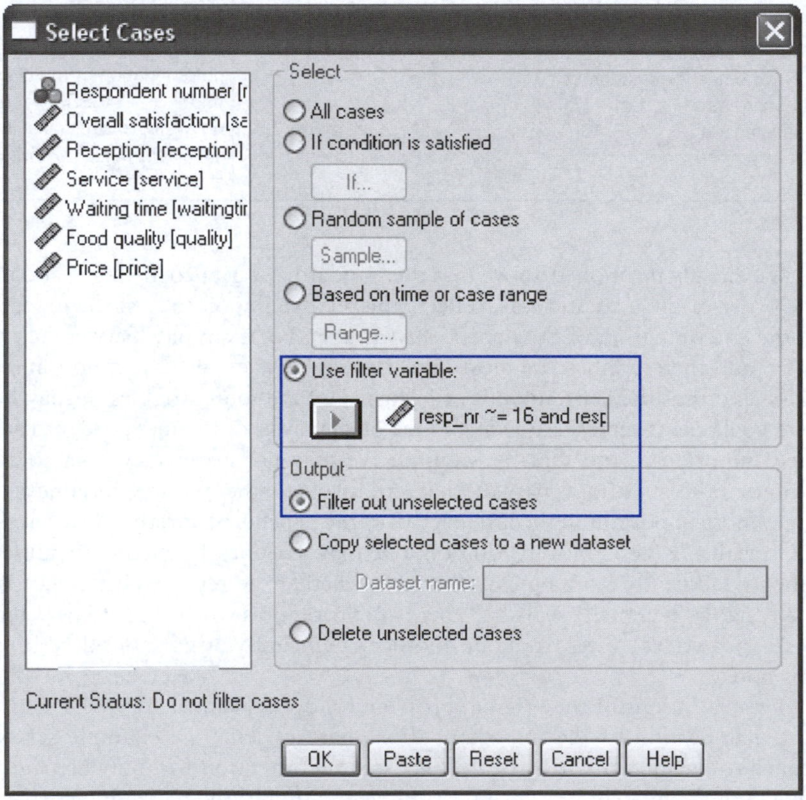

Solution

SPSS commands

Figure 5.50

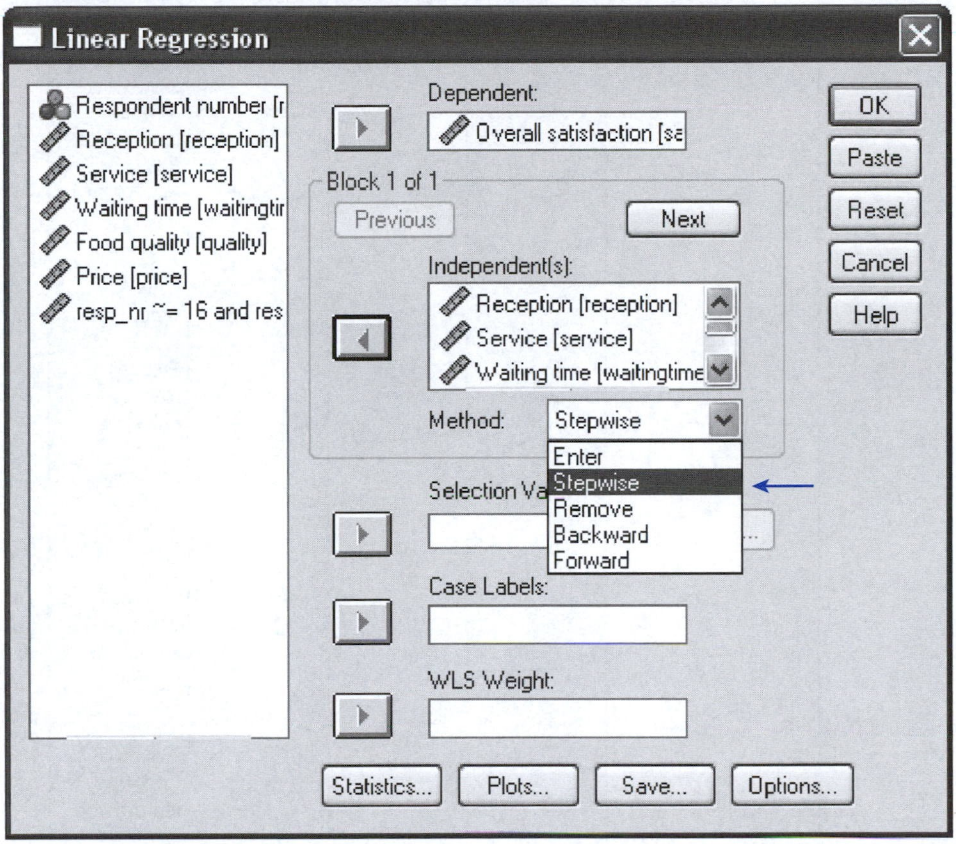

Move the variable 'Overall satisfaction' to the 'Dependent' box, and the variables 'Reception', 'Service', 'Waiting time', 'Food quality', and 'Price' to the 'Independent(s)' box. For method, choose 'Stepwise' and click on 'OK' (Figure 5.50).

Interpretation of the SPSS output

STEP 2: Check the meaningfulness of the model
Before showing the 'Model Summary' and the 'ANOVA' and 'Coefficients' tables, the SPSS output provides an insight into the step-by-step structure of the regression model (Figure 5.51).

Figure 5.51

	Variables Entered/Removed[a]		
Model	Variables Entered	Variables Removed	Method
1	Service		Stepwise (Criteria: Probability -of-F-to- enter <= .050, Probability -of-F-to- remove >= .100).
2	Food quality		Stepwise (Criteria: Probability -of-F-to- enter <= .050, Probability -of-F-to- remove >= .100).
3	Price		Stepwise (Criteria: Probability -of-F-to- enter <= .050, Probability -of-F-to- remove >= .100).
4	Reception		Stepwise (Criteria: Probability -of-F-to- enter <= .050, Probability -of-F-to- remove >= .100).

[a]Dependent Variable: Overall satisfaction

The first variable which is added to the model is 'Service' (see column 'Variables Entered'), since of all five of the independent variables, this one contributes the most to the explanation of the dependent variable 'Overall satisfaction'. In a next step, 'Food quality' is added to the model as the second most explanatory variable. Next, 'Price' is included in the 'Service-Quality' model. Finally, the fourth model contains the variable 'Reception' in addition to the variables 'Service', 'Quality' and 'Price'. The explanatory value of the variable 'Waiting time' is insufficient to justify inclusion in a fifth model.[6] Figure 5.52 confirms this statement considering the p-value of the variable 'Waiting time' in model 4 exceeds the 'probability of F to enter' $(.356 > .05)$.

Figure 5.52

						Collinearity Statistics
Model		Beta In	t	Sig.	Partial Correlation	Tolerance
1	Reception	.283[a]	3.755	.000	.353	.901
	Food quality	.396[a]	5.498	.000	.484	.862
	Price	.382[a]	5.091	.000	.455	.820
	Waiting time	.289[a]	3.206	.002	.307	.651
2	Reception	.237[b]	3.521	.001	.335	.886
	Price	.285[b]	3.933	.000	.369	.744
	Waiting time	.172[b]	2.020	.046	.200	.597
3	Reception	.167[c]	2.421	.017	.239	.782
	Waiting time	.108[c]	1.303	.196	.131	.568
4	Waiting time	.076[d]	.928	.356	.094	.552

Excluded Variables[e]

[a]Predictors in the Model: (Constant), Service
[b]Predictors in the Model: (Constant), Service, Food quality
[c]Predictors in the Model: (Constant), Service, Food quality, Price
[d]Predictors in the Model: (Constant), Service, Food quality, Price, Reception
[e]Dependent Variable: Overall satisfaction

None of the steps has led to the removal of the variables included previously in the model, since the column 'Variables Removed' (Figure 5.51) does not state any of the variable names.

Figure 5.53

Model Summary

Model	R	R Square	Adjusted R Square	Std. Error of the Estimate
1	.649[a]	.422	.416	.907
2	.746[b]	.557	.548	.798
3	.786[c]	.617	.606	.745
4	.800[d]	.639	.624	.728

[a]Predictors: (Constant), Service
[b]Predictors: (Constant), Service, Food quality
[c]Predictors: (Constant), Service, Food quality, Price
[d]Predictors: (Constant), Service, Food quality, Price, Reception

'Model Summary' (Figure 5.53) indicates that Model 1, which only contains one independent variable, 'Service', explains 41.6% of the variation in the dependent variable 'Overall satisfaction' (see 'Adjusted R Square'). Model 4 on the other hand, explains 62.4% of the variation by including four of the five original independent variables.

Before we can interpret the 'Adjusted R Square', it is best to first find out whether or not there is a good fit between the model and the data, or, in other words, if this statistic differs significantly from zero.

Figure 5.54

ANOVA[e]

Model		Sum of Squares	df	Mean Square	F	Sig.
1	Regression	60.042	1	60.042	72.945	.000[a]
	Residual	82.311	100	.823		
	Total	142.353	101			
2	Regression	79.296	2	39.648	62.249	.000[b]
	Residual	63.056	99	.637		
	Total	142.353	101			
3	Regression	87.892	3	29.297	52.719	.000[c]
	Residual	54.461	98	.556		
	Total	142.353	101			
4	Regression	90.996	4	22.749	42.967	.000[d]
	Residual	51.357	97	.529		
	Total	142.353	101			

[a]Predictors: (Constant), Service
[b]Predictors: (Constant), Service, Food quality
[c]Predictors: (Constant), Service, Food quality, Price
[d]Predictors: (Constant), Service, Food quality, Price, Reception
[e]Dependent Variable: Overall satisfaction

This does appear to be the case for each of the four models, since the p-values in the 'ANOVA' table are all less than .05 (Figure 5.54).

STEP 3: *Interpretation of the regression coefficients from Model 4*

Figure 5.55

Coefficients[a]

Model		Unstandardized Coefficients		Standardized Coefficients	t	Sig.
		B	Std. Error	Beta		
1	(Constant)	1.157	.486		2.381	.019
	Service	.770	.090	.649	8.541	.000
2	(Constant)	.314	.454		.691	.491
	Service	.596	.085	.502	6.975	.000
	Food quality	.512	.093	.396	5.498	.000
3	(Constant)	.618	.431		1.433	.155
	Service	.490	.084	.413	5.820	.000
	Food quality	.402	.091	.311	4.403	.000
	Price	.193	.049	.285	3.933	.000
4	(Constant)	.191	.456		.418	.677
	Service	.461	.083	.388	5.543	.000
	Food quality	.398	.089	.308	4.462	.000
	Price	.150	.051	.222	2.954	.004
	Reception	.183	.076	.167	2.421	.017

[a]Dependent Variable: Overall satisfaction

Model 4 of the 'Stepwise' procedure is identical to the final model of the 'Enter' method: the four variables which make a significant contribution to the model are 'Service', 'Food Quality', 'Price' and 'Reception' (p-values $< .05$), and this sequence also indicates the degree of importance in the determination of the overall satisfaction (see order of the betas from large to small). Note that the absolute beta values are in addition identical for both methods (Figure 5.55).

Example 3

The presence of a nominal variable in the regression model

Problem

The model to be estimated differs from that for the original problem, given the fact that an extra independent variable is added: 'Gender'. Since this is not an interval or ratio-scaled variable, but instead a nominal variable, one of the assumptions for a regression analysis has been violated. Nevertheless, it is possible to calculate values for the b's in the following model:

$$\text{Overall satisfaction} = b_0 + b_1\,\text{reception} + b_2\,\text{service} + b_3\,\text{waiting time} + b_4\,\text{quality} + b_5\,\text{price} + \mathbf{b_6\,gender} + \varepsilon \qquad (2)$$

Just like with the original problem, the 'Enter' method is used, however the dataset used is now *Pizza incl gender.sav*.

Solution

SPSS commands

Figure 5.56

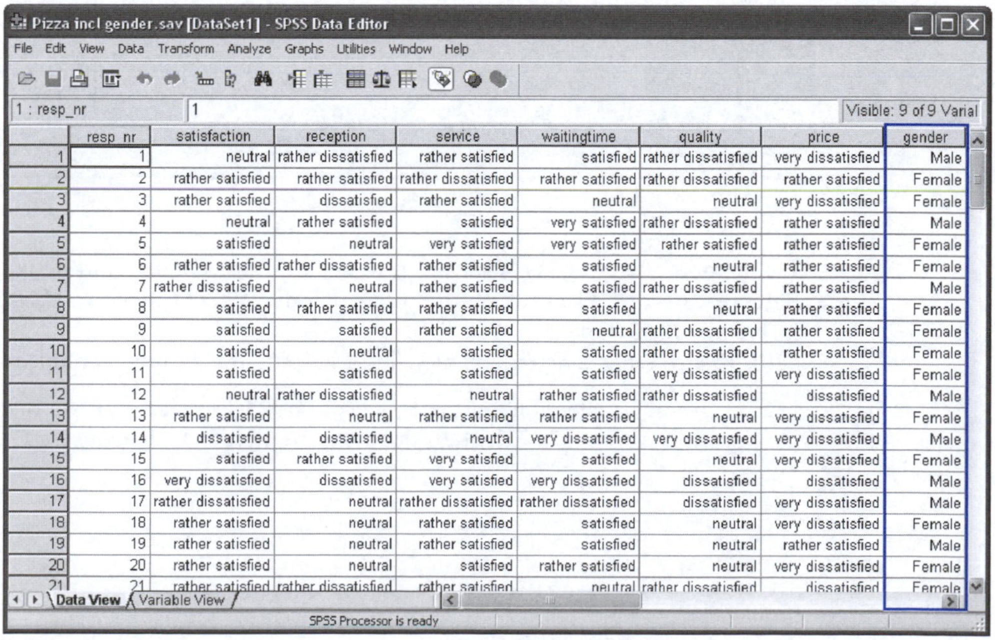

	resp_nr	satisfaction	reception	service	waitingtime	quality	price	gender
1	1	neutral	rather dissatisfied	rather satisfied	satisfied	rather dissatisfied	very dissatisfied	Male
2	2	rather satisfied	rather satisfied	rather dissatisfied	rather satisfied	rather dissatisfied	rather satisfied	Female
3	3	rather satisfied	dissatisfied	rather satisfied	neutral	neutral	very dissatisfied	Female
4	4	neutral	rather satisfied	satisfied	very satisfied	rather dissatisfied	rather satisfied	Male
5	5	satisfied	neutral	very satisfied	very satisfied	rather satisfied	rather satisfied	Female
6	6	rather satisfied	rather dissatisfied	rather satisfied	satisfied	neutral	rather satisfied	Female
7	7	rather dissatisfied	neutral	rather satisfied	satisfied	rather dissatisfied	rather satisfied	Male
8	8	satisfied	rather satisfied	rather satisfied	satisfied	neutral	rather satisfied	Female
9	9	satisfied	satisfied	rather satisfied	neutral	rather dissatisfied	rather satisfied	Female
10	10	satisfied	neutral	satisfied	satisfied	rather dissatisfied	rather satisfied	Female
11	11	satisfied	satisfied	satisfied	satisfied	very dissatisfied	very dissatisfied	Female
12	12	neutral	rather dissatisfied	neutral	rather satisfied	rather dissatisfied	dissatisfied	Male
13	13	rather satisfied	neutral	rather satisfied	rather satisfied	neutral	very dissatisfied	Female
14	14	dissatisfied	dissatisfied	neutral	very dissatisfied	very dissatisfied	very dissatisfied	Male
15	15	satisfied	rather satisfied	very satisfied	satisfied	neutral	very dissatisfied	Female
16	16	very dissatisfied	dissatisfied	very satisfied	very dissatisfied	dissatisfied	dissatisfied	Male
17	17	rather dissatisfied	neutral	rather dissatisfied	rather dissatisfied	dissatisfied	very dissatisfied	Male
18	18	rather satisfied	neutral	rather satisfied	satisfied	neutral	very dissatisfied	Female
19	19	rather satisfied	neutral	rather satisfied	satisfied	neutral	rather satisfied	Male
20	20	rather satisfied	neutral	satisfied	rather satisfied	neutral	very dissatisfied	Female
21	21	rather satisfied	rather dissatisfied	rather satisfied	neutral	rather dissatisfied	dissatisfied	Female

The variable 'Gender' has been added to the dataset (Figure 5.56). This is a nominal variable with two possible answers: 'Male' and 'Female', coded respectively as '1' and '2'.

Working with nominal variables involves the creation of dummy variables. The number of dummies to be created is equal to the number of possible answers for the nominal variable minus 1. Therefore in the current example, it is sufficient to create one dummy (e.g., on the basis of Transform/Recode into Different Variables). This variable, which has already been added to the dataset *Pizza incl gender.sav*, will be named 'female' and is coded as follows: 0 = 'No' and 1 = 'Yes' (Figure 5.57).

Figure 5.57

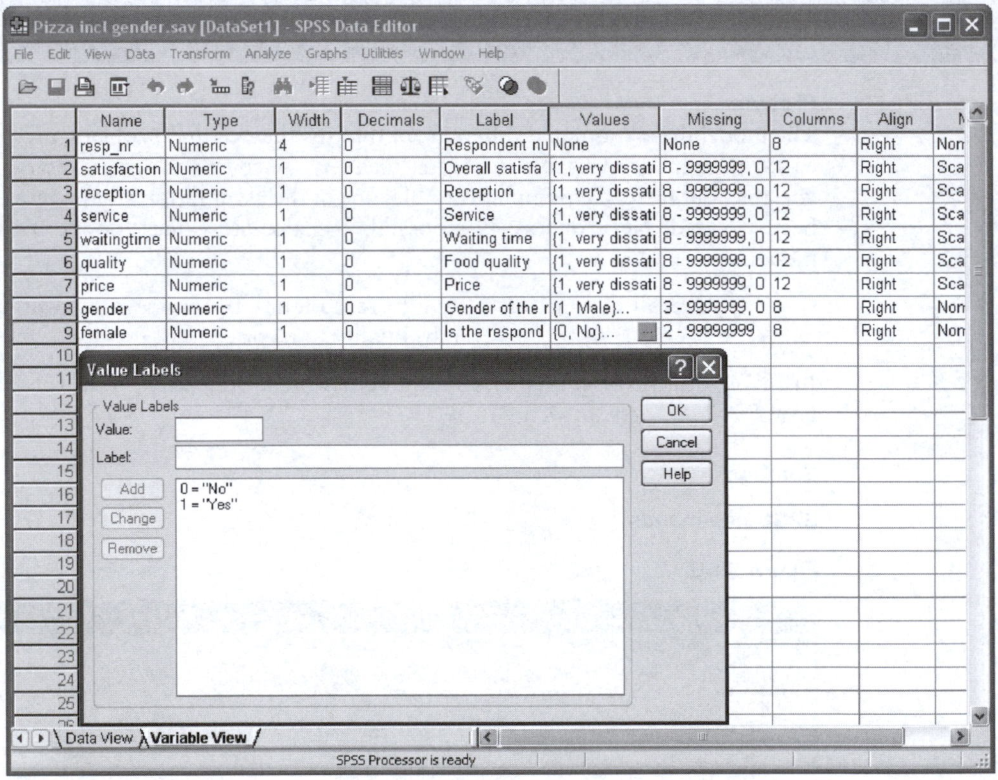

This method of coding is also referred to as 'indicator coding' and designates the male as reference category. Please note, the original coding (1,2) (linked to 'Gender') is therefore replaced by (0,1) (linked to 'Female').

It is best to replace regression model (2), keeping the dummy variable in mind, by:

$$\text{Overall satisfaction} = b_0 + b_1 \text{ reception} + b_2 \text{ service} + b_3 \text{ waiting time} + b_4 \text{ quality} + b_5 \text{ price} + \mathbf{b_6 \text{ female}} + \varepsilon$$

Figure 5.58

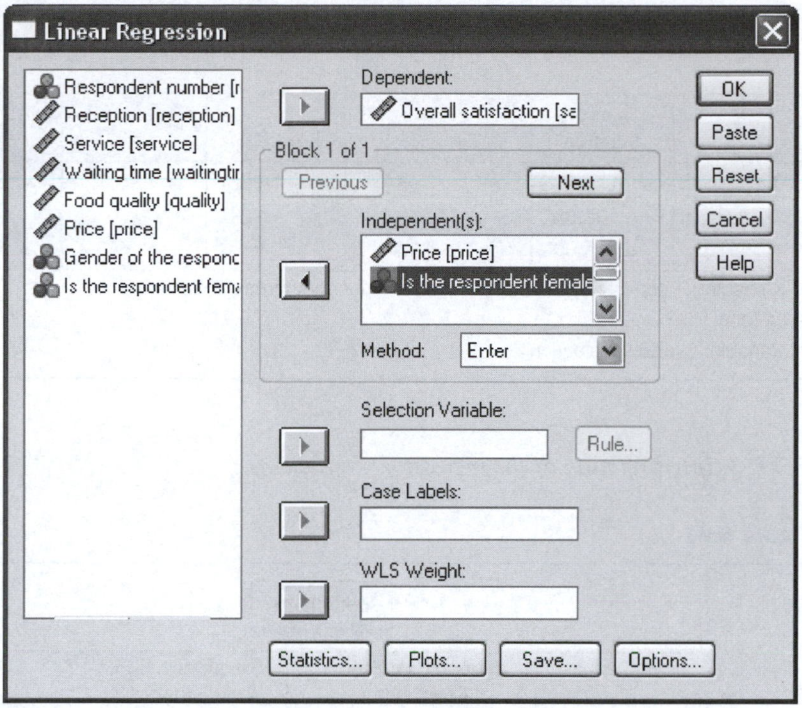

In the 'Linear Regression' window (Figure 5.58), choose 'Overall satisfaction' as the dependent variable and 'Reception', 'Service', 'Waiting time', 'Food quality', 'Price' and 'Is the respondent female' (and not the variable 'Gender of the respondent') as the independent variables. Select the 'Enter' method and then click 'OK'.

Interpretation of the SPSS output

STEP 2: *Check the meaningfulness of the model*
The six independent variables together explain 62.7% of the variation in the dependent variable 'Overall satisfaction' (Figure 5.59).

Figure 5.59

Model Summary				
Model	R	R Square	Adjusted R Square	Std. Error of the Estimate
1	.805[a]	.648	.627	.785

[a]Predictors: (Constant), Food quality, Reception, Is the respondent female?, Service, Price, Waiting time

This 'Adjusted R Square' value differs significantly from zero, since the p-value from the 'ANOVA' table (Figure 5.60) is less than .05. The model is therefore meaningful and an interpretation of the regression coefficients is thus the next step (Figure 5.61).

Figure 5.60

		Sum of Squares	df	Mean Square	F	Sig.
				ANOVA[b]		
Model						
1	Regression	113.738	6	18.956	30.732	.000[a]
	Residual	61.682	100	.617		
	Total	175.421	106			

[a]Predictors: (Constant), Food quality, Reception, Is the respondent female?, Service, Price, Waiting time
[b]Dependent Variable: Overall satisfaction

STEP 3: Interpretation of the regression coefficients

Figure 5.61

Coefficients[a]

		Unstandardized Coefficients		Standardized Coefficients		
Model		B	Std. Error	Beta	t	Sig.
1	(Constant)	−.013	.502		−.026	.979
	Price	.110	.054	.150	2.027	.045
	Is the respondent female?	.752	.165	.290	4.559	.000
	Service	.229	.091	.177	2.521	.013
	Reception	.199	.082	.168	2.410	.018
	Waiting time	.210	.078	.205	2.683	.009
	Food quality	.329	.100	.233	3.303	.001

[a]Dependent Variable: Overall satisfaction

Considering the p-value for each of the six variables is less than .05, each makes a significant contribution to the model, and this also includes the variable 'Is the respondent female'.

The non-standardized regression coefficient b from the variable 'Is the respondent female' is .752: the overall satisfaction score for the women is thus a mean of .752 points higher than that for the men.

Further reading

Cohen, J. and Cohen, P. (1983), *Applied Multiple Regression/Correlation Analysis for the Behavioral Sciences*. 2nd ed. Hillsdale: Erlbaum.

Cohen, J., Cohen, P., West, S., and Aiken, L. (2003), *Applied Multiple Regression/Correlation Analysis for the Behavioral Sciences*. 3rd ed. Hillsdale: Erlbaum.

Gujarati, D. (2003), *Basic Econometrics*. 4th ed. New York McGraw-Hill, Inc.

Gupta, V. (1999), *SPSS for Beginners*. 1st ed. Author House Vijay Gupta.

Tacq, J. (1997), *Multivariate Analysis Techniques in Social Science Research: From Problem to Analysis*. 1st ed. London: Sage Publications.

Endnotes

1 See Gujarati (2003).
2 See Gupta (1999), point 7.5 (Checking formally for heteroscedasticity: White's test).
3 See Gupta (1999), points 8.2.a and 8.2.b (WLS when the exact nature of heteroscedasticity is not known; Weight estimation when the weight is known). See also Cohen and Cohen (1983), p. 129 for a more theoretical approach.
4 The intention is now to stop including row numbers '1', '5', '7', '10' and '16' in the analysis. In order to do this, the condition for selection will have to be stated as follows: resp_nr ~=16 and resp_nr ~=7 and resp_nr ~=29 and resp_nr ~=50 and resp_nr ~=4. Please note the use of the respondent number instead of the row number.
5 See Cohen and Cohen, (1983), pp. 479–80.
6 The 'Stepwise' method will never include the 'Waiting time' variable in the model. With the 'Enter' method on the other hand, this variable will first be included, and then later removed by the researcher.

Chapter 6

Logistic regression analysis

Chapter objectives

This chapter will help you to:

- Understand how and when to use logistic regression analysis
- Carry out logistic regressions with categorical and interval-scaled independent variables
- Deal with interaction terms in a logistic regression model
- Apply and interpret a stepwise logistic regression model (next to the enter method), including more than one 'block' of variables
- Apply and interpret a logistic regression model including a categorical independent variable with more than 2 categories

Technique

The goal of logistic regression is to explain a categorical variable, divided into two groups, on the basis of interval-, ratio-scaled and/or categorical variables. This specific combination of measurement levels of the dependent and the independent variables is what makes logistic regression the recommended technique, instead of linear regression, variance analysis, discriminant analysis, or multinomial logistic regression. Table 6.1 shows how differences in the level of measurement can affect the technique chosen.

Table 6.1

Measurement level of the dependent variable	Standard measurement level of the independent variable	Technique
Interval/ratio	Interval/ratio *Additional:* categorical (Chapter 5)	Linear regression
Interval/ratio	Categorical *Additional:* interval/ratio (Chapter 4)	Variance analysis
Categorical (2 or more categories)	Interval/ratio	Discriminant analysis
Categorical (2 categories)	Interval, ratio and/or categorical	Logistic regression
Categorical (more than 2 categories)	Interval, ratio and/or categorical	Multinomial logistic regression

With regard to the difference between discriminant analysis and logistic regression, one may say that the first technique must satisfy stricter assumptions. For example, (1) the fact that the independent variables are not 'multivariate' normally distributed and (2) a difference in the variance-covariance matrix for the two groups will exclude the application of discriminant analysis, whereas logistic regression still qualifies to predict group membership.

Due to the dichotomous dependent variable, the goal of logistic regression is 'the prediction of an "event" which may or may not occur', as well as 'the identification of variables which play an important role in allowing this prediction to be made'. This event may involve the response to a direct-mail campaign, for example, and the response or lack thereof to the campaign may then be predicted on the basis of the variables 'involvement with the product' and 'loyalty to the company', which are interval and categorically scaled, respectively.

Predicting whether or not an event will occur requires the calculation of the probability that the event 'takes place' and this may be done using the following formula:

■ In the event of **one independent variable**:

$$\text{Probability (event)} = \frac{e^{B_0 + B_1 X}}{1 + e^{B_0 + B_1 X}}$$

where B_0 and B_1: coefficients estimated on the basis of the data, making use of the 'maximum likelihood' method. This method chooses the coefficients in such a way that the observed values for the dependent variable are those which are most likely to occur.

X: independent variable

$e = 2.718$

■ In the event of **more than one independent variable**:

$$\text{Probability (event)} = \frac{e^z}{1 + e^z}$$

where $Z = B_0 + B_1 X_1 + B_2 X_2 + \cdots + B_n X_n$

B_i : coefficient estimated on the basis of the data, making use of the 'maximum likelihood' method

X_i: i^{th} independent variable

$e = 2.718$

The relationship between Z and the probability of the event occurring is presented visually on the basis of an S-shaped curve (Figure 6.1), which is typical of a logistic regression. An increase in Z therefore is accompanied by a 'non-linear' increase in probability.

Just as is the case with linear regression, with logistic regression it is important to pay attention to the presence of outliers, the suitability of the model, the significance or lack

Figure 6.1

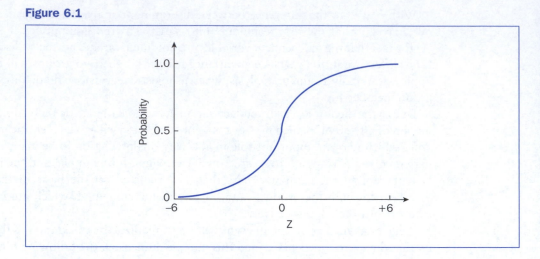

thereof and the interpretation of the coefficients. In addition, the method used to code the categorically independent variables is of vital importance in order to answer the relevant research questions, and the introduction of interaction terms is accompanied by extra 'complications'. All of these points will be explained further using examples, and both theoretical aspects as well as concrete interpretations will also be discussed. This chapter presents four examples, and Table 6.2 lists the focus of each of these examples.

Table 6.2

	Focus
Example 1	■ Coding the categorical independent variable ■ Detecting outliers ■ Determining the suitability of the model ■ Determining the significance of the coefficients and their meaning
Example 2	■ Introduction of the interaction terms ■ Coding the categorical independent variables ■ Rescaling the interval-scaled independent variables ■ Finding and interpreting the relevant coefficients
Example 3	■ Defining two 'blocks' of independent variables, whereby one block uses the 'enter' method and the other the 'stepwise' procedure
Example 4	■ Coding and interpreting, in the case of a categorical independent variable which contains more than two groups

For a more detailed discussion of this technique, the reader may consult the reference works which are listed at the end of this chapter.

Example 1

Interval-scaled and categorical independent variables, without interaction term

Managerial problem

Researchers would like to find out whether an anonymous mail survey leads to a higher rate of response in comparison with a non-anonymous version, and additionally, they wonder whether or not an increase in the level of involvement with the subject of the survey would result in a higher probability of response. In order to achieve this, they have drawn up two versions of a survey on milk consumption, an anonymous and non-anonymous version, and have sent these by post to 304 students. Some three weeks prior to receiving this mail survey, these students had completed a list of questions, the goal of which was to determine their involvement in the subject 'milk consumption'. For each of the students, the response to the mail survey ([response]: sent back (1) or not (0)), the version received ([anonymity]: anonymous (1) vs. non-anonymous (2)), and the level of involvement with the subject ([involvement][1]: 1 = no involvement, . . . 7 = high involvement) were all registered in a dataset, a copy of which is shown in Figure 6.2.

Figure 6.2

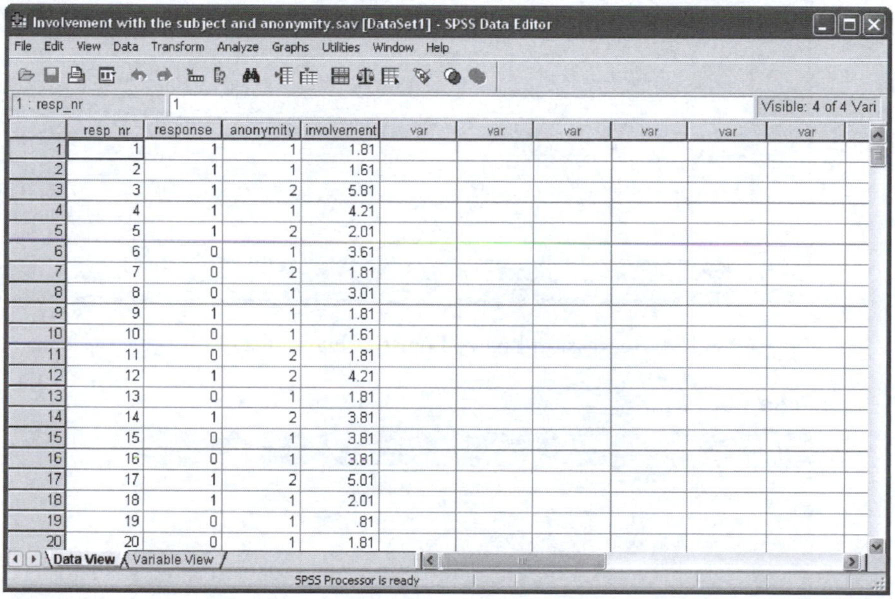

	resp_nr	response	anonymity	involvement
1	1	1	1	1.81
2	2	1	1	1.61
3	3	1	2	5.81
4	4	1	1	4.21
5	5	1	2	2.01
6	6	0	1	3.61
7	7	0	2	1.81
8	8	0	1	3.01
9	9	1	1	1.81
10	10	0	1	1.61
11	11	0	2	1.81
12	12	1	2	4.21
13	13	0	1	1.81
14	14	1	2	3.81
15	15	0	1	3.81
16	16	0	1	3.81
17	17	1	2	5.01
18	18	1	1	2.01
19	19	0	1	.81
20	20	0	1	1.81

Problem

Develop the following model on the basis of the data above (*Involvement with the subject and anonymity.sav*):

$$\text{Response} \cong Z = b_0 + b_1 \text{ Anonymity} + b_2 \text{ Involvement with the subject}$$

Use the 'Enter' method to estimate the model. Take the extremely influential outliers into account, and calculate the values 'Leverage' and 'DfBeta'. Find out if the model is suitable for the data on the basis of (1) 'Model Chi-square', (2) 'Nagelkerke R square', (3) 'R square adjusted count' and (4) the 'Classification Plot'. Calculate the probability that a student who received a non-anonymous survey and has an involvement score of 5.8 will respond.

Find out if the variables 'anonymity' and 'involvement with the subject' exert a significant influence on whether or not the person will return the survey and in which direction, and finally, interpret the regression coefficients in terms of 'odds' and 'log odds'.

Solution

SPSS commands

Figure 6.3

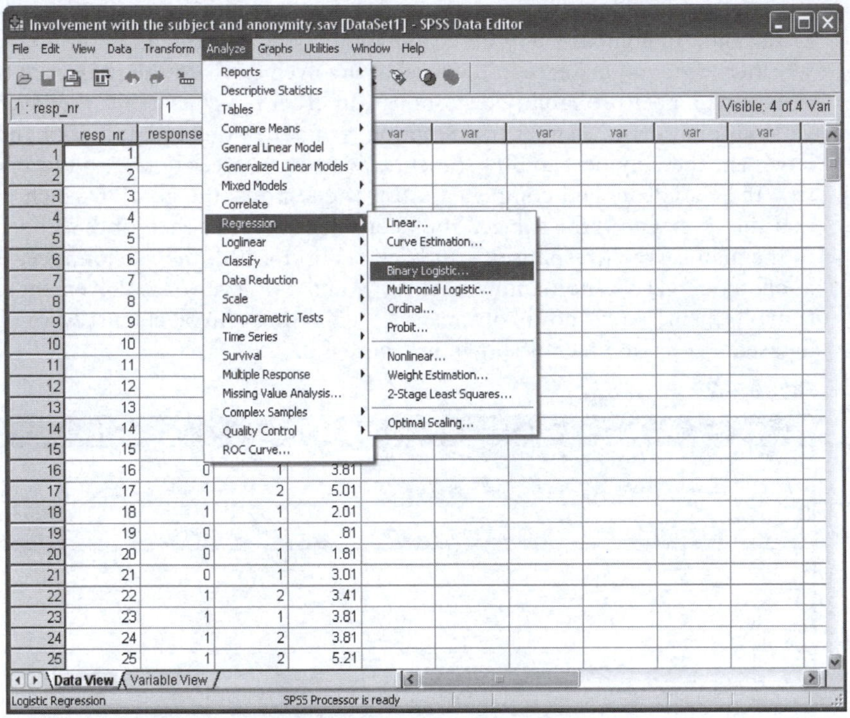

Go to Analyze/Regression/Binary Logistic (Figure 6.3)

Figure 6.4

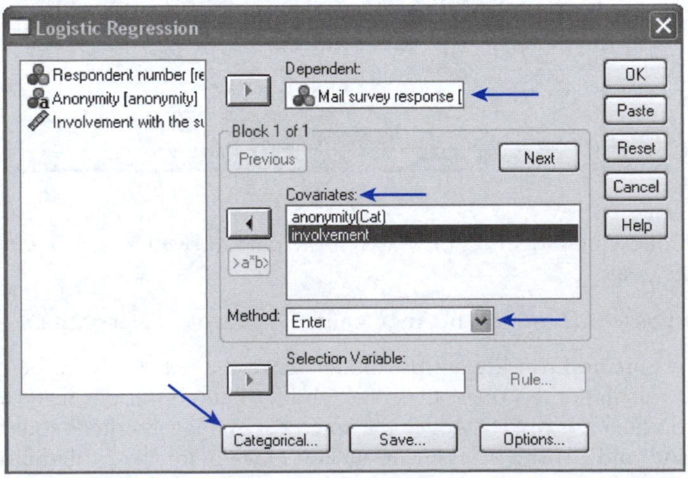

Select the dependent variable [response] from the list of variables, and move it to the 'Dependent' box (Figure 6.4).

The dependent variable comprises two groups, which are coded as '0' and '1' (not as '1' and '2'), whereby '1' corresponds to the group for which the probability is calculated. The variable 'Response to the mail survey' is thus coded as follows: 1 = Response, and 0 = No response. The calculation of the probability that the 'event' takes place will then ultimately involve the calculation of the probability that the mail survey is 'answered'.

The definition of the different 'blocks' will be set out in Example 3. For method, choose the 'Enter' method (see specification of the problem section).

In the 'Logistic Regression' window, choose the independent variables for the model from the list on the left, and move these to the 'Covariates' box. You will notice that the variable 'involvement with the subject' is a ratio-scaled variable, while the variable 'anonymity' is categorically scaled. Given that this last variable in the dataset, 'Variable View' tab, is defined as a 'string', SPSS automatically sees this variable as a categorical variable, and the label 'Cat' is added in the 'Covariates' box. Clicking on the 'Categorical' button at the bottom of the 'Logistic Regression' window will indicate how the categorical variable is coded.

Figure 6.5

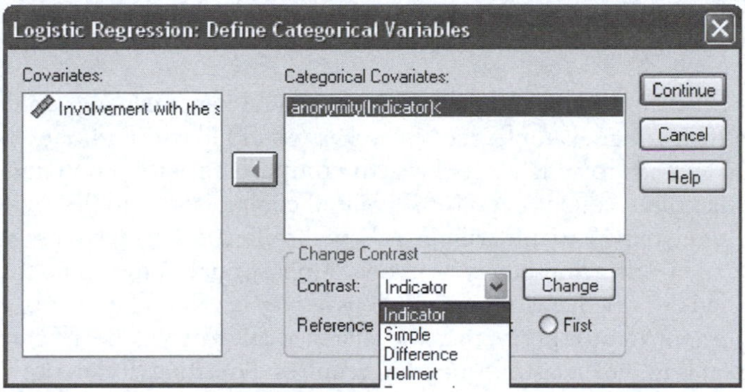

The 'involvement' variable may be found in the 'Covariates' box (Figure 6.5) because it is ratio-scaled. The 'anonymity' variable is automatically included in the 'Categorical Covariates' box because of the 'string' character of this variable. Suppose the categorical variable in the dataset is defined as a 'numerical' variable (see Example 2), then the researcher must indicate in the 'Logistic Regression: Define Categorical Variables' window that the variable is 'categorical' by moving it from the 'Covariates' box to the 'Categorical Covariates' box using the arrow ▶.

Figure 6.6

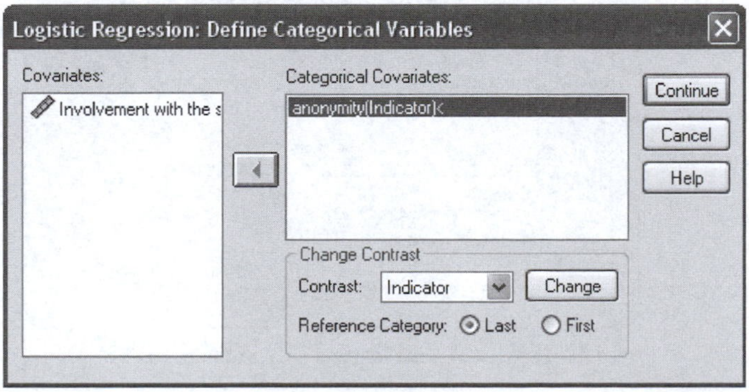

In the 'Categorical Covariates' box (Figure 6.5), the 'anonymity' variable is supplemented by 'Indicator'. This refers to the method used to code this variable, and may be changed under 'Change Contrast – Contrast', e.g., in 'Deviation' (see Example 2). The choice of the reference category (Figure 6.6) is also important, and this may be the first (Reference Category – First) or the last group (Reference Category – Last) of the categorical variable. What does this now mean for the 'anonymity' variable in concrete terms?

'Indicator coding' refers to the fact that the two groups 'Anonymous survey' and 'Non-anonymous survey' will be coded using a '1' and a '0', whereby the last group is the reference category (see 'Reference Category – Last' in Figure 6.6), and thus associated with the '0':

Table 6.3

	Coding in dataset	Coding for performing a logistic regression
Anonymous survey	1	1
Non-anonymous survey	2	0

The choice between the first and the last group as a reference depends on the research question asked. In the current example, the researchers would like to find out whether an anonymous mail survey leads to a higher response in comparison with a non-anonymous version, which means that this second version is the point of comparison, and the regression coefficient linked to the 'anonymity' variable will then show the effect on the response of an anonymous survey as compared with a non-anonymous one. Suppose on the other hand that the researchers would like to find out whether a non-anonymous survey leads to a higher response rate in comparison with an anonymous survey, then the reference category will be the anonymous version, which corresponds to the first group and thus requires the setting 'Reference Category – First'.

Figure 6.7

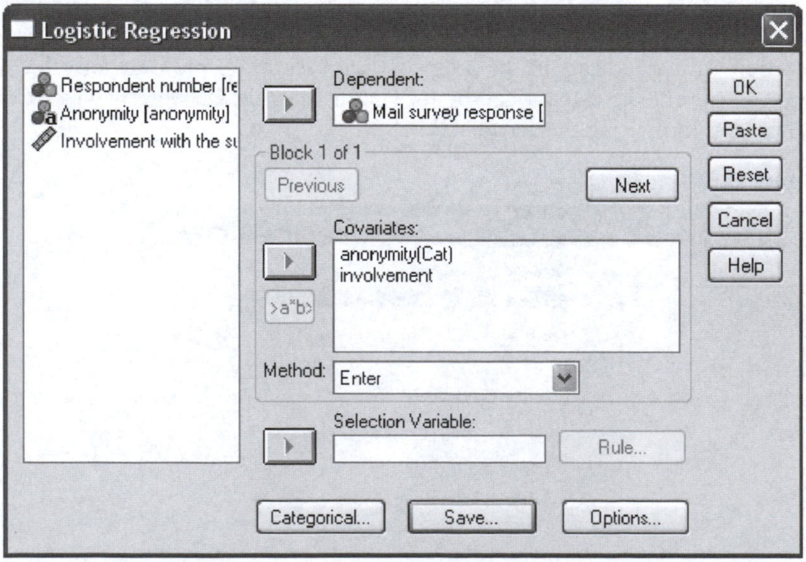

Return to the main window (Figure 6.7) and you can see 'Selection variable'. If the researcher would like to estimate the model on the basis of part of the data only (e.g., the first 150 respondents in the dataset), then he can input a variable under 'Selection Variable' and via the 'Rule' button, define a 'condition' which the cases must satisfy if they are to be part of this estimate (e.g., Rule: 'resp_nr <= 150'). This is applied when the researcher would like to work with a 'training' and a 'test' dataset, whereby the first is used to estimate the model and the second for the estimation of the quality of the model which results. This option is not used in the current application.

From the above, you will notice that the calculation of the probability that a student will respond to the mail survey (see the variable [pre_1] which has been added to the dataset) is not calculated exclusively for those who satisfy the condition (and thus are part of the estimate; e.g. the first 150 respondents in the dataset), but for every student in the dataset.

Return to the main window (Figure 6.4) and click on the 'Save' button. In the 'Logistic Regression: Save window (Figure 6.8), select the options 'Probabilities', 'Group membership', 'Leverage values' and 'DfBeta(s)'.

Figure 6.8

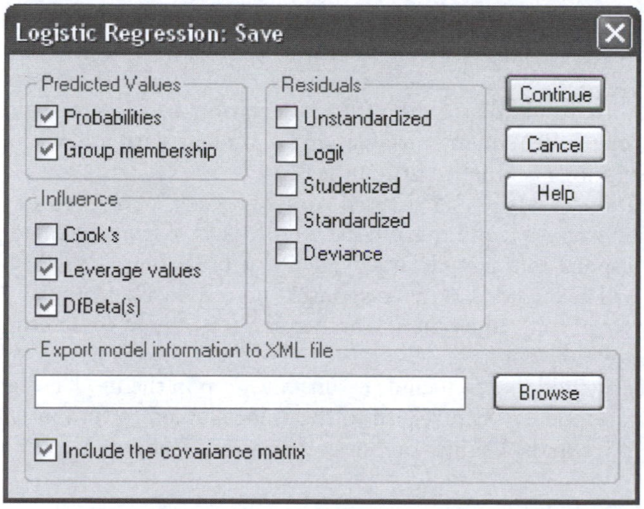

The options 'Probabilities' and 'Group membership' result in two extra variables which are added to the dataset (see [pre_1] and [pgr_1] in Figure 6.11), whereby the first shows the probability that the student will respond to the survey, and the second indicates the predicted group membership ('person who responds' vs. 'person who doesn't respond'), based on this probability.

The 'Residuals' indicate which students are 'outliers', while 'Leverage values' and 'DfBeta(s)' are an indication whether or not the outliers are 'influential'.

There are also extra variables added to the dataset for the detection of influential outliers (Figure 6.11): [lev_1], [dfb0_1], [dfb1_1], and [dfb2_1].

Return to the main window (Figure 6.4) and click 'Options'. The 'Logistic Regression: Options' window (Figure 6.9) will appear.

Select the option 'Classification plots' and you will see a histogram created using the observed and predicted values for the dependent variable, 'mail survey response'. This graph

Figure 6.9

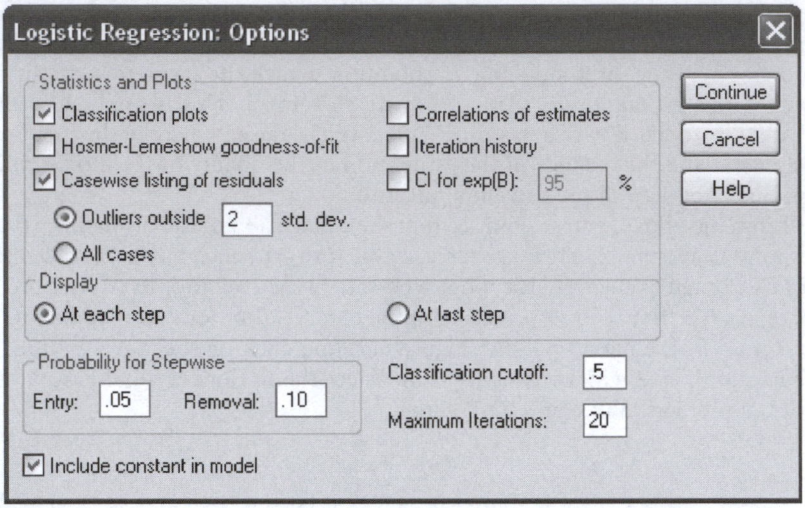

will provide an insight into the quality of the model, just like the 'Hosmer-Lemeshow goodness-of-fit' statistic. This statistic is not asked for in the current application.

Tick the box for 'Casewise listing of residuals', and choose the option 'Outliers outside 2 std. dev.'. A 'residual' stands for the deviation between the observed and the predicted value for the dependent variable, and a student with a deviation of more than two standard deviations is labelled an 'outlier'.

The 'Classification cutoff' of '.5' is used to assign each student to one of two groups ('response' vs. 'no response'), and this is done on the basis of the calculated probability that the student will respond to the mail survey: (1) if this probability is higher (lower) than .5, then the student will be included in the 'response' ('no response') group; and (2) if this probability is exactly equal to .5, then the researcher can toss a coin to determine the group to which the student will belong.

If the researcher would like to include a constant term in the model, then he will choose 'Include constant in model'. With regard to the values linked to 'Probability for Stepwise: Entry/Removal', refer to the chapter on linear regression (Chapter 5).

Interpretation of the SPSS output

The SPSS output contains an entire series of tables, but initially, only the 'Casewise List' table (Figure 6.10) is important.

Figure 6.10

		Observed			Temporary Variable	
Case	Selected Status[a]	Mail Survey Response	Predicted	Predicted Group	Resid	ZResid
294	S	N**	.868	R	−.868	−2.567

Casewise List[b]

[a]S = Selected, U = Unselected cases, and ** = Misclassified cases
[b]Cases with studentized residuals greater than 2.000 are listed

This table indicates which students are outliers, and this appears to be the person in row '294' of the dataset. Table 6.4 provides a more in-depth look at the 'Casewise List'.

Table 6.4

Case = 294	Corresponds to the row number in the dataset, and **not** with the respondent number (which are actually identical in the current application)
Selected Status = S	This student is part of the estimation of the model (an example would be a previously indicated training and test set)
Observed = N**	The observed response to the mail survey appears to be 'No response'. The '**' indicates a misclassification for this student, in other words, there is a difference between the observed and the predicted group membership
Predicted = .868	The probability according to the model that the student will respond to the mail survey, and this appears to be .868 (>.5)
Predicted Group = R	Refers to the predicted group membership, which corresponds to 'Response'
Resid = −.868; ZResid = −2.567	'Resid' (−.868) shows the difference between the observed and the predicted value (0 − .868), whereas 'ZResid' (−2.567) corresponds to the 'studentized residual'. This last value is linked to the option 'Casewise listing of residuals – Outliers outside 2 std. dev.' in the 'Logistic Regression: Options' window: because |−2.567| > 2 the student is labelled as an 'outlier' and included in the 'Casewise List' table.

Is the student in row 294 an 'influential' outlier? In order to determine this, there are four extra variables added to the dataset (Figure 6.11): [lev_1], [dfb0_1], [dfb1_1], and [dfb2_1].

Figure 6.11

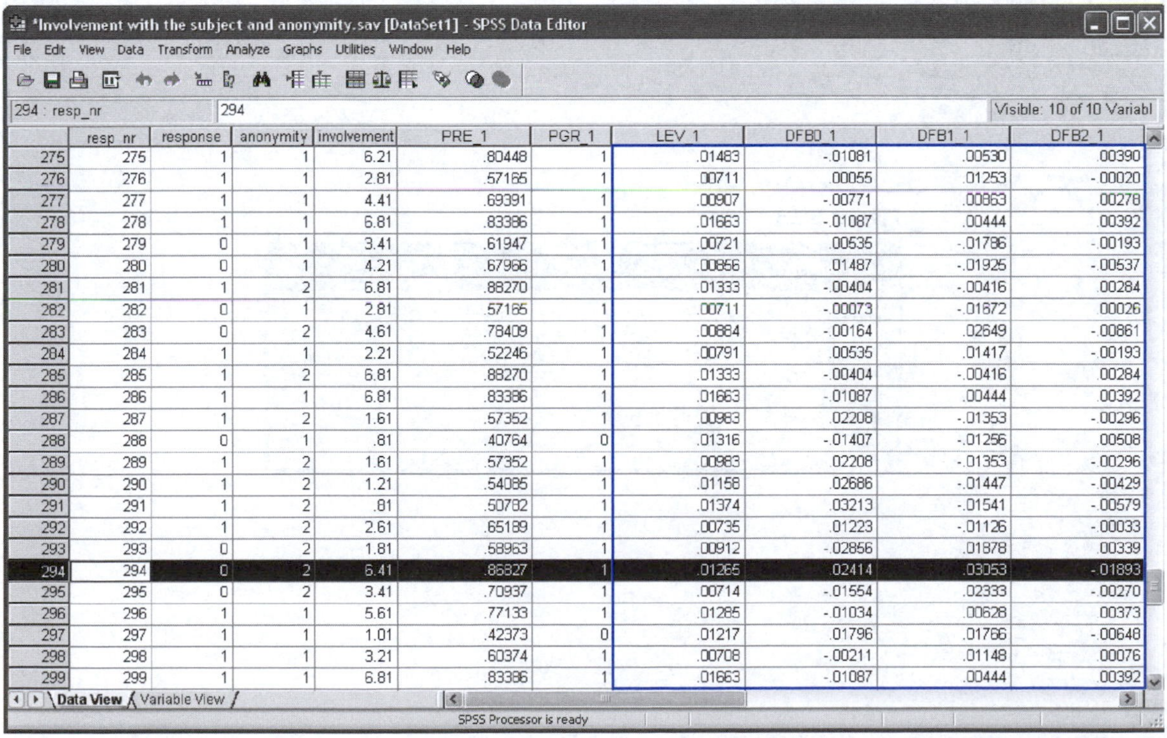

	resp_nr	response	anonymity	involvement	PRE_1	PGR_1	LEV_1	DFB0_1	DFB1_1	DFB2_1
275	275	1	1	6.21	.80448	1	.01483	-.01081	.00530	.00390
276	276	1	1	2.81	.57165	1	.00711	.00055	.01253	-.00020
277	277	1	1	4.41	.69391	1	.00907	-.00771	.00863	.00278
278	278	1	1	6.81	.83386	1	.01663	-.01087	.00444	.00392
279	279	0	1	3.41	.61947	1	.00721	.00535	-.01786	-.00193
280	280	0	1	4.21	.67966	1	.00856	.01487	-.01925	-.00537
281	281	1	2	6.81	.88270	1	.01333	-.00404	-.00416	.00284
282	282	0	1	2.81	.57165	1	.00711	-.00073	-.01672	.00026
283	283	0	2	4.61	.78409	1	.00884	-.00164	.02649	-.00861
284	284	1	1	2.21	.52246	1	.00791	.00535	.01417	-.00193
285	285	1	2	6.81	.88270	1	.01333	-.00404	-.00416	.00284
286	286	1	1	6.81	.83386	1	.01663	-.01087	.00444	.00392
287	287	1	2	1.61	.57352	1	.00983	.02208	-.01353	-.00296
288	288	0	1	.81	.40764	0	.01316	-.01407	-.01256	.00508
289	289	1	2	1.61	.57352	1	.00983	.02208	-.01353	-.00296
290	290	1	2	1.21	.54085	1	.01158	.02686	-.01447	-.00429
291	291	1	2	.81	.50782	1	.01374	.03213	-.01541	-.00579
292	292	1	2	2.61	.65189	1	.00735	.01223	-.01126	-.00033
293	293	0	2	1.81	.58963	1	.00912	-.02856	.01878	.00339
294	294	0	2	6.41	.86827	1	.01265	.02414	.03053	-.01893
295	295	0	2	3.41	.70937	1	.00714	-.01554	.02333	-.00270
296	296	1	1	5.61	.77133	1	.01265	-.01034	.00628	.00373
297	297	1	1	1.01	.42373	0	.01217	.01796	.01766	-.00648
298	298	1	1	3.21	.60374	1	.00708	-.00211	.01148	.00076
299	299	1	1	6.81	.83386	1	.01663	-.01087	.00444	.00392

[lev_1] is related to the 'Leverage' statistic, the goal of which is to discover the 'observations' which have a major 'impact' on the predicted value. The value of this statistic lies between '0' and '1', and is on average equal to the number of parameters to be estimated divided by the sample size (for the present application: 3/304 = .0099 ≅ .01). In order to gain a quick idea of whether or not 'row' 294 is influential, the researcher may retrieve a figure whereby the 'respondent number' may be found on the X-axis and the 'Leverage' value is represented on the Y-axis (Figure 6.17).

Supporting technique

Go to Graphs/Legacy Dialogs/Scatter Dot (Figure 6.12)

Figure 6.12

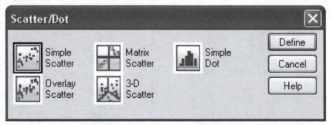

Figure 6.13

In the 'Scatter/Dot' window (Figure 6.13), select 'Simple Scatter', and then click on 'Define'.

Figure 6.14

Select the variables 'Leverage value' and 'Respondent number' from the list on the left, and move these to the boxes 'Y Axis' and 'X Axis'. Click 'OK' (Figure 6.14).

Figure 6.15

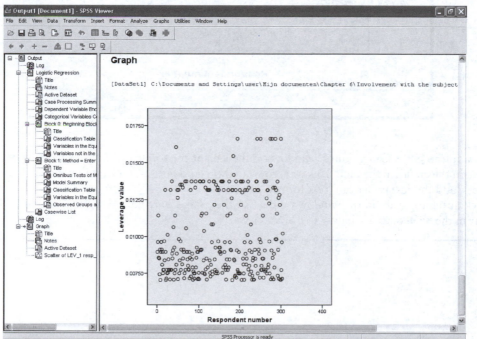

With the left mouse button, double click the figure in the output window (Figure 6.15), and a new window will be opened: the 'SPSS Chart Editor' (Figure 6.16).

Figure 6.16

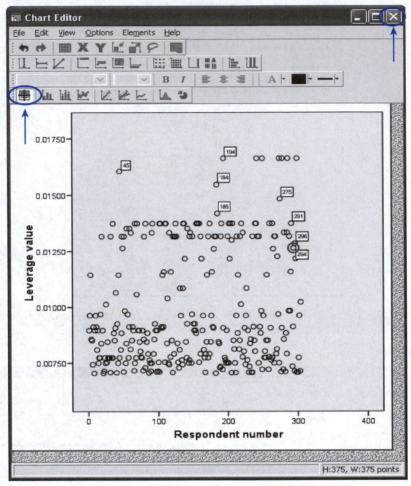

Click in the 'SPSS Chart Editor' window on the icon at the top left, the 'Data Label Mode' button, and then on the circles in the plot. This way, row numbers (and *not* respondent numbers) will be linked to the points, and the researcher can look for row '294'.

Click at the top right in the window on the '×'; the 'SPSS Chart Editor' will close and the figure will reappear in the SPSS output window (see SPSS Viewer).

Figure 6.17

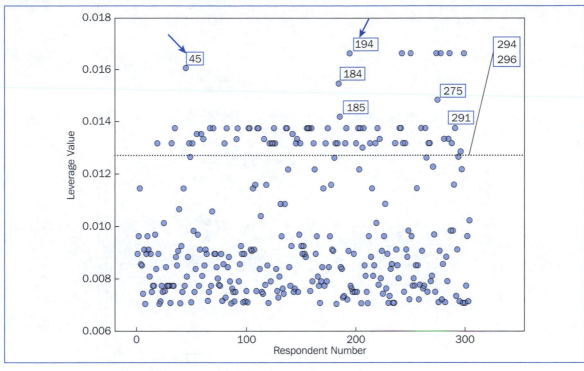

For row '294', the 'Leverage' value is approximately .013 (Figure 6.17). This value is larger than the previously calculated mean (.010), leading the researcher to conclude that this outlier is 'influential'. There are however rows which are even more 'influential' (e.g., rows '194' and '45'), since the 'Leverage' value for these cases is even higher.

[dfb0_1], [dfb1_1], and [dfb2_1] are 'DfBeta' statistics, and show the change in the logistic regression coefficients b_0, b_1 and b_2 respectively after the removal of the relevant case from the model. This way, the regression coefficients linked to the constant, the 'anonymity' variable and the 'involvement with the subject' variable will change by .024, .031, and respectively −.019 once row '294' is no longer included in the estimate of the model (Figure 6.11). Are these changes considerable? In order to get an idea, it is recommended to retrieve a figure similar to the one retrieved for the 'Leverage' values, however which now places the 'dfb' variable on the Y-axis (Figure 6.18).

Both charts indicate that row '294' exerts a considerable influence on the determination of the regression coefficients linked to the variables 'anonymity' and 'involvement with the subject' since point '294' occupies an extreme position for each of the graphs.

Therefore, the 'Leverage' value as well as the 'DfBetas' indicate that row '294' is an 'influential' outlier, which may best be removed from the dataset.[2] You will note here that an outlier which is not influential will not be eliminated.

The next step is the removal of row '294' (which corresponds to respondent number '294') from the dataset (Data/Select Cases – If condition is satisfied: resp_nr ~ = 294), and to re-estimate the regression model (Analyze/Regression/Binary Logistic).

Figure 6.18

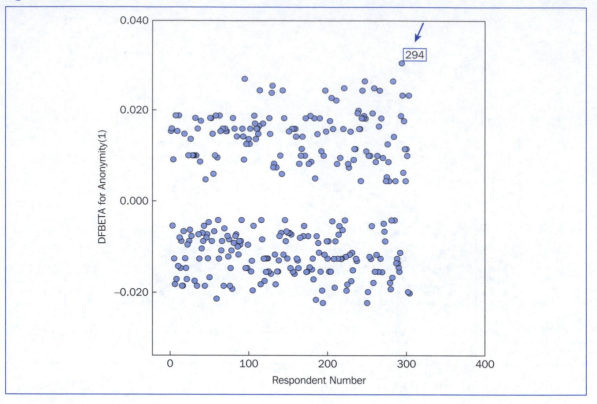

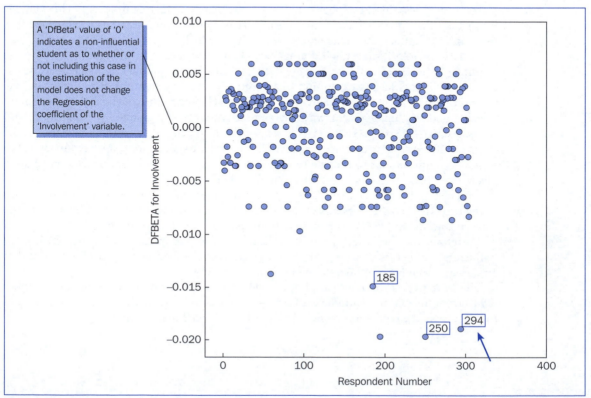

A 'DfBeta' value of '0' indicates a non-influential student as to whether or not including this case in the estimation of the model does not change the Regression coefficient of the 'Involvement' variable.

We must also examine 'Casewise List' in the output window first (Figure 6.19), and there are no outliers found in the current model.

Figure 6.19

Casewise List[a]
[a]The casewise plot is not produced because no outliers were found

The model has been estimated on the basis of 303 cases. The number 'Unselected Cases' is equal to '0', because neither a training nor test set is used (Figure 6.20).

Figure 6.20

Case Processing Summary

Unweighted Cases[a]		N	Percent
Selected cases	Included in analysis	303	100.0
	Missing cases	0	.0
	Total	303	100.0
Unselected cases		0	.0
Total		303	100.0

[a]If weight is in effect, see classification table for the total number of cases

The tables 'Dependent Variable Encoding' and 'Categorical Variables Codings' (Figures 6.21 and 6.22) are linked to the coding of the dependent and the categorical independent variables.

Figure 6.21

Dependent Variable Encoding

Original Value	Internal Value
No response	0
Response	1

Figure 6.22

Categorical Variables Codings

		Frequency	Parameter Coding (1)
Anonymity	Anonymous survey	152	1.000
	Non-anonymous survey	151	.000

This method of coding is necessary in order to be able to perform a 'logistic regression' analysis (dependent variable coded as '0' and '1', and not as '1' and '2', for example) and to answer the relevant research question (what is the effect of an anonymous survey on the response in comparison with a non-anonymous version?).

The coding of the categorical independent variable 'anonymity' corresponds to the definition in the input-window 'Logistic Regression: Define Categorical Variables' (see 'Indicator coding' and 'Last' as reference category in Figure 6.6).

The output is comprised of two blocks: 'block 0' corresponds to the zero-model (there is no knowledge with regard to the independent variables 'anonymity' and 'involvement with the subject', and the model is only created on the basis of the constant), and 'block 1' is related to the 'full' model (there is knowledge with regard to both independent variables, such that the model is not solely based on the constant, but also on the variables 'anonymity' and 'involvement').

Before delving deeper into the significance and the meaning of the regression coefficients, it is important to determine the suitability of the model. There are a number of statistics the researcher may consult to do this, including: 'Model Chi-square', 'Nagelkerke R square', 'R square adjusted count' and the 'Classification plot'.

An often-used criterion for the determination of the quality of a model and the comparison of models is '−2LL' which stands for:

$$-2*\ln \text{ (the likelihood of the observations, given the parameter estimates).}$$

A good (ideal) model corresponds to a high likelihood of the observations ('1'), and a low '−2LL' value ('0'). Given that this last value for the current model is 372.799 (Figure 6.24), the quality could be described as being rather low.

Figure 6.23

Omnibus Tests of Model Coefficients			
		Chi-Square	df	Sig.
Step 1	Step	25.329	2	.000
	Block	25.329	2	.000
	Model	25.329	2	.000

The 'Model Chi-square', which may be found in Figure 6.23, is linked to the '−2LL' value, and shows the difference between the '−2LL' values of the null model and the 'full' model. In the current application, the transition from the null model to the 'full' model seems to be accompanied by a drop in the '−2LL' of 25.329 (for the null model, the '−2LL' value is therefore 398.128). This drop appears to be significant (p-value < .001), which leads to two conclusions: (1) the 'full' model is a 'better' model than the null model; and (2) at least one of the regression coefficients of the variables 'anonymity' and 'involvement' differs from zero (H_0: all of the regression coefficients in the 'full' model, excluding the constant, are zero).

Furthermore, it may be said that (a) a 'df' of '2' corresponds to a difference of two in the number of parameters to be estimated for the 'full' and the null model (see b_1 and b_2), and (b) the 'Step Chi-square', the 'Block Chi-square' and the 'Model Chi-square' are all equal in the current application. By defining 'blocks' of variables in the input window and the application of the 'Stepwise' method, Example 3 will show that this latter situation is not always the case.

Figure 6.24

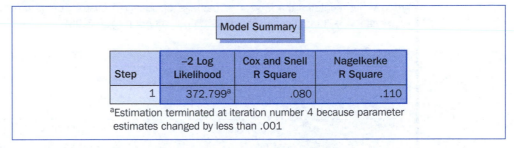

| | Model Summary | | | |
Step	−2 Log Likelihood	Cox and Snell R Square	Nagelkerke R Square
1	372.799[a]	.080	.110

[a]Estimation terminated at iteration number 4 because parameter estimates changed by less than .001

'Cox & Snell R Square' is comparable to 'R Square' in linear regression, in the sense that a higher value corresponds to a better fit of the model. A dissimilarity between the two is however that the first cannot accept the maximum value, the value '1'. 'Nagelkerke R Square' does meet this requirement, considering it falls within a range running from '0' to '1'. Figure 6.24 indicates that this criterion is .11, which is on the low side and points to the lesser quality of the 'full' model.

Figure 6.25

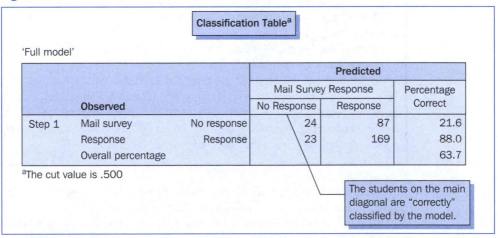

Classification Table[a]

'Full model'

			Predicted		
			Mail Survey Response		Percentage Correct
	Observed		No Response	Response	
Step 1	Mail survey	No response	24	87	21.6
	Response	Response	23	169	88.0
	Overall percentage				63.7

[a]The cut value is .500

The students on the main diagonal are "correctly" classified by the model.

In the 'Classification Table' (Figure 6.25), it appears that 192 (23 + 169) students had actually responded to the mail survey, and that 111 (24 + 87) did not send the survey back. Of the 192 observed 'respondents', the 'full' model classifies 169 as being correct (88.0%), therefore as 'respondents', whereas 23 were incorrectly included in the 'non-respondents' group. For the 111 observed 'non-respondents', 87 appear to have been assigned to the 'respondents' group, and only 24 were correctly included in the 'non-respondents' category (21.6%). In overall terms, the researcher may therefore decide that 63.7% of the students {(24 + 169)/(24 + 169 + 87 + 23)} were correctly classified, which, on the surface, does not appear to be a poor score.

Digging Deeper

This 'Overall Percentage Correct' (63.7%), also referred to as 'R^2_{Count}', can however be misleading. On the basis of a binary model, it is after all possible, without knowledge of the independent variables, to classify at least 50% of the cases correctly, by including them in that group which contains the largest percentage of observed cases. This is now precisely what happens in the 'Classification Table' of the null model (Figure 6.26).

Figure 6.26

Classification Table[a,b]

'Null model'

Observed			Predicted		
			Mail Survey Response		Percentage Correct
			No Response	Response	
Step 0	Mail survey	No response	0	111	.0
	Response	Response	0	192	100.0
	Overall percentage				63.4

[a]Constant is included in the model
[b]The cut value is .500

The 'answer' group contains the largest percentage of observed cases, namely 63.4% (192/303), and the assignment of all 303 cases to this group will lead to a percentage of correct predictions of 63.4.

Therefore, the 'full' model results in an 'Overall Percentage Correct' of 63.7, whereas this percentage is still 63.4 for the null model.

In order to avoid incorrect conclusions, it is advisable not to interpret 'R^2_{Count}' but instead '$R^2_{Adjusted\ Count}$'. The latter criterion corrects 'R^2_{Count}' with the largest row total, and is calculated as follows: $\{(24 + 169) - 192\}/\{303 - 192\} = .009$. The 'full' model will, in comparison with the null model, reduce the prediction error by .9%, which is actually very little and once again, is indicative of the poor quality of the 'full' model.

In addition to the criteria above, there is also a figure which provides insight into the quality of the model: the 'Classification plot' (Figure 6.27).

This figure shows the observed response (in the plot) and the predicted response (at the bottom of the plot) for each of the students. The predicted response is a function of the probability the student will respond to the mail survey, and corresponds to 'response' if the probability is higher than .5 (see 'Classification cutoff'; defined in Figure 6.9) and corresponds to 'no response' if the probability is less than .5. In an ideal case, the observed 'R's are to the right of the .5 mark, and the 'N's to the left of it. This is certainly not the case in the current application, which is indicative of the low quality of the model.

Figure 6.27

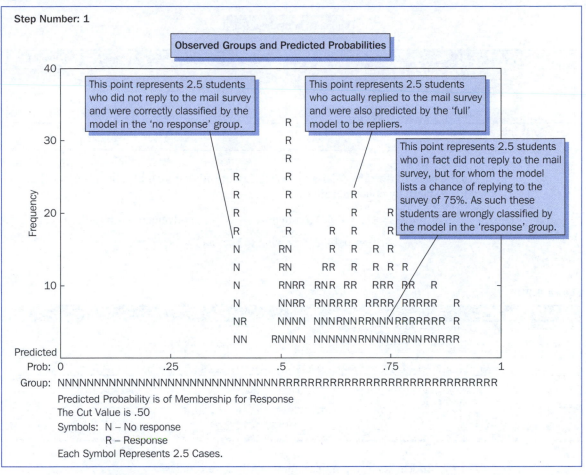

The next step involves the discussion of the logistic regression coefficients, and provides answers to the following questions: (a) on the basis of the coefficients, how may the probability of a response be calculated; (b) when are the coefficients significantly different from zero, meaning the independent variables do have an influence on the response; and (c) how does one interpret the coefficients in terms of 'odds' and 'log odds'?

Under the 'Technique' section, an indication is provided of how **the probability of replying** may be calculated **using regression coefficients**. An example follows below in which the probability that the mail survey will be sent back is calculated for a student (see respondent number '3' in the dataset) who had received a non-anonymous version ([anonymity]: 2, recoded to 0), and is highly involved with the subject ([involvement]: 5.81).

Figure 6.28

Variables in the Equation

		B	S.E.	Wald	df	Sig.	Exp(B)
Step 1[a]	Anonymity(1)	−.436	.249	3.057	1	.080	.647
	Involvement	.350	.078	20.040	1	.000	1.420
	Constant	−.261	.280	.872	1	.350	.770

[a]Variable(s) entered on step 1: Anonymity, involvement

On the basis of the table 'Variables in the Equation' (Figure 6.28), the b's in the Z-model may be replaced by concrete values:

$$Z = (-.261) + (-.436)^{*} \text{ anonymity} + .350^{*} \text{ involvement with the subject,}$$

$$\text{with probability (replying to the mail survey)} = \frac{e^{z}}{1 + e^{z}}$$

Figure 6.29

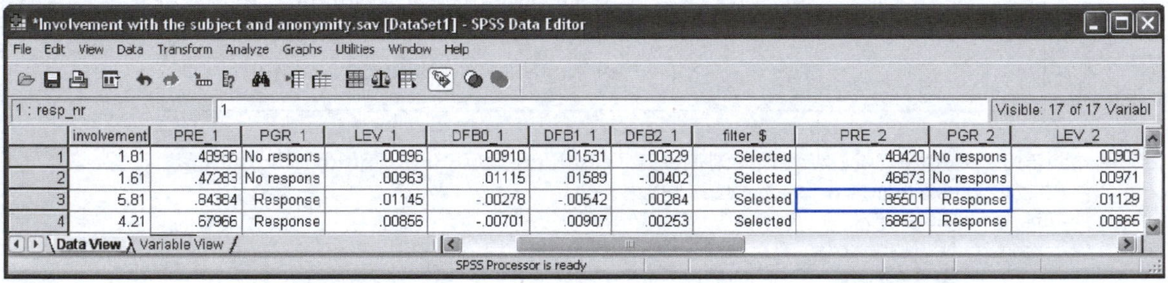
*Involvement with the subject and anonymity.sav [DataSet1] - SPSS Data Editor

File Edit View Data Transform Analyze Graphs Utilities Window Help

1 : resp_nr 1 Visible: 17 of 17 Variabl

	involvement	PRE_1	PGR_1	LEV_1	DFB0_1	DFB1_1	DFB2_1	filter_$	PRE_2	PGR_2	LEV_2
1	1.81	.48936	No respons	.00896	.00910	.01531	-.00329	Selected	.48420	No respons	.00903
2	1.61	.47283	No respons	.00963	.01115	.01589	-.00402	Selected	.46673	No respons	.00971
3	5.81	.84384	Response	.01145	-.00278	-.00542	.00284	Selected	.85601	Response	.01129
4	4.21	.67966	Response	.00856	-.00701	.00907	.00253	Selected	.68520	Response	.00865

Data View Variable View

SPSS Processor is ready

For the student with respondent number '3', this becomes:

$$Z = (-.261) + (-.436)^{*}\ 0 + .350\ ^{*}\ .581 = 1.7725,$$

$$\text{with probability (replying to the mail survey)} = \frac{e^{1.7725}}{1 + e^{1.7725}} = .8547 > .5$$

Therefore, according to the model, the probability is high that this student will respond to the survey, and he or she will be included in the 'response' group, since the probability is higher than .5 (Figure 6.29).

Figure 6.30

Variables in the Equation

		B	S.E.	Wald	df	Sig.	Exp(B)
Step 1[a]	Anonymity(1)	−.436	.249	3.057	1	.080	.647
	Involvement	.350	.078	20.040	1	.000	1.420
	Constant	−.261	.280	.872	1	.350	.770

[a]Variable(s) entered on step 1: Anonymity, Involvement

The 'Wald' statistic (Figure 6.30) which is Chi-square distributed, or the p-value linked to it, is used to determine whether **the regression coefficients differ significantly from zero or not** with H_0: b = 0. The coefficient, linked to 'anonymity' thus does not appear to differ significantly from zero (p-value = .080 > .05), whereas the opposite is true for the 'involvement' coefficient (p-value < .001). In concrete terms, this means that only the 'involvement with the subject' exerts an influence on the response, and this influence also appears to be positive ($b_2 > 0$).

It is worth noting here that in the case of only one degree of freedom (df = 1), the 'Wald' statistic may be calculated on the basis of the regression coefficient (B) and the corresponding standard error (S.E.): Wald = $(B/S.E.)^2$. For the 'anonymity' variable, for example, this would be: $(-.436/.249)^2 = 3.066 \cong 3.057$.

It is also important to know that in the event of a 'large' coefficient, the 'Wald' statistic is no longer reliable[3]. In that case, it is recommended to first construct a model without the relevant variable, to note the '−2LL' value, and then to build a model using this variable, and then once again to note the '−2LL' value. The next step is then to compare these two '−2LL' values: if the change in '−2LL' differs significantly from zero, then the model 'with the variable' is significantly better than the one 'without', and the variable therefore makes an important contribution to the explanation of the response (see Example 3, for the definition of two 'blocks'[4] in this context). Finally, the interpretation of the coefficients is examined in terms of 'odds' and 'log odds'.

The '**log odds**' is defined as follows:

$$Z = B_0 + B_1X_1 + B_2X_2 + \cdots B_nX_n = \text{Logit} = \textbf{Log odds}$$

$$= \text{Log}\, \frac{\text{Probability (Event)}}{\text{Probability (No event)}}$$

The coefficient 'B_n' shows the change in the 'log odds' for a change in the independent variable X by one unit. To be exact: given the coefficient linked to the 'anonymity' variable is equal to −.436 (see B for the 'anonymity' variable in Figure 6.30), the 'log odds' for the responses to the mail survey will decrease by .436 points in the transition from a non-anonymous (coding: 0) to an anonymous (coding: 1) version, all other things being equal.

The above formula may be transformed as a function of '**odds**' in the following manner:

$$\textbf{Odds} = \frac{\text{Probability (Event)}}{\text{Probability (No event)}} = e^{B_0 + B_1X_1 + \cdots + B_nX_n} = e^{B_0}e^{B_1X_1} \cdots e^{B_nX_n}$$

Then 'e^{B_n}', also referred to as 'odds ratio', will be the factor by which the 'odds' changes as variable X_n increases by one unit. Additionally, it may be said that if the regression coefficient B_n is greater (less) than zero, the 'odds ratio' is greater (less) than one, then the 'odds' will thus increase (decrease). A coefficient equal to zero sets the factor equal to 1, and leaves the 'odds' unchanged. Specifically: the transition from a non-anonymous (coding: 0) to an anonymous (coding: 1) version will cause the 'odds' to decrease by a factor of .647 (see Exp(B) for the 'anonymity' variable in Figure 6.30).

The decrease in 'log odds' by .436 points, and the decrease in 'odds' by a factor of .647 as a result of changing the mail survey version from non-anonymous to anonymous also appears from the example worked out below (Table 6.5).

Table 6.5 The calculation of 'odds' and 'log odds', for a person with a low level of involvement with the subject ([involvement]:2) and those who receive an anonymous/non-anonymous survey

Non-anonymous version (coding: 0)	Anonymous version (coding: 1)
Z = (−.261) + .350*2 + (−.436)*0 = .439	Z = (−.261) + .350*2 + (−.436)*1 = .003
Probability (Response) = $e^{.439}/(1 + e^{.437})$ = .608 Probability (No response) = 1 − .608 = .392	Probability (Response) = $e^{.003}/(1 + e^{.003})$ = .501 Probability (No response) = 1 − .501 = .499
Odds = .608/.392 = 1.551	Odds = .501/.499 = 1.004
An increase in the 'anonymity' variable by one unit causes the 'odds' to decrease by a factor of .647 (1.004/1.551), the Exp(B) value for this variable.	
Log odds = ln 1.551 = .439	Log odds = ln 1.004 =.003
An increase in the 'anonymity' variable by one unit causes the 'log odds' to decrease by .436 (.003 − .439), the B value for this variable.	

Example 2

Interval-scaled and categorical independent variables, with interaction term

Managerial problem

The research involved in Example 2 is an extension of that found in Example 1 in two respects: (1) in addition to the 'anonymity' of the version, there is now also 'personalization' involved, meaning that there are now four versions; and (2) not only is the 'involvement with the subject' measured beforehand, but the 'sensitivity to the subject', the 'privacy,' 'helpfulness' and 'social responsibility' of the students are also measured. On the basis of this research structure, the researchers would like to answer the following questions: is the effect of the involvement with the subject on the response different in the case of an anonymous versus a non-anonymous survey; is the effect of the involvement with the subject on the response different depending on whether the person has received a personalized or a non-personalized version; does the sensitivity of the subject have a different effect on the response for an anonymous and non-anonymous survey; and is the effect of the sensitivity of the subject on the response different in the case of a personalized versus a non-personalized version? They are therefore interested in whether or not interaction effects are present between the 'involvement with the subject' or the 'sensitivity of the subject' and the version received.

To this end, a dataset has been made which records the response to the mail survey for each of the students (304 in total) ([response]: answer or no answer), the version received ([anonymity]: anonymous vs. non-anonymous; [personal]: personalized vs. non-personalized), the involvement with the subject ([sinvolv]:' 1 = no involvement with the subject, . . . , 7 = high involvement with the subject), the sensitivity of the subject ([ssensit]: 1 = the subject is not sensitive, . . . 7 = the subject is sensitive), the need for privacy ([sprivacy]: 1 = does not attach a lot of importance to his privacy, . . . , 7 = attaches a lot of importance to his privacy), the helpfulness ([shelp]: 1 = not very helpful, . . . 7 = very helpful), and the feeling of social responsibility ([sresp]: 1 = has no sense of social responsibility, . . . , 7 = has a sense of social responsibility)[5]. Figure 6.31 is a partial representation of this dataset.

Figure 6.31

	respons	sprivacy	sprivcen	shelp	shelpcen	sresp	srespcen	anonymity	personal	sinvolv
1	response	3,80	-,33	5,00	-,22	3,00	-1,75	Anonymou	Personalis	1,81
2	response	5,00	,87	5,75	,53	4,50	-,25	Anonymou	Personalis	1,61
3	response	3,80	-,33	5,00	-,22	5,25	,50	Non anony	Non person	5,81
4	response	5,20	1,07	3,25	-1,97	5,25	,50	Anonymou	Non person	4,21
5	response	3,60	-,53	5,75	,53	3,75	-1,00	Non anony	Non person	2,01
6	no respons	4,00	-,13	4,50	-,72	5,25	,50	Anonymou	Non person	3,61
7	no respons	3,00	-1,13	2,75	-2,47	5,50	,75	Non anony	Non person	1,81
8	no respons	4,00	-,13	5,00	-,22	5,50	,75	Anonymou	Non person	3,01
9	response	4,80	,67	3,75	-1,47	5,25	,50	Anonymou	Personalis	1,81
10	no respons	4,00	-,13	5,00	-,22	5,25	,50	Anonymou	Non person	1,61
11	no respons	3,20	-,93	4,00	-1,22	4,25	-,50	Non anony	Personalis	1,81
12	response	2,60	-1,53	5,00	-,22	4,00	-,75	Non anony	Personalis	4,21
13	no respons	5,80	1,67	5,25	,03	4,75	,00	Anonymou	Personalis	1,81
14	response	1,40	-2,73	6,25	1,03	6,50	1,75	Non anony	Personalis	3,81
15	no respons	4,60	,47	3,25	-1,97	2,00	-2,75	Anonymou	Non person	3,81
16	no respons	2,60	-1,53	1,25	-3,97	2,00	-2,75	Anonymou	Non person	3,81
17	response	3,20	-,93	5,00	-,22	4,75	,00	Non anony	Non person	5,01
18	response	4,20	,07	4,75	-,47	5,25	,50	Anonymou	Personalis	2,01
19	no respons	3,80	-,33	5,25	,03	5,00	,25	Anonymou	Personalis	,81
20	no respons	2,60	-1,53	4,50	-,72	4,50	-,25	Anonymou	Personalis	1,81
21	no respons	4,20	,07	2,75	-2,47	4,50	-,25	Anonymou	Personalis	3,01

Problem

Use the data above (*Involvement with the subject, anonymity and personalization.sav*) to create the following regression model, which is distinct due to the interaction terms present:

$$\text{Response} \cong Z = b_0 + b_1 \text{ privacy} + b_2 \text{ helpfulness} + b_3 \text{ social responsibility}$$
$$+ b_4 \text{ anonymity} + b_5 \text{ personalization} + b_6 \text{ involvement} + b_7 \text{ sensitivity}$$
$$+ b_8 \text{ anonymity} \times \text{involvement} + b_9 \text{ anonymity} \times \text{sensitivity}$$
$$+ b_{10} \text{ personalization} \times \text{involvement} + b_{11} \text{ personalization}$$
$$\times \text{ sensitivity} \tag{1}$$

Why is the model constructed in this way? The terms, linked to the coefficients b_8, b_9, b_{10} and b_{11} refer to the study of possible interaction effects between the 'involvement with the subject', or 'sensitivity of the subject' and the version received. The inclusion of these interaction terms makes it necessary to include the terms with coefficients b_4, b_5, b_6 and b_7 because **for each interaction term, every one of its components** must also be **included separately in the model.** Even if it were to appear from later calculations that these components do not make a significant contribution to the model, they must still be retained. A correct interpretation of the interaction effect is only possible if both the interaction term as well as each of its components is included in the model. Due to a possible effect of the variables 'privacy', 'helpfulness', and 'sense of responsibility' on the response, they are also added to the model (they play the role of covariate here).

Use the 'Enter' method to estimate the model, and determine whether or not the following effects are present: (1) the involvement with the subject has a significant effect on the response in the case of an anonymous (personalized) version; (2) the involvement with the subject has a significant effect on the response in the case of a non-anonymous (non-personalized) version; (3) the effect of involvement on response is different for an anonymous (personalized) and a non-anonymous (non-personalized) version; and (4) independent of the version, the involvement with the subject has a positive effect on the response. Questions linked to the sensitivity of the subject are therefore not answered, and this is done to limit the discussion below somewhat.

In the current example, the focus lies on the interaction effects and their implications, and this latter factor is determined more as it relates to the coding of the variables and the interpretation of the correct regression coefficients and significances. There is thus no attention dedicated to aspects such as the detection of outliers and the determination of the suitability of the model (see Example 1), which in practice will be part of every analysis.

Solution

A number of research questions were included in the previous section entitled 'Problem', which essentially all gauge the effect of the involvement with the subject on the response (in one case in the event of an anonymous version, and another time in the case of a personalized version, . . .). **In Model (1), this effect is shown by coefficient b_6, and this is only in the event the other variables** ('privacy', 'helpfulness', 'feeling of social responsibility', 'sensitivity of the subject', 'anonymity', and 'personalization') **have the value 'zero'**. Logit comparison (1) is then reduced to:

$$\text{Response} \cong Z = b_0 + b_6 \text{ involvement} \tag{2}$$

It should be noted here that the coefficient b_6, and the corresponding tests have little or no meaning if the value 'zero' does not belong to the collection of possible answers for the independent variable. In the current application, this appears to be a problem for the ratio ('privacy', 'helpfulness', 'feeling of social responsibility', and 'sensitivity of the subject'), as well as for the categorical variables ('anonymity' and 'personalization'): the possible values for the ratio variables lie between '1' and '7' and are equal to '1' or '2' for the categorical variables (see coding in the dataset, 'Variable View' tab). What are the implications of this now for the independent variables?

A **first implication** involves the rescaling of the ratio variables, in order to then use these rescaled scores for the estimation of the model. The rescaling may occur by subtracting from the original scores for a certain variable, for example, the mean score for this variable: e.g. [sprivcen] = [sprivacy] − 4.13, where 4.13 is the mean score for the 'privacy' variable (see commands in SPSS: Transform/Compute). The rescaled variables ([sprivcen], [shelpcen], [srespcen], [sinvolvcen] and [ssenscen]) will represent input for the model to be estimated, so that Model (1) may be reformulated as follows:

$$\begin{aligned} \text{Response} \cong Z = b_0 &+ b_1 \text{ privacy}_{cen} + b_2 \text{ helpfulness}_{cen} + b_3 \text{ responsibility}_{cen} + b_4 \text{ anonymity} \\ &+ b_5 \text{ personalization} + b_6 \text{ involvement} + b_7 \text{ sensitivity}_{cen} + b_8 \text{ anonymity} \\ &\times \text{ involvement} + b_9 \text{ anonymity} \times \text{ sensitivity}_{cen} + b_{10} \text{ personalization} \\ &\times \text{ involvement} + b_{11} \text{ personalization} \times \text{ sensitivity}_{cen} \end{aligned} \tag{3}$$

The coefficient b_6 will show the effect of involvement on the response, if the 'new' variables ('privacy$_{cen}$', . . .) are made equal to zero, which in terms of the 'original' scores ('privacy', . . .) amounts to them being equal to the mean value (4.13, . . .). **The effect of involvement on the response will therefore be interpreted within a context of a mean attachment to privacy, a mean helpfulness, a mean sense of social responsibility, and a mean sensitivity of the subject** (and for example not in a context in which people are very attached to their privacy, are not very helpful, have a weak sense of social responsibility, and do not find the subject very sensitive; another rescaling, other than that which is based on the mean, also makes this type of interpretation possible).

A **second implication** is the recoding of the categorical variables, so that the 'zero' value for these variables obtains a concrete meaning. The **recoding** may occur on the basis of 'indicator coding' (0, 1) and 'deviation coding' (−1, 1), and the choice between the two **depends on the specific research problem which must be answered**. A variety of these questions will be asked below, and the appropriate coding will be defined in the SPSS input window (see Analyze/Regression/Binary Logistic – Categorical).

Before focusing on the coding, the outputs and their interpretations for the various research questions, it is important to note that an outlier analysis performed beforehand has shown that **the student with respondent number '585' is an 'influential' outlier, and can best be removed from the dataset**.

Supporting technique

Figure 6.32

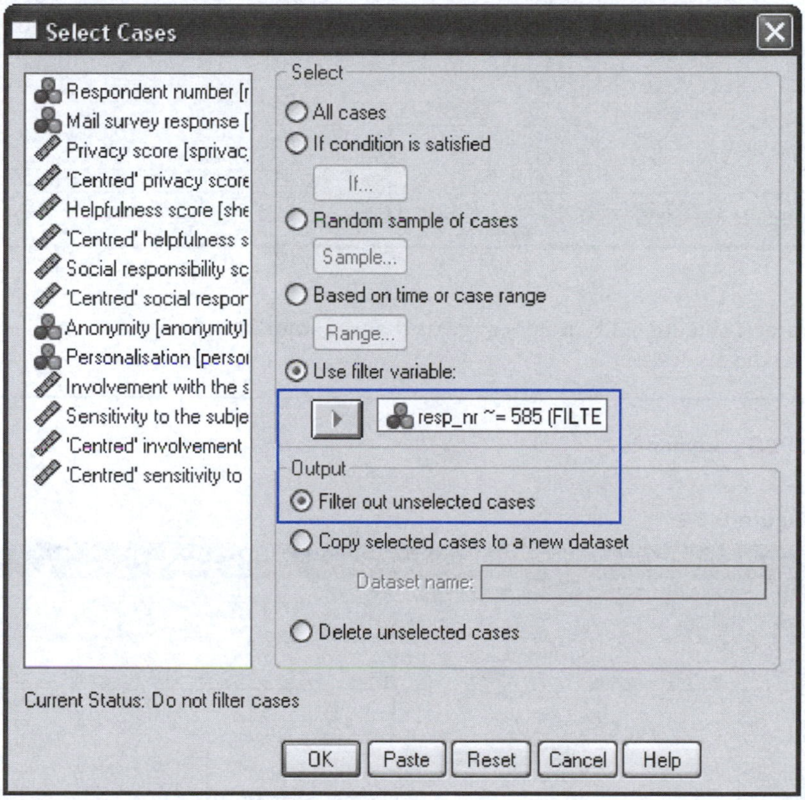

In the main menu, go to Data/Select Cases and choose the option 'Use filter variable' in the 'Select Cases' window which will appear (Figure 6.32). Now move the variable [outliers] (which assigns the status 'selected' to each of the respondents in the dataset, except to the respondent with number '585') from the left column to the box corresponding to this option. In this way, the previously defined selection 'select those students for which the respondent number is not '585' (using the option 'If condition is satisfied' in the 'Select Cases' window) will be retrieved.

Make sure that the option 'Filter out unselected cases' under 'Output' is selected and not the option 'Delete unselected cases', if the researcher does not wish to permanently eliminate the student with number '585' from the dataset.

Figure 6.33

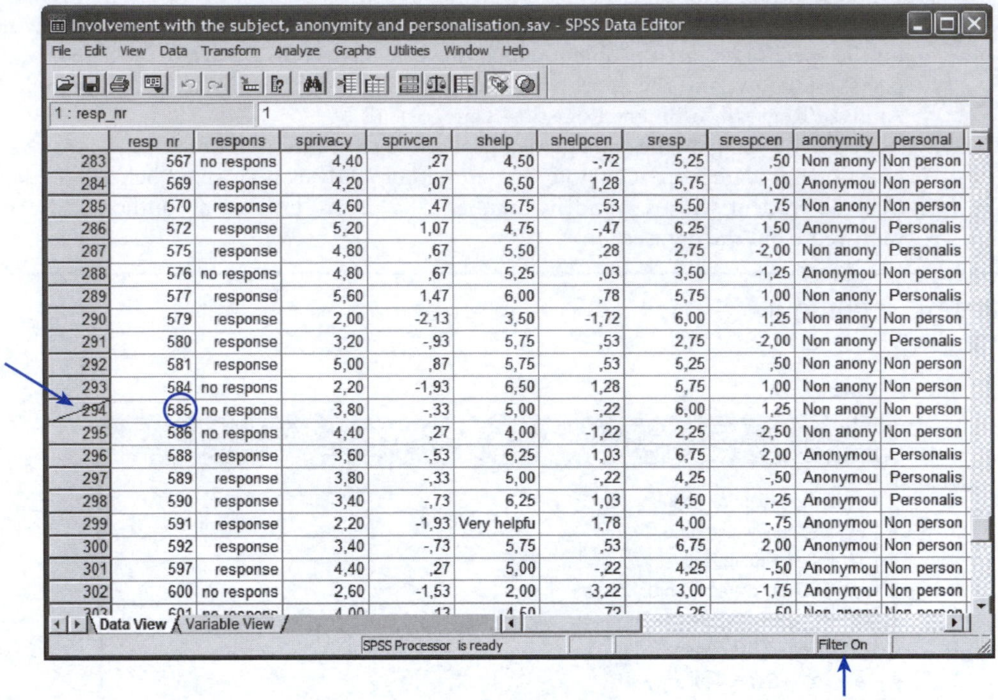

From the dataset (Figure 6.33), it now appears that the student with number '585' will 'temporarily' be excluded from the analysis.

SPSS commands

Figure 6.34

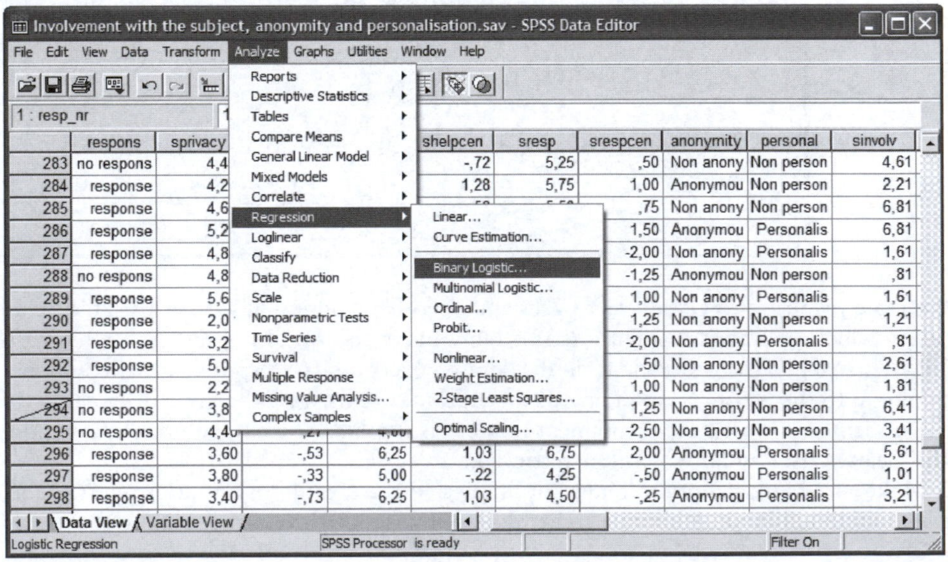

Go to Analyze/Regression/Binary Logistic (Figure 6.34).

Figure 6.35

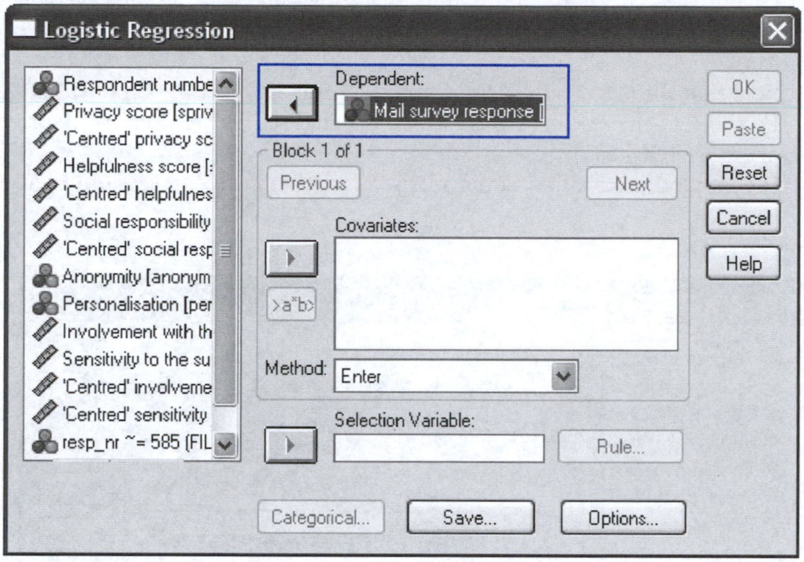

In the 'Logistic Regression' window (Figure 6.35), move the variable [respons] from the list on the left-hand side to the 'Dependent' box.

You will note that a binary variable is involved here, which is coded as '0' and '1': the value '1' is linked to the category 'Response', while '0' corresponds to 'No response' (see 'SPSS Data Editor' – 'Variable View' tab). Through the use of logistic regression, the researcher will then be able to predict the probability that the student will 'answer' the mail survey.

Figure 6.36

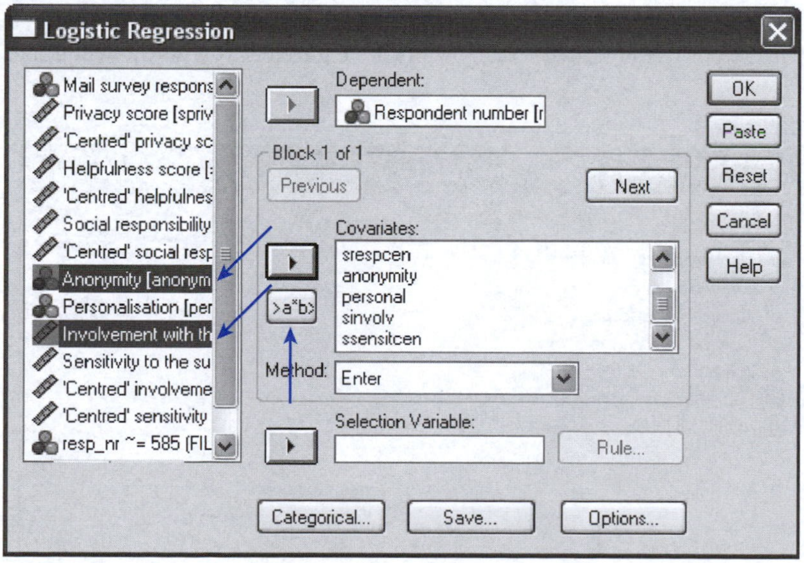

Define the previously mentioned Model (3) in the box under the title 'Covariates' by first including the individual and then the interaction terms (Figure 6.36).

To add the interaction 'Anonymity * Involvement' to the 'covariates' list for example, the researcher first clicks the 'anonymity' variable and then the 'involvement' variable, while also pressing the CTRL key. After selecting both variables, he now must click the '>a*b>' button.

Note that for the variables 'privacy', 'helpfulness', 'social responsibility', and 'sensitivity to the subject', the rescaled, and not the original scores are used (see [sprivcen], [shulpcen], [srespcen], [ssensitcen]).

The method used is the 'Enter' method (see the 'Problem' section; Figure 6.37).

Figure 6.37

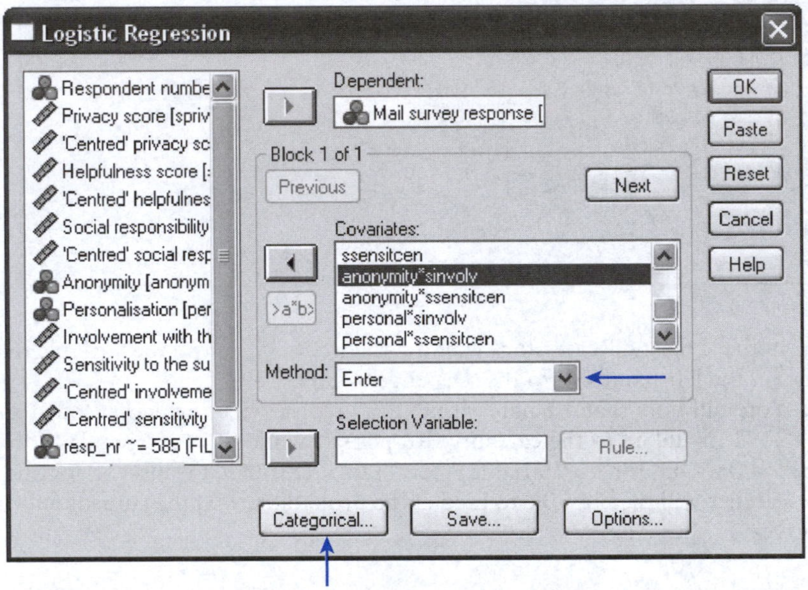

Click on the 'Categorical' button in the main window (Figure 6.37) and the 'Logistic Regression: Define Categorical Variables' (Figure 6.38) window will appear.

Figure 6.38

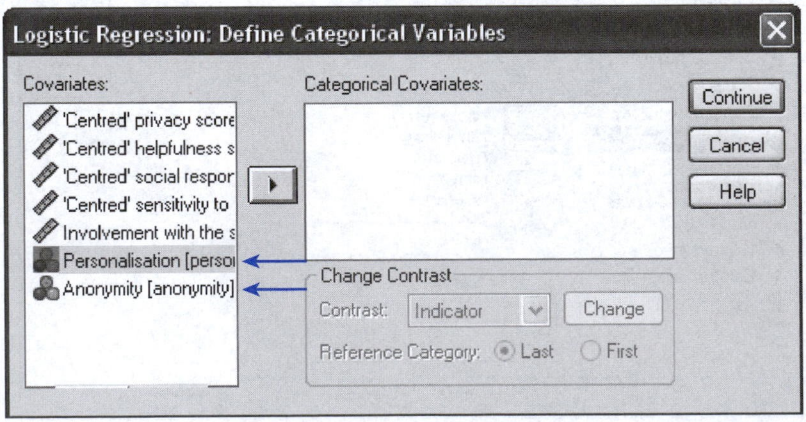

This window indicates which of the independent variables are categorical, and for the current example, these are the variables 'anonymity' and 'personalization'. Both variables must therefore be moved from the list on the left-hand side to the 'Categorical Covariates' box.

Figure 6.39

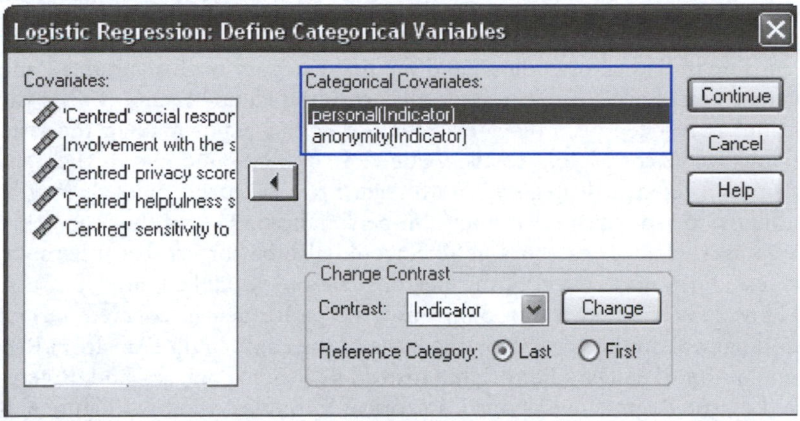

In contrast with Example 1, the categorical variables are not automatically found in the 'Categorical Covariates' box (Figure 6.39). The measurement level of the variables 'anonymity' and 'personalization' is thus also defined in the 'Variable View' tab in the 'SPSS Data Editor' as 'numeric' and not as a 'string'.

After defining 'anonymity' and 'personalization' as 'categorical' covariates, it is important to focus sufficient attention on the method used for coding these variables. Previously we mentioned that this coding may be done on the basis of 'indicator coding' (0, 1) and 'deviation coding' (−1, 1) and that the choice between the two depends on the specific research question which must be answered.

Research question 1: Does the involvement with the subject have a significant effect on the response in the case of an anonymous version?

The coefficient b_6 from comparison (3) will show the effect of involvement on the response, if the other variables, including 'anonymity' and 'personalization', have a 'zero' value. Considering the value of zero for these last two variables does not have a concrete meaning (see 'SPSS Data Editor', 'Variable View' tab; 1: anonymous vs. 2: non-anonymous; 1: personalized vs. 2: non-personalized), recoding becomes necessary.

Table 6.6

	Original coding	Coding as a function of research question
Variable 'anonymity'		
Anonymous	1	0
Non-anonymous	2	1
Variable 'personalization'		
Personalized	1	1
Non personalized	2	−1

Given the fact the researcher would like to find out the effect of involvement on the response in the event of an 'anonymous' survey, the answering category 'anonymous' is linked to the value '0', and 'non-anonymous' is linked to the value '1'. Because the research question makes an abstraction of the fact whether the survey is personalized or not, the response possibilities 'personalized' and 'non-personalized' are recoded as '1' and '−1'. The mean effect of the variable 'personalization' is then '0' (Table 6.6).

In technical terms, this means the following: (1) the variable 'anonymity' is recoded according to 'indicator coding', and the first category of this variable ('anonymous') is the reference category, since it is associated with the value '0'; and (2) the variable 'personalization' is recoded according to 'deviation coding', and making the last category ('non-personalized') correspond to the value '−1' in SPSS amounts to the defining of this last group as a reference category.[6] With regard to the second point, it may be noted that the coding of 'personalized: −1' and 'non-personalized: 1', and thus the definition of the first group as a reference category in SPSS would also be correct, because the researcher is only interested in a mean effect of the 'personalization' variable, that is '0'.

How may the above 'recodings' now be performed in concrete terms in SPSS? These recodings are not performed on the basis of the commands Transform/Recode in the main menu of the 'SPSS Data Editor', but instead by using 'Contrast' and 'Reference Category' in the 'Logistic Regression: Define Categorical Variables' window (Figure 6.40).

Figure 6.40

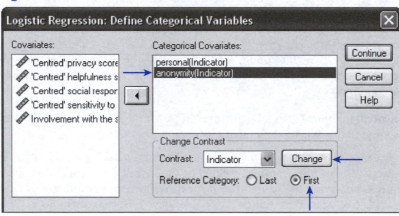

In the 'Categorical Covariates' box, click on the variable 'anonymity'. Change the reference category at the bottom from 'Last' to 'First', and click on the 'Change' button.

Figure 6.41

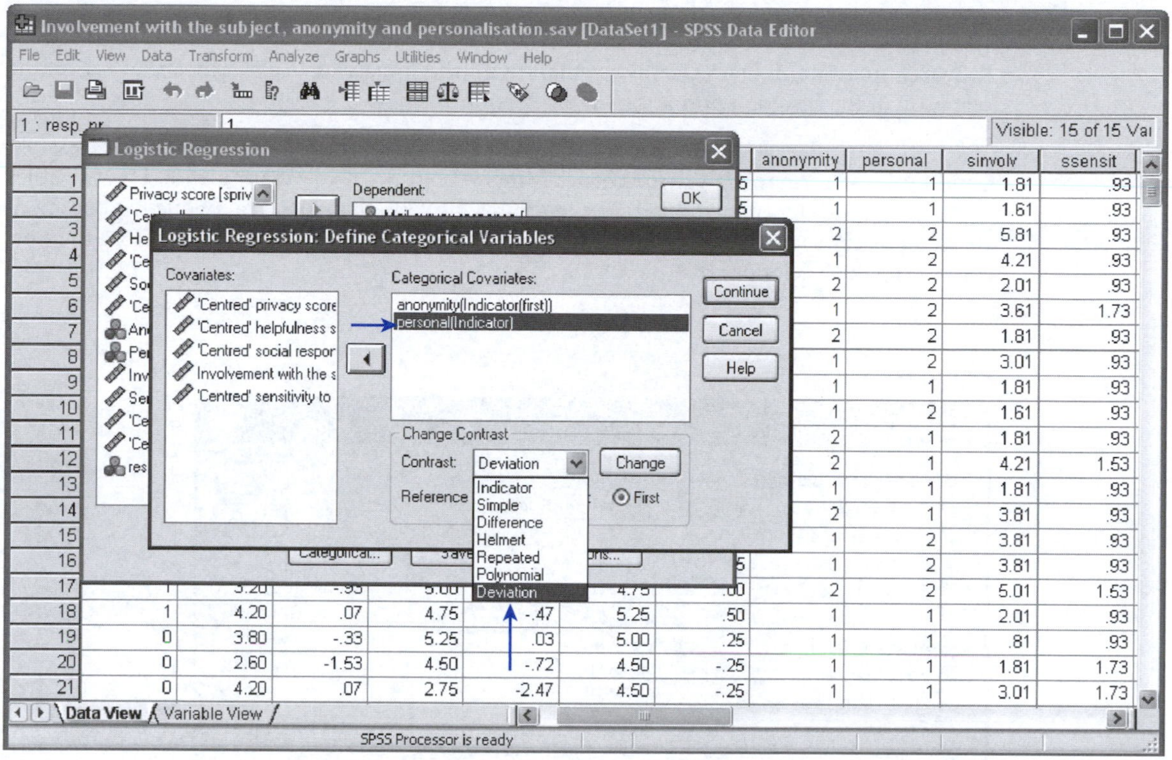

Go to the 'personalization' variable and click on it. Now change the contrast from 'indicator coding' to 'deviation coding'. Indicate 'Last' as reference category, and click on the 'Change' button (Figure 6.41).

Figure 6.42

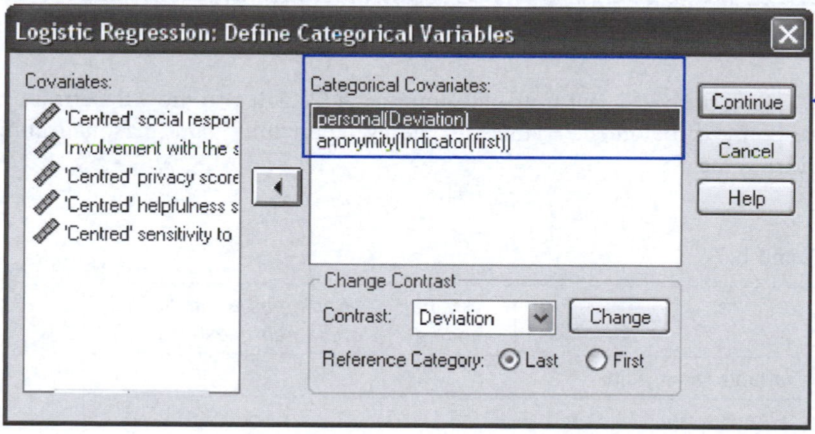

The final recoding appears as shown in Figure 6.42. Now click 'Continue'.

The contents under the buttons 'Save' and 'Options' (Figure 6.37) are not relevant within the context of this example, and the SPSS output may then also be retrieved immediately by clicking 'OK' in the main window. After this output and its interpretation have been generated (see 'Interpretation of the SPSS output' later in this chapter), the researcher may focus on the second research question.

Research question 2: Does the involvement with the subject have a significant effect on the response in the case of a non-anonymous version?

In order to answer this question, the researcher must return to the 'Logistic Regression' window by selecting Analyze/Regression/Binary Logistic in the main menu. The variables included in the 'Dependent' and the 'Covariates' box are then identical, while the coding of the categorical variable 'anonymity' will change. To do this, click 'Categorical' at the bottom of the main window (Figure 6.43).

Figure 6.43

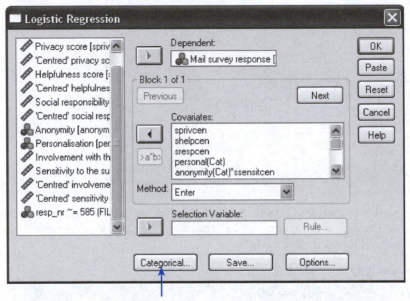

Here, the coefficient b_6 from Comparison (3) will also show the effect of involvement on response if the other variables, including 'anonymity' and 'personalization', have zero as their value.

Table 6.7

	Original coding	Coding as a function of research question
Variable 'anonymity'		
Anonymous	1	1
Non-anonymous	2	0
Variable 'personalization'		
Personalized	1	1
Non-personalized	2	−1

Table 6.7 therefore indicates that as a result of the recoding, which occurs as a function of the specific research question, the zero-value for the variable 'anonymity' will have a concrete meaning namely 'non-anonymous' (the researcher will estimate the effect of involvement on response in the case of a non-anonymous version). The recoding of the 'personalization' variable is identical to that from the previous research questions, given the fact that this question does not specify whether this involves a personalized or non-personalized version either, and thus makes an abstraction of the 'personalization' variable.

Figure 6.44

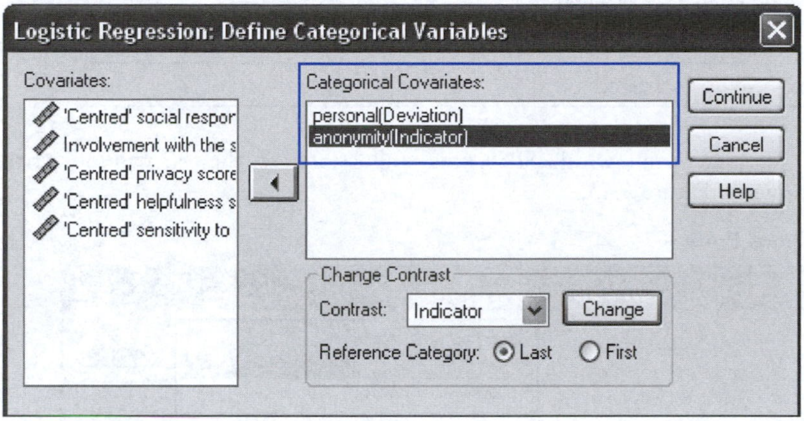

In terms of SPSS input (Figure 6.44), the above means that the variable 'anonymity' is still recoded according to 'indicator coding', but that now the last group, 'non-anonymous', becomes the reference category. In addition, the recoding remains unchanged for the 'personalization' variable (Contrast: 'Deviation'; Reference Category: 'Last').

Click on 'Continue' and then on 'OK' in the main window (Figure 6.43) to see the SPSS output.

Research question 3: Is the effect of involvement on response different for an anonymous and a non-anonymous version?

In order to answer this question, the researcher may call upon the model and the recoding as these were defined in research questions 1 and 2. The difference between research questions 2 and 3 (or 1) thus lies neither in the included individual and interaction terms, nor in the manner of coding, but instead in the interpretation of the correct regression coefficient. This will be clarified further under 'Interpretation of the SPSS output'.

Research question 4: Does the involvement with the subject have a significant effect on the response in the case of a personalized version?

In comparison with the previous three research questions, from now on, the personalization level is the central theme in the survey, and no longer whether or not it is anonymous. Since the approach is identical, it is only the differences which crop up, for example, in coding, which will be examined.

Given the fact the researcher will now try to determine the effect of involvement on the response for a personalized survey, the category 'personalized' will be associated with the value of zero after recoding of the variable 'personalization'. 'Indicator coding' is thus used for this variable, and the 'first' group is the reference category. This research question makes an abstraction of whether or not the questionnaire is anonymous, and this is why 'deviation coding' will be input for the 'anonymity' variable, with the 'last' group, 'non-anonymous' as reference (Table 6.8).

Table 6.8

	Original coding	*Coding as a function of research question*
Variable 'anonymity'		
Anonymous	1	1
Non-anonymous	2	−1
Variable 'personalization'		
Personalized	1	0
Non-personalized	2	1

In concrete terms within SPSS, this is illustrated in the top window of the two windows shown in Figure 6.45.

Figure 6.45

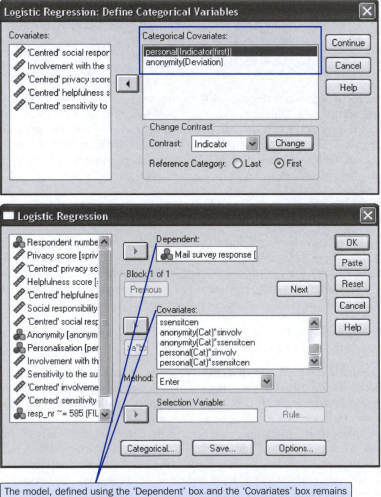

The model, defined using the 'Dependent' box and the 'Covariates' box remains unchanged by focusing on the personalized and unpersonalized version in the research question, instead of on the anonymous/non-anonymous version.

Research question 5: Does the involvement with the subject have a significant effect on the response in the case of a non-personalized version?

In comparison with research question 4, the researcher is not trying to find out the effect in the case of a 'personalized' version, but instead in the case of a 'non-personalized' version. With regard to the coding, this will only result in a change of reference category, namely, from 'personalized' ('First') to 'non-personalized' ('Last') for the 'personalization' variable (Table 6.9 and Figure 6.46).

Table 6.9

	Original coding	Coding as a function of research question
Variable 'anonymity'		
Anonymous	1	1
Non-anonymous	2	−1
Variable 'personalization'		
Personalized	1	1
Non-personalized	2	0

Figure 6.46

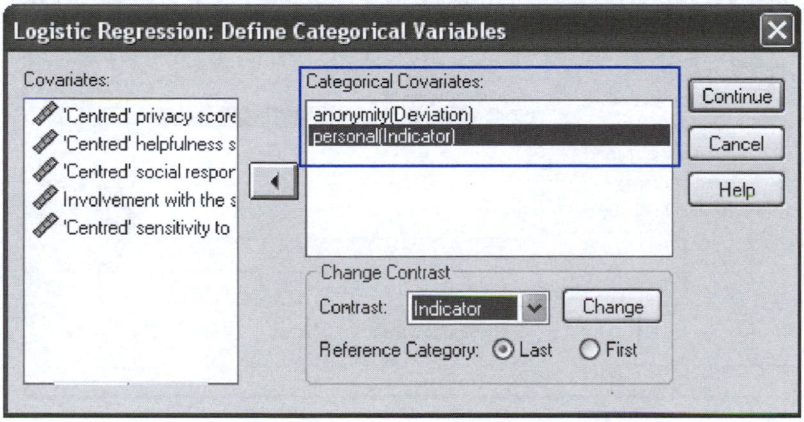

Research question 6: Is the effect of involvement on response different for a personalized version and a non-personalized version?

Formulating an answer to this question may be done on the basis of the coding for research question 4, as well as that for research question 5.

Research question 7: Does the involvement with the subject have a positive effect on the response?

The current research question makes an abstraction of whether or not the survey is anonymous, as well as whether or not it is personalized. Both variables, 'anonymity' and 'personalization', will then have to be coded according to 'deviation coding', in which 'non-anonymous' ('Last') and 'non-personalized' ('Last') are used as a reference ('anonymous' and 'personalized' may also serve just as well as a reference here). The mean effect on each of the categorical independent variables is thus '0' (Table 6.10).

Table 6.10

	Original coding	Coding as a function of research question
Variable 'anonymity'		
Anonymous	1	1
Non-anonymous	2	−1
Variable 'personalization'		
Personalized	1	1
Non-personalized	2	−1

In terms of SPSS input, the above ultimately results in the window as shown in Figure 6.47.

Figure 6.47

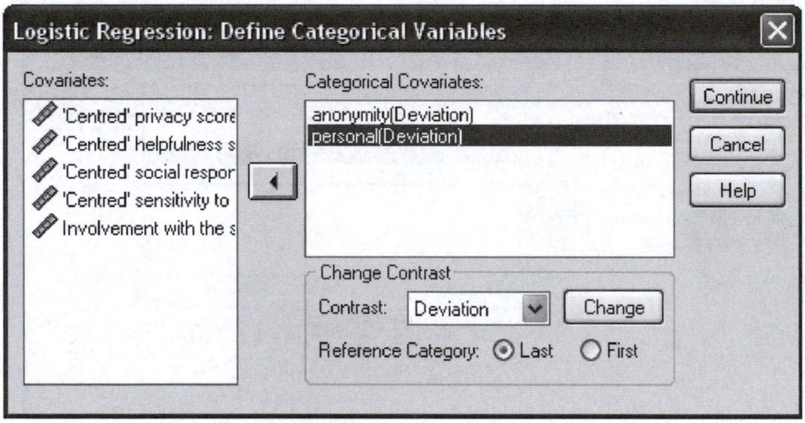

Interpretation of the SPSS output

The SPSS output will be shown and interpreted as a function of the seven specific research questions.

Research question 1: Does the involvement with the subject have a significant effect on the response in the case of an anonymous version?

In total, 303 students are included in the analysis (respondent number '585' was deleted on the basis of the outlier analysis) (Figure 6.48).

Figure 6.48

Case Processing Summary			N	Percent
Selected cases	Included in analysis		303	100.0
	Missing cases		0	.0
	Total		303	100.0
Unselected cases			0	.0
Total			303	100.0

Unweighted Cases[a]

[a]If weight is in effect, see classification table for the total number of cases

With regard to the dependent variable 'mail survey response', the category 'response' is coded as '1' and 'no response' as '0'. The model thus calculates the probability of 'responses' to the survey (Figure 6.49).

Figure 6.49

Dependent Variable Encoding

Original Value	Internal Value
No response	0
Response	1

The coding of the categorical variables 'personalization' and 'anonymity' corresponds to those which are indicated in Table 6.6, and ensures that the regression coefficient b_6 may be interpreted in the context of an anonymous survey, making an abstraction of the fact whether or not it is personalized (Figure 6.50).

Figure 6.50

Categorical Variables Codings

		Frequency	Parameter Coding (1)
Personalization	Personalized survey	152	1.000
	Non personalized survey	151	−1.000
Anonymity	Anonymous survey	152	.000
	Non anonymous survey	151	1.000

The effect of 'the involvement with the subject of the survey' on 'the response' may be seen in regression coefficient b_6 (the B-coefficient linked to the variable [sinvolv]), which is equal to .180 (Figure 6.51).

Figure 6.51

		B	S.E.	Wald	df	Sig.	Exp(B)
Step 1[a]	sprivcen	−.087	.137	.396	1	.529	.917
	shelpcen	.242	.131	3.420	1	.064	1.274
	srespcen	.153	.116	1.737	1	.188	1.165
	anonymity(1)	−.531	.540	.969	1	.325	.588
	personal(1)	.283	.269	1.102	1	.294	1.327
	sinvolv	.180	.109	2.741	1	.098	1.197
	ssensitcen	−.197	.184	1.147	1	.284	.821
	anonymity(1) by sinvolv	.360	.173	4.339	1	.037	1.433
	anonymity(1) by ssensitcen	−.070	.281	.062	1	.804	.933
	personal(1) by sinvolv	−.010	.085	.014	1	.906	.990
	personal(1) by ssensitcen	−.068	.141	.233	1	.629	.934
	Constant	−.186	.364	.262	1	.609	.830

Variables in the Equation

[a]Variable(s) entered on step 1: sprivcen, shelpcen, srespcen, anonymity, personal, sinvolv, ssensitcen, anonymity * sinvolv, anonymity * ssensitcen, personal * sinvolv, personal * ssensitcen

This value indicates a positive relationship, if the coefficient differs significantly from zero. In order to determine this, the researcher will examine the p-value (Sig.), and will have to conclude that this is not the case (.098 > .05). Therefore, involvement does not have a significant effect on the response in the case of an anonymous version. Here, an abstraction is made of the personalization level, and the non-significant effect takes place in a context of a mean attachment to privacy, a mean helpfulness, a mean sense of social responsibility, and a mean sensitivity to the subject. It is important to note that all of the following effects must be interpreted within a context of a mean attachment to privacy, a mean helpfulness, a mean sense of social responsibility, and a mean sensitivity to the subject, however this will not be repeated each time.

On the basis of Figure 6.51, Logit-comparison (2) may be shown as follows:

$$\text{Response} \cong Z = -.186 + .180 \text{ Involvement}$$

This comparison shows the relationship between involvement and response in the event of an anonymous survey, and may be visualized on the basis of a straight line with slope .180 and intercept −.186. Fill in two concrete values for 'involvement' (e.g., the two most extreme values, '1' and '7'), calculate the corresponding Z-values[7] (Table 6.11), and draw (e.g., using Excel) the straight line as shown in Figure 6.55.

Table 6.11

Anonymous version	
Logit-comparison	Z = −.186 + .180*Involvement
Involvement = 1	−.006
Involvement = 7	1.074
Probability of responses to mail survey	Probability(Response) = $e^z/(1 + e^z)$
Involvement = 1	.499
Involvement = 7	.745

Research question 2: Does the involvement with the subject have a significant effect on the response in the case of a non-anonymous version?

Make sure to clearly indicate the coding for the categorical variables each time. This is of vital importance since the regression coefficients are interpreted each time within a specific context, for example, the non-anonymous survey, making abstraction of the personalization level (Figure 6.52).

Figure 6.52

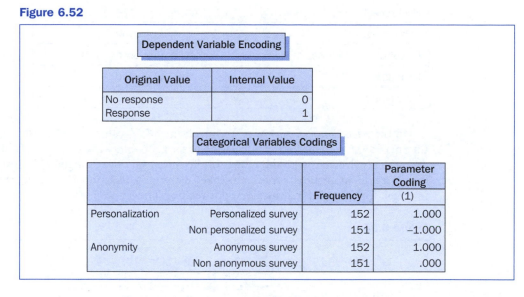

Dependent Variable Encoding

Original Value	Internal Value
No response	0
Response	1

Categorical Variables Codings

		Frequency	Parameter Coding (1)
Personalization	Personalized survey	152	1.000
	Non personalized survey	151	−1.000
Anonymity	Anonymous survey	152	1.000
	Non anonymous survey	151	.000

In the case of a non-anonymous survey, the involvement with the subject has a significant effect on the response (p-value < .001), and this is in a positive direction (b_6 = .540 > 0) (Figure 6.53).

Figure 6.53

Variables in the Equation

		B	S.E.	Wald	df	Sig.	Exp(B)
Step 1[a]	sprivcen	−.087	.137	.396	1	.529	.917
	shelpcen	.242	.131	3.420	1	.064	1.274
	srespcen	.153	.116	1.737	1	.188	1.165
	anonymity(1)	.531	.540	.969	1	.325	1.701
	personal(1)	.283	.269	1.102	1	.294	1.327
	sinvolv	.540	.137	15.572	1	.000	1.715
	ssensitcen	−.267	.216	1.526	1	.217	.766
	anonymity(1) by sinvolv	−.360	.173	4.339	1	.037	.698
	anonymity(1) by ssensitcen	.070	.281	.062	1	.804	1.072
	personal(1) by sinvolv	−.010	.085	.014	1	.906	.990
	personal(1) by ssensitcen	−.068	.141	.233	1	.629	.934
	Constant	−.718	.406	3.122	1	.077	.488

[a]Variable(s) entered on step 1: sprivcen, shelpcen, srespcen, anonymity, personal, sinvolv, ssensitcen, anonymity * sinvolv, anonymity * ssensitcen, personal * sinvolv, personal * ssensitcen

Concrete values for Logit-comparison (2) may also be filled in here (Table 6.12), which leads to the straight line visualized in Figure 6.55 under the 'Non-anonymous' label.

Table 6.12

Non-anonymous version	
Logit-comparison	Z = −.718 + .540*Involvement
Involvement = 1	−.178
Involvement = 7	3.062
Probability of responses to mail survey	Probability(Response) = $e^z/(1 + e^z)$
Involvement = 1	.456
Involvement = 7	.955

On the basis of concrete values for 'involvement', Z-values may be calculated, which in turn may serve as input for the calculation of the probability of a response (Table 6.12). This way, the involvement with the subject of the survey and the probability of response, in this case to a non-anonymous survey, are linked directly to one another, and Figure 6.54 (drawn in Excel, for example) indicates that this relationship is non-linear.

Figure 6.54

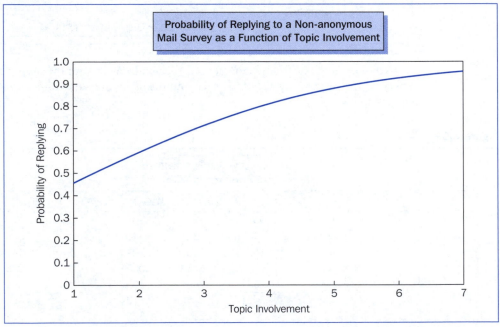

An increase in the involvement with the subject corresponds to an increase in the probability of a response to the non-anonymous version, however this increase in probability weakens as the score for involvement increases.

Research question 3: Is the effect of involvement on response different for an anonymous and a non-anonymous version?

Figure 6.55

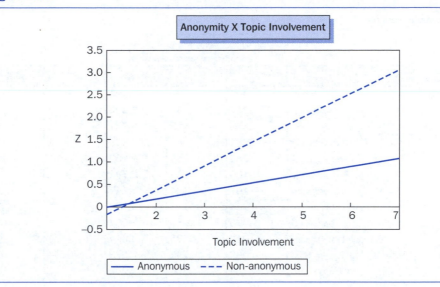

Figure 6.55 leads to the assumption that the effect of involvement on the response will be different for both versions, since the slopes of both curves differ considerably from one another. In addition, the researcher has learned in answering research questions 1 and 2 that in the event of the anonymous version, there is no significant relationship between involvement and response (slope = 0), whereas this relationship is present for the non-anonymous version (slope > 0). If the researcher would now specifically like to find out whether this difference in slopes differs significantly from zero (and therefore whether the effect of involvement on response is different for an anonymous and a non-anonymous version), then he may use the SPSS outputs included previously, namely Figures 6.51 and 6.53 (linked to research questions 1 and 2). These SPSS outputs are re-examined in Figure 6.56.

Instead of the regression coefficient linked to the 'involvement' variable (b_6), it is the coefficient now linked to the interaction term 'anonymity × involvement' (b_8) which is crucial. In this case, b_8 indicates the difference in slope between the anonymous and the non-anonymous version, and this appears to be .360. In addition, this difference differs significantly from zero since the p-value is less than .05 (.037). The researcher may then conclude the following: 'a significant interaction exists between the variables "involvement" and "anonymity"', or, to put it another way, 'the variable "anonymity" moderates the relationship between the involvement with the subject of the survey and the response'.

It may be noted here that with regard to coefficient b_8 and its p-value, the researcher may consult Figure 6.51 as well as Figure 6.53 (that is, both the upper and the lower table in Figure 6.56): the p-values are after all identical, and the coefficients only differ from one another in sign. In Figure 6.51, coefficient b_8 shows that the slope of the 'non-anonymous' version is .360 points steeper than that of the 'anonymous' version. In Figure 6.53, coefficient b_8 shows that the slope of the 'anonymous' version is .360 points flatter than that of the 'non-anonymous' version. Both numbers thus lead to the same conclusion. In comparison with the previous three research questions, from now on, the personalization level of the survey is what will be significant, and no longer the fact of whether or not the survey is anonymous. Since the approach is identical, only the differences which arise will be the object of focus, such as variations in coding.

Figure 6.56

Anonymous Version

Variables in the Equation

		B	S.E.	Wald	df	Sig.	Exp(B)
Step 1[a]	sprivcen	−.087	.137	.396	1	.529	.917
	shelpcen	.242	.131	3.420	1	.064	1.274
	srespcen	.153	.116	1.737	1	.188	1.165
	anonymity(1)	−.531	.540	.969	1	.325	.588
	personal(1)	.283	.269	1.102	1	.294	1.327
	sinvolv	.180	.109	2.741	1	.098	1.197
	ssensitcen	−.197	.184	1.147	1	.284	.821
	anonymity(1) by sinvolv	.360	.173	4.339	1	.037	1.433
	anonymity(1) by ssensitcen	−.070	.281	.062	1	.804	.933
	personal(1) by sinvolv	−.010	.085	.014	1	.906	.990
	personal(1) by ssensitcen	−.068	.141	.233	1	.629	.934
	Constant	−.186	.364	.262	1	.609	.830

[a]Variable(s) entered on step 1: sprivcen, shelpcen, srespcen, anonymity, personal, sinvolv, ssensitcen, anonymity * sinvolv, anonymity * ssensitcen, personal * sinvolv, personal * ssensitcen

Non-anonymous Version

Variables in the Equation

		B	S.E.	Wald	df	Sig.	Exp(B)
Step 1[a]	sprivcen	−.087	.137	.396	1	.529	.917
	shelpcen	.242	.131	3.420	1	.064	1.274
	srespcen	.153	.116	1.737	1	.188	1.165
	anonymity(1)	.531	.540	.969	1	.325	1.701
	personal(1)	.283	.269	1.102	1	.294	1.327
	sinvolv	.540	.137	15.572	1	.000	1.715
	ssensitcen	−.267	.216	1.526	1	.217	.766
	anonymity(1) by sinvolv	−.360	.173	4.339	1	.037	.698
	anonymity(1) by ssensitcen	.070	.281	.062	1	.804	1.072
	personal(1) by sinvolv	−.010	.085	.014	1	.906	.990
	personal(1) by ssensitcen	−.068	.141	.233	1	.629	.934
	Constant	−.718	.406	3.122	1	.077	.488

[a]Variable(s) entered on step 1: sprivcen, shelpcen, srespcen, anonymity, personal, sinvolv, ssensitcen, anonymity * sinvolv, anonymity * ssensitcen, personal * sinvolv, personal * ssensitcen

Research question 4: Does the involvement with the subject have a significant effect on the response in the case of a personalized version?

Figure 6.57

		B	S.E.	Wald	df	Sig.	Exp(B)
			Variables in the Equation				
Step 1[a]	sprivcen	−.087	.137	.396	1	.529	.917
	shelpcen	.242	.131	3.420	1	.064	1.274
	srespcen	.153	.116	1.737	1	.188	1.165
	anonymity(1)	.266	.270	.969	1	.325	1.304
	personal(1)	−.565	.538	1.102	1	.294	.568
	sinvolv	.350	.128	7.475	1	.006	1.419
	ssensitcen	−.300	.217	1.911	1	.167	.741
	anonymity(1) by sinvolv	−.180	.086	4.339	1	.037	.835
	anonymity(1) by ssensitcen	.035	.140	.062	1	.804	1.035
	personal(1) by sinvolv	.020	.169	.014	1	.906	1.020
	personal(1) by ssensitcen	.136	.283	.233	1	.629	1.146
	Constant	−.169	.394	.185	1	.667	.844

[a]Variable(s) entered on step 1: sprivcen, shelpcen, srespcen, anonymity, personal, sinvolv, ssensitcen, anonymity * sinvolv, anonymity * ssensitcen, personal * sinvolv, personal * ssensitcen

The involvement with the subject of the survey has a significant effect on the response (p-value = .006 < .05), and this effect is positive (b_6 = .350 > 0): an increase in involvement represents an increase in response, in the case of a personalized version (Figure 6.57).

Figure 6.59 will present a visualization of the relationship which has been found, and is based on the following Logit-comparison:

$$\text{Response} \cong Z = -.169 + .350 * \text{Involvement}$$

Research question 5: Does the involvement with the subject have a significant effect on the response in the case of a non-personalized version?

Figure 6.58

		B	S.E.	Wald	df	Sig.	Exp(B)
			Variables in the Equation				
Step 1[a]	sprivcen	−.087	.137	.396	1	.529	.917
	shelpcen	.242	.131	3.420	1	.064	1.274
	srespcen	.153	.116	1.737	1	.188	1.165
	anonymity(1)	.266	.270	.969	1	.325	1.304
	personal(1)	.565	.538	1.102	1	.294	1.760
	sinvolv	.370	.116	10.104	1	.001	1.447
	ssensitcen	−.164	.184	.790	1	.374	.849
	anonymity(1) by sinvolv	−.180	.086	4.339	1	.037	.835
	anonymity(1) by ssensitcen	.035	.140	.062	1	.804	1.035
	personal(1) by sinvolv	−.020	.169	.014	1	.906	.980
	personal(1) by ssensitcen	−.136	.283	.233	1	.629	.872
	Constant	−.734	.376	3.815	1	.051	.480

[a]Variable(s) entered on step 1: sprivcen, shelpcen, srespcen, anonymity, personal, sinvolv, ssensitcen, anonymity * sinvolv, anonymity * ssensitcen, personal * sinvolv, personal * ssensitcen

In the case of the non-personalized survey, the involvement also has a significant effect on the response (p-value = .001 < .05), which is positive (b_6 = .370 > 0) (Figure 6.58). The Logit-comparison for the non-personalized version is the following:

$$\text{Response} \cong Z = -.734 + .370*\text{Involvement}$$

This comparison is also shown in Figure 6.59.

Figure 6.59

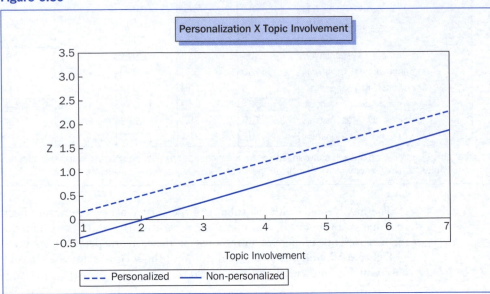

Research question 6: Is the effect of involvement on response different for a personalized version and a non-personalized version?

Figure 6.59 shows that the curves linked to the personalized and the non-personalized survey run nearly parallel, which leads to the strong suspicion that the relationship between involvement and response is identical for both versions. The researcher can test this explicitly by examining the coefficient linked to the interaction term 'personalization $\times$ involvement' (b_{10}) in Figure 6.57 or Figure 6.58, and the corresponding p-value (see grey-coloured squares): b_{10} = .02 (or $-.02$) and p-value = .906 (> .05). Since b_{10} indicates the difference in slope between both curves, and this difference does not appear to differ significantly from zero, the researcher may conclude that the effect of involvement on the response is no different for a personalized than for a non-personalized version of the survey. In this context, one also says that the interaction between involvement and personalization is not significant, or that personalization is not a moderator of the relationship between involvement and response.

Research question 7: Does the involvement with the subject have a positive effect on the response?

One may in fact conclude that there is a significant (p-value < .001), positive (b_6 = .360 > 0) effect of involvement on response (Figure 6.60).

Figure 6.60

Variables in the Equation

	B	S.E.	Wald	df	Sig.	Exp(B)
Step 1[a] sprivcen	−.087	.137	.396	1	.529	.917
shelpcen	.242	.131	3.420	1	.064	1.274
srespcen	.153	.116	1.737	1	.188	1.165
anonymity(1)	.266	.270	.969	1	.325	1.304
personal(1)	.283	.269	1.102	1	.294	1.327
sinvolv	.360	.088	16.636	1	.000	1.433
ssensitcen	−.232	.143	2.618	1	.106	.793
anonymity(1) by sinvolv	−.180	.086	4.339	1	.037	.835
anonymity(1) by ssensitcen	.035	.140	.062	1	.804	1.035
personal(1) by sinvolv	−.010	.085	.014	1	.906	.990
personal(1) by ssensitcen	−.068	.141	.233	1	.629	.934
Constant	−.452	.275	2.698	1	.101	.636

[a]Variable(s) entered on step 1: sprivcen, shelpcen, srespcen, anonymity, personal, sinvolv, ssensitcen, anonymity * sinvolv, anonymity * ssensitcen, personal * sinvolv, personal * ssensitcen

Important guidelines

In performing a logistic regression with interaction terms, the researcher must always take the following three points into consideration:

- Report the method used to code the categorical independent variables and the manner in which the continuous independent variables are scaled (e.g., centring them around the mean), and use this information to interpret the regression coefficients and the tests related to this.

- Code the categorical independent variables and rescale the continuous independent variables so that interesting theoretical and practical questions may be answered.

- If an interaction term is part of the regression model, be sure to include each of its components in the model (even if it appears from later analyses that they are not significant). In applying the 'stepwise' method (Example 3 examines this method in more depth), check the sequence in which interaction terms and their components are added/deleted to/from the model. In this way, the interaction term is not included until each of its components have been included, and none of the components are eliminated as long as the interaction is still part of the model.

One last remark

Strange behaviour on the part of regression coefficients (B) or the standard errors (S.E.) such as the presence of large values may be caused by: (1) multicollinearity, or (2) a sample which is too small. When running a logistic regression analysis the number of cases is preferred to be larger than the number of parameters to be estimated times 10.

Example 3

The 'stepwise' method, in addition to the 'enter' method, and more than one 'block'

Managerial problem

The current example assumes the same datasets as the one used in Example 2[8], however only applies to the variables 'sensitivity of the subject', 'involvement with the subject', 'anonymity', and 'personalization'. The objective of Example 3 is to define more than one block of independent variables, and to use the 'Stepwise' method in addition to the 'Enter' method. The focus will then primarily be on the interpretation of the 'Step Chi-square', 'Block Chi-square' and 'Model Chi-square' statistics.

Problem

Develop the model below on the basis of the data in the dataset *Involvement with the subject, anonymity and personalization .sav*:

$$\text{Response} \cong Z = b_0 + b_1 \text{ Sensitivity} + b_2 \text{ Involvement} + b_3 \text{ Personalization} + b_4 \text{ Anonymity}$$

Include the 'sensitivity' variable as the only variable in the first block of independent variables, and select the 'Enter' method (this allows the variable 'sensitivity' to still be part of the model, even when it later proves to have an insignificant influence on the response; see Chapter 5). Add the variables 'involvement', 'personalization' and 'anonymity' to the model in a second phase, by assigning them to the second block, and select the 'Stepwise' method (the three variables are then added to/deleted from the model step-by-step, and the variables which are ultimately included all have a significant influence on the response). This way, the researcher will be able to determine the effect of 'involvement', 'personalization' and 'anonymity' on the response, 'controlled' for the variable 'sensitivity'.

Solution

SPSS commands

Figure 6.61

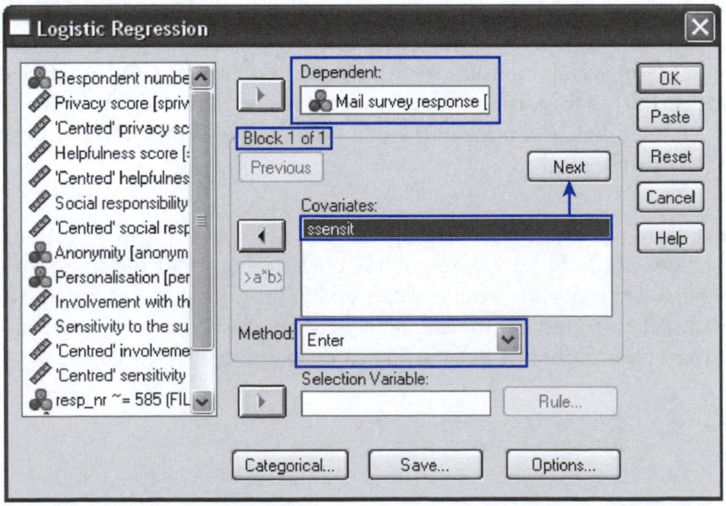

In the main menu, go to Analyze/Regression/Binary Logistic, and the 'Logistic Regression' window (Figure 6.61) will appear. Move the variable 'response' from the list on the left-hand side to the 'Dependent' box, and move the 'sensitivity' variable to the 'Covariates' box. This last variable will automatically become part of the first block, and will be subjected to the 'Enter' method.

Define the second block of independent variables by clicking 'Next' and then to move the three variables 'involvement', 'personalization' and 'anonymity' from the list on the left-hand side to the 'Covariates' box.

Figure 6.62

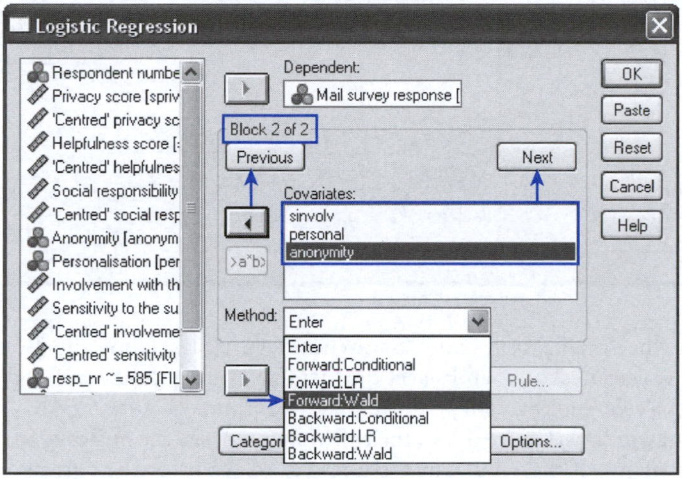

The 'Stepwise' method is applicable to the variables 'involvement', 'personalization' and 'anonymity', and more specifically, the 'Forward: Wald' procedure (Figure 6.62). This last procedure will, unlike the other 'Forward' procedures, base the elimination of a variable from the model on the relevant p-value, which is related to the 'Wald' statistic.

The researcher may alternate between blocks 1 and 2 by using the 'Previous' and 'Next' buttons (Figure 6.62). After clicking the 'Previous' button for example, the first block will appear again in the 'Logistic Regression' window (Figure 6.63).

Figure 6.63

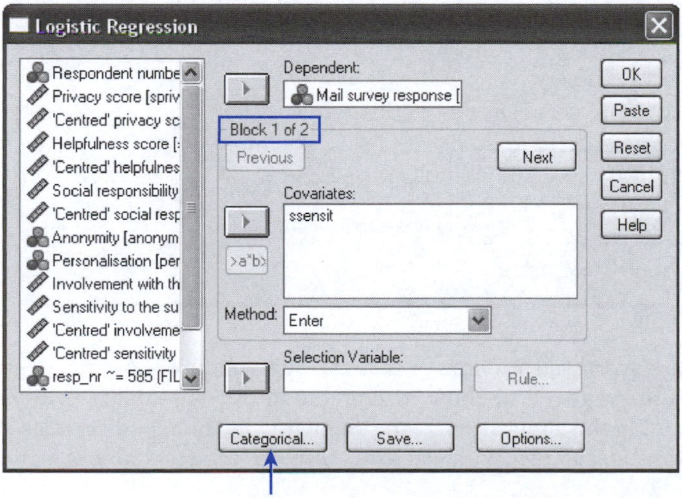

Click 'Categorical' to define the variables 'personalization' and 'anonymity' as 'categorical' independent variables. For this definition, it does not matter whether the contents of block 1 or block 2 are shown in the 'Logistic Regression' window.

Figure 6.64

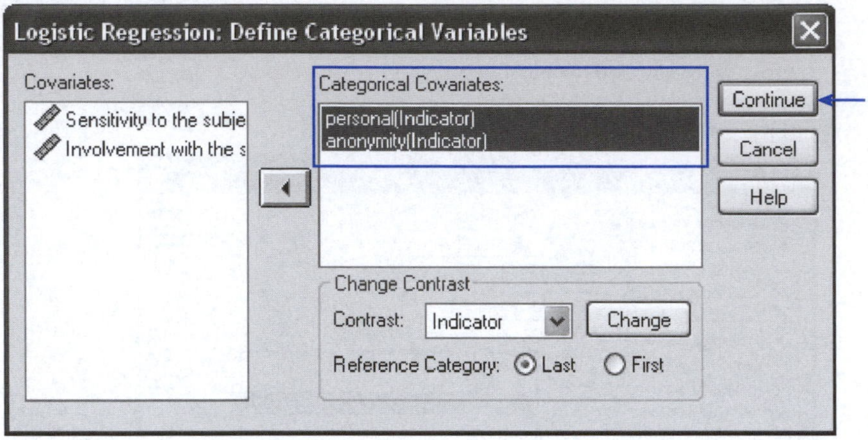

Move the 'personalization' and 'anonymity' variables from the 'Covariates' to the 'Categorical Covariates' box, and select the 'default' coding ('indicator coding' with the last category as the reference category). Now click 'Continue' (Figure 6.64).

In the main window (Figure 6.63), the researcher will see the buttons 'Save' and 'Options' again. The contents of these buttons are not very relevant for the current example, and we will not discuss them any further here.

Figure 6.65

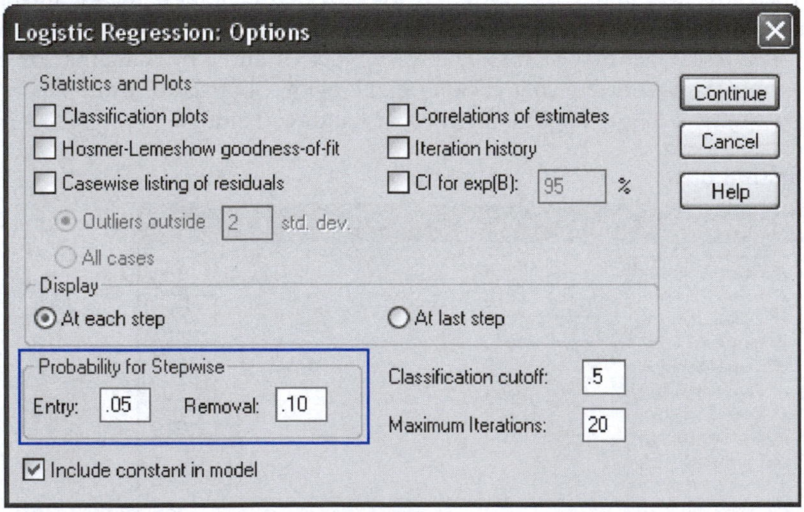

One remark worth mentioning is that the sub-window 'Logistic Regression: Options' (Figure 6.65) shows the 'Probability-to-Enter' and the 'Probability-to-Remove'. These values are relevant in the application of the 'Stepwise' method, and serve as critical values for the 'Score' statistic, and the 'Wald' statistic, respectively: a variable is included in the model if the p-value linked to the 'Score' statistic is less than .05, and a variable is eliminated if the p-value linked to the 'Wald' statistic is greater than .10.

Interpretation of the SPSS output

Figure 6.66

Omnibus Tests of Model Coefficients		Chi-Square	df	Sig.
Step 1	Step	1.866	1	.172
	Block	1.866	1	.172
	Model	1.866	1	.172

Figure 6.67

Variables in the Equation		B	S.E.	Wald	df	Sig.	Exp(B)
Step 1[a]	ssensit	−.168	.123	1.861	1	.173	.846
	Constant	.775	.211	13.504	1	.000	2.171

[a]Variable(s) entered on step 1: ssensit

'Block 0' refers to the null-model, which only includes a constant term. 'Block 1' will add the 'sensitivity' variable to the null model according to the 'Enter' method. Even if the 'Model Chi-square' indicates an insignificant improvement in the current model with respect to the null model (p-value = .172 > .05), and the regression coefficient linked to the 'sensitivity' variable (−.168) does not differ significantly from zero (p-value = .173 > .05), and the sensitivity thus has no significant effect on the response, this variable will still be part of the model (Figures 6.66 and 6.67).

Figure 6.68

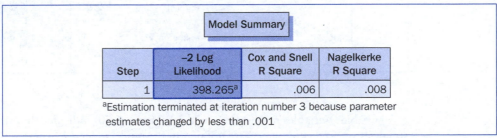

Model Summary			
Step	−2 Log Likelihood	Cox and Snell R Square	Nagelkerke R Square
1	398.265[a]	.006	.008

[a]Estimation terminated at iteration number 3 because parameter estimates changed by less than .001

The '−2LL' for the current model ('constant-sensitivity' model) is 398.265 (Figure 6.68) whereas this is 400.131 for the null model (398.265 + 1.866).

'Block 2' stands for the step-by-step addition or deletion of the variables 'involvement', 'personalization' and 'anonymity' to or from the model, and which initially only contains a constant and the 'sensitivity' variable.

Figure 6.69

		B	S.E.	Wald	df	Sig.	Exp(B)
Step 1[a]	ssensit	−.249	.136	3.389	1	.066	.779
	sinvolv	.348	.078	19.848	1	.000	1.416
	Constant	−.147	.292	.252	1	.615	.864
Step 2[b]	ssensit	−.237	.139	2.883	1	.090	.789
	sinvolv	.354	.079	20.029	1	.000	1.425
	personal(1)	.588	.251	5.491	1	.019	1.801
	Constant	−.467	.326	2.051	1	.152	.627

Variables in the Equation

[a]Variable(s) entered on step 1: sinvolv
[b]Variable(s) entered on step 2: personal

The second block contains two steps: in a first step, the variable 'involvement' is added to the model, and in a second step, the variable 'personalization' is included (Figure 6.69). The regression coefficient of the variable 'sensitivity' does not differ significantly from zero in steps 1 and 2 (p-values = .066 and .090 > .05), yet this variable is part of the model. The 'Enter' method, which includes a variable in the model independent of significance, is responsible for this. It may be noted here that if the variable 'sensitivity' were to be subjected to the 'Stepwise' procedure and would have ever achieved a p-value less than .05 ('Probability-to-Enter'), it would also continue to be part of the model, given the fact that the p-values (.066 and .090) are less than the 'Probability-to-Remove' (.10).

Figure 6.70

Variables not in the Equation

			Score	df	Sig.
Step 1	Variables	personal(1)	5.544	1	.019
		anonymity(1)	2.597	1	.107
	Overall statistics		8.274	2	.016
Step 2	Variables	anonymity(1)	2.783	1	.095
	Overall statistics		2.783	1	.095

The table 'Variables not in the Equation' (Figure 6.70) indicates that the variables 'personalization' and 'anonymity' are not part of the model in Step 1, whereas the 'involvement' variable is included. The p-values related to the 'personalization' (.019) and 'anonymity' (.107) variables in Step 1 indicate that the 'personalization' variable, and not the 'anonymity' variable may be added to the model in a subsequent step {p-value$_{\text{Personalization (anonymity)}}$ = .019 (.107) <(>) 'Probability-to-Enter' = .05}. In Step 2, only the 'anonymity' variable is not included, nor will this variable be added in a third step, since the p-value (.095) is greater than the 'Probability-to-Enter' value (.05).

Figure 6.71

	Model Summary		
Step	**−2 Log Likelihood**	**Cox and Snell R Square**	**Nagelkerke R Square**
1	376.133[a]	.076	.104
2	370.568[a]	.093	.127

[a]Estimation terminated at iteration number 4 because parameter estimates changed by less than .001

The researcher has been able to derive the '−2LL' values from Block 1 which are related to the null-model and the 'constant-sensitivity' model. The 'Model Summary' from Block 2 (Figure 6.71) shows these values for the 'constant-sensitivity-involvement' and 'constant-sensitivity-involvement-personalization' models. Table 6.13 summarizes these values in a comprehensible manner.

Table 6.13

Model	*Formation*	*−2LL*
Null model ('constant' model)	Block 0	400.131
'Constant-sensitivity' model	Block 1	398.265
'Constant-sensitivity-involvement' model	Block 2 − Step 1	376.133
'Constant-sensitivity-involvement-personalization' model	Block 2 − Step 2	370.568

The addition of variables to the model leads to a drop in '−2LL' which indicates a 'probable' improvement in the quality of the model.

Figure 6.72

		Omnibus Tests of Model Coefficients		
		Chi-Square	**df**	**Sig.**
Step 1	Step	22.132	1	.000
	Block	22.132	1	.000
	Model	23.998	2	.000
Step 2	Step	5.565	1	.018
	Block	27.697	2	.000
	Model	29.563	3	.000

The decrease in '−2LL' which occurs in the transition from one model to another and the significance of this increase in quality of the model may be seen in the statistics 'Step

Chi-square', 'Block Chi-square' and 'Model Chi-square', and the corresponding p-values (Sig.) (Figure 6.72). These statistics are explained further in Table 6.14.

Table 6.14

Step 1 'Step Chi-square'	The decrease in '−2LL' during the transition from the **'constant-sensitivity' model** to the **'constant-sensitivity-involvement' model**. This decrease appears to be significant (p-value = .000 < .05), which indicates that the addition of the variable 'involvement' to the model in Step 1 significantly improves its quality.
Step 1 'Block Chi-square'	The decrease in '−2LL' during the transition from Block 1 (the **'constant-sensitivity' model**) to Block 2 (the **'constant-sensitivity-involvement' model**), which has now only added the variable 'involvement' to the model. This value is identical to that shown for 'Step 1 − Step Chi-square'.
Step 1 'Model Chi-square'	The decrease in '−2LL' during the transition from the null-model (the **'constant' model**) to Block 2 (the **'constant-sensitivity-involvement' model**), which has now only added the variable 'involvement' to the model.
Step 2 'Step Chi-square'	The decrease in '−2LL' during the transition from the **'constant-sensitivity-involvement' model** to the **'constant-sensitivity-involvement-personalization' model**. This decrease appears to be significant (p-value = .018 < .05), which indicates that the addition of the variable 'personalization' to the model in Step 2 significantly improves its quality.
Step 2 'Block Chi-square'	The decrease in '−2LL' during the transition from Block 1 (the **'constant-sensitivity' model**) to Block 2 (the **'constant-sensitivity-involvement-personalization' model**), which has now added the variables 'involvement' and 'personalization' to the model. This value is no longer identical to that shown for 'Step 2 − Step Chi-square'.
Step 2 'Model Chi-square'	The decrease in '−2LL' during the transition from the null-model (the **'constant' model**) to Block 2 (the **'constant-sensitivity-involvement-personalization' model**), that has now added the variables 'involvement' and 'personalization' to the model.

The 'df' values in Figure 6.72 show the difference in the number of parameters to be estimated between the two models for which the difference in '−2LL' value is calculated. The number of degrees of freedom related to the 'Step 2 – Model Chi-square' statistic is equal to '3', given the decrease in '−2LL' is determined during the transition from the 'constant' model (1 parameter to be estimated) to the 'constant-sensitivity-involvement-personalization' model (4 parameters to be estimated).

Conclusion: the researcher will opt for the 'constant-sensitivity-involvement-personalization' model, for which two points may be noted: (1) 'sensitivity' does not have a significant effect on the response (p-value = .090; Figure 6.69), however it is part of the model because of the choice to use the 'Enter' method; and (2) the 'anonymity' variable does not correspond to this model, given it is subjected to the 'Stepwise' procedure and its p-value (.107; .095; Figure 6.70) is never less than the 'Probability-to-Enter' (.05).

Example 4

Categorical independent variables with more than two categories

Managerial problem

The researchers would like to find out what the effect is of 'different types of incentives' on 'the response to a mail survey'. To do so, they sent a survey to 524 students, the topic of which was 'the increasing power of the extreme right in the government', and which was accompanied by: (1) no incentive whatsoever; (2) a lottery ticket (direct incentive); or (3) the promise to send a lottery ticket later once the researcher received the completed survey back from the respondent (indirect incentive). In a previous phase, these students had shared their involvement with the subject with the researchers. For each of the students, the response to the mail survey ([response]: response (1) or no response (0)), the type of incentive ([incent]: no incentive (1), a direct incentive (2) or an indirect incentive (3)), and the involvement with the subject of the survey ([involv]: low involvement (0), . . . , high involvement (6)) was recorded in a dataset, part of which is shown in Figure 6.73.

Figure 6.73

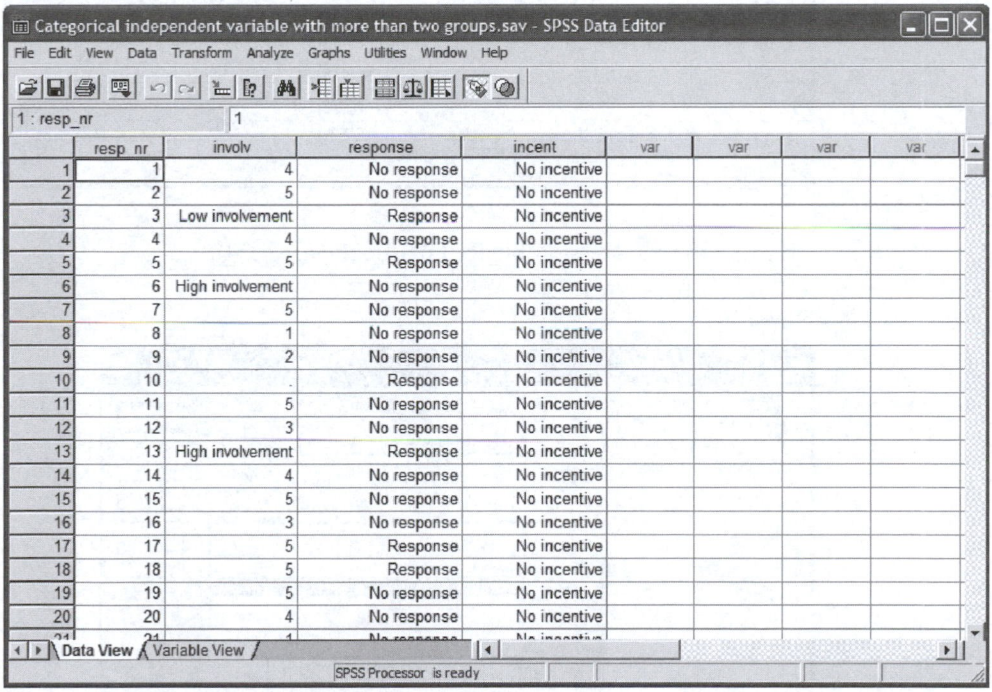

	resp nr	involv	response	incent	var	var	var	var
1	1	4	No response	No incentive				
2	2	5	No response	No incentive				
3	3	Low involvement	Response	No incentive				
4	4	4	No response	No incentive				
5	5	5	Response	No incentive				
6	6	High involvement	No response	No incentive				
7	7	5	No response	No incentive				
8	8	1	No response	No incentive				
9	9	2	No response	No incentive				
10	10	.	Response	No incentive				
11	11	5	No response	No incentive				
12	12	3	No response	No incentive				
13	13	High involvement	Response	No incentive				
14	14	4	No response	No incentive				
15	15	5	No response	No incentive				
16	16	3	No response	No incentive				
17	17	5	Response	No incentive				
18	18	5	Response	No incentive				
19	19	5	No response	No incentive				
20	20	4	No response	No incentive				

Problem

On the basis of the data above (*Categorical independent variable with more than two groups.sav*), develop the following model:

$$\text{Response} \cong Z = b_0 + b_1 \text{ Involvement} + b_2 \text{ Incentive}$$

To estimate the model, use the 'Enter' method. Find out what the effect is on the 'log odds' (response) of the use of : (1) a direct incentive compared with no incentive at all; (2) an indirect incentive compared with no incentive; and (3) no incentive/direct incentive/ indirect incentive compared with the mean effect of the three types of incentive.

Solution

SPSS commands

Figure 6.74

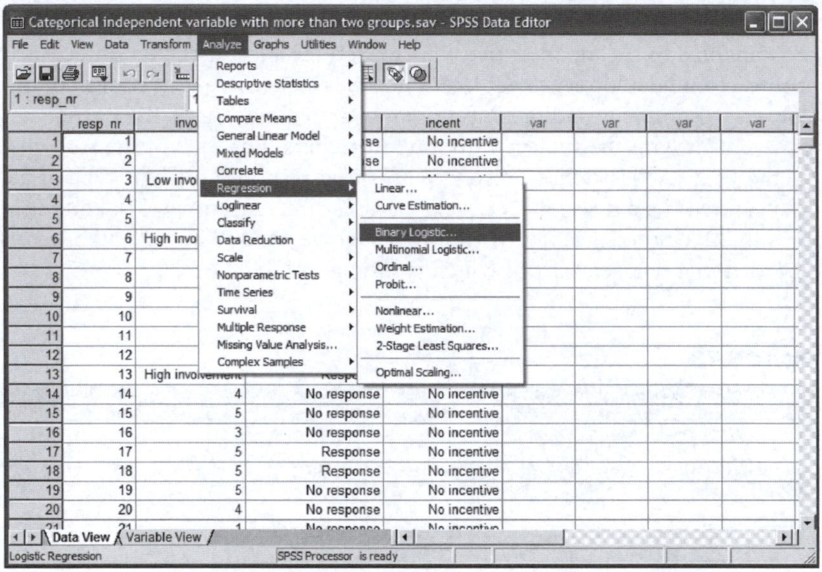

Go to Analyze/Regression/Binary Logistic (Figure 6.74).

Figure 6.75

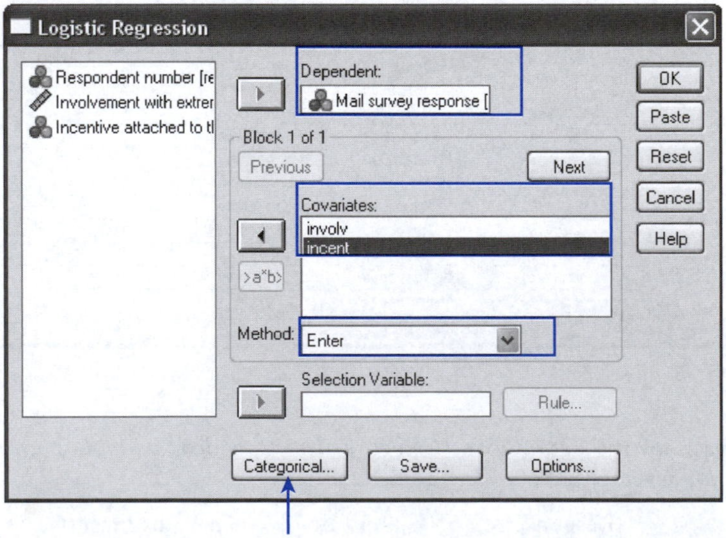

Move the 'response' variable to the 'Dependent' box, and the 'involvement' and 'incentive' variables to the 'Covariates' box (Figure 6.75).

Select the 'Enter' method, and click on 'Categorical' at the bottom of the window to indicate that the variable 'incentive' is a categorical one.

After defining the 'Logistic Regression: Define Categorical Variables' window (Figure 6.76), click 'Continue'. The 'Save' and 'Options' buttons will not be discussed in further depth here as they are not the focus of the current example.

Figure 6.76

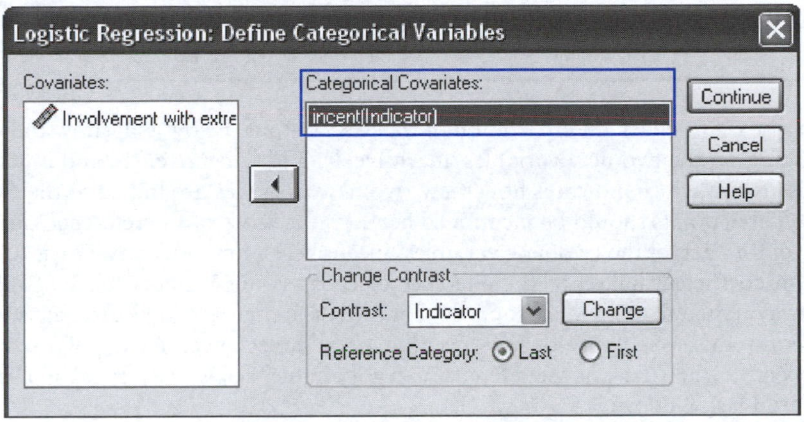

Move the 'incentive' variable in the 'Logistic Regression: Define Categorical Variables' window (Figure 6.76) from the 'Covariates' box to the 'Categorical Covariates' box.

The 'incentive' variable contains three groups: none, direct, and indirect incentives. The result of defining this variable as a 'categorical' independent variable is that SPSS will create two new variables ('incentive(1)' and 'incentive(2)'), one fewer than the number of groups. The way in which these two new variables will be linked to the original variable is a function of the coding (Contrast: Indicator/Deviation; Reference Category: Last/First), which in turn is a function of the research question being asked. This will be explained in more detail on the basis of the two research questions below.

Research question 1: What is the effect of the use of: (1) a direct incentive compared with no incentive at all; and (2) an indirect incentive compared with no incentive on the 'log odds' (response)?

If the regression coefficients for the two new variables are expected to show the effect on the 'log odds' (response) of the use of a certain type of incentive (direct/indirect) **in comparison with a reference category** (no incentive), then 'indicator coding' (1/0) is the recommended method of coding. Considering that 'no incentive' is the reference in the current question, and this category represents the 'first' group of the original variable 'incentive' (see 'SPSS Data Editor', 'Variable View' tab), the researcher sets the 'Reference Category' in the 'Logistic Regression: Define Categorical Variables' window equal to 'First' (Figure 6.77).

Figure 6.77

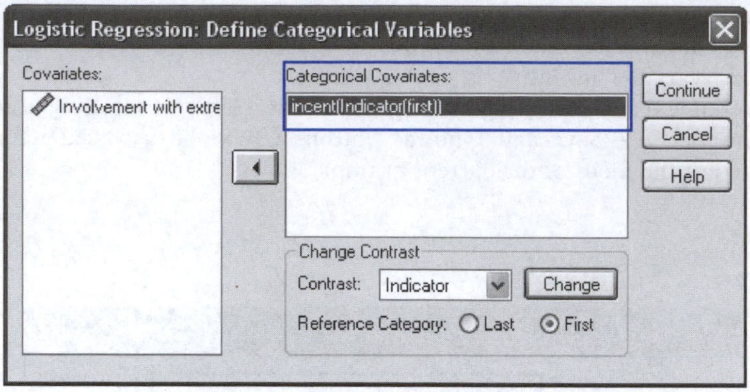

Figure 6.80, under 'Interpretation of the SPSS output' below will show the influence of this coding on the two new variables 'incentive(1)' and 'incentive(2)', and is accompanied by a discussion which indicates how these two new variables are linked to the original variable.

Three points should be mentioned here: (a) the score of the reference category 'no incentive' for each of the two new variables 'incentive(1)' and 'incentive(2)' is '0'; (b) the regression coefficient linked to the reference category is not included in the SPSS output and is always equal to '0'; and (c) suppose that the researcher would like to determine the effect on the response of the use of 'no' incentive or a 'direct' incentive as opposed to an 'indirect' incentive, then 'Last' is the reference category in the 'Logistic Regression: Define Categorical Variables' window.

An in-depth discussion on working with the 'Logistic Regression: Define Categorical Variables' window may be found under Example 2 of this chapter.

Research question 2: What is the effect of the use of no incentive/direct incentive/indirect incentive as compared with the mean effect of the three types of incentive on the 'log odds' (response)?

If the regression coefficients for the two new variables are expected to show the effect on the 'log odds' (response) of the use of a certain type of incentive (none/direct/indirect) **in comparison with the mean effect of the three types of incentive**, then 'deviation coding' ($1/-1$) is the recommended method of coding. 'No' incentive ('First') is also defined as the reference category here (Figure 6.78), however the question here also allows the groups 'direct' and 'indirect' incentive to be specified as the reference.

Figure 6.78

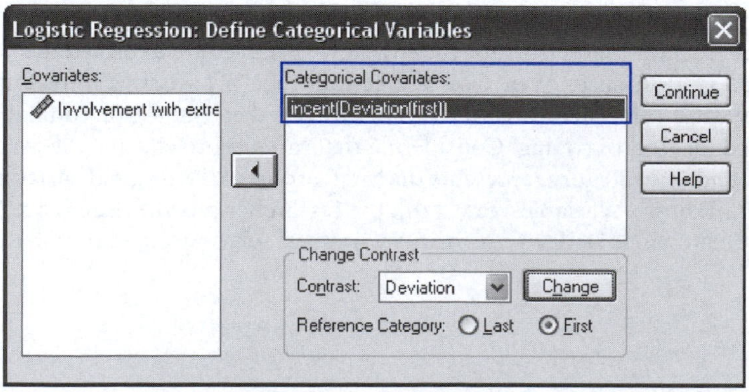

Figure 6.82 under the 'Interpretation of the SPSS output' below will show the influence of this coding on the two new variables 'incentive(1)' and 'incentive(2)', and is also accompanied by a discussion which indicates how these two new variables are linked to the original variable.

Two remarks should be mentioned here: (a) the score of the reference category 'no incentive' for each of the two new variables 'incentive(1)' and 'incentive(2)' is '-1'; (b) the regression coefficient linked to the reference category is not included in the SPSS output yet is no longer equal to '0'. It will be equal to: $-\{\text{coefficient}_{\text{incentive}(1)} + \text{coefficient}_{\text{incentive}(2)}\}$.

Interpretation of the SPSS output

Research question 1: What is the effect of the use of: (1) a direct incentive compared with no incentive at all; and (2) an indirect incentive compared with no incentive on the 'log odds' (response)?

Figure 6.79

Dependent Variable Encoding	
Original Value	Internal Value
No response	0
Response	1

The dependent categorical variable 'response' is coded as '0' in the event of 'no response' and as '1' in the event of a 'response' (Figure 6.79). The regression model will then also calculate the probability of receiving 'responses' to the mail survey.

Figure 6.80

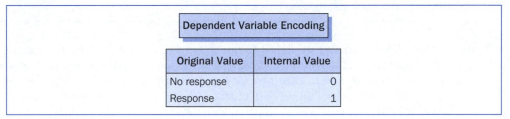

Categorical Variables Coding				
			Parameter Coding	
		Frequency	(1)	(2)
Incentive attached to the survey	No incentive	168	.000	.000
	Direct incentive (independent of sending the survey back)	167	1.000	.000
	Indirect incentive (dependent on sending the survey back)	161	.000	1.000

The 'Frequency' column (Figure 6.80) indicates that 168 students received 'no' incentive, 167 students received a 'direct' incentive, and 161 students received an 'indirect' incentive. The columns 'Parameter coding (1)' and 'Parameter coding (2)' correspond with the two new variables 'incentive(1)' and 'incentive(2)', which are automatically created by SPSS, and which will be part of Figure 6.81, but which are not added to the 'Data View' window in the 'SPSS Data Editor'. Additionally, the 'no incentive' group, as a reference category, will receive the value '0' for each of these two new variables. Students who have received a 'direct' ('indirect') incentive are assigned the code '1' ('0') for the new variable 'incentive(1)', and the code '0' ('1') for 'incentive(2)'.

Figure 6.81

Variables in the Equation

		B	S.E.	Wald	df	Sig.	Exp(B)
Step 1ᵃ	involv	.344	.072	22.769	1	.000	1.410
	incent			1.150	2	.563	
	incent(1)	.235	.229	1.059	1	.303	1.265
	incent(2)	.057	.229	.061	1	.804	1.059
	Constant	−1.927	.364	27.957	1	.000	.146

ᵃVariable(s) entered on step 1: involv, incent

The coefficient (B) linked to the 'incentive(1)' variable indicates that the 'log odds' will increase by .235 points if a 'direct' incentive is added to the mail survey instead of 'no' incentive (Figure 6.81). This increase does not appear to be significant however (p-value = .303 >.05) which means that adding a 'direct' incentive to the mail survey will not lead to a higher response when compared with the cases in which 'no' incentive is added. The coefficient linked to the 'incentive(2)' variable indicates an increase in the 'log odds' by .057 points for the use of an 'indirect' incentive when compared with cases with 'no' incentive. However, this increase may also be attributed to coincidence, and does not differ significantly from zero, given the fact that the p-value (.804) here is also greater than .05. The use of an 'indirect' incentive as compared with 'no' incentive will thus not lead to a higher response.

The reader may find further information on the 'log odds' under Example 1 of this chapter.

Research question 2: What is the effect of the use of no incentive/direct incentive/indirect incentive as compared with the mean effect of the three types of incentive on the 'log odds' (response)?

Figure 6.82

Categorical Variables Codings

		Frequency	Parameter Coding	
			(1)	(2)
Incentive attached to the survey	No incentive	168	−1.000	−1.000
	Direct incentive (independent of sending the survey back)	167	1.000	.000
	Indirect incentive (dependent on sending the survey back)	161	.000	1.000

The interpretation of Figure 6.82 is identical to that for Figure 6.80, with the difference that as a 'reference category', the 'no incentive' group is assigned the value '−1' for each of the two new variables, 'incentive(1)' and 'incentive(2)'.

Figure 6.83

		B	S.E.	Wald	df	Sig.	Exp(B)
Step 1[a]	involv	.344	.072	22.769	1	.000	1.410
	incent			1.150	2	.563	
	incent(1)	.138	.132	1.085	1	.298	1.148
	incent(2)	−.041	.133	.093	1	.760	.960
	Constant	−1.830	.337	29.520	1	.000	.160

Variables in the Equation

[a]Variable(s) entered on step 1: involv, incent

The coefficient linked to the 'incentive(1)' variable indicates that due to the addition of a 'direct' incentive, the 'log odds' will be .138 points higher than the mean effect of the three types of incentive on the 'log odds' (Figure 6.83). The corresponding p-value (.298 > .05) indicates however that this difference in effect does not differ significantly from zero. The effect of the 'indirect' incentive on the 'log odds' would be .041 points lower than the mean effect of the 'incentive' variable (see coefficient 'incentive(2)'), however, the p-value here (.760 > .05) also indicates that this difference in effect may be attributed to coincidence. The degree to which the effect of 'not' adding an incentive to the mail survey deviates from the mean effect of the three types of incentive may be calculated as follows: $−\{.138 + (−.041)\} = −.097$. In comparison with the mean effect, 'not' providing an incentive would serve to lower the 'log odds' the most of all of the three types of incentive, namely by .097 points.

A difference in coding (Figures 6.80 and 6.82) leads to different regression coefficients and p-values for the variables 'incentive(1)' and 'incentive(2)' (Figures 6.81 and 6.83), but the final conclusions are identical: the coefficients lead one to conclude that a 'direct' incentive is the best choice to drive the response rate to the mail survey upwards, followed by an 'indirect' incentive, and finally by 'no' incentive; the p-values make it clear however that there is no difference in effect for these three types of incentive, and that the choice for 'no' incentive may be made (the response is identical for all three types, however the 'no incentive' option is less expensive).

Further reading

Irwin, J. and McClelland, G. (2001), 'Misleading Heuristics and Moderated Multiple Regression Models', *Journal of Marketing Research*, 38(1), 100–9.

Menard, S. (1995), *Applied Logistic Regression Analysis*. Thousand Oaks, California: Sage Publications, Inc.

Norušis, M. (1994), *SPSS for Windows: Advanced Statistics, Release 6.1*. Chicago, Illinois: SPSS, Inc.

Endnotes

1   The 'involvement' variable is a scale score which is based on five items.

2   If after seeing the 'Leverage' value and the 'DfBetas', the researcher doubts the impact of a certain outlier, he may calculate the model with and without this respondent and then determine whether the influence on the model is considerable (e.g., a regression coefficient which is not significant if the outlier is included in the model, yet is significant after the elimination of this respondent).

3   In the event of a 'large' coefficient, the standard error takes on a value which is too high and the 'Wald' statistic takes on a value which is too low, which will cause the researcher to fail to reject the null hypothesis (coefficient is equal to zero), whereas he should have in fact rejected it.

4   'Block 1', in the SPSS input window, contains the model without the relevant variable, and 'Block 2' only contains the relevant variable; the values 'Block Chi-square' and 'Sig.', related to 'Block 2', indicate the change in '−2LL' as a result of the addition of this variable to the model, and whether or not this change is significant.

5   The scores for [sinvolv], [ssensit], [sprivacy], [shelp] and [sresp] are mean scores, each of which are calculated on the basis of a number of items.

6   In the 'Logistic Regression: Define Categorical Variables' window, the 'Non-personalized' category is indicated as the reference category. The researcher must also keep in mind that in terms of the interpretation of the SPSS output, in the case of 'deviation coding', the mean effect of the two types of personalization ('Personalized' and 'Non-personalized') will serve as a reference (see Example 4).

7   Z-values stand for 'Logit' values here and not for 'standardized' values.

8   Note that the respondent number '585' is not an outlier in Example 3.

Chapter 7

Exploratory factor analysis

Chapter objectives

This chapter will help you to:

- Understand how and when to use exploratory factor analysis
- Decide whether it is useful to conduct a factor analysis
- Decide upon the number of factors and their definition
- Interpret factor results
- Compute factor scores
- Compute summated scales and this after performing a reliability analysis (Cronbach's Alpha)

Technique

Exploratory factor analysis is a general term for a class of multivariate analysis techniques whose goal is to decrease the size of a dataset, and to reduce it to an actual underlying dimensionality. This means that a large quantity of variables will be reduced to a smaller amount of previously unknown dimensions which are also referred to as factors. This chapter will focus on one of these techniques, namely principal components analysis (PCA).

Contrary to regression analysis for example, factor analysis does not lead to the categorization of the data into dependent and independent variables. It is only the strength of the association between the variables which is important, to the extent that it is possible to define a smaller set of dimensions, each of which is based on a number of the original variables, while still keeping the majority of the information. This therefore involves an exploratory description of the data, or the preparation of the data material for further analysis, such as regression or cluster analysis for example. It is also useful to note here that in addition to the exploratory form, confirmatory factor analysis may also be involved. This last technique makes a priori statements about the expected number of underlying dimensions and the nature of these, and will be discussed in Chapter 8.

Digging Deeper

Figure 7.1 Exploratory vs. confirmatory factor analysis

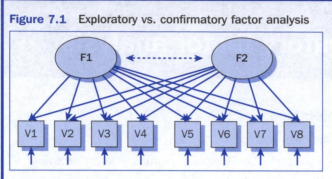

Exploratory factor analysis

- Paths from every factor to every variable
- Uncorrelated measurement errors
- Factors are often not correlated (unless oblique rotation is applied)
- The presence of a good fit between model and data is not tested
- No unique solution: rotation leads to a simpler interpretation

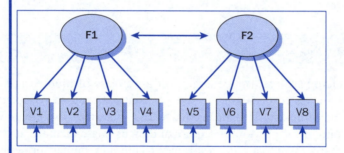

Confirmatory factor analysis

- Paths from every factor to only a few variables
- Measurement errors may be correlated
- Factors are usually correlated
- Paths may be limited to specific values
- The values for paths may be set equal to one another
- The presence of a good fit between model and data is tested

Performing a factor analysis is based on three assumptions:

1 As far as the **measurement levels** of the variables are concerned, **interval or ratio variables** form the input for a classical factor analysis. A Likert scale, which registers the degree of agreement with a particular statement on the basis of a limited number of response categories (5, 7 or 9), will, strictly speaking, produce an ordinal variable and thus does not qualify for this type of analysis. Research has shown that the use of these types of scales in factor analysis does not lead to unreliable results per se,

and that the bias decreases as the number of response categories increases. Non-metric principal components analysis may be performed in SPSS on the basis of 'CATPCA'. This procedure is part of the 'add-on' module, 'Categories'.

2 The use of variables, which are described in **different measurement units** for example, 5-, 7- and 9-point scales, may be used in the same factor analysis after the raw data have been standardized. In this way, the mean will be 0 and the standard deviation will be 1 for each variable, and the response scales will be comparable to one another. It is important to note that choosing the 'correlation matrix' as input for the factor analysis (Figure 7.7) means that it is unnecessary to standardize the variables beforehand in the case of different measurement units; the standardization occurs automatically in this case. It must be noted here that even if all of the variables have **the same level of measurement**, the choice will also be made for an analysis of the correlation matrix, and thus the standardization of the variables, if the objective of the analysis is to discover an underlying dimensionality and to create 'indices' (factors).

3 With regard to the **number of observations** necessary for the performance of a factor analysis, one may say that **for every variable there are at least ten times as many observations** (respondents) necessary. This is however a rule of thumb, and may be applied less strictly. There is however an absolute minimum of one hundred respondents required.

In performing a factor analysis, there are a number of steps which must be taken, during which it is important to pay sufficient attention to the following five points:

1 *Find out whether it is meaningful to perform a factor analysis on the variables chosen*
Given the fact that factor analysis is focused on finding a number of underlying dimensions on the basis of the correlation between the variables, a first step may be the calculation of the 'Pearson' correlation coefficient for each pair of variables. The resulting correlation matrix will then have to contain a considerable number of correlations greater than .30 in order for the factor analysis to make sense. Supplemental indications may be obtained by examining the anti-image correlation matrix, for example, 'Bartlett's test of sphericity' and 'Kaiser-Meyer-Olkin measure of sampling adequacy' (MSA). These will be discussed later in the chapter under the section 'Interpretation of the SPSS output'.

2 *Choose a method to extract factors*
The factor analysis techniques (e.g. 'Image factoring', 'Principal axis factoring', 'Principal components' and 'Unweighted least squares') differ from one another with regard to the calculation of the weighting coefficients (see a_{ij} in Comparison (1)). In the case of the principal components analysis, this calculation will lead to factor scores which explain a maximum possible share of the variance. This means that the first factor explains the largest possible part of the total variance, the second factor explains the largest possible portion of the remaining variance, . . . Moreover, the factors obtained will not be correlated (orthogonal), and in terms of the number, will be equal to no more than the number of original variables.

3 *Determine the number of factors*
Given the fact that, in addition, an increasingly smaller portion of the variance in the original data is explained as more factors are extracted, the researcher may limit the number of relevant factors, at the expense of the smallest possible loss of explanatory

power. This limitation of the number of factors is a subjective procedure. The researcher may, for example, use a number of criteria to determine this number: (1) the 'Kaiser criterion', which will only retain those factors for which the Eigenvalue is greater than one, and thus only those factors which explain a minimal portion of the variance; (2) the 'Scree plot', which shows the evolution of the Eigenvalue for successive factors, and recommends retaining that amount of factors which corresponds to the 'elbow' in the curve; and (3) an amount of expected factors stated a priori.

4 *Choose an orthogonal or oblique rotation or no rotation at all*

An ideal factor structure would involve a situation in which every factor has a strong correlation to a number of original variables, and correlates either insignificantly or not at all with all of the others. In this way, a meaningful interpretation may be given to every factor and every underlying dimension of the data set. This means that the goal must be to ensure that the factor loadings for some of the variables are as close as possible to 1 for some of the factors, and as close as possible to 0 for the other factors. A rotation of the factors is thus recommended. There are two important types of rotation: the orthogonal (the factors are also uncorrelated after rotation) and the oblique (the factors are correlated after rotation, and thus no longer independent from one another) rotation. Moreover, each type may be subdivided even further: 'varimax', 'quartimax' and 'equamax' are examples of the orthogonal rotation while 'direct oblimin' and 'promax' will lead to an oblique rotation. In practice, the varimax rotation will be used often, whereby the number of variables which have high loads on each of the factors is minimized, thus simplifying the interpretation of the factors.

5 *Calculate factor scores*

If the researcher is satisfied with the factor structure found, he or she may calculate factor scores on the basis of linear combinations of the original scores for the input variables, which may be shown in their general form as follows:

$$F_j = a_{1j}X_1 + a_{2j}X_{2 + \ldots + } a_{nj}X_n \tag{1}$$

where F_j = factor j
X_i = original variable
a_{ij} = weighting coefficient

Filling in concrete values for these original variables and weighting coefficients will then lead to the calculation of factor scores: scores for each respondent for each of the factors. These scores, which possess the interesting feature of being uncorrelated, will often serve as input for regression analysis in order to compensate for the multicollinearity problem present with regard to the original variables (see Chapter 5).

Given the fact that, according to Equation (1), the calculation of factor scores for factor j includes each of the original variables and thus also those which have a low factor loading on this, the scores obtained will be less 'pure'. The calculation of a 'summated scale' for factor j may offer a solution here, considering it may be limited to those variables which score high enough for this factor, and thus typify it. A summated scale may therefore be calculated as the sum or the mean of the qualifying variables, but not until these variables have been subjected to a reliability analysis: the calculation of 'Cronbach's Alpha' (Figure 7.40 and subsequent figures). In a cluster analysis, this 'summated scale' may serve as a basis for the clustering (see Chapter 9).

For a further theoretical discussion of the factor analysis technique, the reader is advised to consult the literature listed at the end of this chapter.

Example

Exploratory factor analysis

Managerial problem

A supermarket chain asked 500 of its customers to fill in a questionnaire which contained the following 12 questions (items), among others, which are measured according to 7-point Likert scales (Table 7.1):

Table 7.1

How do you view doing the shopping? (Check one answer only for each statement)	totally disagree	disagree	somewhat disagree	neither agree nor disagree	rather agree	agree	totally agree
a) It is very important to me to organize the shopping well.	☐	☐	☐	☐	☐	☐	☐
b) When I leave to go shopping, I know exactly what I am going to buy.	☐	☐	☐	☐	☐	☐	☐
c) By doing the shopping, I fulfil my duty and take my responsibility.	☐	☐	☐	☐	☐	☐	☐
d) I enjoy doing the shopping.	☐	☐	☐	☐	☐	☐	☐
e) I do the shopping at a leisurely pace.	☐	☐	☐	☐	☐	☐	☐
f) I enjoy the atmosphere while shopping.	☐	☐	☐	☐	☐	☐	☐
g) Doing the shopping is a drag.	☐	☐	☐	☐	☐	☐	☐
h) I try to keep the time that I spend doing the shopping to a minimum.	☐	☐	☐	☐	☐	☐	☐
i) I like seeing familiar faces in a supermarket.	☐	☐	☐	☐	☐	☐	☐
j) I usually take a list with me when I go to do the shopping.	☐	☐	☐	☐	☐	☐	☐
k) I enjoy shopping with the entire family.	☐	☐	☐	☐	☐	☐	☐
l) I like to have a stock of several products on hand at home.	☐	☐	☐	☐	☐	☐	☐

If one reads these questions carefully, one would expect that there are two underlying dimensions here: the degree of pleasure experienced during shopping (items c, d, e, f, g, h, i and k), and the degree to which shopping is planned (items a, b, j and l). In order to find this out, the marketing research department of the chain would like to perform a factor analysis on the dataset, an excerpt of which is shown in Figure 7.2.

Figure 7.2

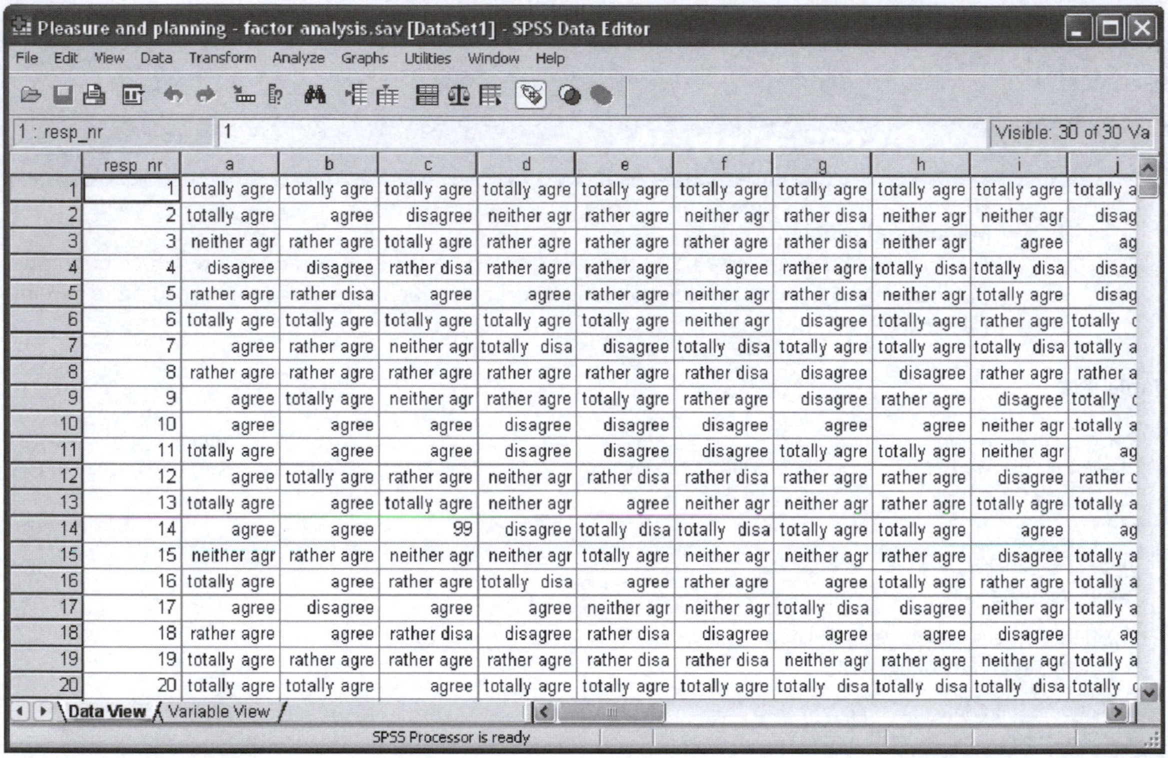

	resp_nr	a	b	c	d	e	f	g	h	i	j
1	1	totally agre	totally agre	totally agre	totally agre	totally agre	totally agre	totally agre	totally agre	totally agre	totally a
2	2	totally agre	agree	disagree	neither agr	rather agre	neither agr	rather disa	neither agr	neither agr	disag
3	3	neither agr	rather agre	totally agre	rather agre	rather agre	rather agre	rather disa	neither agr	agree	ag
4	4	disagree	disagree	rather disa	rather agre	rather agre	agree	rather agre	totally disa	totally disa	disag
5	5	rather agre	rather disa	agree	agree	rather agre	neither agr	rather disa	neither agr	totally agre	disag
6	6	totally agre	totally agre	totally agre	totally agre	totally agre	neither agr	disagree	totally agre	rather agre	totally c
7	7	agree	rather agre	neither agr	totally disa	disagree	totally disa	totally agre	totally agre	totally disa	totally a
8	8	rather agre	rather agre	rather agre	rather agre	rather agre	rather disa	disagree	disagree	rather agre	rather a
9	9	agree	totally agre	neither agr	rather agre	totally agre	rather agre	disagree	rather agre	disagree	totally c
10	10	agree	agree	agree	disagree	disagree	disagree	agree	agree	neither agr	totally a
11	11	totally agre	agree	agree	disagree	disagree	disagree	totally agre	totally agre	neither agr	ag
12	12	agree	totally agre	rather agre	neither agr	rather disa	rather disa	rather agre	rather agre	disagree	rather c
13	13	totally agre	agree	totally agre	neither agr	agree	neither agr	neither agr	rather agre	totally agre	totally a
14	14	agree	agree	99	disagree	totally disa	totally disa	totally agre	totally agre	agree	ag
15	15	neither agr	rather agre	neither agr	neither agr	totally agre	neither agr	neither agr	rather agre	disagree	totally a
16	16	totally agre	agree	rather agre	totally disa	agree	rather agre	agree	totally agre	rather agre	totally a
17	17	agree	disagree	agree	agree	neither agr	neither agr	totally disa	disagree	neither agr	totally a
18	18	rather agre	agree	rather disa	disagree	rather disa	disagree	agree	agree	disagree	ag
19	19	totally agre	rather agre	rather agre	rather agre	rather disa	rather disa	neither agr	rather agre	neither agr	totally a
20	20	totally agre	totally agre	agree	totally agre	totally agre	totally agre	totally disa	totally disa	totally disa	totally c

Problem

Perform a factor analysis for the 12 statements above and find two possible underlying dimensions or factors: 'Pleasure' and 'Planning'. The data for this analysis is included in the dataset *Pleasure and planning – factor analysis.sav*.

Several guidelines should be followed: (1) at the start of the analyses, calculate the anti-image correlation matrix, 'Bartlett's test of sphericity' and 'Kaiser-Meyer-Olkin measure of sampling adequacy'; (2) choose principal components analysis as the method; (3) use the 'Kaiser criterion' and the 'Scree plot' to determine the number of factors; (4) perform a varimax rotation; and (5) calculate 'summated scales' after performing the necessary reliability analyses.

Solution

SPSS commands

Figure 7.3

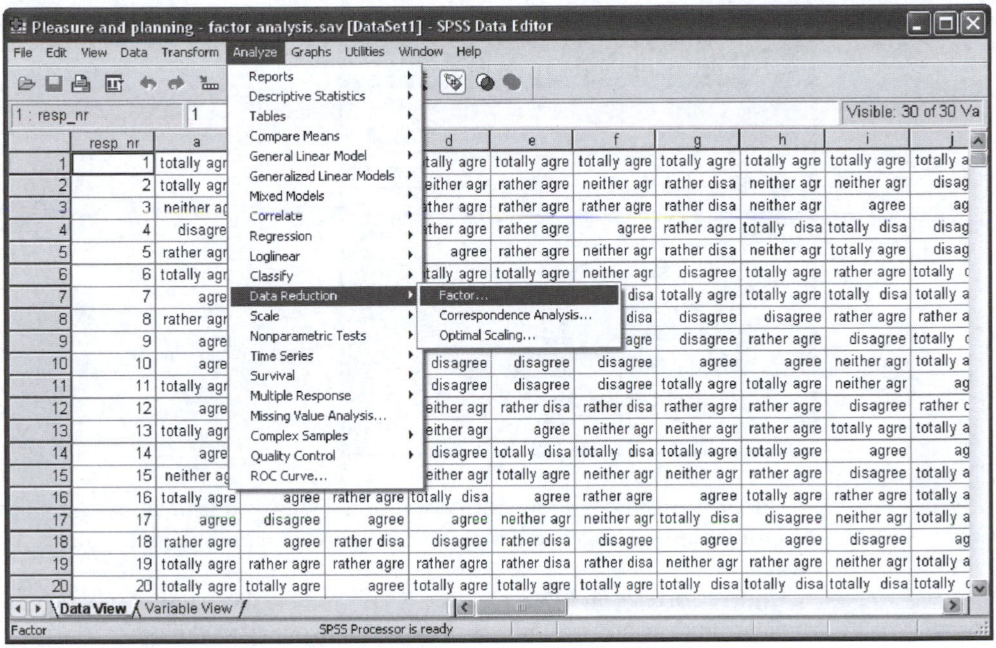

Go to Analyze/Data Reduction/Factor (Figure 7.3).

Figure 7.4

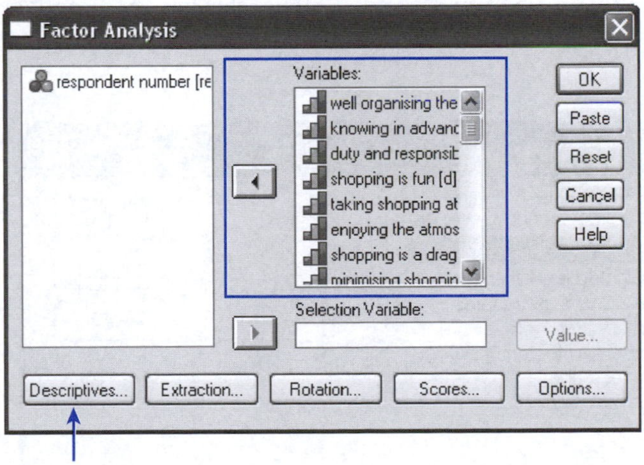

Move the variables which serve as input for the factor analysis to the 'Variables' box. Use the ▶ arrow to do this, at the top of the dialogue window (Figure 7.4).

Click the 'Descriptives' button at the bottom of the dialogue window and the 'Factor Analysis: Descriptives' window (Figure 7.5) will appear.

Figure 7.5

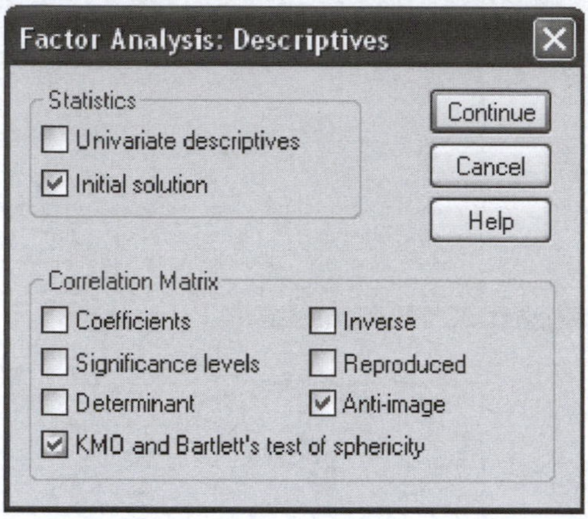

Under 'Statistics', choose 'Initial solution'. This results in an output window with 'Initial Communalities', 'Eigenvalues', and the percentages linked to these for the explained variance.

Under 'Correlation Matrix', select 'KMO and Bartlett's test of sphericity' and 'Anti-image' to determine the meaningfulness of performing a factor analysis.

Although they are not selected, the following are still worth mentioning: 'Univariate descriptives' (indicates the number of valid observations, the mean and the standard deviation for each variable), 'Coefficients' (results in a correlation matrix for the variables included), and 'Significance levels' (one-sided testing to determine whether the correlation coefficient differs from zero).

Return to the main window (Figure 7.4) by clicking on 'Continue' and click on 'Extraction'. The window 'Factor Analysis: Extraction' (Figure 7.6) will appear.

Figure 7.6

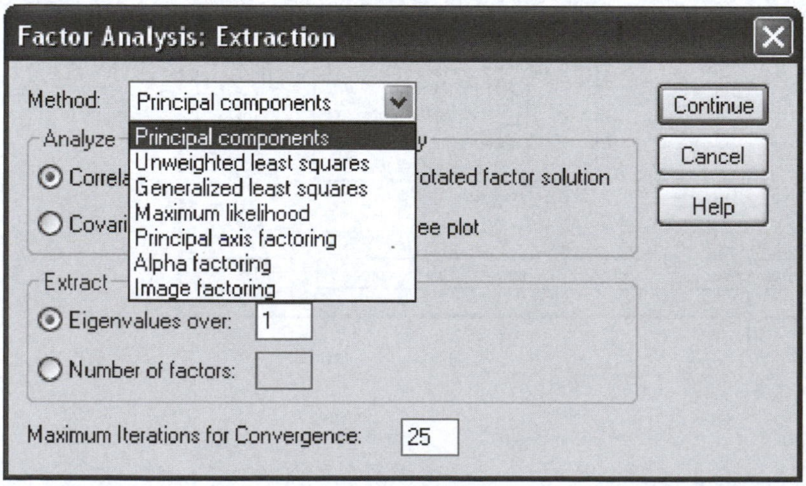

As was mentioned earlier, a factor analysis may be based on different methods. The instructions advise choosing the principal components analysis, therefore the default option 'Principal components' must be selected here.

Figure 7.7

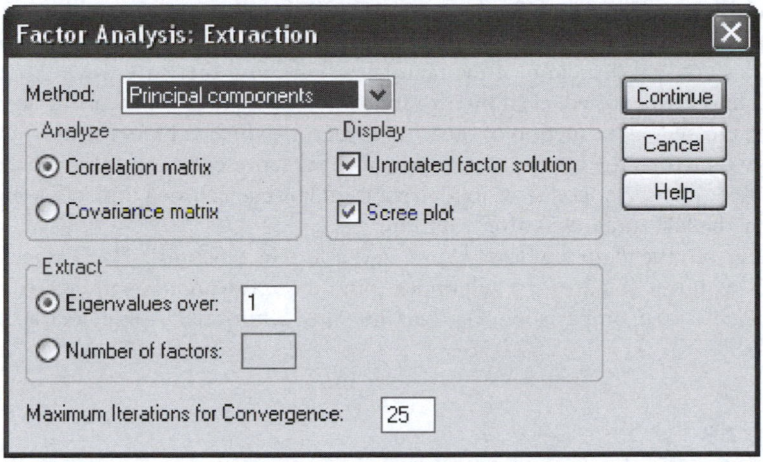

Under 'Analyze' (Figure 7.7), choose the default option 'Correlation matrix'. The underlying dimensions are then determined on the basis of the correlation between the original variables.

Under 'Display', select 'Unrotated factor solution' to include the 'Extraction communalities', the 'Extraction Sums of Squared Loadings' and the 'Component Matrix' in the output, and 'Scree plot' to produce a graph which displays the quantity of explained variance per factor.

The instructions also mention the use of the 'Kaiser criterion' for the determination of the number of factors. Choose the option 'Eigenvalues over: 1'. If the researcher has a clear picture beforehand of the number of dimensions sought, for example '2' in the present example, then the choice may be made for 'Number of factors: 2'.

Return to the main window (Figure 7.4) by clicking on 'Continue' and click 'Rotation'. In the 'Factor Analysis: Rotation' window (Figure 7.8), check 'Varimax'.

Figure 7.8

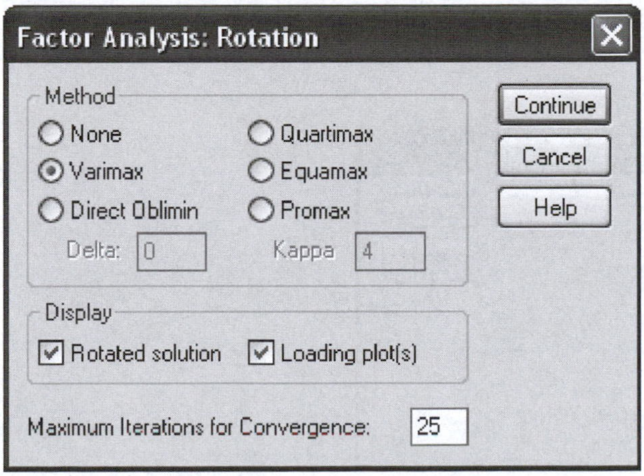

Starting from a two-factor solution, it is recommended to implement a rotation in order to simplify the interpretation of the factors. In this case, an orthogonal rotation was selected instead of an oblique one, since the factors have been assumed to be independent of one another.

Under 'Display', choose 'Rotated solution' and 'Loading plot(s)'. This first option leads to the 'Rotated Sums of Squared Loadings', the 'Rotated Component Matrix' and the 'Component Transformation Matrix' in the output window. The 'Loading plot(s)' option provides a visual depiction of the factor loadings, and there are three different possibilities which may be identified: (1) if three or more factors are present, then a three-dimensional plot will be created, as a function of those three factors which explain the most variance; (2) with only two factors, the result is a two-dimensional representation; (3) with one factor, no plot is created. If an orthogonal or oblique rotation has been chosen under 'Method', the plot will display the factor loadings **after** rotation.

Return to the main window (Figure 7.4) and select 'Scores'. The 'Factor Analysis: Factor Scores' window (Figure 7.9) will appear, and if the researcher is interested in the weighting coefficients of Comparison (1), then he must choose 'Display factor score coefficient matrix'.

Figure 7.9

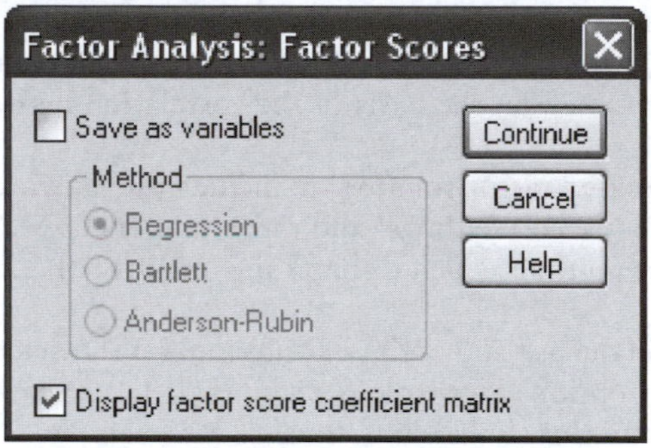

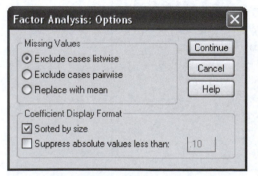

The 'Save as variables/Regression' option is checked if the factor structure is definite and the researcher would like to use the factor scores for further analyses. For every final factor, a new variable will be added to the dataset which shows the score for every respondent for the respective factor.

Figure 7.10

In the main window (Figure 7.4), click 'Options' and the 'Factor Analysis: Options' window (Figure 7.10) will appear. The 'Exclude cases listwise' option is checked as the default option in SPSS, and indicates that a case (a row from the dataset) will not be part of the analysis, if it has a 'system missing' or a 'user missing' (see Chapter 1) for one or more of the variables included in the analysis.

Under 'Coefficient Display Format', choose the option 'Sorted by size'. This will place the items in the 'Rotated Component Matrix' which load on the same factor directly under one another and also arrange them according to the size of their factor loadings, with the highest loadings coming first.

The 'Suppress absolute value less than: .10' option will omit factor loadings in the 'Rotated Component Matrix' which are less than .10 in absolute value.

Return now to the main window (Figure 7.4) and click 'OK' now that all of the specifications have been entered.

Interpretation of the SPSS output

Before starting with the interpretation of the SPSS output, it is a good idea to stop and review the three assumptions which were made at the beginning of this chapter: (1) the measurement level is interval or ratio (the questionnaire contained 7-point Likert scales which, strictly speaking, have an ordinal measurement level, yet in practice are often treated as being interval-scaled because of the 'assumption of equal appearing intervals'); (2) the presence of different measurement units necessitates a standardization of the variables, and in the event of identical measurement levels, standardization is also used, if the objective is the discovery of an underlying dimensionality (given the fact the researcher would like to find a number of underlying dimensions for the original variables, the choice has been made for the analysis of the correlation matrix, and thus for the standardization of the variables); (3) the number of respondents present is at least 10 times the number of variables (500 respondents $> 10*12$ items, so the dataset contains enough respondents for the analysis to be performed).

The three assumptions have been satisfied in the present example. In the next step, we try to determine if it is meaningful to perform a factor analysis.

A factor analysis is only significant if the variables involved are sufficiently correlated to one another. 'Bartlett's test of sphericity', the anti-image correlation matrix and 'Kaiser-Meyer-Olkin measure of sampling adequacy' provide insight into the degree of correlation and will be explained further below.

Figure 7.11

KMO and Bartlett's Test		
Kaiser-Meyer-Olkin measure of sampling adequacy.		.818
Bartlett's test of sphericity	Approx. Chi-square	2155.802
	df	66
	Sig.	.000

'Bartlett's test of sphericity' attempts to determine whether there is a high enough degree of correlation between at least a number of the variables included, in other words, states that H_0: correlation matrix = identity matrix (in other words, that the variables are uncorrelated). In the current example, the null hypothesis is rejected (p-value $< .001$; see '1' in Figure 7.11), therefore making a factor analysis meaningful.

Figure 7.12

Anti-image correlation													
Well organizing the shopping trip	.676ᵃ	−.394	−.233	−.020	.095	−.033	−.002	−.018	−.019	−.293	.083	−.152
Knowing in advance what to buy	−.394	.659ᵃ	−.104	.047	−.057	−.081	.074	−.260	.052	−.170	−.126	.057
Duty and responsibility	−.233	−.104	.671ᵃ	−.226	−.083	−.027	−.181	−.039	−.093	.044	.037	−.021
Shopping is fun	−.020	.047	−.226	.832ᵃ	−.045	−.250	.510	.126	−.011	.028	−.161	−.039
Taking shopping at ease	.095	−.057	−.083	−.045	.919ᵃ	−.243	.179	.113	.002	.033	−.045	−.032
Enjoying the atmosphere	−.033	−.081	−.027	−.250	−.243	.890ᵃ	.226	.132	−.195	.013	−.084	−.034
Shopping is a drag	−.002	.074	−.181	.510	.179	.226	.818ᵃ	−.255	.020	−.064	−.008	−.115
Minimizing shopping time	−.018	−.260	−.039	.126	.113	.132	−.255	.869ᵃ	−.140	.095	−.017	.040
Like familiar faces	−.019	.052	−.093	−.011	.002	−.195	.020	−.140	.776ᵃ	−.002	−.084	−.108
Shopping list most of the time	−.293	−.170	.044	.028	.033	.013	−.064	.095	−.002	.733ᵃ	−.109	−.103
Like shopping with the whole family	.083	−.126	.037	−.161	−.045	−.084	−.008	−.017	−.084	−.109	.861ᵃ	−.153
Like having a stock of products	−.152	.057	−.021	−.039	−.032	−.034	−.115	.040	−.108	−.103	−.153	.702ᵃ

ᵃMeasures of Sampling Adequacy(MSA)

The anti-image correlation matrix (Figure 7.12) shows the negative value for the partial correlations[1] between the variables. Underlying dimensions will exist, and a factor analysis will therefore be relevant, if the partial correlations and thus also the values in the anti-image correlation matrix are close to zero. Figure 7.12 shows the anti-image correlation matrix and it is sufficient to only study the values under (or above) the main diagonal (see '2'). Since only the value for the variables 'shopping is a drag' and 'shopping is fun' is high (.510), the factor analysis is considered to be relevant.

Another criterion used to determine the degree of correlation between the variables and thus the applicability of factor analysis is the 'Kaiser-Meyer-Olkin measure of sampling adequacy' statistic. Before interpreting the global MSA value, it is advisable to study the MSA linked to each individual variable (see main diagonal in Figure 7.12, '3') and to eliminate those variables for which this value is 'unacceptable'. MSA lies between 0 and 1, and will be 'unacceptable' if the value is less than .50. Since the lowest MSA value is .659, not a single variable will be eliminated, and the global statistic may be examined in a subsequent step (see Figure 7.11, '4'). This is .818 (> .50), and therefore demonstrates that a factor analysis may be performed.

The 'Bartlett's test of sphericity', the anti-image correlation matrix and 'Kaiser-Meyer-Olkin measure of sampling adequacy' all indicate that a factor analysis is meaningful, and a principal components analysis may be caried out. The output of this analysis is discussed hereafter.

The original variables are standardized, and this is why the variance for each of the variables is equal to 1. Since the principal components analysis applies to the total variance of the variables, and not only that part of the variance which is in common with the other variables, for example, such as in 'Principal Axis Factoring', the 'Communalities – Initial' column contains the value 1 (Figure 7.13).

Figure 7.13

Communalities		
	Initial	Extraction
Well organizing the shopping trip	1.000	.703
Knowing in advance what to buy	1.000	.652
Duty and responsibility	1.000	.332
Shopping is fun	1.000	.797
Taking shopping at ease	1.000	.604
Enjoying the atmosphere	1.000	.759
Shopping is a drag	1.000	.815
Minimizing shopping time	1.000	.607
Like familiar faces	1.000	.495
Shopping list most of the time	1.000	.431
Like shopping with the whole family	1.000	.408
Like having a stock of products	1.000	.575

Extraction Method: Principal component analysis.

The values in the 'Communalities – Extraction' column show which part of the variance of each variable is explained by a given number of factors, in this case, three (see the discussion regarding the columns under the heading 'Extraction Sums of Squared Loadings' in Figure 7.14). One may therefore say that 70.3% of the total variance in the variable 'organizing the shopping well' is explained by the three underlying dimensions.

If there are as many factors as there are variables, twelve in this application, then all of the communalities are equal to 1, and for each variable the variance is fully explained.

A low value for these communalities indicates that the variable in question is not very relevant for the definition of the factors in that particular configuration, and therefore may be eliminated. The determination of this 'low' value is subjective, however, given the fact that the lowest communality for the present example is .332, the researcher may decide that all of the variables are relevant.

Figure 7.14

	Total Variance Explained								
	Initial Eigenvalues			Extraction Sums of Squared Loadings			Rotation Sums of Squared Loadings		
Component	Total	% of Variance	Cumulative %	Total	% of Variance	Cumulative %	Total	% of Variance	Cumulative %
1	3.830	31.913	31.913	3.830	31.913	31.913	3.667	30.557	30.557
2	2.316	19.302	51.215	2.316	19.302	51.215	2.132	17.763	48.321
3	1.031	8.592	59.807	1.031	8.592	59.807	1.378	11.486	59.807
4	.968	8.070	67.877						
5	.812	6.763	74.640						
6	.723	6.026	80.665						
7	.615	5.123	85.788						
8	.500	4.167	89.955						
9	.390	3.253	93.209						
10	.360	2.996	96.205						
11	.280	2.333	98.538						
12	.175	1.462	100.000						

Extraction Method: Principal component analysis.

Figure 7.14 contains three important components: 'Initial Eigenvalues', 'Extraction Sums of Squared Loadings' and 'Rotation Sums of Squared Loadings'. These will each be explained in sequence. The maximum variance to be explained for all of the variables together is equal to the total number of variables, so in this case, this is 12. The part of this total variance which is explained by each of the factors is indicated by the Eigenvalues (see

'Initial Eigenvalues – Total' column in Figure 7.14). If we divide this eigenvalue for each factor by the number of variables (= the total variance = 12), then we will obtain insight into the part of the total variance that is explained by every factor. For instance, the first factor explains 31.91% of the total variance in the twelve variables. Previously it was said that the first factor explains the largest possible part of the total variance, the second factor the largest possible part of the remaining variance, etc. The decreasing values in the 'Initial Eigenvalues – % of Variance' column now show this clearly. The cumulative explained proportion of the variance may now also be calculated (see 'Initial Eigenvalues – Cumulative %' column). The first three factors together for example explain 59.81% of the total variance, and the variance is fully explained if the number of factors is equal to the number of variables, namely 12.

The columns under the heading 'Extraction Sums of Squared Loadings' in Figure 7.14 contain the same values as those under the heading 'Initial Eigenvalues', yet these values are only shown for the first three components. The 'Kaiser criterion' (see instructions) determines this number, by only keeping those factors for which the Eigenvalue is greater than 1.

Figure 7.15

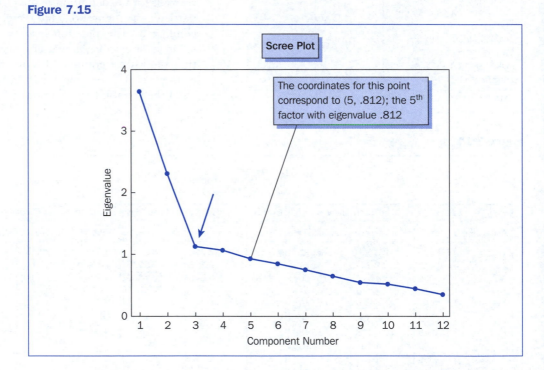

The 'Scree plot' (Figure 7.15) also provides an indication in this regard, and in the present example also refers to three relevant factors since the 'elbow' is located at this point. Nonetheless, it must be said here that the 'Kaiser criterion' as well as the 'Scree plot' only provide an 'indication', and that the ultimate decision with regard to the number of factors to be retained is left up to the researcher. He has indicated in the instructions that he only expects two instead of three underlying dimensions, namely 'Pleasure' and 'Planning'. Further investigation of the factor loadings (see 'Rotated Component Matrix', Figure 7.17) will show that 'two' factors is the right number for this analysis.

Previously, we indicated that a rotation of the relevant factors simplifies the interpretation of the underlying dimensions. The columns under the heading 'Rotation Sums of Squared

Loadings' in Figure 7.14 relate to this rotation, and then it appears that the total variance explained by the three rotated factors (59.81%) is as large as it is in the non-rotated case. The distribution of the explanatory power of each of the factors has however changed (31.91%, 19.30% and 8.59% before rotation versus 30.56%, 17.76% and 11.49% after rotation). The sequence of the rotated factors is therefore no longer meaningful. Not only does the rotation change nothing in terms of the total explained variance, it also has no impact on the communality of each variable (see 'Communalities – Extraction' column in Figure 7.13): equal portions of the variance for each variable are thus explained.

Figure 7.16

Component Matrix[a]

	Component		
	1	2	3
Shopping is fun	.888	.004	−.091
Shopping is a drag	−.880	.130	.157
Enjoying the atmosphere	.868	.062	−.035
Taking shopping at ease	.769	−.056	−.097
Minimizing shopping time	−.722	.270	.111
Like shopping with the whole family	.491	.262	.313
Well organizing the shopping trip	−.031	.807	−.224
Knowing in advance what to buy	−.004	.743	−.316
Shopping list most of the time	−.064	.648	−.081
Duty and responsibility	.185	.527	−.142
Like having a stock of products	.129	.430	.612
Like familiar faces	.323	.254	.571

Extraction Method: Principal component analysis.
[a] 3 components extracted

The 'Component Matrix' (Figure 7.16) only contains values for the three relevant factors, and these values are also referred to as 'factor loadings'. A factor loading corresponds to the correlation between a set of factor scores and a set of scores for an original variable. It must also be noted here that equating factor loading to correlation is only justified if the factors are independent of one another and are therefore orthogonal.

On the basis of this matrix, the researcher can calculate the communalities (see 'Communalities – Extraction' column in Figure 7.13) and the Eigenvalues indicated previously (see 'Extraction Sums of Squared Loadings – Total' column in Figure 7.14). For example, the communality or the explained variance for the variable 'shopping is a drag' is equal to the sum of the squared correlation coefficients between this variable and each factor $\{.82 = (-.88)^2 + (.13)^2 + (.16)^2\}$, and the Eigenvalue or the variance explained by the first factor for example is equal to the sum of the squared correlation coefficients between that particular factor and each of the original variables $\{3.83 = (.89)^2 + (-.88)^2 + (.87)^2 + (.77)^2 + \cdots + (.13)^2 + (.32)^2\}$.

The correlation between the variables and the factors is however not exclusive; all of the variables are correlated to a greater or lesser degree with all of the factors, although this may be much less applicable to one factor than another. In order to better guarantee the exclusivity of the relationship between a variable and a factor, it is advisable to work with the 'rotated' factor structure. For example, the variable 'prefer to see familiar faces' in the non-rotated solution (see 'Component Matrix', Figure 7.16) loads primarily on the third factor (.571), however the loadings on the first and the second factor are not insignificant (.323 and .254).

After rotation (see 'Rotated Component Matrix', Figure 7.17), the relationship between this variable and the third factor is however more exclusive, considering the fact that the loadings on the factors 1 through 3 are .154, .025, and .686 respectively.

Figure 7.17

Rotated Component Matrix[a]

	Component		
	1	2	3
Shopping is a drag	–.901	.041	–.035
Shopping is fun	.879	.058	.143
Enjoying the atmosphere	.841	.090	.211
Taking shopping at ease	.772	.002	.087
Minimizing shopping time	–.755	.191	.015
Well organizing the shopping trip	–.072	.831	.084
Knowing in advance what to buy	–.018	.807	–.015
Shopping list most of the time	–.119	.629	.146
Duty and responsibility	.150	.546	.110
Like having a stock of products	–.063	.168	.737
Like familiar faces	.154	.025	.686
Like shopping with the whole family	.374	.135	.500

Eliminate

Extraction Method: Principal component analysis.
Rotation Method: Varimax with Kaiser normalization.
[a]Rotation converged in 4 iterations

The following question now arises: 'Shouldn't one assume a minimum loading on one factor and a maximum loading on every other factor in order to guarantee a purer definition of the factors?', or, in other words, 'When can one clearly assign a variable to one specific factor on the basis of the factor loadings?' In the first place, this assignment of variables to factors is subjective, however the researcher may apply a number of guidelines, including the statistical and practical significance of the factor loadings. The size of the sample is determinative for this first form of significance, and for the present example in which the sample size is 500, a factor loading will be statistically significant if it is greater than or equal to .30. This value is based on Table 7.2.

The practical significance on the other hand indicates that the factor loading must be at least .50 before a variable may be assigned to a certain factor, and this rule requires a minimum sample size of 100.

It must also be mentioned here that the sign of the factor loading in the 'Rotated Component Matrix' (Figure 7.17) is not an indication of the size of the relationship between variable and factor. Opposite signs of factor loadings for different variables for the same

Table 7.2 Identification of significant factor loading on the basis of the sample size

Factor loading	Sample size necessary for significance (at the .05 level)
.30	350
.35	250
.40	200
.45	150
.50	120
.55	100
.60	85
.65	70
.70	60
.75	50

factor only reflect that the various variables are related with the same factor but in opposite directions (this involves the two poles of the same dimension). In order to simplify the interpretation, it is sometimes recommended to formulate or code all of the variables in the same direction before performing the analysis. In fact, this is necessary in order to calculate Cronbach's Alpha and the 'summated scale'.

Bearing in mind the above rules of statistical and practical significance and the meaning of opposite signs for factor loadings, the following assignment may be made for the twelve variables to the three factors:

■ 'Shopping is a drag' and 'minimizing shopping time' versus 'shopping is fun', 'enjoying the atmosphere', 'shopping at a leisurely pace' represent the opposite poles of the first dimension, 'Pleasure'.

■ 'Organizing the shopping well', 'knowing in advance what to buy', 'shopping list most of the time' together define the second dimension, 'Planning'.

According to the output of the factor analysis, 'duty and responsibility' also belongs to the dimension 'Planning', however the researcher had previously expressed the suspicion that this variable belongs to the 'Pleasure' factor on the basis of its contents, which implies a considerable and negative loading on the first factor. The actual loading on the first factor (.150) is however positive and too low to be of any significance. Considering content takes precedence over 'numbers' obtained via analysis, the variable 'duty and responsibility' will not be attributed to the second factor, and will furthermore be removed from later analyses. Other researchers could make the conjecture that 'duty and responsibility' belongs to the 'Planning' instead of the 'Pleasure' dimension. In that case, the item loads on the correct factor (.546 for the second factor in comparison with .150 and .110 for the first and the third factors), and will not be removed from later analyses but will be attributed to this second factor, the factor 'Planning'. Once again, this is an indication of the subjective formation of the ultimate factors.

■ 'Like having a stock of products' and 'prefer to see familiar faces' clearly load on the third factor, however their content is so different that it is impossible to name this third dimension. Therefore, these two variables will also be eliminated.

■ 'Like shopping with the whole family' loads statistically significantly on the first and the third factor, whereas only the loading on the third factor may be described as being practically significant. The researcher may elect to make an abstraction of these statistical and practical significances and eliminate the variable, since the loadings of .374 and .500 on both factors do not vary substantially from one another, and the relationship between variable and factor is thus not sufficiently exclusive.

We may add to the above that in addition to the guidelines for statistical and practical significance, the researcher may apply the following 'stricter' rule in order to guarantee a purer definition of the factors: items are only suitable for interpretation of a factor result if their loading on one factor is at least .75, and no more than .25 for all other factors.

Figure 7.18

Component	1	2	3
Component Transformation Matrix			
1	.967	.022	.253
2	−.116	.925	.362
3	−.226	−.380	.897

Extraction Method: Principal component analysis.
Rotation Method: Varimax with Kaiser normalization.

Component	1	2	3
Component Score Covariance Matrix			
1	1.000	.000	.000
2	.000	1.000	.000
3	.000	.000	1.000

Extraction Method: Principal component analysis.
Rotation Method: Varimax with Kaiser normalization.

The 'Component Transformation Matrix' (Figure 7.18) provides insight into the manner in which the orthogonal rotation is performed, and the fact that the three factors are also independent of one another after rotation may be seen in the 'Component Score Covariance Matrix' (Figure 7.18): the values which do not lie on the main diagonal are equal to zero.

Figure 7.19

Component Score Coefficient Matrix

	Component 1	Component 2	Component 3
Well organizing the shopping trip	.001	.405	−.071
Knowing in advance what to buy	.031	.413	−.159
Duty and responsibility	.051	.264	−.029
Shopping is fun	.244	.040	−.020
Taking shopping at ease	.218	.018	−.042
Enjoying the atmosphere	.224	.043	.037
Shopping is a drag	−.263	−.011	.099
Minimizing shopping time	−.220	.063	.091
Like familiar faces	−.056	−.107	.558
Shopping list most of the time	−.031	.288	.026
Like shopping with the whole family	.042	−.008	.346
Like having a stock of products	−.123	−.053	.608

Extraction Method: Principal component analysis.
Rotation Method: Varimax with Kaiser normalization.

The 'Component Score Coefficient Matrix' (Figure 7.19) shows the weighting coefficients which are used to calculate the factor scores on the basis of Equation (1).

It appeared earlier from the 'Rotated Component Matrix' that it would be best to eliminate the variables 'duty and responsibility', 'like having a stock of products', 'prefer to see familiar faces' and 'like shopping with the whole family', and for this reason in a next step, the researcher will perform the factor analysis once again on the basis of the eight remaining variables.

In comparison with the previous analysis, the choice will now be made to use '2' factors as the basis for the extraction (see 'Pleasure' and 'Planning'), instead of an Eigenvalue greater than '1'. The researcher only expects two dimensions and the previous interpretation of the factor loadings also indicates a 'two factor' solution. Moreover, factor scores will be retrieved since this now involves the final factor structure. Figure 7.20 contains the input screens which show these modifications.

Figure 7.20

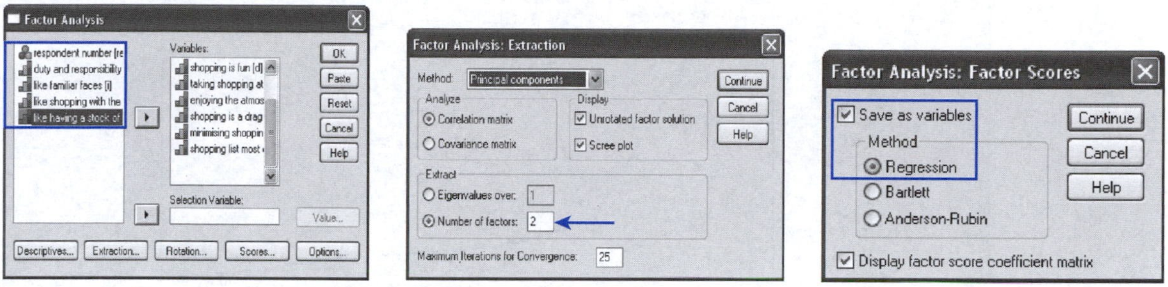

Given the interpretation of the output runs parallel to that of the previous analysis, the explanation will be limited to a number of observations. It is only the discussion of the 'Component Plot in Rotated Space' (Figure 7.24) and the explicit calculation of the factor scores on the basis of the weighting coefficients included in the 'Component Score Coefficient Matrix' (Figure 7.25) that makes an added contribution.

Figure 7.21

Total Variance Explained

Component	Initial Eigenvalues			Extraction Sums of Squared Loadings			Rotation Sums of Squared Loadings		
	Total	% of Variance	Cumulative %	Total	% of Variance	Cumulative %	Total	% of Variance	Cumulative %
1	3.584	44.802	44.802	3.584	44.802	44.802	3.560	44.494	44.494
2	1.907	23.833	68.635	1.907	23.833	68.635	1.931	24.141	68.635
3	.724	9.045	77.680						
4	.504	6.295	83.975						
5	.425	5.315	89.290						
6	.387	4.832	94.122						
7	.280	3.496	97.618						
8	.191	2.382	100.000						

Extraction Method: Principal component analysis.

In Figure 7.21, the window 'Extraction Sums of Squared Loadings' shows a number of statistics for the two factors requested: as expected, the first factor explains the largest part of the total variance, namely 44.80%, and the second factor explains 23.83%, or when taken together, they explain 68.64% of the total variance. It may also be remarked here that the application of the 'Kaiser criterion' (Eigenvalue > 1) would also have led to the extraction of two factors. It is however possible that both criteria 'Eigenvalues over:' and 'Number of factors:' in other examples lead to a different number of factors.

Figure 7.22

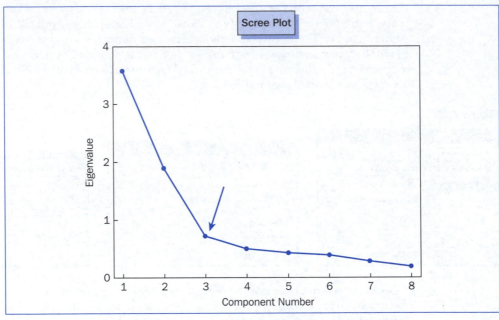

In spite of the fact that two factors are expected a priori, and the 'Kaiser criterion' also calls for two factors, the 'Scree plot' (Figure 7.22) indicates three factors.

Figure 7.23

Rotated Component Matrix[a]

	Component	
	1	2
Shopping is a drag	−.905	.054
Shopping is fun	.889	.026
Enjoying the atmosphere	.871	.087
Taking shopping at ease	.788	−.030
Minimizing shopping time	−.755	.215
Well organizing the shopping trip	−.018	.840
Knowing in advance what to buy	−.013	.810
Shopping list most of the time	−.056	.715

Extraction Method: Principal component analysis.
Rotation Method: Varimax with Kaiser normalization.
[a]Rotation converged in 3 iterations

For each variable, the 'Rotated Component Matrix' (Figure 7.23) shows a high absolute loading on one of the two factors and a low loading on the remaining factor. The correlation between variable and factor is thus sufficiently exclusive to be able to guarantee a pure definition of both factors.

Figure 7.24

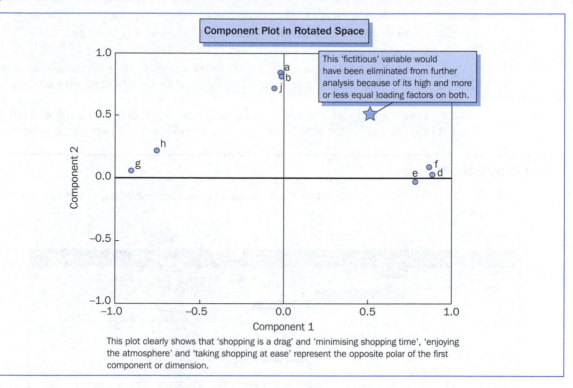

Component Plot in Rotated Space

This 'fictitious' variable would have been eliminated from further analysis because of its high and more or less equal loading factors on both.

This plot clearly shows that 'shopping is a drag' and 'minimising shopping time', 'enjoying the atmosphere' and 'taking shopping at ease' represent the opposite polar of the first component or dimension.

This exclusive relationship between variable and factor which is often the result of rotating the factors obtained initially, is also evidenced visually in the 'Component Plot in Rotated Space' (Figure 7.24): an 'extreme' score on the one axis often implies a 'zero' score on the other axis.

Figure 7.25

Component Score Coefficient Matrix

	Component		
	1	2	
Well organizing the shopping trip	.020	.437	a
Knowing in advance what to buy	.020	.422	b
Shopping is fun	.252	.040	d
Taking shopping at ease	.222	.008	e
Enjoying the atmosphere	.249	.071	f
Shopping is a drag	−.254	.001	g
Minimizing shopping time	−.207	.090	h
Shopping list most of the time	.005	.371	j

Extraction Method: Principal component analysis.
Rotation Method: Varimax with Kaiser normalization.
Component scores.

It had already been mentioned previously that the values in the 'Component Score Coefficient Matrix' (Figure 7.25), the weighting coefficients, may be used for the calculation of the factor scores on the basis of Equation (1). Filling this comparison in with concrete values for the first factor leads to the following equality:

$$F_1 = \text{'Pleasure'} = .020*a + .020*b + .252*d + .222*e + .249*f$$
$$+ (-.254)*g + (-.207)*h + .005*j$$

If we replace the letters a, b, d, e, f, g, h and j by the scores obtained for the second respondent for each of these original variables, for example, then we will obtain the score for the second respondent for the first factor. It must be mentioned here that the 'standardized' values for the original variables will be used, since the factor scores obtained via SPSS (see [fac1_1] and [fac2_1] in the SPSS 'Data View' window; Figure 7.29) are also standardized.

Supporting technique

For the addition of standardized values for original variables to the SPSS dataset, the researcher may follow the steps below:

Figure 7.26

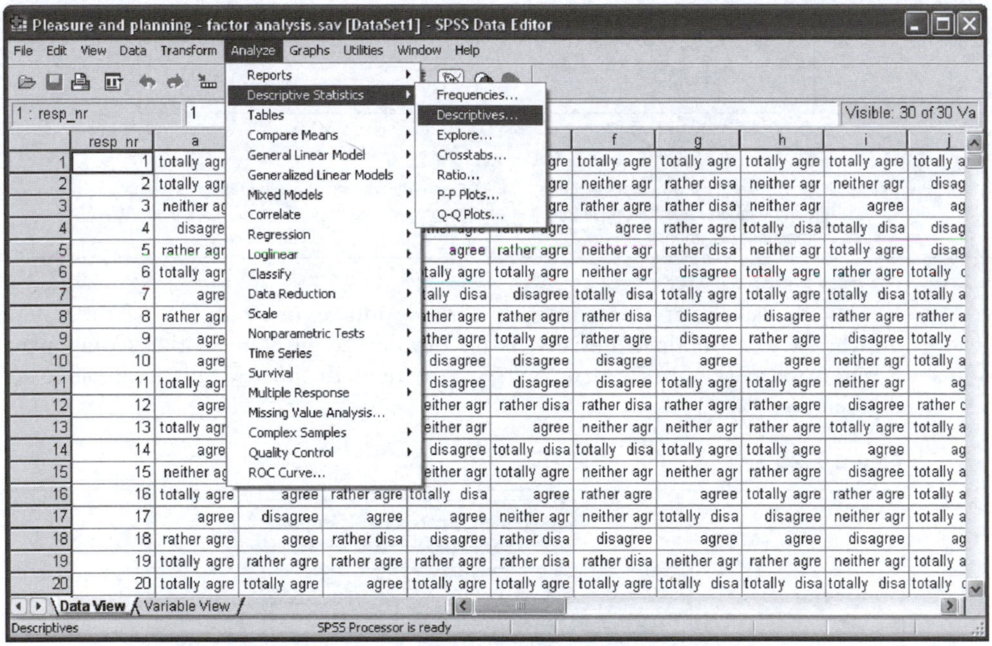

Go to Analyze/Descriptive Statistics/Descriptives (Figure 7.26).

Figure 7.27

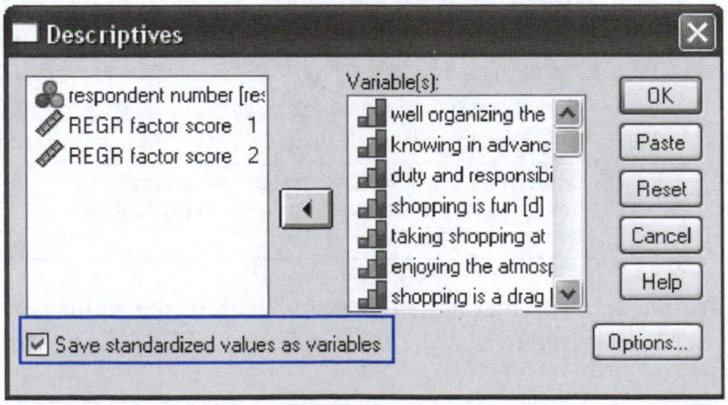

Select the variables to be standardized in Figure 7.27 and select 'Save standardized values as variables'. A number of statistics may be found under the 'Options' button (mean, standard deviation, etc.), however these are not relevant here.

Figure 7.28

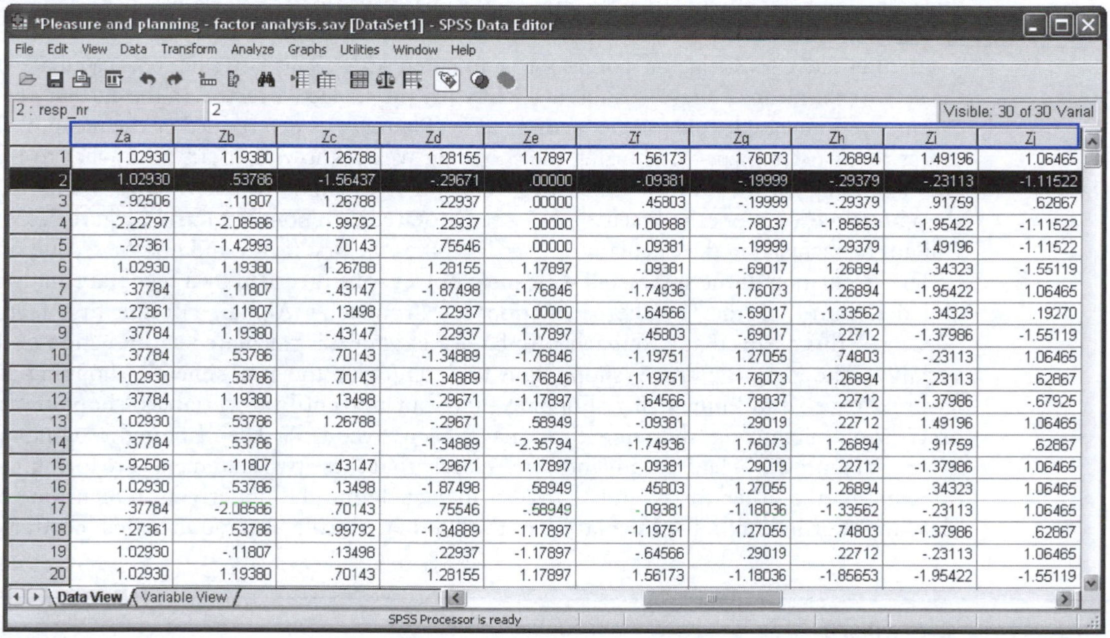

	Za	Zb	Zc	Zd	Ze	Zf	Zg	Zh	Zi	Zj
1	1.02930	1.19380	1.26788	1.28155	1.17897	1.56173	1.76073	1.26894	1.49196	1.06465
2	1.02930	.53786	-1.56437	-.29671	.00000	-.09381	-.19999	-.29379	-.23113	-1.11522
3	-.92506	-.11807	1.26788	.22937	.00000	.45803	-.19999	-.29379	.91759	.62867
4	-2.22797	-2.08586	-.99792	.22937	.00000	1.00988	.78037	-1.85653	-1.95422	-1.11522
5	-.27361	-1.42993	.70143	.75546	.00000	-.09381	-.19999	-.29379	1.49196	-1.11522
6	1.02930	1.19380	1.26788	1.28155	1.17897	-.09381	-.69017	1.26894	.34323	-1.55119
7	.37784	-.11807	-.43147	-1.87498	-1.76846	-1.74936	1.76073	1.26894	-1.95422	1.06465
8	-.27361	-.11807	.13498	.22937	.00000	-.64566	-.69017	-1.33562	.34323	.19270
9	.37784	1.19380	-.43147	.22937	1.17897	.45803	-.69017	.22712	-1.37986	-1.55119
10	.37784	.53786	.70143	-1.34889	-1.76846	-1.19751	1.27055	.74803	-.23113	1.06465
11	1.02930	.53786	.70143	-1.34889	-1.76846	-1.19751	1.76073	1.26894	-.23113	.62867
12	.37784	1.19380	.13498	-.29671	-1.17897	-.64566	.78037	.22712	-1.37986	-.67925
13	1.02930	.53786	1.26788	-.29671	.58949	-.09381	.29019	.22712	1.49196	1.06465
14	.37784	.53786	.	-1.34889	-2.35794	-1.74936	1.76073	1.26894	.91759	.62867
15	-.92506	-.11807	-.43147	-.29671	1.17897	-.09381	.29019	.22712	-1.37986	1.06465
16	1.02930	.53786	.13498	-1.87498	.58949	.45803	1.27055	1.26894	.34323	1.06465
17	.37784	-2.08586	.70143	.75546	-.58949	-.09381	-1.18036	-1.33562	-.23113	1.06465
18	-.27361	.53786	-.99792	-1.34889	-1.17897	-1.19751	1.27055	.74803	-1.37986	.62867
19	1.02930	-.11807	.13498	.22937	-1.17897	-.64566	.29019	.22712	-.23113	1.06465
20	1.02930	1.19380	.70143	1.28155	1.17897	1.56173	-1.18036	-1.85653	-1.95422	-1.55119

Twelve new columns are added to the original dataset: Za, Zb, Zc, . . . , Zk and Zl. These contain the standardized scores for each of the respondents to each of the original variables (Figure 7.28).

Figure 7.29

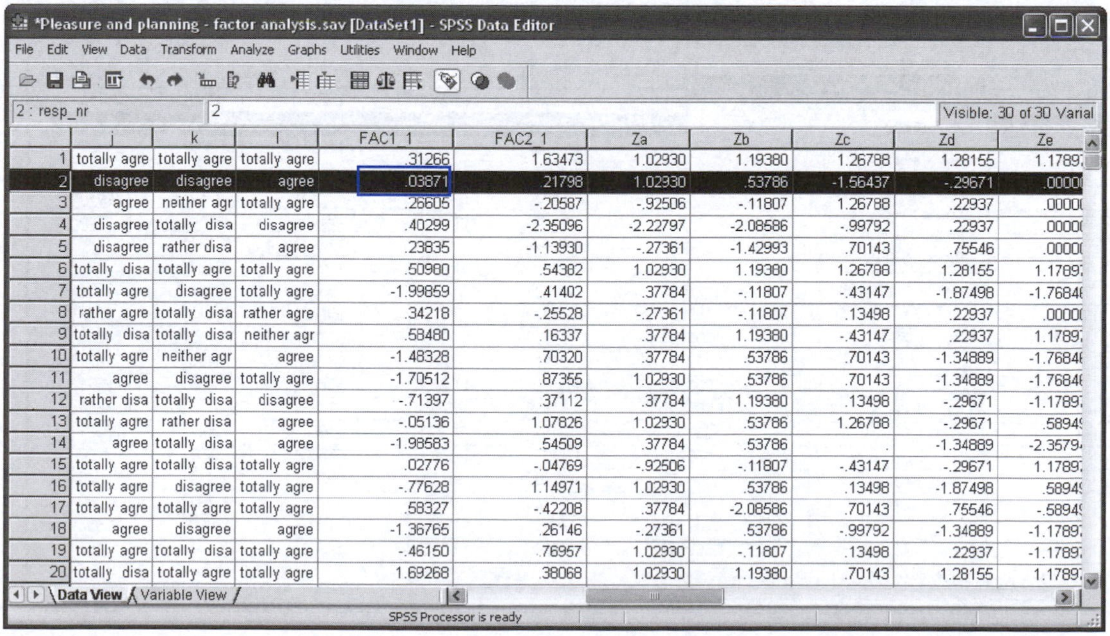

	j	k	l	FAC1_1	FAC2_1	Za	Zb	Zc	Zd	Ze
1	totally agre	totally agre	totally agre	.31266	1.63473	1.02930	1.19380	1.26788	1.28155	1.1789
2	disagree	disagree	agree	.03871	.21798	1.02930	.53786	-1.56437	-.29671	.0000
3	agree	neither agr	totally agre	.26605	-.20587	-.92506	-.11807	1.26788	.22937	.0000
4	disagree	totally disa	disagree	.40299	-2.35096	-2.22797	-2.08586	-.99792	.22937	.0000
5	disagree	rather disa	agree	.23835	-1.13930	-.27361	-1.42993	.70143	.75546	.0000
6	totally disa	totally agre	totally agre	.50980	.54382	1.02930	1.19380	1.26788	1.28155	1.1789
7	totally agre	disagree	totally agre	-1.99859	.41402	.37784	-.11807	-.43147	-1.87498	-1.7684
8	rather agre	totally disa	rather agre	.34218	-.25528	-.27361	-.11807	.13498	.22937	.0000
9	totally disa	totally disa	neither agr	.58480	.16337	.37784	1.19380	-.43147	.22937	1.1789
10	totally agre	neither agr	agree	-1.48328	.70320	.37784	.53786	.70143	-1.34889	-1.7684
11	agree	disagree	totally agre	-1.70512	.87355	1.02930	.53786	.70143	-1.34889	-1.7684
12	rather disa	totally disa	disagree	-.71397	.37112	.37784	1.19380	.13498	-.29671	-1.1789
13	totally agre	rather disa	agree	-.05136	1.07826	1.02930	.53786	1.26788	-.29671	.5894
14	agree	totally disa	agree	-1.98583	.54509	.37784	.53786	.	-1.34889	-2.3579
15	totally agre	totally disa	totally agre	.02776	-.04769	-.92506	-.11807	-.43147	-.29671	1.1789
16	totally agre	disagree	totally agre	-.77628	1.14971	1.02930	.53786	.13498	-1.87498	.5894
17	totally agre	totally agre	totally agre	.58327	-.42208	.37784	-2.08586	.70143	.75546	-.5894
18	agree	disagree	agree	-1.36765	.26146	-.27361	.53786	-.99792	-1.34889	-1.1789
19	totally agre	totally disa	totally agre	-.46150	.76957	1.02930	-.11807	.13498	.22937	-1.1789
20	totally disa	totally agre	totally agre	1.69268	.38068	1.02930	1.19380	.70143	1.28155	1.1789

Therefore, the second respondent has the following score for the first factor: .020*1.03 + .020*.54 + .252*(−.30) + .222*0 + .249*(−.09) + (−.254)*(−.20) + (−.207)*(−.29) + .005*(−1.12) = .04. This score corresponds to the factor score which was calculated directly by SPSS and which is shown in the 'Data View' window (Figure 7.29).

If, for example, the researcher would like to base a regression analysis on the dimensions 'Pleasure' and 'Planning', then he may make direct use of the variables [FAC1_1] and [FAC2_1].

An alternative to the factor score is the 'summated scale'. This latter figure is calculated as the sum or the mean of those variables which typify the respective factor. In the current application, the summated scale for the second factor 'Planning' is determined as the mean of the scores for the statements 'organizing the shopping well', 'knowing in advance what to buy' and 'shopping list most of the time'. Regardless of the loading of the variable 'minimizing shopping time' on the second factor (.215 – see 'Rotated Component Matrix', Figure 7.23), it will not be included in the calculation, since it typifies the first factor and not the second one.

The calculation of the summated scale must however be preceded by a reliability analysis, and determined further by the calculation of 'Cronbach's Alpha'. For the first factor, 'Pleasure', this means that Cronbach's Alpha, for example, is calculated as a function of the variables 'shopping is a drag', 'shopping is fun', 'enjoying the atmosphere', 'shopping at a leisurely pace', and 'minimizing shopping time' but not until the variables 'shopping is a drag' and 'minimizing shopping time' have been 'recoded'. The 'Rotated Component Matrix' (Figure 7.23) had already indicated clearly that these two statements are formulated opposite to the other three, and that they in fact define the underlying dimension 'No pleasure'. Furthermore, the calculation of the summated scale also requires this recoding.

Supporting technique

Recoding

Figure 7.30

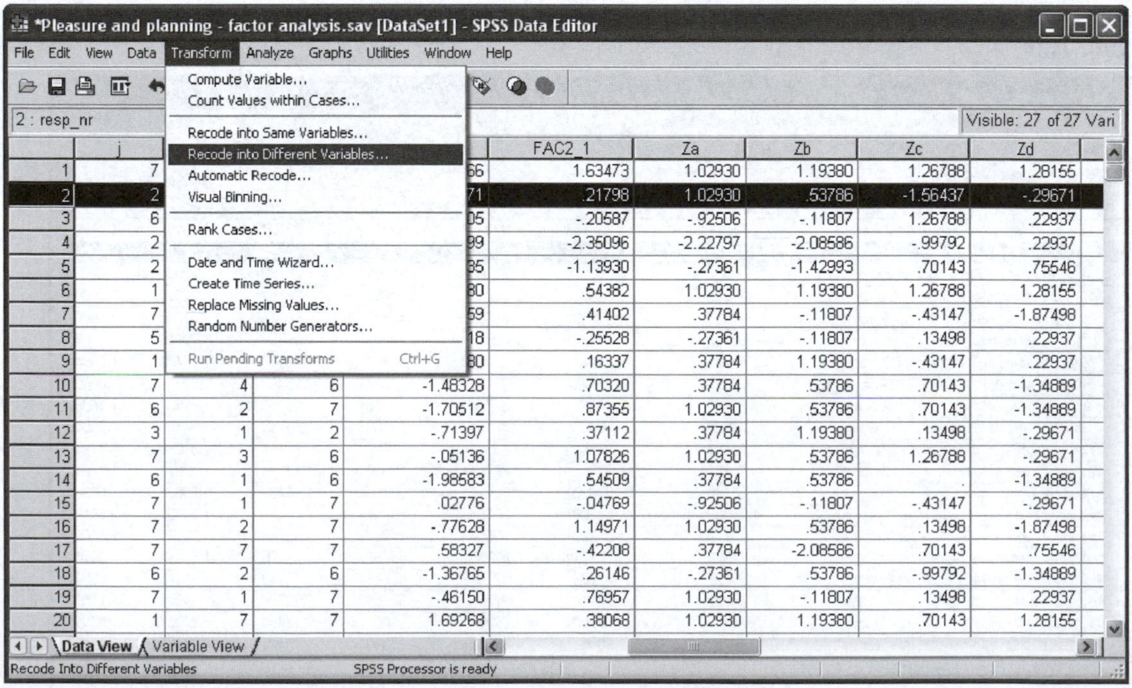

Go to Transform/Recode Into Different Variables (Figure 7.30).

Figure 7.31

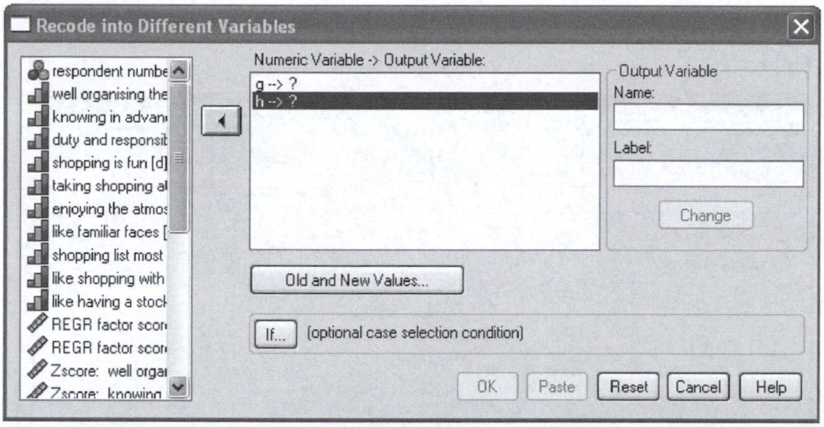

In the left-hand column, select the variables 'shopping is a drag' [g] and 'minimizing shopping time' [h] and move them to the box under 'Numeric Variable -> Output Variable' (Figure 7.31).

Figure 7.32

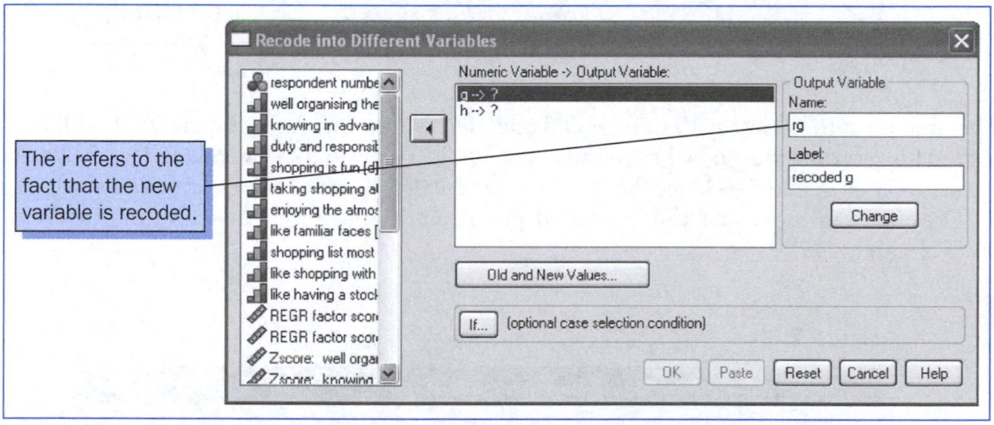

The r refers to the fact that the new variable is recoded.

Click 'g' and determine the name and label of the recoded variable under 'Output Variable' (Figure 7.32).

Figure 7.33

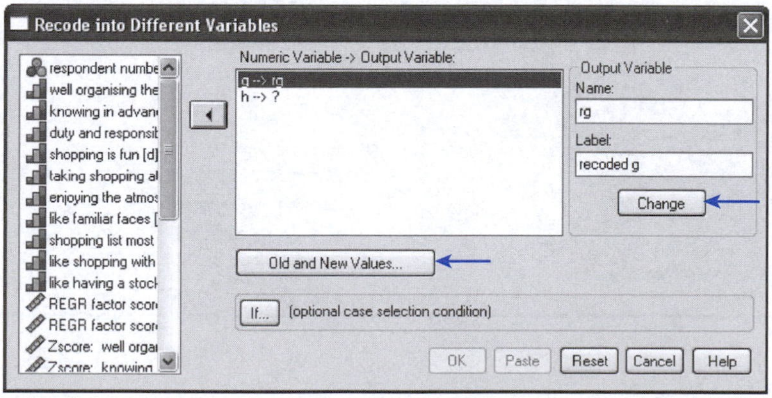

Now click on the 'Change' button and the expression 'g -> rg' will appear. Follow the same procedure for the variable 'h' and then click on the button 'Old and New Values' (Figure 7.33).

Figure 7.34

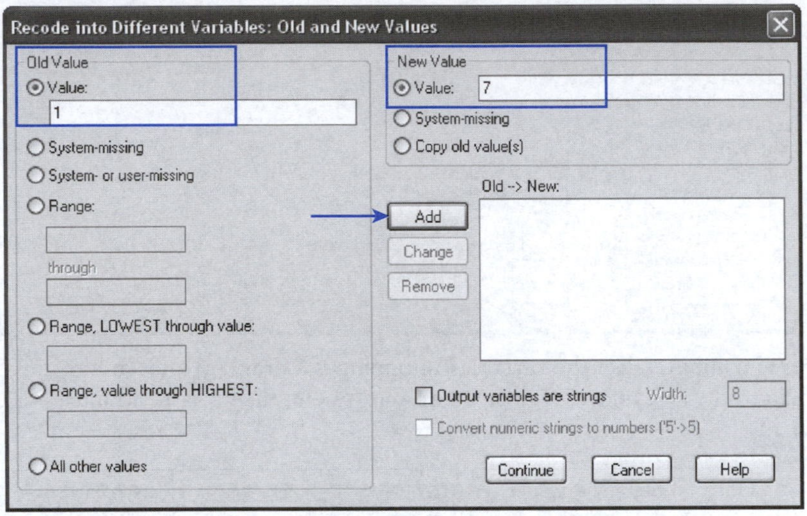

The 'Recode into Different Variables: Old and New Values' window (Figure 7.34) will appear, and the method for recoding must now be indicated under 'Old Value' and 'New Value': 1 -> 7, 2 -> 6, 3 -> 5, 4 -> 4, 5 -> 3, 6 -> 2, and 7 ->1 (see the 7-point Likert scales). Each of these conversions will be included in the 'Old -> New' box, and thus recorded permanently, once the 'Add' button has been clicked (Figures 7.34 and 7.35).

Figure 7.35

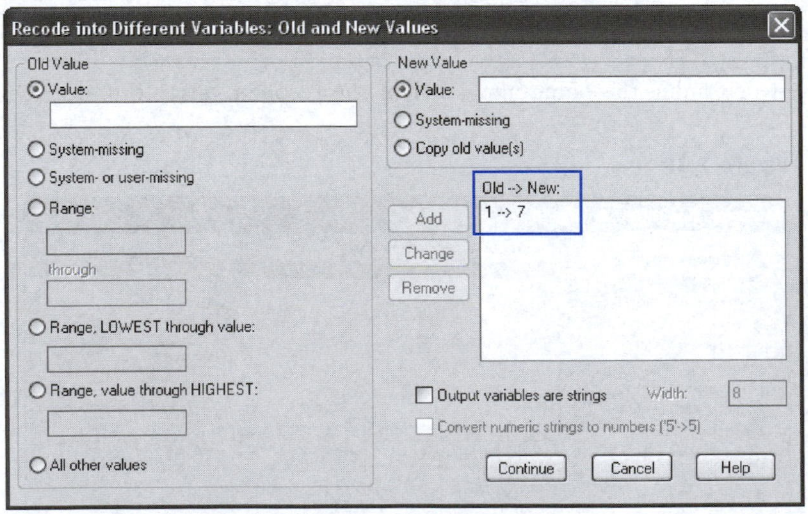

Figure 7.36

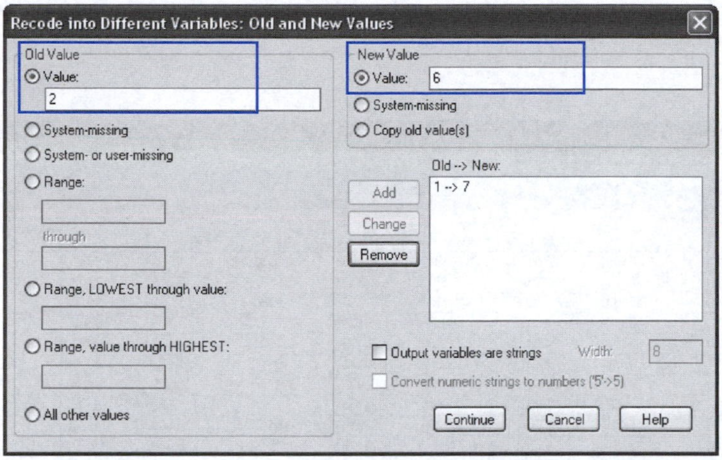

The conversion of '2' to '6' and the final list with the recodings are shown with the aid of two screens (Figures 7.36 and 7.37).

Figure 7.37

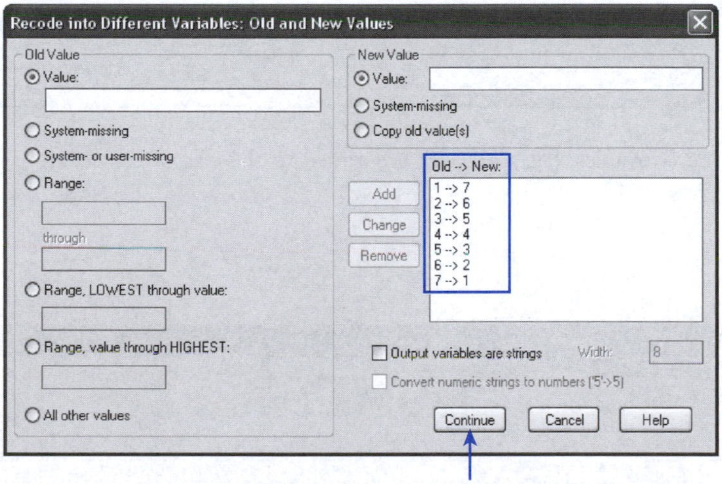

Figure 7.38

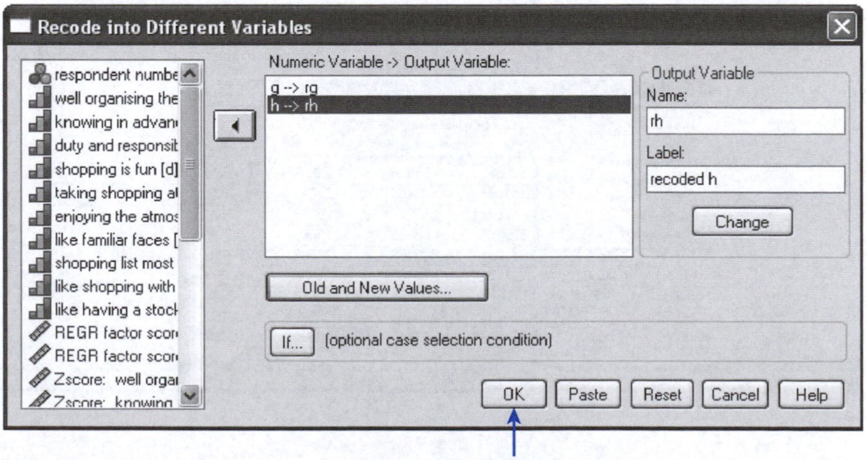

After clicking 'Continue' (Figure 7.37), the 'Recode into Different Variables' window (Figure 7.38) will reappear. The previous definition of 'Old and New Values' is immediately applicable to both variables, and the next step is to click 'OK'.

Figure 7.39

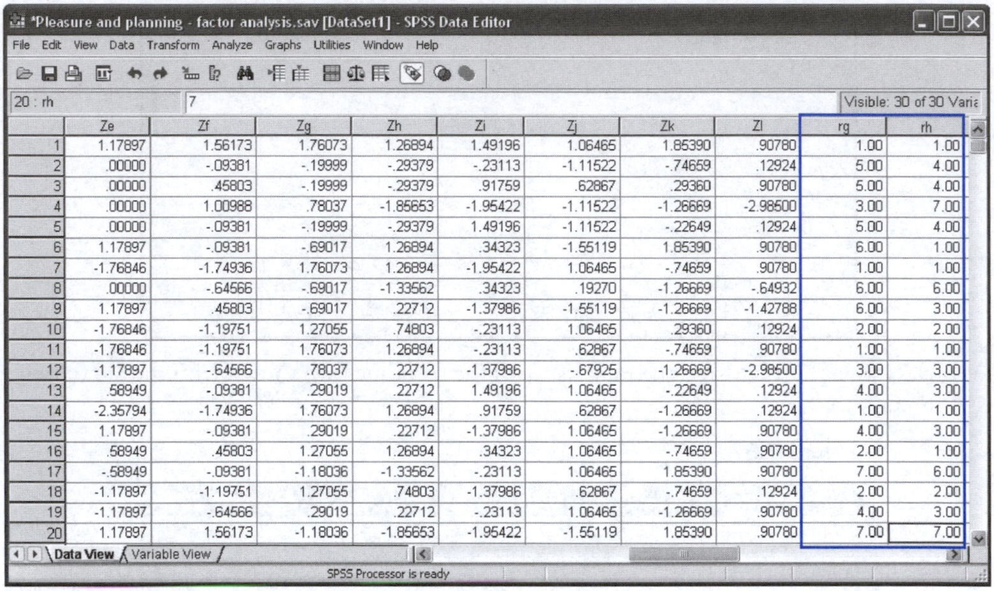

The two 'recoded' variables, [rg] and [rh], are added to the end of the columns in the 'Data View' window (Figure 7.39).

Cronbach's Alpha

Figure 7.40

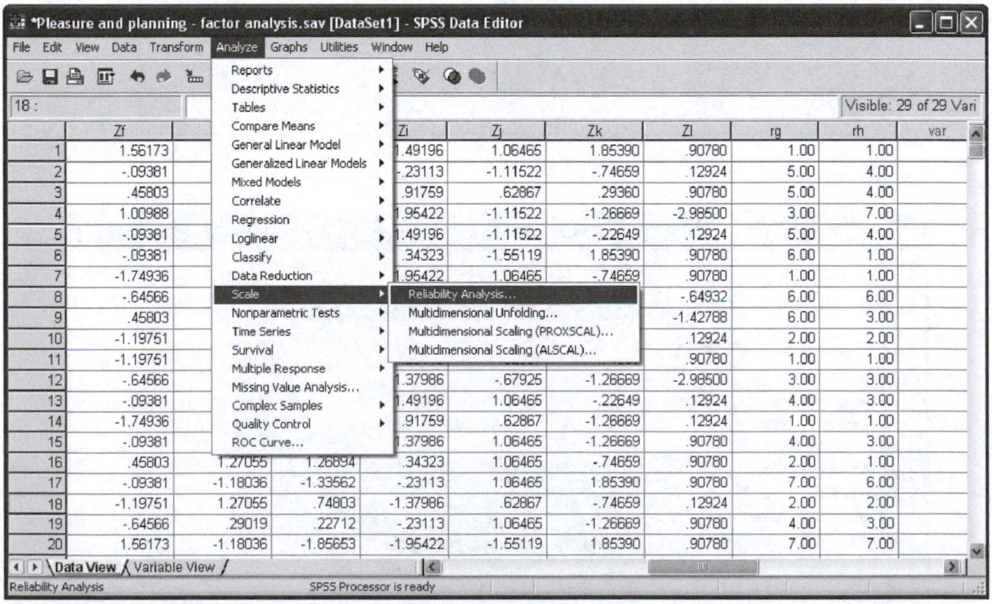

Go to Analyze/Scale/Reliability Analysis (Figure 7.40).

Figure 7.41

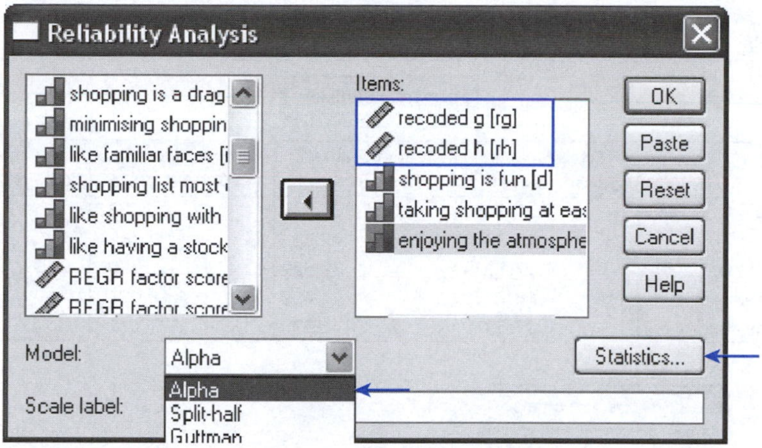

Move the variables which typify the first factor to the box 'Items' and do not select the variables 'shopping is a drag' [g] or 'minimizing shopping time' [h], but now choose **the recoded variables** [rg] and [rh] instead (Figure 7.41).

Under 'Model', select: the desired reliability analysis. The calculation of Cronbach's Alpha corresponds to the 'Alpha' option, which is also the default setting in SPSS. Now click 'Statistics'.

Figure 7.42

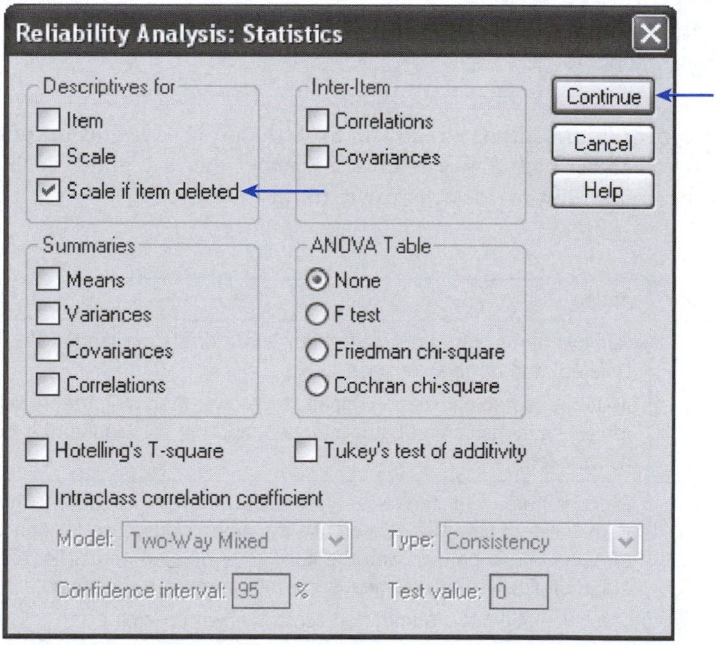

In the 'Reliability Analysis: Statistics' window (Figure 7.42), choose the option 'Scale if item deleted'. This will result in the following statistics: (1) the mean and the variance for the underlying dimension after the elimination of the respective statement; (2) the correlation between the relevant statement and one factor, consisting of the other statements; and (3) Cronbach's Alpha for the scale after the removal of the respective statement.

Now click 'Continue', and 'OK' in the main window (Figure 7.41).

Figure 7.43

Item-Total Statistics

	Scale Mean if Item Deleted	Scale Variance if Item Deleted	Corrected Item-Total Correlation	Cronbach's Alpha if Item Deleted
Recoded g	17.1700	37.476	.837	.854
Recoded h	18.3260	42.553	.651	.897
Shopping is fun	17.1980	39.622	.807	.862
Taking shopping at ease	16.7620	44.402	.675	.891
Enjoying the atmosphere	17.5920	41.220	.776	.870

Case Processing Summary

		N	%
Cases	Valid	500	100.0
	Excluded[a]	0	.0
	Total	500	100.0

[a]Listwise deletion based on all variables in the procedure

Reliability Statistics

Cronbach's Alpha	N of Items
.898	5

The results will appear in the output window in SPSS (Figure 7.43). This output contains an Alpha value of .898, and the researcher may now ask himself whether this is a 'good' or 'bad' result, and what the next step should be. Table 7.3 provides an answer to this question.

Table 7.3

Cronbach's Alpha value	Action
smaller than .60	Remove items with the lowest 'Item-Total Correlation' and/or the highest 'Alpha if Item Deleted' and do this stepwise.
	If after repeated elimination, Alpha stays lower than .60, then a scale based on the remaining items cannot be constructed, and the calculation of a 'summated scale' is not allowed.
between .60 and .80	Remove items with the lowest 'Item-Total Correlation' and/or the highest 'Alpha if Item Deleted' stepwise to increase the Alpha value. Carefully consider the increase of Alpha in comparison with the number of deleted items. For example, a rise in Alpha of .02, with an elimination of four items is not justified.
	The calculation of a summated scale is always permitted.
larger than .80	An elimination of items with the purpose to increase Alpha is not necessary and the summated scale can be calculated immediately.

In general: the calculation of Chronbach's Alpha preferably needs a minimum of three items, and is sensitive for the number of items comprised. For example, increasing the number of items will inflate this statistic and will possibly lead to a 'good' score while the items are heterogeneous among themselves. Hence, running a factor analysis before calculating Cronbach's Alpha (per Factor) is recommended.

Therefore, given the fact the Alpha value of .898 is greater than .80, the result should be considered 'very good', and an elimination of one of the five statements is unnecessary. The column 'Alpha if Item Deleted' indicates that the elimination of none of the items will lead to an increase in Alpha considering the fact that all of the values in this column are less than .898. In the next step, a summated scale may be calculated on the basis of these five items.

Performing the same reliability analysis on the three statements which typify the 'Planning' dimension leads to the results shown in Figure 7.44:

Figure 7.44

Item-Total Statistics

	Scale Mean if Item Deleted	Scale Variance if Item Deleted	Corrected Item-Total Correlation	Cronbach's Alpha if Item Deleted
Well organizing the shopping trip	9.74	10.065	.574	.493
Knowing in advance what to buy	9.98	10.719	.497	.579
Shopping list most of the time	10.60	7.166	.455	.694

Case Processing Summary

		N	%
Cases	Valid	500	100.0
	Excluded[a]	0	.0
	Total	500	100.0

[a]Listwise deletion based on all variables in the procedure

Reliability Statistics

Cronbach's Alpha	N of Items
.672	3

The Alpha value of .672 lies between .60 and .80, which indicates a 'good' result. The elimination of statements, the goal of which is to increase the Alpha value, is an option, and may lead here to an increase in Alpha to .694 through the elimination of item 'shopping list most of the time'. This elimination will however not be performed since it would lead to a scale which is based on only two statements, 'well organizing the shopping trip' and 'knowing in advance what to buy'. Moreover, the increase in Alpha would only be marginal.

Summated scale

Figure 7.45

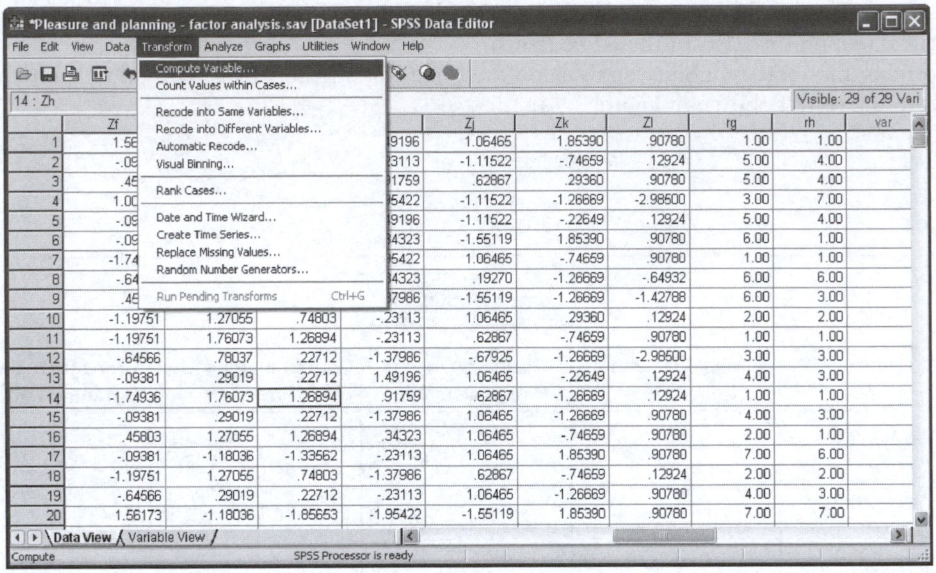

Go to Transform/Compute Variable (Figure 7.45).

Figure 7.46

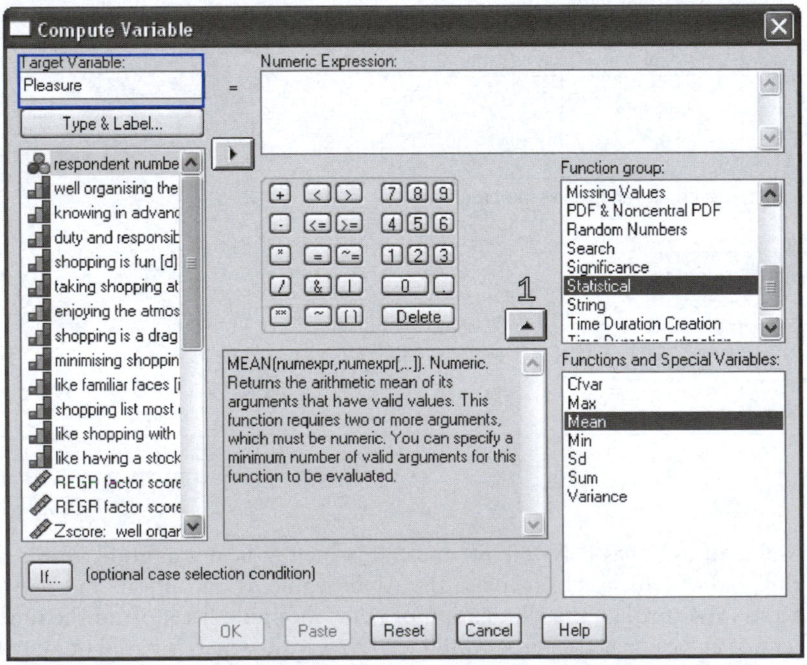

Under 'Target Variable' in Figure 7.46, fill in the name of the new variable, the 'summated scale'. Under 'Function Group', select the function which will serve as the basis upon which the 'summated scale' will be calculated. In the present example, the 'summated scale' is defined as a mean. For this reason, choose the option 'Mean' in the 'Functions and Special Variables' window (make sure that 'All' (default setting) or 'Statistical' is selected for 'Function group').

Figure 7.47

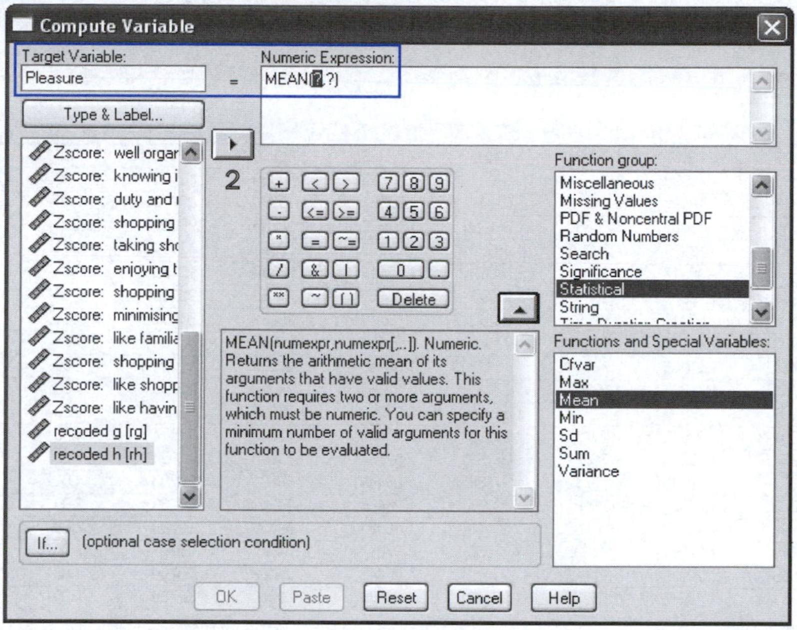

From the list of variables, select those which load on the factor 'Pleasure', and move them using the arrow indicated by a '2' to the box 'Numeric Expression' (Figure 7.47). Make sure that the recoded variables ([rg] and [rh]) are included instead of the statements 'shopping is a drag' [g] and 'minimizing shopping time' [h].

Figure 7.48

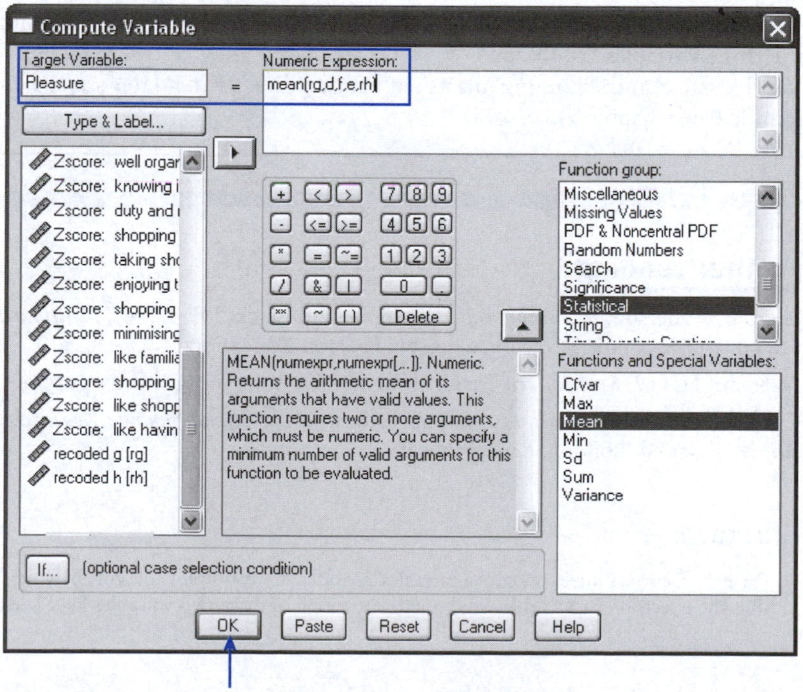

After completing the numeric expression, click ‘OK’ (Figure 7.48).

Figure 7.49

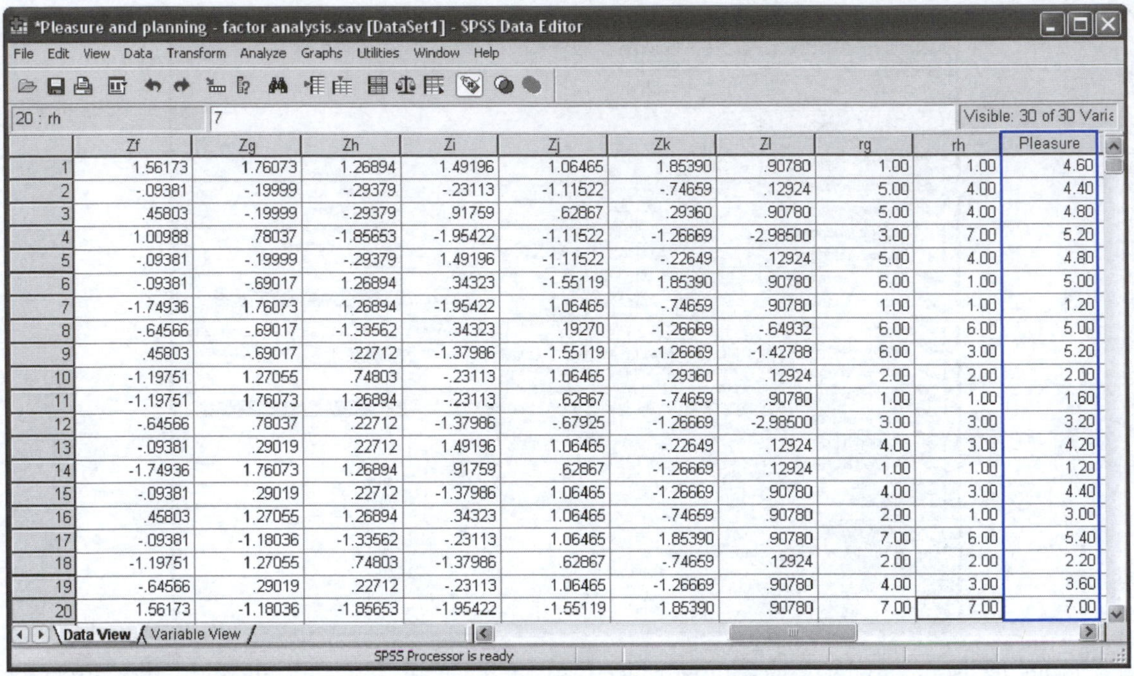

	Zf	Zg	Zh	Zi	Zj	Zk	Zl	rg	rh	Pleasure
1	1.56173	1.76073	1.26894	1.49196	1.06465	1.85390	.90780	1.00	1.00	4.60
2	-.09381	-.19999	-.29379	-.23113	-1.11522	-.74659	.12924	5.00	4.00	4.40
3	.45803	-.19999	-.29379	.91759	.62867	.29360	.90780	5.00	4.00	4.80
4	1.00988	.78037	-1.85653	-1.95422	-1.11522	-1.26669	-2.98500	3.00	7.00	5.20
5	-.09381	-.19999	-.29379	1.49196	-1.11522	-.22649	.12924	5.00	4.00	4.80
6	-.09381	-.69017	1.26894	.34323	-1.55119	1.85390	.90780	6.00	1.00	5.00
7	-1.74936	1.76073	1.26894	-1.95422	1.06465	-.74659	.90780	1.00	1.00	1.20
8	-.64566	-.69017	-1.33562	.34323	.19270	-1.26669	-.64932	6.00	6.00	5.00
9	.45803	-.69017	.22712	-1.37986	-1.55119	-1.26669	-1.42788	6.00	3.00	5.20
10	-1.19751	1.27055	.74803	-.23113	1.06465	.29360	.12924	2.00	2.00	2.00
11	-1.19751	1.76073	1.26894	-.23113	.62867	-.74659	.90780	1.00	1.00	1.60
12	-.64566	.78037	.22712	-1.37986	-.67925	-1.26669	-2.98500	3.00	3.00	3.20
13	-.09381	.29019	.22712	1.49196	1.06465	-.22649	.12924	4.00	3.00	4.20
14	-1.74936	1.76073	1.26894	.91759	.62867	-1.26669	.12924	1.00	1.00	1.20
15	-.09381	.29019	.22712	-1.37986	1.06465	-1.26669	.90780	4.00	3.00	4.40
16	.45803	1.27055	1.26894	.34323	1.06465	-.74659	.90780	2.00	1.00	3.00
17	-.09381	-1.18036	-1.33562	-.23113	1.06465	1.85390	.90780	7.00	6.00	5.40
18	-1.19751	1.27055	.74803	-1.37986	.62867	-.74659	.12924	2.00	2.00	2.20
19	-.64566	.29019	.22712	-.23113	1.06465	-1.26669	.90780	4.00	3.00	3.60
20	1.56173	-1.18036	-1.85653	-1.95422	-1.55119	1.85390	.90780	7.00	7.00	7.00

A column with the heading ‘Pleasure’ has been added to the dataset (Figure 7.49). This column assigns a score between 1 and 7 to each of the respondents, in which a high score indicates experiencing a great deal of ‘pleasure’ during shopping and a low score indicates that very little ‘pleasure’ is experienced during shopping.

This same method may be used to calculate a summated scale for the factor ‘Planning’, and this may be done using the three variables ‘a’, ‘b’, and ‘j’.

The variables ‘Pleasure’ and ‘Planning’ may then be used directly in a later step as input for a cluster analysis, for example (see Chapter 9).

Further reading

Hair, J., Anderson, R., Babir, B., Tatham, R. and Black, W. (2006), *Multivariate Data Analysis*. 6th ed. Upper Saddle River, New Jersey: Pearson Education.

Harman, H. (1976), *Modern Factor Analysis*. 3rd ed. Chicago: University of Chicago Press.

Tacq, J. (1997), *Multivariate Analysis Techniques in Social Science Research: From Problem to Analysis*. 1st ed. London: Sage Publications.

Endnote

1 The partial correlation between the variables ‘a’ and ‘b’ for example is the correlation between these variables after the effects of the variables ‘c’ through ‘l’ on each of these two variables have been taken into account.

Chapter 8

Confirmatory factor analysis and path analysis using SEM

Chapter objectives

This chapter will help you to:

- Understand how and when to use confirmatory factor analysis and path analysis
- Build a measurement model using AMOS
- Build a structural equation (path) model using AMOS
- Optimize estimation results
- Assess the validity and reliability of the model
- Interpret the model results

Technique

Structural Equation Modelling (SEM) is a method used to estimate a set of regression equations simultaneously. SEM is therefore also suitable for the estimation of traditional models (e.g. regression analysis) as well as more complex relationships (e.g. confirmatory factor analysis). This chapter will discuss two specific fields of application: confirmatory factor analysis and path analysis. The former involves the testing of a measurement model with latent (not immediately observable) variables; path analysis involves the estimation of structural relationships between latent variables. The general idea behind the SEM method is to estimate the model in such a way that the sample covariance matrix corresponds as closely as possible to the model covariance matrix. The (extra) SPSS module which is used to perform SEM is AMOS.

SEM uses some specific terminology and agreements. There are three types of variables which are used and discussed in this chapter (see also Figure 8.1 in which each of the concepts covered is displayed in graphic form).

- Observed or manifest variables are variables which are measured effectively (e.g., score on 7-point scale). They are presented as square or rectangular (v1, v2, v3 and v4 in Figure 8.1).
- Non-observed variables or latent variables are variables which are not measured directly, but may be derived/estimated on the basis of the score for and the variance of the observed variables. They are presented as circles or ovals (Factor 1 and Factor 2 in Figure 8.1).

Figure 8.1

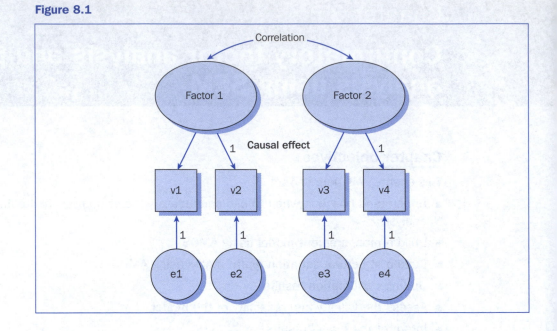

- Error terms (which determine the unique variance of a variable) are non-observable and are therefore always indicated with a circle (e1, e2, e3 and e4 in Figure 8.1).

In addition, there are still the mutual relationships which must be established.

- Double-pointed arrows are used to indicate correlations and covariances.
- Single-pointed arrows are used to indicate causal effects.

The numbers '1' in the figures are necessary in order to assign a measurement scale to the latent factors and error terms. This results in unique solutions.

In the sections that follow, the researcher will attempt to estimate a model. In order to do this, there are two consecutive steps necessary: first we need to find out if and which variables actually determine underlying dimensions (example 1: confirmatory factor analysis), in order to be able to determine in the next step which relationships may be found between these dimensions (example 2: path analysis).

If the reader would like to use the files immediately such as those supplied on the CD, then it is recommended to first copy them to the hard drive (or to another recordable information carrier) since AMOS creates extra files during the analysis, including the output file. If the user starts up the program from a non-recordable information carrier such as a CD-ROM, AMOS will report an error.

For a more in-depth discussion of this technique, the reader is advised to consult the reference works which appear at the end of this chapter.

Example 1

Confirmatory factor analysis

Managerial problem

The researcher would like to find out to what degree time pressure and price consciousness can have an influence on the level of involvement in shopping behaviour. During the first phase, the researcher should try to find out whether the different variables measured measure the underlying dimensions in a correct manner. The variables are defined as follows (variable name may be found between parentheses after the statement), and are included in the file *involvement.sav*.

Involvement (involv)

With regard to my weekly shopping time . . .

I am not interested	1 2 3 4 5 6 7	I am very interested (involv1)
Does not mean anything to me	1 2 3 4 5 6 7	Means a lot to me (involv2)
Is not important to me	1 2 3 4 5 6 7	Is important to me (involv3)

Price Consciousness (prcon) (totally disagree (1) – totally agree (7))

The money that I save by finding low prices is usually worth the time and effort (prcon1)

I will shop in more than one store to find low prices (prcon2)

I will shop in more than one supermarket to take advantage of low prices (prcon3)

I will always visit more than one supermarket to find low prices (prcon4)

I enjoy going to different stores to be able to compare prices (prcon5)

Time Pressure (tpress) (totally disagree (1) – totally agree (7))

I always feel rushed when I shop (tpress1)

When I shop, I have to get it done quickly (tpress2)

I only have a limited time available to do the shopping (tpress3)

I try to finish my shopping as quickly as possible because I have other things to do (tpress4)

I don't have enough time to do my weekly shopping properly (tpress5)

Figure 8.2 shows the results of an exploratory factor analysis (EFA, see Chapter 7). This allows us to get an initial idea of the dimensionality of the measurements, in other words whether the different items really do belong to a certain underlying dimension. If the items from the above scales load effectively on three different factors, this already indicates exploratively that they measure different dimensions (see also the introduction in Chapter 7).

Confirmatory factor analysis (CFA) should not be confused with EFA. The essential difference is that in performing an EFA, it is not yet known which variables will determine a certain factor/dimension, whereas with CFA, it is assumed (hypothesis) that certain variables correctly measure a certain factor. On the basis of a hypothesis test, CFA may then be used to find out to which degree the different assumed variables also truly do measure that certain factor.

Figure 8.2

Rotated Component Matrix[a]			
	Component		
	1	**2**	**3**
involv1	.153	−.175	.904
involv2	.119	−.123	.938
involv3	.146	−.047	.910
prcon1	.261	.015	.140
prcon2	.833	.012	.052
prcon3	.956	−.059	.086
prcon4	.940	−.079	.072
prcon5	.953	−.047	.108
tpress1	−.026	.746	−.003
tpress2	.047	.849	−.031
tpress3	−.077	.788	−.133
tpress4	−.051	.858	−.177
tpress5	−.017	.815	−.054

Extraction Method: Principal component analysis.
Rotation Method: Varimax with Kaiser normalization.
[a]Rotation converged in 5 iterations

Figure 8.2 shows that all of the items load high on the expected three underlying dimensions. If the rule is applied which requires that there be a minimum loading of .50 on a certain factor, but at the same time no more than .30 on another factor, then from Figure 8.2, we may conclude that all of the items satisfy this requirement, except for 'prcon1'. This may be an indication that this item should be kept out of the analysis. For the time being, this item will continue to be included in the CFA.

Problem

Create a confirmatory factor analysis model in AMOS for the three constructs (time pressure, price consciousness and level of involvement). Estimate this model and make the necessary adjustments in order to arrive at a good model.

Solution

AMOS commands

First, the confirmatory factor model must be created. To do this, 'AMOS Graphics' must be opened (component of the AMOS module). A start screen will be obtained such as that shown in Figure 8.3. The idea now is to draw the confirmatory factor model in the grey centre screen via the drawing options which may be found on the right-hand side of the screen, and to label the various parameters.

A number of steps are described below which must be followed. The ultimate goal is to generate a diagram such as that shown in Figure 8.16. This involves a model with three factors.

Figure 8.3

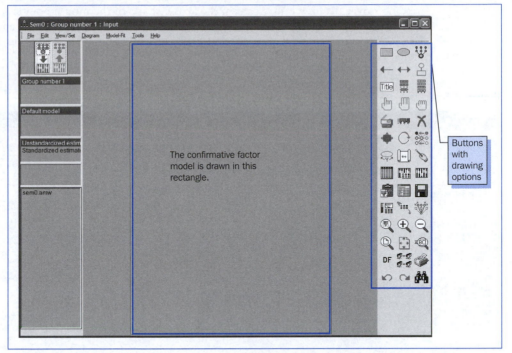

 In order to draw the first construct, namely the latent variable 'time pressure', including five underlying variables, click the **Draw Latent Variables and Indicators** square. (Figure 8.4)

Figure 8.4

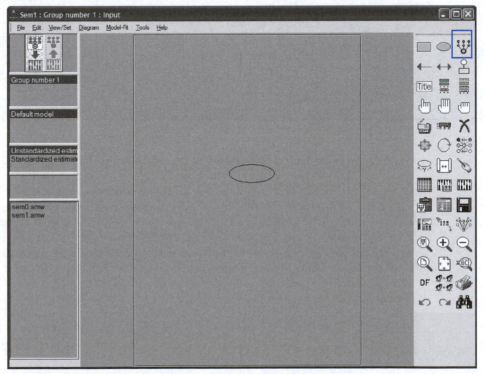

In Figure 8.4 you will see that this button is now 'depressed'. When you move the mouse pointer over the grey centre screen, the arrow shape of the mouse pointer will change into the icon of the depressed button. You may now click the grey centre screen, while keeping the left mouse button depressed, and draw an oval. The image shown in Figure 8.4 was created using this method.

Figure 8.5

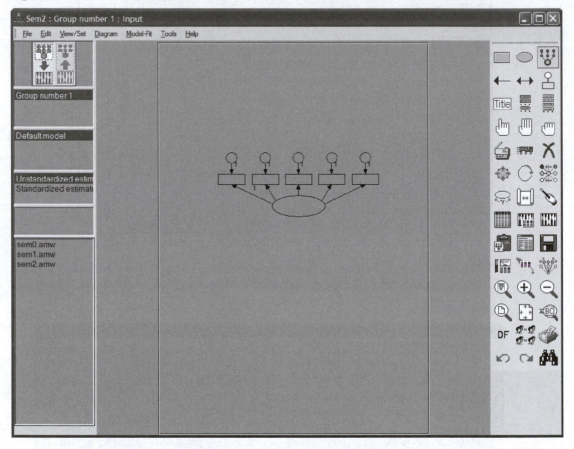

Move the (modified) mouse pointer to the oval. This will then light up red. Now click in this oval. You will see that a variable is created which is attached to this oval. Click a total of five times in this oval, so that five variables will now be attached to the oval (see Figure 8.5). The number '1' which you will (automatically) see appear next to some of the arrows relates to the model identification. A model is identified when it is impossible for two different parameter sets (estimates) to produce the same covariance matrix. To a certain extent, this may be compared to the impossibility of estimating the unknowns in an algebraic equation system, if there are more unknowns than equations. In order to arrive at this identification, it is necessary to fix certain relationships to be 1 (this amounts to providing a measurement scale). AMOS does this automatically while creating the constructs. A model which does not satisfy these conditions is referred to as an 'underidentified' model. A 'just identified' model indicates a model which is just barely capable of being estimated, but for which there is no extra information (degrees of freedom) left to evaluate the estimated model. This is the case with an 'overidentified model'. It is this last type of model which much be targeted. In addition, it is also recommended to have at least three different indicators for each construct. This way, another condition (rank condition) is always satisfied.

Figure 8.6

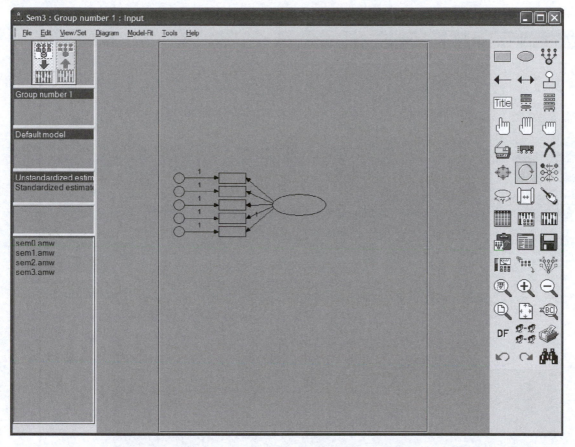

 When the additional variables created (indicators) on the left-hand side of the oval are desired, the variables attached to the oval may be rotated. To do this, click the **Rotate Indicators** button. (Figure 8.6)

The indicators may be rotated 90 degrees to the right each time, by placing the mouse pointer in the oval drawn previously and clicking three times with the left mouse button (= 270 degrees). You will then generate the image seen in Figure 8.6.

If a portion of the drawing falls outside of the grey centre screen, this may be corrected as follows. Click on **Resize the Path Diagram To Fit On A Page** (white page with four red arrows) to fit the figure to the page.

An alternative method is to click on the **Select All Objects** button (hand with extended fingers).

The figure will light up blue (the figure is selected). Now click the **Move Objects** button (truck).

Move the mouse pointer to the figure, click on it and hold it there while the figure is dragged. Release it when it has arrived at the desired location. The figure is still selected (blue). Make a copy of this construct first (since the same structure with five underlying variables is needed twice for a latent variable, namely for price consciousness and for time pressure) before turning this selection off.

Figure 8.7

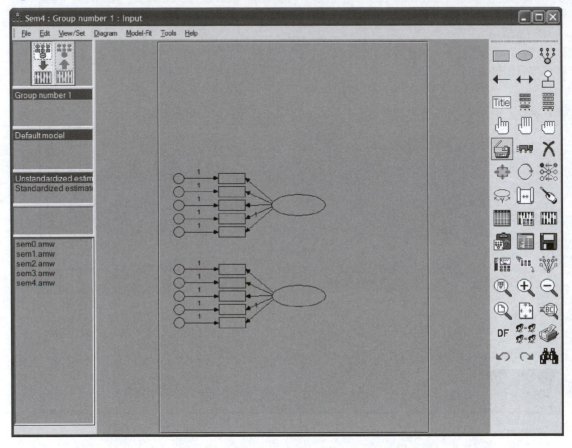

To make a copy, you must make sure that the object to be copied is selected (which is already the case here). Now click the **Duplicate Objects** button. (Figure 8.7)

Click the previously drawn oval now with the left mouse button, hold it down and you will see that a copy of the existing figure has now been created and may be dragged. Moving the copy to a specific location may be done by releasing the mouse button. If you hold the shift key down at the same time, this ensures that the copy will be moved parallel to the original. In this example, this occurs downwards, so that an image is obtained such as the one shown in Figure 8.7.

Next, a third latent variable with three underlying variables is added to Figure 8.7 in a manner analogous to that described above. This will be placed to the right of the two other latent variables with the indicators to the right of the oval (this means you only have to click once, to turn them 90 degrees to the right; see also Figures 8.5 and 8.6). The measurement model as shown in Figure 8.8 is now complete.

Figure 8.8

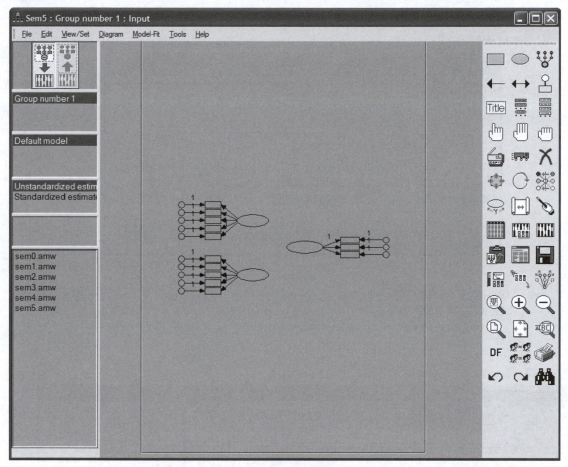

The next step is to read in the data.

Figure 8.9

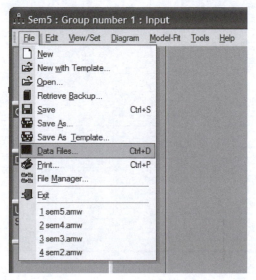

Go to File/Data Files (Figure 8.9).

Figure 8.10

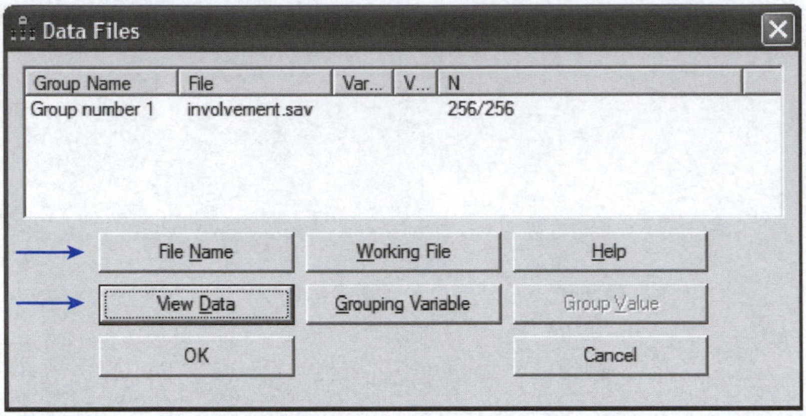

Click on 'File Name', select the required file in the subwindow (here: *involvement.sav*), and click 'Open'. This will produce an image such as the one seen in Figure 8.10. Click on 'View Data' to view the data (not required).

Figure 8.11

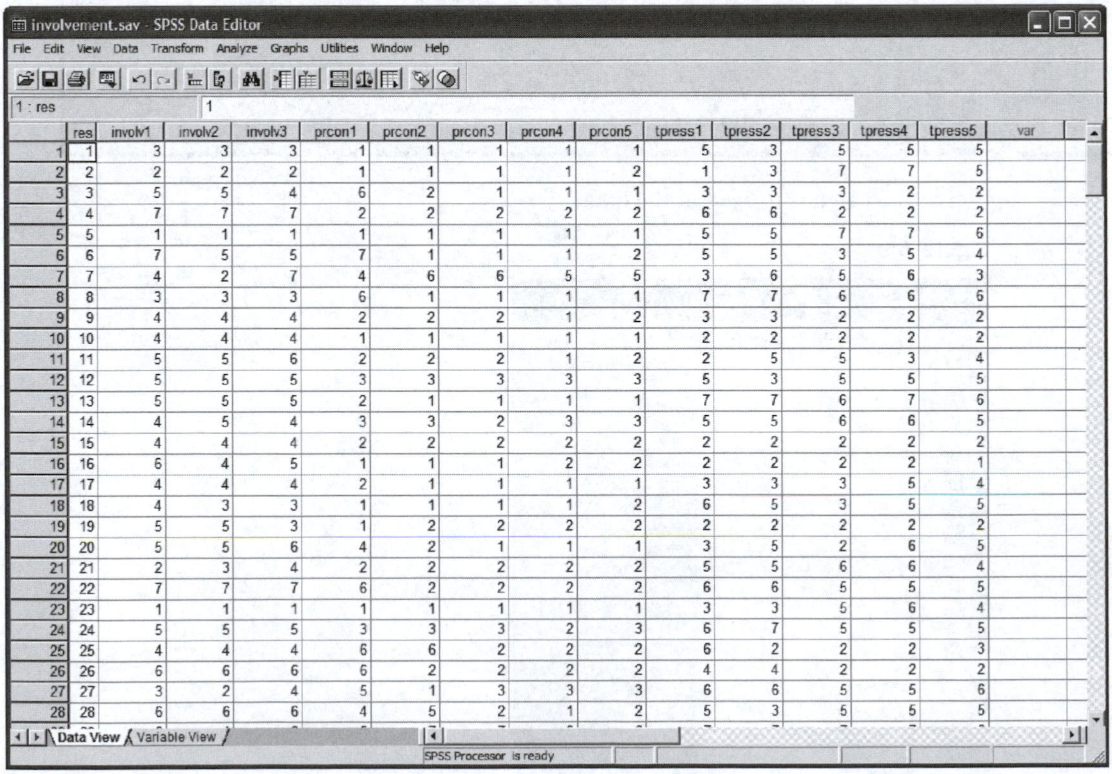

	res	involv1	involv2	involv3	prcon1	prcon2	prcon3	prcon4	prcon5	tpress1	tpress2	tpress3	tpress4	tpress5	var
1	1	3	3	3	1	1	1	1	1	5	3	5	5	5	
2	2	2	2	2	1	1	1	1	2	1	3	7	7	5	
3	3	5	5	4	6	2	1	1	1	3	3	3	2	2	
4	4	7	7	7	2	2	2	2	2	6	6	2	2	2	
5	5	1	1	1	1	1	1	1	1	5	5	7	7	6	
6	6	7	5	5	7	1	1	1	2	5	5	3	5	4	
7	7	4	2	7	4	6	6	5	5	3	6	5	6	3	
8	8	3	3	3	6	1	1	1	1	7	7	6	6	6	
9	9	4	4	4	2	2	2	1	2	3	3	2	2	2	
10	10	4	4	4	1	1	1	1	1	2	2	2	2	2	
11	11	5	5	6	2	2	2	1	2	2	5	5	3	4	
12	12	5	5	5	3	3	3	3	3	5	3	5	5	5	
13	13	5	5	5	2	1	1	1	1	7	7	6	7	6	
14	14	4	5	4	3	3	2	3	3	5	5	6	6	5	
15	15	4	4	4	2	2	2	2	2	2	2	2	2	2	
16	16	6	4	5	1	1	1	2	2	2	2	2	2	1	
17	17	4	4	4	2	1	1	1	1	3	3	3	5	4	
18	18	4	3	3	1	1	1	1	2	6	5	3	5	5	
19	19	5	5	3	1	2	2	2	2	2	2	2	2	2	
20	20	5	5	6	4	2	1	1	1	3	5	2	6	5	
21	21	2	3	4	2	2	2	2	2	5	5	6	6	4	
22	22	7	7	7	6	2	2	2	2	6	6	5	5	5	
23	23	1	1	1	1	1	1	1	1	3	3	5	6	4	
24	24	5	5	5	3	3	3	2	3	6	7	5	5	5	
25	25	4	4	4	6	6	2	2	2	6	2	2	2	3	
26	26	6	6	6	6	2	2	2	2	4	4	2	2	2	
27	27	3	2	4	5	1	3	3	3	6	6	5	5	6	
28	28	6	6	6	4	5	2	1	2	5	3	5	5	5	

Had SPSS not yet been active, SPSS would then be started up and the data would be displayed in the Data Editor screen (Figure 8.11). There are no missing values in this data file. If a researcher finds him or herself confronted with 'missing values', some of the output will not be generated. The researcher may then take appropriate action: for example, to continue working with limited output or modify the data file by removing the respondents with the missing values for example or to replace them by the respective mean.

Figure 8.12

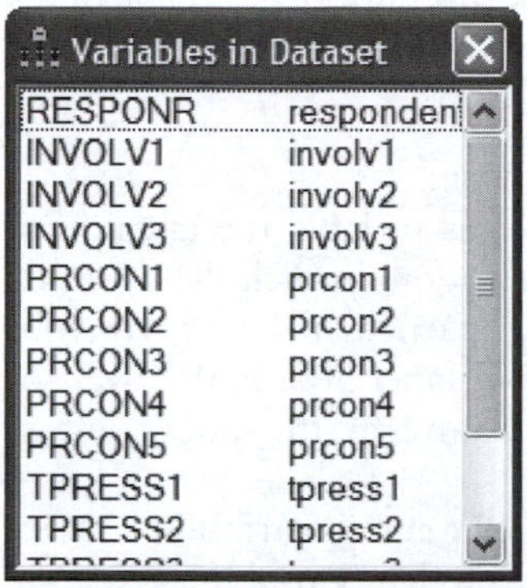

AMOS can read different types of files. In addition to SPSS data files, AMOS can also read Excel, Access and Lotus files.

Via the Windows toolbar, go back to the AMOS window and click in Figure 8.10 on 'OK' so that the data will be available for an analysis in AMOS.

An overview of the variables used to label the indicators may be obtained by clicking the **List Variables in Data Set** button.

The first variable in Figure 8.12 is the respondent number which is not used in this analysis. The next variable, 'involv1', is the first of the three potential variables which determine the underlying construct 'involvement'. Click this variable holding the button down, and drag it to the top indicator square (see Figure 8.13).

Figure 8.13

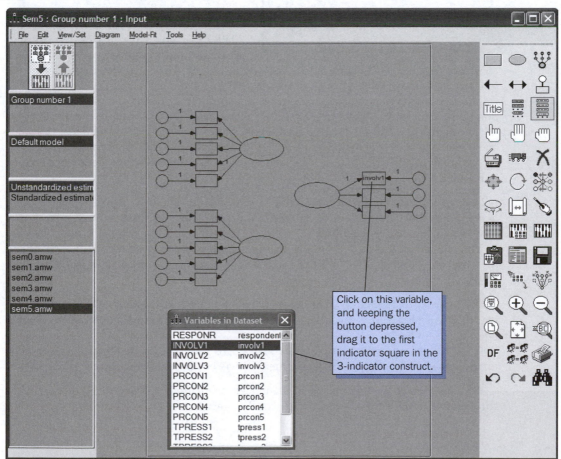

Repeat this step for each variable for the corresponding constructs.

🖐 Here is a tip which can prove useful when the lay-out needs to be adapted. When the variable name does not fit entirely in the square, click the **Select Single Objects** button.

Use the pointer which has now been modified by the button to indicate those squares whose shapes (sizes) must be changed.

⊡ This may be done using the **Shape Change** button. Click this button, go to one of the squares with the pointer, click it and hold the button down. The shape of the squares will change with the motion of the mouse pointer.

🖐 You may deselect objects using the **Deselect Objects** button.

Figure 8.14

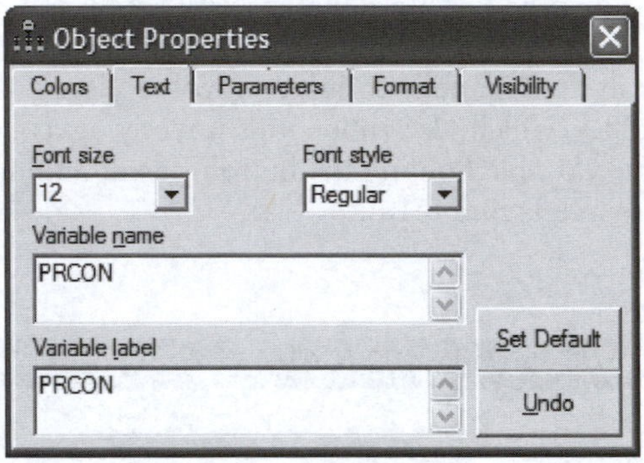

The next step is to label the latent variables. To do this, double-click the oval that represents that particular latent variable. The first we will label here is the oval for the construct found at the upper left in Figure 8.13.

For the latent variable 'Price Consciousness', under 'Variable name' and 'Variable label', we will fill in 'PRCON'. This will result in an image such as that seen in Figure 8.14.

Apply the same method to 'Tpress' ('TPRESS', construct lower left in Figure 8.13) and 'Involvement' ('INVOLV', construct right centre in Figure 8.13). You will also notice that it is possible to change the font size in Figure 8.14.

The next step in the graphic portrayal of the confirmatory factor analysis is the designation of the error terms (circles for each observed variable). In this example, the designations 'e1' through 'e13' are used. Double-click on one of the attached circles and under 'Variable name' type the corresponding name (e.g., 'e1' in the first circle under 'prcon1').

A number of aesthetic changes were made in order to obtain an image identical to the one in Figure 8.15.

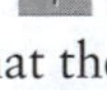

🚚 If the ovals are located too close to the squares, click the **Move Objects** button (truck), then move the pointer to an oval and drag the squares further away from it. The arrows will automatically adjust.

You will notice that the numbers '1' (between the arrows between the latent variable and the observed variables) for 'TPRESS' and 'PRCON' are not located next to one specific arrow.

🔍 In order to correct this, you can move the numbers corresponding to the arrows so that they are placed in a more logical location by clicking the **Move Parameter Values** button.

Click this button and then click the arrow and the number (loading) corresponding to this arrow will be selected so that the number may be dragged to the more logical location.

↔ The last step in the building of the model for the time being is the admission of the correlations between the various constructs. This means that the correlation arrows in the

Figure 8.15

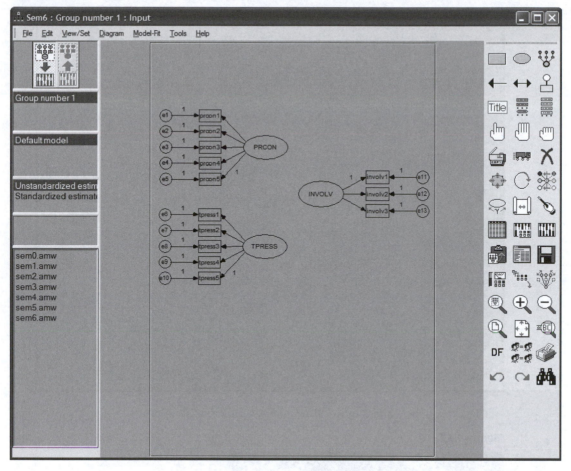

model must be drawn between the different latent variables. This may be done using the **Draw Covariances button**.

Click this button, go with the pointer to the oval of a latent variable, click it and hold the button down while moving the pointer to another oval. Release the button once you have the arrived at the other oval. A double-arrow will now be drawn between the two ovals. Use the same method for the two remaining relationships (correlations). You will now see an image like the one shown in Figure 8.16.

The curvature of the covariance arrows may be adjusted using the **Shape Change** button. Click this button, use the modified pointer to go to the arrow to be modified so that it lights up, click and adjust the curvature as desired and then release.

This model may also be found on the CD-ROM as *sem7.amw* (It is recommended to copy this file to the hard drive and then to open this file in AMOS). Sometimes it is best to read the data in again via File/Data Files because AMOS cannot find the path back to the data file.

The model may now be estimated. Before actually performing the estimation, several preferences may first be set so that a better interpretation of the output is possible. This may be done via the **View Analysis Properties** icon.

Figure 8.16

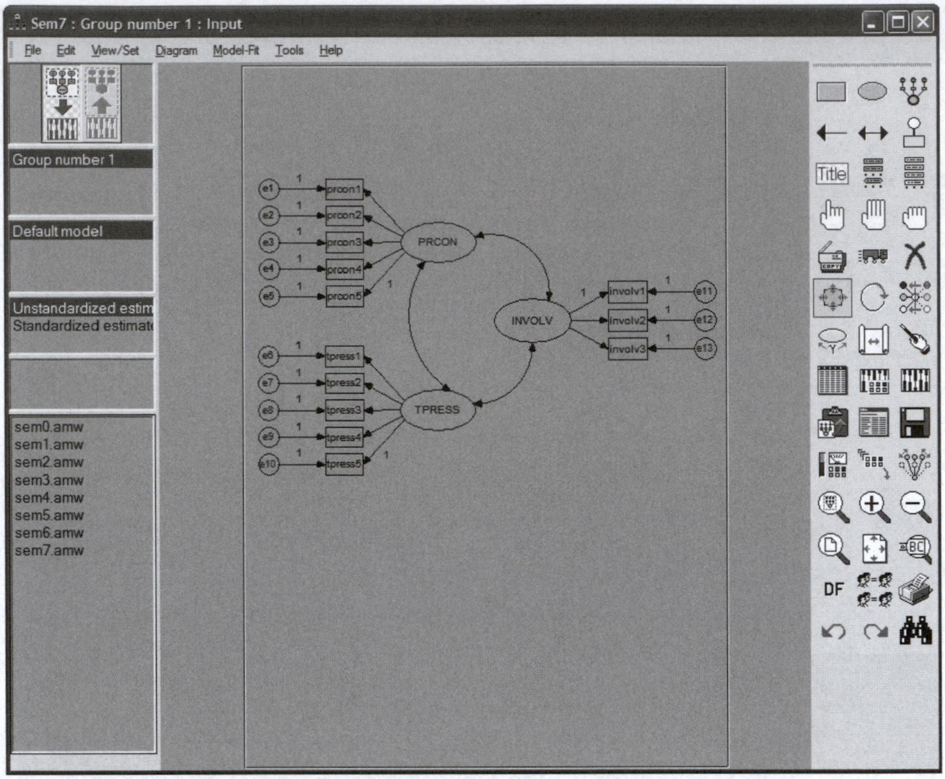

Click this button and a subwindow with several tabs will appear.

Figure 8.17

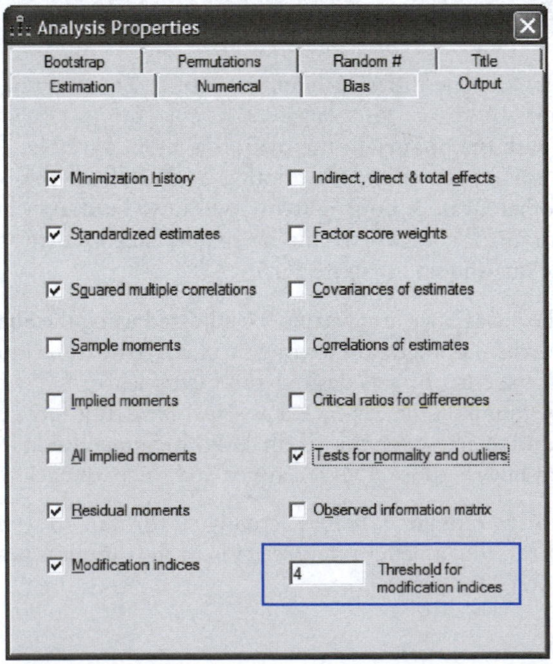

Using these tabs, the output may be adjusted or certain methods of estimation may be chosen. The 'Minimization history' and 'Test for normality and outliers' options are always checked. In the 'Output' tab, also indicate the options 'Standardized estimates', 'Squared multiple correlations', 'Residual moments', and 'Modification indices' (Figure 8.17). For this last option, the limit is four, which indicates that AMOS will only show those changes which each lead to a decrease of at least four units in the Chi-square value.

Figure 8.18

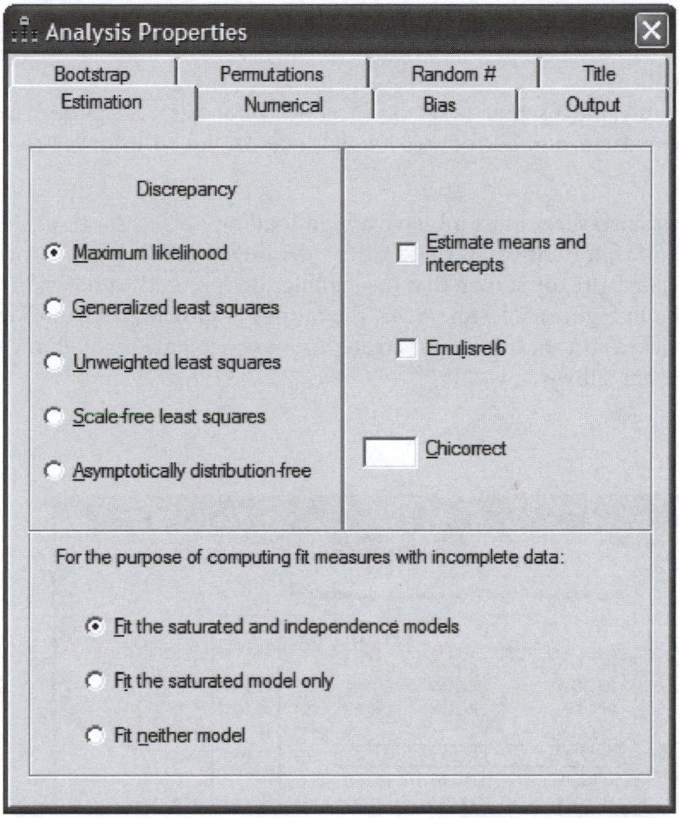

The Estimation tab may be used to choose one of the different estimation techniques. The standard setting is the Maximum Likelihood (ML) estimation (Figure 8.18), which assumes that the underlying variables are multivariate normally distributed. ML estimations are fairly robust when the multivariate normal assumption is only violated to a limited degree. A sufficient number of observations (at least 100) are necessary. The Chi-square value and the standard errors may however be more biased. Other estimation techniques do not have this underlying normality assumption, yet demonstrate other limitations and/or certain characteristics. For further information on this topic, please see the specialized literature.

Although the variables in this example are not all normally distributed (and therefore certainly not multivariate normally distributed), the example is calculated further using the ML estimation method. Determining (Multivariate) Normality may be done through descriptive statistics, univariate and multivariate testing. This is not discussed here however.

▓▓ Next, close this subwindow. Estimating the model may be done by clicking the **Calculate Estimates** icon.

▦ In order to view the analysis results, click the **View Text Output** icon. A tab system is used in order to simplify the selection of partial output.

Interpretation of the AMOS output

In order to be able to make decisions regarding reliable constructs, the following features of the solution must be studied: unidimensionality, convergent validity, reliability and discriminant validity.

Unidimensionality

Unidimensionality means that a set of variables only has one underlying dimension in common. There are a number of steps which may be taken in order to study unidimensionality:

1 The variables measures must all have a high loading ($>.50$) on the latent variables and must be significant (Critical Ratio = C.R. = t-value > 1.96). Exploratory factor analysis (Figure 8.2) had already shown that the loadings on 'prcon1' were very low (highest loading = .261). In Figures 8.19 and 8.20, the output is shown (after the **View Text Output** icon was clicked). In the left menu screen, one may navigate through the output by clicking the relevant subwindow.

Figure 8.19

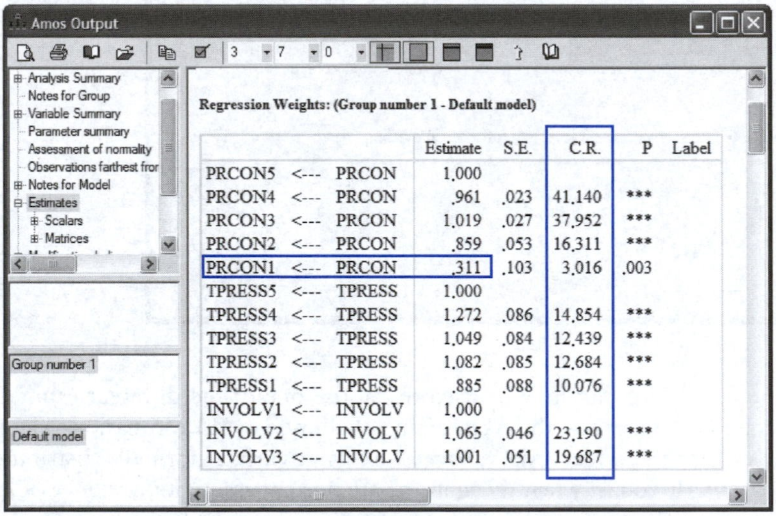

In Figure 8.19, the suboutput 'Regression Weights' and in Figure 8.20 the suboutput 'Standardized Regression Weights' were chosen. Figure 8.19 shows that all of the unstandardized loadings (regression weights) differ significantly from zero (in the C.R. [Critical Ratio] column, there is not a single value that is less than 1.96). The loading for 'prcon1' does however appear to be low (.311).

Figure 8.20

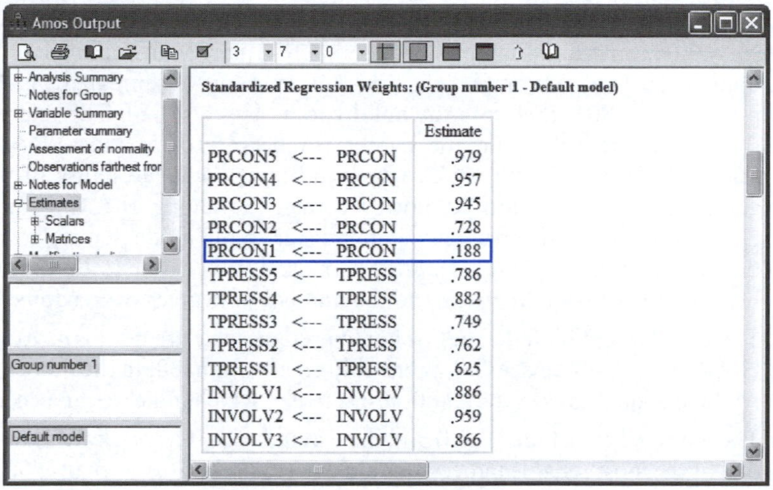

Standardized Regression Weights: (Group number 1 - Default model)

			Estimate
PRCON5	<---	PRCON	.979
PRCON4	<---	PRCON	.957
PRCON3	<---	PRCON	.945
PRCON2	<---	PRCON	.728
PRCON1	<---	PRCON	.188
TPRESS5	<---	TPRESS	.786
TPRESS4	<---	TPRESS	.882
TPRESS3	<---	TPRESS	.749
TPRESS2	<---	TPRESS	.762
TPRESS1	<---	TPRESS	.625
INVOLV1	<---	INVOLV	.886
INVOLV2	<---	INVOLV	.959
INVOLV3	<---	INVOLV	.866

In Figure 8.20, it appears that the standardized Regression Weight for 'prcon1' is equal to .188, which is less than the required minimum of .50, and in a review of the model, this variable will have to be removed. It is incidentally worth noting that due to the fact that comparable measurement scales are involved here, there is very little difference between the non-standardized and the standardized solutions. If the measurement levels of the various variables do differ significantly from one another, both results may differ considerably. The standardized loadings then provide a better image. The unstandardized loadings are only examined in order to learn the significance of the measured variables.

Figure 8.21

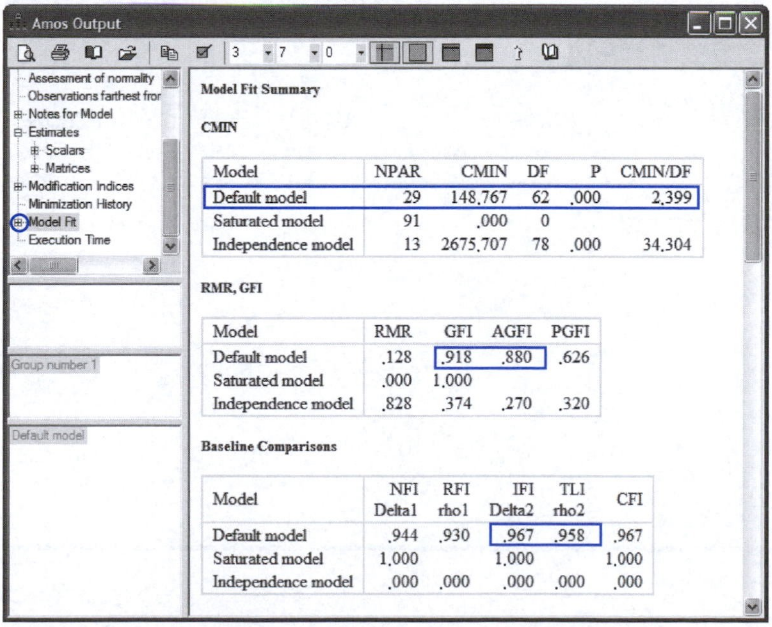

Model Fit Summary

CMIN

Model	NPAR	CMIN	DF	P	CMIN/DF
Default model	29	148.767	62	.000	2.399
Saturated model	91	.000	0		
Independence model	13	2675.707	78	.000	34.304

RMR, GFI

Model	RMR	GFI	AGFI	PGFI
Default model	.128	.918	.880	.626
Saturated model	.000	1.000		
Independence model	.828	.374	.270	.320

Baseline Comparisons

Model	NFI Delta1	RFI rho1	IFI Delta2	TLI rho2	CFI
Default model	.944	.930	.967	.958	.967
Saturated model	1.000		1.000		1.000
Independence model	.000	.000	.000	.000	.000

2 Determining the 'overall fit' (general quality) of the measurement model.

There are different criteria used to determine the general quality of the model. A number of them will be discussed below (Figure 8.21):

- The overall fit determines to what degree the covariance matrix generated by the model corresponds to the actual (observed) covariance matrix. The null hypothesis of equal covariance matrices would therefore actually not be allowed to be rejected (p > 0.05, or if large samples are used: Chi-square value/number of degrees of freedom < 2). In the example, the Chi-square value (discrepancy) is 148.767 with a p-value of <.001, therefore the null hypothesis is rejected. The relationship between the Chi-square value and the number of degrees of freedom does not satisfy the assumed criterion (2.399 > 2), which indicates that the quality of the model is not good. It should be noticed however that examining the Chi-square value (and corresponding significance) alone often leads to the model having to be rejected (particularly with larger samples). For this reason, it is better to look at the relationship between the Chi-square value and the number of degrees of freedom.

- The Goodness of Fit Index (GFI) should preferably be greater than .90 and the Adjusted Goodness of Fit Index (AGFI) preferably greater than .80. In the model, the GFI and the AGFI are equal to .919 and .880, respectively, which indicates an acceptable model.

- The Tucker-Lewis Index (TLI) and the Comparative Fit Index (CFI) (each of which are one of the most reliable indices) should preferably be greater than .90. These are in this case .958 and .967, respectively. These values are also greater than the .95 cut-off which is recommended by Hu and Bentler (1999).

Two other indicators which are frequently used in determining the overall fit of an SEM model are the RMSEA (Root Mean Square Error of Approximation) and the SRMR (Standardized Root Mean Square Residual). The RMSEA may be obtained by scrolling down through Figure 8.21 or by clicking the '+' sign for 'Model Fit' and clicking RMSEA. An image such as the one shown in Figure 8.22 will then appear.

Figure 8.22

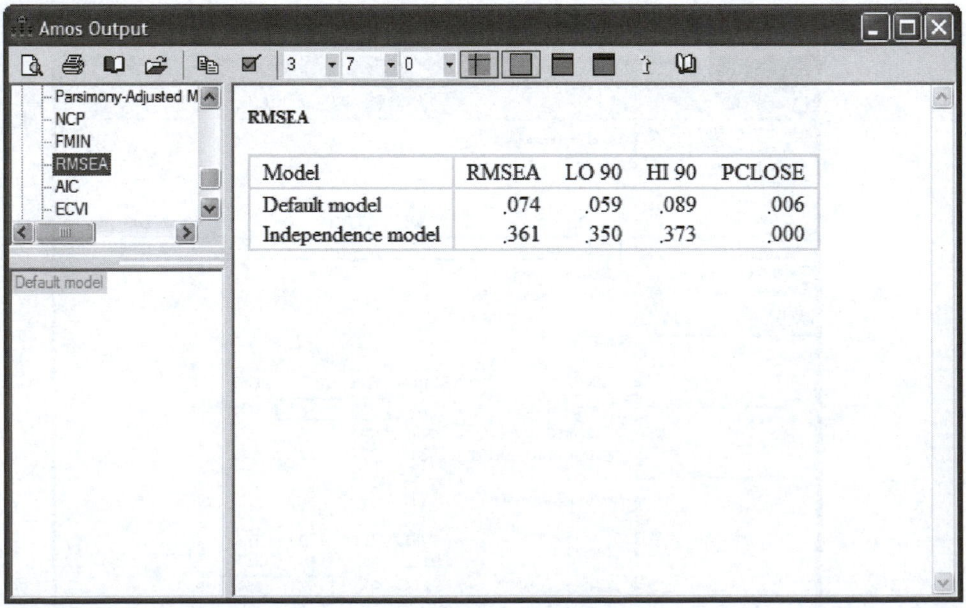

RMSEA

Model	RMSEA	LO 90	HI 90	PCLOSE
Default model	.074	.059	.089	.006
Independence model	.361	.350	.373	.000

The RMSEA is .074 here. Hu and Bentler (1999) place the cut-off at .06, whereas Browne and Cudeck (1993) assert that values less than or equal to .05 indicate a good fit and values up to .08 indicate an acceptable fit. The value .074 in our example indicates that the fit may be viewed as acceptable.

One last fit index which will be discussed here is the SRMR. This value must be calculated additionally in AMOS. Go to Tools/Macro/Standardized SRMR (Figure 8.23).

Figure 8.23

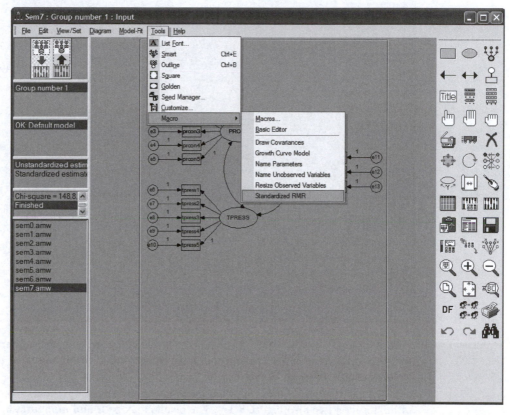

Figure 8.24

The researcher will then see a window such as the one shown in Figure 8.24. The value here is .0455 which is lower than the usual cut-off of .08 (Hu and Bentler, 1999), which indicates a good fit. Given that the loading for 'prcon1' is too low and that the Chi-square value is still too high (p-value too low) to conclude that the model is good the variable 'prcon1' is removed from the analysis. Graphically, this is done as follows.

Go back to the path diagram which was drawn (via the Windows menu bar) and click the Erase Objects button.

When the mouse pointer is moved over the diagram, the 'x' mark indicated moves along with it across the screen. Use this to click on the object (in this case, the variable 'prcon1') which must be deleted. You will notice that both the arrow and the variable square will disappear.

After this, click on the corresponding residual (circle with 'e1') so that this also disappears. An image such as the one in Figure 8.25 will appear.

Figure 8.25

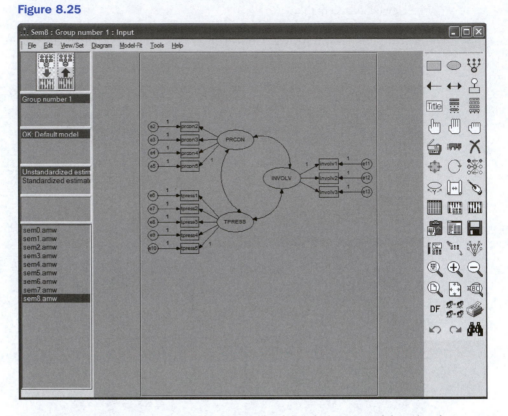

Should 'prcon5' (arrow with '1') also have to be deleted, then one of the other four construct arrows would have to be clicked and a parameter value of '1' input so that the model remains identifiable (see above).

After that, the model may be estimated once again by clicking on the **Calculate Estimates** icon (see also Figure 8.17). The results may be found in Figures 8.26 and 8.27.

Figure 8.26

Regression Weights: (Group number 1 - Default model)

			Estimate	S.E.	C.R.	P	Label
PRCON5	<---	PRCON	1.000				
PRCON4	<---	PRCON	.961	.023	41.189	***	
PRCON3	<---	PRCON	1.019	.027	37.955	***	
PRCON2	<---	PRCON	.858	.053	16.292	***	
TPRESS5	<---	TPRESS	1.000				
TPRESS4	<---	TPRESS	1.272	.086	14.854	***	
TPRESS3	<---	TPRESS	1.049	.084	12.439	***	
TPRESS2	<---	TPRESS	1.082	.085	12.684	***	
TPRESS1	<---	TPRESS	.885	.088	10.076	***	
INVOLV1	<---	INVOLV	1.000				
INVOLV2	<---	INVOLV	1.065	.046	23.189	***	
INVOLV3	<---	INVOLV	1.001	.051	19.686	***	

Figure 8.27

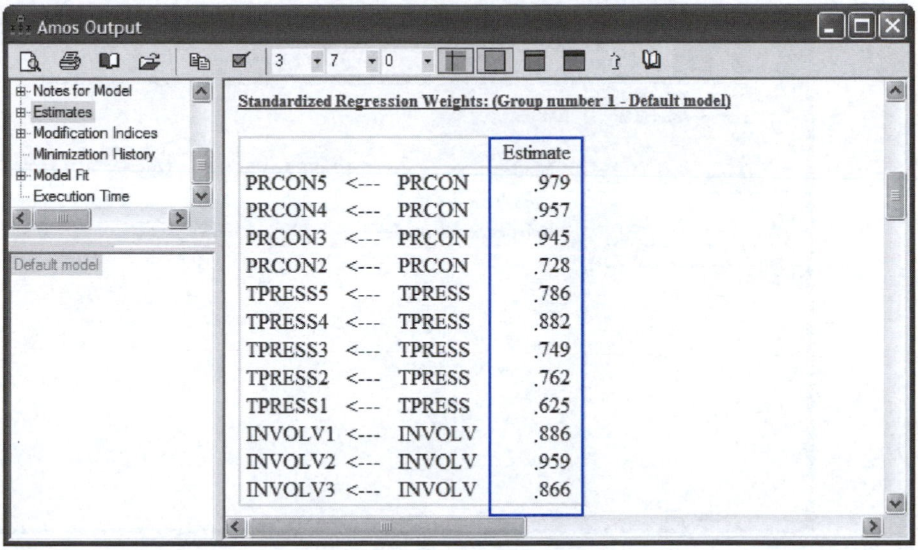

Amos Output

Standardized Regression Weights: (Group number 1 - Default model)

			Estimate
PRCON5	<---	PRCON	.979
PRCON4	<---	PRCON	.957
PRCON3	<---	PRCON	.945
PRCON2	<---	PRCON	.728
TPRESS5	<---	TPRESS	.786
TPRESS4	<---	TPRESS	.882
TPRESS3	<---	TPRESS	.749
TPRESS2	<---	TPRESS	.762
TPRESS1	<---	TPRESS	.625
INVOLV1	<---	INVOLV	.886
INVOLV2	<---	INVOLV	.959
INVOLV3	<---	INVOLV	.866

From these figures, it appears that all of the loadings are significant and larger than .50. The fact that the solutions are acceptable may be concluded from Figure 8.27 in which all of the standardized regression weights lie between -1 and 1.

Figure 8.28

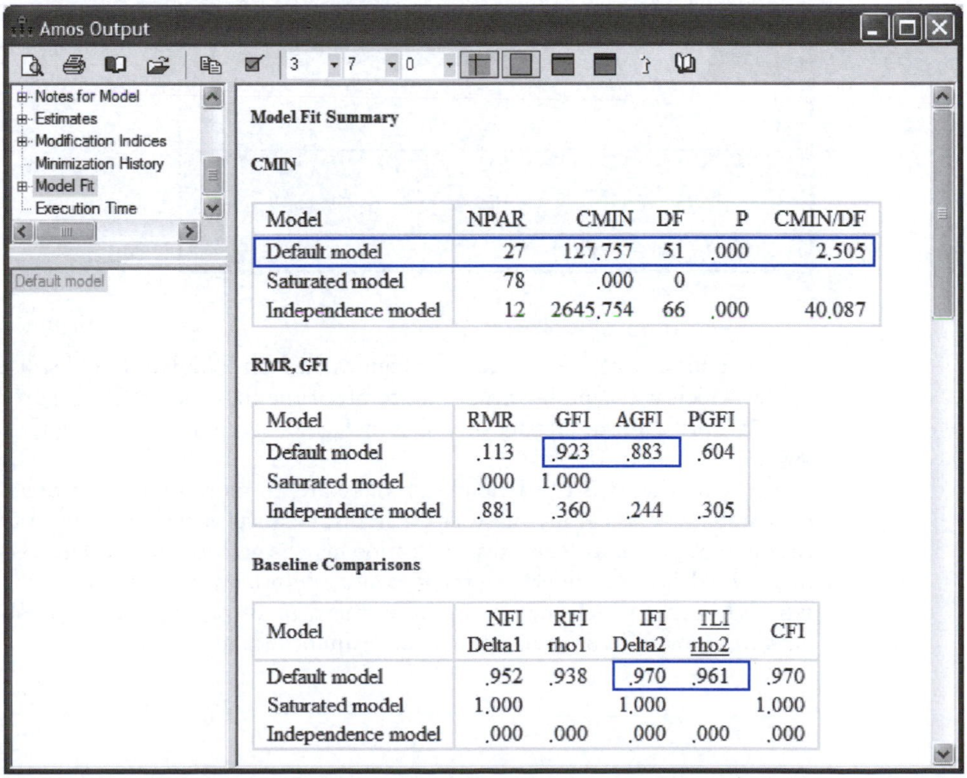

Amos Output

Model Fit Summary

CMIN

Model	NPAR	CMIN	DF	P	CMIN/DF
Default model	27	127.757	51	.000	2.505
Saturated model	78	.000	0		
Independence model	12	2645.754	66	.000	40.087

RMR, GFI

Model	RMR	GFI	AGFI	PGFI
Default model	.113	.923	.883	.604
Saturated model	.000	1.000		
Independence model	.881	.360	.244	.305

Baseline Comparisons

Model	NFI Delta1	RFI rho1	IFI Delta2	TLI rho2	CFI
Default model	.952	.938	.970	.961	.970
Saturated model	1.000		1.000		1.000
Independence model	.000	.000	.000	.000	.000

Figure 8.29

Model	RMSEA	LO 90	HI 90	PCLOSE
Default model	.077	.060	.094	.005
Independence model	.392	.379	.404	.000

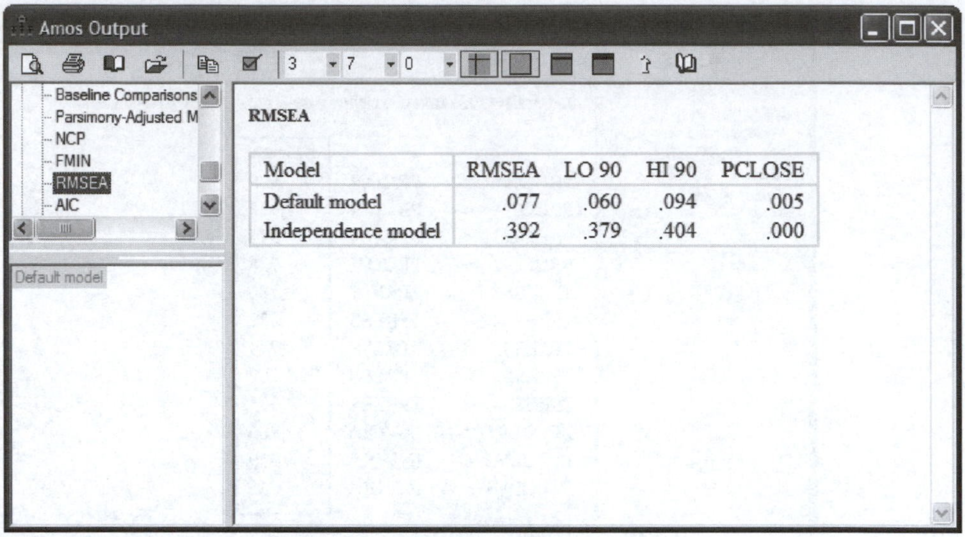

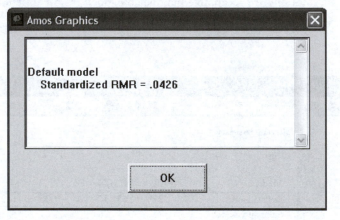

Figure 8.30

The 'goodness of fit' indicators in Figures 8.28 and 8.29 and 8.30 still do not indicate a model which is acceptable according to all of the indicators (Chi-square (discrepancy) = 127.757, $p < .001$; discrepancy/number of degrees of freedom = 2.505; GFI = .923; AGFI = .883; TLI = .961; CFI = .97).

Since, on the basis of the loadings, there are no more reasons to remove variables, the next step must be a study of other criteria. It is however necessary for a theoretical justification to be present before a respecification may be performed. The latter obviously depends to a great degree on underlying theories and interpretation by the researcher. There are two types of output which may be useful in this type of respecification. First of all, the standardized (normalized) residuals may be examined (Figure 8.31).

Figure 8.31

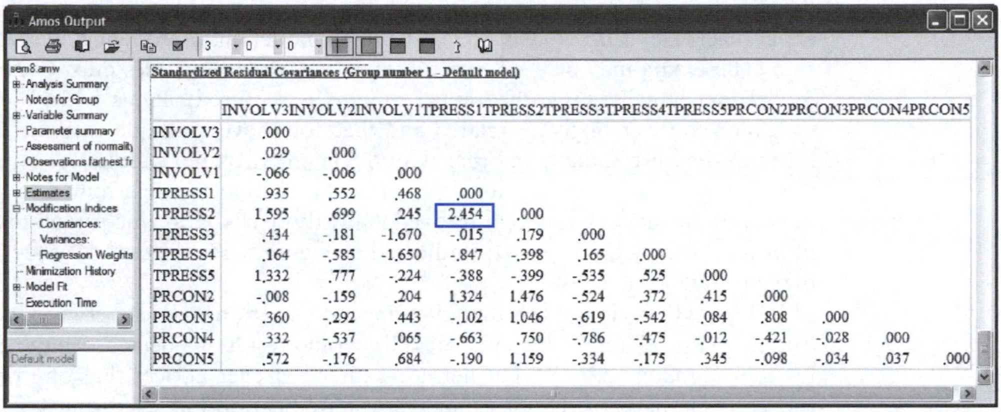

Standardized Residual Covariances (Group number 1 - Default model)

	INVOLV3	INVOLV2	INVOLV1	TPRESS1	TPRESS2	TPRESS3	TPRESS4	TPRESS5	PRCON2	PRCON3	PRCON4	PRCON5
INVOLV3	,000											
INVOLV2	,029	,000										
INVOLV1	-,066	-,006	,000									
TPRESS1	,935	,552	,468	,000								
TPRESS2	1,595	,699	,245	2,454	,000							
TPRESS3	,434	-,181	-1,670	-,015	,179	,000						
TPRESS4	,164	-,585	-1,650	-,847	-,398	,165	,000					
TPRESS5	1,332	,777	-,224	-,388	-,399	-,535	,525	,000				
PRCON2	-,008	-,159	,204	1,324	1,476	-,524	,372	,415	,000			
PRCON3	,360	-,292	,443	-,102	1,046	-,619	-,542	,084	,808	,000		
PRCON4	,332	-,537	,065	-,663	,750	-,786	-,475	-,012	-,421	-,028	,000	
PRCON5	,572	-,176	,684	-,190	1,159	-,334	-,175	,345	-,098	-,034	,037	,000

These are the residuals of the observed and estimated covariance matrix divided by their asymptotic standard errors. Values larger than |2.58| indicate model misspecification. There is no single value which is larger, however the value 2.454 ('tpress2' and 'tpress1') does attract some attention and deserves to be studied further.

Figure 8.32

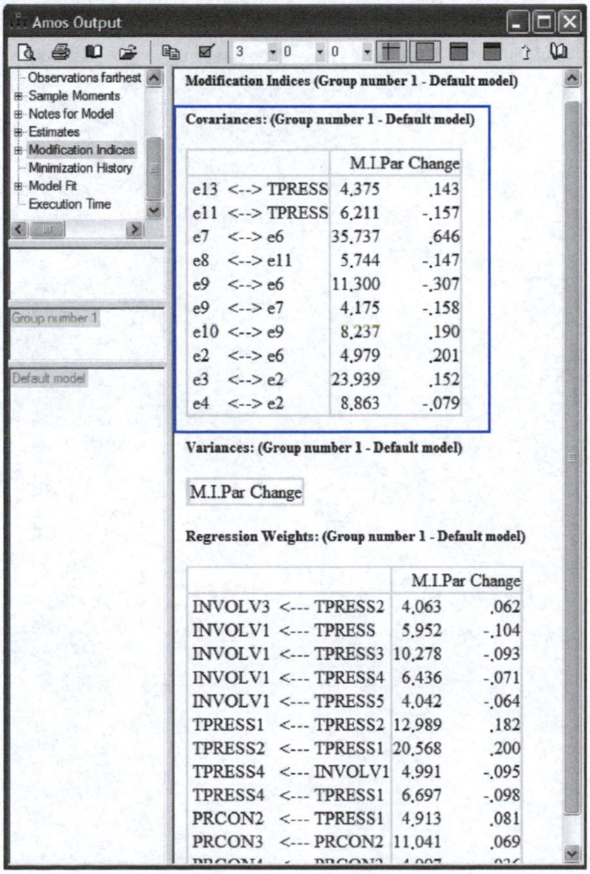

Modification Indices (Group number 1 - Default model)

Covariances: (Group number 1 - Default model)

	M.I.	Par Change
e13 <--> TPRESS	4,375	,143
e11 <--> TPRESS	6,211	-,157
e7 <--> e6	35,737	,646
e8 <--> e11	5,744	-,147
e9 <--> e6	11,300	-,307
e9 <--> e7	4,175	-,158
e10 <--> e9	8,237	,190
e2 <--> e6	4,979	,201
e3 <--> e2	23,939	,152
e4 <--> e2	8,863	-,079

Variances: (Group number 1 - Default model)

M.I.	Par Change

Regression Weights: (Group number 1 - Default model)

	M.I.	Par Change
INVOLV3 <--- TPRESS2	4,063	,062
INVOLV1 <--- TPRESS	5,952	-,104
INVOLV1 <--- TPRESS3	10,278	-,093
INVOLV1 <--- TPRESS4	6,436	-,071
INVOLV1 <--- TPRESS5	4,042	-,064
TPRESS1 <--- TPRESS2	12,989	,182
TPRESS2 <--- TPRESS1	20,568	,200
TPRESS4 <--- INVOLV1	4,991	-,095
TPRESS4 <--- TPRESS1	6,697	-,098
PRCON2 <--- TPRESS1	4,913	,081
PRCON3 <--- PRCON2	11,041	,069

In order to gain a better idea of the relationships between these variables, the 'modification indices' may be used (Figure 8.32). These indices (with covariances) indicate what the effect (decrease) is on the Chi-square value in modelling or allowing an additional relationship. These data may be used here to determine which variables must be removed from the model (once again, some theoretical support is required). Items which belong to a latent variable yet are strongly correlated and therefore have a unique variance (in other words, together measure something other than the latent variable) should not both be included in the analysis. After every removal of a variable, it may be determined to what degree the quality of the model has been improved. Only those changes which result in an index change of at least 4 may be displayed (indicated in Figure 8.16, if desired, other threshold values may be given).

In Figure 8.32, it appears that allowing a connection to exist between 'e6' (error term in 'tpress1') and 'e7'(error term in 'tpress2'), would result in a decrease in the Chi-square value by approximately 35.737. Furthermore, the researcher notices that omitting 'e6' from the total (on the basis of the most important modification indices displayed), causes the Chi-square value to decrease by approximately (35.737 + 11.300 + 4.979) = 52.016. There is no other variable which may be omitted and cause an effect that is higher than this 52.016. Apparently, 'e6' (tpress1) is responsible for most problems and the researcher also feels that there are sufficient theoretical reasons to support the removal of this variable.

Figure 8.33

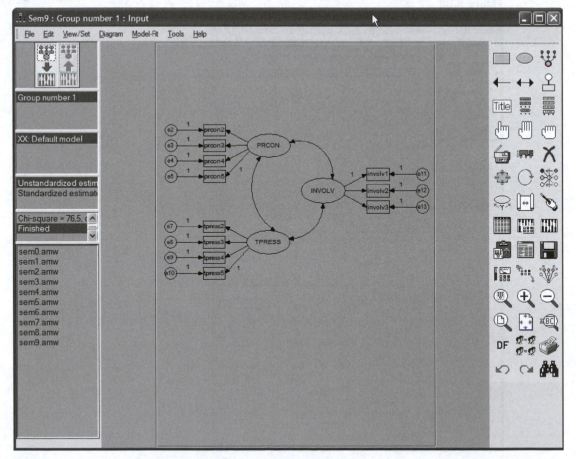

When 'tpress1' is removed, the model appears as shown in Figure 8.33.

Through the additional elimination of 'tpress1', the model is improved considerably (see Figures 8.34, 8.35 and 8.36).

Figure 8.34

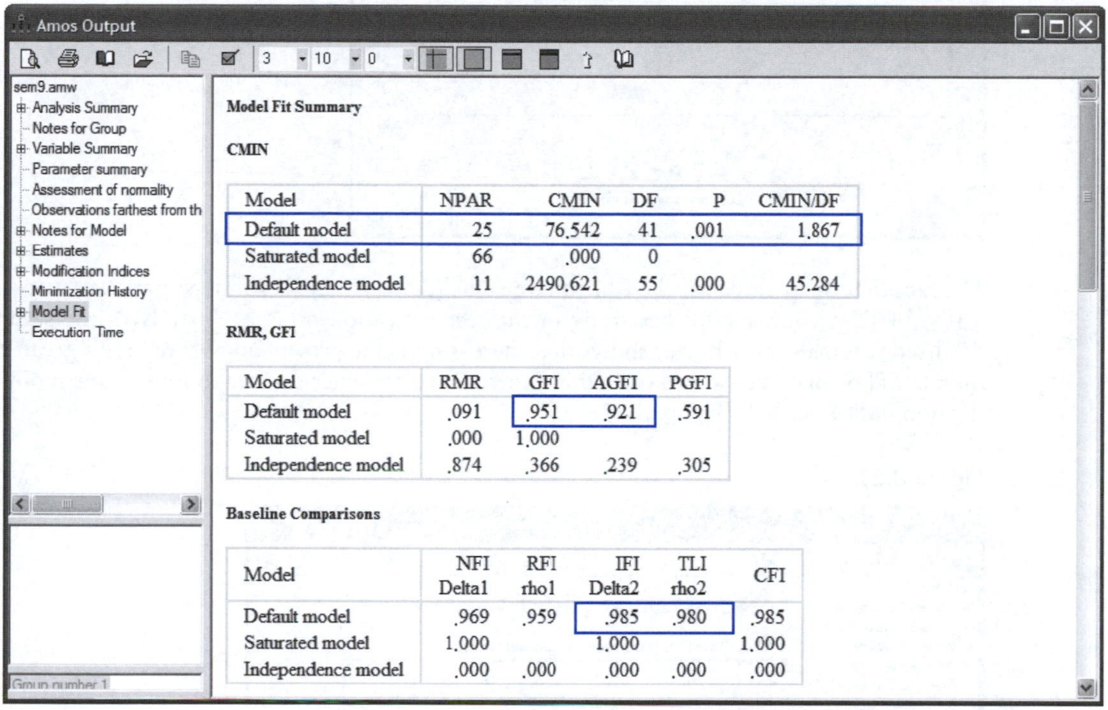

Model Fit Summary

CMIN

Model	NPAR	CMIN	DF	P	CMIN/DF
Default model	25	76.542	41	.001	1.867
Saturated model	66	.000	0		
Independence model	11	2490.621	55	.000	45.284

RMR, GFI

Model	RMR	GFI	AGFI	PGFI
Default model	.091	.951	.921	.591
Saturated model	.000	1.000		
Independence model	.874	.366	.239	.305

Baseline Comparisons

Model	NFI Delta1	RFI rho1	IFI Delta2	TLI rho2	CFI
Default model	.969	.959	.985	.980	.985
Saturated model	1.000		1.000		1.000
Independence model	.000	.000	.000	.000	.000

Figure 8.35

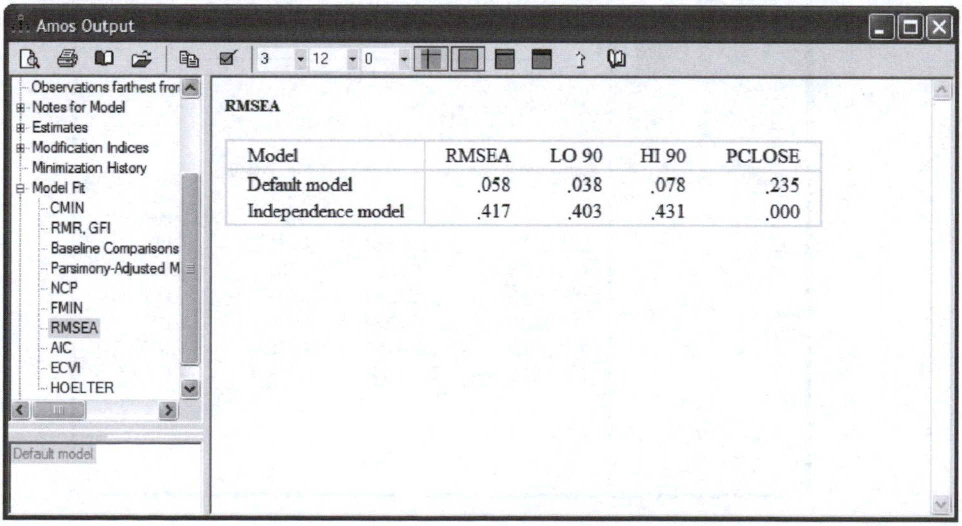

RMSEA

Model	RMSEA	LO 90	HI 90	PCLOSE
Default model	.058	.038	.078	.235
Independence model	.417	.403	.431	.000

Figure 8.36

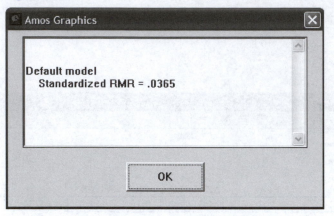

The fact that the p-value for the Chi-square value (discrepancy) is still less than .05 (specifically .001), encourages further study of the respecification criteria. A study of the standardized residuals (not shown) shows that there is no value present anywhere that is greater than |2.58| or that even approaches this figure. The researcher decides to look at the modification indices as well (Figure 8.37).

Figure 8.37

Amos Output

sem9.amw
- Analysis Summary
- Notes for Group
- Variable Summary
- Parameter summary
- Assessment of normality
- Observations farthest from th
- Notes for Model
- Estimates
- Modification Indices
- Minimization History
- Model Fit
- Execution Time

Default model

Modification Indices (Group number 1 - Default model)

Covariances: (Group number 1 - Default model)

		M.I.	Par Change
e13 <-->	TPRESS	4.447	.143
e11 <-->	TPRESS	7.159	-.168
e8 <-->	e11	4.638	-.133
e8 <-->	e7	4.443	.210
e3 <-->	e2	23.932	.152
e4 <-->	e2	8.866	-.079

Variances: (Group number 1 - Default model)

	M.I.	Par Change

Regression Weights: (Group number 1 - Default model)

		M.I.	Par Change
INVOLV3 <---	TPRESS2	4.051	.062
INVOLV1 <---	TPRESS	6.789	-.111
INVOLV1 <---	TPRESS3	10.205	-.092
INVOLV1 <---	TPRESS4	6.238	-.070
PRCON3 <---	PRCON2	11.038	.069
PRCON4 <---	PRCON2	4.099	-.036

In Figure 8.37, it may be determined that by allowing a connection to exist between 'e2' ('prcon2') on the one hand, and 'e3' ('prcon3') and 'e4' ('prcon4') on the other, this will cause a decrease in the Chi-square value by 23.932 and 8.886 respectively. Elimination of the 'e2' ensures an effect of 23.932 + 8.666 = 32.598. The researcher also feels here that there are sufficient theoretical reasons to remove the variable 'prcon2' from the model (Figure 8.38).

Figure 8.38

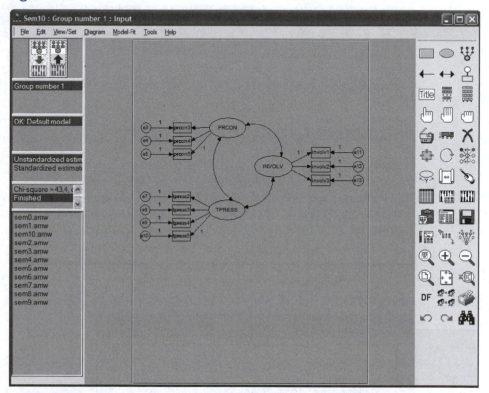

Figure 8.39

Model Fit Summary

CMIN

Model	NPAR	CMIN	DF	P	CMIN/DF
Default model	23	43.406	32	.086	1.356
Saturated model	55	.000	0		
Independence model	10	2272.408	45	.000	50.498

RMR, GFI

Model	RMR	GFI	AGFI	PGFI
Default model	.092	.969	.946	.564
Saturated model	.000	1.000		
Independence model	.899	.387	.250	.316

Baseline Comparisons

Model	NFI Delta1	RFI rho1	IFI Delta2	TLI rho2	CFI
Default model	.981	.973	.995	.993	.995
Saturated model	1.000		1.000		1.000
Independence model	.000	.000	.000	.000	.000

The p-value for 'Discrepancy' (Figure 8.39) is now .086, which is greater than .05 which means that the null hypothesis that the covariance matrix generated by the model is equal to the actual (observed) covariance matrix may no longer be rejected. The other criteria which were used prior to this (Figures 8.39, 8.40 and 8.41) all provide an indication of a very good fit.

Figure 8.40

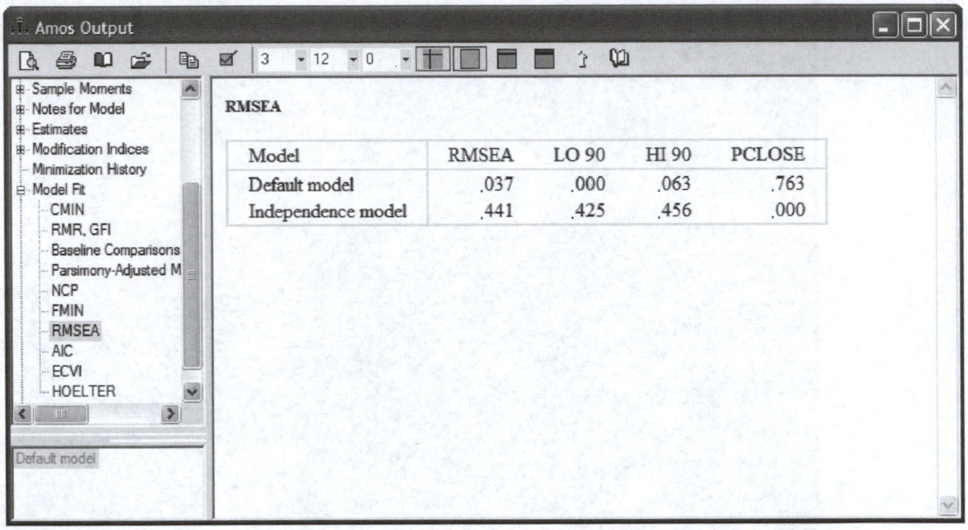

Model	RMSEA	LO 90	HI 90	PCLOSE
Default model	.037	.000	.063	.763
Independence model	.441	.425	.456	.000

Figure 8.41

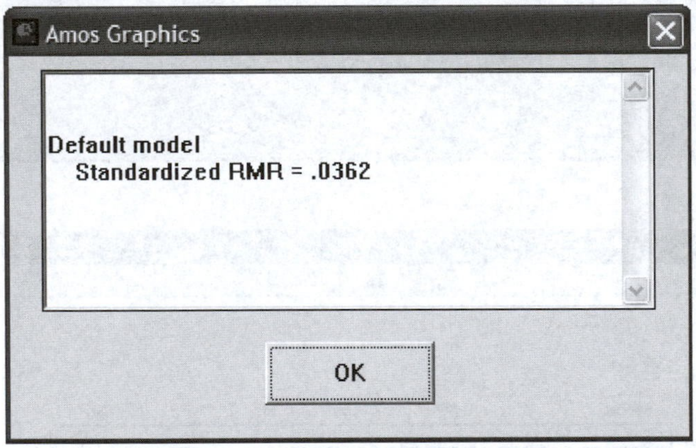

The following characteristics which must be studied will be evaluated on the basis of the results from this last model.

Convergent validity

Convergent validity indicates the degree to which two different indicators of a latent variable confirm one another. A first (weak) condition is that each of the loadings is significant. In Figure 8.42, this is shown to be the case (all of the C.R. >1.96).

Figure 8.42

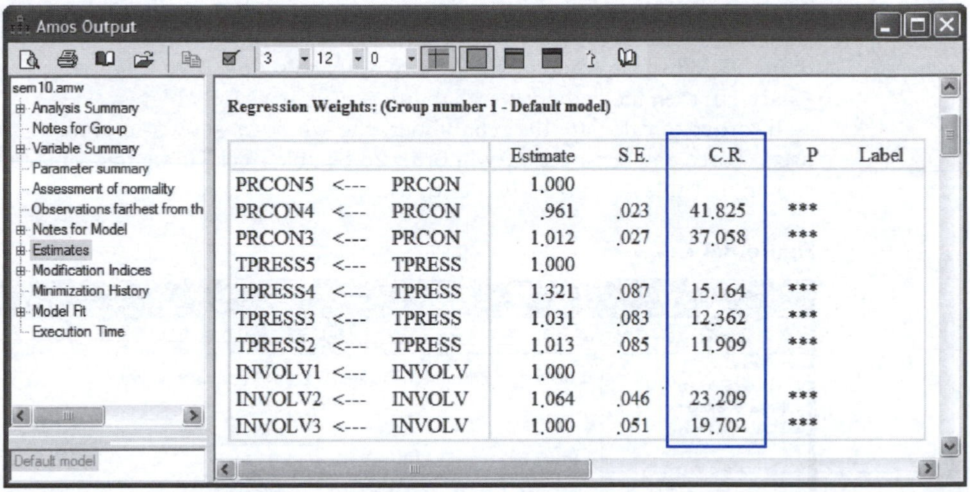

Regression Weights: (Group number 1 - Default model)

			Estimate	S.E.	C.R.	P	Label
PRCON5	<---	PRCON	1.000				
PRCON4	<---	PRCON	.961	.023	41.825	***	
PRCON3	<---	PRCON	1.012	.027	37.058	***	
TPRESS5	<---	TPRESS	1.000				
TPRESS4	<---	TPRESS	1.321	.087	15.164	***	
TPRESS3	<---	TPRESS	1.031	.083	12.362	***	
TPRESS2	<---	TPRESS	1.013	.085	11.909	***	
INVOLV1	<---	INVOLV	1.000				
INVOLV2	<---	INVOLV	1.064	.046	23.209	***	
INVOLV3	<---	INVOLV	1.000	.051	19.702	***	

A stricter condition is that the correlation between each indicator and the corresponding latent variable is greater than .50 (see standardized regression coefficients in Figure 8.43) together with a good fit (quality) of the model (see Figure 8.32). Both conditions are satisfied.

Figure 8.43

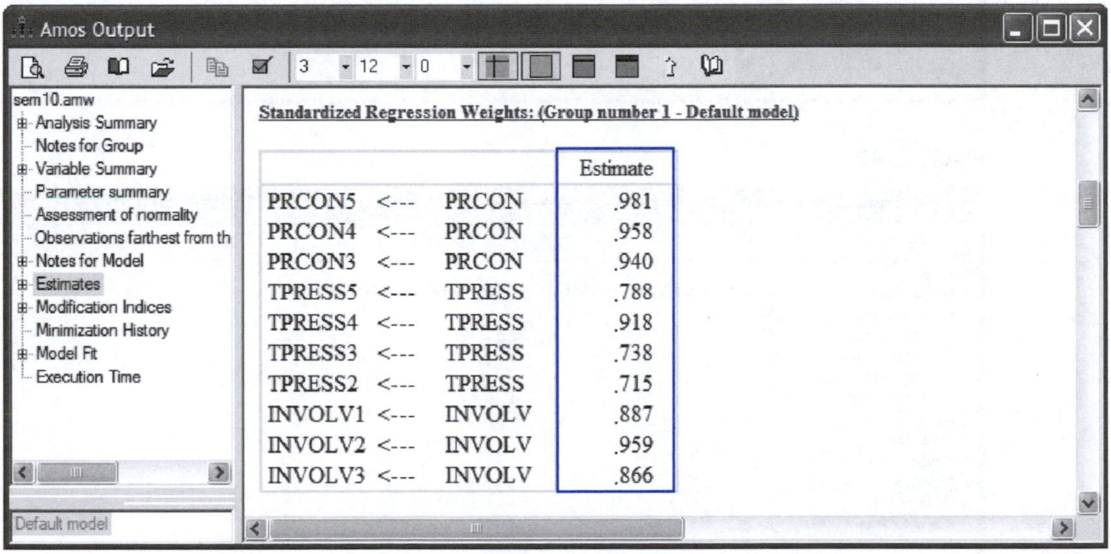

Standardized Regression Weights: (Group number 1 - Default model)

			Estimate
PRCON5	<---	PRCON	.981
PRCON4	<---	PRCON	.958
PRCON3	<---	PRCON	.940
TPRESS5	<---	TPRESS	.788
TPRESS4	<---	TPRESS	.918
TPRESS3	<---	TPRESS	.738
TPRESS2	<---	TPRESS	.715
INVOLV1	<---	INVOLV	.887
INVOLV2	<---	INVOLV	.959
INVOLV3	<---	INVOLV	.866

Reliability

Reliability must always be verified after convergent validity, because a model may be reliable without it being convergent valid. A criterion for reliability may however not be extracted directly from the output. The reliability may however be determined on the basis of the 'composite reliability' which must be calculated manually for every latent variable.

$$\textit{Composite reliability} = \frac{\left(\sum \textit{standardized loadings}\right)^2}{\left(\sum \textit{standardized loadings}\right)^2 + \sum \textit{measurement errors}}$$

The measurement error is equal to one minus the reliability of the indicator. This latter figure is the square of the standardized loading of the indicator, or also known as the 'squared multiple correlation'. The guideline is that the composite reliability must be higher than .70. When we compare this with Cronbach's alpha (see Chapter 7, Exploratory Factor Analysis), then the composite reliability is usually slightly higher.

In order to calculate the reliabilities, the windows shown in Figures 8.44 and 8.45 are used. These data are necessary in order to be able to calculate the composite reliabilities as shown in Table 8.1 (no AMOS output).

Figure 8.44

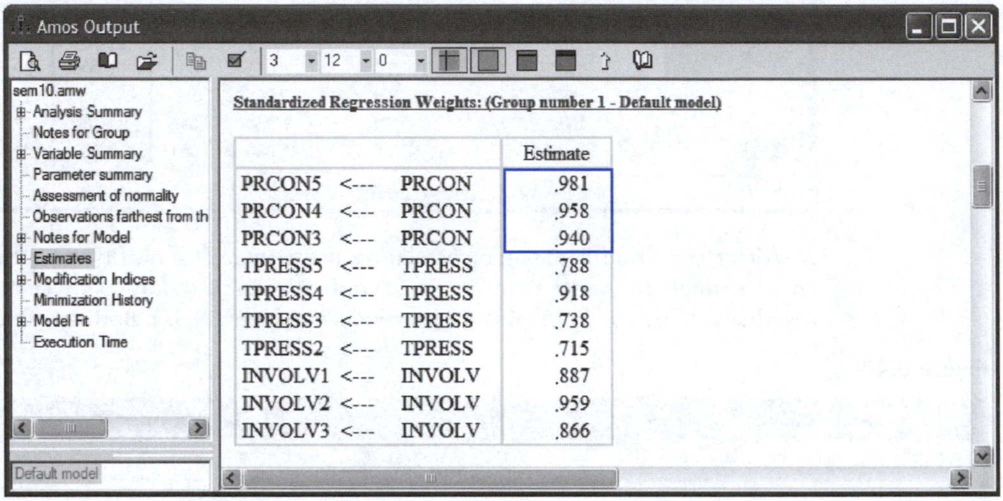

			Estimate
PRCON5	<---	PRCON	.981
PRCON4	<---	PRCON	.958
PRCON3	<---	PRCON	.940
TPRESS5	<---	TPRESS	.788
TPRESS4	<---	TPRESS	.918
TPRESS3	<---	TPRESS	.738
TPRESS2	<---	TPRESS	.715
INVOLV1	<---	INVOLV	.887
INVOLV2	<---	INVOLV	.959
INVOLV3	<---	INVOLV	.866

Figure 8.45

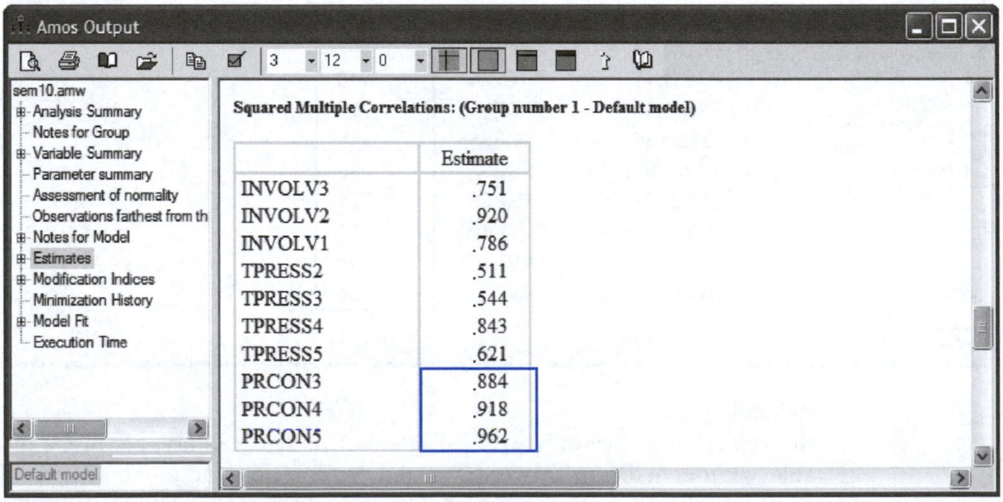

	Estimate
INVOLV3	.751
INVOLV2	.920
INVOLV1	.786
TPRESS2	.511
TPRESS3	.544
TPRESS4	.843
TPRESS5	.621
PRCON3	.884
PRCON4	.918
PRCON5	.962

In order to calculate the reliability of 'PRCON' for example, the standardized loadings for the numerator in the above formula are first added up: .940 + .958 + .981 = 2.879.

The square of this sum is 8.289. We must also calculate the sum of the measurement errors for the denominator, which is the sum of each 1-squared multiple correlation, which is .236 (.116 + .082 + .038). The reliability for the construct 'PRCON' may then be calculated as 8.289/ (8.289 + .236) = .972.

Table 8.1

		Standardized regression weight	Squared multiple correlation	1-squared multiple correlation	Construct reliability
PRCON	PRCON3	0.940	0.884	0.116	
	PRCON4	0.958	0.918	0.082	
	PRCON5	0.981	0.962	0.038	
	sum	2.879			
	sum^2	8.289	sum	0.236	**0.972**
TPRESS	TPRESS2	0.715	0.511	0.489	
	TPRESS3	0.738	0.544	0.456	
	TPRESS4	0.918	0.843	0.157	
	TPRESS5	0.788	0.621	0.379	
	sum	3.159			
	sum^2	9.979	sum	1.481	**0.871**
INVOLV	INVOLV1	0.887	0.786	0.214	
	INVOLV2	0.959	0.92	0.080	
	INVOLV3	0.866	0.751	0.249	
	sum	2.712			
	sum^2	7.355	sum	0.543	**0.931**

Another criterion for the reliability of a latent variable is the variance extracted criterion. This criterion shows which part of the collective variance of the indicators may be found in the latent variable. In terms of calculations, the formula used here does not differ that much from the one used for construct reliability, except that instead of the square of the sum of the standardized loadings, it uses the sum of the squares of the standardized loadings.

$$Variance\ extracted = \frac{\sum \left(standardized\ loadings\right)^2}{\sum (standardized\ loadings)^2 + \sum measurement\ errors}$$

The guideline here is that each construct should have a value greater than .50. The variance extracted for each latent variable is calculated in Table 8.2.

Table 8.2

		Standardized regression weight	Squared multiple correlation	1-squared multiple correlation	Variance extracted
PRCON	PRCON3	0.940	0.884	0.116	
	PRCON4	0.958	0.918	0.082	
	PRCON5	0.981	0.962	0.038	
	sum		2.764	0.236	**0.921**
TPRESS	TPRESS2	0.715	0.511	0.489	
	TPRESS3	0.738	0.544	0.456	
	TPRESS4	0.918	0.843	0.157	
	TPRESS5	0.788	0.621	0.379	
	sum		2.520	1.481	**0.630**
INVOLV	INVOLV1	0.887	0.786	0.214	
	INVOLV2	0.959	0.92	0.080	
	INVOLV3	0.866	0.751	0.249	
	sum		2.456	0.543	**0.819**

Because the construct reliability for all three of the constructs is greater than .60, and the 'Variance extracted' criteria are greater than .50, the researcher may decide that all of the individual indicators have been measured consistently.

Discriminant validity

Discriminant validity is achieved when the correlation between constructs differs significantly from 1 or when the Chi-square difference test indicates that two constructs are not perfectly correlated. This means that it must be determined (for two constructs each time) whether the change in the Chi-square value between the restrictive model (model in which the correlation between two constructs is set equal to one) and the accepted model is significant. The latter is the desired outcome, since a non-significant difference would indicate that we cannot be sure that both constructs are not perfectly correlated with one another. In AMOS however it is only possible to fix covariances (assign a certain fixed value to them) and it is not possible to do this for correlation as well, meaning that it is not possible to determine discriminant validity this way in AMOS.

AMOS does present the correlations between the constructs (Figure 8.46) but it does not give the corresponding confidence intervals (when -1 or 1 is not included in the confidence interval of the estimated correlation, this would be an indication for discriminant validity). AMOS gives these confidence intervals, but only when the bootstrapping estimation procedure is used. However, this technique is not covered by this book. Another procedure to check for discriminant validity was developed by Fornell and Larcker (1981). They advance that for each couple of constructs the square of the correlation between these two constructs should be smaller than their corresponding AVE.

Figure 8.46

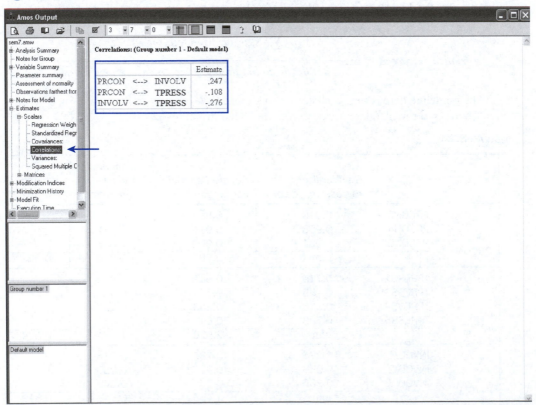

Table 8.3 presents the mutual variances between the latent variables and can be used to check for the presence of discriminant validity. For the elements on the diagonal (bold), this corresponds with the AVE of the constructs. The non-diagonal elements are calculated as the square of the correlations between the constructs (e.g., the value .012 between the variables 'PRCON' and 'TPRESS' is the square of the correlation between both variables which is −.108 (Figure 8.46). As shown in Table 8.3, none of the variances that is shared by two constructs (squared correlation) is higher than the average variance extracted of these constructs. This finding indicates discriminant validity for the three constructs that were formed.

Table 8.3

	PRCON	TPRESS	INVOLV
PRCON	**0.921**		
TPRESS	0.012	**0.630**	
INVOLV	0.061	0.076	**0.819**

In conclusion, the measurement model proves to be unidimensional, reliable, and indicates convergent and discriminant validity.

Example 2

Path analysis

Problem

Find out what the effect is of price consciousness and time pressure on the degree of involvement during shopping.

Solution

AMOS commands

Now that it is certain that the constructs have been measured in the proper manner, the covariance arrows from Figure 8.37 are removed (via the **Erase Objects** button).

Expected causal relationships may be depicted in AMOS by drawing causal arrows (arrow pointing in one direction). To do this, click the **Draw Paths** button. The researcher may draw an arrow from one construct to the other.

When another unique variance must be given to a (latent) variable, this may be done via the **Draw Unique Variables** button.

This allows the researcher to indicate that another variance may be present in the latent variable which may not be explained by the underlying indicators for that latent variable.

Click this button, then go to the latent variable and click here once again with the left mouse button. You will notice that an object is attached to the variable (circle with an arrow). By clicking on this once again, the position of this new variable may be rotated 45 degrees with each click. Click the **Draw Unique Variables** button once again to turn off this function. By double-clicking the new variable (circle), a variable name may be given.

The researcher would like to find out what the effect of 'PRCON' and 'TPRESS' is on 'INVOLV' and must therefore draw a causal arrow from 'PRCON' to 'INVOLV' and from 'TPRESS' to 'INVOLV'. Another unique variable is added to the dependent variable ('e14'). This results in an image such as the one seen in Figure 8.47 (*sem11.amw*).

Figure 8.47

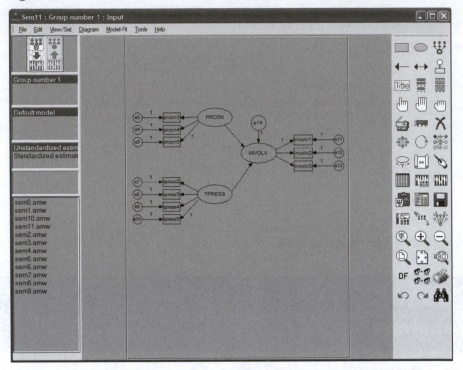

The model is then estimated by clicking the **Calculate Estimates** button.

Interpretation of the AMOS output

Initially, we examine the fit of the solution. In Figures 8.48, 8.49 and 8.50, indications are provided that the model is good.

Figure 8.48

Model Fit Summary

CMIN

Model	NPAR	CMIN	DF	P	CMIN/DF
Default model	22	46.051	33	.065	1.395
Saturated model	55	.000	0		
Independence model	10	2272.408	45	.000	50.498

RMR, GFI

Model	RMR	GFI	AGFI	PGFI
Default model	.126	.967	.945	.580
Saturated model	.000	1.000		
Independence model	.899	.387	.250	.316

Baseline Comparisons

Model	NFI Delta1	RFI rho1	IFI Delta2	TLI rho2	CFI
Default model	.980	.972	.994	.992	.994
Saturated model	1.000		1.000		1.000
Independence model	.000	.000	.000	.000	.000

Figure 8.49

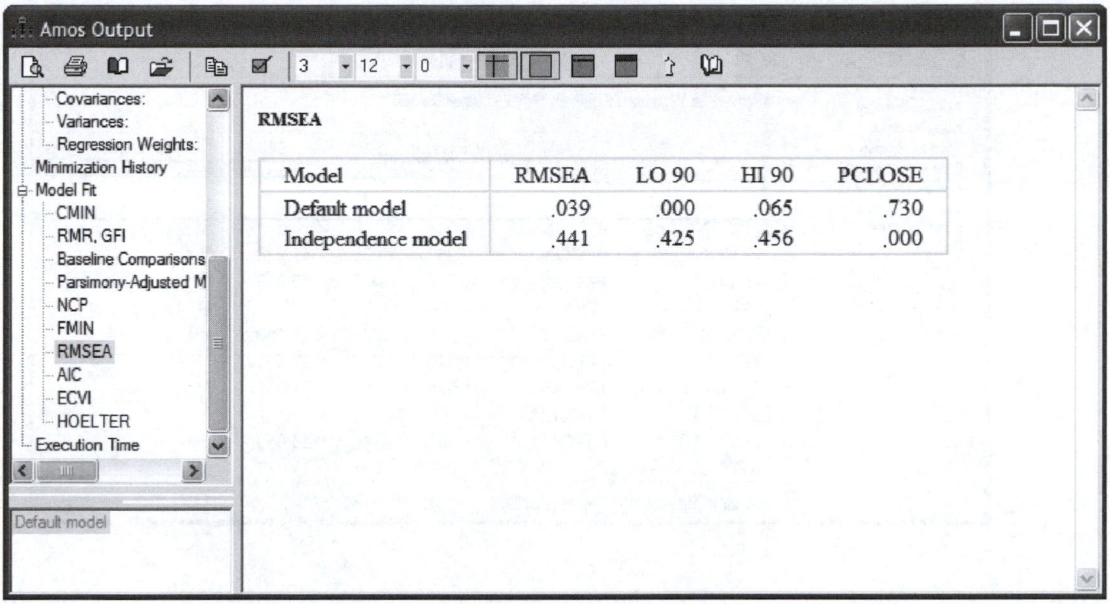

Figure 8.50

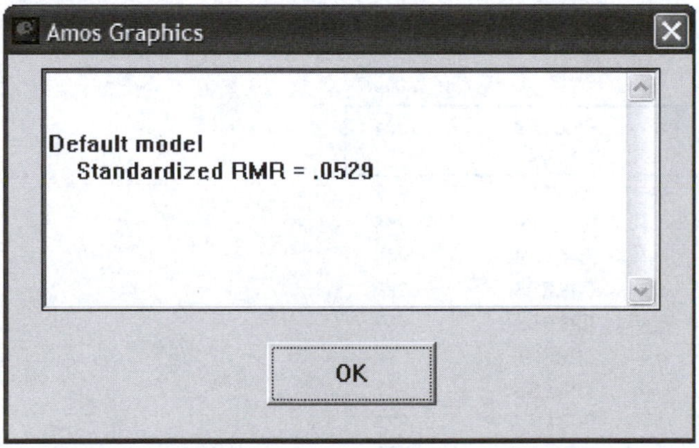

The Chi-square value is 46.051 with a p-value of .065 >.05, and the null hypothesis that the covariance matrix generated by the model is equal to the actual (observed) covariance matrix cannot be rejected. The fact that the model is a qualitatively good one is also evidenced by the good scores for GFI (.967), AGFI (.945), TLI (.992), CFI (.994), RMSEA (0.39) and SRMR (.0529).

Figure 8.51

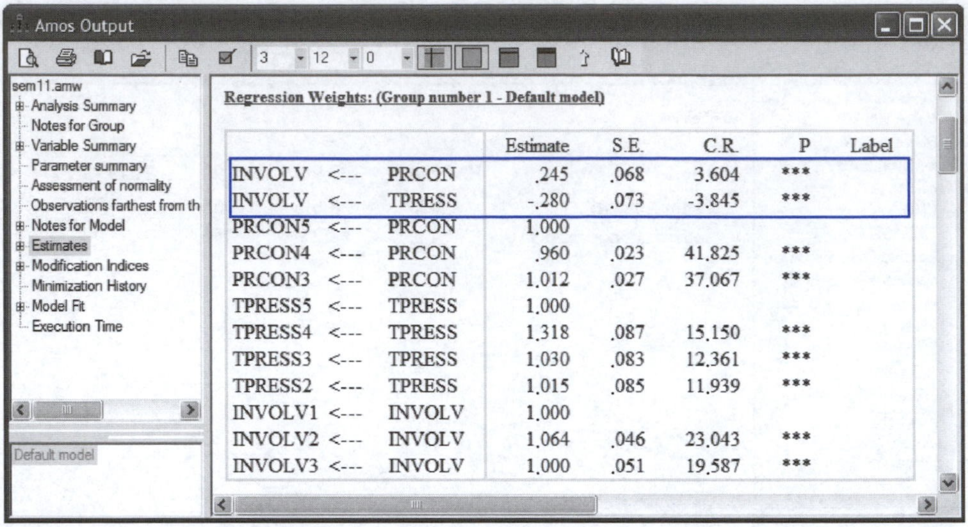

Regression Weights: (Group number 1 - Default model)

			Estimate	S.E.	C.R.	P	Label
INVOLV	<---	PRCON	.245	.068	3.604	***	
INVOLV	<---	TPRESS	-.280	.073	-3.845	***	
PRCON5	<---	PRCON	1.000				
PRCON4	<---	PRCON	.960	.023	41.825	***	
PRCON3	<---	PRCON	1.012	.027	37.067	***	
TPRESS5	<---	TPRESS	1.000				
TPRESS4	<---	TPRESS	1.318	.087	15.150	***	
TPRESS3	<---	TPRESS	1.030	.083	12.361	***	
TPRESS2	<---	TPRESS	1.015	.085	11.939	***	
INVOLV1	<---	INVOLV	1.000				
INVOLV2	<---	INVOLV	1.064	.046	23.043	***	
INVOLV3	<---	INVOLV	1.000	.051	19.587	***	

Figure 8.52

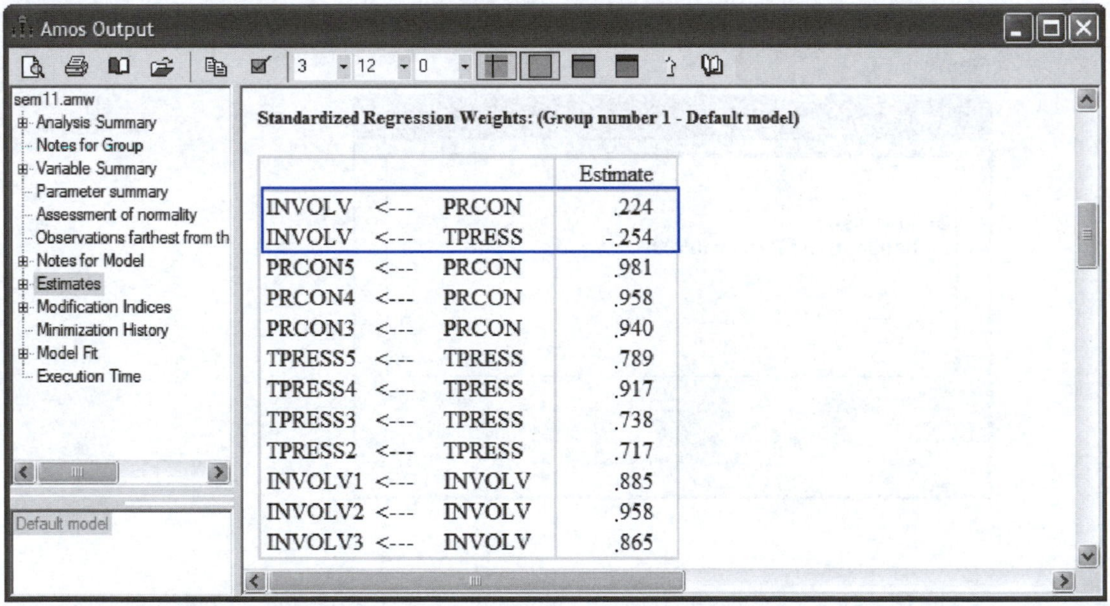

Standardized Regression Weights: (Group number 1 - Default model)

			Estimate
INVOLV	<---	PRCON	.224
INVOLV	<---	TPRESS	-.254
PRCON5	<---	PRCON	.981
PRCON4	<---	PRCON	.958
PRCON3	<---	PRCON	.940
TPRESS5	<---	TPRESS	.789
TPRESS4	<---	TPRESS	.917
TPRESS3	<---	TPRESS	.738
TPRESS2	<---	TPRESS	.717
INVOLV1	<---	INVOLV	.885
INVOLV2	<---	INVOLV	.958
INVOLV3	<---	INVOLV	.865

In Figures 8.51 and 8.52, the unstandardized and standardized regression coefficients are shown, respectively. Both price consciousness 'PRCON' and time pressure 'TPRESS' appear to have a significant influence on the degree of involvement 'INVOLV' (C.R. or t-values are 3.604 and −3.845 respectively, both have a significance of <.001). In other words, the null hypothesis that the path coefficient is equal to zero is rejected every time.

Figure 8.53

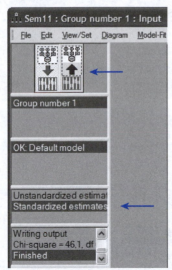

The influence of price consciousness is positive (correlation = .224) and the influence of time pressure is negative (correlation = −.254). This latter figure is also logical since people who do not have much time probably also do not have much time to be (substantially) involved during shopping. On the other hand, it appears that when consumers are price conscious, this translates partially into their degree of involvement during shopping.

AMOS also offers the possibility to display the coefficients obtained in the 'structural model' proposed (Figure 8.47). Suppose that the researcher would like to show the standardized values in this diagram.

First indicate 'Standardized estimates'. Then click the **View the output path diagram** button (icon with the wide arrow pointing from the estimation toward the diagram) (see left of the indicator arrow in Figure 8.53). To remove the coefficients again (and therefore to return to Figure 8.47), click the button directly adjacent to it (with the wide arrow pointing from the diagram toward the estimation).

Figure 8.54

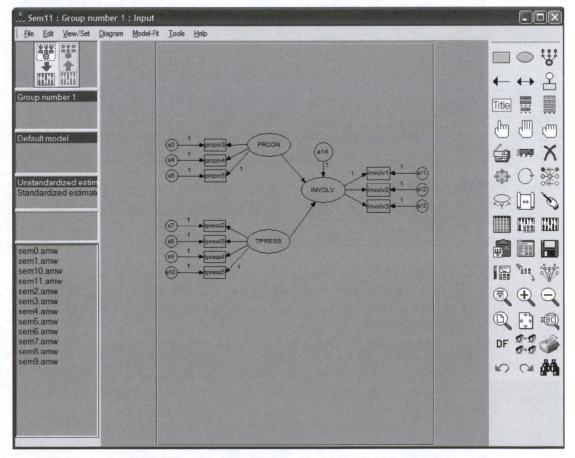

In our example, we opted for displaying the standardized estimates. The path diagram itself may be easily copied (Edit/Copy (to Clipboard)), in order to move it to a word processing program, for example (Figure 8.54).

Figure 8.55

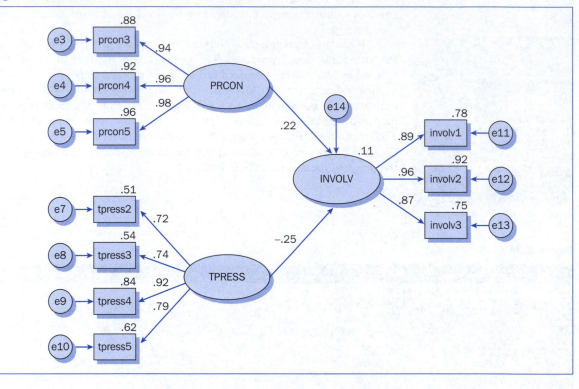

Further reading

Arbuckle, J.L. and Wothke, W. (1999), *Amos 4.0 User's Guide*. Chicago, Illinois: SmallWaters Corporation.

Bollen, K.A. and Long, J.S. [Eds.] (1993), *Testing Structural Equation Models*. Newbury Park, CA: Sage.

Browne, M. W. and Cudeck, R. (1993), 'Alternative ways of assessing model fit' in Bollen, K. A. and Long, J. S. [Eds.], *Testing structural equation models* (pp. 136–62). Newbury Park, CA: Sage.

Byrne, B.M. (2001), *Structural equation modeling with Amos – Basic Concepts, Applications, and Programming*. Mahwah, N.J.: Erlbaum.

Formell, C. and Larcker, D.F. (1981), Evaluating structural equation models with unobservable variables and measurement error, *Structural Equation Modeling*, 3, 62–72.

Hu, L.-T. and Bentler, P.M. (1999), 'Cut-off criteria for fit indexes in covariance structure analysis: Conventional criteria versus new alternatives', *Structural Equation Modeling*, 6, 1–55.

Chapter 9

Cluster analysis

Chapter objectives

This chapter will help you to:

- Understand when and how to use cluster analysis
- Assess the appropriateness of the data to carry out a cluster analysis
- Carry out an hierarchical cluster analysis based on binary data and interpret the results
- Carry out a two-step cluster analysis (hierarchical followed by K means) based on metric data and interpret the results

Technique

The objective of cluster analysis is to take a sample of n individuals or objects, each of which is measured for p variables, and group it into g classes, where g is less than n. In other words, the goal is to sort cases (individuals, products, brands, stimuli) into groups so that a high degree of similarity exists between cases in the same group, and a low degree of similarity between cases belonging to different groups. This similarity is evaluated on the basis of the value of each case (individual, product, etc.) for the variables (characteristics, attributes) upon which the cluster analysis is performed.

In performing a cluster analysis, the following four steps are taken:

1 **Select the variables or attributes, and in doing so pay attention to the measurement level, an even distribution of the attributes across the underlying dimensions and the comparability**

In terms of measurement level, a distinction is made between binary and continuous attributes. A binary attribute is an attribute that is either present or absent for an individual, and may be obtained via the 'pick any' method for example. A continuous attribute may assume different values, and may be the result of a semantic differential, a Likert scale or a stapel scale. Later on, this distinction in measurement level will demonstrate its importance in terms of the choice of (1) the similarity, dissimilarity or distance index and (2) the cluster algorithm.

The variables for which the cases will be clustered must be evenly distributed in terms of number across the underlying dimensions. If this is not done, then the underlying dimension measured on the basis of many variables will weigh more heavily in the clustering process than the dimension for which only one or several variables have been measured. In order to cope with this problem, it is recommended to first perform a factor analysis (see Chapter 7) on the clustering variables and then to include the resulting factors as clustering variables, if they are 'pure' factors, or the 'summated scales'. This way, every (underlying) dimension of variables will weigh equally in the clustering process.

Attributes are comparable if they are expressed in the same unit of measurement. If this is not the case (e.g., age expressed in years and income expressed in Euros), then the variables must be made comparable by giving them the same weight: for example, by standardizing them so that every variable will have a mean of 0 and a standard deviation of 1.

2 Choose a similarity, dissimilarity or distance index

In similarity indices, the two individuals (or clusters) with the highest association are agglomerated in the cluster algorithm. In dissimilarity indices, the respondents with the lowest dissimilarity are agglomerated. And finally, in distance indices, the two individuals are agglomerated who are closest to one another with regard to the variables or attributes for which the clustering is being performed.

The importance of the measurement level of the attributes is evidenced in the fact that with similarity indices, a distinction may be made between 'matching coefficients' for binary data, and correlation coefficients for continuous data. Distance indices exist for binary as well as continuous data.

3 Choose a cluster algorithm

An initial distinction is made between hierarchical clustering and partition methods. Characteristic of the hierarchical methods is that (1) in every step of the analysis, only two individuals or groups of individuals are considered and (2) once an individual has been assigned to a cluster, the cluster may no longer change for this person. These two restrictions are not applicable to the partition methods. As far as measurement level is concerned, the hierarchical methods can handle binary as well as continuous variables, while the partition methods can only process continuous data. Whereas partition methods can only process continuous data in SPSS, they can handle both continuous as well as binary data in other software packages (e.g., Clustan). It is important to emphasize that this discussion concerns the ability to process binary as well as continuous variables, and that this does not aim for a combination of both measurement levels in the same analysis. Should the researcher wish to combine different measurement levels in a single analysis, then he may use the 'TwoStep Cluster' procedure which may be found under the 'Classify' analyses in SPSS. However, be careful not to confuse this 'TwoStep Cluster' procedure with the method set out under Example 2, which applies a hierarchical clustering followed by a K-means clustering.

The hierarchical methods contain agglomerative methods (departure of n individuals which each represent one cluster, and then agglomerate these two clusters with the highest similarity or lowest dissimilarity or distance until all of the individuals have been included in one cluster) and divisive methods (departure of one cluster which contains all of the *n* individuals, and divides those into two groups, after which these groups are further divided up into two groups until n clusters result). The examples set out below concentrate on the agglomerative methods, and more specifically, the Ward method. This last method is also referred to as the minimum variance method, since it will attempt to generate clusters with the least possible amount of variance within each cluster.

The partition methods assume the distribution of n individuals in *k* (k < n) clusters or partitions determined beforehand. The individuals are reallocated from the one cluster to the other until a certain stopping criterion has been optimally met.

There are two types of partition methods: K-means and hill-climbing. In the second example described below, the first type is applied, which amounts to every individual being reallocated to that cluster for which the distance to the centre is the shortest. The procedure stops when this has been accomplished for all of the individuals.

Studies show that the K-means methods are superior to the hierarchical methods when the choice is made for an initial configuration based on the results of a hierarchical method. Moreover, the K-means method is most efficient when the same optimum criterion is used as that used to generate the initial configuration. With the K-means methods, this criterion consists of minimizing the distances within each cluster to the centre of that cluster. This is the same as the criterion used in Ward's hierarchical method. Therefore, for continuous variables, a good procedure will first perform a hierarchical cluster analysis using Ward's method and then use the results generated from this as input for the K-means method.

4 Determine the number of clusters and evaluate the cluster structure

Research performed previously, preparatory qualitative research, and intuition may all be used to determine the number of clusters and the evaluation of the cluster structure. In addition to this rather subjective approach, there is also the more objective approach which uses for example, Calinski and Harabasz's index, the C-index, the increase in error sum of squares, the split-run procedure, etc. This last, objective approach will however not be described in the examples below. Within SPSS, objective criteria for the determination of the optimum number of cluster groups may only be found in the 'TwoStep Cluster' module. For a further discussion of the cluster analysis technique, the reader is advised to consult reference works listed at the end of this chapter.

Two examples will be worked out in this chapter. Example 1 illustrates a hierarchical clustering of binary attributes, while Example 2 uses the hierarchical cluster analysis as input for a K-means clustering, and does this for continuous attributes.

Example 1

Cluster analysis with binary attributes – hierarchical clustering

Managerial problem

A market research firm has been asked to group 235 commercials into various clusters. To do this, six experts have subjected each of the commercials to a content analysis, which contained an evaluation which determined the absence or presence of aspects of eroticism [erotic], humour [humour] and warmth [warmth][1]. Additionally, the ability or failure to arouse feelings of fear [fear] and the presence or absence of professionalism [profes] and originality [original] in the commercials was also determined. Finally, the experts were asked to indicate whether the commercial focused on the creation of an image or whether the supply of information was central to the ad [imagedom]. Each of these seven criteria was linked to a binary variable: the characteristic is present (1: Yes), or the characteristic is not present (0: No), and these variables were included in an SPSS dataset (Figure 9.1).

Figure 9.1

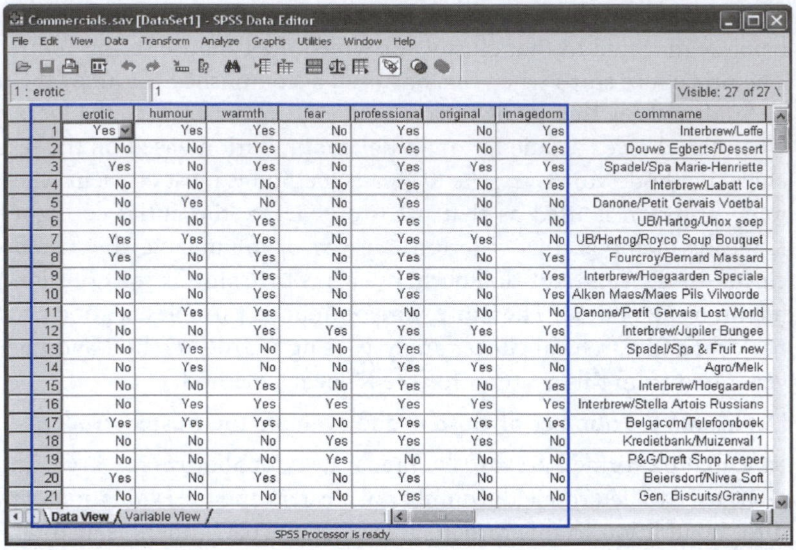

Problem

Perform a cluster analysis on the dataset above (*Commercials.sav*), using the seven binary variables 'eroticism', 'humour', 'warmth', 'fear', 'professionalism', 'originality', and 'image vs. information dominance'. Choose a hierarchical clustering, based on Ward's method and the distance index 'Squared Euclidean Distance', and allow the number of cluster groups to vary from three to six. Find an interesting cluster solution on the basis of criteria such as the number of commercials within each group and the possibility to typify the groups.

Important: in the case of binary data, the application of a K-means clustering is not allowed within SPSS; hierarchical methods are the only ones that lead to a correct output.

Solution

SPSS Commands

Figure 9.2

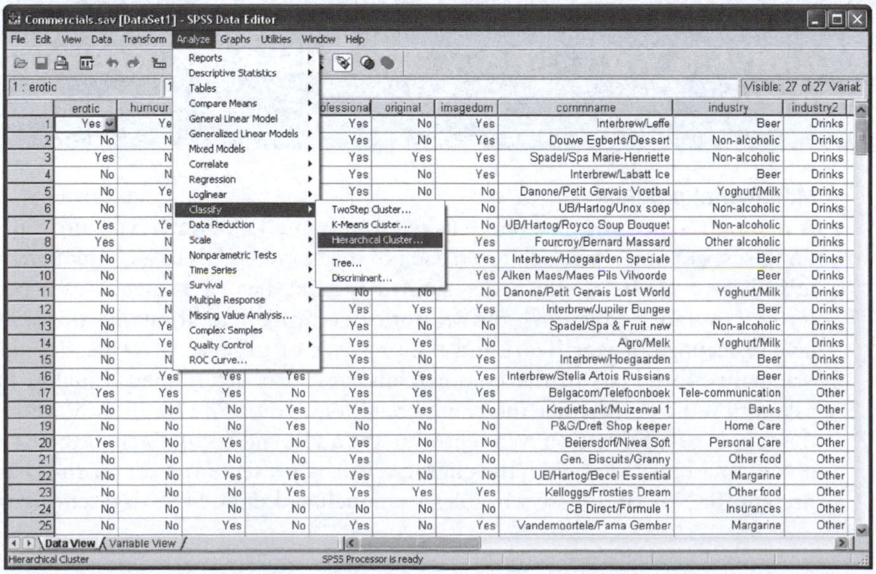

Go to Analyze/Classify/Hierarchical Cluster (Figure 9.2).

Figure 9.3

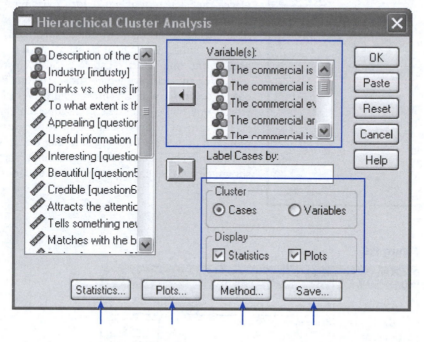

Select the seven binary variables from the list on the left-hand side which lie at the foundation of the cluster analysis: [erotic], [humour], [warmth], [fear], [professional], [original], and [imagedom] and move them to the 'Variable(s)' box using the top arrow (Figure 9.3).

Since the objective is for the clustering to group the commercials, choose the option 'Cluster: Cases'.

Tick the options 'Display: Statistics' and 'Display: Plots', and then define the content of the buttons at the bottom of the main window: 'Statistics', 'Plots', 'Method' and 'Save'.

Figure 9.4

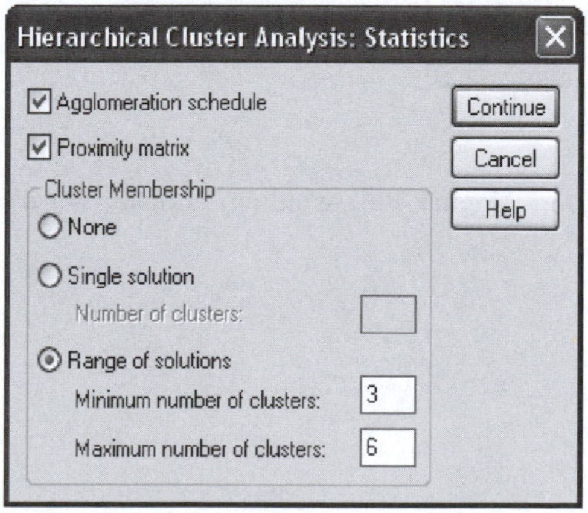

In the 'Hierarchical Cluster Analysis: Statistics' window (Figure 9.4), choose 'Agglomeration schedule' and 'Proximity matrix'. The first table provides an insight into the manner in which the commercials are clustered; the last indicates the 'distance' per pair of commercials, namely the 'Binary Squared Euclidean Distance' between them.

In the SPSS output, the 'Cluster Membership' option results in a table which indicates the cluster group to which each commercial belongs. If the researcher is only interested in one cluster solution (e.g., with three cluster groups), then he may opt for 'Single solution: 3 clusters'. If, however, he chooses a more exploratory approach and he would like to obtain insight into the manner in which commercials switch cluster groups when a three through six cluster solution is requested, then the option 'Range of solutions: from 3 through 6 clusters' is the most recommended one.

Figure 9.5

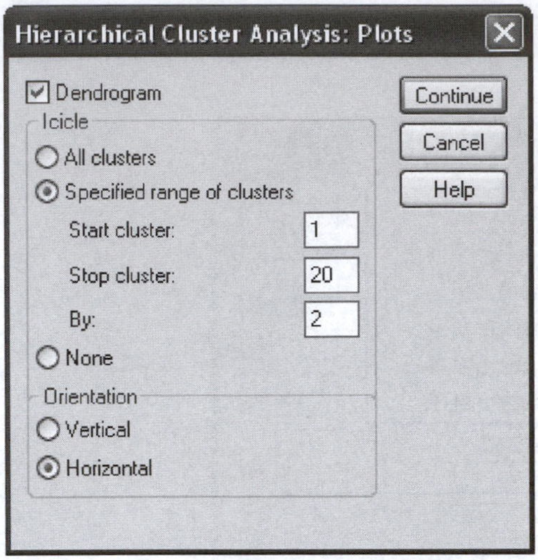

In the window 'Hierarchical Cluster Analysis: Plots' (Figure 9.5), choose the option 'Dendrogram' which will result in a visual display of the formation of cluster groups, supplemented by the distance at which the combination took place. The icicle plot also provides a visual representation of the sequential combinations, and does this for all of the possible cluster solutions, 'All clusters', or only for a limited number, 'Specified range of clusters'. With regard to this last option, the line 'Start cluster: 1, Stop cluster: 20, By: 2' stands for an icicle plot which shows the one through twenty cluster solution, with an intermediate step of two (in other words, one, three, five, seven, . . . nineteen cluster groups).

The vertical or horizontal orientation relates to the icicle plot, and in the case of a large number of cases, 'Horizontal' is chosen. This means that the commercials will not be shown next to each other, but under one another.

Figure 9.6

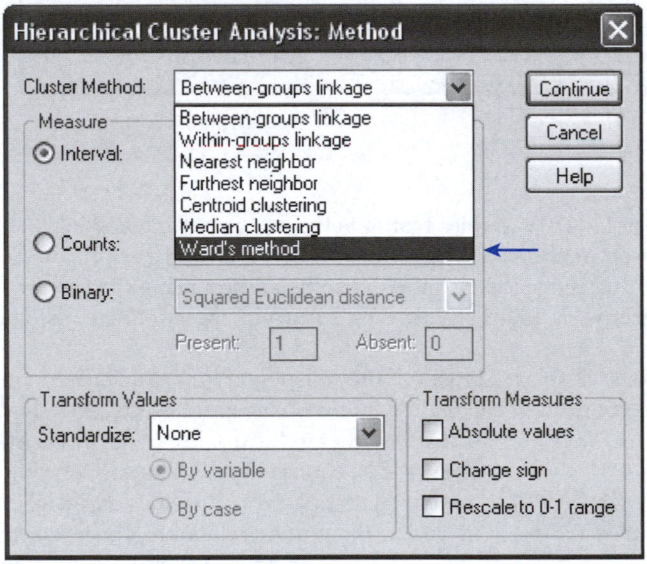

In the 'Hierarchical Cluster Analysis: Method' (Figure 9.6) window, choose 'Ward's method' for cluster method (see instructions).

Figure 9.7

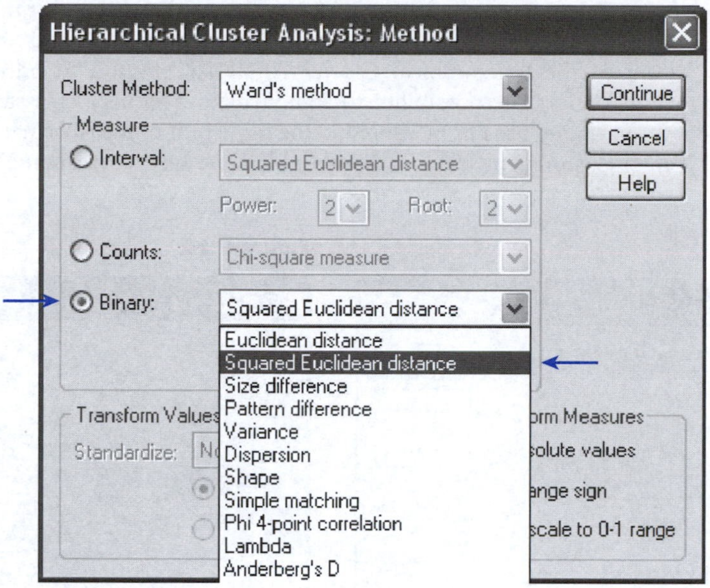

Base the forming of cluster groups on the distance index 'Squared Euclidean distance' (see instructions), however do not forget to first change the measurement level from interval-scaled to binary (Figure 9.7).

Figure 9.8

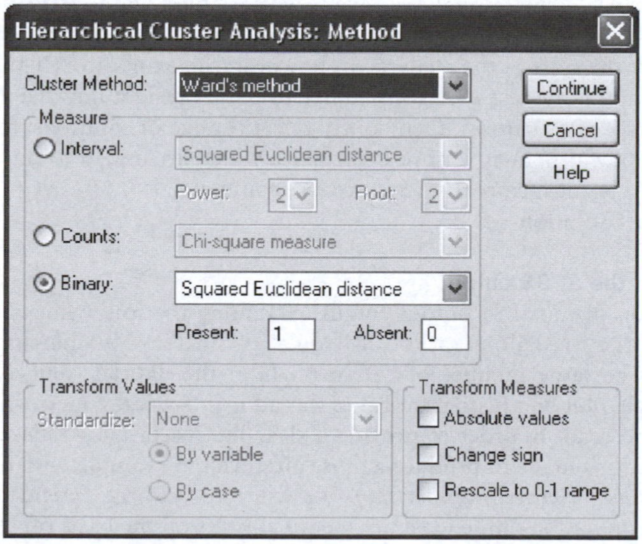

The seven binary variables have been coded in such a manner that the value one indicates the presence of the characteristic, whereas a zero indicates the absence of the characteristic. For this reason, 'Present' and 'Absent' (Figure 9.8) are defined as '1' and '0'.

At the bottom of the 'Hierarchical Cluster Analysis: Method' window (Figure 9.9), 'Transform Values' offers the possibility to standardize variables. This standardization is meaningful if the variables are not measured in the same unit of measurement, and may only be applied if the measurement level of the variables involved corresponds to 'Interval' or 'Counts'.

Figure 9.9

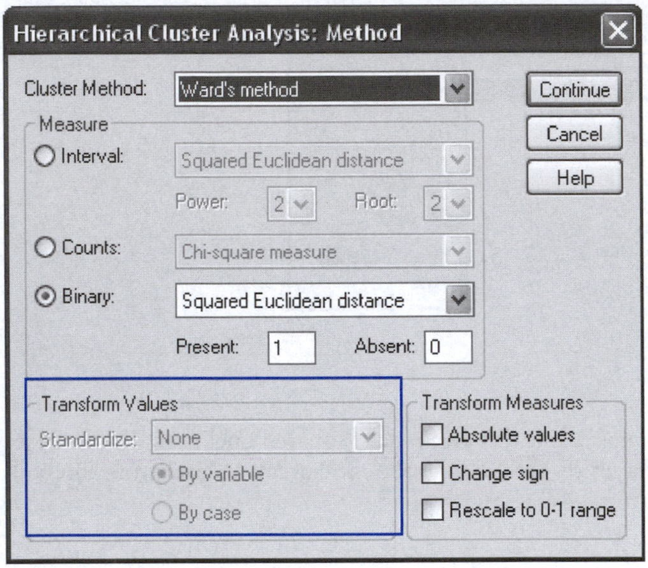

Figure 9.10

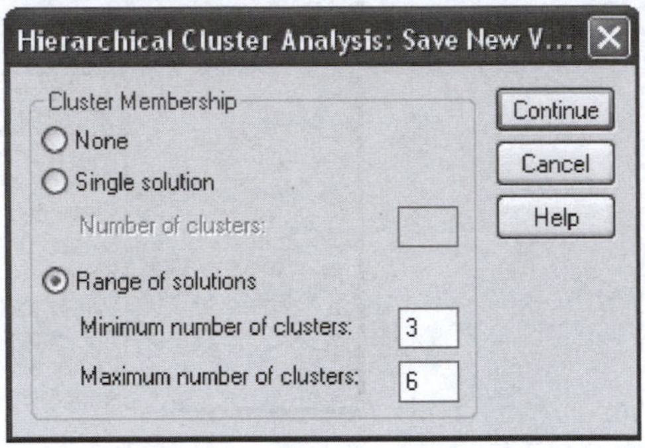

In the 'Hierarchical Cluster Analysis: Save New Variables' window (Figure 9.10), choose the option 'Single solution', if the number of groups into which the commercials may be divided is clear at the start of the analysis. If, however, the exploratory nature of the analysis is important, and if the researcher would like to obtain insight into the three through six cluster solution (see instructions), then he will select 'Range of solutions: from 3 through 6 clusters'. This choice generates four new variables which are added to the dataset, each of which shows the cluster membership for the 235 commercials in the event of a three, four, five and six cluster solution.

Interpretation of the SPSS output

The interpretation of the SPSS output entails examining the following tables and graphs: 'Proximity Matrix', 'Agglomeration Schedule', 'Cluster Membership', 'Icicle' and 'Dendrogram'. **The large number of commercials in the dataset (namely 235) however results in the icicle plot and histogram being spread over several pages, which makes these graphs difficult to read. In order to provide a clear interpretation of these graphs and the tables, the choice was made to produce a more abbreviated example with only 10 commercials (*Commercials – limited number.sav*).** We will return to the extended example again later for the determination of the ideal number of clusters on the basis of: (1) the number of commercials within each group; and (2) the characterization of each group, using cross tabulation of the cluster membership variable (e.g., [clu3_1]) with the basic variables 'erotic', 'humour', 'warmth', 'fear', 'professional', 'original', and 'image vs. information dominant'.

Figure 9.11

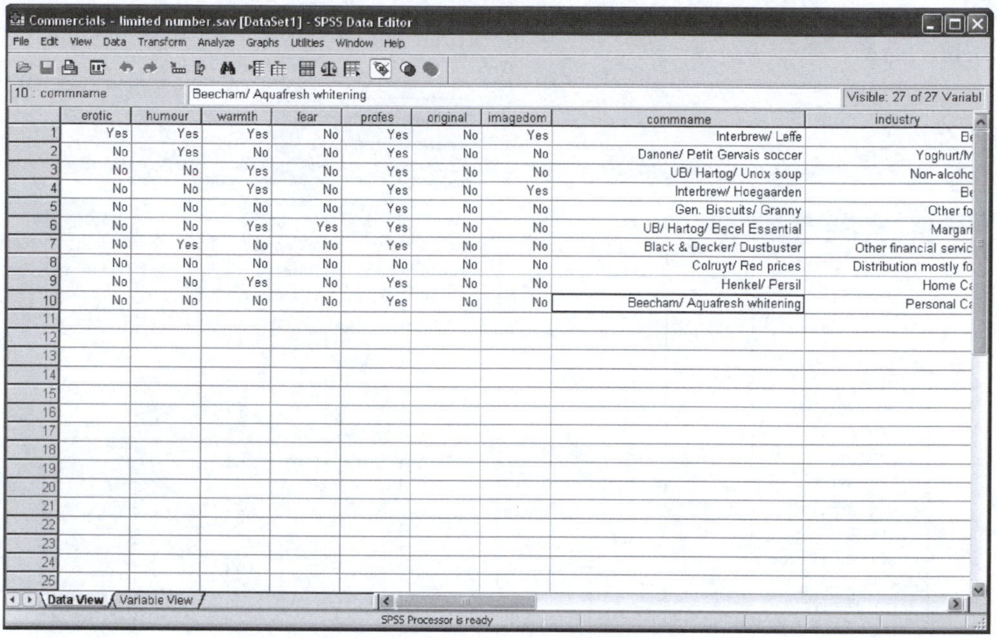

Open the dataset *Commercials – limited number.sav* (Figure 9.11) next to the dataset *Commercials.sav* by starting up the SPSS software a second time, and perform the SPSS commands mentioned above once again. Be sure to note that with regard to the labelling of the commercials in the output window and the drawing of the icicle plot, several changes have been made (Figures 9.12 and 9.13).

Figure 9.12

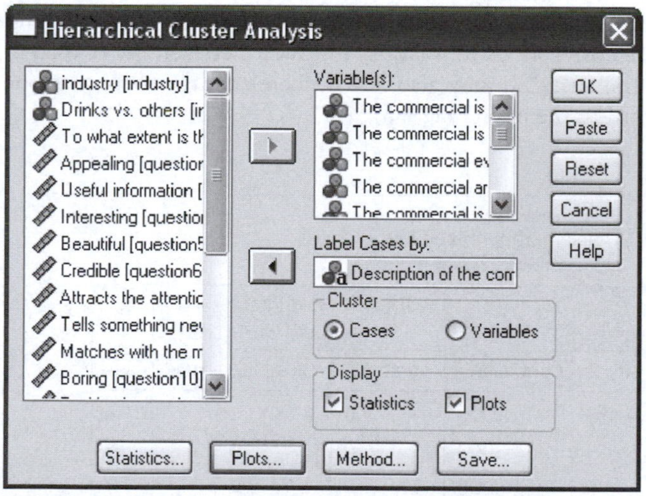

In the dataset the variable [commname] is defined as string and not as numerical. Because of this, the variable may be moved to the 'Label Cases by:' box. This will result in the commercials having a name in the output window (and not just a number).

Figure 9.13

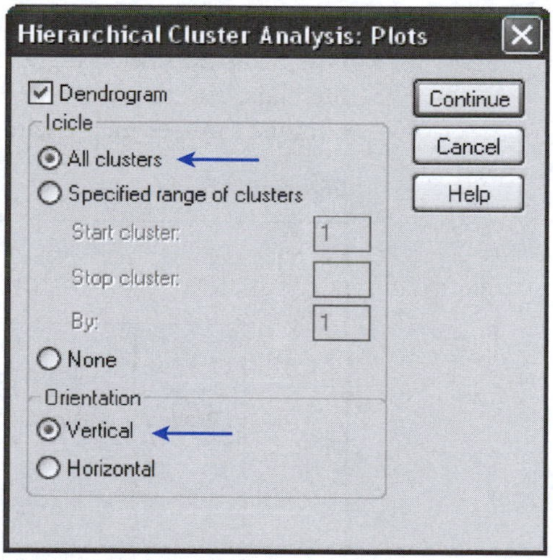

With regard to the icicle plot, the one through ten cluster solutions are presented visually (see 'Icicle – All clusters'), and the orientation is vertical (see 'Orientation – Vertical') (Figure 9.13).

This last characteristic implies that the ten commercials are shown next to one another, not under one another.

Figure 9.14

					Binary Squared Euclidean Distance					
Case	1: Interbrew/ Leffe	2: Danone/ Petit Gervais	3: UB/Hartog/ Unox soup	4: Interbrew/ Hoegaarden	5: Gen. Biscuits/ Granny	6: UB/Hartog/ Becel Essential	7: Black and Decker/ Dustbuster	8: Colruyt/ Red prices	9: Henkel/ Persil	10: Beecham/ Aquafresh whitening
1: Interbrew/Leffe	0	3	3	2	4	4	3	5	3	4
2: Danone/Petit Gervais	3	0	2	3	1	3	0	2	2	1
3: UB/Hartog/ Unox soup	3	2	0	1	1	1	2	2	0	1
4: Interbrew/ Hoegaarden	2	3	1	0	2	2	3	3	1	2
5: Gen. Biscuits/ Granny	4	1	1	2	0	2	1	1	1	0
6: UB/Hartog/Becel Essential	4	3	1	2	2	0	3	3	1	2
7: Black and Decker/ Dustbuster	3	0	2	3	1	3	0	2	2	1
8: Colruyt/Red prices	5	2	2	3	1	3	2	0	2	1
9: Henkel/Persil	3	2	0	1	1	1	2	2	0	1
10: Beecham/Aqua- fresh whitening	4	1	1	2	0	2	1	1	1	0

Proximity Matrix

This is a dissimilarity matrix

SPSS starts with the display of the 'Proximity Matrix' (Figure 9.14) which calculates the 'Binary Squared Euclidean Distance' for each pair of commercials. This matrix is a dissimilarity matrix, since a higher score corresponds to a larger 'distance' between the two commercials, and thus a greater 'dissimilarity'. It may also be said here that the scores are one another's mirror image with regard to the main diagonal.

Figure 9.15

Agglomeration Schedule

	Cluster Combined			Stage Cluster First Appears		
Stage	Cluster 1	Cluster 2	Coefficients	Cluster 1	Cluster 2	Next Stage
1	5	10	.000	0	0	4
2	3	9	.000	0	0	5
3	2	7	.000	0	0	7
4	5	8	.667	1	0	7
5	3	6	1.333	2	0	6
6	3	4	2.167	5	0	8
7	2	5	3.500	3	4	9
8	1	3	5.600	0	6	9
9	1	2	8.900	8	7	0

The 'Agglomeration Schedule' (Figure 9.15) indicates how cluster groups are formed, in order to arrive at a single cluster solution in step 9.

The columns 'Cluster Combined' indicate which commercials or groups of commercials have been in a certain step. It may also be noted here that a group of commercials will be given a name which corresponds to the number of the first commercial which was added. In other words, group {5, 10} which is formed after the first step will return in the fourth step as '5'.

'Coefficients' represents the distance index and when two cluster groups are combined, the distance between the two most 'different' or 'dissimilar' commercials will be indicated. Characteristic is that the values in this column become larger after steps 1 through 9 have been completed. This is logical, since first those commercials or groups of commercials are combined which are the least 'dissimilar', or in other words, are the most homogeneous.

The columns 'Stage Cluster First Appears' indicate in which previous step a group of commercials had already appeared. The 'Next Stage' column on the other hand indicates the subsequent step during which a commercial or group of commercials will be added to the relevant group.

What does the explanation above mean in concrete terms? In the first step, commercials '5' and '10' are clustered; neither commercial had been involved in a previous clustering and this new cluster group {5, 10} will be involved in the clustering process once again in step 4. In a later step, commercials '3' and '9' will be grouped, neither of which had been involved in a previous clustering and this new cluster group {3, 9} will be included in the clustering process once again in step 5. In step 4, commercials '5' and '8' will be agglomerated, however commercial '5' had already been linked to commercial '10' in step 1. Therefore the new cluster group will contain the commercials '5' and '10' and '8', and will once again be involved in the process in step 7. This way, step 7 will thus lead to the formation of the new group {2, 7, 5, 8, 10}. Finally, step 9 will lead to a single cluster group which contains the 10 commercials.

Figure 9.16

Cluster Membership				
Case	6 Clusters	5 Clusters	4 Clusters	3 Clusters
1: Interbrew/Leffe	1	1	1	1
2: Danone/Petit Gervai	2	2	2	2
3: UB/Hartog/Unox sou	3	3	3	3
4: Interbrew/Hoegaarde	4	4	3	3
5: Gen. Biscuits/Grann	5	5	4	2
6: UB/Hartog/Becel Es	6	3	3	3
7: Black and Decker/Dust	2	2	2	2
8: Colruyt/Red prices	5	5	4	2
9: Henkel/Persil	3	3	3	3
10: Beecham/Aquafresh w	5	5	4	2

The table 'Cluster Membership' (Figure 9.16) displays the three through six cluster solutions requested, and for each commercial, shows to which specific group of commercials it belongs. This information may also be found in the dataset (Figure 9.17) via the variables [clu6_1], [clu5_1], [clu4_1], and [clu3_1].

Figure 9.17

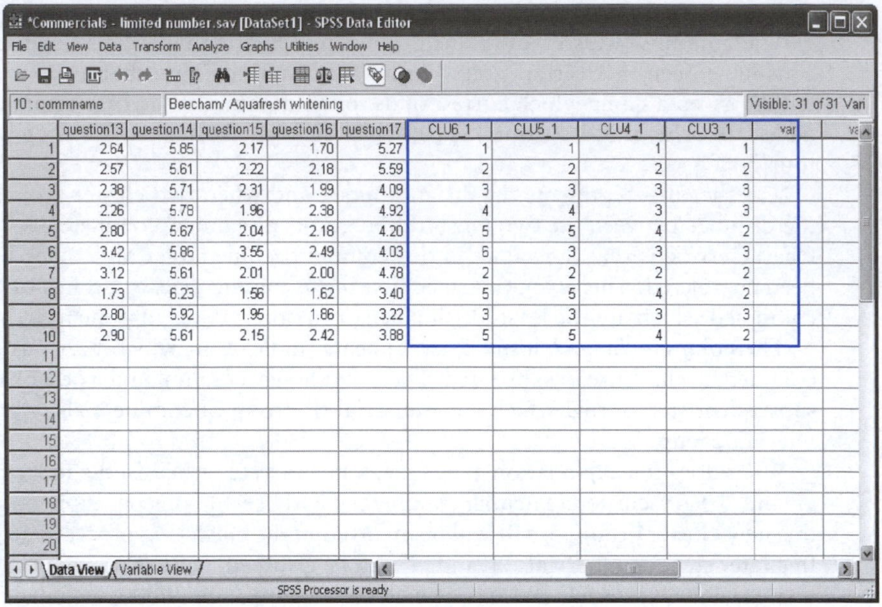

Commercials - limited number.sav [DataSet1] - SPSS Data Editor

File   Edit   View   Data   Transform   Analyze   Graphs   Utilities   Window   Help

10 : commname   Beecham/ Aquafresh whitening   Visible: 31 of 31 Vari

	question13	question14	question15	question16	question17	CLU6_1	CLU5_1	CLU4_1	CLU3_1	var
1	2.64	5.85	2.17	1.70	5.27	1	1	1	1	
2	2.57	5.61	2.22	2.18	5.59	2	2	2	2	
3	2.38	5.71	2.31	1.99	4.09	3	3	3	3	
4	2.26	5.78	1.96	2.38	4.92	4	4	3	3	
5	2.80	5.67	2.04	2.18	4.20	5	5	4	2	
6	3.42	5.86	3.55	2.49	4.03	6	3	3	3	
7	3.12	5.61	2.01	2.00	4.78	2	2	2	2	
8	1.73	6.23	1.56	1.62	3.40	5	5	4	2	
9	2.80	5.92	1.95	1.86	3.22	3	3	3	3	
10	2.90	5.61	2.15	2.42	3.88	5	5	4	2	
11										
12										
13										
14										
15										
16										
17										
18										
19										
20										

Data View / Variable View /

SPSS Processor is ready

In the case of a three-cluster solution for example, 'Leffe' represents the first group; 'Petit Gervais', 'Granny', 'Dustbuster', 'Red prices', and 'Aquafresh whitening' form the second group; and 'Unox soup', 'Hoegaarden', 'Becel Essential' and 'Persil' form the last group.

It may be said here that 'Leffe' will still belong to the first group of commercials after the six through three cluster solution has been completed, whereas 'Aquafresh whitening' which originally belonged to group '5' for example, will then move to group '4' and finally to group '2'.

Figure 9.18

Vertical Icicle

Number of Clusters	8: Colruyt/Red prices		10: Beecham/Aquafresh w		5: Gen. Biscuits/Grann		7: Black and Decker/Dust		2: Danone/Petit Gervai		4: Interbrew/Hoegaarde		6: UB/Hartog/Becel Es		9: Henkel/Persil		3: UB/Hartog/Unox sou		1: Interbrew/Leffe
1	X	X	X	X	X	X	X	X	X	X	X	X	X	X	X	X	X	X	X
2	X	X	X	X	X	X	X	X	X	X	X	X	X	X	X	X	X		X
3	X	X	X	X	X	X	X	X	X		X	X	X	X	X	X	X		X
4	X	X	X	X	X		X	X	X		X	X	X	X	X	X	X		X
5	X	X	X	X	X		X	X	X		X		X	X	X	X	X		X
6	X	X	X	X	X		X	X	X		X		X		X	X	X		X
7	X	X	X	X	X		X	X	X		X		X		X		X		X
8	X	X	X	X	X		X		X		X		X		X		X		X
9	X	X	X		X		X		X		X		X		X		X		X

Case

The icicle plot (Figure 9.18) provides a visual representation of each step in the clustering process. Initially, each commercial forms a separate cluster, while after nine steps, the ten commercials are agglomerated to form one group. The diagram is also read from bottom to top, in which each commercial is represented by a column of ×'s and the blank spaces indicate that these commercials do **not** belong to the same group.

In concrete terms: there were originally 10 clusters, one for each commercial, and all of the commercials are separated from one another by a blank space. This situation is not shown in the icicle plot, yet would be found all the way at the bottom. In the first step, commercials '5' (Granny) and '10' (Aquafresh) are agglomerated, leaving nine clusters remaining. The next step groups commercials '9' (Persil) and '3' (Unox soup). Commercials '7' (Dustbuster) and '2' (Petit Gervais) follow next. Then, commercial '8' (Red prices) is added to the previously formed group {10, 5}, and so on. In the final step, the groups {8, 10, 5, 7, 2} and {4, 6, 9, 3, 1} are agglomerated to form a single cluster group.

By reading the dendrogram (Figure 9.19) from left to right, the researcher gains insight into the way in which the commercials are agglomerated, in order to ultimately arrive at a single group which contains all ten commercials. Compared with the icicle plot, the disadvantage of the dendrogram is that the sequence of formation of the first groups of commercials is unclear, however the advantage is that the distance at which the agglomeration has taken place is indicated, and this is done using the 'Rescaled Distance Cluster Combine' function. This distance criterion is linked to 'Coefficients' in the 'Agglomeration Schedule' (Figure 9.15), and lies between '1' and '25'. This means that the shortest distance between two commercials at the time of agglomeration corresponds to '0' in the

Figure 9.19

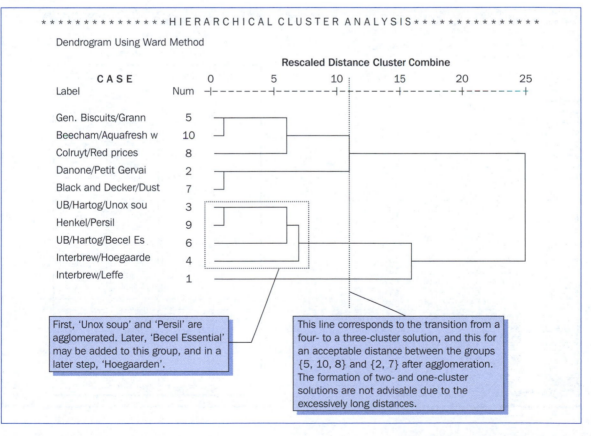

***************HIERARCHICAL CLUSTER ANALYSIS***************

Dendrogram Using Ward Method

Rescaled Distance Cluster Combine

First, 'Unox soup' and 'Persil' are agglomerated. Later, 'Becel Essential' may be added to this group, and in a later step, 'Hoegaarden'.

This line corresponds to the transition from a four- to a three-cluster solution, and this for an acceptable distance between the groups {5, 10, 8} and {2, 7} after agglomeration. The formation of two- and one-cluster solutions are not advisable due to the excessively long distances.

'Agglomeration Schedule' and to '1' in the dendrogram; for the largest distance, these values are '8.9' and '25' respectively. These distances provide an indication regarding the appropriate number of clusters: for the current example, the researcher may decide to create three groups of commercials ({5, 10, 8, 2, 7}, {3, 9, 6, 4}, {1}), given the further agglomerations are accompanied by large distances between the groups.

In addition to the distance index, the number of commercials in each cluster group and the ability to assign a meaningful description to each of the clusters on the basis of the basic variables 'erotic', 'humour', 'warmth', 'fear', 'professional', 'original', and 'image vs. information dominant' provide an indication regarding the ideal number of groups. It is important to remember that the ultimate number chosen is subjective, and may thus vary from one researcher to the next. **For a further elaboration on the material in this paragraph, we will return to the extensive example, and it is primarily the four variables [clu3_1], [clu4_1], [clu5_1] and [clu6_1] which had already been added to the dataset *Commercials.sav* as a result of the previous cluster analysis, which are important.**

Go to the dataset *Commercials.sav* (Figure 9.20) and calculate frequency tables for the variables [clu3_1], [clu4_1], [clu5_1] and [clu6_1] (Analyze/Descriptive Statistics/ Frequencies; see Chapter 2). Using cross tabulation, link each of these cluster membership variables to the seven basic variables (Analyze/Descriptive Statistics/Crosstabs, whereby the cluster membership variable is placed in the columns and the basic variable in the rows, and whereby the 'Pearson Chi-Square' statistic and the column percentage are requested; see Chapter 3).

Figure 9.20

	question11	question12	question13	question14	question15	question16	question17	CLU6_1	CLU5_1	CLU4_1	CLU3_1	var
1	4.96	5.52	2.64	5.85	2.17	1.70	5.27	1	1	1	1	
2	4.66	5.36	2.94	5.67	2.28	2.17	3.83	2	2	2	2	
3	3.40	3.07	4.10	4.31	4.67	3.84	3.72	1	1	1	1	
4	5.04	5.48	2.56	5.27	2.70	2.25	5.70	3	3	3	3	
5	4.94	5.79	2.57	5.61	2.22	2.18	5.59	3	3	3	3	
6	4.71	5.50	2.38	5.71	2.31	1.99	4.09	4	4	2	2	
7	5.00	5.37	3.13	6.19	2.34	1.97	5.15	5	1	1	1	
8	5.34	5.04	3.58	5.83	3.44	2.33	4.85	2	2	2	2	
9	5.09	5.82	1.86	6.04	1.70	1.80	5.35	2	2	2	2	
10	5.24	5.89	2.44	6.32	1.89	1.90	5.29	2	2	2	2	
11	4.21	5.41	2.66	5.59	3.17	2.71	5.14	4	4	2	2	
12	4.03	5.04	2.35	5.07	2.16	2.19	5.48	1	1	1	1	
13	4.83	4.79	3.54	5.36	3.79	3.49	5.04	3	3	3	3	
14	3.38	3.99	3.68	4.45	3.82	4.35	4.60	5	1	1	1	
15	5.20	5.78	2.26	5.78	1.96	2.38	4.92	2	2	2	2	
16	4.47	5.12	3.80	5.81	4.44	3.12	5.61	1	1	1	1	
17	4.84	5.21	2.49	5.51	2.39	2.33	4.75	1	1	1	1	
18	3.74	5.11	3.28	5.38	3.36	2.98	3.90	6	5	4	3	
19	3.08	5.22	3.15	5.22	2.53	2.28	2.82	6	5	4	3	
20	4.33	5.18	2.69	5.43	2.25	2.22	4.03	2	2	2	2	
21	4.74	5.51	2.80	5.67	2.04	2.18	4.20	3	3	3	3	
22	5.08	5.65	3.42	5.86	3.55	2.49	4.03	4	4	2	2	
23	4.64	5.37	3.81	5.34	3.58	2.58	5.14	1	1	1	1	
24	3.87	4.17	4.35	5.27	4.12	3.80	4.34	3	3	3	3	
25	4.01	5.28	3.27	5.37	3.26	2.59	3.59	2	2	2	2	
26	3.87	5.33	3.21	4.95	3.38	3.21	4.91	6	5	4	3	
27	4.91	5.94	3.12	5.61	2.01	2.00	4.78	3	3	3	3	
28	3.88	5.23	4.05	4.59	3.22	2.90	5.17	6	5	4	3	

The four frequency tables (Figure 9.21) provide an insight into the number of commercials per group by examining the frequencies and the 'valid percentages'. The rejection of a certain cluster solution may then be based on the low number of commercials for one or more groups. It is not interesting to draw conclusions for a certain type of commercial if this group only contains four commercials, for example.

Figure 9.21

Six Cluster Solution

		Frequency	Percent	Valid Percent	Cumulative Percent
Valid	1	33	14.0	14.5	14.5
	2	23	9.8	10.1	24.7
	3	59	25.1	26.0	50.7
	4	36	15.3	15.9	66.5
	5	23	9.8	10.1	76.7
	6	53	22.6	23.3	100.0
	Total	227	96.6	100.0	
Missing	System	8	3.4		
Total		235	100.0		

Cluster groups '1' and '5' and not '1' and '2' are agglomerated by the transition from the six- to the five-cluster solution. Inspection of the columns [clu6_1] and [clu5_1] in the dataset (Figure 9.22) show this clearly.

Five Cluster Solution

		Frequency	Percent	Valid Percent	Cumulative Percent
Valid	1	56	23.8	24.7	24.7
	2	23	9.8	10.1	34.8
	3	59	25.1	26.0	60.8
	4	36	15.3	15.9	76.7
	5	53	22.6	23.3	100.0
	Total	227	96.6	100.0	
Missing	System	8	3.4		
Total		235	100.0		

Four Cluster Solution

		Frequency	Percent	Valid Percent	Cumulative Percent
Valid	1	56	23.8	24.7	24.7
	2	59	25.1	26.0	50.7
	3	59	25.1	26.0	76.7
	4	53	22.6	23.3	100.0
	Total	227	96.6	100.0	
Missing	System	8	3.4		
Total		235	100.0		

During the transition from a four- to the three-cluster solution, the groups '3' and '4' are agglomerated to one new group, '3'.

Figure 9.21 *Continued*

		Frequency	Percent	Valid Percent	Cumulative Percent
	Three Cluster Solution				
Valid	1	56	23.8	24.7	24.7
	2	59	25.1	26.0	50.7
	3	112	47.7	49.3	100.0
	Total	227	96.6	100.0	
Missing	System	8	3.4		
Total		235	100.0		

In the current application, the four frequency tables indicate that there is not a single group that only consists of a low number of commercials, and therefore may not be considered a criterion for the rejection of one or more of the four possible cluster solutions.

Figure 9.22

question17	CLU6_1	CLU5_1	CLU4_1	CLU3_1
5.27	1	1	1	1
3.83	2	2	2	2
3.72	1	1	1	1
5.70	3	3	3	3
5.59	3	3	3	3
4.09	4	4	2	2
5.15	5	1	1	1
4.85	2	2	2	2

Another criterion for making a choice between the six, five, four and three cluster solution is the ability to assign a significant meaning to each of the cluster groups, or, in other words, to be able to derive unambiguous types of commercials. In order to find this out, it is necessary to perform a crosstab analysis (Figure 9.23) on the cluster membership variable, [clu6_1], [clu5_1], [clu4_1] or [clu3_1], with each of the basic variables, 'erotic', 'humour', 'warmth', 'fear', 'professional', 'original', and 'image vs. information dominant'. In order to limit the quantity of analyses and characterizations, we may start with one of the four cluster membership variables, for example, the four cluster solution [clu4_1].

Figure 9.23

Crosstab

			Four Cluster Solution				Total
			1	2	3	4	
The commercial is erotic	No	Count	36	45	59	29	169
		% within four cluster solution	64.3%	76.3%	100.0%	54.7%	74.4%
	Yes	Count	20	14	0	24	58
		% within four cluster solution	35.7%	23.7%	.0%	45.3%	25.6%
Total		Count	56	59	59	53	227
		% within four cluster solution	100.0%	100.0%	100.0%	100.0%	100.0%

Crosstab

			Four Cluster Solution				Total
			1	2	3	4	
The commercial is humorous	No	Count	18	45	50	46	159
		% within four cluster solution	32.1%	76.3%	84.7%	86.8%	70.0%
	Yes	Count	38	14	9	7	68
		% within four cluster solution	67.9%	23.7%	15.3%	13.2%	30.0%
Total		Count	56	59	59	53	227
		% within four cluster solution	100.0%	100.0%	100.0%	100.0%	100.0%

Crosstab

			Four Cluster Solution				Total
			1	2	3	4	
The commercial evokes warmth	No	Count	33	0	55	53	141
		% within four cluster solution	58.9%	.0%	93.2%	100.0%	62.1%
	Yes	Count	23	59	4	0	86
		% within four cluster solution	41.1%	100.0%	6.8%	.0%	37.9%
Total		Count	56	59	59	53	227
		% within four cluster solution	100.0%	100.0%	100.0%	100.0%	100.0%

Crosstab

			Four Cluster Solution				Total
			1	2	3	4	
The commercial arouses fear	No	Count	33	33	59	7	132
		% within four cluster solution	58.9%	55.9%	100.0%	13.2%	58.1%
	Yes	Count	23	26	0	46	95
		% within four cluster solution	41.1%	44.1%	.0%	86.8%	41.9%
Total		Count	56	59	59	53	227
		% within four cluster solution	100.0%	100.0%	100.0%	100.0%	100.0%

Figure 9.23 *Continued*

Crosstab

			Four Cluster Solution				Total
			1	2	3	4	
The commercial is well developed (professional)	No	Count	11	20	46	41	118
		% within four cluster solution	19.6%	33.9%	78.0%	77.4%	52.0%
	Yes	Count	45	39	13	12	109
		% within four cluster solution	80.4%	66.1%	22.0%	22.6%	48.0%
Total		Count	56	59	59	53	227
		% within four cluster solution	100.0%	100.0%	100.0%	100.0%	100.0%

Crosstab

			Four Cluster Solution				Total
			1	2	3	4	
The commercial is original	No	Count	2	53	59	48	162
		% within four cluster solution	3.6%	89.8%	100.0%	90.6%	71.4%
	Yes	Count	54	6	0	5	65
		% within four cluster solution	96.4%	10.2%	.0%	9.4%	28.6%
Total		Count	56	59	59	53	227
		% within four cluster solution	100.0%	100.0%	100.0%	100.0%	100.0%

Crosstab

			Four Cluster Solution				Total
			1	2	3	4	
Image dominant versus information dominant	No	Count	18	31	43	45	137
		% within four cluster solution	32.1%	52.5%	72.9%	84.9%	60.4%
	Yes	Count	38	28	16	8	90
		% within four cluster solution	67.9%	47.5%	27.1%	15.1%	39.6%
Total		Count	56	59	59	53	227
		% within four cluster solution	100.0%	100.0%	100.0%	100.0%	100.0%

The results from these crosstabs are summarized in an overview table (Table 9.1) which will be used for the characterization of each of the four groups of commercials.

It should also be noted here that the relationship between the cluster membership variable and each of the seven basic variables appears to be significant (p-value$_{\text{Pearson Chi-Square}} <$ .001), and that the two conditions for the interpretation of the 'Pearson Chi-Square' statistic have been satisfied (less than 20% of the cells have an expected count of less than 5, and the minimum theoretical expected frequency is greater than 1; Figure 9.24 illustrates this for the basic variable 'erotic'). This means that for each of the basic variables, there are differences present between two or more groups.

Table 9.1 Overview table: 4 clusters

Basic-variable	Sig./ Insig.	Group 1	Group 2	Group 3	Group 4
The commercial is erotic	Sig.	Rather few	Rather few	**None**	**Approximately half**[3]
The commercial is humorous	Sig.	Quite a few	Rather few	Rather few	Rather few
The commercial evokes warmth	Sig.	Approximately half	All	Few	None
The commercial arouses fear	Sig.	Approximately half	Approximately half	**None**	**Quite a few**
The commercial is well developed (professional)	Sig.	Quite a few	Quite a few	Rather few	Rather few
The commercial is original	Sig.	Many	Few	None	Few
Image dominant versus information dominant	Sig.	Quite a few	Approximately half	Rather few	Rather few
The typical commercial for this group . . .		is humorous, evokes warmth, is professional and **original**, and strives to create an image	**evokes warmth**, is professional but **not original**, and its primary focus is on creating an image	**is not erotic, does not radiate any warmth, does not arouse feelings of fear, is not original** and its primary focus is on providing information	is erotic, **does not radiate** warmth, arouses feelings of fear, is **not original**, and its primary focus is on providing information
Example		Swan sausages with ET creatures	Douwe Egberts dessert coffee	Black & Decker Dustbuster	

Figure 9.24

Chi-Square Tests			
	Value	df	Asymp. Sig. (2-sided)
Pearson Chi-square	34.241[a]	3	.000
Likelihood ratio	47.356	3	.000
Linear-by-linear association	.000	1	.984
N of valid cases	227		

[a]0 cells (.0%) have expected count less than 5. The minimum expected count is 13.54

The overview table Table 9.1 indicates that a meaningful interpretation may be attached to the groups '1', '2', and '3', whereas the description for group '4' is ambiguous. This indicates that the four-cluster solution is not a good choice, and that the suitability of the other cluster solutions, namely the six, five and three-cluster solution should be investigated. In this context, the four frequency tables used previously (see Figure 9.21) would lead us to believe that the three-cluster solution is the most recommended. The identical group of commercials which may not be clearly characterized in the case of the four-cluster solution, is also present in the five and the six-cluster solution (see the 23.3% which corresponds to group '4' in the four-cluster solution and which returns in the five and the six-cluster solution, linked to the groups '5' and '6'). In the case of the three-cluster solution on the other hand, this group (23.3%) is combined with group '3' from the four-cluster solution (26%), and the 'new' group '3' (49.3%) is potentially unambiguous. In order to find this out, cross tabulation is requested once again, however these will now determine the relationship between the seven basic variables and the cluster membership variable [clu3_1] instead of [clu4_1]. Only the overview table (Table 9.2) is included below.

In the overview table each of the clusters may now be clearly characterized: group '1' stands for the original, emotional commercial, group '2' coincides with the warm, image-dominated commercial, and group '3' corresponds to the cool, informational commercial. This indicates that this solution is a good final solution. With regard to the transition from the four to the three-cluster solution, two points may be made: (1) the basic variables 'erotic' and 'fear', which are significant in the four-cluster solution are no longer significant in the three-cluster solution (these significances were primarily based on the differences between the groups '3' and '4', and it is precisely these two groups which have been agglomerated in

Table 9.2 Overview table: 3 clusters

Basic-variable	Sig./ Insig.	Group 1	Group 2	Group 3
The commercial is erotic	Insig.	Rather few	Rather few	Rather few
The commercial is humorous	Sig.	Quite a few	Rather few	Rather few
The commercial evokes warmth	Sig.	Approximately half	All	Few
The commercial arouses fear	Insig.	Approximately half	Approximately half	Approximately half
The commercial is well developed (professional)	Sig.	Quite a few	Quite a few	Rather few
The commercial is original	Sig.	Many	Few	Few
Image dominant versus information dominant	Sig.	Quite a few	Approximately half	Rather few
The typical commercial for this group . . .		is humorous, evokes warmth, is professional and **original**, and strives to create an image	**evokes warmth**, is professional but **not original**, and its primary focus is on creating an image	**does not radiate any warmth, is not original** and its primary focus is on providing information

the three cluster solution); and (2) in terms of the number of commercials and the characterization, the groups '1' and '2' from the four-cluster solution are identical to the clusters '1' and '2' from the three-cluster solution.

Supporting technique

The next step is to further explore the three-cluster solution on the basis of two types of variables: (1) descriptive variables (e.g., the product category to which the commercial belongs, [industry2]); and (2) criterion variables (these are variables which the researcher would like to explain on the basis of the cluster membership). This last group of variables is based on a questionnaire, the topic of which was one of the 235 commercials, completed by some 40 people for each commercial, an excerpt from which is shown below:

Commercial ID [   ]

- To what extent is this commercial pleasant to watch? Please use a score from 1 to 10.

Not at all pleasant				Neutral					Very pleasant
1	2	3	4	5	6	7	8	9	10

- Below you will find a list of statements regarding this commercial. Please indicate the degree to which you agree with each.

	totally disagree	disagree	more or less disagree	neutral	more or less agree	agree	totally agree
The commercial provides useful information [question 3]	1	2	3	4	5	6	7
The commercial is pretty [question 5]	1	2	3	4	5	6	7
The commercial attracts the attention [question 7]	1	2	3	4	5	6	7
The commercial is boring [question 10]	1	2	3	4	5	6	7
Watching the commercial gave me a positive impression of the brand [question 11]	1	2	3	4	5	6	7
The commercial communicates a clear message [question 12]	1	2	3	4	5	6	7
It takes a long time before you know what it is about [question 15]	1	2	3	4	5	6	7
The commercial is remarkable [question 17]	1	2	3	4	5	6	7

Figure 9.25

	imagedom	commname	industry	industry2	question1	question2	question3	question4	question5	question6	quest
1	Yes	Interbrew/Leffe	Beer	Drinks	7.85	5.45	4.40	4.53	6.13	5.09	
2	Yes	Douwe Egberts/Dessert	Non-alcoholic	Drinks	6.79	4.54	4.39	4.17	5.14	5.04	
3	Yes	Spadel/Spa Marie-Henriette	Non-alcoholic	Drinks	5.42	3.79	3.19	3.53	4.19	3.75	
4	Yes	Interbrew/Labatt Ice	Beer	Drinks	7.48	5.22	4.03	4.87	5.59	4.72	
5	No	Danone/Petit Gervais Voetbal	Yoghurt/Milk	Drinks	7.50	5.24	5.07	4.79	5.61	4.76	
6	No	UB/Hartog/Unox soep	Non-alcoholic	Drinks	6.63	4.83	5.04	4.61	5.12	4.66	
7	No	UB/Hartog/Royco Soup Bouquet	Non-alcoholic	Drinks	7.68	5.40	4.55	4.45	5.55	4.74	
8	Yes	Fourcroy/Bernard Massard	Other alcoholic	Drinks	8.17	5.23	3.92	4.17	5.99	4.65	

The value 7.85 equals the average of the scores of 40 persons on 'question1' for the 'Leffe' commercial

The values in the dataset (Figure 9.25) for the variables [question 1], [question 3], [question 5], ... and [question 17] are aggregated scores at the commercial level.

Furthermore, the exploration is done on the basis of cross tabulation or 'one-way analysis of variance, depending on the measurement level of the descriptive and the criterion variables: if the measurement level is nominal, then the cross table with the Chi-Square test is the recommended technique (Analyze/Descriptive Statistics/Crosstabs), whereas an interval/ratio measurement level requires an analysis of variance (Analyze/Compare Means/One-Way ANOVA). Considering Chapters 3 and 4 treat these techniques in detail, the description below will only report and discuss the results.

Cluster membership and product category to which the commercial belongs

Figure 9.26

Chi-Square Tests

	Value	df	Asymp. Sig. (2-sided)
Pearson Chi-square	14.309[a]	2	.001
Likelihood ratio	14.754	2	.001
Linear-by-linear association	7.429	1	.006
N of valid cases	227		

[a] 0 cells (.0%) have expected count less than 5. The minimum expected count is 7.65

The Chi-Square test (Figure 9.26) may be interpreted, since the two conditions have been satisfied: less than 20% of the cells have an expected count of less than 5 (0%), and the minimum expected count is greater than 1 (7.65). This test therefore indicates that a significant relationship exists between the three-cluster solution and the product category to which the commercial belongs (p-value = .001 < .05).

Figure 9.27

Drinks vs. Others * Three Cluster Solution Cross Tabulation

			Three Cluster Solution			Total
			1	2	3	
Drinks vs. others	Drinks	Count	10	15	6	31
		% within three cluster solution	17.9%	25.4%	5.4%	13.7%
	Other	Count	46	44	106	196
		% within three cluster solution	82.1%	74.6%	94.6%	86.3%
Total		Count	56	59	112	227
		% within three cluster solution	100.0%	100.0%	100.0%	100.0%

The cross table (Figure 9.27) clarifies the relationship found. A horizontal comparison of the column percentages demonstrates that the greatest difference is located between the warm, image-dominated commercial (cluster 2) and the cool informational commercial (cluster 3): of the 100 warm, image-dominated commercials, 25 belong to the product category 'Drinks' while this amount is only 5 in the case of the cool informational commercial.

Cluster membership and criterion variables: pleasant to watch, provides useful information, etc.

Are the original, emotional commercials (cluster 1) more pleasant to watch in comparison with the cool, informational commercials (cluster 3)? Do the warm, image-dominant commercials (cluster 2) grab one's attention more than the two other types? Do the cool, informational commercials make a more positive impression than the original, emotional or the warm, image-dominant commercials? The researcher will find an answer to these types of questions in Figures 9.28, 9.29 and 9.30.

Figure 9.28

Descriptives

		N	Mean	Std. Deviation	
To what extent is the commercial pleasant to watch?	1	56	6.6758	1.11288	4
	2	59	6.2489	.91799	
	3	111	5.4132	1.07986	
	Total	226	5.9442	1.17760	
Useful information	1	56	4.2727	.80337	5
	2	59	4.4035	.54554	
	3	111	4.3063	.79905	
	Total	226	4.3234	.74101	
Beautiful	1	42	4.7129	.84038	
	2	43	4.7744	.69940	
	3	76	3.8207	.92318	
	Total	161	4.3082	.96080	
Attracts the attention	1	42	5.0127	.68906	
	2	43	4.5791	.63688	
	3	76	4.1002	.93233	
	Total	161	4.4662	.88376	
Boring	1	42	2.9420	.70308	
	2	43	3.1008	.60172	
	3	76	3.7674	.81608	
	Total	161	3.3740	.82249	
Positive impression of the mark	1	42	4.2921	.62628	
	2	43	4.4096	.57183	
	3	76	3.8754	.72804	
	Total	161	4.1268	.70249	
Clear	1	42	4.5756	.72827	
	2	43	5.0406	.65274	
	3	76	4.9320	.72437	
	Total	161	4.8680	.72533	
It takes a long time before you know what it is about	1	56	3.6572	.94530	
	2	59	3.0263	.85033	
	3	111	2.9492	.87255	
	Total	226	3.1448	.93002	
Remarkable	1	42	4.6822	.60617	
	2	43	4.1292	.65397	
	3	76	3.8135	.84598	
	Total	161	4.1244	.81823	

The mean (Figure 9.28, 4) scores would lead us to believe that the original, emotional commercial is the most pleasant to watch, followed by the warm, image-dominated commercial, and the cool, informational commercial would score the poorest. Are these assumptions correct, or in other words are the differences statistically significant?

Figure 9.29

		Sum of Squares	df	Mean Square	F	Sig.
To what extent is the commercial pleasant to watch?	Between groups	66.751	2	33.375	30.346	.000
	Within groups	245.265	223	1.100		
	Total	312.016	225			
Useful information	Between groups	.555	2	.278	.503	.605
	Within groups	122.992	223	.552		
	Total	123.547	225			
Beautiful	Between groups	34.281	2	17.140	23.878	.000
	Within groups	113.420	158	.718		
	Total	147.701	160			
Attracts the attention	Between groups	23.268	2	11.634	18.075	.000
	Within groups	101.696	158	.644		
	Total	124.964	160			
Boring	Between groups	22.814	2	11.407	21.099	.000
	Within groups	85.423	158	.541		
	Total	108.237	160			
Positive impression of the mark	Between groups	9.389	2	4.695	10.662	.000
	Within groups	69.568	158	.440		
	Total	78.958	160			
Clear	Between groups	5.183	2	2.591	5.183	.007
	Within groups	78.994	158	.500		
	Total	84.177	160			
It takes a long time before you know what it is about	Between groups	19.776	2	9.888	12.612	.000
	Within groups	174.834	223	.784		
	Total	194.610	225			
Remarkable	Between groups	20.417	2	10.208	18.603	.000
	Within groups	86.704	158	.549		
	Total	107.121	160			

ANOVA (1) (6)

The ANOVA table (Figure 9.29, 1) indicates that significant differences do in fact exist between the three types of commercials in terms of the degree to which it is pleasant to watch them (p-value < .001). In a subsequent step, the 'Multiple Comparisons' (Figure 9.30) indicate between which types these differences may be found[4].

The degree to which commercials falling under type '3', the cool informational commercial, are pleasant to watch appears to differ significantly from that corresponding to the two other types, the original, emotional and the warm, image-dominated commercials (p-value < .001 for groups '3' and '1', and '3' and '2'; Figure 9.30, 2). The scores for the original, emotional and the warm, image-dominated commercials on the other hand, appear not to differ significantly from one another (p-value = .090 > .05, for groups '1' and '2'; Figure 9.30, 3).

Figure 9.30

Multiple Comparisons

Bonferroni

Dependent Variable	(I) Three Cluster Solution	(J) Three Cluster Solution	Mean Difference (I-J)	Std. Error	Sig.
To what extent is the commercial pleasant to watch?	1	2	.42691	.19566	.090
		3	1.26262*	.17190	.000
	2	1	-.42691	.19566	.090
		3	.83571*	.16897	.000
	3	1	-1.26262*	.17190	.000
		2	-.83571*	.16897	.000
Useful information	1	2	-.13080	.13855	1.000
		3	-.03356	.12173	1.000
	2	1	.13080	.13855	1.000
		3	.09725	.11965	1.000
	3	1	.03356	.12173	1.000
		2	-.09725	.11965	1.000
Beautiful	1	2	-.06150	.18381	1.000
		3	.89213*	.16290	.000
	2	1	.06150	.18381	1.000
		3	.95362*	.16168	.000
	3	1	-.89213*	.16290	.000
		2	-.95362*	.16168	.000
Attracts the attention	1	2	.43355*	.17405	.041
		3	.91241*	.15425	.000
	2	1	-.43355*	.17405	.041
		3	.47886*	.15309	.006
	3	1	-.91241*	.15425	.000
		2	-.47886*	.15309	.006
Boring	1	2	-.15880	.15952	.963
		3	-.82547*	.14137	.000
	2	1	.15880	.15952	.963
		3	-.66667*	.14031	.000
	3	1	.82547*	.14137	.000
		2	.66667*	.14031	.000
Positive impression of the mark	1	2	-.11748	.14396	1.000
		3	.41670*	.12758	.004
	2	1	.11748	.14396	1.000
		3	.53418*	.12662	.000
	3	1	-.41670*	.12758	.004
		2	-.53418*	.12662	.000
Clear	1	2	-.46497*	.15340	.009
		3	-.35639*	.13595	.029
	2	1	.46497*	.15340	.009
		3	.10857	.13493	1.000
	3	1	.35639*	.13595	.029
		2	-.10857	.13493	1.000
It takes a long time before you know what it is about	1	2	.63083*	.16519	.001
		3	.70798*	.14513	.000
	2	1	-.63083*	.16519	.001
		3	.07715	.14266	1.000
	3	1	-.70798*	.14513	.000
		2	-.07715	.14266	1.000
Remarkable	1	2	.55298*	.16071	.002
		3	.86874*	.14243	.000
	2	1	-.55298*	.16071	.002
		3	.31576	.14136	.081
	3	1	-.86874*	.14243	.000
		2	-.31576	.14136	.081

*The mean difference is significant at the .05 level

Therefore, the cool, informational commercial is, compared with the original, emotional and the warm, image-dominated commercials less pleasant to watch (mean$_{group3}$ = 5.41 < mean$_{group1}$ = 6.68 and mean$_{group2}$ = 6.25), whereas these last two types mentioned both score equally well (Figure 9.28, 4).

With regard to the degree to which the commercial provides useful information, one would expect that the cool, informational commercial would score the highest, however the mean scores would lead us to believe that the warm, image-dominated commercial occupies first place (Figure 9.28, 5). The ANOVA table provides the answer here: the degree to which useful information is provided is identical for the three types of commercials (p-value = .605 > .05; Figure 9.29, 6).

For the other characteristics, on the basis of the 'Descriptives', the ANOVA table, and the 'Multiple Comparisons' table, the researcher may draw the following conclusions: (1) the cool, informational commercial appears to be less appealing, grabs the viewer's attention less, is more boring, and leaves a less positive impression of the brand behind than the two other types; and (2) the original, emotional commercial is the least clear and must be watched longer in order to determine what it is about, however it is the most remarkable. On the basis of the second conclusion, the advertising agency may make the decision, for example, to make the advertising message more explicit.

Example 2

Cluster analysis with continuous attributes – hierarchical clustering as input for K-means clustering

Managerial problem

A supermarket would like to find out if there are groups of customers who differ from one another in terms of the 'degree of pleasure they experience during shopping' and the 'degree to which doing the shopping is planned'. In order to research this, the marketing department drew up a survey which contained the following questions, among others: eight items (7-point Likert scale) gauging the dimension of pleasure, [c] through [i], and [k], and four items (7-point Likert scale) to identify the degree of planning involved in doing the shopping [a], [b] [j] and [l] (see Chapter 7 on exploratory factor analysis for a concrete description of the items). This survey was completed by 500 customers, and a partial representation of the data is included in Figure 9.31.

Moreover, the marketers expect that there are four distinct groups of customers (Table 9.3).

Problem

Perform a cluster analysis on the dataset *Pleasure and planning – cluster analysis.sav*, on the basis of the eight 'pleasure' and four 'planning' items, and use a 4-cluster solution. Use a hierarchical cluster analysis, performed via Ward's method, and then use the results from this as input for the K-means method (also known as Quick clustering).

Figure 9.31

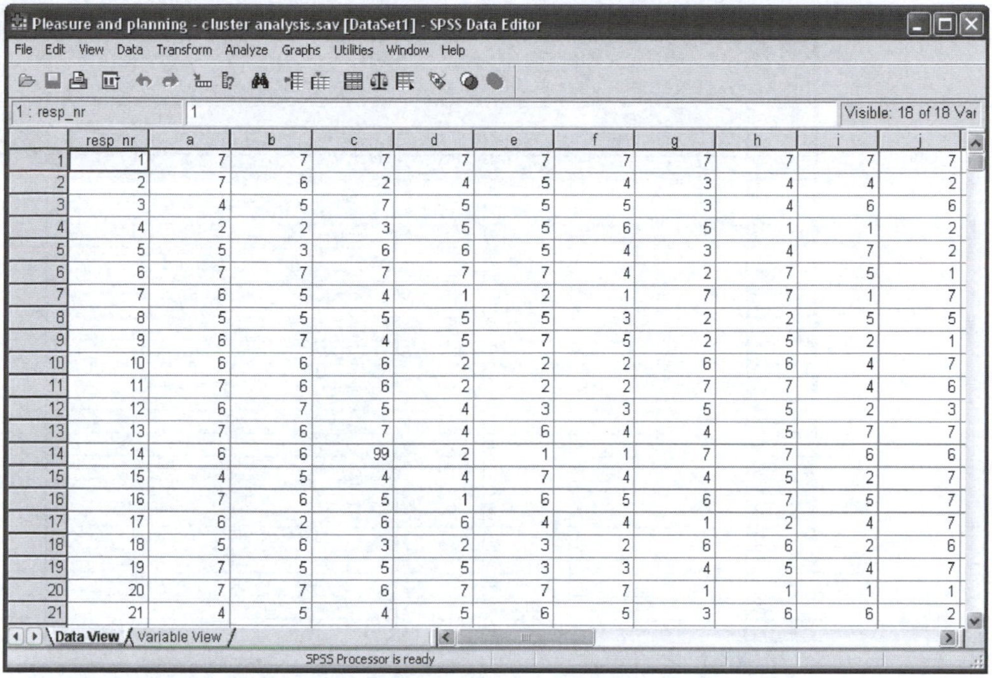

	resp nr	a	b	c	d	e	f	g	h	i	j
1	1	7	7	7	7	7	7	7	7	7	7
2	2	7	6	2	4	5	4	3	4	4	2
3	3	4	5	7	5	5	5	3	4	6	6
4	4	2	2	3	5	5	6	5	1	1	2
5	5	5	3	6	6	5	4	3	4	7	2
6	6	7	7	7	7	7	4	2	7	5	1
7	7	6	5	4	1	2	1	7	7	1	7
8	8	5	5	5	5	5	3	2	2	5	5
9	9	6	7	4	5	7	5	2	5	2	1
10	10	6	6	6	2	2	2	6	6	4	7
11	11	7	6	6	2	2	2	7	7	4	6
12	12	6	7	5	4	3	3	5	5	2	3
13	13	7	6	7	4	6	4	4	5	7	7
14	14	6	6	99	2	1	1	7	7	6	6
15	15	4	5	4	4	7	4	4	5	2	7
16	16	7	6	5	1	6	5	6	7	5	7
17	17	6	2	6	6	4	4	1	2	4	7
18	18	5	6	3	2	3	2	6	6	2	6
19	19	7	5	5	5	3	3	4	5	4	7
20	20	7	7	6	7	7	7	1	1	1	1
21	21	4	5	4	5	6	5	3	6	6	2

Table 9.3

	Plans the shopping	*Doesn't plan the shopping*
Lots of pleasure during shopping	1	2
Little pleasure during shopping	3	4

Solution

Before discussing the SPSS commands and the interpretation of the output, it is advisable to take a moment to examine Step 1 of the cluster analysis: the measurement level of the variables, the comparability and an even distribution of the variables over the underlying dimensions. Since the twelve items which form the basis of the cluster analysis fall under the Likert scale category, the measurement level is continuous. A standardization of these items is not necessary, since they are expressed in the same unit of measurement: 7-point scale. With regard to the criterion 'an even distribution of the variables over the underlying dimensions', a problem may occur since the dimension 'pleasure' is measured on the basis of eight items and the dimension 'planning' is based on only four items. This unequal distribution of the items over the two dimensions is not extreme, however factor analysis may be used to then work further in the cluster analysis with the two resulting factors. A detailed description of the conversion of the twelve items in the two underlying dimensions or factors may be found in Chapter 7. Both factors, 'pleasure' and 'planning' have already been added to the dataset *Pleasure and planning – cluster analysis.sav* (Figure 9.32).

Figure 9.32

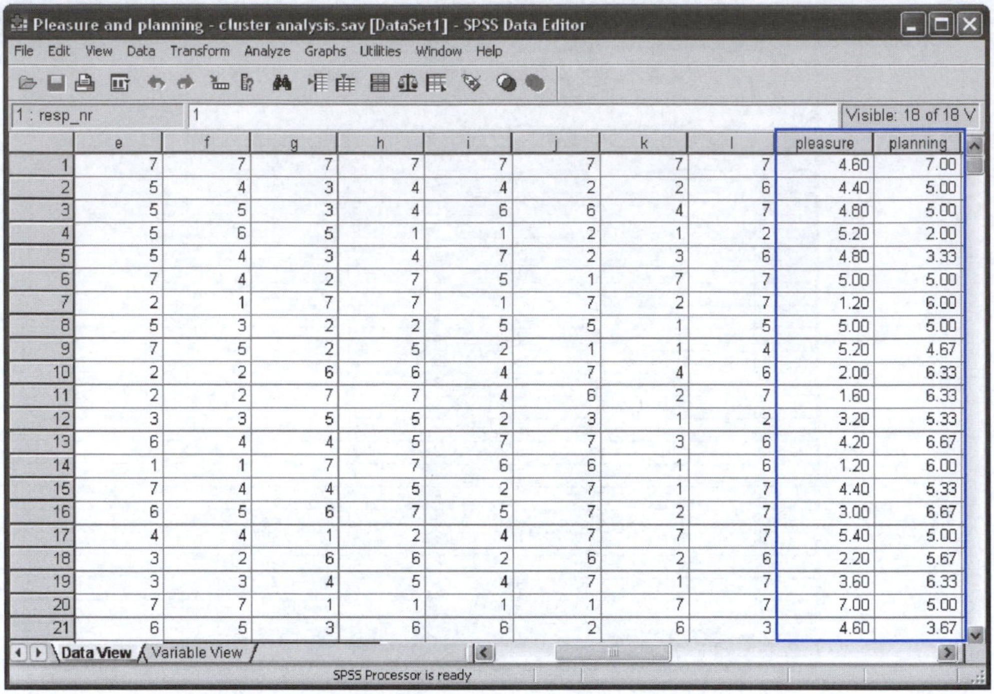

SPSS commands: Hierarchical clustering

Figure 9.33

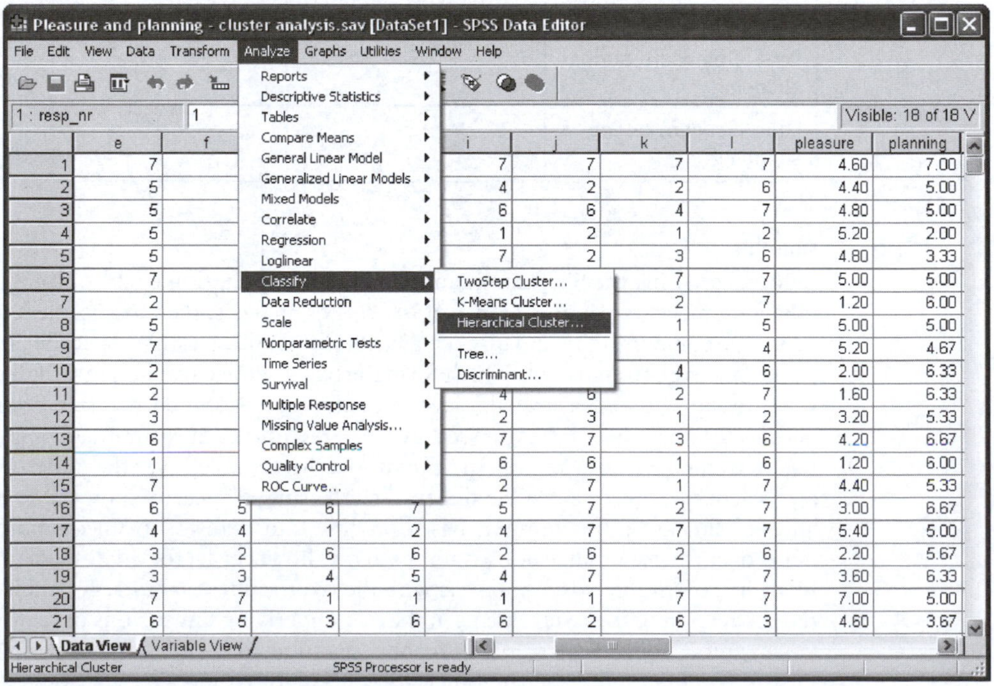

Go to Analyze/Classify/Hierarchical Cluster (Figure 9.33).

Figure 9.34

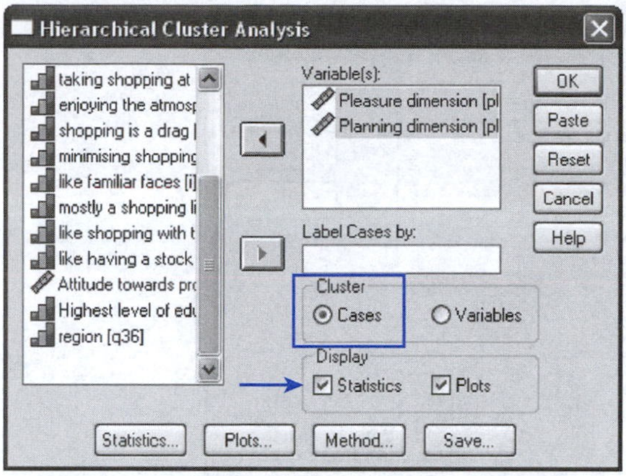

In the 'Hierarchical Cluster Analysis' window (Figure 9.34), select the characteristics from the list on the left-hand side on the basis of which the customers are to be divided into groups, [pleasure] and [planning], and move these to the 'Variable(s)' box using the top arrow.

Under 'Cluster', choose the 'Cases' option, since the analysis groups the respondents and not the variables. The latter would actually amount to a factor analysis.

Under 'Display', 'Statistics' and 'Plots' are checked as default settings. They will however have to be unchecked since the researcher is only interested in the cluster membership (see the 'Save' button) which will serve as input for the K-means clustering.

Figure 9.35

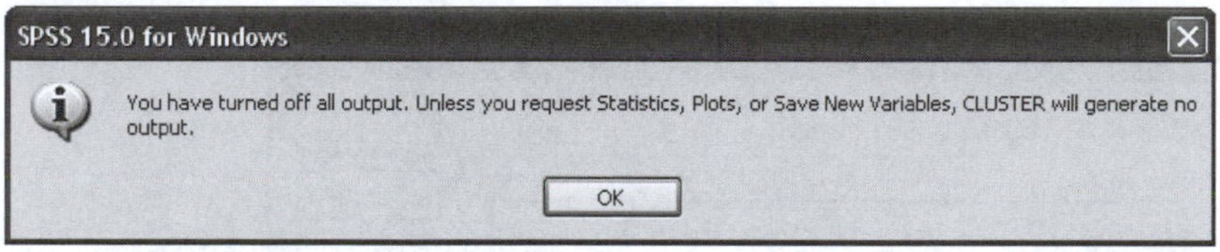

Deselecting the 'Statistics' and 'Plots' options will lead to the following message: 'You have turned off all output.

Unless you request Statistics, Plots, or Save New Variables, CLUSTER will generate no output' (Figure 9.35). Click 'OK' here, and define the buttons 'Method' and 'Save' in the main window (Figure 9.36).

Figure 9.36

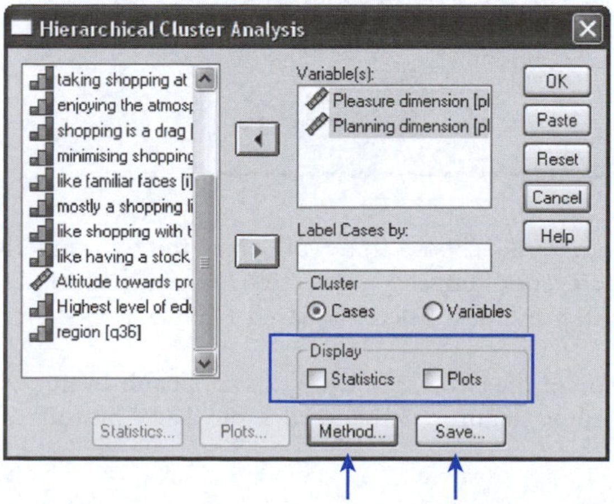

Figure 9.37

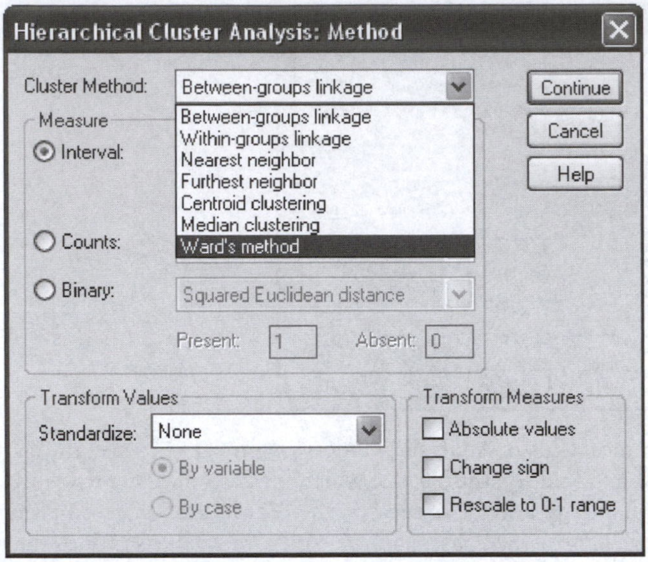

In the 'Hierarchical Cluster Analysis: Method' window (Figure 9.37), choose 'Ward's method' as cluster method (see instructions).

Figure 9.38

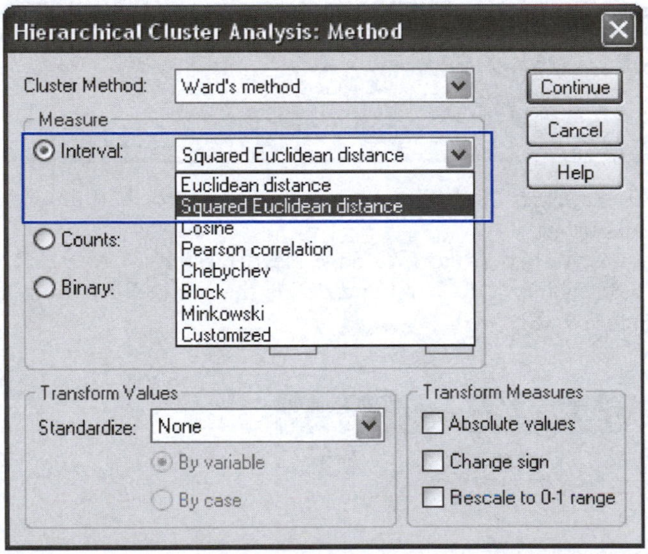

Under 'Measure' (Figure 9.38), choose 'Interval', since the two underlying dimensions 'pleasure' and 'planning' are 'continuously' scaled (two 'summated scales' based on 7-point Likert scales). For the distance index, select 'Squared Euclidean Distance' from the pull-down menu.

A further transformation of the two variables is not applicable in this example.

Return to the main window (Figure 9.36) and click the 'Save' button.

Figure 9.39

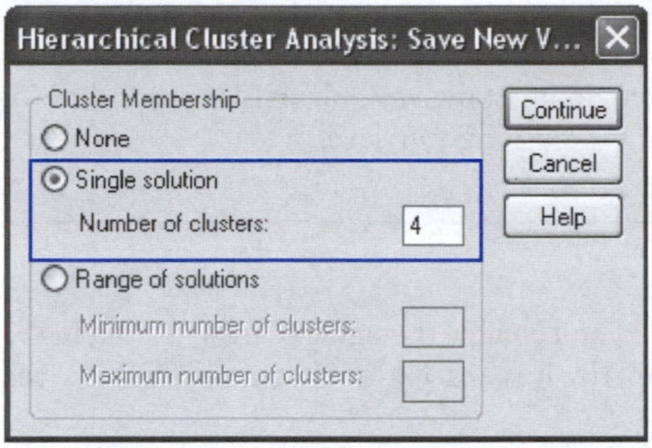

In the 'Hierarchical Cluster Analysis: Save New Variables' window (Figure 9.39), choose the option 'Single solution: 4 clusters'. This will cause a new variable to be added to the dataset which shows the group to which each respondent belongs, and it is this variable which will serve as input for the K-means clustering. The number of clusters is set at '4', since the marketers assume four different groups of customers (see instructions).

Return to the main window (Figure 9.36) and click 'OK'.

Interpretation of the SPSS output: Hierarchical clustering

Figure 9.40

Case Processing Summary[a,b]					
Cases					
Valid		**Missing**		**Total**	
N	Percent	N	Percent	N	Percent
500	100.0	0	.0	500	100.0

[a]Squared Euclidean distance used
[b]Ward linkage

Since the researcher did not request any 'statistics' or 'plots', the SPSS output is very brief. Only the number of respondents used in the analysis and the number of 'missings' are shown (Figure 9.40).

Figure 9.41

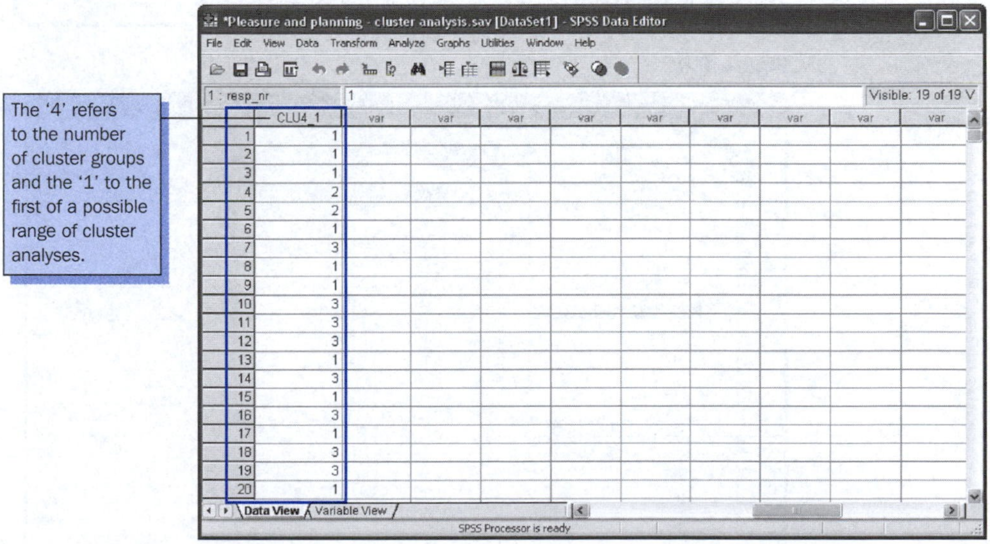

The '4' refers to the number of cluster groups and the '1' to the first of a possible range of cluster analyses.

The addition of the variable [CLU4_01] to the dataset (Figure 9.41), which shows the cluster membership on the basis of the hierarchical clustering, as such respondents '1' through '3' belong to the first group, respondents '4' and '5' to the second group, etc.

The analysis thus results in four groups, and it is the mean scores for each of these groups for the two underlying dimensions 'pleasure' and 'planning' that will serve as input for the K-means clustering. Before this K-means clustering may be performed, it is necessary to complete a number of steps, such as the renaming of the variable [CLU4_1] and the aggregating of the scores for the two dimensions at the cluster group level.

Supporting technique

Go to the 'Variable View' window (Figure 9.42) and change the name 'CLU4_1' to 'cluster_'. **In order for the remaining SPSS procedure to proceed properly, it is crucial for the name 'cluster_' to be chosen.**

Figure 9.42

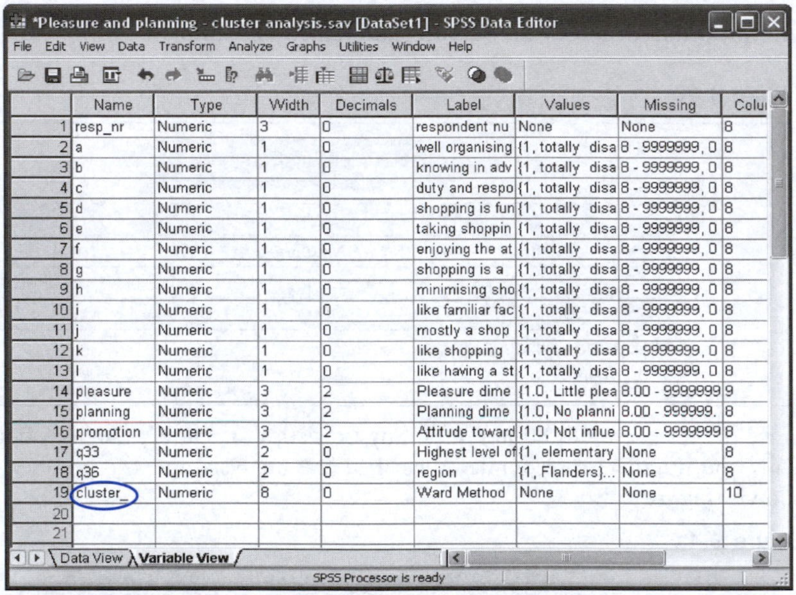

Figure 9.43

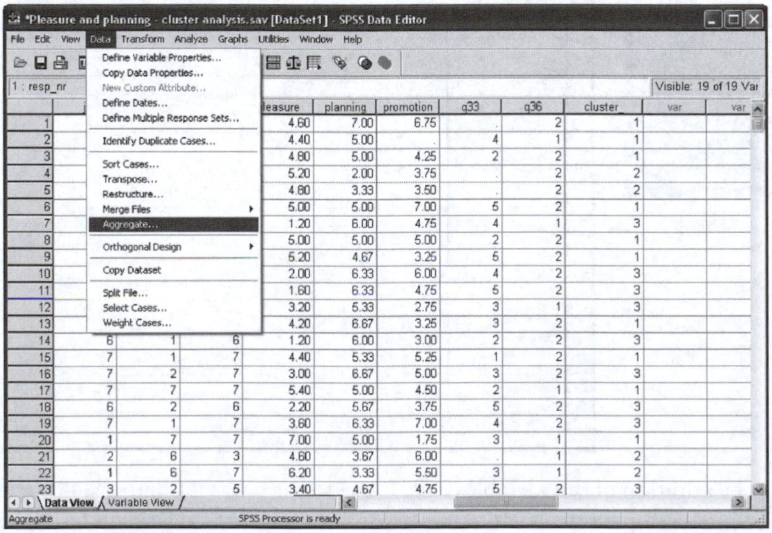

Go to Data/Aggregate (Figure 9.43).

Figure 9.44

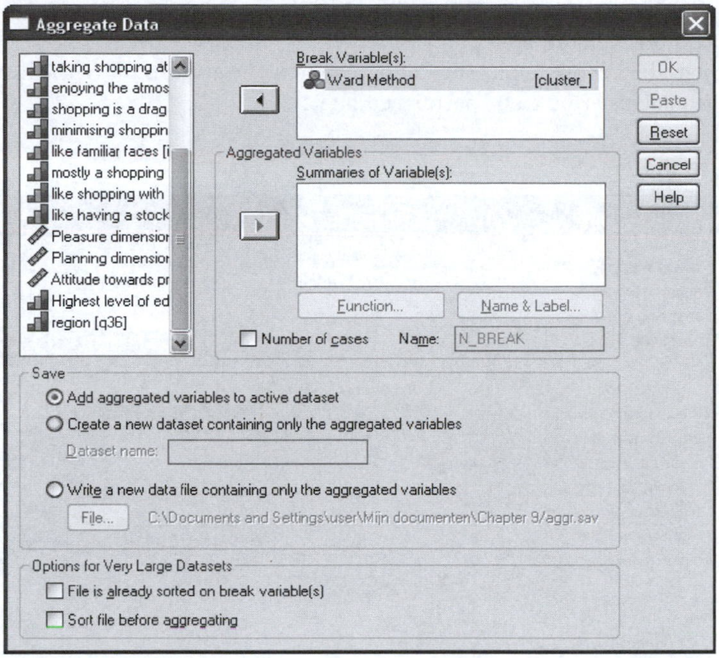

In the 'Aggregate Data' window (Figure 9.44), select the variable from the list on the left-hand side on the basis of which the customers are to be divided into groups, and move this to the 'Break Variable(s)' box. In the current application the division will occur according to the cluster membership, and therefore according to the variable [cluster_].

Figure 9.45

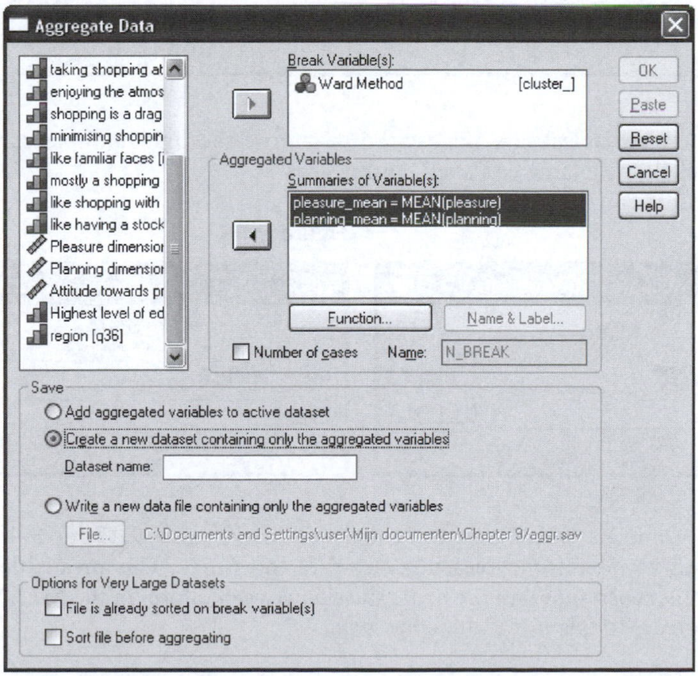

From the list on the left side, choose the variables for which an aggregated score (a mean in the current example) must be calculated. This will move the variables 'pleasure' and 'planning' to the 'Aggregated Variables' box (Figure 9.45).

Notice that the variables chosen, 'pleasure' and 'planning', lie at the basis of the hierarchical clustering, and also of the K-means clustering to be performed later.

Figure 9.46

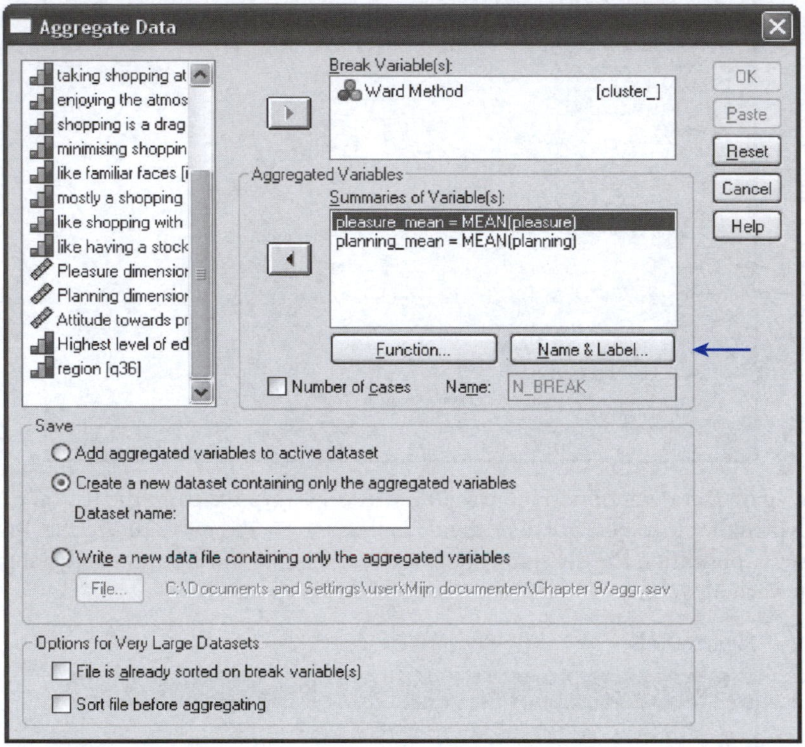

In the 'Aggregated Variables' box (Figure 9.46), choose the first line 'pleasure_mean = MEAN (pleasure)' and then click the 'Name & Label' button.

Figure 9.47

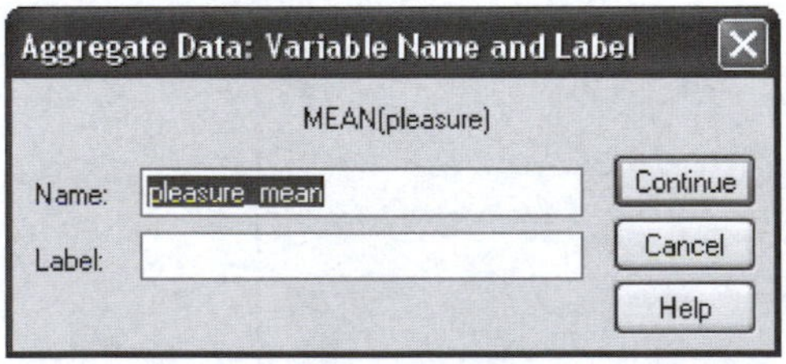

Figure 9.48

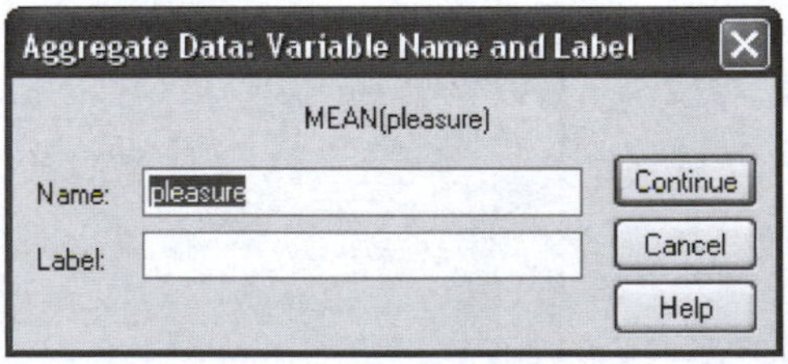

In the 'Aggregate Data: Variable Name and Label' window (Figures 9.47 and 9.48), change the name of the new aggregated variable from 'pleasure_mean' to 'pleasure'. **This means that the name of the aggregated variable must correspond to the name shown between quotes in the MEAN function.** Change the name 'planning_mean' to 'planning' the same way.

Figure 9.49

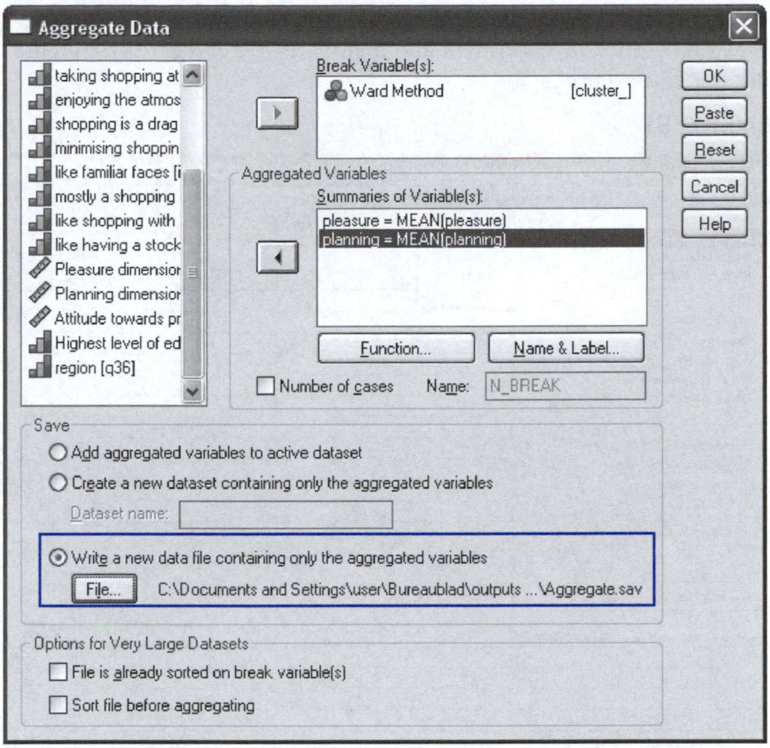

On the basis of the aggregated variables, create a new dataset named *Aggregate.sav*. To do this, choose the option 'Write a new data file containing only the aggregated variables' (Figure 9.49), and then click the 'File' button.

Figure 9.50

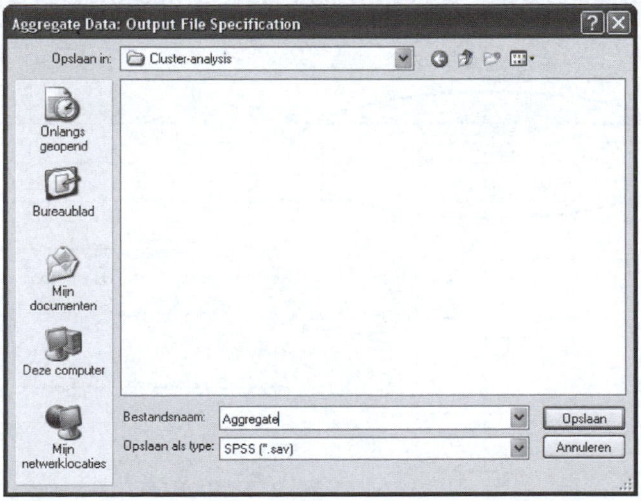

In the 'Aggregate Data: Output File Specification' window (Figure 9.50), choose the folder in which the new dataset is to be saved (e.g., 'Cluster–analysis') and give the dataset an appropriate name (e.g., 'Aggregate'). Click 'Save'.

In the main window (Figure 9.49), click 'OK' and the aggregated dataset will be created.

Creating the aggregated dataset does not result in extra SPSS output, nor the addition of variables to the original *Pleasure and planning – cluster analysis.sav* dataset. However, a new dataset, *Aggregate.sav* will be created, which will be opened by choosing **File/Open/Data** – *Aggregate.sav* (Figure 9.51). Make sure that the original dataset is saved first.

Figure 9.51

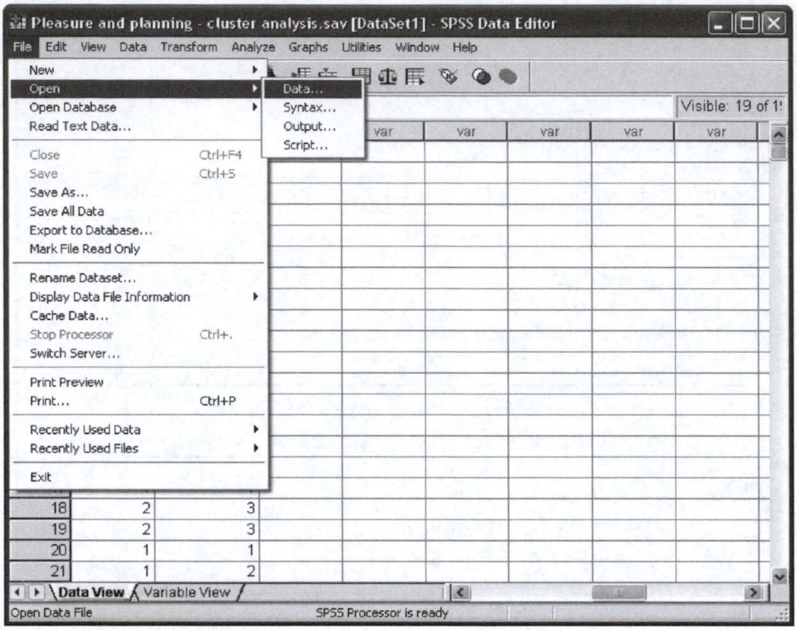

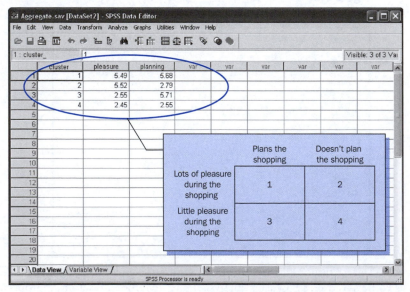

The *Aggregate.sav* dataset (Figure 9.52) indicates the mean score for the dimensions 'pleasure' and 'planning' for each of the four cluster groups.

Figure 9.52

For example, the first group has scores of 5.49 and 5.68, respectively. These mean scores also demonstrate that the distribution of the customers over the four quadrants included in the instructions is realistic.

These scores serve as an initial configuration for the K-means clustering. The final scores for this last technique will vary from these initial scores because of the reallocation of 'customers' from one cluster group to the other.

If the *Aggregate.sav* dataset contains 'missing values', indicated by a **'comma' under the 'cluster_'** **column,** then it is necessary to **select the corresponding row and to delete it.**

After saving any changes to the *Aggregate.sav* dataset, return to the original *Pleasure and planning – cluster analysis.sav* dataset, and perform the K-means clustering using the *Aggregate.sav* dataset as input.

SPSS commands: K-means clustering

Figure 9.53

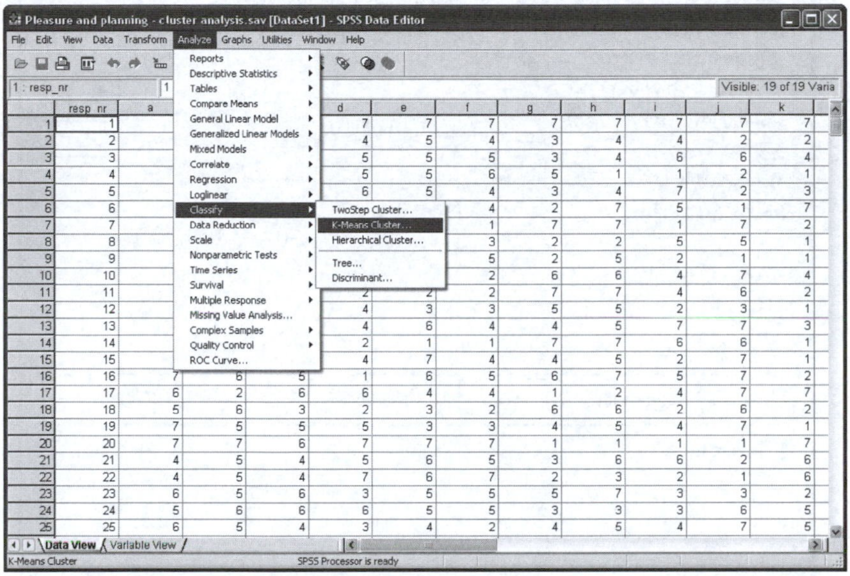

Go to Analyze/Classify/K-Means Cluster (Figure 9.53).

Figure 9.54

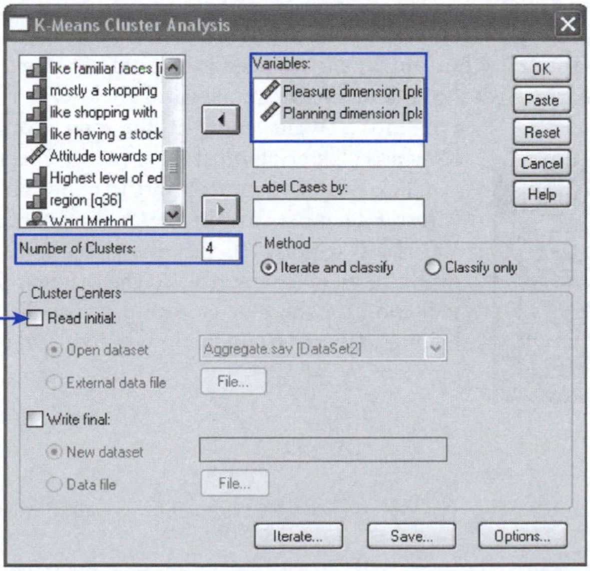

In the 'K-Means Cluster Analysis' window (Figure 9.54), select the variables which also lie at the foundation of the hierarchical clustering, namely 'pleasure' and 'planning', and move these to the 'Variables' box using the top arrow.

Next to 'Number of Clusters', fill in the number '4'. This number corresponds to the number of cluster groups input under the hierarchical clustering.

Figure 9.55

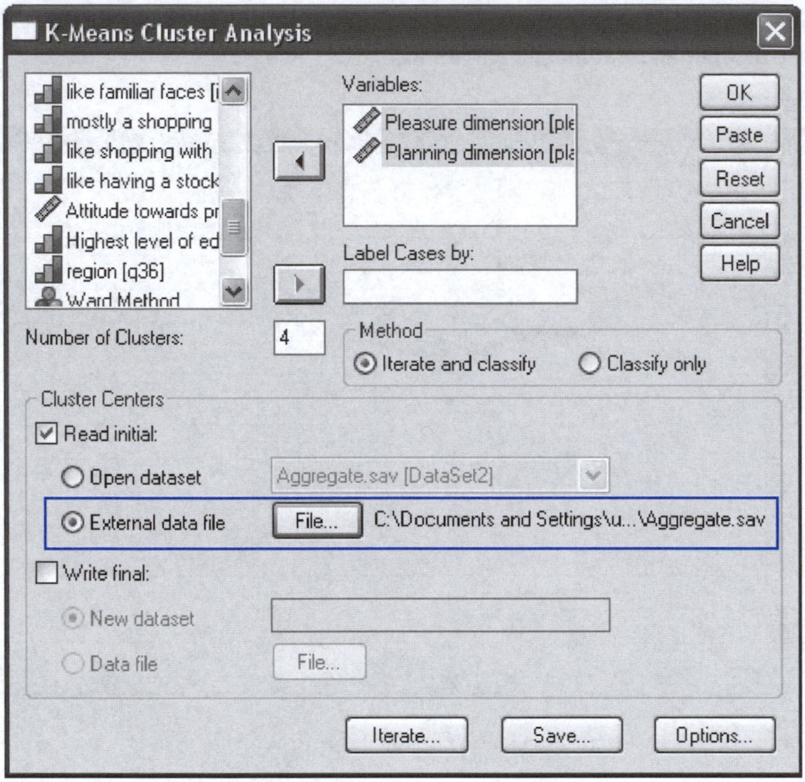

Under 'Cluster Centers' (Figure 9.55), choose 'Read Initial', next choose 'External data file' and then click the 'File' button. In the 'K-Means Cluster Analysis: Read from File' window which appears, select the *Aggregate.sav* dataset and click 'Open'.

Figure 9.56

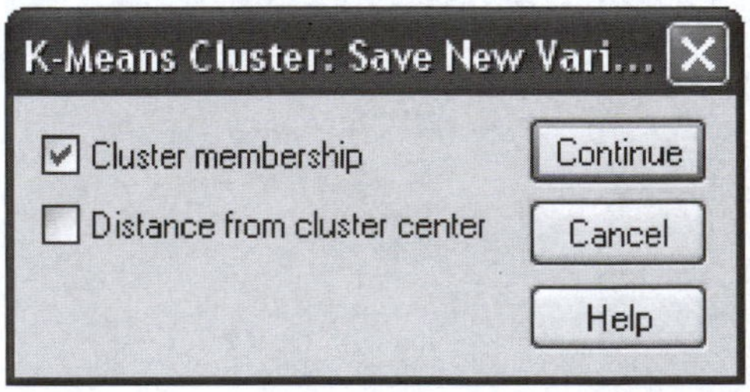

Choose 'Write final' if the final configuration of the K-means clustering must be saved in a separate dataset.

Click the 'Save' button in the main window, and choose 'Cluster membership' in the 'K-Means Cluster: Save New Variables' window (Figure 9.56). This will result in the addition of an extra variable to the original dataset and which will indicate the cluster group to which every respondent belongs. Return to the main window and click the 'Options' button.

Figure 9.57

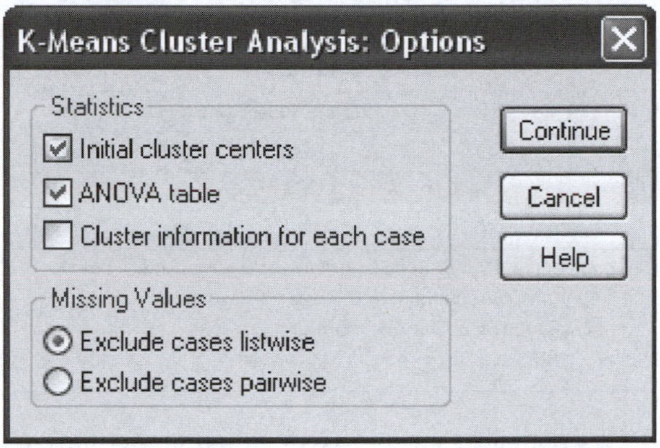

In the 'K-Means Cluster Analysis: Options' window (Figure 9.57), choose 'Initial cluster centers' under 'Statistics'. This will result in SPSS output which corresponds to the contents of the 'Aggregate' dataset.

Also check the box for 'ANOVA table'. This table provides an indication regarding the existence of differences between the cluster groups in terms of the cluster variables, 'pleasure' and 'planning' in the current application.

The option 'Exclude cases listwise' is checked as a default setting in SPSS and indicates that a case (one row from the dataset) will not be part of the analysis if it has a 'system missing' or a 'user missing' (see Chapter 1) for one or more of the variables included in the analysis.

Return to the main window (Figure 9.55) and under 'Method' choose the default option 'Iterate and classify'[5]. Now click 'OK' and the output of the K-means clustering will appear.

Interpretation of the SPSS output: K-means clustering

Figure 9.58

Initial Cluster Centers				
	Cluster			
	1	2	3	4
Pleasure dimension	5.49	5.52	2.55	2.45
Planning dimension	5.68	2.79	5.71	2.55

Input from FILE subcommand

The output from the K-means clustering starts with the display of the initial 'cluster centers' (Figure 9.58), for which the scores for the two underlying dimensions 'pleasure' and 'planning' correspond to the values stated in the *Aggregate.sav* dataset (Figure 9.52).

Figure 9.59

	Iteration History[a]			
	Change in Cluster Centers			
Iteration	1	2	3	4
1	.008	.017	.013	.056
2	.000	.000	.000	.000

[a]Convergence achieved due to no or small change in cluster centers. The maximum absolute coordinate change for any center is .000. The current iteration is 2. The minimum distance between initial centers is 2.889.

After two iterations, the stopping criterion has already been optimized, putting a stop to the further reallocation of customers from one cluster group to the other (Figure 9.59).

Figure 9.60

	Final Cluster Centers			
	Cluster			
	1	2	3	4
Pleasure dimension	5.48	5.52	2.55	2.48
Planning dimension	5.69	2.81	5.72	2.60

A comparison of the scores for the final (Figure 9.60) and the initial cluster centers (Figure 9.58) for the dimensions 'pleasure' and 'planning' only produces slight differences. In the current application, the hierarchical clustering has therefore already resulted in an optimum solution. However this is more the exception than the rule.

Figure 9.60 shows that with regard to doing the shopping in a supermarket, there are in fact four distinct customer groups. These groups clearly differ from one another according to their score for the two underlying dimensions 'pleasure' and 'planning', which is presented visually on the basis of Figure 9.61 (by using the program Excel). Each group in this figure is accompanied by a characteristic name.

Figure 9.61

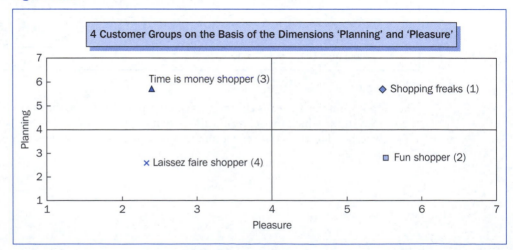

The ANOVA table (Figure 9.62) indicates that at least two of the four customer groups score significantly different for the pleasure dimension, and that the same conclusion applies to the planning dimension (p-value < .001).

Figure 9.62

	ANOVA					
	Cluster		Error			
	Mean Square	df	Mean Square	df	F	Sig.
Pleasure dimension	345.853	3	.425	496	813.206	.000
Planning dimension	250.623	3	.497	496	504.022	.000

The F tests should be used only for descriptive purposes because the clusters have been chosen to maximize the differences among cases in different clusters. The observed significance levels are not corrected for this and thus cannot be interpreted as tests of the hypothesis that the cluster means are equal.

It may also be said here that the cluster groups are formed in such a way that the differences between them in terms of the dimensions 'pleasure' and 'planning' are maximum, and that the p-values in principle may not be linked to the fact whether the null hypothesis is rejected or not (H_0:the four customer groups have identical scores for the pleasure dimension, respectively the planning dimension). If the researcher finds a p-value here which is greater than .05, then he may conclude that that particular dimension is not a good basis for the formation of clusters.

Figure 9.63

Number of Cases in Each Cluster		
Cluster	1	230.000
	2	77.000
	3	160.000
	4	33.000
Valid		500.000
Missing		.000

Finally, the SPSS output (Figure 9.63) provides insight into the number of customers per cluster group, and then it appears that the 'shopping freaks' and the 'time is money shoppers' are the best represented. The 'laissez-faire shopper' who does not plan the shopping and who does not experience pleasure in the shopping is in the minority.

In addition to the SPSS output, there is the extra variable [QCL_1] which is added to the dataset by SPSS (Figure 9.64). This variable indicates the cluster membership which results from the K-means clustering. As such, respondent '27' belongs to cluster group '1' for example.

The reallocation of respondents may be seen from the columns 'cluster_' and 'QCL_1', which indicate the membership resulting from the hierarchical and the K-means clustering: respondent '28' moves from group '1' to group '2', and respondent '29' jumps from '3' to '4'.

Figure 9.64

	k	l	pleasure	planning	promotion	q33	q36	cluster_	QCL_1	var
1	7	7	4.60	7.00	6.75	.	2	1	1	
2	2	6	4.40	5.00	.	4	1	1	1	
3	4	7	4.80	5.00	4.25	2	2	1	1	
4	1	2	5.20	2.00	3.75	.	2	2	2	
5	3	6	4.80	3.33	3.50	.	2	2	2	
6	7	7	5.00	5.00	7.00	5	2	1	1	
7	2	7	1.20	6.00	4.75	4	1	3	3	
8	1	5	5.00	5.00	5.00	2	2	1	1	
9	1	4	5.20	4.67	3.25	5	2	1	1	
10	4	6	2.00	6.33	6.00	4	2	3	3	
11	2	7	1.60	6.33	4.75	5	2	3	3	
12	1	2	3.20	5.33	2.75	3	1	3	3	
13	3	6	4.20	6.67	3.25	3	2	1	1	
14	1	6	1.20	6.00	3.00	2	2	3	3	
15	1	7	4.40	5.33	5.25	1	2	1	1	
16	2	7	3.00	6.67	5.00	3	2	3	3	
17	7	7	5.40	5.00	4.50	2	1	1	1	
18	2	6	2.20	5.67	3.75	5	2	3	3	
19	1	7	3.60	6.33	7.00	4	2	3	3	
20	7	7	7.00	5.00	1.75	3	1	1	1	
21	6	3	4.60	3.67	6.00	.	1	2	2	
22	6	7	6.20	3.33	5.50	3	1	2	2	
23	2	5	3.40	4.67	4.75	5	2	3	3	
24	5	7	5.20	5.67	5.50	3	1	1	1	
25	5	5	3.20	6.00	4.25	3	1	3	3	
26	4	6	4.80	5.67	5.00	3	1	1	1	
27	2	6	5.40	6.00	5.50	3	1	1	1	
28	2	6	6.00	4.00	5.00	1	2	1	2	
29	4	7	3.60	4.00	2.67	2	1	3	4	
30	4	3	3.60	4.33	6.25	.	1	3	3	

Supporting technique

A next step may involve the description of the cluster groups on the basis of socio-demographic characteristics, attitudes, etc. The marketers have added a number of extra questions to the original questionnaire in this regard, which gauge the highest diploma received, for example [q33], the region in which they live [q36], and the attitude with respect to promotions [promotion]. The measurement level of these variables (nominal, ordinal, interval or ratio), as well as the number of cluster groups, determines the choice of the appropriate analysis technique:

- The existence of a relationship between the cluster membership variable and the highest diploma received (or the region in which the customer lives) may be researched on the basis of cross tabulation, supplemented by the Chi-Square test, given the variable 'diploma' (or 'region') is nominally scaled.

- Determining whether the four cluster groups have a different attitude towards promotions may be done using a 'one-way analysis of variance' since the 'promotion' variable is interval-scaled (summated scale after factor analysis on a 7-point Likert scale) and the 'cluster group' variable contains more than two groups.

Since cross tabulation and 'one-way analysis of variance' have been treated at length in Chapters 3 and 4, the description here will be limited to a report and discussion of the results.

Cluster membership and highest diploma received

Determining the existence of a relationship between the cluster group to which a person belongs and the highest diploma received may be done on the basis of a cross table analysis, supplemented by the Chi-Square test (Figure 9.65). These statistics may be found in SPSS under Analyze/Descriptive Statistics/Crosstabs.

Figure 9.65

Chi-Square Tests

	Value	df	Asymp. Sig. (2-sided)
Pearson Chi-square	15.170[a]	12	.232
Likelihood ratio	15.577	12	.211
Linear-by-linear association	6.947	1	.008
N of valid cases	439		

[a]3 cells (15.0%) have expected count less than 5. The minimum expected count is 1.65

The interpretation of the Chi-square value is allowed, since less than 20% of the cells have an expected count of less than 5 (15%), and the minimum expected count is greater than 1 (1.65).

The analysis does not show a significant relationship between membership and diploma (p-value = .232 > .05).

Cluster membership and region where person lives

Determining the existence of a relationship between the cluster group to which a person belongs and the region in which he or she lives may also be done using cross table analysis, supplemented by the Chi-Square test. Place the cluster membership in the columns and the region in the rows, and request column percentages.

Figure 9.66

Chi-Square Tests

	Value	df	Asymp. Sig. (2-sided)
Pearson Chi-square	11.394[a]	3	.010
Likelihood ratio	11.240	3	.010
Linear-by-linear association	.248	1	.618
N of valid cases	498		

[a]0 cells (.0%) have expected count less than 5. The minimum expected count is 11.63

The SPSS output (Figure 9.66) now shows a significant relationship between membership and region (p-value = .01 < .05), and an interpretation of the Chi-square value is also permitted here (0% < 20%, and 11.63 > 1).

Figure 9.67

| | | | Cluster Number of Case | | | | |
			1	2	3	4	Total
Region	Flanders	Count	148	38	113	18	317
		% within cluster number of case	64.3%	49.4%	71.1%	56.3%	63.7%
	Wallonia or Brussels	Count	82	39	46	14	181
		% within cluster number of case	35.7%	50.6%	28.9%	43.8%	36.3%
Total		Count	230	77	159	32	498
		% within cluster number of case	100.0%	100.0%	100.0%	100.0%	100.0%

Region * Cluster Number of Case Crosstabulation

A concrete interpretation of the relationship found may be done on the basis of the cross table (Figure 9.67). A horizontal comparison of the column percentages thereby demonstrates that the greatest difference may be found between cluster groups '2' (fun shoppers) and '3' (time is money shoppers). Out of 100 'fun shoppers', 49 are Flemish, while this figure is 71 out of 100 for 'time is money shoppers'.

Cluster membership and attitude towards promotions

The determination of different attitudes held by the four cluster groups with regard to promotions may be done on the basis of a 'one-way analysis of variance' which may be found in SPSS under Analyze/ Compare Means/One-way ANOVA.

Figure 9.68

Descriptives

Attitude towards promotion dimension

	N	Mean	Std. Deviation	Std. Error	95% Confidence Interval for Mean		Minimum	Maximum
					Lower Bound	Upper Bound		
1	226	4.7695	1.28863	.08572	4.6006	4.9385	1.3	7.0
2	77	4.3279	1.30489	.14871	4.0317	4.6241	1.3	7.0
3	160	4.5547	1.42685	.11280	4.3319	4.7775	1.0	7.0
4	32	3.9896	1.45801	.25774	3.4639	4.5153	1.3	7.0
Total	495	4.5810	1.36239	.06123	4.4607	4.7013	1.0	7.0

The means in Figure 9.68 already lead us to believe that there are in fact different attitudes, and that the 'laissez-faire shopper' has the least positive (3.99), and the 'shopping freak' the most positive (4.77) attitude towards promotions. Are actual differences between the cluster groups involved here, or may these differences only be attributed to coincidence? The ANOVA table (Figure 9.69) provides an answer.

Figure 9.69

ANOVA

Attitude towards promotion dimension

	Sum of Squares	df	Mean Square	F	Sig.
Between groups	24.269	3	8.090	4.450	.004
Within groups	892.645	491	1.818		
Total	916.914	494			

Given the fact that the p-value (.004) is less than .05, there are thus significant differences present between the groups with regard to their attitudes towards promotions.

Figure 9.70

Multiple Comparisons

Dependent Variable: Attitude towards promotion dimension
Bonferroni

(I) Cluster Number of Case	(J) Cluster Number of Case	Mean Difference (I-J)	Std. Error	Sig.
1	2	.44162	.17792	.080
	3	.21486	.13931	.742
	4	.77996*	.25467	.014
2	1	−.44162	.17792	.080
	3	−.22677	.18701	1.000
	4	.33834	.28359	1.000
3	1	−.21486	.13931	.742
	2	.22677	.18701	1.000
	4	.56510	.26110	.186
4	1	−.77996*	.25467	.014
	2	−.33834	.28359	1.000
	3	−.56510	.26110	.186

*The mean difference is significant at the .05 level

The 'Post Hoc' test (Figure 9.70) then shows the cluster groups in which these differences in attitude may be found. The attitudes regarding promotions vary only significantly from one another for the groups '1' and '4', so for the 'shopping freaks' and the 'laissez-faire shoppers' (p-value = .014 < .05, for groups 1 and 4). As far as the 'fun shoppers' (group 2) and the 'time is money shoppers' (group 3) are concerned for example, we cannot say that this last group has a more positive attitude toward promotions (p-value = 1 > .05; mean$_{group3}$ = 4.55 versus mean$_{group2}$ = 4.33).

Further reading

Everitt, B., Landau, S. and Leese, M. (2001), *Cluster Analysis*. 4th ed. London: Edward Arnold.

Kaufman, L. and Rousseeuw, P. (2005), *Finding Groups in Data: An Introduction to Cluster Analysis*. 10th ed. New York: John Wiley & Sons.

Norušis, M. (1993), *SPSS for Windows: Professional Statistics, Release 6.0*. Chicago, Illinois: SPSS, Inc.

Endnotes

1 'Warmth' may be defined here as a certain degree of cosiness and comfort, a friendly atmosphere (e.g., a family situation, grandparents and child).

2 Out of 100 commercials which belong to the first cluster group, 36 were considered to be erotic, which is 'rather few'.

3 Out of 100 commercials which belong to the fourth cluster group, 45 were considered to be erotic, which is 'approximately half'.

4 For the statements 'attracts the attention' and 'remarkable' it would have been more correct to interpret the 'Tamhane's T2' test instead of the 'Bonferroni' test. After all, the 'Test of Homogeneity of Variances' shows that for each of these statements the assumption of equal variances does not hold.

5 It is recommended to put the 'Maximum Iterations' equal to 100 c instead of 10). This can be done in the 'K-Means Cluster Analysis: 'Iterate' window, obtained after clicking the 'Iterate' button at the bottom of the main window (Figure 9.55).

Chapter 10

Multidimensional scaling techniques

Chapter objectives

This chapter will help you to:

- Understand when and how to use multidimensional scaling
- Understand the different types of MDS techniques, the underlying data structure, data collection methods and presentation formats
- Carry out a two-way, two-mode MDS analysis (correspondence analysis) and interpret its results
- Carry out a three-way, two-mode MDS analysis (two-way, one-mode MDS with replications in PROXSCAL) and interpret its results

Technique

Multidimensional scaling (MDS) is a collection of techniques, the objective of which is to visualize the underlying, hidden structure in a data matrix. To do this, an association is calculated between one or more sets of objects. This association provides an indication of how alike (similar) or unalike (dissimilar) the two sets of objects to be compared are. On the basis of these associations, one or more spatial diagrams are created which contain a point configuration or a vector configuration or both. Each point or each vector, which corresponds to a line which travels in a certain direction from the origin, represents one of the objects. The input for the model is therefore a matrix of 'distance measurements' (dissimilarities) or of 'proximity data' (similarities). In the output, the spatial diagram (map), the points are visualized in such a manner that the more similar (or less dissimilar) the objects in the matrix are, the closer they are to one another. The map forms a visual representation, successful or unsuccessful, of the hidden structure present in the data.

MDS is a generic term for a whole range of techniques which do not all have the same characteristics and may be categorized on the basis of the following three criteria: (1) the shape of the data matrix; (2) the technique to compose the map; and (3) the data collection method used. Each of these criteria is discussed in further detail below.

The form of the data matrix: the number of ways and the number of modes

Ways

A square matrix ($n \times n$) with the same objects (e.g. brands) in both the rows and the columns or a rectangular matrix ($m \times n$) with m attributes in the rows and n brands in the columns are examples of a two-way matrix, since there is a number of rows present horizontally and a number of columns vertically. Either a (n × n) or (m × n) matrix may be developed for each of k respondents. If we put these matrices one after the other like slices of cake, a three-way matrix is created (m × n × k), with the respondents representing the third 'way'.

Modes

If the data originate from a single source, for example the n brands in a square matrix (n × n), then this is referred to as 'one-mode' data. If they originate from two sources, for example the m attributes and the n brands in an (m × n) matrix, then this is 'two-mode' or bimodal data. If they originate from three sets, e.g., the m attributes and the n brands, yet are collected to be analysed for k respondents, the (m × n × k) matrix, then this is referred to as 'three-mode' or trimodal data.

Ways × Modes

Table 10.1

		Number of ways	
		2	3
Number of modes	1	Two-way, one-mode (1)	Three-way, one-mode (4)
	2	Two-way, two-mode (2) **Example 1**	Three-way, two-mode (5) **Example 2**
	3	Two-way, three-mode (3)	Three-way, three-mode (6)

The six cases as illustrated in Table 10.1 are described as follows:

(1) In a 'two-way, one-mode' matrix the brands are compared with one another. This may be done for example on the basis of 'the triads method', which will result in a similarity matrix for a certain respondent. On the basis of this matrix, the researcher may attempt to develop a visual space, also referred to as a 'perceptual map', which shows these similarities as well as possible. If the distances between the brands in the map are measured afterwards, they will observe the 'ranking' on the whole which may also be found in the similarities. Below is an example to illustrate 'the triads method'.

Suppose that every brand is printed on a separate card. The researcher takes three cards from the pile and asks: 'On these cards, you see three car makes. Please indicate which two makes, in your opinion, resemble one another the most, and which two show the most significant differences?' This procedure will be repeated for each of the combinations of the three makes. Each time that two makes are evaluated as 'resembling one another the most', they will be assigned the value '1', and the resulting total score will then be converted to a 'ranking' (e.g., 10: most similar, 1: least similar, and this will be used to map five makes).

(2) In 'two-way, two-mode' MDS, the data matrix consists of m rows (e.g., preferences of m respondents or scores for m attributes) and n columns (e.g., n products or n brands), and the relationship between two different sets of objects is studied. The objective of the analysis is to find a common space for both rows **and** columns.

Here, a distinction may be made between 'external' and 'internal' analysis. **External analysis** relates to putting (mapping) preferences (also named 'dominance') in a 'pre-existing' map which is based on similarities. This way the external analysis may be viewed as an extension of a 'two-way, mode' MDS analysis. In the previously discussed car example, not only was a (n × n) similarity matrix calculated between the cars themselves, but the respondents were also asked to rank the cars by preference. If we assume m respondents and n makes, a (m × n) preference matrix will be created. For each of the m individuals, an ideal point will be calculated in the pre-existing map of the n makes on the basis of its ranking of the makes. This ideal point is put so that the relative distance to the brand coordinates corresponds to the ranking assigned by the consumer. This is referred to as a 'preferential space'. **Internal analysis** on the other hand creates a visual diagram using a single analysis containing both rows (m) as well as columns (n). This type of space is often referred to as a 'joint space'.

(3) A 'two-way, three-mode' matrix is created by the concatenation of two modes in one way. For example, individuals stand for one mode and one way, and the combinations of the car makes and the attributes represent the other two modes and the second way. In the case of ten car makes and eight attributes, this would result in eighty elements.

(4) 'Three-way, one-mode' data do not occur in practice very often. The registration of a person's voter behaviour in the years 1990, 1995 and 2000 may serve as an example for this type of data. The researcher may then make an estimate of the probability that a person will vote for party X **and** party Y **and** party Z in the subsequent years.

(5) A 'three-way, two-mode' data matrix is an extension of a 'two-way, one-mode' dataset. If k respondents are asked to compare m car makes on the basis of their similarity, then this will result in a (k × m × m) matrix, which consists of three ways (k, m, and m) and two sets, namely respondents and car makes (k and m). For the processing of this matrix, the researcher may use one of the following three techniques:

a) 'Two-way, one-mode' MDS, after averaging: one common data matrix will be calculated (m × m) for all k respondents, and there will be only one map created and this will be for the so-called 'mean' respondent. The respondents will be used as the chance factor in this case.

b) 'Two-way, one-mode' MDS per subgroup: the k respondents will first be grouped into homogeneous subgroups, and a separate map will be drawn for each of these subgroups.

c) 'Two-way, one-mode' MDS per respondent: for each of the k respondents, one data matrix (m × m) will be calculated; the data will therefore not be aggregated. In addition to a joint map, a separate map will also be created for each respondent; this type of analysis is named 'individual difference' MDS.

(6) 'Three-way, three-mode' MDS arises from the evaluation of a number of objects on different features by several people, or from the preferential ranking of objects by people at different times. In this context, this is also referred to as 'weighted or replicated unfolding'.

The technique: the measurement level of the input and output and the representation of the data

Measurement level of input and output

Table 10.2

			Output (map)	
			Vector model	Distance model
Input (data)	Non-metrical data	Nominal	Non-metrical MDS	Example 1
		Ordinal	↕	Example 2
	Metrical data	Interval/ ratio	Metrical MDS	

Table 10.2 indicates that with regard to the input of an MDS analysis, a distinction may be made between 'nominal' (classified data) and 'ordinal' (ranked data) on the one hand, and 'interval' and 'ratio' data (measured data) on the other hand. With regard to the output of MDS, two cases may also be identified: (1) the vector model, which includes points (e.g., makes) and vectors (e.g., individuals) in a visual diagram, and whereby the 'orthogonal projections' of the points onto the vectors reflect the individuals' preferences for the makes; and (2) the distance model, which only includes points (e.g., makes) in the map, and whereby the 'distances' between the various points in the map are measurable with Euclidean algebra (see Formula (1) for d (x_i, x_j) later in this chapter) and correspond to the empirically observed dissimilarities for the makes.

Interval- or ratio-scaled data may be processed using metrical as well as non-metrical MDS, since interval or ratio data may also be processed on an ordinal level. Ordinal data on the other hand may only be analysed using non-metrical MDS.

The difference between non-metrical and metrical MDS will be explored further below.

Suppose that the point of departure is a square 'two-way, one-mode' matrix with associations between n objects (e.g., makes) measured on an ordinal, interval or ratio level as input, and suppose also that a_{ij} shows the degree of association between object i and object j. The output configuration may then be represented as X, containing the points $x_1, \ldots x_n$, which represent the objects, and in an R-dimensional space, every point may be represented by its coordinates: $x_1 = (x_{11}, \ldots x_{1R}), \ldots, x_n = (x_{n1}, \ldots x_{nR})$. The Euclidean distance between two points x_i and x_j is then equal to:

$$d (x_i, x_j) = d_{ij} = \sqrt{\sum_{R=1}^{R} (x_{in} - x_{jn})^2} \tag{1}$$

MDS procedures will look for a configuration in which the distance d_{ij} between the points x_i and x_j correspond as much as possible to the association between the objects i and j. The equation below plays a crucial role in this:

$$A^t = T = D + E$$

where A: associations between the n objects, the input matrix
   t: transformation function
   T: transformed associations or 'pseudo distances' between the n objects
   D: distances between the objects in the R-dimensional space or 'distances-in-the-solution'
   E: 'error', difference between the pseudo distances and the distances-in-the-solution

The associations between the n objects are therefore first converted into pseudo distances on the basis of the transformation function t, and MDS then tries to minimize the difference between the distances-in-the-solution and these pseudo distances. The degree to which this attempt is successful determines the 'fit' of the solution.

The transformation function t may take on different forms, and this is closely related to the assumed measurement level of the associations:

Metrical MDS procedures assume interval- or ratio-scaled data which correspond to the 'real' distances between the objects via an exact function. Examples of functions are: $t(A) = b + c*A$ and $t(A) = d*A$. This first type of function is called a linear function, or also an 'interval' transformation (straight line with intercept). The second type is a multiplicative function, and is also called a 'ratio' transformation (straight line through the origin). The objective of the procedure thus consists of finding a space with a number of coordinates so that the distance between the points corresponds as much as possible (proportionally) to the 'distance' between the input values themselves.

For example, a person Y divides 100 points among 4 brands as follows: brand A: 50; brand B: 25; brand C: 20; and brand D: 5. In the spatial representation of a metrical MDS solution, with 'ratio' transformation, the distance to A for person Y will be **25/50 times as 'great'** as the distance to B, and the distance to D **20/5 times as great** as the distance to C. In other words, the relationship between the input values is respected.

Non-metrical MDS procedures are based on ordinal data, which express the relationships between the objects in numbers for which only the sequence contains meaningful information. These numbers will then be subjected to a monotonous transformation, which is also called an 'ordinal' transformation, since they retain the sequence information. These techniques therefore do not attempt to find a certain 'proportional' relationship, but strive to cause the 'ranking' of the distances between the points to correspond as much as possible with the 'ranking' which results from the empirically recorded associations.

If we re-examine the example of the division of 100 points between four brands, then the data can be read as follows: person Y first chooses brand A, then brand B, then brand C and finally brand D. In the ideal situation, the distance from person Y to A in the map would then be less than that to B, which in turn will be less than the distance from person Y to C. Respecting the ranking is therefore central to this procedure, not retaining the relationship between the input values.

In the analysis of ordinal data, the researcher will therefore opt for a monotone transformation, and he will also choose a 'discrete or a continuous treatment of ties'. What does this amount to? In a matrix with associations between objects, items known as 'ties' may occur. This indicates that different pairs of objects are characterized by similar associations. If the researcher would like for these pairs to be at equal distances from one another in the final MDS image, then the 'ties' may not be split, and this is known as a 'discrete' treatment of the 'ties' ($a_{ij} = a_{hk} \rightarrow t(a_{ij}) = t(a_{hk})$; 'Kruskals secondary approach'). If, on the other hand, he or she does not require the pairs to be at equal distances from one another and the 'ties' may in fact be split, then a 'continuous' approach to the 'ties' is central here ($a_{ij} = a_{hk} \rightarrow t(a_{ij})$ or $t(a_{ij}) > t(a_{hk}) <$ $t(a_{hk})$; 'Kruskals primary approach').

Representation of the data

In the case of a representation of two sets in one visual space ('two-mode' data), there are several possible options, namely point-vector and point-point representations.

MDPREF is software which is specially designed for the analysis of ratio-scaled preference data and will produce **point-vector representations**. Using this technique, points will stand for brands, for example, and the vectors for individuals, and in a two-dimensional space, the orthogonal projections of the points onto a vector will reflect a person's preference for the various brands. MDPREF's counterpart in SPSS is CATPCA[1] (Categorical Principal Components Analysis), a component of the 'Categories' module. CATPCA can process variables from different levels of measurement.

In a **point-point representation**, subjects (e.g. individuals) as well as objects (e.g. brands) are represented by points. A subject point like this is also called an ideal point, and the distance from every object point to this ideal point is then an indication of the preference: the shorter the distance from brand to individual, the greater the preference of that individual for the particular brand.

Data collection method: direct or indirect measurement

Many types of data collection procedures are available for MDS. In the specific case of a square input matrix, the associations between the row and the column elements may be collected in a direct or indirect manner.

Direct data collection

With direct measurement, the respondent is presented with a set of objects and is asked to compare each with one another (see Example 2, 'question 1'; Table 10.4), and is thus not required to answer on the basis of criteria which were determined by the researcher beforehand. After an analysis of 'directly' collected data, the researcher does not know immediately however which attributes played a role in the comparison of the objects. The importance of the attributes may only be determined indirectly after the map has been drawn up; for example, this may be done by finding out which stimuli occupy extreme positions on the dimensions of the map, or by examining related groups of objects. The respondent may be asked additional questions to simplify the interpretation of the axes, for example by using them as input for an external analysis. The method of direct data collection is moreover limited in terms of the number of objects to be studied: at least 7 or 8 objects are required to construct a perceptual map in two or three dimensions; if the number of objects to be studied is greater than 20, then it will be nearly impossible for the consumer to compare all of the objects. Data collection which is done using the direct method will usually require a great deal of the respondent's time and can lead to exhaustion and boredom.

Indirect data collection

With indirect measurement, the respondent is asked for example to evaluate every car make on the basis of twenty items about the bodywork, the price, the motor performance, the prestige, the usage, etc. and this is done using one or more scale methods (e.g., Semantic differential, Likert scale or Stapel scale). The scores collected in this manner may then be used directly as input for a rectangular matrix which places the makes in the columns and the attributes in the rows ('two-mode' data), however they may also be converted into associations between the makes themselves and this will serve indirectly as input for a square matrix ('one-mode' data). However, two problems can occur when this method of data collection is used, both of which are linked to the fact that the visual space derived from this is a function of the attributes used. First of all, the scales must be exhaustive; in other words, no relevant attributes may be omitted. One of the greatest disadvantages of the method is that exhaustiveness of the collected items or attributes is actually difficult to guarantee. Secondly, all of the attributes included must be relevant.

From the above, it may be clear that MDS contains a whole spectrum of techniques. Before examining the results produced from two examples, we will provide a short indication of where certain techniques may be found in SPSS (Table 10.3). After all, there is not a single common denominator 'MDS' in SPSS. It may also be said that many MDS techniques, including correspondence analysis and the PROXSCAL analyses are not included in the standard SPSS package, but are part of the add-on module, 'Categories'.

Table 10.3

MDS technique				Location in SPSS	
Categorical regression (CATREG)				Analyze/Regression/Optimal Scaling	
Categorical principal components analysis (CATPCA)				Analyze/Data reduction/Optimal Scaling	
Nonlinear canonical correlation analysis (OVERALS)					
Homogeneity analysis (HOMALS)					
Correspondence analysis (FCA)				Analyze/Data reduction/Correspondence Analysis **Example 1**	
Multidi mensional scaling	ALSCAL			Analyze/Scale/Multidimensional Scaling (ALSCAL)	
	PROXSCAL	Non-individual difference model: basic model		Analyze/Scale/Multidimensional Scaling (PROXSCAL) **Example 2**	Identity model
		Individual difference model	INDSCAL		Weighted Euclidean model
			IDEOSCAL		Generalized Euclidean model
			IDEOSCAL with minimal rank of matrix		Reduced rank model

Note PROXSCAL was added to SPSS since SPSS 10, and performs the 'same'[2] analyses (e.g. INDSCAL) as the more familiar ALSCAL. Nonetheless, PROXSCAL is preferable to ALSCAL for the following reasons: (1) an improved algorithm; (2) the ability to use one's own initial configuration; (3) the option to 'fix' certain points in the visual model; (4) the ability to specify a linear combination of independent variables which drives the mapping of the points; and (5) the minimization of 'Normalized Raw Stress' (which is based on 'distances') instead of 'S-Stress' (which is based on 'squared distances', and is the criterion which is to be minimized in the case of ALSCAL).

For a more in-depth discussion of the MDS techniques, the reader may consult reference works listed at the end of this chapter.

The current chapter contains two examples. 'Example 1' treats a 'two-way, two-mode' MDS analysis, the input for which is a rectangular matrix of nominally scaled data. More specifically, this involves a correspondence analysis. A 'three-way, two-mode' dataset, with in essence ordinal data, forms the basis of 'Example 2'. This dataset, which contains many square symmetrical matrices, will be worked out according to a 'two-way, one-mode' MDS analysis with replications, and this will be done in the SPSS module PROXSCAL. Both examples will be explained and worked out in detail below.

Example 1

'Two-way, two-mode' MDS – correspondence analysis

Technique: supplement

Correspondence analysis (CA) is a non-metrical 'two-way, two-mode' procedure. The data which are nominal in nature are collected indirectly, and the output, which is produced after an internal analysis, is a point-point visual representation in a Euclidean space. The objective of CA consists of visually representing of m rows (e.g., attributes, characteristics of shopping centres) and n columns (e.g., clusters, groups of fashion-sensitive consumers) from a contingency table or cross table as a set of m row and n column points in a space ('joint space') with as few (preferably two) dimensions as possible, in order to gain insight into the interrelationships which exist between the clusters and between the attributes, and all of the elements together (clusters **and** attributes).

The technique places very few demands on the data. In principle, the only strict condition is a rectangular matrix with non-negative cells, which represent similarities (a high cell value corresponds to a small difference or, in other words, to a great similarity between both categories). In addition, the following three points are deserving of sufficient attention: (1) the data matrix must be large enough, so that the structure will not be apparent to the naked eye or via simple statistical techniques; (2) the variables must be homogeneous; and (3) the data must be heterogeneous. What do the points (2) and (3) mean in concrete terms? The 'variables' in point (2) correspond to the elements in the rows (attributes) and in the columns (clusters), and these data in the rows and/or columns must be comparable with one another. For example, it is not meaningful to place an attribute, measured via a semantic differential, in the same matrix next to an attribute measured via the 'pick any' method. The word 'data' in point (3) refers to that which is found in the cells of the matrix. If there is no variance present within the dataset, then a visual representation is also not meaningful, since the representation is not designed to result in the visual expression of the variance within the dataset.

Managerial problem

The problem here involves a manufacturer of fashionable women's apparel which sells its products via exclusive clothing boutiques. On the basis of extensive research, the company has discovered who its final customer is and has learned what her needs and preferential clothing are. Via the study performed here, the manufacturer would like to find out in which neighbourhoods (shopping centres) in Brussels it should target to set up points of distribution to sell its collection. The study conducted here will therefore have to provide an answer to the following two questions: (1) where does the fashion-sensitive shopper in Brussels buy her clothing; and (2) what is according to this fashion-sensitive consumer the image and profile of each shopping centre in Brussels? To accomplish this, the researcher decides to segment the fashion-sensitive consumers using the relationship which they develop with one or more shopping centres as criterion. The purpose will then be to find a range of variables which permit the creation of the best possible insight and provide an explanation for the relationship the consumer has with her shopping centres.

First, an exploratory qualitative study will be performed to collect the relevant datasets. To that end, the literature and the pre-existing market studies on this topic will be perused. Then, a number of women from the target group will be interviewed individually via an in-depth interview, using projective techniques. In total, 18 consumers will be interviewed. These consumers satisfy the following three criteria: (1) female, between the ages of 18 and 60; (2) regular patron (at least once a month) of a Brussels shopping centre; and (3) purchases clothing from this shopping centre. The goal is representativeness as far as the shopping centres are concerned. The respondents are asked each time to draw up the relevant list of shopping centres and to supplement this list.

On the basis of the results from the exploratory phase (the desk research and the in-depth interviews mentioned above), lists will be drawn up which contain 64 important characteristics (23 rational statements, 18 emotional statements, and 23 personality statements) and 10 relevant shopping centres.

Secondly, the data will be collected on a large scale, so that quantitative conclusions may be drawn. To do this, 302 respondents who satisfied the criteria set previously (see exploratory phase) will be asked to complete a questionnaire, in person. These criteria will be put into operation as follows:

- In order to ensure that the person being interviewed belongs to the target group, she must buy designer clothing from the company or one of its competitor, in other words those brands which are available in the distribution points where the client's brand is also available. A list of 41 brands which qualify is drawn up.

- When it appears that the person being interviewed satisfies the age criterion set previously and during a certain period of time has bought one of the brands, she will be invited to participate in a personal interview.

The selection of the respondents will occur proportionally in each of the ten shopping centres.

A number of behavioural and identification questions will be asked first. Then, the respondent will select five words or statements from each of the lists of rational, emotional and personality traits which apply the most to their **most preferred** shopping centre. The method used is the 'pick k out of m' data collection, and will result in an image of each respondent's wishes with regard to shopping centres.

On the basis of the interviews, a data matrix will be created consisting of 302 rows (the respondents) and 64 columns (the characteristics). This data matrix only contains the numbers '1' and '0': a '1' indicates the 'selection' of a certain attribute by the respondent, and a '0' represents 'non-selection'. The objective now consists in finding consumer segments which are as homogeneous as possible internally and as heterogeneous as possible externally with regard to their relationship to the preferred shopping centres. To do this, a cluster analysis (see Chapter 9, 'Cluster analysis with binary attributes') will be performed on the dataset which will attempt to find groups of respondents whose response patterns to the 64 characteristics run as parallel to one another as possible. This analysis will produce four clusters and therefore four groups of fashion-conscious women, with similar desires with regard to shopping centres within each group. Cluster '1' contains 77 people, cluster '2' 53 people, cluster '3' 81 and finally, cluster '4' contains 91 persons.

In the next step, the researcher would like to gain insight into the differences between the four segments on the basis of each of the three sets of characteristics. For this reason, all of the characteristics will be cross-tabulated with the four segments and tested for significant differences. Each of the characteristics which display these significant differences between the clusters will be accepted ($\alpha = .05$). This way, 46 of the original 64 attributes will remain.

For each of the 302 respondents, the most preferred shopping centre is also indicated, which makes it possible to calculate the distribution for each shopping centre across the four clusters (e.g., of the 37 respondents who chose '1' as the most preferred centre, 5 belong to cluster '1', 7 to cluster '2', 5 to cluster '3' and 20 to cluster '4'). As is the case with the characteristics, it is only meaningful to continue to work with those shopping centres for which there are significant differences in the preferences between the four clusters, and this amount appears to be seven after the cross tabulation analysis ($\alpha = .05$).

Up until now, the results have been fairly abstract. The researcher can attempt to visually represent what the clusters mean using CA. This graphic model or map has the advantage of making it easier to allow interpretations, and to show clearly the interrelationships between the consumer segments and the shopping centre characteristics. The output from the cluster analysis is therefore input for the CA, and in the current example, this is a data matrix (Figure 10.1) consisting of 46 rows (the characteristics) and 4 columns (the clusters).

Figure 10.1

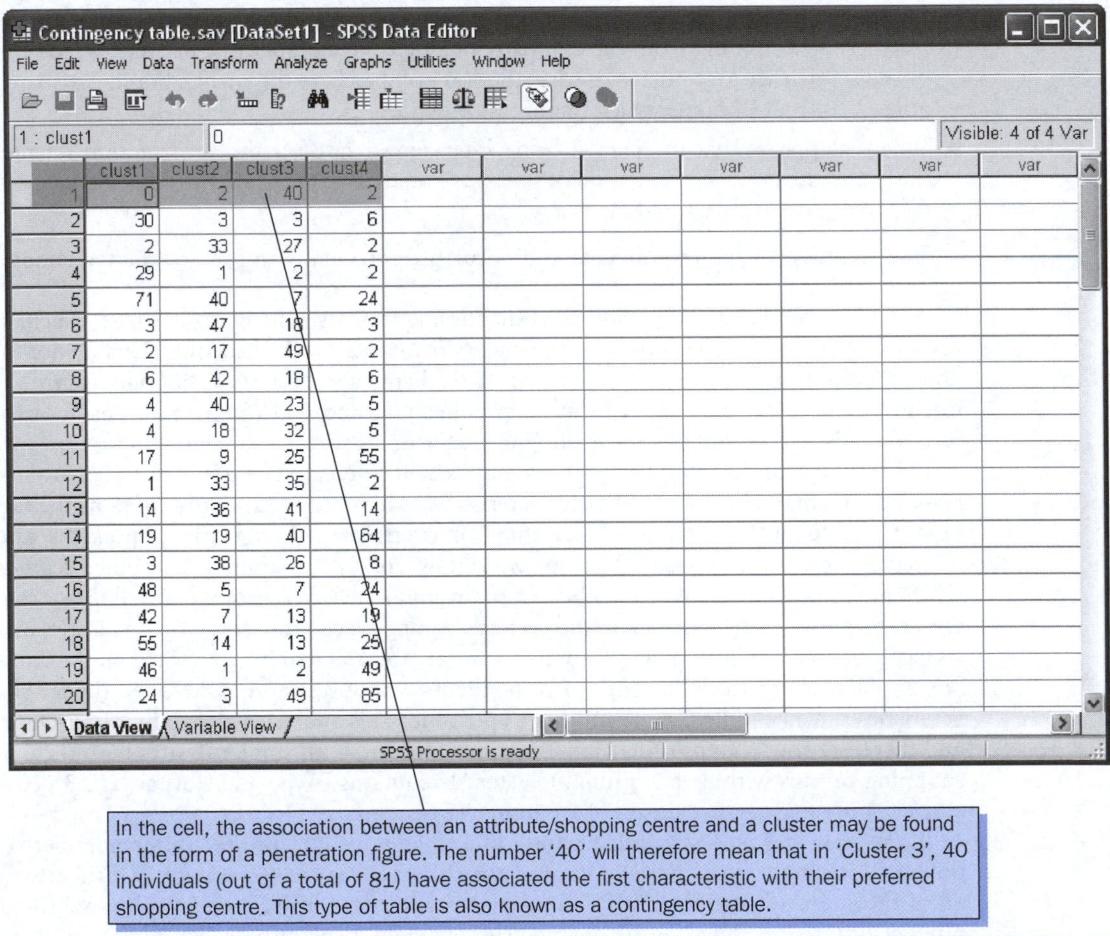

	clust1	clust2	clust3	clust4
1	0	2	40	2
2	30	3	3	6
3	2	33	27	2
4	29	1	2	2
5	71	40	7	24
6	3	47	18	3
7	2	17	49	2
8	6	42	18	6
9	4	40	23	5
10	4	18	32	5
11	17	9	25	55
12	1	33	35	2
13	14	36	41	14
14	19	19	40	64
15	3	38	26	8
16	48	5	7	24
17	42	7	13	19
18	55	14	13	25
19	46	1	2	49
20	24	3	49	85

In the cell, the association between an attribute/shopping centre and a cluster may be found in the form of a penetration figure. The number '40' will therefore mean that in 'Cluster 3', 40 individuals (out of a total of 81) have associated the first characteristic with their preferred shopping centre. This type of table is also known as a contingency table.

Seven extra rows corresponding to the shopping centres have been added to this matrix at the bottom. **These centres will be added to the map afterwards as additional external information to the map (formed on the basis of the segments and the characteristics).**

Problem

Perform a correspondence analysis, focusing on the following points: (1) redesign the contingency table (*Contingency table.sav*) to create a dataset that can serve as input for CA in SPSS (*Input correspondence analysis.sav*); (2) perform the CA so that the clusters and the characteristics which are compared with one another in the map; (3) request a 3-dimensional solution, and find out if the visual representation leads to a satisfying result in two dimensions. If so, assign a meaning to both axes; and (4) calculate the coordinates of the preferred shopping centres, and also include these in the visual representation which was created previously on the basis of the clusters and the characteristics.

The contingency table may also serve directly as input for CA, however the researcher must employ syntax. Additional attention will be focused on this aspect at the end of the discussion (see the subsection 'Contingency table as input for factorial correspondence analysis: Syntax'.

Solution

SPSS Commands

If the researcher would like to work with the input windows in SPSS, he will have to convert the dataset *Contingency table.sav* (Figure 10.1) to a dataset which looks like the one shown in Figure 10.2.

Figure 10.2

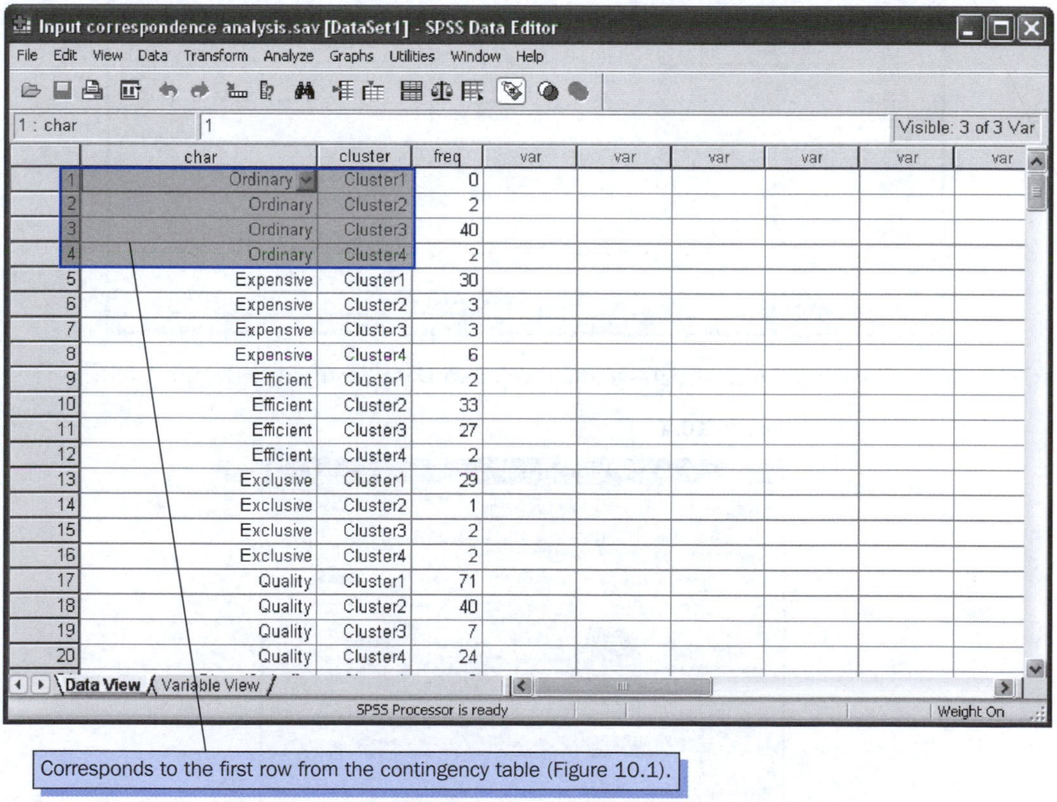

Corresponds to the first row from the contingency table (Figure 10.1).

This dataset contains three variables: (1) the variable 'characteristic' contains 53 categories (46 characteristics and 7 shopping centres), which correspond to the 53 rows from the contingency table; (2) the variable 'cluster' contains 4 categories (4 cluster groups) which correspond to the 4 columns from the contingency table; and (3) the variable 'frequency' which stands for the values from the contingency table, the so-called 'penetration figures'.

The transformation of the dataset *Contingency table.sav* to the dataset *Input correspondence analysis.sav* may be done using the 'Restructure' module in SPSS. This module offers many options, however in the next section, only those windows are shown which lead to the desired dataset, namely *Input correspondence analysis.sav*.

Supporting technique

Figure 10.3

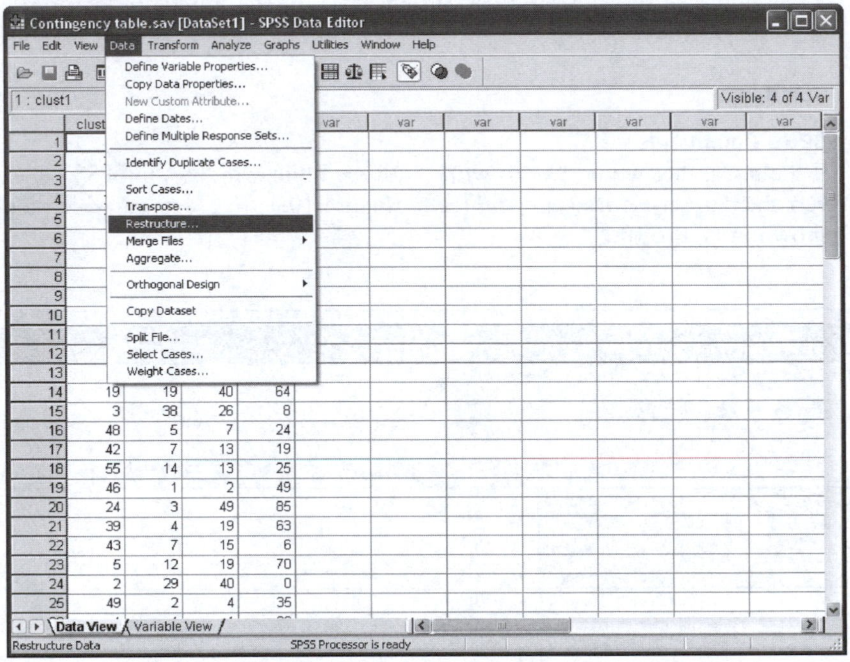

Open the *Contingency table.sav* dataset and then go to Data/Restructure (Figure 10.3).

Figure 10.4

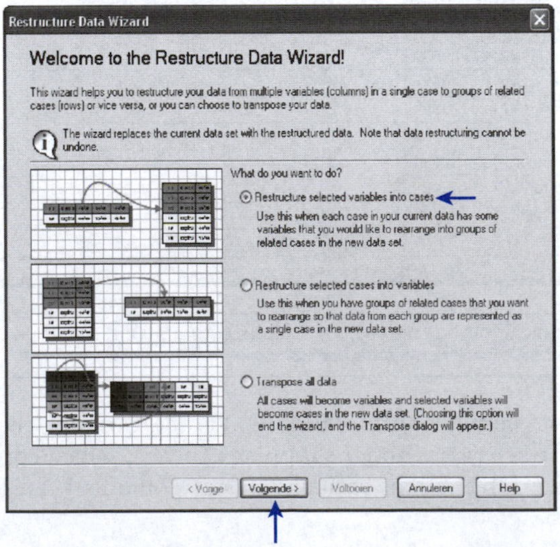

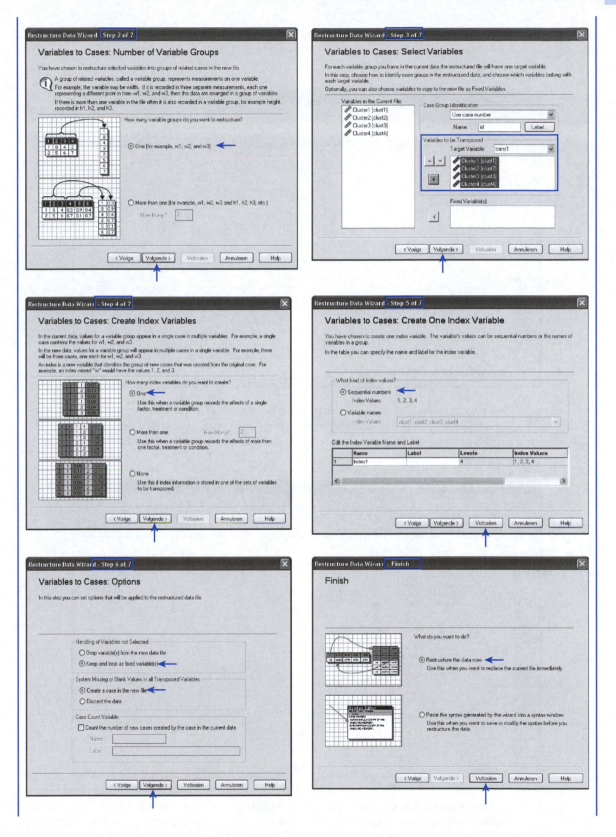

The 'Restructure Data Wizard' (Figure 10.4) will appear, the seven windows of which will have to be run through in sequence.

Figure 10.5

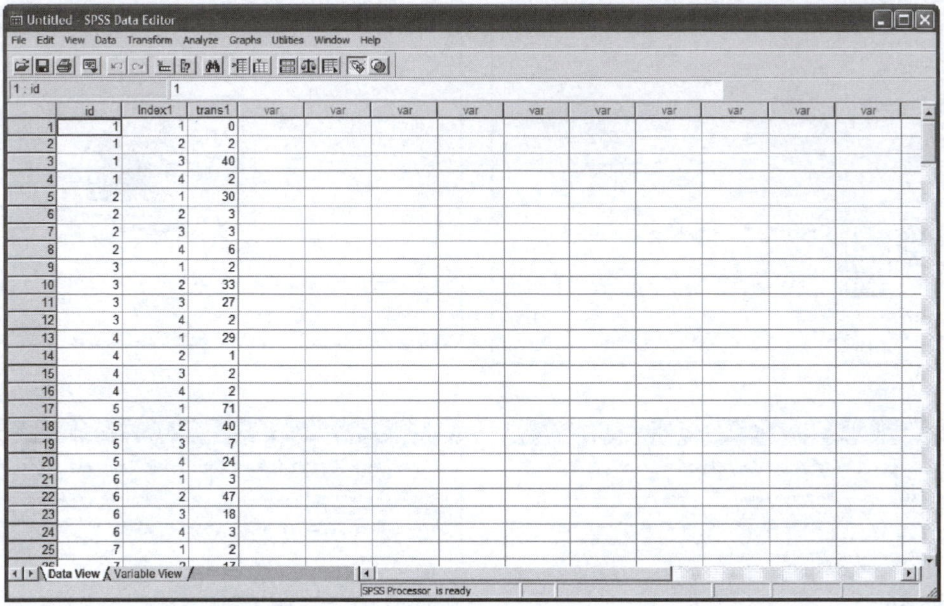

Untitled - SPSS Data Editor

	id	Index1	trans1
1	1	1	0
2	1	2	2
3	1	3	40
4	1	4	2
5	2	1	30
6	2	2	3
7	2	3	3
8	2	4	6
9	3	1	2
10	3	2	33
11	3	3	27
12	3	4	2
13	4	1	29
14	4	2	1
15	4	3	2
16	4	4	2
17	5	1	71
18	5	2	40
19	5	3	7
20	5	4	24
21	6	1	3
22	6	2	47
23	6	3	18
24	6	4	3
25	7	1	2

The result is a new dataset (Figure 10.5) which, after the variables have been renamed ([id] → [char]; [index1] → [cluster]; [trans1] → [freq]) and the 'value labels' have been assigned, will correspond to the dataset *Input correspondence analysis.sav* (Figure 10.6) (see Chapter 1 for the definition of variables).

Figure 10.6

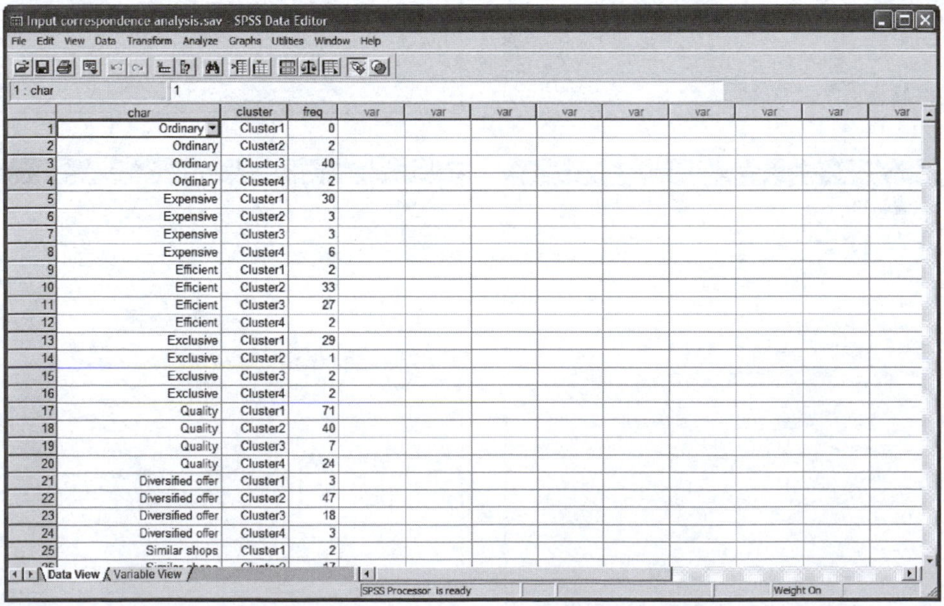

Input correspondence analysis.sav - SPSS Data Editor

	char	cluster	freq
1	Ordinary	Cluster1	0
2	Ordinary	Cluster2	2
3	Ordinary	Cluster3	40
4	Ordinary	Cluster4	2
5	Expensive	Cluster1	30
6	Expensive	Cluster2	3
7	Expensive	Cluster3	3
8	Expensive	Cluster4	6
9	Efficient	Cluster1	2
10	Efficient	Cluster2	33
11	Efficient	Cluster3	27
12	Efficient	Cluster4	2
13	Exclusive	Cluster1	29
14	Exclusive	Cluster2	1
15	Exclusive	Cluster3	2
16	Exclusive	Cluster4	2
17	Quality	Cluster1	71
18	Quality	Cluster2	40
19	Quality	Cluster3	7
20	Quality	Cluster4	24
21	Diversified offer	Cluster1	3
22	Diversified offer	Cluster2	47
23	Diversified offer	Cluster3	18
24	Diversified offer	Cluster4	3
25	Similar shops	Cluster1	2

Before the researcher may start with performing a correspondence analysis on the dataset *Input correspondence analysis.sav*, he must first assign a weight to each of the cases (to each specific combination of a characteristic/shopping centre with a cluster group) and must do this according to the 'penetration figure' variable.

Figure 10.7

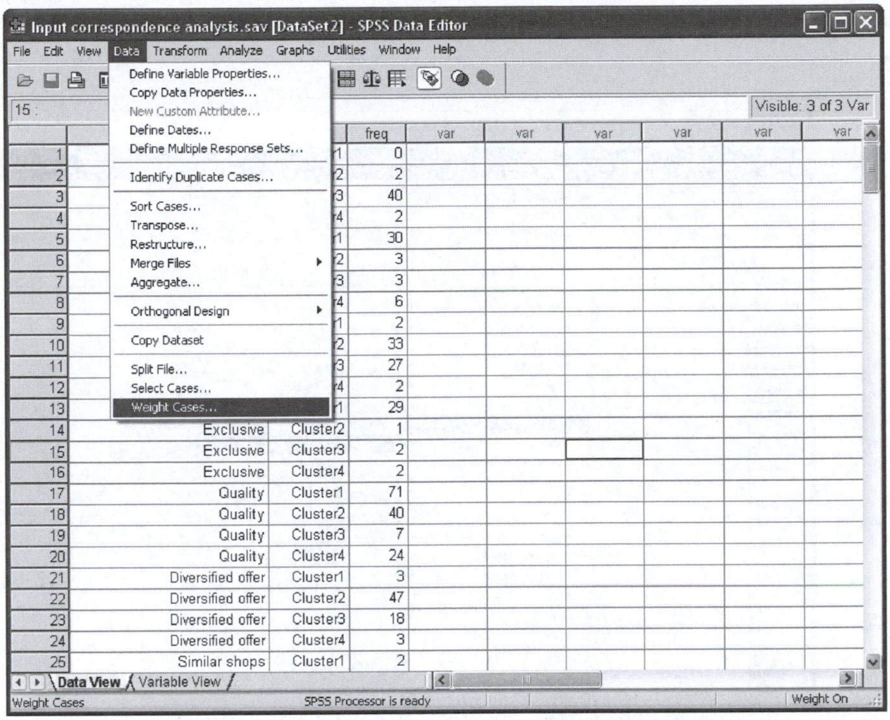

Supporting technique

Go to Data/Weight Cases (Figure 10.7). The value '0' for this variable figure (see for instance first row in Figure 10.7) will lead to the inclusion of the following 'Log' in the output window:

> Warning # 3211

> On at least one case, the value of the weight variable was zero, negative,

> or missing. Such cases are invisible to statistical procedures and graphs

> which need positively weighted cases, but remain on the file and are

> processed by non-statistical facilities such as LIST and SAVE.

This 'warning' will however not lead to a distortion of the results under the subsection 'Interpretation of the SPSS output' below.

Figure 10.8

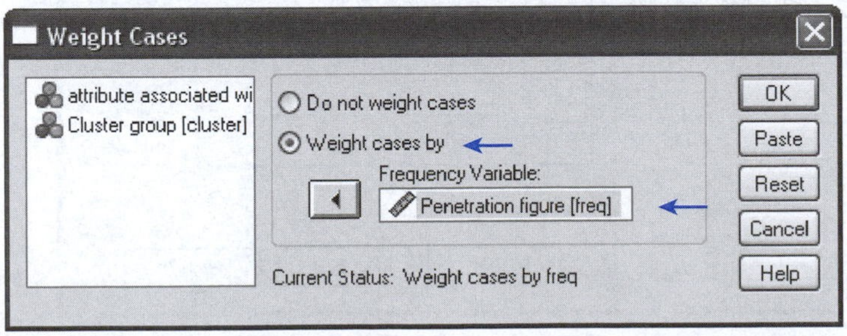

In the 'Weight Cases' window (Figure 10.8), choose the option 'Weight cases by' and move the variable [freq] from the list with variables on the left-hand side to the box 'Frequency Variable'. Click 'OK'.

After the transformation of the dataset and the assignment of weights to the cases, the researcher may finally get started with the performance of the correspondence analysis.

Figure 10.9

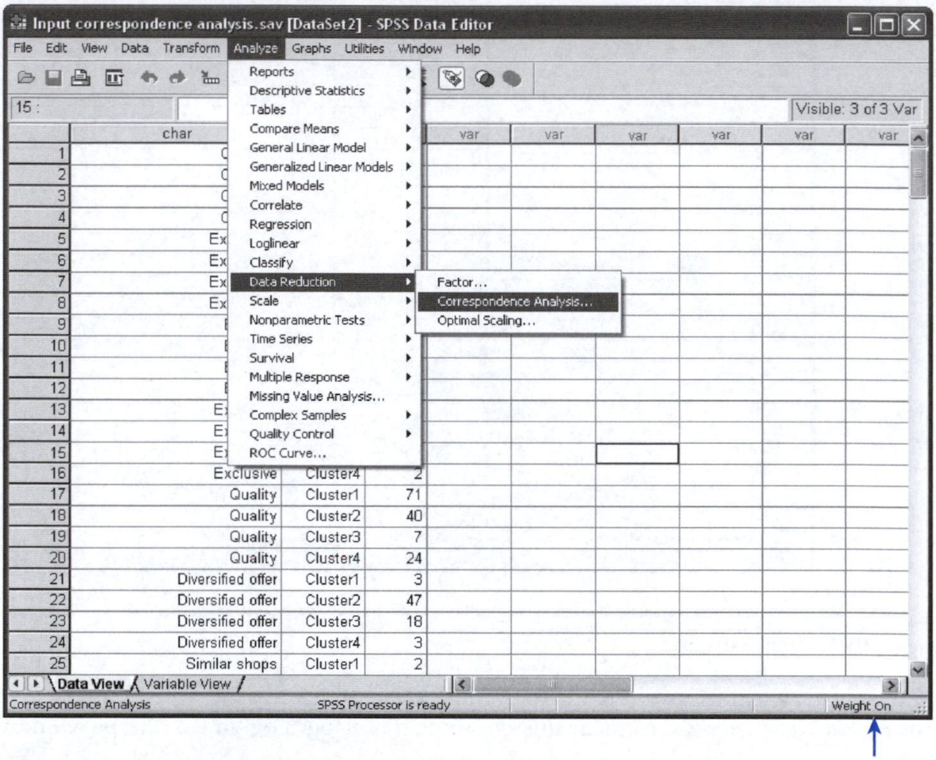

Go to Analyze/Data Reduction/Correspondence Analysis (Figure 10.9).

Notice that at the bottom of the screen the text 'Weight On' has been included, which indicates that a weighting is applicable.

Figure 10.10

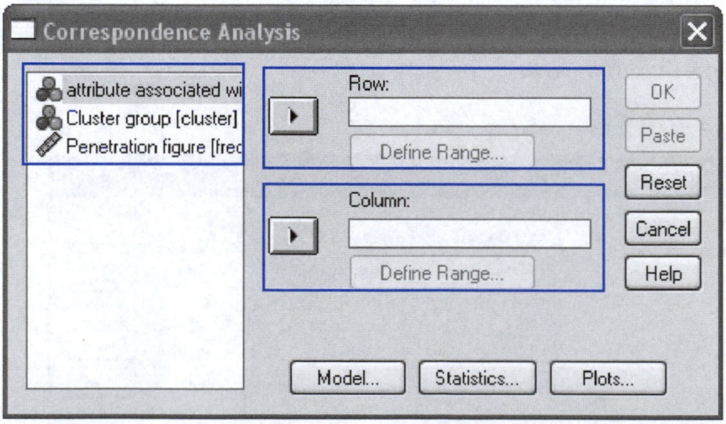

The characteristics of the shopping centres constitute the rows of the contingency table, and the cluster groups the columns (Figure 10.1). For this reason, the 'char' variable in the 'Correspondence Analysis' window (Figure 10.10) must be moved from the list on the left-hand side with variables to the 'Row' box using the top arrow and the 'cluster' variable to the box 'Column'.

Figure 10.11

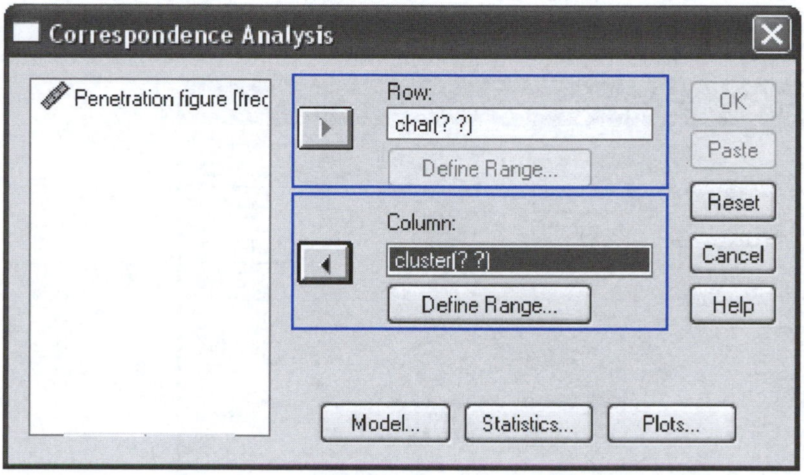

Correspondence Analysis

- Penetration figure [freq

Row:
char(? ?)

Define Range...

Column:
cluster(? ?)

Define Range...

OK

Paste

Reset

Cancel

Help

Model...   Statistics...   Plots...

In the next step, define the categories of the 'char' and 'cluster' variables by clicking the 'Define Range' buttons (Figure 10.11).

Figure 10.12

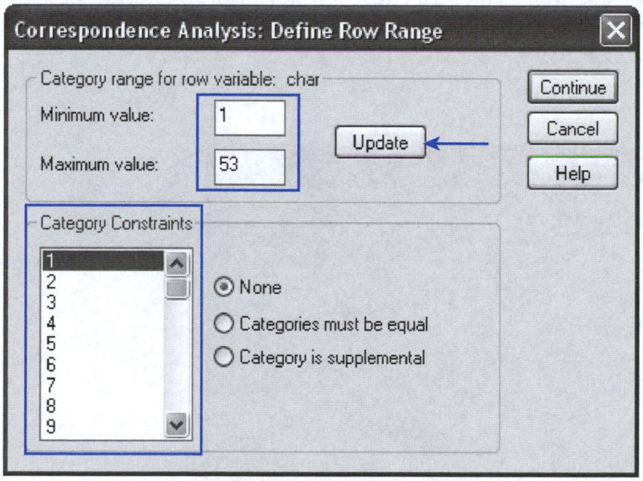

Correspondence Analysis: Define Row Range

Category range for row variable: char

Minimum value: 1

Maximum value: 53

Update

Continue

Cancel

Help

Category Constraints
1
2
3
4
5
6
7
8
9

- None
- Categories must be equal
- Category is supplemental

In the 'Correspondence Analysis: Define Row Range' window (Figure 10.12), input '1' for the minimum value for the 'char' variable, and '53' as the maximum value. This corresponds to the coding for the 'char' variable in the 'Variable View' tab in the 'SPSS Data Editor'. Click the 'Update' button and the box under 'Category Constraints' will be filled in with '53' categories.

The 'None' option which is now applicable to each of the 53 categories, indicates that no restriction has been placed on the categories. They are thus all (characteristics **and** shopping

centres) defined as 'active rows' and such will all guide the visual representation of characteristics and cluster groups. This is however not what the researcher wants.

The researcher would only like to add the shopping centres to the map as additional
external information afterwards, and does not want these centres to control the configuration of characteristics and cluster groups, as well as the orientation of the axes. In order to
achieve this goal, the researcher must define the shopping centres as 'supplementary rows'
and thus place the restriction 'Category is supplemental' on the categories 47 through 53.

Figure 10.13

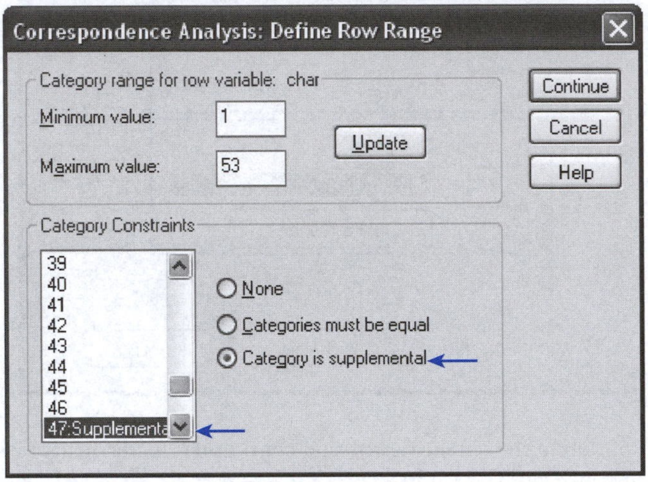

In the list with 53 categories, find category 47 (shop '1'), and choose the option
'Category is supplemental'. Apply this procedure to the categories 48 through 53 (shop '2'
through shop '7') (Figure 10.13).

Figure 10.14

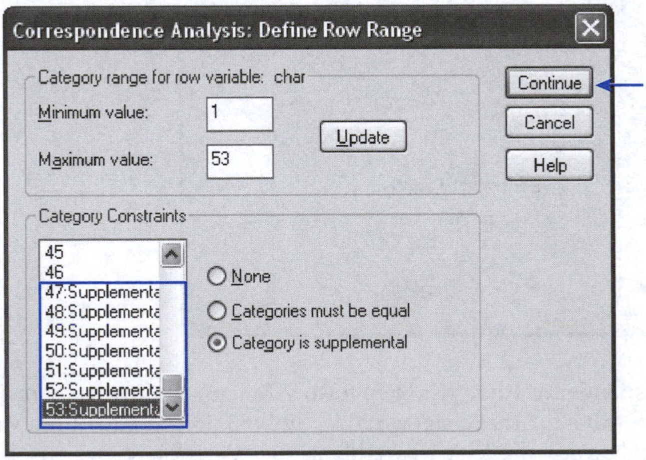

After defining the seven shopping centres as supplemental rows, click 'Continue'
(Figure 10.14).

Digging Deeper

The above method implies that the visual representation of characteristics and cluster groups, in which the researcher was originally interested exclusively, will also contain the shopping centres. It is however possible to only assign characteristics and cluster groups to this initial plot by defining the shopping centres as 'missing'.

Figure 10.15

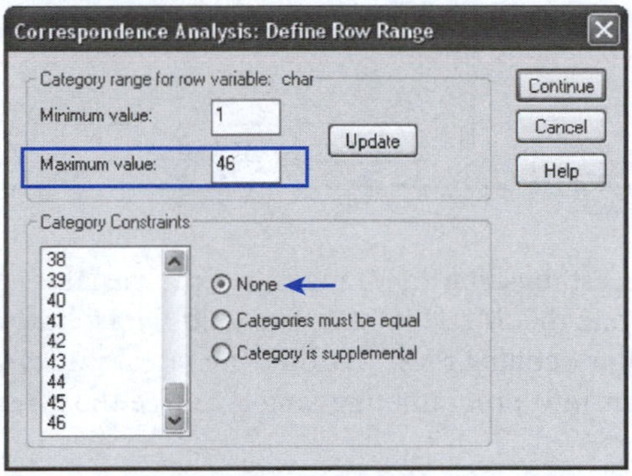

To do this, the researcher will also have to assign a minimum value of '1' to the title 'Category range for row variable: char' however the maximum value will have to be '46' instead of '53' (Figure 10.15). If he would also like to include the centres as additional external information in the map afterwards, he will have to follow the procedure with 'supplemental rows' as described above.

Figure 10.16

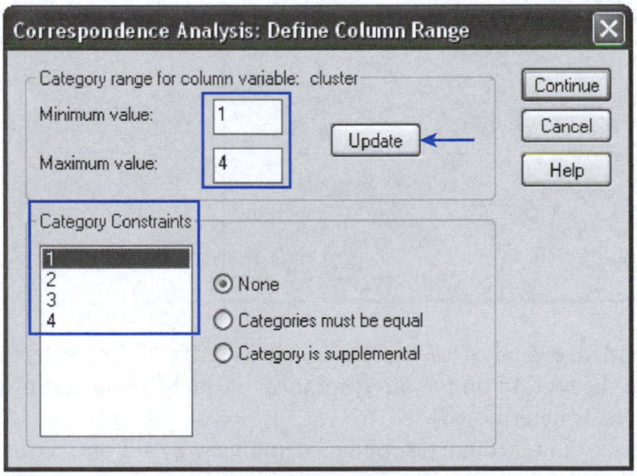

After establishing the 'Category range' for the 'char' variable, the researcher will follow the same procedure for the 'cluster' variable. The four cluster groups correspond with the codes '1' through '4' (see 'SPSS Data Editor', 'Variable View' tab), and this is why the minimum and maximum values in the 'Correspondence Analysis: Define Column Range' window (Figure 10.16) are '1' and '4' respectively. Since each of the four groups helps to determine the visual representation and the orientation of the axes, and therefore corresponds to an 'active column', no restriction applies to these categories.

Figure 10.17

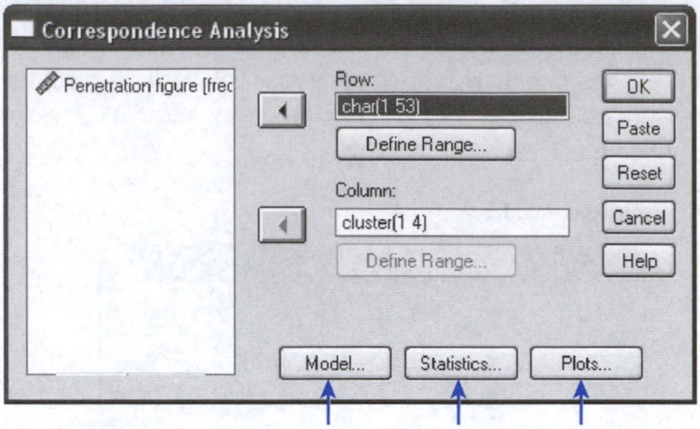

After establishing the 'ranges' for the variables 'char' and 'cluster', the researcher may now define the 'Model', 'Statistics' and 'Plots' buttons in sequence (Figure 10.17).

If, after defining these buttons, the researcher would like to transform the commands he has input into programming language (see the syntax in Figure 10.36), then he must click 'Paste'.

Figure 10.18

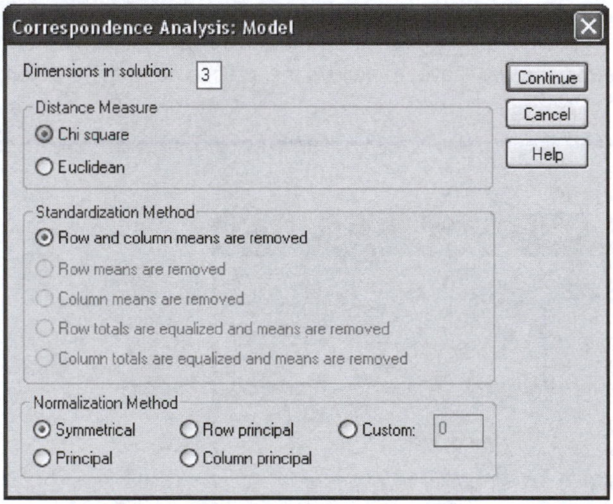

In the 'Correspondence Analysis: Model' window (Figure 10.18), select a 3-dimensional solution (see later in the section on the interpretation of the SPSS output how the maximum number of dimensions is determined).

Since this involves a standard correspondence analysis, based on a contingency table, it would be best for the researcher to choose the 'Chi-square' distance measure. This automatically means that the option 'Row and column means are removed' will be checked as the standardization method.

Choose 'Symmetrical' as the normalization method. The main goal of the analysis is after all the comparison between row (characteristics) and column (clusters) points. If the researcher however is primarily interested in comparisons between all of the column points and between all of the row points themselves, and not in the comparison between row and column points, then it would be best for him to choose 'Principal'. If the goal is to determine the differences or similarities between the categories of the row variable 'characteristic' (column variable 'cluster'), then he would be better off opting for 'Row principal' ('Column principal'). And finally, 'Custom' offers the possibility to create an intermediate solution, by specifying a value between '−1' and '1'. In this way, the value '1' corresponds to 'Row principal', the value '0' corresponds with 'Symmetrical' and the value '−1' with 'Column principal'. It may be said here that the choice of the normalization method will influence the later choice of plots. With the 'Principal' normalization for example, it is not possible to retrieve a 'Biplot' (a map which includes both row and column points). This last visual representation is actually only meaningful in the case of a 'Symmetrical' normalization. If the researcher chooses a 'Row principal' ('Column principal') normalization, then the only recommended option is a scatterplot with row points (column points).

Figure 10.19

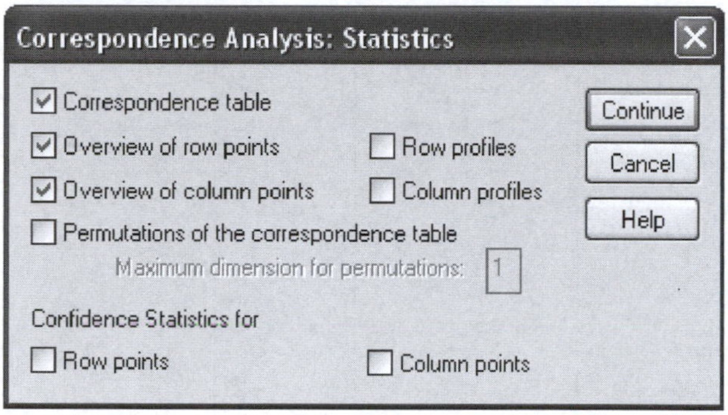

Figure 10.20

In the 'Correspondence Analysis: Statistics' window (Figure 10.19), choose 'Correspondence table', 'Overview of row points' and 'Overview of column points'. This will result in a contingency table in the output window of SPSS, and for each of the row and column points the following statistics: 'Mass', 'Score in Dimension', 'Inertia', 'Contribution of Point to Inertia of Dimension' and 'Contribution of Dimension to Inertia of Point'. A 'Summary' table which provides insight for each dimension into values such as 'Singular value', 'Inertia' and 'Proportion of Inertia Accounted for' will be added to the output automatically.

In the 'Correspondence Analysis: Plots' window (Figure 10.20), choose 'Biplot'. As was indicated above, this will include row as well as column points in the same configuration. The options 'Row points' and 'Column points' will only result in a visual representation of the row points or the column points, respectively.

'ID label width for scatterplots' results in the assignment of labels to the points in the visual representation. The value to be filled in lies between '0' and '20'. The value '0' will link the row or column number to the point (e.g., '1' for the first row point 'ordinary'), and the value '5' for example will assign a label consisting of five characters (e.g., 'ordin' for the row point 'ordinary'). In the current application, the value '0' was chosen, since the assignment of sizeable labels makes the map illegible.

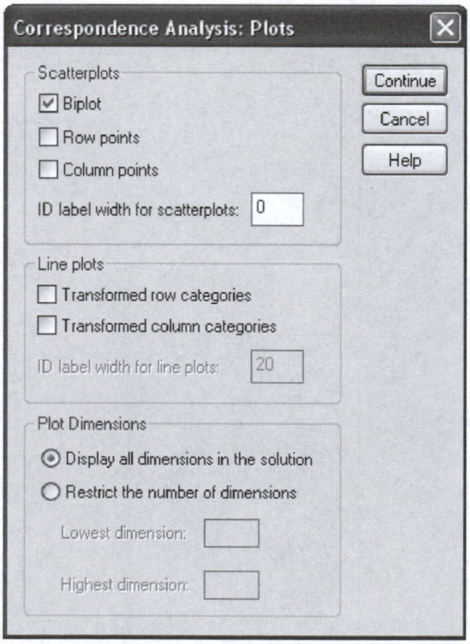

Interpretation of the SPSS output

Figure 10.21

Correspondence Table

Attribute Associated With The Preferred Shopping Centre	Cluster Group				
	Cluster1	Cluster2	Cluster3	Cluster4	Active Margin
Ordinary	0	2	40	2	44
Expensive	30	3	3	6	42
Efficient	2	33	27	2	64
Exclusive	29	1	2	2	34
Quality	71	40	7	24	142
Diversified offer	3	47	18	3	71
Similar shops	2	17	49	2	70
Habit	6	42	18	6	72
Good price quality ratio	4	40	23	5	72
Clothes for more than one season	4	18	32	5	59
Small shops	17	9	25	55	106
To buy	1	33	35	2	71
Availability of parking space	14	36	41	14	105
To look around	19	19	40	64	142
Bargains	3	38	26	8	75
Trendsetting	48	5	7	24	84
Shop fidelity	42	7	13	19	81
Well known brands	55	14	13	25	107
Enjoyment	46	1	2	49	98
Good atmosphere	24	3	49	85	161
A long time shopping	39	4	19	63	125
Fashion-conscious	43	7	15	6	71
Relaxing	5	12	19	70	106
Superficial	2	29	40	0	71
Personal	49	2	4	35	90
Noisy	1	1	1	22	25
Quiet	4	20	50	4	78
Standing	63	2	6	9	80
Pastime	13	6	26	72	117
For everybody	2	15	64	43	124
Decent	0	12	46	0	58
Business class	60	0	2	10	72
Chique	61	2	5	11	79
Busy	6	2	32	52	92
Simple	2	10	57	18	87
Normal	2	10	49	2	63
Young	9	0	44	72	125
Classic	59	24	4	9	96
Social	0	12	26	2	40
Athletic	29	0	5	29	63
Sympathetic	20	2	9	86	117
Demanding	45	0	4	5	54
Smooth	14	2	37	69	122
Popular	0	11	42	0	53
Friendly	8	1	46	42	97
Self-assured	52	0	17	2	71
Shop 1[a]	5	7	5	20	
Shop 2[a]	1	2	13	26	
Shop 3[a]	43	1	1	1	
Shop 4[a]	28	2	1	8	
Shop 5[a]	0	4	32	3	
Shop 6[a]	0	37	26	3	
Shop 7[a]	0	0	3	30	
Active Margin	1008	594	1139	1135	3876

[a]Supplementary row

The associations between the clusters and the shopping makes do not influence the 'Active Marginal'. This is why the addition of the makes to the three-dimensional representation of the clusters and the characteristic will not influence the location of these points.

The interpretation of the output of an CA always starts with an inspection of the 'Correspondence Table' or contingency table (Figure 10.21). The values in this table must agree with the numbers in the original dataset, *Contingency table.sav* (Figure 10.1). This way the researcher can ascertain that the analysis is in fact based on the correct data.

The SPSS output will contain two figures at the end (Figures 10.22 and 10.23), which show the interrelationships between the clusters and the attributes in two dimensions, and do this for the combination of the dimensions '1' and '2', as well as for the combination '1' and '3'[3].

Figure 10.22

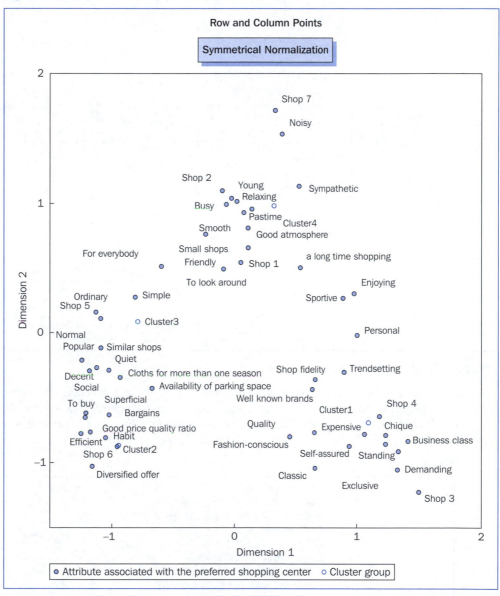

Figure 10.22 *Continued*

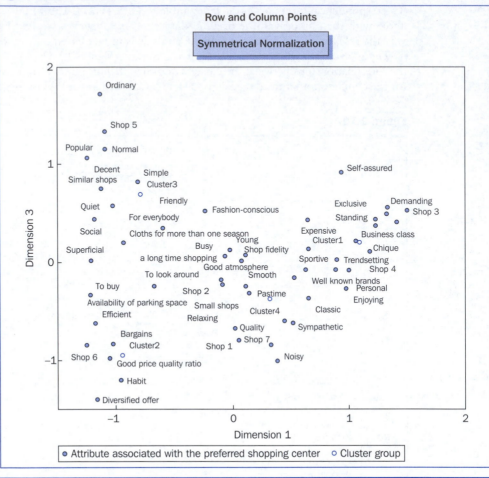

Supporting technique

In this context it is interesting to know that the coordinates of the points and the corresponding labels may be written to a separate data file (*coordinates.sav*) by including the 'OUTFILE = SCORE (*coordinates.sav*)' command in the syntax. This syntax may be obtained by clicking 'Paste' before clicking 'OK' in Figure 10.17. This modified syntax is shown in Figure 10.23.

Figure 10.23

```
CORRESPONDENCE
    TABLE = char(1 53) BY cluster(1 4)
    /SUPPLEMENTARY = char(47,48,49,50,51,52,53)
    /DIMENSIONS = 3
    /MEASURE = CHISQ
    /STANDARDIZE = RCMEAN
    /NORMALIZATION = SYMMETRICAL
    /PRINT = TABLE RPOINTS CPOINTS
    /PLOT = NDIM(1,MAX) BIPLOT(0)
    /OUTFILE=SCORE
```

How would one then describe the dataset (*c: coordinates.sav*) (Figure 10.24)? In total, it contains 57 rows (46 characteristics, 7 shopping centres and 4 clusters).

Figure 10.24

	ROWTYPE	LEVEL_	VARNAME_	DIM1	DIM2	DIM3	var	var	var
34	ROW	Busy	attribute assoc	-.07	.99	.06			
35	ROW	Simple	attribute assoc	-.81	.27	.82			
36	ROW	Normal	attribute assoc	-1.09	-.12	1.15			
37	ROW	Young	attribute assoc	-.03	1.04	.13			
38	ROW	Classic	attribute assoc	.65	-1.04	-.37			
39	ROW	Social	attribute assoc	-1.18	-.30	.44			
40	ROW	Sportive	attribute assoc	.89	.27	-.08			
41	ROW	Sympathic	attribute assoc	.52	1.13	-.62			
42	ROW	Demanding	attribute assoc	1.33	-.91	.56			
43	ROW	Smooth	attribute assoc	.08	.93	.02			
44	ROW	Popular	attribute assoc	-1.24	-.21	1.06			
45	ROW	Friendly	attribute assoc	-.24	.76	.52			
46	ROW	Self-assured	attribute assoc	.94	-.87	.92			
47	ROW	Shop 1	attribute assoc	.05	.54	-.79			
48	ROW	Shop 2	attribute assoc	-.10	1.10	-.18			
49	ROW	Shop 3	attribute assoc	1.50	-1.23	.53			
50	ROW	Shop 4	attribute assoc	1.18	-.64	.11			
51	ROW	Shop 5	attribute assoc	-1.09	.11	1.33			
52	ROW	Shop 6	attribute assoc	-1.25	-.78	-.84			
53	ROW	Shop 7	attribute assoc	.33	1.72	-.84			
54	COLUMN	Cluster1	Cluster group	1.09	-.69	.20			
55	COLUMN	Cluster2	Cluster group	-.95	-.87	-.95			
56	COLUMN	Cluster3	Cluster group	-.79	.09	.69			
57	COLUMN	Cluster4	Cluster group	.32	.98	-.37			

'Rowtype_' indicates whether a row or a column from the original contingency table is involved. 'Level_' shows the 'labels'. 'Varname_' refers to the description of the two variables which are used as input for the CA in SPSS (see [char] and [cluster] in the dataset *Input correspondence analysis.sav*), and finally 'Dimn' corresponds to the scores at the points for the nth dimension.

Figure 10.25

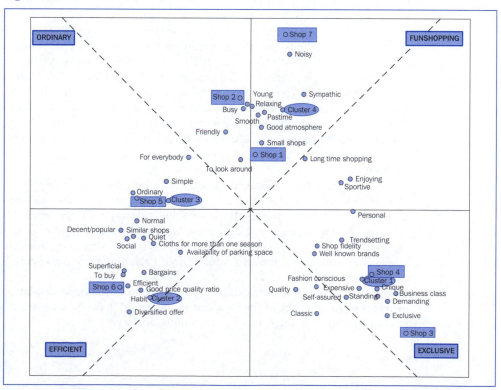

Figure 10.25 shows that there are four separate groups of attributes, each of which situates itself around one of the four clusters. In the first step, the clusters are described on the basis of the characteristics, and in the second step, these characteristics are used to name the two 'subjective' axes.

'Cluster 1' represents those in search of high class, exclusive products and who are very fashion-conscious. The relationship to shopping and shopping centres is characterized by attraction to the chic and expensive and an aversion to everything that is ordinary and less expensive. This type of consumer wishes to clearly distance herself from the 'ordinary' consumer in her relationship with her preferred shopping centre.

'Cluster 2' distances itself completely from everything that has to do with shopping. Shopping should be done as quickly, efficiently and cheaply as possible. The shopping centre must have a broad range of products and ample, convenient parking facilities, so that all of the shopping may be done at one time and quickly. Shopping is not a pleasant activity for this type of consumer, it is a necessity. For this reason, 'Cluster 2' may be found in the map faraway from all of the 'positive' characteristics. You will notice that this also involves fashion-sensitive women.

The consumers in 'Cluster 3' are in search of ordinary, everyday products. These people have a positive attitude with regard to shopping yet in contrast with 'Cluster 1', are definitely not looking for high class and exclusive products. They do not care to distinguish themselves from the others and are comfortable among the masses.

For 'Cluster 4', shopping is considered to be 'funshopping'. They enjoy strolling and browsing around and look at everything. They enjoy shopping for long periods of time. For them, shopping is clearly a pleasant and relaxing way to pass the time. They enjoy a friendly, young, dynamic and fun shopping environment.

On the basis of the interrelationships between the attributes in the visual representation, an attempt may now be made to name the axes. It may be mentioned briefly here that in the case of 'Symmetrical normalization', the axis system will be rotated and the location of the origin may be shifted, without changing the Euclidean distance between the points. This simplifies the interpretation of the output. The **first axis** runs from 'Cluster 4' to 'Cluster 2'. The attributes around 'Cluster 2' are the opposite of those around 'Cluster 4'. The attributes round 'Cluster 2' and the distance to all of the other attributes allow the researcher to conclude that in its relationship with shopping and shopping centres, this cluster group is in search of 'efficiency'. The other pole of the axis is formed by 'Cluster 4' and may be described via the attributes located there. 'Cluster 4' is in search of the opposite of 'Cluster 2', namely 'funshopping'. The first axis could then be called: 'efficient' versus 'funshopping'. The **second axis** runs from 'Cluster 3' to 'Cluster 1'. The consumers in 'Cluster 1' are in search of exclusivity and distance themselves from the masses. 'Cluster 3' is located on the opposite side, and unlike the others, likes to conform and is in search of ordinary, everyday products. The second axis could be named: 'exclusive' versus 'ordinary'.

However, a visual representation alone is insufficient for creating a complete and correct interpretation of the results. After all, the visual representation does not allow the researcher to know (1) if a display in two dimensions provides a 'good' image of the data, (2) what the importance is of each axis, (3) which points have the greatest impact in the orientation of the axes, (4) how 'well' a point is represented in the space, and (5) what can be done with additional external information. Each of these five points is discussed in more depth below.

The first point concerns the question of whether or not a **visual display in two dimensions provides a 'good' image of the data matrix**. A second question may be asked straight away to enquire about the importance of each individual axis.

Figure 10.26

| | | | | | Proportion of Inertia | | Confidence Singular Value | | |
| | | | | | | | | Correlation | |
Dimension	Singular Value	Inertia	Chi-square	Sig.	Accounted for	Cumulative	Standard deviation	2	3
1	.661	.436			.532	.532	.010	.192	.085
2	.525	.275			.336	.868	.013		.186
3	.330	.109			.132	1.000	.017		
Total		.820	3179.255	.000[a]	1.000	1.000			

Summary

[a]135 degrees of freedom

The algorithm calculates the 'inertia' of the solution (.436 for dimension '1', .275 for dimension '2', and .109 for dimension '3'; Figure 10.26), also referred to as 'principal inertia'. This inertia provides a general image of the quality of the solution, in the sense that this criterion indicates what each axis' contribution is to the total solution. This way, the inertia of each axis indicates how much of the total variance in the data is explained by that respective axis. It is expressed as compared to the 'total inertia' (.820), which produces a 'Proportion of Inertia Accounted For'. This proportion is .532, .336 and .132 for the dimensions '1', '2', and '3', respectively. The first dimension thus has the highest percentage of explained variance (53%), followed by the second dimension (34%), followed by the third dimension (13%). It may be said that 100% of the variance is always explained by the minimum of the number of 'active' rows and 'active' columns in the matrix −1. This means that a matrix consisting of 46 active rows and 4 active columns may always be presented perfectly in three dimensions {Mim (46, 4) − 1}. In the current example, the three axes together therefore explain 100% of the inertia (.532 + .336 + .132 = 1).

If the researcher only considers the 2-dimensional solution (dimension '1', dimension '2'), he will lose information. After all, both axes together 'only' explain 87% of the total variance in the data. An added third axis would, in this example, therefore have additionally explained 13% of the variance. Still, the researcher may decide that the data matrix is displayed 'well' in two dimensions. How 'well' it will have to be examined on a case-by-case basis, but the following guideline may be followed: if an axis with a relatively high explained variance (20% or more) is omitted, then the effect of this on the visual representation will have to be studied closely.

Those points which have the greatest impact in the orientation of the axes are determined via the contribution each point makes to the inertia of each axis, or the 'Contribution of Point to Inertia of Dimension' (Figures 10.27 and 10.28, 1 and 2). In this way, the points with a high contribution play the largest role in the determination of the orientation of the axes, and therefore also in the naming and the interpretation thereof.

This type of information is extremely relevant to determining the stability of the solution. After all, if the contribution to an axis is determined nearly entirely by one point, then leaving the relevant row (characteristic) or column (cluster) out of the data matrix and reanalyzing the remaining rows and columns can produce a totally different configuration. If, on the other hand, a point contributes little, then leaving the respective row or column out will have very little influence on the ultimate configuration.

Figure 10.27

Overview Row Points[b]

Attribute Associated With The Preferred Shopping Centre	Mass	Score in Dimension			Inertia	Contribution						Total
						Of Point to Inertia of Dimension			Of Dimension to Inertia of Point			
		1	2	3		1	2	3	1	2	3	
Ordinary	.011	-1.130	.159	1.721	.021	.022	.001	.102	.460	.007	.532	1.000
Expensive	.011	1.063	-.782	.217	.012	.019	.013	.002	.689	.296	.014	1.000
Efficient	.017	-1.176	-.765	-.620	.022	.035	.018	.019	.678	.228	.094	1.000
Exclusive	.009	1.327	-1.055	.492	.016	.023	.019	.006	.637	.320	.044	1.000
Quality	.037	.446	-.801	-.596	.021	.011	.045	.039	.225	.575	.200	1.000
Diversified offer	.018	-1.161	-1.029	-1.400	.038	.037	.037	.109	.426	.266	.309	1.000
Similar shops	.018	-1.124	-.271	.750	.019	.035	.003	.031	.788	.036	.175	1.000
Habit	.019	-.956	-.877	-1.202	.028	.026	.027	.081	.407	.272	.321	1.000
Good price quality ratio	.019	-1.052	-.809	-.978	.026	.031	.023	.054	.526	.247	.227	1.000
Clothes for more than one season	.015	-.933	-.346	.201	.010	.020	.003	.002	.883	.096	.021	1.000
Small shops	.027	.111	.658	-.241	.007	.001	.023	.005	.032	.893	.075	1.000
To buy	.018	-1.218	-.653	-.331	.023	.041	.015	.006	.791	.180	.029	1.000
Availability of parking space	.027	-.673	-.429	-.241	.011	.019	.009	.005	.722	.232	.046	1.000
To look around	.037	-.091	.492	-.225	.005	.000	.017	.006	.036	.852	.112	1.000
Bargains	.019	-1.023	-.633	-.831	.022	.031	.015	.041	.612	.186	.202	1.000
Trendsetting	.022	.898	-.304	.027	.013	.026	.004	.000	.916	.083	.000	1.000
Shop fidelity	.021	.655	-.362	.137	.007	.014	.005	.001	.791	.192	.017	1.000
Well known brands	.028	.630	-.437	-.074	.010	.017	.010	.000	.720	.275	.005	1.000
Enjoying	.025	.978	.303	-.267	.018	.037	.004	.005	.898	.069	.034	1.000
Good atmosphere	.042	.109	.811	.076	.015	.001	.052	.001	.022	.972	.005	1.000
A long time shopping	.032	.531	.504	-.155	.011	.014	.016	.002	.568	.407	.024	1.000
Fashion-conscious	.018	.649	-.769	.432	.012	.012	.021	.010	.428	.478	.094	1.000
Relaxing	.027	.019	1.017	-.671	.019	.000	.054	.037	.000	.785	.215	1.000
Superficial	.018	-1.212	-.620	.019	.021	.041	.013	.000	.828	.172	.000	1.000
Personal	.023	1.003	-.020	-.080	.015	.035	.000	.000	.997	.000	.003	1.000
Noisy	.006	.383	1.535	-1.005	.011	.001	.029	.020	.058	.742	.200	1.000
Quiet	.020	-1.024	-.290	.576	.017	.032	.003	.020	.819	.052	.129	1.000
Standing	.021	1.232	-.858	.438	.030	.047	.029	.012	.690	.266	.043	1.000
Pastime	.030	.140	.957	-.312	.016	.001	.053	.009	.025	.914	.061	1.000
For everybody	.032	-.597	.513	.349	.013	.017	.016	.012	.570	.334	.097	1.000
Decent	.015	-1.245	-.212	1.064	.021	.035	.001	.051	.721	.017	.263	1.000
Business class	.019	1.412	-.835	.409	.032	.056	.025	.009	.758	.211	.032	1.000
Chique	.020	1.233	-.790	.372	.028	.047	.024	.009	.729	.238	.033	1.000
Busy	.024	-.068	.993	.065	.012	.000	.045	.000	.006	.992	.003	1.000
Simple	.022	-.811	.275	.820	.016	.022	.003	.046	.625	.057	.319	1.000
Normal	.016	-1.090	-.117	1.154	.020	.029	.000	.066	.637	.006	.357	1.000
Young	.032	-.025	1.041	.128	.019	.000	.067	.002	.001	.990	.009	1.000
Classic	.025	.654	-1.042	-.365	.022	.016	.051	.010	.315	.636	.049	1.000
Social	.010	-1.183	-.295	.439	.011	.022	.002	.006	.894	.044	.062	1.000
Sportive	.016	.888	.267	-.075	.009	.019	.002	.000	.930	.067	.003	1.000
Sympathetic	.030	.519	1.135	-.617	.030	.012	.074	.035	.182	.690	.128	1.000
Demanding	.014	1.335	-.914	.558	.024	.038	.022	.013	.685	.255	.060	1.000
Smooth	.031	.075	.930	.016	.014	.000	.052	.000	.008	.992	.000	1.000
Popular	.014	-1.245	-.213	1.061	.019	.032	.001	.047	.722	.017	.261	1.000
Friendly	.025	-.238	.763	.523	.011	.002	.028	.021	.086	.706	.208	1.000
Self-assured	.018	.939	-.875	.916	.023	.024	.027	.047	.462	.319	.219	1.000
Shop 1[a]	.010	.051	.543	-.793	.003	.000	.000	.000	.005	.426	.570	1.000
Shop 2[a]	.011	-.102	1.100	-.177	.007	.000	.000	.000	.011	.974	.016	1.000
Shop 3[a]	.012	1.500	-1.226	.528	.028	.000	.000	.000	.628	.333	.039	1.000
Shop 4[a]	.010	1.182	-.644	.111	.012	.000	.000	.000	.806	.190	.004	1.000
Shop 5[a]	.010	-1.091	.109	1.335	.014	.000	.000	.000	.570	.005	.426	1.000
Shop 6[a]	.017	-1.252	-.776	-.843	.027	.000	.000	.000	.653	.199	.148	1.000
Shop 7[a]	.009	.328	1.717	-.840	.016	.000	.000	.000	.038	.836	.126	1.000
Active Total	1.000				.820	1.000	1.000	1.000				

[a]Supplementary point
[b]Symmetrical normalization

These values correspond with the scores from the characteristics and the shops for the three dimensions, and the values for dimensions '1' and '2' have been plotted out in Figure 10.25. These coordinates may also be found in the dataset 'COORDINATES.SAV' (obtained using the syntax in Figure 10.25).

The shops represent additional external information, and will not influence the positions of the characteristics and the clusters in Figure 10.23. The 'Contribution of Point to Inertia of Dimension' is then also '0' for these shops; in other words, they do not play a role in the determination of the orientation of the axes.

The sum of the contributions of the three dimensions to each characteristic and each shop is equal to '1'. 100% of the variance in the specific point is explained using these three dimensions. If the researcher asks for a two-dimensional solution in SPSS, then many 'Total' values will be less than '1': only a limited percentage of the variance in a point may be explained using two dimensions.

The sum of the contributions for the 46 characteristics (active rows in the contingency table) is of equal to '1' for each dimension.

Figure 10.28

		Score in Dimension				Contribution						
						Of Point to Inertia of Dimension			Of Dimension to Inertia of Point			
Cluster Group	Mass	1	2	3	Inertia	1	2	3	1	2	3	Total
Cluster1	.260	1.093	−.693	.201	.274	.470	.238	.032	.749	.239	.013	1.000
Cluster2	.153	−.946	−.867	−.950	.197	.208	.219	.420	.461	.307	.232	1.000
Cluster3	.294	−.790	.086	.690	.168	.278	.004	.424	.719	.007	.274	1.000
Cluster4	.293	.317	.982	−.374	.181	.045	.539	.124	.107	.818	.074	1.000
Active Total	1.000				.820	1.000	1.000	1.000				

Overview Column Points[a]

[a]Symmetrical normalization

What does the above imply for the current application? Which characteristics/clusters carry a large weight in the explanation of the axes? For the characteristics, the 'natural weight' appears to be approximately .020 (1/46 = .022), and for the clusters this is equal to .25 (1/4 = .25). The points for which the contribution is higher than this natural weight play an important role in the orientation and interpretation of the axes, and the characteristics/ clusters with the highest contributions are the most important in determining the axes. In particular the characteristics 'to buy' (.041), 'superficial' (.041), 'standing' (.047), 'business class' (.056), and 'chic' (.047) appear to be responsible for the orientation of the X-axis, and the attributes 'quality' (.045), 'good atmosphere' (.052), 'relaxing' (.054), 'pastime' (.053), 'busy' (.045), 'young' (.067), 'classic' (.051), 'sympathetic' (.074) and 'smooth' (.052) appear to determine the direction of the Y-axis. With regard to the clusters, the groups '1' and '4' in particular appear to be important in the orientation of the X-axis ('Cluster 1' with .470) and the Y-axis ('Cluster 4' with .539). Each of these points occupies a fairly extreme position in Figure 10.25.

In addition to the 'subjective' (intuitive) designation of the axes (see two axes 'ordinary versus exclusive' and 'funshopping versus efficient', which follow from the study of Figure 10.25), there is also the 'objective' (based on numbers) interpretation such as that explained above (see 'the contribution of each point to the inertia of each axis'). In this example, it would be best for the researcher to choose the 'subjective' interpretation since it allows the definition of two clearly distinct axes, which also makes it possible to clearly distinguish the four clusters from one another and to characterize them.

How well a row (characteristic or shop) **or a column** (cluster group) of the contingency table is **displayed in a space** formed by dimensions '1' and '2' for example (see Figure 10.25) may be seen in the columns entitled 'Contribution of Dimension to Inertia of Point' (Figures 10.27 and 10.28, 3 and 4). This is evidenced by 'ordinary' and 'shop1' which appear to be less well represented in this 2-dimensional solution. The third axis, after all, explains 53.2% and 57% respectively of the variance in these points. They may also best be represented and interpreted in a 3-dimensional space. If the researcher still wishes to choose a 2-dimensional map, then it is advisable to use the necessary care in interpreting the location of these two points in the visual representation. This location is the result of a straight line projection of both 'points' onto the (dimension '1', dimension '2') surface.

An interesting feature of correspondence analysis is that **additional external information** may be introduced into an existing visual representation without the location of the previously included points changing. This occurs via the 'transition formula' and is also referred to as the 'passive cell' option. In SPSS terms, this amounts to the following: the 'supplementary' rows or columns from the contingency table are added to a pre-existing map, which is based on the 'active' rows and columns.

In the current example, the different shopping centres will be introduced into the visual representation of characteristics and clusters as points. These shopping centres are part of the original contingency table after all, and have been labelled as 'supplementary' (Figures 10.29 and 10.30).

Figure 10.29

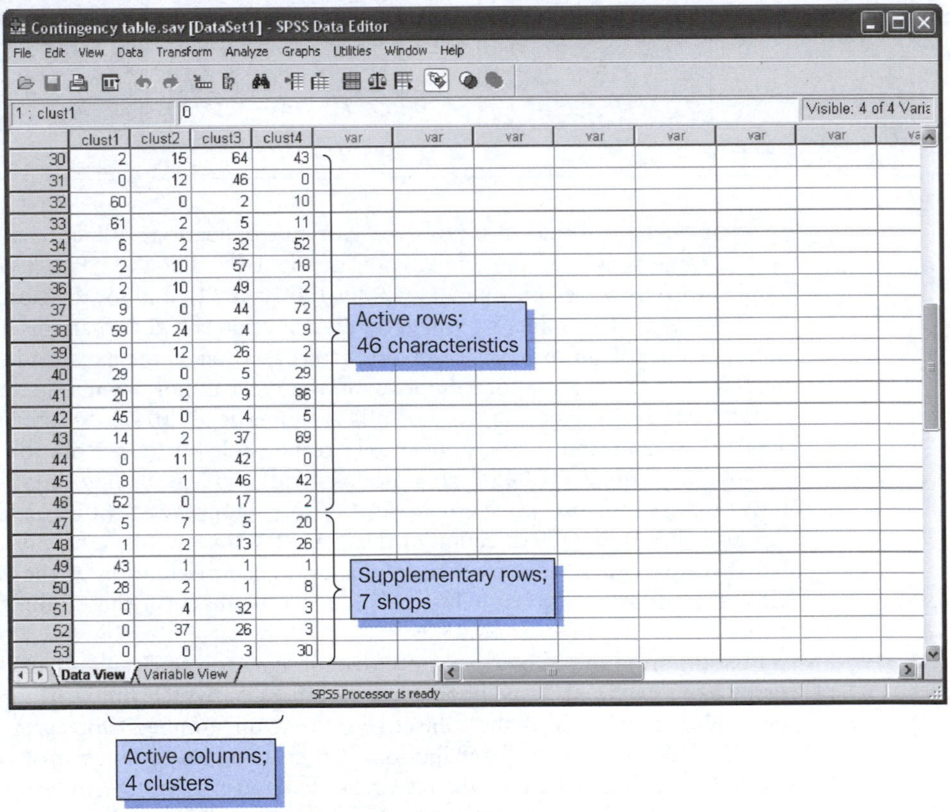

Once again, it may be studied how 'well' or 'poorly' this additional information is shown in the visual representation. It was already mentioned in the previous section that shop '1' is not displayed as well in the 2-dimensional solution, since only 43% of the variance in this point (Figure 10.27, 3) is explained by the axes X and Y from Figure 10.25.

The coordinates for the shops may be found at the bottom of Figure 10.27, in the columns 'Score in Dimension'. Figure 10.25 contains the shops and allows the relationships between the clusters, the characteristics and the shops to be determined.

The respondents in 'Cluster 1' have a clearly expressed preference for shopping centres '3' and '4', to which the other clusters are much less attracted. These two shopping centres are very exclusive and expensive. 'Cluster 2' has a clear relationship with shopping centre '6', which is in fact a general centre with a large car park. 'Cluster 3' demonstrates a preference for shopping centre '5' which may be described as being popular. And finally the consumers in 'Cluster 4' like to shop in shopping centres '1', '2', and '7' which are very lively and geared towards young shoppers.

Figure 10.30

Decent	0	12	46	0	58
Business class	60	0	2	10	72
Chique	61	2	5	11	79
Busy	6	2	32	52	92
Simple	2	10	57	18	87
Normal	2	10	49	2	63
Young	9	0	44	72	125
Classic	59	24	4	9	96
Social	0	12	26	2	40
Sportive	29	0	5	29	63
Sympathetic	20	2	9	86	117
Demanding	45	0	4	5	54
Smooth	14	2	37	69	122
Popular	0	11	42	0	53
Friendly	8	1	46	42	97
Self-assured	52	0	17	2	71
Shop 1[a]	5	7	5	20	
Shop 2[a]	1	2	13	26	
Shop 3[a]	43	1	1	1	
Shop 4[a]	28	2	1	8	
Shop 5[a]	0	4	32	3	
Shop 6[a]	0	37	26	3	
Shop 7[a]	0	0	3	30	
Active Margin	1008	594	1139	1135	3876

[a] Supplementary row

43 of the 77 respondents in 'Cluster 1' have indicated shop '3' as their preferred shopping centre. This shop will therefore have to lie close to 'Cluster 1' in Figure 10.25.

The preference patterns for the clusters with regard to the shopping centres differ significantly from one another.

The visual representation also allows an estimation of the degree of competition between the different shopping centres. The conclusion which may be drawn from the map is that the different shopping centres in Brussels do, in fact, anticipate the individual consumer demand patterns. Not one of the shopping centres assumes a true middle position ('stuck in the middle').

Next, cross tables may be created between the clusters and all of the other questions from the questionnaire (such as age, language, brands purchased, visits – in the past and present – to shopping centres). These data serve to allow a better identification of the segments found. A number of significant results are retrieved. The clusters appear to differ significantly in terms of socio-demographic characteristics such as age and language. 'Cluster 1' is relatively older (45–60: 28%), French-speaking (66%) and only 19% are buyers of the client's brand; 'Cluster 2' is also relatively older (45–60: 19%), French-speaking (66%), and contains the largest number of buyers of the client's brand (36%); 'Cluster 3' is relatively young (18–44: 40%), less French-speaking (50%), and 30% are buyers of the client's brand; 'Cluster 4' is also relatively young (18–44: 43%), with a very high percentage which are French-speaking (84%), and not very interested in the client's brand (16%). For confidentiality reasons, the results from other cross tables are not shown in this application.

Contingency table as input for factorial correspondence analysis: Syntax

In a previous section, it was discussed that a contingency table can serve as direct input for CA. The researcher cannot make use of the input screens from SPSS however, but will have to use the following syntax instead (Figure 10.31).

Figure 10.31

```
CORRESPONDENCE
    TABLE = ALL (53, 4)
    /SUPPLEMENTARY ROW (47,48,49,50,51,52,53)
    /DIMENSIONS = 3
    /MEASURE = CHISQ
    /STANDARDIZE = RCMEAN
    /NORMALIZATION = SYMMETRICAL
    /PRINT = TABLE RPOINTS CPOINTS
    /PLOT = NDIM(1,MAX) BIPLOT(0)
    /OUTFILE = SCORE (c: coordinates.sav) .
```

Clarification of the syntax:

- TABLE = ALL (53, 4): refers to the use of a contingency table with 53 rows (46 characteristics and 7 shopping centres) and 4 columns (4 clusters);

- /SUPPLEMENTARY ROW (47, 48, 49, 50, 51, 52, 53): refers to the fact that the last 7 rows of the contingency table (the 7 shopping centres) are supplementary rows, and will therefore be added to the map as additional external information;

- /DIMENSIONS = 3: refers to a 3-dimensional solution;

- /MEASURE = CHISQ and /STANDARDIZE = RCMEAN: default values for the distance criterion and the method of standardization. It may be said here that only a RCMEAN standardization (row and column averages are removed) can correspond to a Chi-square distance, and not a RMEAN, for example (in which only row means are removed) or a CMEAN (in which only column means are removed);

- /NORMALIZATION = SYMMETRICAL: refers to the fact that the main goal of the analysis is the comparison between row (characteristics) and column points (clusters);

- /PRINT = TABLE RPOINTS CPOINTS: TABLE produces the contingency table complete with 'active margins' (Figure 10.21), RPOINTS is linked to the rows from the contingency table (characteristics and shops) and shows 'Mass', 'Score in Dimension', 'Inertia', 'Contribution of Point to Inertia of Dimension' and 'Contribution of Dimension to Inertia of Point' (Figure 10.27), and CPOINTS shows the same statistics as RPOINTS, but then for the columns (clusters) of the contingency table (Figure 10.28). The 'Summary' table (Figure 10.26) is always included;

- /PLOT = NDM (1, MAX) BIOPLOT (0): NDIM (1, MAX) refers to the fact that each of the three dimensions is included in the visual representation (Figure 10.22). If the following command NDIM (1, 2) is given, then only a 2-dimensional plot will be included, and this will show the dimensions '1' and '2'. BIPLOT indicates that both row and column elements are included in the plot. (0) refers to the fact that column and row numbers are assigned to the points in the map (e.g., the point that corresponds to the first row from the contingency table will be labelled '1'). If this value is greater than '0' (with a maximum of '20'), for example '5', then the points will be labelled with the corresponding labels up to and including '5' characters;

- /OUTFILE = SCORE (c: Coordinates.sav): results in an extra dataset (coordinates.sav; Figure 10.24), which shows the labels and scores of each of the row and column points for the three dimensions.

Supporting technique

How does one actually run this syntax?

Figure 10.32

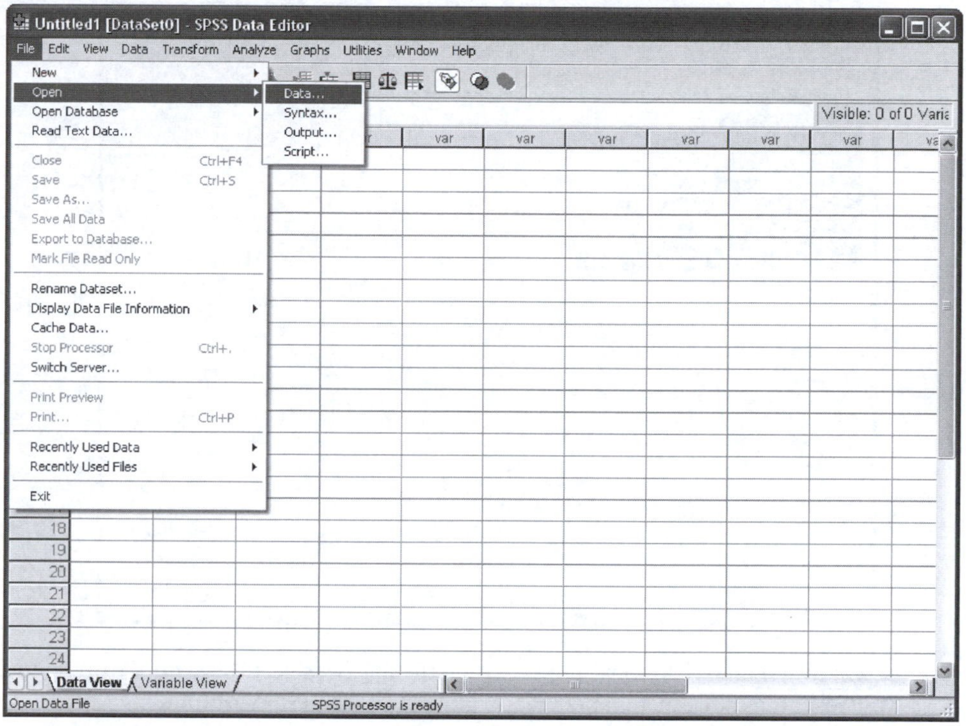

Go to File/Open/Data (Figure 10.32), and choose the *Contingency table.sav* dataset.

Figure 10.33

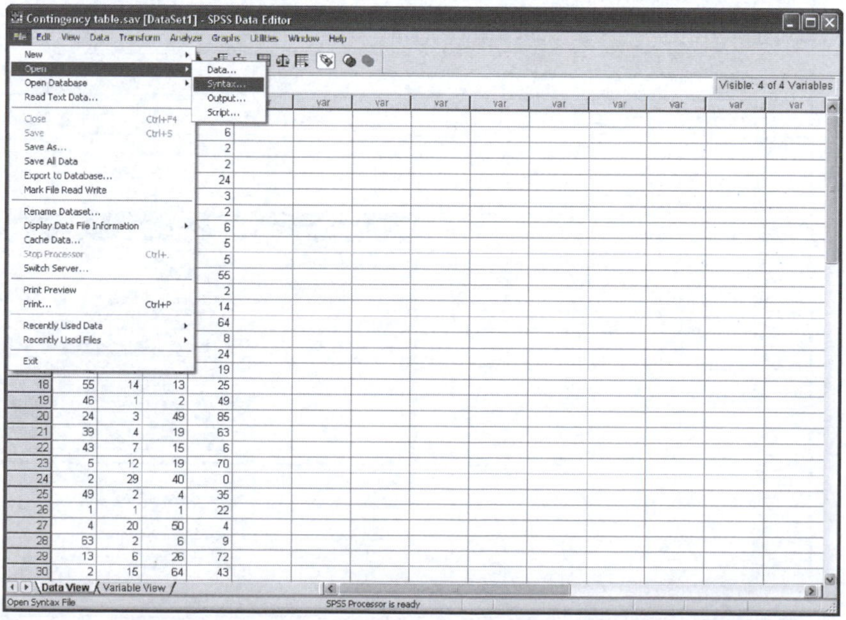

After opening the dataset, go to File/Open/Syntax (Figure 10.33), and request the existing syntax *Without restructure option.sps*.

Figure 10.34

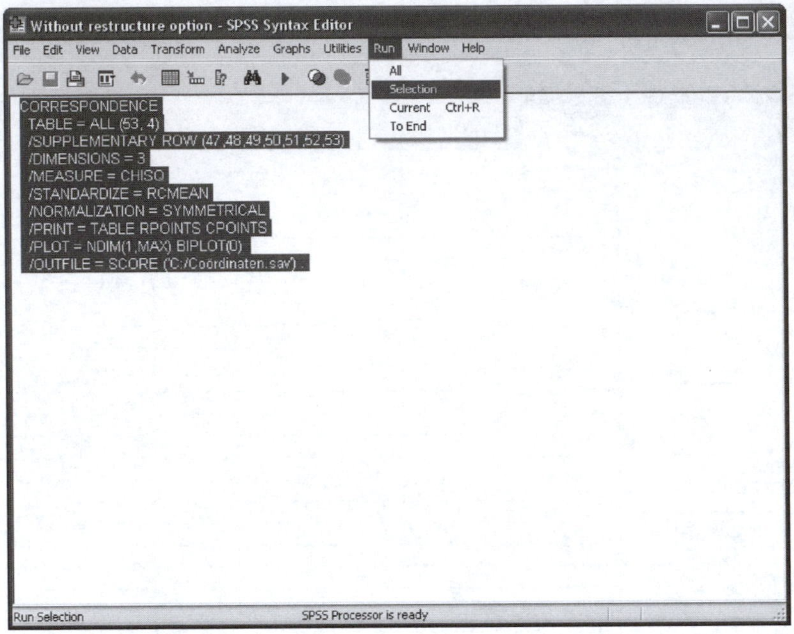

The syntax window (Figure 10.34) will open. Using the mouse, select the syntax from Figure 10.31. Then choose Run/Selection in the menu and SPSS will produce the desired output.

Figure 10.35

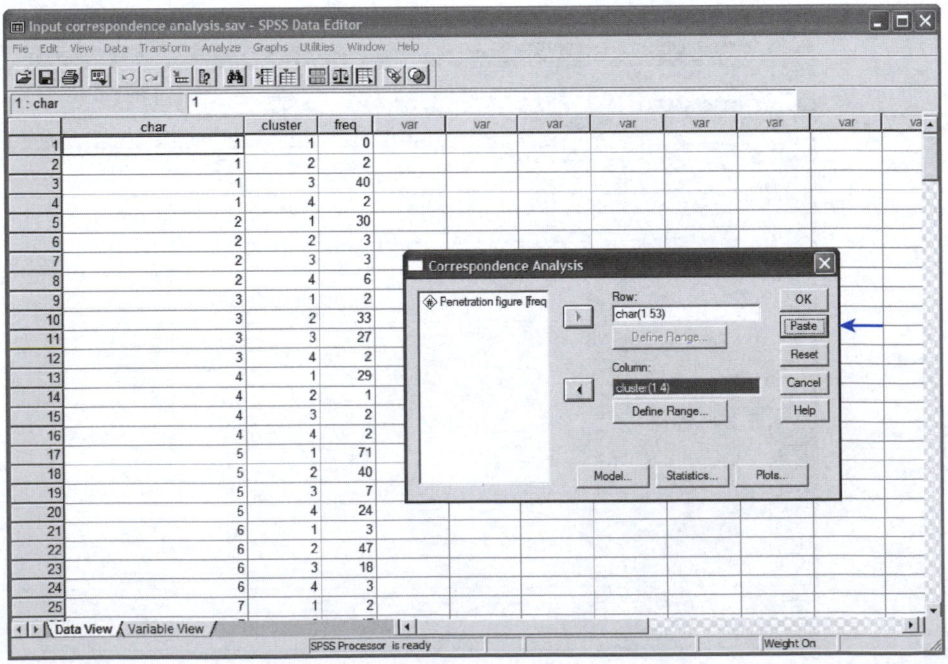

If the researcher works directly with input screens, and does so for the dataset *Input correspondence analysis.sav*, he may use the 'Paste' button in the 'Correspondence Analysis' window (Figure 10.35) to convert the input commands into a syntax which will appear in the 'SPSS Syntax Editor' window (Figure 10.36) and will resemble the syntax shown in Figure 10.37.

Figure 10.36

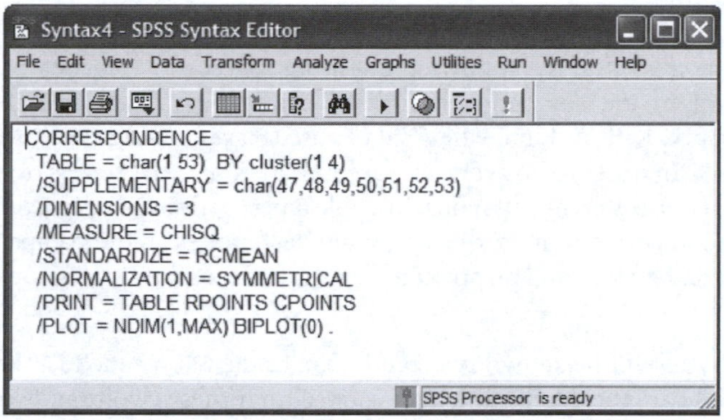

```
CORRESPONDENCE
  TABLE = char(1 53)  BY cluster(1 4)
  /SUPPLEMENTARY = char(47,48,49,50,51,52,53)
  /DIMENSIONS = 3
  /MEASURE = CHISQ
  /STANDARDIZE = RCMEAN
  /NORMALIZATION = SYMMETRICAL
  /PRINT = TABLE RPOINTS CPOINTS
  /PLOT = NDIM(1,MAX) BIPLOT(0) .
```

Figure 10.37

```
CORRESPONDENCE
  TABLE = char(1 53) BY cluster(1 4)
  /SUPPLEMENTARY = char(47,48,49,50,51,52,53)
  /DIMENSIONS = 3
  /MEASURE = CHISQ
  /STANDARDIZE = RCMEAN
  /NORMALIZATION = SYMMETRICAL
  /PRINT = TABLE RPOINTS CPOINTS
  /PLOT = NDIM(1, MAX) BIPLOT(0).
```

How do the two syntaxes in Figures 10.31 and Figure 10.37 differ from one another?

■ TABLE = char(1 53) BY cluster(1 4): refers to the fact that the contingency table is formed by the inclusion of all of the possible combinations of the variables 'characteristic' and 'cluster', whereby this first variable contains 53 categories and the last contains 4.

■ /SUPPLEMENTARY = char(47, 48, 49, 50, 51, 52, 53): indicates that the variable 'characteristic' contains 7 supplementary, and therefore non-active categories. These correspond to the different shopping centres, and will therefore be input in the map as additional external information.

■ /OUTFILE = SCORE (*Coordinates.sav*): this command is missing from Figure 10.37. The retrieval of an extra dataset which contains labels and coordinates for each of the row and column points is then also possible only through the addition of an extra command line to the syntax (and not via the input screens in SPSS).

If the researcher would like to apply the syntax from Figure 10.37 directly to the dataset *Input correspondence analysis.sav* (and therefore does not want to use the input screens), then he must not forget to first assign a weight to every case according to the 'frequency' variable (Figures 10.7, 10.8 and 10.9).

Example 2

'Three-way, two-mode' MDS – 'two-way, one-mode' MDS using replications in PROXSCAL

Managerial problem

The manufacturer of Mars candy bars would like to conduct an image study. More specifically, the company is interested in the following question: where is Mars located in a perceptual space with regard to the competing brands of candy bars, such as Balisto (Korn-Mix, Cereal-Mix), Bounty, KitKat, Lion, Milka Lila Pause (Hazelnut – Praline), Milky Way, Nuts, Snickers and Twix. In order to answer this question, and, in other words, to gain insight into how alike (similar) or different (dissimilar) people's perceptions are regarding Mars in comparison with the competing brands, the marketing department of the company has drawn up the list of questions below, and has presented this questionnaire to 50 people to answer.

Question 1

In this question, you will be shown two candy bar brands at a time (Table 10.4). For each pair, you must indicate the degree to which you feel that these two brands of candy bars are alike or different. There are no pre-set criteria for this comparison task; you may evaluate them on the basis of your own insight.

The following applies to all of the comparisons:

1 = the candy bar brands bear a strong resemblance to one another

9 = the candy bar brands differ greatly from one another

Fill your responses in at your own pace. It is important that you think carefully about each comparison before giving your answer.

Table 10.4

		Very similar 1	2	3	4	5	6	7	8	Very different 9
Balisto	Bounty	☐	☐	☐	☐	☐	☐	☐	☐	☐
Twix	KitKat	☐	☐	☐	☐	☐	☐	☐	☐	☐
Nuts	Lion	☐	☐	☐	☐	☐	☐	☐	☐	☐
Milka Lila Pause	Balisto	☐	☐	☐	☐	☐	☐	☐	☐	☐
Snickers	Bounty	☐	☐	☐	☐	☐	☐	☐	☐	☐
KitKat	Milky Way	☐	☐	☐	☐	☐	☐	☐	☐	☐
Lion	Twix	☐	☐	☐	☐	☐	☐	☐	☐	☐
Milka Lila Pause	Mars	☐	☐	☐	☐	☐	☐	☐	☐	☐
Balisto	Snickers	☐	☐	☐	☐	☐	☐	☐	☐	☐
Milky Way	Lion	☐	☐	☐	☐	☐	☐	☐	☐	☐
Nuts	Milka Lila Pause	☐	☐	☐	☐	☐	☐	☐	☐	☐
Mars	Balisto	☐	☐	☐	☐	☐	☐	☐	☐	☐

. . .

'Question 1' contains a total of 45 pairs of candy bar brands, since ten brands are compared with one another and it is assumed that the degree of similarity is identical for pairs such as 'Balisto-Bounty' and 'Bounty-Balisto'. The formula which lies at the basis of the number '45' is the following: 10*(10 − 1)/2. From this, we can see that the creation of a perceptual map for more than ten brands on the basis of a 'direct' collection of associations quickly leads to the scoring of a large number of brand pairs, which requires a great deal of effort on the part of the respondent.

The scores which are recorded in this way are defined as 'dissimilarities' instead of as 'similarities' since a higher score corresponds to a greater dissimilarity, a greater difference, or less of a similarity between the two brands of the pair in question.

After presenting this question to the 50 people participating in the study, the answers are input in the 'SPSS Data Editor', which will lead to the creation of a dataset such as the one shown in Figure 10.38.

Figure 10.38

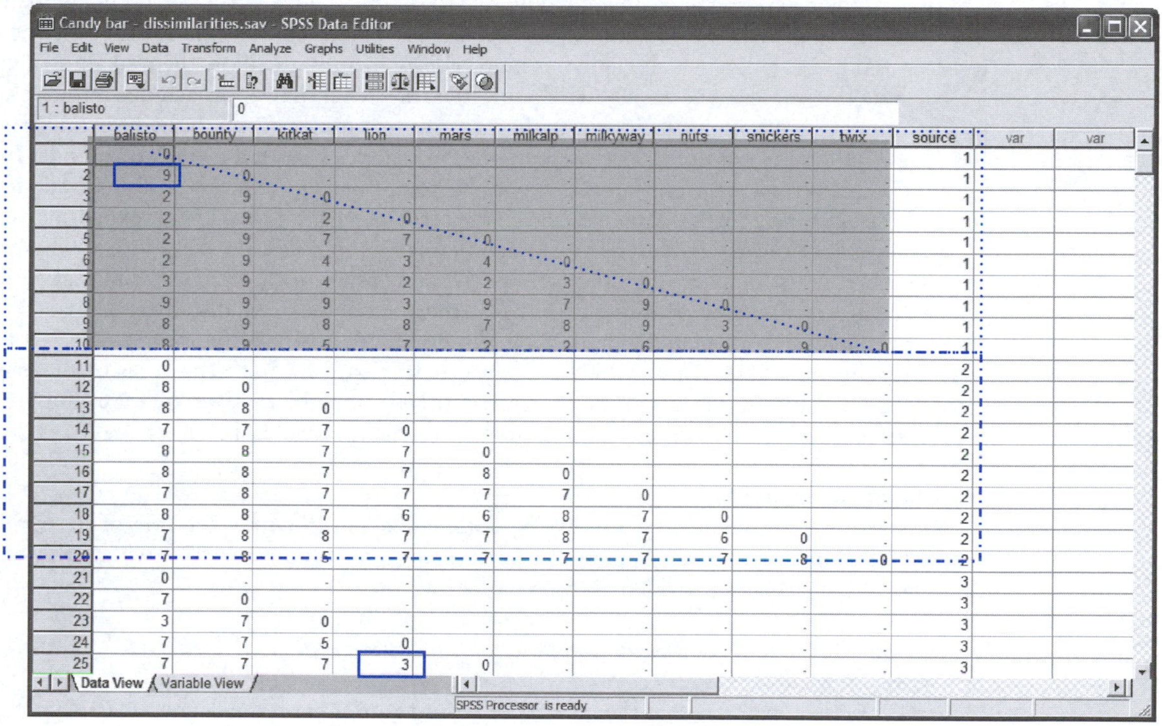

A number of points may be made with regard to the dataset above:

- Ten successive rows will be assigned to each of the 50 respondents. In other words, the first ten rows are linked to respondent '1' and the rows '11' through '20' are linked to respondent '2'. This is shown by the variable [source].

- Just like the columns (with the exception of the [source] column), the rows also correspond to the ten candy bar brands. So, row '1' stands for Balisto, row '2' for Bounty, row '3' for KitKat, row '4' for Lion, row '5' for Mars, row '6' for Milka Lila Pause, row '7' for Milky Way, row '8' for Nuts, row '9' for Snickers and row '10' for Twix. Row '11' stands for Balisto again, row '12' for Bounty, etc.

- The first respondent perceives Balisto and Bounty to be very different from one another since he assigns the value '9' to the first pair in the question (see second row, first column in the dataset). According to the third respondent, the Lion-Mars pair is more or less the same, since he notes the value '3' in the dataset (see 25th row and fourth column).

■ For each respondent, the 45 answers together form the 'bottom triangle' of a square, symmetrical matrix (see for respondent '1' the grey area in the dataset). The cells above the main diagonal[4] which are thus a mirror image of those below it must not be filled in for a PROXSCAL analysis. Even the cells on the main diagonal may remain empty. It must be said that if the researcher has asymmetrical data, the completion of the entire matrix is necessary. A brief example of asymmetrical data: ten people indicate on a scale of 1 to 9 how nice they feel the other nine people are. For example, person A may feel that person B is very nice and score a 9, while person B might want nothing to do with A and gives that person a score of 3.

■ For each respondent, the values on the main diagonal are equal to zero. This is logical since the scores are for dissimilarities, and the perceived difference is obviously nil for pairs such as Balisto-Balisto, Bounty-Bounty, etc.

Initially, the marketing department would like to obtain an idea of the perceptual map of the ten candy bar brands. In addition, they would also like to gain insight into the characteristics of the candy bars which guide this map. This will, after all, allow them to adjust the Mars candy bars image, if necessary. To do this, the researcher may approach this intuitively by examining the map, and to interpret the axes, for example, on the basis of candy bar brands which obtain extreme scores or by going in search of related groups of brands. In addition to an intuitive approach, it is also possible to perform an 'external analysis' of additional data, and specifically to analyze the characteristics of candy bars (e.g., expensive vs. inexpensive, for children vs. for everyone, high in calories vs. low-calorie). These attributes may also be used to impose a 'restriction' on the perceptual map, which should make an interpretation of the axes possible in terms of these attributes. Finally, there is also the 'Procrustes analysis' in which the map is compared with a known configuration, which follows from previous research or which is derived beforehand from a hypothesis or theory. The external analysis, the imposition of restrictions upon the perceptual map and the Procrustes analysis will however not be examined further in this book.

Technique: supplement
Before starting with the display of the SPSS commands and the interpretation of the SPSS outputs, an explanation of a number of theoretical concepts is necessary. We will do this on the basis of the example provided above.

Underlying model, and transformation function used: per individual matrix or for the entire 'three-way, two-mode' dataset
Figure 10.38 demonstrates that the researcher has information on the degree of association between ten candy bar brands, and has this data for each of the 50 respondents. This type of data may be analysed in different ways, which will be explained below.

If the researcher assumes that the distance relationships of all 50 individual matrices all have the same underlying structure and the numbers in the one matrix may be compared with the numbers in another matrix, and he would like to refrain from averaging the 50 matrices regardless, he may choose to employ **Replicated Multidimensional Scaling (RMDS)**[5] in which the data are considered to be **'Unconditional'**[6]. This last term is directly linked to the second assumption, namely the fact that all of the numbers from the 'three-way, two-mode' dataset may be compared with one another. If this is not the case and the researcher drops the second assumption, then this is referred to as **'Matrix-Conditionality'**[7]. This means that it is possible that all 50 respondents 'observe' or 'have in mind' the same relationships between the brands, yet all assign numbers in their own, individual manner to the relationships in scoring the brands-pairs in 'question 1'. Where the one person may use an eight, another person may give a score of five in indicating the same degree of association for one and the same pair of candy bars. It may also occur that the one respondent assigns a seven to brands which only differ slightly from one another, while another uses this seven for brands with a large difference between them (one person's seven therefore does not have the same meaning as the other person's seven). In these types of cases, there is of course no point in comparing the numbers assigned by one respondent with these assigned by another RP. This implies that, in terms of transformation functions (see 'Measurement level of input and output' for further explanation), every individual matrix will have to have its own function, whereas in the 'unconditional' case, a single function for the entire 'three-way, two-mode' dataset is sufficient. The ultimate goal of RMDS is to arrive at an x-dimensional solution, which describes the distance data for the 50 individual matrices 'collectively' in the best manner possible, and thus will be a 'compromise' solution. **The current example will be worked out further on the basis of RMDS, with a matrix-conditional approach to the data.**

Multiplicative, linear or monotone transformation, and discrete or continuous treatment of ties

In the section 'Measurement level of input and output', different transformation functions were presented, and it was demonstrated that the choice of a certain function is closely related to the measurement level of the collected associations. In the current example, the associations are scored on a 9-point scale (see question 1 asked under the 'Managerial problem' section), which is seen as ordinal data in strict methodological terms, however is sometimes nonetheless treated by researchers as interval data when equal intervals are assumed. **The scores will be viewed as being 'ordinal' here, which implies a monotone transformation function. Moreover, a 'continuous' instead of 'discrete' approach to the ties will be chosen.** The associations are recorded between 45 pairs of candy bar brands and this is done on the basis of only a limited number of categories, namely nine (possible score per pair goes from 1, 'very similar' to 9, 'very different'). Brand pairs with the same score do not necessarily have to be at the same distance from one another in the perceptual map.

Minimum requirements for a PROXSCAL analysis

It is important to know that PROXSCAL requires a minimum of three variables, in this case, three brands. In the current example, this requirement has been satisfied since a perceptual map has been requested for ten candy bar brands.

Definitions

In performing the SPSS commands, the terms 'proximity', 'transformed proximity' and 'distance' will appear in the windows. 'Proximity' stands for the similarities or the dissimilarities (dependent on the example, in the current application thus for dissimilarities), and therefore for the values in Figure 10.38. 'Transformed proximity', also referred to as 'disparity', corresponds to the transformed similarities or dissimilarities, and therefore the pseudo distances. 'Distance' finally is translated as the distance-in-the-solution.

Problem

The subsection 'Problem' contains two parts: (1) data specification and (2) dimensionality of the solution. The specific questions for each of these parts are discussed next then shown.

For the dataset *Candy bar – dissimilarities.sav*, indicate the format for the data (proximity – direct collection of the associations) and the number of matrices (multiple), and also define the 'Proximity' and the 'Source' variables.

Determine the optimal dimensionality, taking the 1-dimensional through 8-dimensional solutions into consideration. Base the choice on five points: (1) the stress value; (2) the 'Scree Plot'; (3) the number of points in the perceptual map; (4) the number of original scores; and (5) an intuitive interpretation of the contents of the map.

Each of these will be treated in succession, first showing the SPSS commands and then, if available, the SPSS outputs and their interpretations. Use an 'add-on' module of SPSS, viz. PROXSCAL, to concretize the above.

Solution

SPSS commands: data specification

Figure 10.39

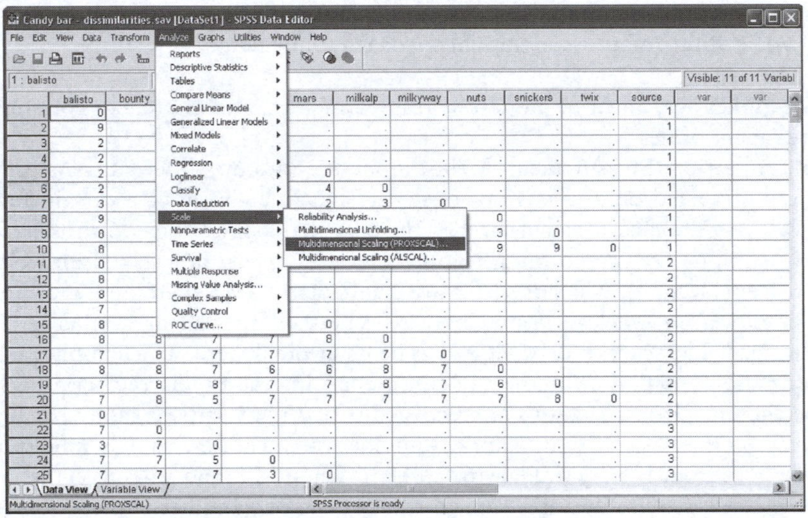

Go to Analyze/Scale/Multidimensional Scaling (PROXSCAL) (Figure 10.39)

Figure 10.40

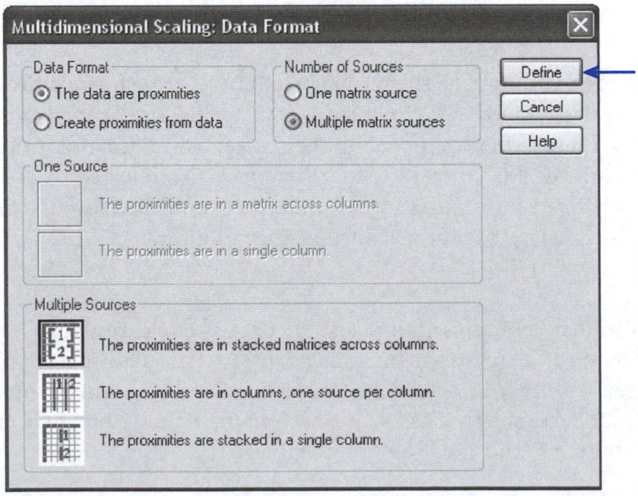

The 'Multidimensional Scaling: Data Format' window (Figure 10.40) will appear, and the researcher must define the contents and the structure of the dataset *Candy bar – dissimilarities.sav* here.

The numbers in the dataset have been obtained by asking 50 people 'question 1', and for each brand-pair, to indicate the degree of dissimilarity directly (a higher score corresponds to a larger perceived difference between the two brands). This is why the option 'The data are proximities' must be chosen instead of 'Create proximities from data'.

Select the option 'Multiple matrix sources', since the dataset contains a dissimilarities matrix for each of the 50 respondents.

Since Figure 10.38 shows that the dissimilarities matrices for successive respondents are placed under one another, choose 'The proximities are in stacked matrices across columns'.

After defining 'Data Format', 'Number of Sources' and 'Multiple Sources', click 'Define', and the 'Multidimensional Scaling (Proximities in Matrices Across Columns)' window (Figure 10.41) will open.

Figure 10.41

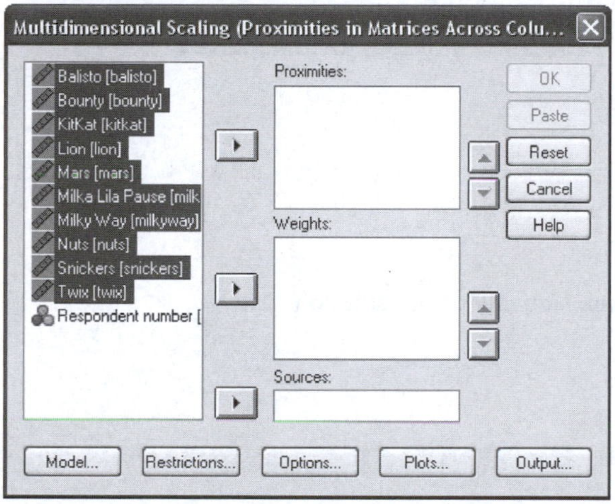

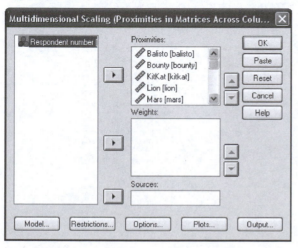

Figure 10.42

Select the ten brands [balisto], [bounty], [kitkat], [lion], [mars], [milkalp], [milkyway], [nuts], [snickers] and [twix] in the left-hand column. To do this click 'Balisto' with the left mouse button, keep it depressed and drag it downwards to 'Twix'. Now move the brands to the 'Proximities' box using the top arrow ▣. An image like the one shown in Figure 10.42 will now appear.

Select the variable 'Respondent number', and move it to the 'Sources' box by clicking on the bottom arrow ▣ (Figure 10.42). If the researcher is working with several matrices (in this case there are 50), then a variable must be indicated in the 'Sources' box which indicates the source to which each row in the dataset belongs (so for every 'case'), and therefore the respondent from which it originated.

Figure 10.43

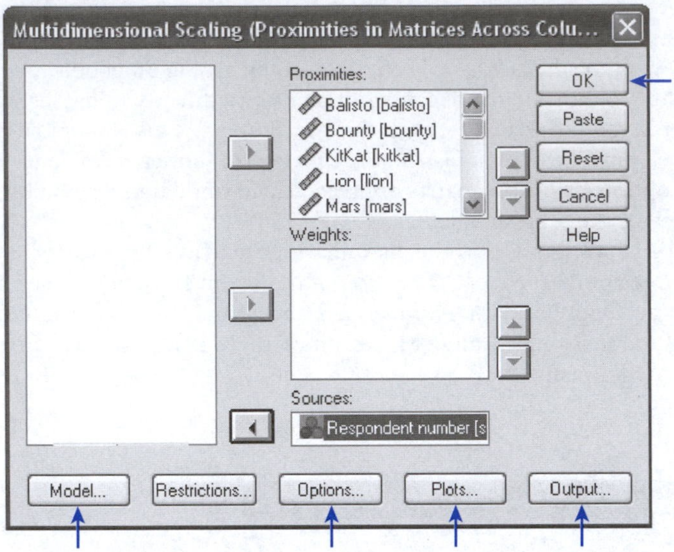

The 'Model', 'Options', 'Plots' and 'Output' buttons will be defined in line with part 2 of the problem definition, after which clicking 'OK' will produce the desired output (Figure 10.43).

SPSS commands: dimensionality of the solution

Figure 10.44

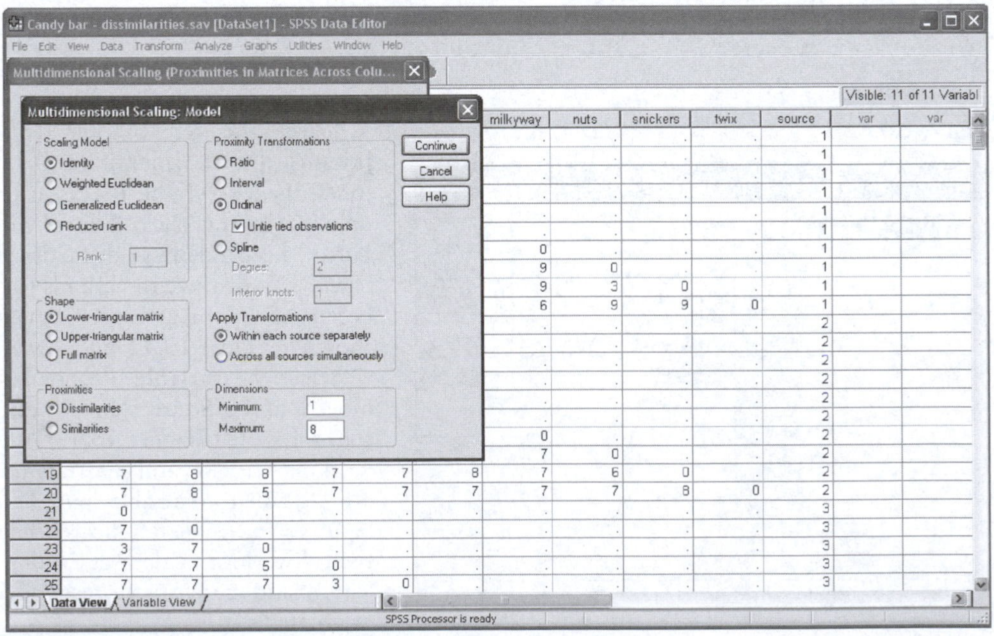

In the main window, 'Multidimensional Scaling (Proximities in Matrices across Columns)' (Figure 10.43), click 'Model', and the 'Multidimensional Scaling: Model' (Figure 10.44) window will appear.

In the sections 'Underlying model, and transformation function used: per individual matrix or for the entire "three-way, two-mode" dataset' and 'Multiplicative, linear or monotone transformation, and discrete or continuous treatment of ties, the following are indicated: (1) this example is being analysed using RMDS, with a matrix-conditional approach to the data, and (2) the data are being subjected to a monotone transformation function, with a continuous treatment of the ties. For this reason, choose the options 'Scaling Model – Identity' and 'Apply Transformations – Within each source separately' to guarantee the first point, and for the option 'Proximity Transformations – Ordinal', supplemented by 'Untie tied observations', to guarantee the second point.

Under 'Shape' choose 'Lower-triangular matrix', since the associations between the brands are included in the 'lowest' triangles of the square symmetrical matrices (see Figure 10.38). Choose 'Full matrix', if the dataset contains asymmetrical matrices.

Under 'Proximities', select the 'Dissimilarities' option. The answers to 'question 1', which form the input for the analysis, are, after all, 'dissimilarities'; a higher score for 'question 1' corresponds to a greater difference between the two brands of the relevant pair. Choose 'Similarities' if a higher score corresponds to a greater similarity between the two brands.

In the current example, an 'appropriate' perceptual map is sought for the ten candy bar brands, and the dimensionality of the configuration plays an important role in this. Since the researcher has no idea of the number of dimensions necessary to display the 'three-way, two-mode' dataset the best way possible, he will analyse the dataset a number of times, and will do this with a different dimensionality each time. He chooses a fairly large number of dimensions for the initial configuration, namely '8' (see discussion on the number of points in the map for the determination of this upper limit), and will look for solutions in '7', '6', '5', '4', '3', and '2' dimensions and finally in '1' dimension in the next steps. In the SPSS window (Figure 10.44) under 'Dimensions', choose '1' as the 'Minimum' and '8' as 'Maximum'. SPSS will then automatically perform the analyses for the different dimensions, starting with the largest and ending with the smallest number of dimensions, and will use the solution from the previous analysis as the initial configuration each time, whereby the last dimension is omitted. The software will then report a number of 'fit' values for each analysis, including the 'Normalized Raw Stress', and plotting these with regard to the number of dimensions (see option 'Plots – Stress' in the 'Multidimensional Scaling: Plots' window, Figure 10.46) will result in a 'Scree Plot'. The course of this curve will then provide an indication of the optimal dimensionality of the solution.

Figure 10.45

Click 'Continue', and then 'Options' in the main window. The 'Multidimensional Scaling: Options' window (Figure 10.45) will appear.

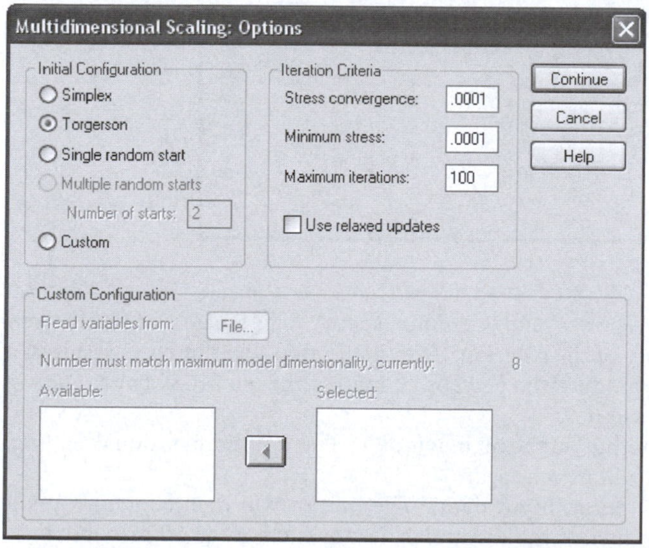

Under 'Initial Configuration', an indication is provided to show how the 'initial configuration' is created. It may be based on the placement of the brands at equal distances from one another (Simplex), on a classical scale solution (Torgerson[8]), on one or more 'random' configurations (Single random start/ Multiple random starts), or on a map indicated at the researcher's own discretion (Custom).

Since the number of dimensions of the solution has not yet been established (see the minimum and the maximum number of dimensions, '1' and '8' respectively, in Figure 10.44), it is not possible to choose the option 'Multiple random starts'. If the researcher does not have his own 'initial configuration', then he may choose 'Torgerson', as is the case here, or 'Single random start'. The option 'Simplex' is not advisable. If, in a later stage of the analysis, the number of dimensions for the solution has been established (for example, '2'), then 'Torgerson', or 'Multiple random starts' should be chosen, or both, by including them in analyses which are performed alongside one another, and in which the goal is to find the solution with the lowest stress value.

The numbers under 'Iteration Criteria' indicate that the algorithm will stop if the difference in the successive 'Normalized Raw Stress' values is less than .0001 (see 'Stress convergence'; falling between 0 and 1) or if the 'Normalized Raw Stress' is less than .0001 (see 'Minimum stress'; falling between 0 and 1). The algorithm will perform 100 iterations unless one of the two previous conditions is satisfied sooner (see 'Maximum iterations').

Click 'Continue', and then on 'Plots' in the main window. The 'Multidimensional Scaling: Plots' window (Figure 10.46) will then appear.

Figure 10.46

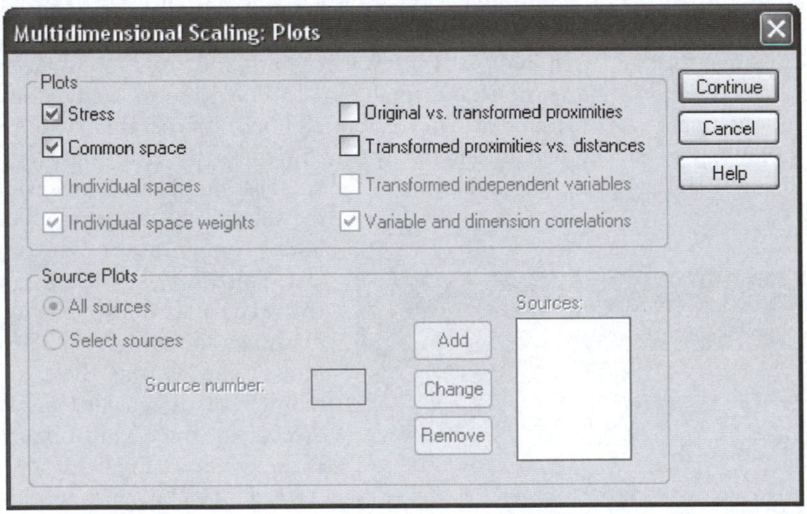

Under 'Plots', select the options 'Stress' and 'Common space', since the goal of the analysis is to determine the dimensionality of the solution. The first option will therefore result in a 'Scree Plot', and the second will produce the perceptual map of the ten candy bar brands in '8' dimensions through '1' dimension.

Click 'Continue', and then 'Output' in the main window. The 'Multidimensional Scaling: Output' window (Figure 10.47) will now appear.

Under 'Display', choose the option 'Input data'. The output will then contain a pivot table which shows the original scores or the dissimilarities for each of the 50 respondents.

Figure 10.47

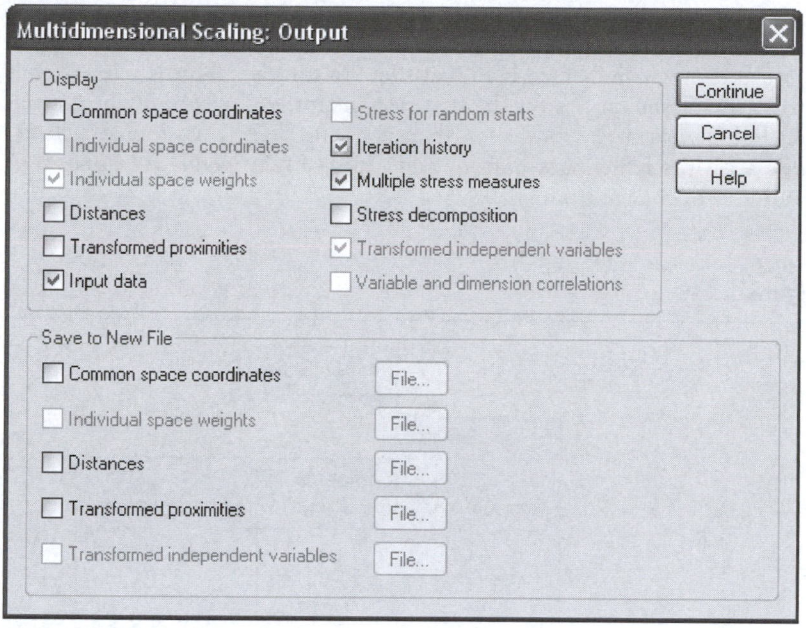

Select the option to display the 'Iteration history'. This option provides an insight into the number of iterations necessary to arrive at a solution and into the progression of the 'Normalized Raw Stress'.

Select 'Multiple stress measures' as well. In addition to the 'Normalized Raw Stress', criteria such as 'Stress-I', 'S-Stress', 'Dispersion Accounted For' and 'Tucker's Coefficient of Congruence' will also be shown in the output window. These all provide an indication of the fit of the solution.

Click 'Continue', and then 'OK' in the main window. The output window will now appear.

Interpretation of the SPSS output: dimensionality of the solution

Figure 10.48

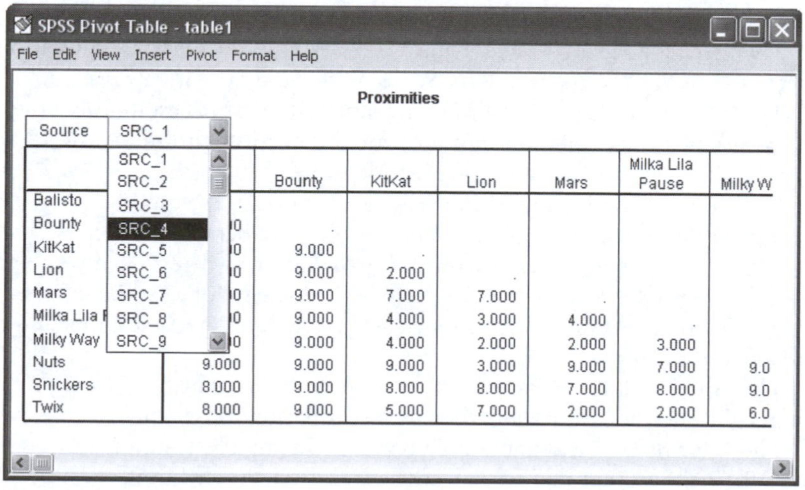

At the beginning of the output, the researcher will find the 'Proximities' table (Figure 10.48). This table will show the original scores for the 45 brand pairs (Figure 10.38) and makes it possible for the researcher to make sure that the analysis is in fact based on the correct data. It must also be commented here that the 'Proximities' table is a 'pivot' table. Figure 10.48 shows the dissimilarities for the first respondent, yet may easily be converted into a figure which shows the scores for the fourth respondent. To do this, double click on the 'Proximities' table with the left mouse button, and a pull-down menu will appear. Click SRC_4 and 'Source' will change from 'SRC_1' to 'SRC_4'.

Figure 10.49

Iteration History

Dimensionality: 1

Iteration	Normalized Raw Stress	Improvement
0	.20246[a]	
1	.14946	.05300
2	.14849	.00097
3	.14840	.00009[b]

[a]Stress of initial configuration: Torgerson start

[b]The iteration process has stopped because improvement has become less than the convergence criterion

The third iteration causes a decrease of .00009 in the 'Normalized Raw Stress', which is less than the predetermined 'Convergence criterion' of .0001 (Figure 10.45). A fourth iteration is thus no longer necessary.

The 'Iteration History' table (Figure 10.49) shows the number of iterations, as well as the 'decrease' in the 'Normalized Raw Stress' with successive iterations.

This table is also a pivot table making it possible to request not only the iteration history for a 1-dimensional solution, but also for the 2- through 8-dimensional solutions. To do this, double click on the 'Iteration History' table.

In comparison with the 1-dimensional solution, the solution in two dimensions, for example (Figure 10.50), requires a much larger number of iterations ('21' vs. '3').

Next, the optimal dimensionality of the solution is determined on the basis of the following five points: (1) the stress value; (2) the 'Scree Plot'; (3) the number of points in the perceptual map; (4) the number of original scores; and (5) an intuitive interpretation of the contents of the map.

The 'Stress and Fit Measures' table (Figure 10.51), which is also a pivot table, provides an insight into the 'fit' of the 2-dimensional solution for example

The 'Normalized Raw Stress' (NRS) is .056 for the solution in two dimensions. Figure 10.50 shows that this value is arrived at after the PROXSCAL algorithm, minimizing the NRS, has run through 21 iterations.

Figure 10.50

Iteration History

Dimensionality: 2

Iteration	Normalized Raw Stress	Improvement
0	.08486[a]	
1	.06239	.02248
2	.06065	.00174
3	.05961	.00103
4	.05897	.00064
5	.05855	.00042
6	.05826	.00029
7	.05804	.00022
8	.05786	.00019
9	.05769	.00017
10	.05753	.00016
11	.05737	.00016
12	.05721	.00016
13	.05705	.00016
14	.05690	.00015
15	.05675	.00015
16	.05661	.00014
17	.05647	.00014
18	.05634	.00013
19	.05622	.00012
20	.05611	.00011
21	**.05602**	.00010[b]

[a]Stress of initial configuration: Torgerson start
[b]The iteration process has stopped because improvement has become less than the convergence criterion

Figure 10.51

Stress and Fit Measures

Dimensionality: 2

Normalized raw stress	**.05602**
Stress-I	.23668[o]
Stress-II	.67483[o]
S-stress	.14912[p]
Dispersion accounted for (D.A.F.)	.94398
Tucker's coefficient of congruence	.97159

PROXSCAL minimizes Normalized Raw Stress.
[o]Optimal scaling factor = 1.059
[p]Optimal scaling factor = .954

If we take the square root of the 'Normalized Raw Stress', we find a value for 'Stress-I':

$$\sqrt{NRS} = \text{Stress-I} = \sqrt{\frac{\text{Kruskal's raw stress}}{\sum(\text{Distance in the solution}^2)}}$$

$$= \sqrt{\frac{\sum(\text{Distance in the solution} - \text{Pseudo distance})^2}{\sum(\text{Distance in the solution}^2)}}$$

The lowest possible value is also desirable here. Technically, this minimization amounts to finding a perceptual map and a transformation for which it applies that the sum of the squares of the differences between the distances-in-the-solution and the transformed dis-similarities (the so-called 'pseudo distances') is as small as possible.

From the above, we have already been able to conclude that it is best for 'Normalized Raw Stress' and 'Stress-I' to take on the lowest possible values, and ideally, they should be equal to '0', the minimum value. A value of .05 for 'Stress-I' corresponds to a good solution, while a value of .20 is actually classified as being a poor solution. In addition to these 'measures of misfit of the data' or 'badness-of-fit' criteria, a higher stress value points to a worse solution, there are also 'measures of fit of the data' or 'goodness-of-fit' criteria. 'Dispersion Accounted For' and 'Tucker's Coefficient of Congruence' are examples of this last type, and will result in a high value for a good solution, with a maximum of '1'. It should be mentioned that these 'goodness-of-fit' criteria often produce numbers higher than .90, even when the stress values are actually too high to arrive at a good solution. Therefore low values for 'Dispersion Accounted For' and 'Tucker's Coefficient of Congruence' clearly indicate that a bad solution is involved, while high values do not always indicate a good solution.

For the current 2-dimensional solution, 'Dispersion Accounted For' and 'Tucker's Coefficient of Congruence' have values of .944 and .972, respectively. These values are not low, such that the solution may not automatically be classified as being 'bad'. 'Stress-I' is equal to .237, a figure that deviates substantially from the minimum value '0', yet on the other hand is a score for an MDS analysis with replications, and is still somewhat acceptable. The stress value in this case will always be (much) greater than with a classic MDS analysis, after averaging, since for each distance-in-the-solution d_{ij}, there are 50 (and not only 1) pseudo distances which can all deviate from d_{ij}.

It was mentioned previously that the researcher has no idea of the number of dimensions that are necessary to best display the data from the 'three-way, two-mode' dataset, which has led to the reanalysis of the same data, on the basis of a different number of dimensions each time. So, just like the 2-dimensional solution, the researcher has 'badness-of-fit' and 'goodness-of-fit' criteria for the 1-, 3-, 4-, 5-, 6-, 7- and 8-dimensional solutions. In order to determine the optimum number of dimensions, the researcher may examine and compare these values in detail, however on the other hand, he may also have a look at the 'Scree Plot' (Figure 10.52).

Figure 10.52

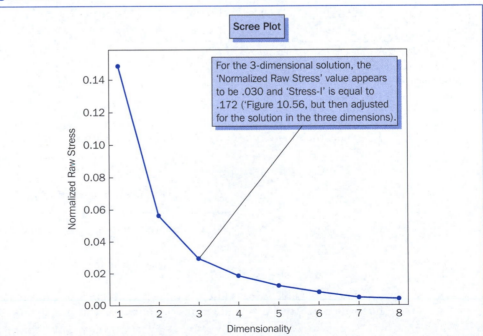

Scree Plot

For the 3-dimensional solution, the 'Normalized Raw Stress' value appears to be .030 and 'Stress-I' is equal to .172 ('Figure 10.56, but then adjusted for the solution in the three dimensions).

This graph places the stress of a solution on the vertical axis, and its dimensionality on the horizontal axis, and allows the course of the stress to be studied; in other words, how much does the stress decrease if solutions with more dimensions are chosen? The following two points should be kept in mind: (1) it generally applies that a higher dimensionality leads to lower stress, which, for the current example, would mean that the 8-dimensional solution is chosen; and (2) a solution with the fewest possible dimensions is desirable, since this type of solution is more economical in terms of the number of parameters to be estimated, and in general, is easier to interpret, which then again favours a 2- or 3- dimensional solution. The researcher must therefore find a solution which has acceptable stress with the lowest possible dimensionality.

In the ideal situation, the 'Scree Plot' (Figure 10.52) would show a monotone decreasing curve, which, in the case of a certain dimensionality, is (nearly) equal to zero. In practice, the researcher must find the typical 'elbow' or bend in the curve (see also Chapter 7, 'Exploratory factor analysis'): in front of the bend, the stress will decrease considerably as a result of the addition of extra dimensions to the solution; after the bend, the inclusion of the new dimensions will result in only a slight reduction in stress. This bend will then indicate the optimal dimensionality of the solution.

For the current application, the bend 'seems' to be located in three[9] dimensions. The causes of this type of 'weak' bend can be coincidental or systematic measurement errors in the data. We will not discuss this in further detail.

The above study of the optimal number of dimensions using the stress values leads us therefore to believe that the 3-dimensional solution is optimal but also that the solution in two dimensions would be fairly acceptable. In addition to stress there are still other factors which play an important role in the determination of the optimal dimensionality, and as was previously summarized, these are: the number of brands included, the number of observations (or original scores), and a number of intrinsic aspects. These will be discussed in more detail below.

The current application assumes that the dissimilarities are ordinally scaled (which means they are non-metrical data), which implies that the ten brands fit perfectly in an 8-dimensional space ($10 - 2$). If the original scores are seen as interval data (metrical data), then there is a perfect display in nine dimensions ($10 - 1$). The objective however is to strive for spaces which are (much) smaller, and it is said that a configuration with more than $\frac{1}{2}*10$ (=5) dimensions actually does not contain that many fewer dimensions than the maximum number, or 8 in this case, and may thus be rejected. The fact always remains that a solution in four, five or more dimensions is not very easy to interpret. This paragraph brings the researcher back to the choice between a 2- or 3-dimensional solution.

If the researcher demands there be at least twice as many observations (e.g., dissimilarities) in classical MDS analyses as parameters to be estimated (the number of objects in the configuration*the dimensionality of the map), then he must take the following rule into consideration as regards the dimensionality of the solution:

dimensionality of the solution $\leq$ (number of objects in the configuration $- 1)/4$

By analogy[10] for the current MDS analysis with 50 replications, the following formula could be proposed:

dimensionality of the solution $\leq 50*($ number of objects in the configuration $- 1)/4$

In concrete terms, this would amount to the number of dimensions being less than or equal to 112 (=$50*\{10 - 1\}/4$). However, it should be mentioned here that, even though there are 50 matrices and the relationship of the number of observations to the number of parameters to be estimated is thus more favourable, the ten objects could never be shown in more than nine, or eight dimensions (see discussion on 'number of brands included' above). A solution in 112 dimensions for example (although it is technically feasible in terms of the relationship between observations and number of parameters to be estimated) is not realistic.

The possibility to be able to understand a perceptual map 'intrinsically' is very closely related to the dimensionality of the solution. Since the 2- and 3-dimensional solutions in this example are the most plausible, the visual representations of these are shown and discussed below.

Before starting with the concrete interpretation, first a few comments: (1) the horizontal and the vertical axes are rescaled to '−1', '+1', and show a sub-division of .2. With the left mouse button, double click the relevant axis in the 'SPSS Chart Editor', and replace the 'Auto Range' with 'Custom Range' values. The purpose of this is to represent both dimensions on the basis of identical axes, so that the scaling of the axes cannot lead to erroneous interpretations; (2) for the conversion of the 'matrix' representation with three dimensions to a figure which only shows two dimensions, double click the matrix plot in the 'SPSS Chart Editor', and a 'Properties' window will pop up. In this window select the 'Variables' tab. Next select 'Marker' instead of 'Matrix' type and define 'Dimension 1' as the 'X Axis' and 'Dimension 3' as the 'Y Axis' to obtain the final plot listed in figure 10.54. Do not forget to click 'Apply' at the bottom of the 'Properties' window.

Figure 10.53

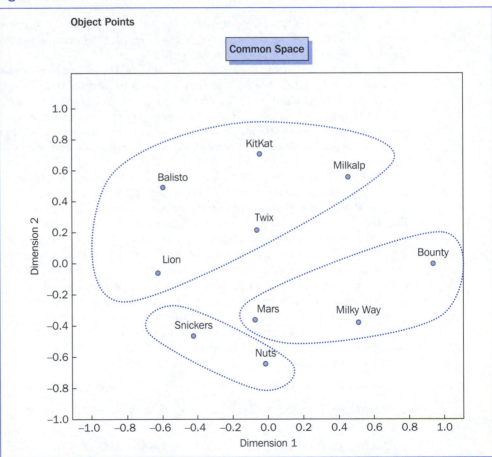

2-dimensional solution
The solution in two dimensions (Figure 10.53) seems to be driven primarily by the following three candy bar attributes: clear presence or absence of nuts, crunchy or non-crunchy, and 'soft' or 'hard'.

Nuts and Snickers are clearly characterized by the presence of nuts. Mars, Milky Way and Bounty are 'soft' candy bars, whereby Bounty lies a bit farther away due the clearly distinct coconut flavour. Lion, Balisto, Twix, KitKat and Milka Lila Pause are then the crunchy 'candies'[11].

It should be remarked at this point that another researcher could possibly interpret this 2-dimensional solution on the basis of other candy bar attributes, and that the analysis here involves a subjective approach.

Whereas one can say that the 2-dimensional solution is influenced by the characteristics 'crunchy', 'soft' and 'nuts', the underlying structure of the 3-dimensional solution (Figure 10.54) is not nearly as obvious.

Figure 10.54

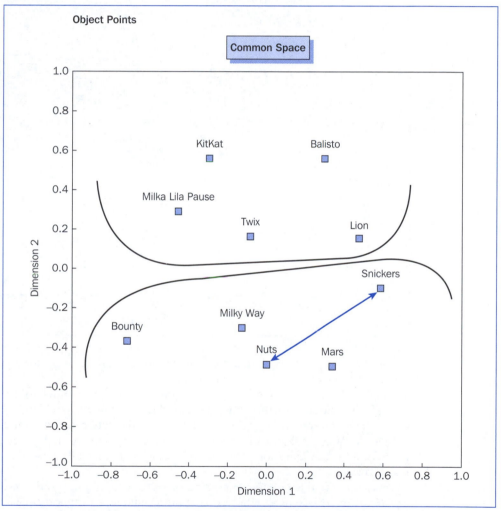

3-dimensional solution
In plotting out the dimensions '1' and '2', the 'crunchy vs. non-crunchy' attribute also appears to play a role here. The fact that Nuts lies closer to Milky Way and Mars than Snickers is strange. One would actually expect on the one hand the candy bars with nuts and on the other, the soft candy bars to stick together.

Figure 10.54 *Continued*

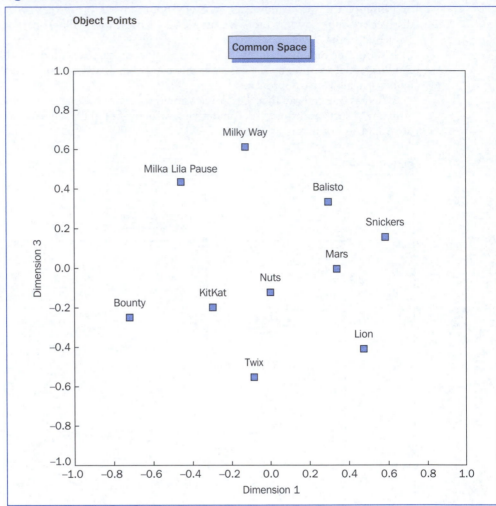

For the perceptual map based on the dimensions '1' and '3', it is not immediately apparent which attributes lie at the foundation.

Finally, if we look at the configuration on the basis of the dimensions '2' and '3', it is possible that the fact whether or not the brand is 'well-known' could be what is steering the map. Mars, Snickers, Bounty, Lion and Twix are the better known brands in comparison with Milky Way, Milka Lila Pause, Balisto and Kitkat, and group themselves in the bottom left part of the configuration. It is perhaps strange that Nuts falls under the category of well-known brands.

In addition to this intuitive interpretation of the configurations, the researcher may also decide to employ the more enforced analysis techniques to support the choice between the 2- and the 3-dimensional solution, such as a 'Procrustes analysis' or an 'external analysis'. As was mentioned previously, these techniques will not be discussed in further detail.

Conclusion: the researcher will choose the 2-dimensional solution here, since this has an acceptable stress value and is intrinsically clear. The 3-dimensional solution may have a lower stress value, but it is not as clear which attributes are responsible for the steering of the map.

Figure 10.54 *Continued*

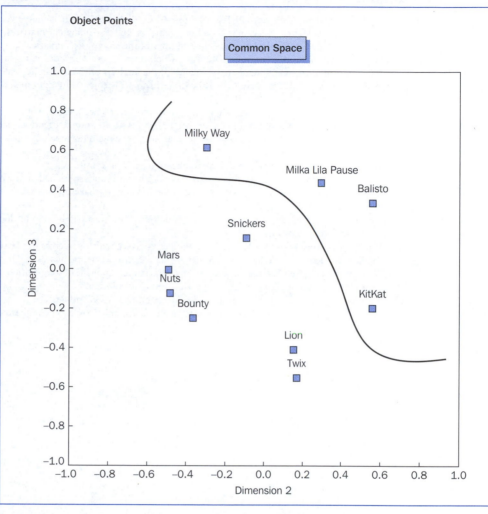

Further reading

Borg, I. and Groenen, P. (2005), *Modern Multidimensional Scaling: Theory and Applications.* 2nd ed. New York: Springer Verlag.

Meulman, J. and Heiser, W. (2004), *SPSS Categories 13.0.* Chicago, Illinois: SPSS, Inc.

Norušis, M. (1993), *SPSS for Windows: Professional Statistics, Release 6.0.* Chicago, Illinois: SPSS, Inc.

Website reference

A website which contains documentation and software for the performance of a whole series of multidimensional scale techniques is NewMDSX: http://www.newmdsx.com/.

Endnotes

1 CATPCA replaces the previous PRINCALS procedure. The latter is still available via syntax.

2 Note that ALSCAL analyses can be based on square as well as rectangular matrices, while PROXSCAL can only be based on square matrices. In addition, in the case of asymmetrical data, ALSCAL has the choice of: (1) finding a compromise solution which fits the best with both parts of the matrix; (2) the application of a row-conditional analysis; and (3) the analysis of the matrix according to a model with asymmetrical weights. PROXSCAL on the other hand will remove any asymmetry in the data matrix prior to the analysis.

3 These plots also contain the seven shopping centres however since the only role they play in this example is to serve as additional external information, there is no additional attention placed on them here.

4 The researcher may also choose to fill in the cells above the main diagonal, and to leave the cells below it open.

5 The 50 respondents are considered to be 'replications' of one another.

6 It may be said here that the perceptual map of the candy bar brands, obtained on the basis of RMDS with an 'unconditional' approach to the data, will often be equal to that obtained via CMDS after averaging of the data.

7 Data may also be interpreted as being 'row-conditional', however, this chapter does not examine this concept in further detail.

8 'Torgerson' corresponds to a Young-Householder analysis, which perceives the associations as real distances, measured at a ratio level, which then, using the cosine rule, calculates scalar products from these distances, to ultimately use them as input for a principal component decomposition.

9 Certain researchers might even defend the 4-dimensional solution.

10 The number of parameters to be estimated is identical for CMDS and RMDS.

11 The dotted lines have been added for educational reasons and are not to be requested in SPSS.

Chapter 11

Conjoint analysis

Chapter objectives

This chapter will help you to:

- Understand when and how to use conjoint analysis
- Understand the different types of conjoint measurements and when to apply them
- Interpret the results of a conjoint analysis

Technique

The objective of conjoint analysis is to estimate the relationship between an ordinally- or interval-scaled variable (e.g., a consumer's preference for a certain type of product) and nominally-scaled independent variables, namely, the characteristics of the product type or the product attributes. Conjoint analysis is often used in marketing as a tool in product development, in order to find out which characteristics a product should have in order to appeal to the target audience.

A conjoint analysis consists of the following steps:

- **Determination of the relevant product attributes**
  First, the applicable product characteristics for the product to be researched must be determined. Only those attributes qualify which are capable of being manipulated and which are relevant for the consumer. In the case of the product 'car', this can include: make, degree of luxury, mileage, etc. The attribute engine (measured in terms of yes/no) is obviously meaningless since all cars have an 'engine'. The consequence of this is that this attribute may not be manipulated and therefore does not qualify for inclusion in the conjoint analysis (unless it is included as 'engine type').

- **Determination of the relevant levels for each product attribute**
  A number of 'levels' must be determined for each attribute (e.g., for make: Renault, Opel, Ford, etc.). Relevance and realism are also important here.

- **Determination of the data collection method and the type of scale**
  The researcher may work with rankings or scores. The second possibility will be used in the example below.

- **Method of estimation**
  Depending on whether non-metrical (rankings) or metrical (scores) independent variables will be used, the researcher will follow a modified procedure (algorithm).

- **Analysis of the result**

In conjoint analysis, the assumption is made that the consumer considers a product as a bundle of attributes with certain levels, whereby a utility score is determined for each level of each attribute. The point of a conjoint analysis is that the researcher can find out how much importance a consumer attaches to a certain product attribute (level), without having to ask this question explicitly. Imagine that the questions are to be asked each time in order of importance on a 7-point scale, then it is very possible that the consumer might find everything equally important. In a conjoint analysis, because of the specific design of the technique, the consumer is required as it were to weigh one aspect against the other.

A further discussion of these techniques may be found in the reference literature listed at the end of this chapter.

Example

Conjoint analysis

Managerial problem

A person interested in starting a new fitness club has organized several focus group meetings and has also performed a comparative study of the fitness clubs in his area. From these studies, it has become clear to him that, no matter what, his new club will have to have a number of features that he foresees as comprising a basic package. He will also indicate this list clearly in his questionnaire. This basic package would be described as follows:

The fitness club would be located along a major approach road in order to guarantee its accessibility and the use of public transport. There will also be sufficient parking available. The class packages will be trend-oriented with a great deal of variation in a modern and well-maintained infrastructure. Clients would have professional supervision available to them. They will of course also have the opportunity to take a relaxing breather complete with a snack and a beverage after having freshened up in the numerous showers and changing rooms.

In addition, there are several characteristics (child care, saunas, etc.) for which he is uncertain what the consumers' preferences would be. He is also unable to offer all of them due to a limited budget. In order to find out which features he should offer, he will perform a conjoint analysis to get an idea of the utility levels of (four) product attributes and their respective levels.

These are shown in Figure 11.1. There are essentially $2 \times 3 \times 2 \times 3 = 36$ combinations possible about which preference indications may be asked to each respondent. This poses several practical problems, however. A respondent might experience difficulties in being able to express a non-biased preference for each combination, let alone that he will be able to rank these 36 combinations adequately in order of preference. Conjoint analysis offers a solution for this problem. In Chapter 4 on analysis of variance, it was indicated that whenever more than one factor is studied at the same time, interaction effects may arise between these factors. Conjoint analysis makes an abstraction of these interaction effects; in other words, it assumes that they do not exist, and that only main effects are possible. If this assumption is made, a fractional (partial) design is constructed (called the orthogonal design) whereby only the main effects are estimated. 'Design' refers to a well-chosen number of combinations of the levels of the different factors (attributes). The advantage is that preference indicators only have to be asked about a (substantially) smaller number of combinations. The disadvantage is that, if interaction effects were present in reality, the results obtained would be biased.

Figure 11.1

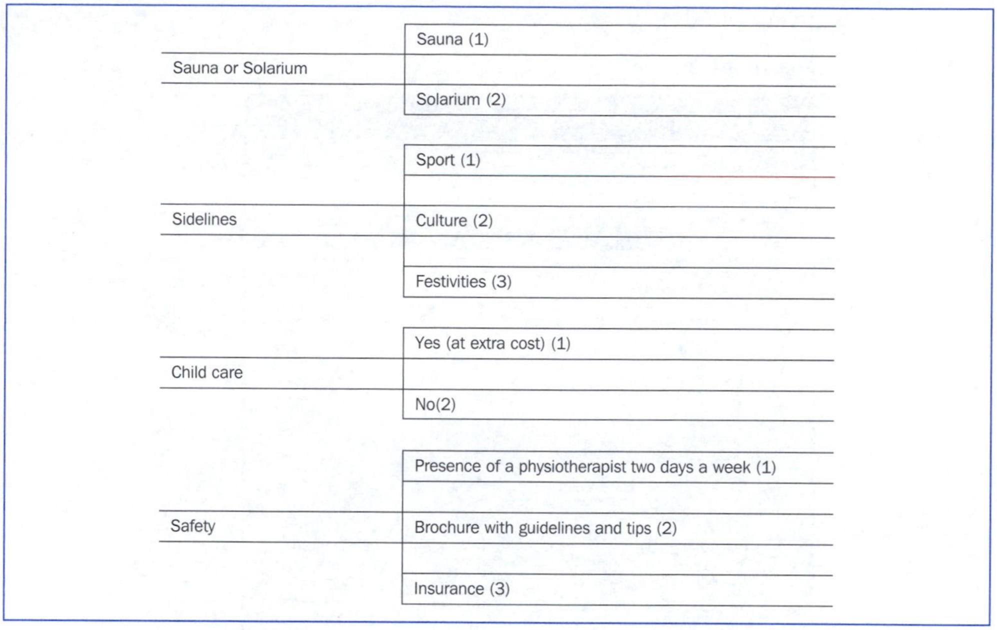

Sauna or Solarium	Sauna (1)
	Solarium (2)
Sidelines	Sport (1)
	Culture (2)
	Festivities (3)
Child care	Yes (at extra cost) (1)
	No (2)
Safety	Presence of a physiotherapist two days a week (1)
	Brochure with guidelines and tips (2)
	Insurance (3)

The first step is therefore to generate an orthogonal design. Next, a preference indication must be obtained for every combination generated. In practical terms, this can mean that a card (situation description) is created for every combination, for which the respondent must then indicate an answer (for example, the degree of preference). After that, the model is estimated.

Problem

Generate an orthogonal design that may be used to create the different combinations for which information must be obtained. Generate three holdout cases (profiles which are not in the orthogonal design), input one holdout case manually (see below) and simulate all 36 combinations. Perform the analysis with the aid of the dataset *fitness.sav* and interpret the results.

Solution

SPSS commands

Figure 11.2

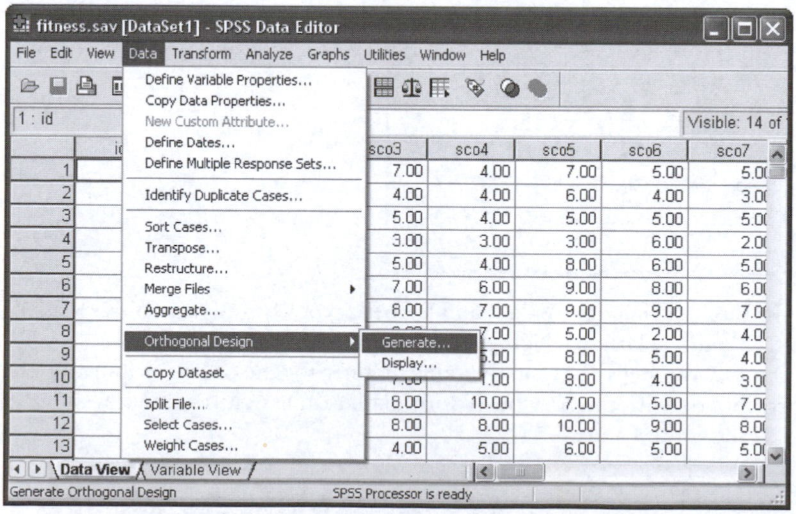

The first step is to generate the orthogonal design via Data/Orthogonal Design/Generate (Figure 11.2).

Figure 11.3

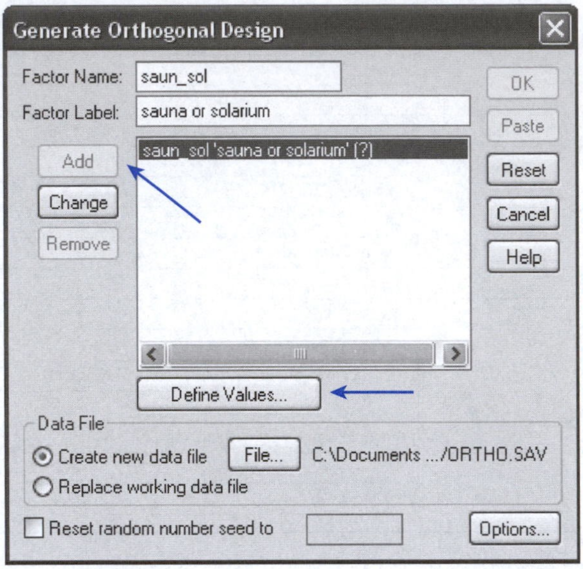

Next, the intention is to input every product characteristic and to indicate the levels. In the 'Factor Name' window, type 'saun_sol' (maximum of 8 characters) and 'sauna or solarium' in 'Factor Label', and then click 'Add'. This allows the factor to be included in the overview window. The next step is to click this factor in the overview window, so that it is selected (Figure 11.3). Then click the 'Define Values' button which has now become active. This way, the underlying attribute may be entered for the different levels.

Figure 11.4

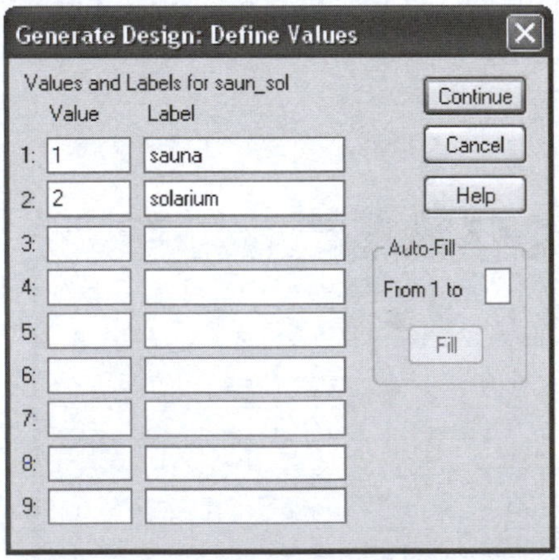

In the first line, for 'Value' and 'Label', type '1' and 'sauna' respectively, on the second line, '2' and 'solarium' (Figure 11.4). Now click 'Continue'.

Follow the steps above in the same manner for the other attributes so that all of the input corresponds with the previously formulated fitness club attributes and their respective levels as shown in Figure 11.1.

Figure 11.5

Generate Orthogonal Design

Factor Name:	[ ]
Factor Label:	[ ]

Add
Change
Remove

saun_sol 'sauna or solarium' (1 'sauna' 2 'sol
sidelines 'sidelines' (1 'sport' 2 'culture' 3 'fes
childcare 'child care' (1 'yes (at extra cost)' 2
safety 'safety' (1 '2 days physiotherapist' 2 'b

OK
Paste
Reset
Cancel
Help

Define Values...

Data File

⦿ Create new data file   [File...]   C:\orthofit.sav
◯ Replace working data file

☑ Reset random number seed to   [3000]   [Options...]

In the 'Data File' subwindow, click 'File' and save the output file (the orthogonal design that was created here) on a data carrier under an arbitrary name (here the C-drive and *orthofit.sav* respectively)(Figure 11.5).

Figure 11.6

Generate Orthogonal Design: Op...

Minimum number of cases to generate: [ ]

Holdout Cases

☑ Number of holdout cases: [3]
☐ Randomly mix with other cases

[Continue] [Cancel] [Help]

Instead of 'the' orthogonal design, it is better to refer to them as 'an' orthogonal design. There are in fact several sets of possible combinations which allow the researcher to measure the main effects. Where SPSS uses other initial values in its determination of an orthogonal design, a fixed initial value must be indicated, if the intention is for the same design to be generated in a subsequent session. This may be done by checking 'Reset random number seed to' and by filling in a whole number between 0 and 2 billion (in this case, 3000). This will result in an image such as the one shown in Figure 11.5. Now click 'Options'.

For 'Holdout Cases', check 'Number of holdout cases' and type '3' (Figure 11.6). Now click 'Continue' and then 'OK' in the main window.

Figure 11.7

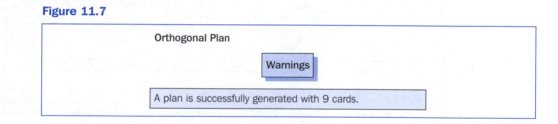

Orthogonal Plan

Warnings

A plan is successfully generated with 9 cards.

In Figure 11.7, the message is shown which then appears in the output window. This informs the user that the orthogonal design requested was generated successfully (*orthofit.sav* on the C-drive) and that the number of possible combinations was reduced from 36 to 9. In other words, each respondent only has to be asked about nine of the thirty-six combinations.

Figure 11.8

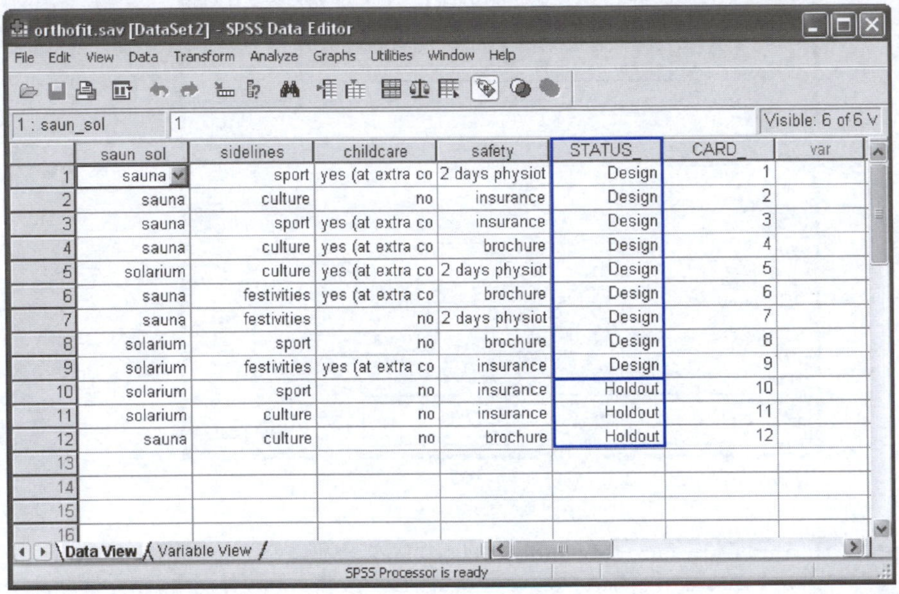

When the file *orthofit.sav* is opened (in the SPSS Data Editor screen), it does in fact become clear that nine 'design' cards have been generated in addition to three holdout cases. The *orthofit.sav* file which may be found on the CD-ROM contains extra lines.

Figure 11.9

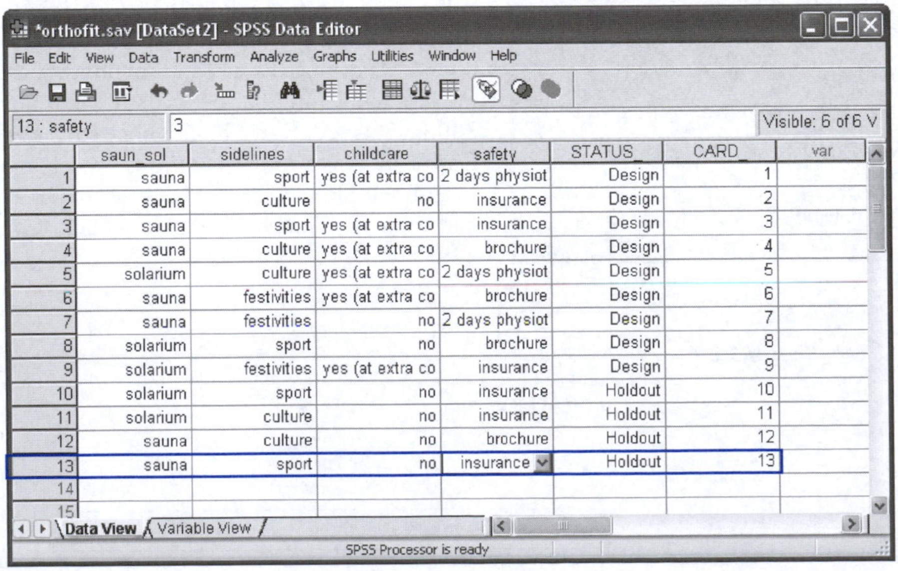

This is due to the fact that the researcher would now like to add an extra 'holdout' case, namely the combination (sauna-sport-no child care and insurance). In the [saun_sol] column, on the 13th line, type a '1' (this '1' stands for the attribute 'sauna'). Apply the same procedure to the other attributes (the 'value labels' may also be used which indicate the possibilities for each cell). For 'status_', choose 'Holdout' and for 'card_' choose '13' (since it is the 13th card) (Figure 11.9). The instructions also specify that a simulation be performed for all 36 combinations, in other words, the researcher would like to know which preference score each combination would obtain, given the parameter estimations which are obtained with the nine profiles in the analysis. As was done with the additional input of the holdout case in Figure 11.9, he will now also input each of the 36 possible combinations (Figure 11.10).

Figure 11.10

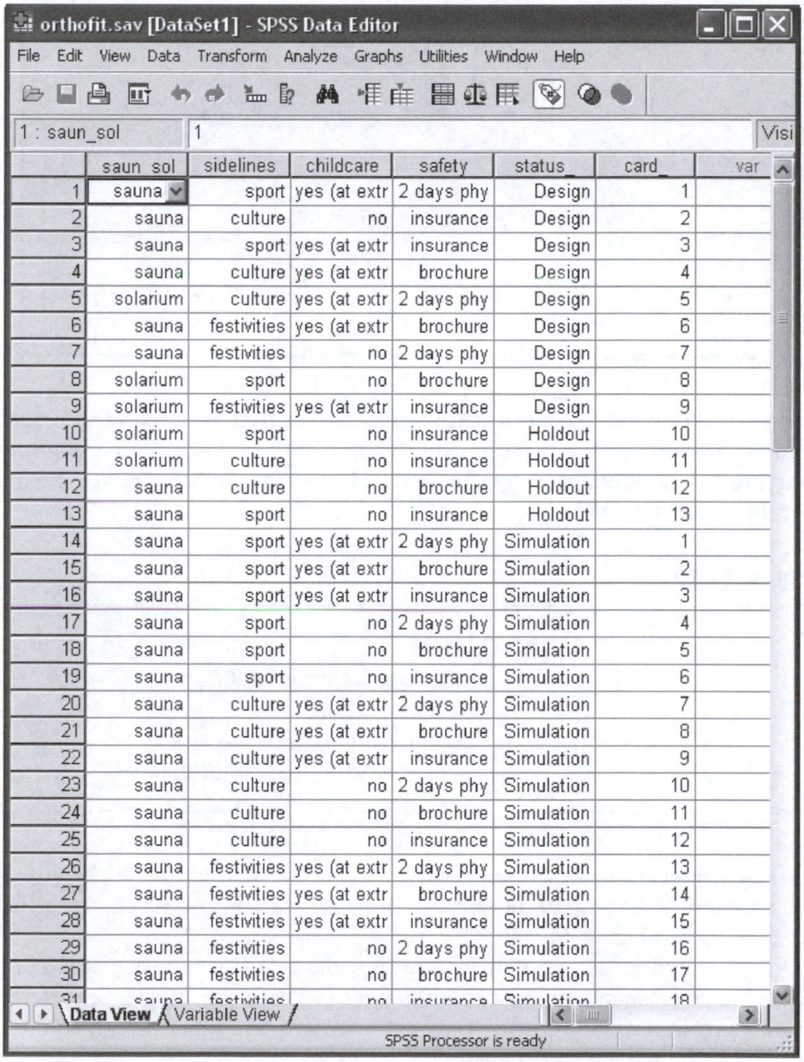

orthofit.sav [DataSet1] - SPSS Data Editor

File Edit View Data Transform Analyze Graphs Utilities Window Help

1 : saun_sol 1

	saun_sol	sidelines	childcare	safety	status_	card_	var
1	sauna	sport	yes (at extr	2 days phy	Design	1	
2	sauna	culture	no	insurance	Design	2	
3	sauna	sport	yes (at extr	insurance	Design	3	
4	sauna	culture	yes (at extr	brochure	Design	4	
5	solarium	culture	yes (at extr	2 days phy	Design	5	
6	sauna	festivities	yes (at extr	brochure	Design	6	
7	sauna	festivities	no	2 days phy	Design	7	
8	solarium	sport	no	brochure	Design	8	
9	solarium	festivities	yes (at extr	insurance	Design	9	
10	solarium	sport	no	insurance	Holdout	10	
11	solarium	culture	no	insurance	Holdout	11	
12	sauna	culture	no	brochure	Holdout	12	
13	sauna	sport	no	insurance	Holdout	13	
14	sauna	sport	yes (at extr	2 days phy	Simulation	1	
15	sauna	sport	yes (at extr	brochure	Simulation	2	
16	sauna	sport	yes (at extr	insurance	Simulation	3	
17	sauna	sport	no	2 days phy	Simulation	4	
18	sauna	sport	no	brochure	Simulation	5	
19	sauna	sport	no	insurance	Simulation	6	
20	sauna	culture	yes (at extr	2 days phy	Simulation	7	
21	sauna	culture	yes (at extr	brochure	Simulation	8	
22	sauna	culture	yes (at extr	insurance	Simulation	9	
23	sauna	culture	no	2 days phy	Simulation	10	
24	sauna	culture	no	brochure	Simulation	11	
25	sauna	culture	no	insurance	Simulation	12	
26	sauna	festivities	yes (at extr	2 days phy	Simulation	13	
27	sauna	festivities	yes (at extr	brochure	Simulation	14	
28	sauna	festivities	yes (at extr	insurance	Simulation	15	
29	sauna	festivities	no	2 days phy	Simulation	16	
30	sauna	festivities	no	brochure	Simulation	17	
31	sauna	festivities	no	insurance	Simulation	18	

Data View / Variable View

SPSS Processor is ready

This may easily be done by first inputting all of the possible combinations (in figures) via a spreadsheet program, and then exporting this to SPSS. Pay attention to the last two columns: 'Simulation' must be shown in the next to last column each time, and the cards are numbered starting from '1'. The *orthofit.sav* file on the CD-ROM contains all (49) of these profiles. This file is the one that will be used from now on.

Next, profile descriptions must be created for the first nine plus four cards (in order to use them in a questionnaire). SPSS also shows the profiles for the simulation cases, but these are not used for the purposes of the questionnaire.

Figure 11.11

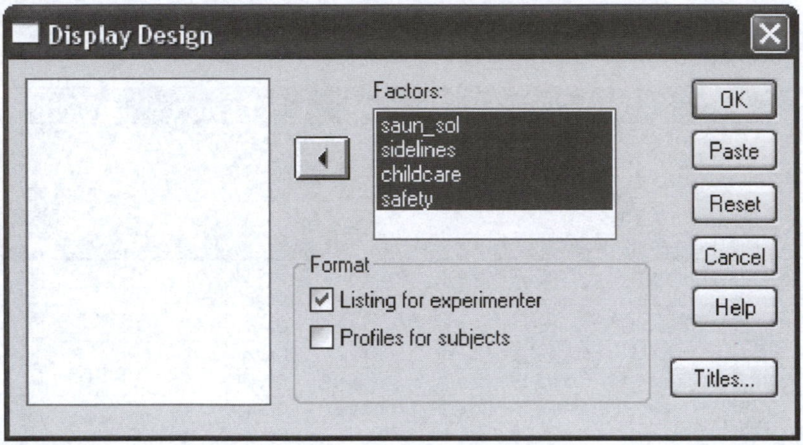

Go to Data/Orthogonal Design/Display. Select all four of the variables in this subwindow and move these to the 'Factors' subwindow. In the 'Format' subwindow, now click the 'Listing for experimenter' option. You will then see an image like the one shown in Figure 11.11. Click 'OK'.

Figure 11.12

Card 1
sauna or solarium sauna
sidelines sport
child care yes (at extra cost)
safety 2 days physiotherapist

The researcher will then see a description of the measurement level for each of the fitness club attributes for each of the combinations generated. This results in the output for the first card as seen in Figure 11.12.

It goes without saying that in a survey, the questions must be made more respondent-friendly. The respondent must be offered the possibility to express a preference for each generated profile (= situation described). The card in Figure 11.12 could be made 'survey ready' by changing it to read as in Figure 11.13:

Figure 11.13

Situation 1

To what degree do you find the situation below appealing? (Circle the appropriate number)

In addition to the existing basic package, clients may also use the sauna. There is also a physiotherapist present two days per week whom you are free to consult. Child care is also available (at an additional cost). There is also the possibility of participating in sports-oriented sidelines such as a mountain-biking, weekend rafting, or a bowling night.

Not appealing at all								Very appealing	
1	2	3	4	5	6	7	8	9	10

This may be done for all of the combinations generated (9 'design' combinations and 4 'holdout' combinations). Next, all thirteen situations may be presented to the respondents. If questions were also asked about several socio-demographic characteristics, subanalyses may then also be performed later in order to determine differences between men and women, for example. The answers from 242 respondents may be found in the *fitness.sav* file (Figure 11.14). 'sco1' stands for the score on the ten-point scale for the first card (situation 1, as shown in Figure 11.13), 'sco2' for the score for the second card, and so on.

Figure 11.14

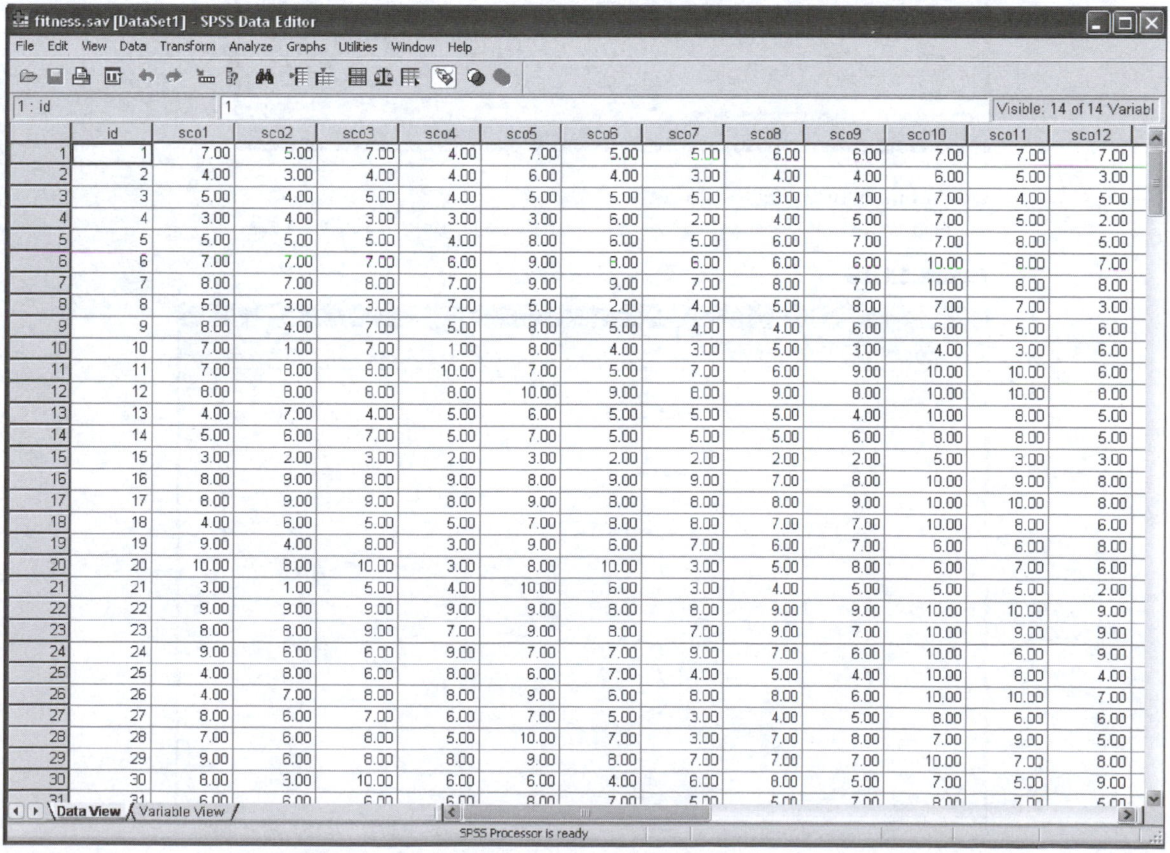

	id	sco1	sco2	sco3	sco4	sco5	sco6	sco7	sco8	sco9	sco10	sco11	sco12
1	1	7.00	5.00	7.00	4.00	7.00	5.00	5.00	6.00	6.00	7.00	7.00	7.00
2	2	4.00	3.00	4.00	4.00	6.00	4.00	3.00	4.00	4.00	6.00	5.00	3.00
3	3	5.00	4.00	5.00	4.00	5.00	5.00	5.00	3.00	4.00	7.00	4.00	5.00
4	4	3.00	4.00	3.00	3.00	3.00	6.00	2.00	4.00	5.00	7.00	5.00	2.00
5	5	5.00	5.00	5.00	4.00	8.00	6.00	5.00	6.00	7.00	7.00	8.00	5.00
6	6	7.00	7.00	7.00	6.00	9.00	8.00	6.00	6.00	6.00	10.00	8.00	7.00
7	7	8.00	7.00	8.00	7.00	9.00	9.00	7.00	8.00	7.00	10.00	8.00	8.00
8	8	5.00	3.00	3.00	7.00	5.00	2.00	4.00	5.00	8.00	7.00	7.00	3.00
9	9	8.00	4.00	7.00	5.00	8.00	5.00	4.00	4.00	6.00	6.00	5.00	6.00
10	10	7.00	1.00	7.00	1.00	8.00	4.00	3.00	5.00	3.00	4.00	3.00	6.00
11	11	7.00	8.00	6.00	10.00	7.00	5.00	7.00	6.00	9.00	10.00	10.00	6.00
12	12	8.00	8.00	6.00	8.00	10.00	9.00	8.00	9.00	8.00	10.00	10.00	8.00
13	13	4.00	7.00	4.00	5.00	6.00	5.00	5.00	5.00	4.00	10.00	8.00	5.00
14	14	5.00	6.00	7.00	5.00	7.00	5.00	5.00	5.00	6.00	8.00	8.00	5.00
15	15	3.00	2.00	3.00	2.00	3.00	2.00	2.00	2.00	2.00	5.00	3.00	3.00
16	16	8.00	9.00	8.00	9.00	8.00	9.00	9.00	7.00	8.00	10.00	9.00	8.00
17	17	8.00	9.00	9.00	8.00	9.00	8.00	8.00	8.00	9.00	10.00	10.00	8.00
18	18	4.00	6.00	5.00	5.00	7.00	8.00	8.00	7.00	7.00	10.00	8.00	6.00
19	19	9.00	4.00	8.00	3.00	9.00	6.00	7.00	6.00	7.00	6.00	6.00	8.00
20	20	10.00	8.00	10.00	3.00	8.00	10.00	3.00	5.00	8.00	6.00	7.00	6.00
21	21	3.00	1.00	5.00	4.00	10.00	6.00	3.00	4.00	5.00	5.00	5.00	2.00
22	22	9.00	9.00	9.00	9.00	9.00	8.00	8.00	9.00	9.00	10.00	10.00	9.00
23	23	8.00	8.00	9.00	7.00	9.00	8.00	7.00	9.00	7.00	10.00	9.00	9.00
24	24	9.00	6.00	6.00	9.00	7.00	7.00	9.00	7.00	6.00	10.00	6.00	9.00
25	25	4.00	8.00	6.00	8.00	6.00	7.00	4.00	5.00	4.00	10.00	8.00	4.00
26	26	4.00	7.00	8.00	8.00	9.00	6.00	8.00	8.00	6.00	10.00	10.00	7.00
27	27	8.00	6.00	7.00	6.00	7.00	5.00	3.00	4.00	5.00	8.00	6.00	6.00
28	28	7.00	6.00	8.00	5.00	10.00	7.00	3.00	7.00	8.00	7.00	9.00	5.00
29	29	9.00	6.00	8.00	8.00	9.00	8.00	7.00	7.00	7.00	10.00	7.00	8.00
30	30	8.00	3.00	10.00	6.00	6.00	4.00	6.00	8.00	5.00	7.00	5.00	9.00
31	31	6.00	6.00	6.00	6.00	8.00	7.00	5.00	5.00	7.00	8.00	7.00	5.00

The final estimation may not be done via the click-method in SPSS. To do this, the researcher will have to program in the syntax mode.

First make sure that the data for the answers have been loaded (in other words, that the data are shown in the active window). The relevant data file may also be read in via the syntax mode (not discussed here). Next:

Figure 11.15

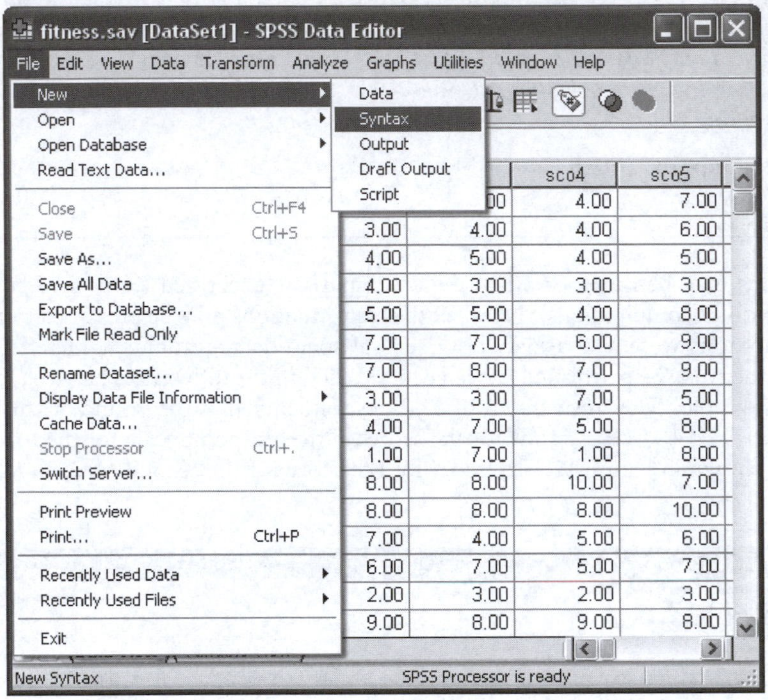

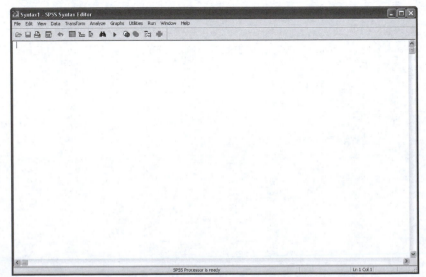

Go to File/New/Syntax (Figure 11.15).

You will then see a window such as the one shown in Figure 11.16.

Figure 11.16

Type the following in this new window (only the text which is shown in front of the arrows). Pay attention to the point after the last (sub-) command (Figure 11.17):

Figure 11.17

Conjoint plan='c:\orthofit.sav'	→ loads the combinations generated
/data=*	→ uses the data found on the current data sheet
/score=sco1 to sco13	→ indicates that scoring values are used
/subject=id	→ the variable name for the respondent number is 'id'
/utility='c:\utilfit.sav'	→ writes the utility scores to the *utilfit.sav* file
/plot summary.	→ plots the mean results

Digging Deeper

■ There is another parameter (/factors) which, if omitted (as is the case here), has the standard value 'discrete'. This means that the factor levels are all categorical and that there are no assumptions about the relationship between the factor and the scores. Use 'linear' when there is reason to suspect a linear relationship between the factor and the scores. The researcher may specify the direction this relationship is expected to take even further by using the words 'more' or 'less' (following the word 'linear' with a space between the two). 'More' indicates the assumption that higher levels are preferred for a factor, while 'less' indicates that lower levels are chosen for a factor. A typical example in the fitness club case could be the additional factor of 'membership fee': the higher the levels, the lower the preference is likely to be. The parameter line would then appear as follows:

/factors=sauna or solarium (discrete) sidelines (discrete) child care (discrete) safety (discrete) membership money (linear less)

Other possibilities for '/factors' are 'ideal' and 'anti-ideal' and relate to expected quadratic relationships between factors and scores.

■ With '/score', an indication may be provided of how the data is gathered. 'sequence' is used when the respondents are asked to order the profiles from the most appealing to the least appealing. 'rank' is used to indicate the ranking for each profile, while 'score' is used to indicate that preference scores are used.

The input in the syntax window would then look like that shown in Figure 11.18 (*fitness.sps*).

Figure 11.18

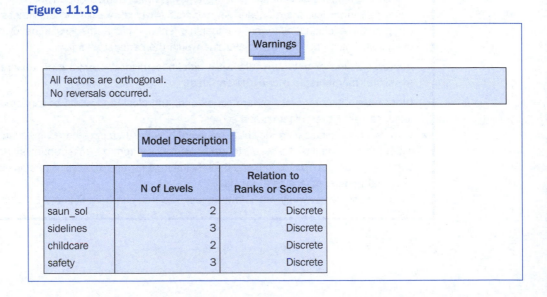

Select the code typed by indicating it with the mouse or by holding down the 'Ctrl' key and the 'a' so that all of the typed code in the Syntax window will be selected. Now click the 'Ctrl' key and the 'r' to run the code selected. This last command may also be executed by clicking the 'Play' button in the Syntax window.

Interpretation of the SPSS output

Figures 11.19 and 11.20 show the sections of the SPSS output. A subanalysis is created for each respondent, however initially it is more important to examine the average results (overall statistics).

Figure 11.19

Warnings

All factors are orthogonal.
No reversals occurred.

Model Description

	N of Levels	Relation to Ranks or Scores
saun_sol	2	Discrete
sidelines	3	Discrete
childcare	2	Discrete
safety	3	Discrete

In Figure 11.19, an indication is provided that the four attributes which were used in this analysis were seen as being 'discrete', which means that there is no relationship believed to exist between the attribute levels and the scores.

Figure 11.20

Utilities			
		Utility Estimate	Std. Error
saun_sol	sauna	−.301	.108
	solarium	.301	.108
sidelines	sport	.121	.144
	culture	.130	.144
	festivities	−.251	.144
childcare	yes (at extra cost)	.266	.108
	no	−.266	.108
safety	2 days physiotherapist	.102	.144
	brochure	−.131	.144
	insurance	.030	.144
(Constant)		6.342	.114

Importance Values

saun_sol	20.725
sidelines	31.013
childcare	18.445
safety	29.400

Averaged importance score

Correlations[a]

	Value	Sig.
Pearson's R	.948	.000
Kendall's tau	.778	.002
Kendall's tau for holdouts	.667	.087

[a]Correlations between observed and estimated preferences

Preference Scores of Simulations[a]

Card Number	ID	Score
1	1	6.530
2	2	6.297
3	3	6.458
4	4	5.997
5	5	5.764
6	6	5.925
7	7	6.538
8	8	6.305
9	9	6.466
10	10	6.006
11	11	5.772
12	12	5.933
13	13	6.158
14	14	5.924
15	15	6.085
16	16	5.625
17	17	5.392
18	18	5.553
19	19	7.133
20	20	6.899
21	21	7.060
22	22	6.600
23	23	6.367
24	24	6.528
25	25	7.141
26	26	6.908
27	27	7.069
28	28	6.608
29	29	6.375
30	30	6.536
31	31	6.760
32	32	6.527
33	33	6.688
34	34	6.228
35	35	5.994
36	36	6.156

[a]Negative simulation scores or all zero simulation scores are found. This subject will not be included in computing preference probabilities using the Bradley-Terry-Luce or Logit methods.

The output with the mean results across all of the respondents as shown in Figure 11.20 may be found under 'Overall Statistics'. It is best to first look at three statistics which give an idea how well the model corresponds to the data. Since both Pearson's R and Kendall's tau are criteria for the correlations between the observed and estimated preferences, it is desirable for both statistics to be as close to the value of one as possible. The significances reported alongside these indicate whether the null hypothesis (no correlation) should be rejected or not (with a 95% confidence level, this means that if the significance is less than .05, the null hypothesis of a null correlation must be rejected). In the example, both the Pearson's R (.948) and the Kendall's tau (.778) are high and both correlations appear to be significant (respectively < .0001 and .0018). In many conjoint analyses the number of parameters is nearly the same as the number of profiles evaluated, which artificially drives the correlation between the observed and estimated scores up. In this type of case, it is a good idea to have an extra correlation indicator on the basis of the 'holdouts', since information on the latter has been asked, yet was not used to estimate the scores. Holdouts, however, typically generate lower correlations, and if holdouts are included it is advisable to ask questions about at least four of them. However, it is important to remember that by including many holdouts, the questionnaire can become too long, and will thus essentially disregard the ultimate objective of a conjoint analysis, namely the reduction in the number of profiles to be questioned. The Kendall's tau for the holdouts is equal to .667 in the example (sig. = .0871 < .10, so significant at the 90% level). If, however, the general opinion is that the correlation criteria found are not high enough, the model may need to be respecified (for example, by asking the question whether all of the relevant attributes and/or measurement levels have been included).

Next, the researcher may look at the importance of the attributes and the utilities of the different levels. In Figure 11.20, he will notice that the sequence of importance is: sidelines, safety, sauna or solarium and child care. Their averaged importance is respectively 31.01, 29.40, 20.73 and 18.45. These importances always add up to 100 when rounded off. Within each attribute we must now try to find out which level or levels have the highest utilities. For instance, we see that for the attribute 'saun_sol', the highest utility (.3014) is assigned to the solarium level, and the lowest to sauna (−.3014). You will also note that the utilities within each attribute add up to zero.

SPSS also offers the possibility of displaying the output from Figure 11.20 in graph form. In Figure 11.21, the mean importance is shown for each attribute.

Figure 11.21

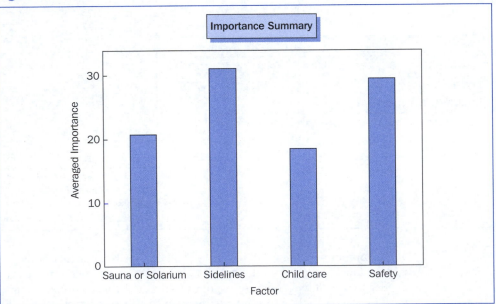

In the Figures 11.22 through 11.25, the relative utility levels are shown for each attribute.

Figure 11.22

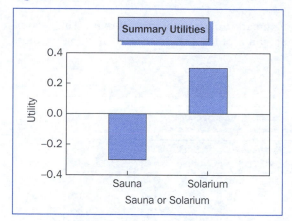

Figure 11.23

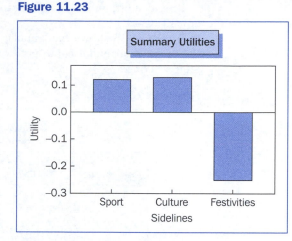

Figure 11.24

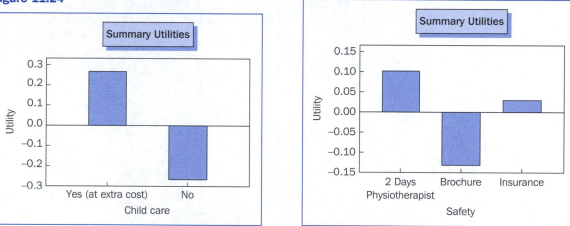

Figure 11.25

From Figures 11.21 through 11.25, it appears that a fitness club which, in addition to the basic package, also offers its clients a solarium, organizes cultural sidelines, provides child care (at an additional cost), and has a physiotherapist available two days a week will generate the highest total utility. To the extent that the other restrictions (e.g., budget) do not have a determinative influence, the entrepreneur would be well-advised to choose this combination. The utility may be calculated as follows (one uses the level with the highest utility for each attribute):

utility (solarium) + utility (cultural sidelines) + utility (child care at extra cost) + utility (2 days physiotherapist) + constant = .3014 + .1296 + .2663 + .1019 + 6.3418 = 7.141.

This last number may also be seen in the 'Simulation results' at the bottom of Figure 11.20. The top combination among the 36 simulated combinations (see also Figure 11.10), is simulation 25. Under 'Simulation results', we also see the (rounded off) number 7.1 for Card 25.

The least appealing combination is that of a sauna, festivities such as sidelines, lack of child care and distribution of a brochure. The combination would generate a total utility of:

utility (sauna) + utility (festivities) + utility (no child care) + utility (brochure) + constant = .3014 + (−.2509) + (−.2663) + (−.1315) + 6.3418 = 5.3917.

Rounded off, this results in 5.4 and this is also the value which may be found in simulation 17 (Card 17).

Figure 11.26 shows the 'Simulation Summary' (part of the text output). This section shows the probability that a specific simulation profile has been selected as being the most preferred one.

Figure 11.26

		Preference Probabilities of Simulations[b]		
Card Number	ID	Maximum Utility[a]	Bradley-Terry-Luce	Logit
1	1	3.7%	2.9%	3.6%
2	2	.1%	2.8%	2.0%
3	3	2.1%	2.8%	2.9%
4	4	.9%	2.6%	1.9%
5	5	.6%	2.5%	1.4%
6	6	.6%	2.6%	1.8%
7	7	4.0%	2.9%	3.3%
8	8	2.1%	2.8%	2.5%
9	9	3.9%	2.8%	3.2%
10	10	1.3%	2.6%	1.9%
11	11	.4%	2.5%	1.7%
12	12	1.5%	2.6%	2.0%
13	13	.7%	2.7%	2.0%
14	14	.1%	2.6%	1.7%
15	15	.2%	2.7%	1.7%
16	16	.4%	2.4%	1.4%
17	17	.3%	2.3%	1.4%
18	18	.5%	2.4%	1.4%
19	19	15.1%	3.2%	6.1%
20	20	3.7%	3.1%	3.8%
21	21	9.2%	3.1%	5.2%
22	22	3.7%	2.9%	3.2%
23	23	1.2%	2.8%	2.5%
24	24	3.2%	2.9%	3.1%
25	25	8.0%	3.2%	4.9%
26	26	4.7%	3.0%	4.1%
27	27	8.6%	3.1%	5.0%
28	28	.8%	2.9%	2.7%
29	29	3.7%	2.8%	2.6%
30	30	3.2%	2.8%	3.0%
31	31	2.9%	3.0%	3.3%
32	32	3.2%	2.9%	3.0%
33	33	.9%	2.9%	3.0%
34	34	.6%	2.7%	2.2%
35	35	2.5%	2.6%	2.4%
36	36	1.6%	2.7%	2.2%

[a]Including tied simulations

[b]y out of x subjects are used in the Bradley-Terry-Luce and Logit methods because these subjects have all nonnegative scores

This BTL (Bradley-Terry-Luce) model calculates the probability of choosing a profile as being the most preferred by dividing the utility of the simulation profile in question by the sum of the total utilities of all of the simulation profiles together. With simulation 25 (the profile that generated the highest utility), this is 3.2%. This would have to be the highest figure that may be found in Figure 11.26. Simulation 19 however also has a percentage of 3.2%. The rounding off performed in SPSS probably plays a role in this. Simulation 17 (the profile that generated the lowest utility) shows a percentage of 2.32%, the lowest value of all of the profiles. This indicates that the probability that this profile is chosen as being the most preferred is the lowest.

If desired, in addition to these summarizing results, the graphic output may also be shown for each respondent by replacing '/plot summary' in the syntax code (see Figures 11.17 and 11.18) by '/plot all'. The numerical results for each respondent will then be saved under the name *utilfit.sav* (arrived at using the command utility=c:\utilfit.sav', also in Figures 11.17 and 11.18). These utility scores for each respondent may be used as input for further analysis, for example a cluster analysis (see Chapter 9).

Further reading

SPSS Conjoint 8.0 (1997), Chicago, Illinois: SPSS, Inc.

Louviere, J.J. (1988), *Analyzing Decision Making – Metric Conjoint Analysis*. Sage University Paper 'Series on Quantitative Applications in the Social Sciences', no. 67, Beverly Hills, CA: Sage Publications.

Index